A STEPHEN CRANE
ENCYCLOPEDIA

D0068901

A STEPHEN CRANE ENCYCLOPEDIA

Stanley Wertheim

Greenwood Press
Westport, Connecticut • London

9.98

Library of Congress Cataloging-in-Publication Data

Wertheim, Stanley.
    A Stephen Crane encyclopedia / Stanley Wertheim.
      p. cm.
    Includes bibliographical references (p.) and index.
    ISBN 0–313–29692–8 (alk. paper)
    1. Crane, Stephen, 1871–1900—Encyclopedias. 2. Authors,
American—19th century—Biography—Encyclopedias. I. Title.
PS1449.C85Z9824   1997
813'.4—dc21   97–5859

British Library Cataloguing in Publication Data is available.

Library of Congress Catalog Card Number: 97–5859
ISBN: 0–313–29692–8

First published in 1997

Greenwood Press, 88 Post Road West, Westport, CT 06881
An imprint of Greenwood Publishing Group, Inc.

Printed in the United States of America

∞

The paper used in this book complies with the
Permanent Paper Standard issued by the National
Information Standards Organization (Z39.48–1984).

10 9 8 7 6 5 4 3 2 1

Copyright Acknowledgment

The editor and publisher gratefully acknowledge permission to reprint the following material:

Excerpts from *The Correspondence of Stephen Crane*, edited by Stanley Wertheim. Copyright ©
1988 by Columbia University Press. Reprinted with permission of the publisher.

To the memory of
William Merriam Gibson

Contents

Preface

Stephen Crane was a meteor. The publication of *The Red Badge of Courage* in September 1895 when he was only twenty-three years old projected him into instant fame; at twenty-eight he was dead. His untimely end made comparison with the tragic fate of Thomas Chatterton or Edgar Allan Poe almost inevitable, but Crane was not, as Amy Lowell would have it, "a boy, spiritually killed by neglect." In the brief span of his literary career, Crane enjoyed a significant measure of renown as well as notoriety, but his contemporary reputation rested almost entirely on the war novel, and he felt that his talent had ultimately been misjudged. *Maggie* in its first printing was all but ignored by reviewers, and *The Black Riders* was ridiculed and parodied. The works of fiction that appeared prior to *The Red Badge* were considered apprentice writing, and those published after it were judged repetitious or inferior. The core of praise remained focused on Crane's one great success, and to this day, even among educated American readers, he is known only as the author of the most realistic Civil War novel ever written, three or four action-packed short stories, and a handful of iconoclastic free verse poems.

A Stephen Crane Encyclopedia seeks to increase the reader's knowledge of Stephen Crane's short but furiously creative life and to encourage a more extensive appreciation of his works. Crane was befriended and admired by some of the most important literary figures of his time, among them Hamlin Garland, William Dean Howells, Willa Cather, and Irving Bacheller in the United States and Harold Frederic, Joseph Conrad, Ford Madox Ford, Edward Garnett, Henry James, and H. G. Wells in England. Crane was a pioneer in the development of a number of genres in modern American fiction and poetry. He was the first literary chronicler of the burgeoning slums of urban America who refused to sentimentalize his materials; his Western stories reveal the steady retreat of the frontier before the encroachments of a modern, Europeanized civilization; his best short stories, like his experimental epigrammatic and lyrical poems, engage the themes of humanity's relationship to God and nature, love, war, and social injustice; and his tales of Whilomville, especially that neglected masterpiece, "The Monster," anticipate the revolt from the village theme of later American writers in questioning the essential goodness of small-town life. Crane has been called a realist, a naturalist, an impressionist, a symbolist, and an existentialist, and this multifaceted taxonomy of his art is an indicator of his modernism. Above all, his objective as a writer was, as his close friend Joseph Conrad expressed his own aesthetic task in the preface to *The Nigger of the "Narcissus,"* "by the power of the written word to make you hear, to make you feel—it is before all, to make you *see*."

From his adolescence until his death in 1900, Crane was a professional journalist, and his range of reporting was extensive. In the early 1890s, he was a freelance feature writer for many New York City newspapers. Later he was employed by William Randolph Hearst and Joseph Pulitzer, the Bacheller and McClure newspaper syndicates, and the leading monthly magazines in the United States and England. He covered the New Jersey shore, the Bowery slums and the Tenderloin underworld of New York, conditions of labor in the coal mines of Pennsylvania, drought and blizzard in Nebraska, quotidian life in the cities of the West and Mexico, war in Greece and Cuba, and a host of other contemporary and historical subjects. *A Stephen Crane Encyclopedia* demonstrates the ineluctable interrelationship between Crane's finest journalism and his best fiction. The same faculty of vision, approximation of immediate sensory experience, pervasive irony, symbolism, and compressed narrative control may be found in parallel reportorial and fictional accounts such as his *New York Press* report "Stephen Crane's Own Story" and "The Open Boat" or his *New York World* dispatches about the battle for the San Juan hills during the Cuban campaign of the Spanish-American War and the thinly fictionalized short stories of *Wounds in the Rain*. Distinctions between fact and fiction, reality and the transformative imagination, are broken down in many of Crane's prose works, and in this sense also he is one of the first modern American writers.

A Stephen Crane Encyclopedia provides separate entries in an alphabetized sequence for the significant aspects of Stephen Crane's life and career as a creative writer and journalist. There are entries for members of his immediate and extended family who were influential in his life; close friends and associates, famous and obscure; educational institutions that he attended; places where he resided; publishers and syndicates by whom he was employed; literary movements with which he is usually associated by critics; and the works of fiction, poetry, and journalism that he wrote. In the controversial world of Crane studies almost any statement is merely an opinion, and entries on Crane's creative writing and journalism are intended to be critical as well as informational.

Individual entries are provided for almost all of Crane's prose works but not for each of his 136 known poems, the greater number of which are epigrammatic and many of which are fragmentary and redundant. For the most part they are discussed under his two books of poetry, *The Black Riders* and *War Is Kind*. Noteworthy uncollected and posthumous poems are accorded separate entries. In Crane's sketches, short stories, and novels, minor characters are often referred to in passing with common names such as Jones, Haines, or Casey or are merely functional and identified only by epithets and descriptive qualities, such as "the sharp lieutenant," "the adjutant," "the officer who rode like a cowboy," "the fat, green Mexican," "a tall German," "a man and a boy," and "a sixteen-year-old girl without any hat and with a roll of half-finished vests under her arm." These characters are usually not given individual entries in the *Encyclopedia*, but entries are provided for minor characters and unnamed characters who play consequential roles in the works in which they appear, including, for example, the man with the cheery voice in *The Red Badge of Courage*, the assassin of "An Experiment in Misery," the gambler and the Swede in "The Blue Hotel," and the lieutenant in "An Episode of War." Entries are selectively cross-referenced with an asterisk. Titles, names of significant characters, and members of Crane's immediate family and his literary agents and commercial publishers (unless they were also personal friends) are presumed to have separate entries and are not so marked. Assumed names and editorially supplied titles for posthumously published or unpublished works are indicated by brackets.

Crane's newspaper reports and sketches were often syndicated, and even those published only in a single newspaper were subjected to editorial procedures over which he usually had little or no control. Since the texts of these works are necessarily eclectic, excerpts from them in *A Stephen Crane Encyclopedia* are taken from volume 8, *Stephen Crane: Tales, Sketches, and Reports* (1973), and volume 9, *Stephen Crane: Reports of War* (1971), of the University Press of Virginia edition of *The Works of Stephen Crane*, 10 vols., edited by Fredson Bowers (1969–75). Quotations of Crane's other fictional works and of his poems are from first American or English book editions or periodical appearances. Typographical errors have been silently corrected. The texts of letters from and to Stephen and Cora Crane are derived from *The Correspondence of Stephen Crane*, edited by Stanley Wertheim and Paul Sorrentino (1988), and much of the biographical information in this volume is based on Stanley Wertheim and Paul Sorrentino, *The Crane Log: A Documentary Life of Stephen Crane*, revised edition (1995). Letters, titles, incidents, and persons whose only source is in Thomas Beer's fictionalized biography, *Stephen Crane: A Study in American Letters* (1923) or in his essays about Stephen and Cora Crane have been excluded from the *Encyclopedia* except for purposes of commentary.

I am grateful to Columbia University Press for permission to quote the text of *The Correspondence of Stephen Crane*. For advice and encouragement, and most of all for the ongoing example of dedication to high standards of scholarship, I thank my colleagues and friends in the Stephen Crane Society of the American Literature Association, notably John Clendenning, James B. Colvert, Jesse Crisler, Patrick K. Dooley, Joseph R. McElrath, Jr., George Monteiro,

Donald Pizer, Gary Scharnhorst, Paul Sorrentino, and Donald Vanouse. My greatest debt, as always, is to my wife, Mary Conroy Wertheim, who, contrary to her expectations, has shared her life with two men, one of whom died at the age of twenty-eight.

Chronology

1871   Stephen Crane born on 1 November in Newark, New Jersey, the fourteenth and last child of Jonathan Townley Crane, presiding elder of Methodist churches in the Newark district, and Mary Helen (Peck) Crane, daughter of a clergyman and niece of Methodist bishop Jesse T. Peck.

1874–80   Jonathan Townley Crane is minister of Methodist churches in Bloomington and then Paterson, New Jersey. Mrs. Crane is active in the Women's Christian Temperance Union. The family moves in April 1878 to Port Jervis, New York, where Crane's father serves as pastor of the Drew Methodist Church until his death on 16 February 1880. Mrs. Crane moves her family temporarily to Roseville, near Newark, but Stephen remains in Sussex County, New Jersey, with his brother Edmund.

1883   The Crane family moves to Asbury Park, a resort town on the New Jersey coast where Stephen's brother Townley has established a shore reporting agency. Another brother, William Howe, practices law in Port Jervis and becomes one of the founders of the Hartwood Club, a private hunting and fishing preserve in nearby Sullivan County.

1884   Crane's sister Agnes Elizabeth dies at the age of twenty-eight.

1885–87   Stephen attends Pennington Seminary (New Jersey), a Methodist boarding school where his father had been principal (1849–58).

1888   In January Crane enrolls in Claverack College and Hudson River Institute, a coeducational school with a military cadet corps for boys in Columbia County, New York. He spends the summer months from 1888 through 1892 in Asbury Park assisting his brother Townley in reporting shore news for local newspapers and the *New York Tribune*.

1890   Crane publishes his first sketch, "Henry M. Stanley," in the Claverack College magazine, the *Vidette*. He becomes a captain in the school's cadet corps but leaves Claverack and in the fall enters Lafayette College as a mining engineering student. He joins Delta Upsilon fraternity, then withdraws from the college in the first month of the second semester.

1891   Crane transfers to Syracuse University in January. He lives in the Delta Upsilon fraternity house and becomes a member of the varsity baseball team. His sketch "The King's Favor" appears in the *University Herald*. He begins a story about a prostitute that evolves into *Maggie: A Girl of the Streets*. In August Crane meets Hamlin Garland at Avon-by-the-Sea on the New Jersey shore and reports his lecture on William Dean Howells in the 18 August issue of the *New York Tribune*. He does not return to college in the fall. He begins to explore the slums of lower Manhattan while living with Edmund in Lake View, New Jersey. His mother dies on 7 December.

1892   Sullivan County tales and sketches appear in the *New York Tribune*. A furor over Crane's satiric report of the annual parade of the Junior Order of United American Mechanics in Asbury Park results in his severance from the *Tribune*. In October he moves into a boarding house on Avenue A in Manhattan with a group of medical students. He shares a room with Frederic M. Lawrence and revises *Maggie*.

1893   *Maggie: A Girl of the Streets* is privately printed under the pseudonym of Johnston Smith. Crane is introduced to Howells by Garland. He begins composition of *George's Mother* and *The Red Badge of Courage* in the spring. He shares a studio room in the old Art Students League building on East Twenty-third Street in Manhattan with illustrator and artist friends at intervals from 1893 to 1895.

1894   Crane writes social studies such as "An Experiment in Misery" and "In the Depths of a Coal Mine," publishes New York City sketches in the *New York Press* 1894–96, and takes some of his poems and the manuscript of *The Red Badge of Courage* to Garland. He completes *George's Mother*. The Bacheller syndicate serializes an abridged and truncated version of *The Red Badge of Courage* in early December.

1895   Crane travels to the West and Mexico as a feature writer for the Bacheller syndicate. He meets Willa Cather in Lincoln, Nebraska. He revises *The Red Badge of Courage* under the direction of Ripley Hitchcock. *The Black Riders* is published in May by Copeland & Day. Crane becomes an active member of the Lantern Club, a convivial group of journalists. *The Red Badge of Courage* is published in book form by Appleton in late September. He begins composition of *The Third Violet* at his brother Edmund's home in Hartwood, New York.

1896 Appleton publishes a variant version of *Maggie* and also *The Little Regiment*. Edward Arnold publishes *George's Mother*. *The Third Violet* is serialized by the McClure syndicate. Crane's career as an investigative reporter in New York is destroyed by his defense of Dora Clark in her suit for false arrest against the New York City Police Department. He leaves for Jacksonville, Florida, at the end of November to report the Cuban insurrection for the Bacheller syndicate. He meets Cora Taylor, the madam of a pleasure resort, the Hotel de Dream.

1897 The *Commodore*, which is carrying men and munitions to Cuba, founders off the coast of Florida on the morning of 2 January. Crane and three crew members spend thirty hours on the sea in a ten-foot dinghy. This experience becomes the factual framework for "The Open Boat." *The Third Violet* is published in May. Crane, accompanied by Cora, covers the Greek-Turkish War as a correspondent for the *New York Journal* and the *Westminster Gazette*. They settle in England at Ravensbrook, Surrey, as Mr. and Mrs. Stephen Crane. In September they visit Ireland with Harold Frederic and Kate Lyon. Crane meets Joseph Conrad in October. Crane writes "The Monster" and "The Bride Comes to Yellow Sky."

1898 *The Open Boat and Other Tales of Adventure* is published. Crane goes to Cuba as a correspondent for Pulitzer's *New York World*. He is discharged from the *World* in July and covers the Puerto Rican campaign for the *New York Journal*. After the Protocol of Peace is signed, Crane slips into Havana and spends four months leading an underground existence. He returns to New York at the end of December.

1899 Crane returns to England in January. He and Cora move to Brede Place, Sussex. Among their friends are Joseph Conrad, Henry James, Ford Madox Ford, and H. G. Wells. *War Is Kind, Active Service,* and *The Monster and Other Stories* are published. "The Ghost" is performed at a holiday party in late December. Afterward, Crane collapses with a tubercular hemorrhage.

1900 Crane suffers new hemorrhages in April. He dies of tuberculosis in a sanitarium at Badenweiler, Germany, on 5 June, and his body is returned to the United States for burial in Hillside, New Jersey. *Whilomville Stories* and *Wounds in the Rain* are published posthumously.

1901 *Great Battles of the World* appears. The book is researched and for the most part written by Kate Lyon.

1902 *Last Words*, an anthology of early and late writings compiled by Cora, is published in England but not in the United States.

1903 *The O'Ruddy*, completed by Robert Barr, is published.

A

["**Above All Things**"]. This untitled essay dealing with the social and economic condition of most of Mexico's Indian population, sometimes referred to by the title of "The Mexican Lower Classes," was written either during or shortly after Crane's two-month sojourn in Mexico as a correspondent for the Bacheller, Johnson and Bacheller newspaper syndicate in the spring of 1895. It remained unpublished in Crane's lifetime, perhaps because Irving Bacheller* considered its speculations unsuitable or too radical for his newspaper readership. It was first printed from the manuscript by R. W. Stallman in "Stephen Crane: Some New Sketches," *Bulletin of the New York Public Library* 71 (1967): 554–62.

In this important social statement, Crane acknowledges the impossibility of evaluating the aspirations of people with whose culture one is not familiar, but he considers it extraordinary that the lower classes of Mexican Indians should value their existence at all. Despite their poverty and ignorance, Crane can perceive no evidence that they are dissatisfied with their squalid condition. Their serenity, impassivity, and apparent contentment strike Crane as integers of their essential morality and are in striking contradistinction to the growing discontent that Crane perceives among the urban poor he had written about in *Maggie* and his New York City sketches:

> The people of the slums of our own cities fill a man with awe. That vast army with its countless faces immovably cynical, that vast army that silently confronts eternal defeat, it makes one afraid. One listens for the first thunder of the rebellion, the moment when this silence shall be broken by a roar of war. Meanwhile one fears this class, their numbers, their wickedness, their might—even their laughter. There is a vast national respect for them. They have it in their power to become terrible. And their silence suggests everything.

More explicitly than in his slum fiction, Crane implies that the growing economic disparities manifest in American society at the end of the nineteenth century might ultimately lead to violent communal upheaval.

"Across the Covered Pit". A suspenseful article, unpublished in Crane's lifetime, dealing with the Reverend H. C. Hovey's exploration of Mammoth Cave in west-central Kentucky. Crane describes how Hovey and a guide negotiated their way over the unstable slabs of stone covering the deep pit that separated the mouth of Mammoth Cave from its interior. Hovey lectured at the Seaside Assembly in Avon-by-the-Sea in July 1890. On 25 July his subject was "Mazes and Marvels of Mammoth Cave." A review of Seaside Assembly activities headed "Avon Seaside Assembly," printed in the *New York Tribune* on 28 July, that mentions Hovey's lectures may have been authored by Crane. This article was first printed in R. W. Stallman, "Stephen Crane: Some New Stories (Part III)," *Bulletin of the New York Public Library* 61 (1957): 36–46.

Active Service. Usually referred to as Crane's novel of the Greek-Turkish War of 1897, *Active Service* is actually a sentimental comedy of manners, interlaced with satire, in which the war serves as a vague backdrop. Crane covered the brief conflict in Greece as a correspondent for the *New York Journal* and the *Westminster Gazette*, although he saw combat only at Velestino. He had sketched out *Active Service* before he left England to report the Cuban War, but he probably did not begin to work seriously on the novel until after his return from Cuba in January 1899. He finished the book in mid-May, when he wrote to Clara Frewen* that it was "now being sent forth to the world to undermine whatever reputation for excellence I may have achieved up to this time and may heaven forgive it for being so bad." *Active Service* was serialized in newspapers by McClure from August through October 1899 and published in book form that fall by Frederick A. Stokes in New York and William Heinemann in London.

   Active Service opens at the home of Professor Harrison B. Wainwright of Washurst College, near New York City. Marjory Wainwright intrudes into the study of her curmudgeonly father, a self-righteous, unworldly pedant, and abruptly announces that she wishes to marry Rufus Coleman, Sunday editor of the *New York Eclipse*, the fictional equivalent of the *New York World*. The professor is astonished and outraged. In his judgment, Coleman, a former student at Washurst, is a drunkard and a gambler, and the newspaper that employs him is "a great outrage on our sensibilities." Indeed, the kind of reporting practiced by the *Eclipse*, whose offices are located "at the top of an immense building on Broadway," seems to be a parodic equivalent of the sensationalist yellow journalism made notorious by two of Crane's employers, Joseph Pulitzer of the *New York World* and William Randolph Hearst of the *New York Journal*. The *Eclipse* features disasters, scandal, and horror stories. One of the pieces Coleman chooses to titillate the depraved readers of the newspaper is illustrated with a half-page drawing of a deformed baby born in Massachusetts. "In place of upper limbs the child had growing from its chest a pair of fin-like hands, mere bits of skin covered bones. Furthermore it had only one eye."

Marjory's father obdurately forbids her to marry Coleman and proposes to separate the lovers by taking her on a field trip to Greece with his class to study antiquities. Marjory, distraught but unwilling to defy her father, bids a seemingly dispassionate farewell to Coleman in the presence of Coke, a wealthy student resembling Jem Oglethorpe in *The Third Violet*, whom Coleman views as a rival for Marjory's affections. Coleman's pride will not allow him to express his despair, and in a comedy of errors, both Coleman and Marjory are led to believe that neither cares for the other.

Six weeks later, Coleman advises Sturgeon, the proprietor of the *Eclipse*, that as a vacation he would like to go to Greece to report the war. Sturgeon, who seems to be a caricature of Pulitzer or Hearst, proposes instead that the newspaper recruit "a battalion of men to go to Cuba and fight the Spaniards under its own flag—the *Eclipse* flag." On 20 June 1898, the *World* had reported that it was the first newspaper "to establish permanent headquarters on Cuban soil." Crane, Alexander Kenealy,* and Sylvester Scovel* had set up a camp "over which floats the Cuban flag, with the World's banner." Sturgeon observes that war correspondence is not very restful and "an idiotic way to take a vacation," but he accedes to Coleman's request.

On the steamship to Liverpool, Coleman encounters Nora Black, a comic-opera performer with whom he had been previously romantically involved, who is on her way to London for an engagement. Nora, an independent, sensuous woman, in contrast to the clinging, virginal Marjory, obviously still cares for Coleman, but he is impervious to her blandishments. In London Coleman finds himself sitting near Nora in the restaurant of his hotel. She is aware of his presence and announces to a group of her admirers that the kind of man she really likes is one she cannot control. "He obliges me to admire him the most when he remains stolid; stolid to my lures."

Coleman travels to Athens, where he calls on the American minister to Greece, the Hon. Thomas M. Gordner of Nebraska, a character based on Eben Alexander,* to whom *Active Service* is dedicated. When Coleman inquires about the Wainwright party, Gordner informs him that they have recklessly gotten themselves into the predicament of being trapped behind Turkish lines at Nikopolis in Epirus and that fighting is imminent in the area. Coleman immediately resolves that he will attempt to rescue them; he is "on active service, an active service of the heart." By a delightful if implausible coincidence, he receives a cable at his hotel from the *Eclipse* ordering him to find the Wainwrights, whose disappearance has made headlines in the United States. Coleman journeys by train, steamer, and diligence to Arta and on the road confronts a disturbing portent of the horrors of war when he and his dragoman come upon a group of soldiers watching the burial of a dead Turk. Coleman, "moved by a strong, mysterious impulse, went forward to look at the poor little clay-coloured body.

At that moment a snake ran out from a tuft of grass at his feet and wriggled wildly over the sod. The dragoman shrieked, of course, but one of the soldiers put his heel upon the head of the reptile and it flung itself into the agonising knot of death.'' To Coleman, this horrible incident, interwoven with his romantic thoughts of Marjory, exemplifies the discord of life.

Coleman succeeds in attaching himself to a Greek cavalry detachment moving toward the front. Their advance is slowed by enemy resistance near Arta, and Coleman and his dragoman set off alone for Nikopolis, some thirty kilometers away. They join a battalion of infantry that flees at the report that the army advancing toward Jannina had been turned back by the Turks and that 500 Circassion cavalry reinforced by Albanian guerrillas are sweeping toward them. Stumbling through a dense forest with volleys of artillery and bullets whistling in their ears, Coleman and his dragoman are caught between two lines of the Turkish army. When they hear stealthy footsteps behind them, they are convinced that the end has come, but when challenged, the trailing group remarkably turns out to be the Wainwrights and the students, who are also fleeing the Turkish advance. The Wainwrights greet Coleman as a rescuer, and his reputation is immediately rehabilitated in the eyes of the professor, although Marjory seems curiously impassive. Coleman leads the party back toward Arta. On the road they encounter another group, among whom, by even greater and less plausible coincidence, is Nora Black, sitting ''on a fat and glossy horse . . . dressed in one of the most correct riding habits which had ever been seen in the East.'' Nora has given up her acting role and become Coleman's rival as special correspondent of the *New York Daylight* in Greece. Like Cora Crane, she endeavors to report war from the woman's point of view, but she admits that her primary motive in coming to Greece was to seek Coleman out. Back in Arta, Nora's presence disconcerts Coleman and causes dissension between him and some of the students. Mrs. Wainwright is convinced that Coleman and Nora arranged the rendevous in Greece and is outraged that he has introduced an infamous actress into Marjory's presence.

After more harrowing incidents and romantic entanglements involving Nora Black's attempts to use Coke in order to undermine Coleman's relationship with Marjory, the Wainwright party, Coleman, and Nora return to Athens. Marjory, convinced that Coleman is caught in the lures of Nora Black and no longer cares for her, goes into a deep depression. Her formerly rigid, impassive father, who now views Coleman as their rescuer and protector, feels her pain deeply. He leaves his despairing daughter, seeks Coleman out, and bluntly informs him that he retracts his opposition to the marriage. The novel ends with an idyllic scene of Coleman and Marjory resting in a secluded cove by the sea and reflecting on their happiness.

The longest novel that Crane completed, *Active Service* is generally dismissed by critics as a potboiler written when Crane was desperately short of funds. With its absurdly contrived plot, stock characterizations, and pretentious and stilted dialogue, *Active Service* often seems to verge on parody, and some critics suggest that the novel is an unsuccessful spoof of the romantic adventure fiction popular at the end of the nineteenth century, such as Kipling's *The Light That Failed* (1890) or Richard Harding Davis's* *Soldiers of Fortune* (1897). Rufus Coleman identifies with chivalric heroic prototypes. "He imagined himself in a way like them. He, too, had come out to fight for love with giants, dragons and witches." The tedious variegations of the flimsy melodramatic love plot, the prolix trivial banter of the students, and the stilted dialogue result in an unevenness of tone that overwhelms the parodic elements. *Active Service* emerges largely as an ineffectual conventional romance, a fragmented melange of disparate and unreconciled elements.

Suggested Reading

Gilkes, Lillian. "*The Third Violet, Active Service,* and *The O'Ruddy*: Stephen Crane's Potboilers." In *Stephen Crane in Transition*. Ed. Joseph Katz. De Kalb: Northern Illinois University Press, 1972. 106–26.
Knapp, Bettina. *Stephen Crane*. New York: Ungar, 1987. 109–20.
Robertson, Michael. "The Cultural Work of Active Service." *American Literary Realism 1870–1910* 28.2 (1996): 1–10.

"Adventures of a Novelist". Crane's account of his initial involvement in the Dora Clark* affair was printed in the *New York Journal* on 20 September 1896. In a prefatory statement, the *Journal* explained that Crane had been hired the previous week to write a series of studies of life in New York for the newspaper and that he "chose the police courts as his first subject." After spending a morning in the Jefferson Market Police Court, where he "observed the machinery of justice in full operation," Crane concluded that "he had seen but a kaleidoscopic view of the characters who passed rapidly before the judicial gaze of the presiding Magistrate. He must know more of that throng of unfortunates; he must study the police court victims in their haunts."

On the evening of 15 September, Crane met two chorus girls by appointment in "a Turkish Smoking Parlor" on West Twenty-ninth Street. Some time before midnight, they walked to the Broadway Garden,* a notorious resort of prostitutes, where he interviewed them. They were joined at their table by Ruby Young, better known by her street names of Dora Clark and Dora Wilkins. In "Adventures of a Novelist" Crane maintains that he "knew nothing whatever" of Dora Clark, but in a 28 August "From the Metropolis" article in the *Port Jervis Evening Gazette*, he had criticized police harassment of prostitutes and had referred obliquely to her claim of false arrest by officer Rosenberg of the Nineteenth Precinct. At 2:00 A.M. Crane left the Broadway Garden with Dora Clark and the two chorus girls. In his *Journal* article, he explains that he escorted one of the chorus girls to an uptown cable car, leaving Dora Clark and the other chorus girl in conversation at the corner of Thirty-first Street and Broadway. As he was returning to them, the young women were suddenly arrested by patrolman Charles Becker* for soliciting two passing men whom they had probably not even noticed. In terror, the chorus girl maintained that Crane was her husband, and when Crane gallantly acknowledged this, Becker released her. She and Crane followed the patrolman and his prisoner to the precinct station house, where Dora Clark was charged and incarcerated. The chorus girl became hysterical during the proceedings, and Crane escorted her home. Afterward, as he wrote in a fragmentary draft of "Adventures of a Novelist," he ruefully began to reflect on the "inopportune arrival of a moral obligation," and he returned to the police station where, against the advice of the desk sergeant, he made a statement confirming Dora Clark's innocence. That evening he told a *Journal* reporter: "I was strongly advised by Sergeant McDermott not to try to help her, for I seemed a respectable sort of man, he said, and it would injure me. I knew well that I was risking a reputation that I have worked hard to build. But . . . she was a woman and unjustly accused, and I did what was my duty as a man." In the morning, "a reluctant witness" at the Jefferson Market Police Court, he "recited what he believed to be a true accounting, and the Magistrate discharged the prisoner."

"Adventures of a Novelist" reveals that Crane did not act impulsively but was aware of the risk to his reputation that defending Dora Clark would entail: "Apparently the united wisdom of the world declared that no man should do anything but throw his sense of justice to the winds in an affair of this description. 'Let a man have a conscience for the daytime,' said wisdom. 'Let him have a conscience for the daytime, but it is idiocy for a man to have a conscience at 2:30 in the morning, in the case of an arrested prostitute.' " Indeed, Crane's involvement proved costly. Praise for his courage in New York newspapers gradually turned to insinuation and derision. At the beginning of October, Dora Clark brought charges of false arrest and prosecution against Becker and patrolman Martin Conway. When it became known that Crane intended to testify in her behalf, the police launched an investigation into his activities and especially his residence during the previous spring and summer in various houses on Twenty-second Street and Twenty-seventh Street that had reputations for opium smoking and prostitution. The seamier side of Crane's life in the Tenderloin was revealed. The *New York Journal* reported on 11 October that "the police of the Thirtieth Street Station have told the novelist that they are prepared to swear that he led a fast life among the women of the Tenderloin, and that he would be prosecuted on the charge of maintaining an opium joint in his rooms if he testified in Dora Clark's behalf against Becker." The police raided Crane's apartment and found a montage of opium-smoking paraphernalia mounted on a wall plaque, a souvenir of his widely read syndicated article, "Opium's Varied Dreams." In the hearing on the night of 15–16 October at police headquarters on Mulberry Street, Crane took the stand as a witness for the prosecution, and in the cross-examination by defense lawyer Louis Grant, his reputation was severely damaged. Grant's questions insinuated that Crane was an opium addict who lived off the earnings of prostitutes. Perhaps more important to his subsequent career, Crane had incurred the wrath of the powerful New York Police

Department, which intensified its campaign of harassment against him. His career as an investigative reporter in the city was clearly finished, and he was glad to accept the Bacheller syndicate's assignment to go to Cuba to report on the growing insurrection against Spanish rule.

Suggested Reading

Fryckstedt, Olov W. "Stephen Crane in the Tenderloin." *Studia Neophilologica* 34 (1962): 135–63.

Stallman, R. W., and E. R. Hagemann, eds. *The New York City Sketches of Stephen Crane*. New York: New York University Press, 1966. 217–63.

Wertheim, Stanley, and Paul Sorrentino. *The Crane Log: A Documentary Life of Stephen Crane*. New York: G. K. Hall, 1994. 200–19.

"Ah, haggard purse, why ope thy mouth". A comic poem, in a tradition going back to Chaucer, of the poet's lament to his empty purse. According to Corwin Knapp Linson,* who preserved the manuscript and published it in his memoir, *My Stephen Crane* (13–14), this dramatic monologue was written in December 1892 when Crane was leading an impoverished, nomadic life in New York. The purse reproaches the poet with its "empty stomach," but, he replies, "I'd sell my steps to the grave / If t'were but honestie."

Alden, Henry Mills (1836–1919). Born in Vermont, a descendant of John Alden, the Pilgrim, Alden worked as a "bobbin boy" in a cotton mill in the manufacturing town of Hoosick Falls, New York. He prepared for the ministry at Williams College and Andover Theological Seminary but was never ordained. In 1861 Alden arrived in New York City with two dollars in his pocket and went into publishing. In 1863 he assisted Alfred H. Guernsey in writing *Harper's Pictorial History of the Great Rebellion*. This began a connection with Harper and Brothers that lasted over fifty years. Alden was managing editor of *Harper's Weekly* from 1863 to 1869 and editor of *Harper's Magazine* from 1869 until his death. Under his editorship, it became the most widely circulated magazine in the United States.

William Dean Howells,* who himself had no love for free verse, could not persuade Alden to publish the poems of Crane's *The Black Riders*, but in August 1898, "The Monster," which had been rejected by *McClure's*, appeared in *Harper's New Monthly Magazine* before being published by Harper and Brothers as the lead story of a book. The thirteen stories that comprise the Harper and Brothers volume *Whilomville Stories* appeared in the magazine from August 1899 through August 1900. Crane's Bowery story "A Desertion" was published posthumously in the November 1900 issue of *Harper's*. Alden may also have played a part in the March 1898 publication of "Death and the Child" in two successive issues of *Harper's Weekly*, although the story was collected in the McClure volume, *The Open Boat and Other Tales of Adventure*.

Alexander, Eben (1851–1911). Educated at Yale, Alexander taught ancient languages there for thirteen years. In 1886 he became professor of Greek at the University of North Carolina. From 1893 through the summer of 1897, he served as envoy extraordinary and minister plenipotentiary to Greece, Romania, and Serbia. After his retirement from government service, he returned to his university position. Alexander met Stephen and Cora Crane in Athens in April 1897 and soon became one of their valued friends. His references to Cora in correspondence as "Mrs. Stewart" indicates that he knew that the Cranes were not married, but his friendship made Cora respectable in Athens. Sylvester Scovel,* a correspondent for the *New York World* in Greece, wrote to his wife on 19 May that "Lady Stewart is received by some of the most prominent people and even the Queen may receive her. How's that for the Greeks who are said to be the only moral people in this part of Europe?" Alexander appears as Thomas M. Gordner in *Active Service*, and the first American edition of the novel is dedicated to him.

Alger, Russell A. (1836–1907). Governor of Michigan and later senator from that state, commander in chief of the Grand Army of the Republic, and secretary of war during the Spanish-American War. On 25 September 1898, when Crane was very nearly incommunicado in Havana, writing only to his agent, Paul Revere Reynolds, and ignoring communications from Cora Crane and friends in England, Cora wrote and sent a cablegram to Alger expressing fears for Crane's safety. Alger passed these communications along to Major General J. F. Wade, chairman of the American Evacuation Commission, who conveyed word to Crane through Otto Carmichael,* but Crane apparently ignored Cora's entreaties.

"All feeling God, hear in the war-night". Crane's longest and most ambitious poem on war was not published in his lifetime. The typescript in the Rare Book and Manuscript Library at Columbia University bears the title "The Battle Hymn" and a notation that "the ms., of above, has just been discovered in saddle-bags used by Stephen Crane during the late war with Spain." The poem was printed for the first time by Daniel Hoffman in *The Poetry of Stephen Crane* (New York: Columbia University Press, 1957, pp. 158–162). Portentous in tone, it is uncharacteristically chauvinistic. While soldiers "grope and bleed apace" in "the forest of the lost standards," there is a Christ-like quality in their suffering and sacrifice that gives war an ethical dimension and ensures final victory for the "long blue corps."

"Along the Shark River". A bantering report in the *New York Tribune*, 15 August 1892, of activities at Avon-by-the-Sea featuring the scientific and artistic work of the Seaside Assembly's summer school. Crane writes of the summer youths and young women "who are inclined to mingle useful lessons in the arts and sciences with the pleasure and expense usually attendant upon seaside life" and the faculty and students of the assembly's School of Biology who "are constantly engaged in inspecting great glass jars filled with strange floating growths in the laboratory on the banks of Shark River."

["Americans and Beggars in Cuba"]. Untitled and unfinished, this is a dispatch from Havana reproduced from a holograph in the Rare Book and Manuscript Library of Columbia University by R. W. Stallman and E. R. Hagemann in *The War Dispatches of Stephen Crane* (New York: New York University Press, 1964, pp. 208–9). Crane wonders why five American commissioners whose health has been carefully protected have died in Cuba, while none of the correspondents, cattle dealers, and others who have lived casually, "with no regard for yellow fever or any other terror of the tropics," have succumbed. He also notes that the hordes of beggars in Havana will readily descend on any American but will rarely approach a Spanish officer.

" 'And If He Wills, We Must Die' ". This is the third in the developmental order of the Spitzbergen tales and the only one from which Lieutenant Timothy Lean is absent. The episode focuses on the annihilation of a squad of the Twelfth Infantry defending an outpost and is a good deal more grim than its predecessors, "The Kicking Twelfth" and "The Shrapnel of Their Friends." The story appeared in the *Illustrated London News* on 28 July 1900 and was collected in *Last Words*.

Sent to occupy a house on a highway in advance of any other Spitzbergen unit, Sergeant Morton and fifteen men of the Twelfth are attacked by Rostina troops they cannot see. All is confusion and disorder in the house as the men are slaughtered, and their deaths are described in horrific detail reminiscent of *The Red Badge of Courage*. A soldier shot in the throat "gurgled and then lay down on the floor. The blood slowly waved down the brown skin of his neck while he looked meekly at his comrades." The men fight so fiercely that when the enemy occupies the house, a subaltern comments that he had estimated them as at least a hundred strong. The final irony is that the sacrifice of the men in attempting to hold an indefensible position was futile. The courier sent to order them to withdraw had been killed before he could deliver his message.

"The Angel Child". Placed first in the volume of *Whilomville Stories*, although "Lynx-Hunting" was composed earlier, "The Angel Child," as well as "The Stove," in which the child Cora, her ineffectual father, and excitable mother are also featured, may be based to some extent on anecdotes Cora Crane told Stephen about her childhood. Apart from the identity of the first name, there are other parallels. Cora Ethel Howorth was an only child whose father, John Howorth, was an artist depicted in one of her stories, "The Lavender Trousers," as an unworldly dreamer with a domineering wife. "The Angel Child" appeared in the August 1899 issue of *Harper's New Monthly Magazine*.

"The Angel Child" opens with a summer visit to Whilomville by Mrs. Trescott's cousin from New York, a "quiet, slow, and misty" painter with his "quick, beautiful, imperious" wife and Cora, their "one child. Perhaps it would be better to say that they had one CHILD." On her birthday, Cora asks her father for a gift of money, and he inattentively hands her a five-dollar bill, not realizing the enormity of the sum. The imperious Cora sallies forth attended by her retinue of children from Whilomville's leading families: Jimmie Trescott, Dan and Ella Earl, the Margate twins, the three Phelps children, and others. They first visit a candy store and indulge in an orgy that leaves them somewhat ill and then proceed to William Neeltje's barbershop, where they all, except Dan Earl, who refuses, have their long hair, fashionable for boys and girls alike at this time, shorn by the barber. Cora's haircut is a satiric rape of the lock, as "To the floor there fell proud ringlets, blazing even there in their humiliation with a full fine bronze light." The children leave the barbershop elated, and only Ella Earl realizes the probable consequences of what they have done and begins to weep while "William Neeltje stood watching them, upon his face a grin of almost inhuman idiocy." The mothers of the children are outraged when they see the results of Neeltje's efforts, but Eldridge Margate, grandfather of the twins, comments that he would "rather see boys look more like boys than like two little wax figgers," and Dr. Trescott, "composed and cool-blooded," acts as a steadying influence on the hysterical women. A few days later, the angel child's mother, trailed by her bewildered husband, leads Cora to the railroad station, cutting short their vacation in Whilomville.

Arbutus Cottage. The house on Fourth Avenue in Asbury Park, New Jersey, where Crane lived with his family at various times from the spring of 1883 until a few months after the death of his mother in December 1891. Arbutus shrubs may still be found growing in the front yard of the cottage.

The Arena. See Flower, Benjamin Orange.

"Artillery Duel Was Fiercely Fought on Both Sides". On 1 July 1898, the opening day of the Battle of San Juan, Crane climbed to the vantage point of El Pozo, where he could observe the attack of General Lawton's troops on El Caney and the shelling of the Spanish trenches by American artillery. In this dispatch, published in the *New York World* on 3 July, he comments on the advance of American troops toward Santiago and two fierce exchanges of artillery fire between the battery commanded by Captain George S. Grimes and Spanish gunners entrenched in the San Juan hills. Grimes's part in the engagement is described more fully in Crane's longer report, "Stephen Crane's Vivid Story of the Battle of San Juan."

"Art in Kansas City". An uncompleted jeu d'esprit that was not published in Crane's lifetime, "Art in Kansas City" was, along with "The Camel," intended as part of a series of tall tales featuring a character named Uncle Clarence. In this sketch, Uncle Clarence relates the story of a cow he "met" in Kansas City that painted remarkably well in watercolors. Her owner squelched her aspirations for a career because "people were beginning to complain that her milk was thin. He would, he said, allow her to paint in oils but for this she had no fancy. This man was a singularly evil person and I believe his sole object in prohibiting his cow to sketch in water-colours was to deliver a stunning blow to the progress of art in Kansas City." The burlesque quality of this sketch seems to date it as an early composition, but it may have been written on Crane's trip to the West in January 1895 when he passed through Kansas City on his way to Nebraska or even later. In either event, Crane seems to be satirizing the quality of artistic production in the American heartland. "Art in Kansas City" was first published by R. W. Stallman in "New Short Fiction by Stephen Crane: II," *Studies in Short Fiction* 1 (1964): 147–52.

Suggested Reading

Katz, Joseph. " 'Art in Kansas City': A New 'Uncle Clarence' Story." *Stephen Crane Newsletter* 2.1 (1967): 3–6.

["The Art Students' League Building"]. This untitled sketch in Crane's notebook in the Alderman Library of the University of Virginia was unpublished in Crane's lifetime and was first printed from the manuscript by R. W. Stallman in the *Bulletin of the New York Public Library* 60 (1956): 457–59. It briefly describes the life of young artists in the rambling building that extended from 143 to 147 East Twenty-third Street before and after the Art Students League moved to its new location in the American Fine Arts Society building at 215 West Fifty-seventh Street in October 1892. Crane used the setting of the old building in "The Silver Pageant," "Stories Told by an Artist," and *The Third Violet*. In "The Art Students' League Building" Crane depicts the interior of the structure, "a place of slumberous corridors rambling in puzzling turns and curves," and the spirited escapades of its inhabitants. The inscription carved on an old beam "in the topmost and remotest studio" that Crane ascribes to Ralph Waldo Emerson, "Congratulate yourselves if you have done something strange and extravagant and broken the monotony of a decorous age," is not found in Emerson's works.

Crane moved into the old Art Students League building in the fall of 1893 and shared a small studio with Nelson Greene,* R. G. Vosburgh,* and William W. Carroll.* Frederick C. Gordon,* who drew the original design for the covers of *The Black Riders*, had a large, well-lighted studio on the flight above, and David Ericson* also lived in the building. In their reminiscences, Greene and Vosburgh recall how three of the men took turns sleeping in the one large bed of the studio, while the fourth slept on a cot. They pooled their resources of food and clothing and, according to Vosburgh, "the first man up was usually the best dressed for the day, unless one of them had a particular reason for wishing to present a good appearance." Humorously describing the life of the artist group, Crane told Hamlin Garland*: "We eat off the floor and paint on towels and wrapping paper." He continued to share studios in the building intermittently until the spring of 1895. Nelson Greene recalled that when Crane stayed there briefly after his return from Mexico, "[t]he studio was an evening hang out for the bunch, with beer, soft drinks, cigarettes and tobacco always on hand. Politics, religion, art, literature, music, social patterns were all discussed and Crane and I were the 'radicals' and we had opinions on everything."

Suggested Reading

Greene, Nelson. "I Knew Stephen Crane." In Stanley Wertheim, "Stephen Crane Remembered." *Studies in American Fiction* 4 (1976): 45–64.
Stallman, Robert, and E. R. Hagemann, eds. *The New York City Sketches of Stephen Crane.* New York: New York University Press, 1966. 14–16.
Vosburgh, R. G. "The Darkest Hour in the Life of Stephen Crane." *Criterion*, n.s. 1 (February 1901): 26–27.

"Asbury Park As Seen by Stephen Crane". Crane's last article on the subject of Asbury Park was printed in the *New York Journal* on 16 August 1896 on a page devoted to news of summer resorts. From the perspective of a newspaperman in search of unusual and entertaining topics, Crane laments the fact that Asbury Park is so conventional a town that it offers no opportunity for sensational journalism. With the exception of its prohibition law and "numerous other laws that prevent people from doing those things which philosophers and economists commonly agree work for the harm of society," Asbury Park is a sane and commonplace summer resort. As in "On the Boardwalk" and some of his earlier Asbury Park reports, Crane cannot resist some sarcastic reflections on founder James A. Bradley,* especially his penchant for decorating the Asbury Park boardwalk with signs expressing moral apothegms. When he is not to be seen on the streets of the town, the natives often imagine that Bradley is in his library, "flying through tome after tome of ancient lore in chase of those beautiful expressions which add so particularly to the effect of the Atlantic."

"Asbury's New Move". Melvin Scholberlin, in his unpublished Crane biography "Flagon of Despair" (George Arents Research Library, Syracuse University), attributes this short sketch, appearing in the *Philadelphia Press* on 12 July 1887, to Crane on the basis of internal evidence. The anecdote in which a Superintendent Snedeker, a kind of beach policeman, breaks up a romantic interlude involving a young couple on the beach at Asbury Park contains impressionistic touches and some sharp ironic contrasts but lacks the essential attributes of Crane's later style. If authored by Crane, it is one of his first known published works, written when he was only fifteen, but Schoberlin attributes an even earlier piece to Crane, "The Summer Tramp," which appeared in an Asbury Park newspaper, the *Daily Spray*, on 20 June 1887.

The Assassin. An otherwise unnamed Bowery derelict in "An Experiment in Misery" who guides the young man to a seven-cent flophouse where they spend the night. The assassin is a habitual tramp who incessantly blames others for his downtrodden condition. In "The Men in the Storm," Crane contrasts such men with those temporarily down on their luck through circumstances beyond their control.

"At Clancy's Wake". A short, satiric playlet first published in the humor magazine *Truth** on 3 July 1893 and collected in *Last Words*. "At Clancy's Wake" is a dated period piece replete with Irish ethnic stereotypes and an overuse of linguistic features that Crane conceived of as being characteristic of Irish-American speech. The playlet consists of a dialogue at Mike Clancy's wake between his widow, intent on singing the praises of her late husband, a recently deceased ward heeler, and Mr. Slick, a reporter for the "Daily Blanket," who is attempting to garner the mundane facts of Clancy's life for an obituary. Mrs. Clancy is drinking heavily, and at her urging the reporter drinks along with her until he is so intoxicated and confused that he cannot recall "who the blazesh is dead here, anyhow?"

"At the Pit Door". A late sketch published posthumously in the September 1900 issue of the *Philistine,** "At the Pit Door" is reminiscent of "The Men in the Storm" in its depiction of a line of people two abreast waiting to enter a building. This structure is a London theater rather than a New York shelter, and the crowd of ticket holders is bored rather than desperate. Street entertainers seek to earn a few pence by amusing the indifferent queue. There is a girl with a guitar, a contortionist, a "melancholy youth" who whistles, and a group of minstrels in blackface. All are clearly needy, and the contortionist reminds the crowd that "a man's got his livin' to make, altho p'raps we may 'ave different ways of doing it." In contrast to "The Men in the Storm," the lighthearted tone of this sketch obviates any serious social implications.

Atkins, Billie. In "Billie Atkins Went to Omaha," he is Crane's satirical depiction of the archetypal American hobo, an impulsive drifter and raconteur who when drunk "tells a tale with indescribable gestures and humorous emotions that makes one feel that, after all, the buffets of fate are rather more comic than otherwise."

"The Auction". A sketch written in 1896 with an indeterminate setting suggestive of New York City, "The Auction" was first published in the "Midnight Sketches" section of the English edition of *The Open Boat*. It is an unsuccessful admixture of pathos and irony dealing with the public sale of the furniture and household goods of a retired sea captain named Jim Ferguson and his wife, who have become bankrupt by his alcoholism. The auction is interrupted by the chatter of their parrot. The parrot's banter causes wild hilarity among the bidders, and for the aged couple "the sale of their home—this financial calamity lost its power in the presence of the social shame contained in a crowd's laughter."

The Authors Club. Founded in 1882 when New York City was displacing Boston as the literary center of America, the Authors Club was organized to bring writers together on a social rather than a professional basis. Membership was restricted to authors of a separately published literary work or a book pertaining to literature. Among the members were Irving Bacheller,* Edward Bellamy, George W. Cable, Eugene Field, Harold Frederic,* Thomas Wentworth Higginson,* William Dean Howells,* Theodore Roosevelt,* and Mark Twain. The club had no house of its own but rented rooms at various locations in the city. At the time Crane became a member in March 1896, the Authors Club was located in a suite donated by Andrew Carnegie on Seventh Avenue between Fifty-sixth and Fifty-seventh Streets. The club's first significant publication, *Liber Scriptorum* (1893), was an elaborate miscellany made up of contributions from each member autographed in pen and ink. A second *Liber Scriptorum* was issued in 1921. Crane was nominated for membership by Howells at the request of Ripley Hitchcock.* He was pleased with this honor and gratefully accepted, but since he left New York permanently in November, he was not active in club activities.

Suggested Reading

Osborne, Duffield. *The Authors Club: An Historical Sketch.* New York: Knickerbocker Press, 1913.

"Avon Seaside Assembly". A short, unsigned report in the *New York Tribune* on 28 July 1890 that may have been authored by Crane of activities and lectures in art, oratory, elocution, and other subjects at the Seaside Assembly and the opening of institutes in music and Christian philosophy in Avon-by-the-Sea. This report mentions a course of lectures by Dr. H. C. Hovey, a prominent cave explorer whose adventures at Mammoth Cave in Kentucky are recounted in Crane's "Across the Covered Pit."

"Avon's School by the Sea". The ironic tenor as well as the subject matter of this unsigned report in the *New York Tribune* on 4 August 1890 about courses given in the Seaside Assembly's summer school at Avon on the New Jersey coast makes Crane's authorship likely. The guests at boardinghouses and hotels can recognize the members of the American Institute of Christian Philosophy "by a certain wise, grave and reverend air that hangs over them from the top of their glossy silk hats to their equally glossy boots. A member gazes at the wild tossing of the waves with a calm air of understanding and philosophy that the poor youthful graduate from college, with only a silk sash and flannel suit to assert his knowledge with, can never hope to acquire." The report contains a paragraph about the tenor Albert G. Thies, whose performance before Chief Cetewayo, the "king" of the Zulus, is the subject of Crane's later sketch, "The King's Favor," in the Syracuse *University Herald* for May 1891.

B

Bacheller, Irving (1859–1950). After graduating from St. Lawrence University, Bacheller worked for a time on a hotel trade journal before joining the staff of the *Brooklyn Daily Times*. In 1883–84, with James W. Johnson, he formed a press syndicate to supply special articles to newspapers and magazines. The firm grew rapidly, and sold fiction and feature articles to most of the metropolitan newspapers in the United States. Besides Stephen Crane, Bacheller introduced Arthur Conan Doyle and Rudyard Kipling to the American reading public. He also supplied material by other contemporary writers, notably Joseph Conrad,* Hamlin Garland,* and Anthony Hope. In 1896 Bacheller sold his syndicate to John Brisben Walker, the owner of *Cosmopolitan*. From 1898 to 1900 he was Sunday editor of the *New York World*. Bacheller wrote many short stories, poems, and essays and more than thirty novels, the most popular of which, *Eben Holden*, a romantic story of pioneers in the St. Lawrence Valley, sold almost a million copies.

Bacheller was one of Crane's personal friends and the most important promoter of his literary career immediately preceding and following the publication of *The Red Badge of Courage*. They first met in October 1894 when Crane brought the manuscript of the war novel to Bacheller for publication in his newspaper syndicate, after it had lain neglected in the offices of S. S. McClure for six months. Bacheller recalls that he and his wife read the manuscript and "were thrilled by its power and vividness." He arranged to publish a condensed and truncated version of the novel in the syndicate's new "Six Day Serial Service," and *The Red Badge* was serialized in a number of newspapers in early December. John Berryman and others have estimated that the novel appeared in some 750 newspapers, but since fewer than ten printings have been observed, this seems unlikely.

Bacheller also took on other work by Crane. In late January 1895, Crane left on an extensive tour of the West and Mexico to write feature articles for the Bacheller syndicate. In the course of his travels and afterward, he wrote sketches of life in Nebraska; Hot Springs, Arkansas; New Orleans; Galveston and San Antonio, Texas; and Mexico City. More consequential to his literary career, he absorbed the geographic and social background for his important Western short stories. On his return to New York City in mid-May, Crane joined the Lantern Club* on William Street, of which Bacheller was the perpetual president. During 1895–96, Bacheller syndicated a number of Crane's sketches and also several short stories, including, among others, "The Pace of Youth," "One Dash— Horses," "A Mystery of Heroism," "An Indiana Campaign," "A Gray Sleeve," "The Snake," "A Tale of Mere Chance," "A Freight Car Incident," and "A Detail." In November 1896, realizing that his defense of Dora Clark* against the New York police establishment had destroyed his career as an investigative reporter in the city, Crane accepted a commission from the Bacheller syndicate to report on the rebellion in Cuba. Crane did not reach Cuba, and in the wreck of the *Commodore* he purportedly jettisoned the chamois-skin belt containing $700 in Spanish gold that Bacheller had given him. In his memoirs, Bacheller accepted Crane's version of how the belt was lost and expressed regret that he could not finance another attempt to get Crane to Cuba. Since Bacheller was giving up his syndicate, they had no further professional relationship following this incident.

Suggested Reading

Bacheller, Irving. *Coming Up the Road*. Indianapolis: Bobbs-Merrill, 1928. 276–79, 292–
    93.
———. *From Stores of Memory*. New York: Farrar and Rinehart, 1933. 110–12.
Katz, Joseph. "Stephen Crane and Irving Bacheller's Gold." *Stephen Crane Newsletter*
    5.1 (1970): 4–5.

Bainbridge. In "The Monster" he is a railway engineer who patronizes Reifsnyder's barbershop and comments on the social implications of Henry Johnson's facelessness.

"Ballydehob". This travel sketch, the second in a series of "Irish Notes," appeared in the *Westminster Gazette* on 22 October 1897 and was collected in *Last Words*. Crane pictures a poor Irish country village with no tourist attractions. Ballydehob has three hundred inhabitants and four constables. In Ireland, Crane sardonically observes, innkeepers die young since they tend to freely imbibe their own wares, but they leave widows capable of running the business. The Irish are so versatile a people that an unschooled Ballydehob farmer nursing his tupenny glass of stout at a pub may have highly sophisticated opinions on political conditions in remote parts of the world and at the same time be convinced "that a hair from a horse's tail when thrown in a brook would turn shortly to an eel."

Barr, Mark (1871–1950). Born in Pennsylvania but a British subject, Barr became assistant editor of *Electrical World* in 1891. In 1895 he received a degree in physics and mathematics from London University and became a frequent contributor of scientific articles to professional journals. His special interest was in electrical calculating machinery. Barr and his wife, Mabel, were occasional visitors to Brede Place* in 1899. Mabel Barr was the niece of Harold Frederic's* mistress, Kate Lyon,* and the elder sister of Edith Richie Jones.* Like his sister-in-law, Barr also slept in the haunted room at Brede Place and found that the mysterious swinging open of the door was caused by a defective latch, which he repaired, and the ghost walked no more.

Suggested Reading

Barr, Mark. "The Haunted House of Brede." In Stanley Wertheim. "Stephen Crane Remembered." *Studies in American Fiction* 4 (1976): 45–64.

Barr, Robert (1850–1912). Born in Glasgow, Scotland, novelist Robert Barr emigrated to Canada with his parents in childhood and was educated in a normal school in Ontario. Until 1876 he worked as a teacher. After that he was an editorial writer for the *Detroit Free Press* and contributed humorous sketches to the newspaper under the name Luke Sharp. Barr moved to London in 1881. With Jerome K. Jerome, he founded the popular monthly, the *Idler*. Barr was associated with the magazine until his death but subordinated his editorial work to writing fiction. He contributed many short stories to English and American magazines and was the author of numerous collections of stories and romantic historical novels, notably *From Whose Bourne* (1893), *The Triumphs of Eugene Valmont* (1896), *Tekla: A Romance of Love and War* (1898), *The Woman Wins* (1904), and *The Watermead Affair* (1906). Barr was a clubman and raconteur; among his friends were Arthur Conan Doyle, Harold Frederic,* and Rider Haggard.*

Barr and Crane met shortly after Stephen and Cora settled at Ravensbrook,* Surrey, in June 1897 near Barr's home, perched on a steep hill in Woldingham and appropriately named Hillhead. Harold Frederic lived nearby at Kenley, and the three writers and their families formed a convivial group, sometimes joined by Joseph and Jessie Conrad.* When Crane disappeared into Havana in the summer of 1898, Cora turned to Barr for help. Through James Creelman,* the *Journal*'s representative in London, Barr tried to make certain that Cora's messages were forwarded to Crane, and he attempted to obtain passage with deferred payment for her to New York from various shipping lines. In an 8 April 1899 *Saturday Evening Post* article, "American Brains in London," Barr called Crane "probably the greatest genius America has produced since Edgar Allan Poe, to whom, I fancy, he bears some resemblance." Barr gave Crane much needed advice in his dealings with publishers, especially Frederick A. Stokes. He contributed a long satirical poem to the composition of "The Ghost," although he did not attend the sole performance of the farce in Brede village or Crane's house party at the end of December 1899. On 19 May 1900, accompanied by Stewart Edward White, Barr paid a last visit to Crane in the Lord Warden Hotel at Dover, where Crane was resting preparatory to taking a steamer to Calais on what would be his final journey to the Black Forest. Barr read the manuscript of *The O'Ruddy*, and he and Crane discussed the completion of the novel. Barr promised that he would finish *The O'Ruddy*, but after Crane's death he developed reservations, and it was not until 1903 that he agreed to write the last eight chapters. An abridged version of *The O'Ruddy* appeared in the *Idler* before the book was published in England.

Suggested Reading

Barr, Robert. "American Brains in London." *Saturday Evening Post* 8 April 1899: 648–
      49.

Barry, John D. (1866–1942). Born in Boston, Barry was graduated from Harvard in 1888. He served a journalistic apprenticeship, holding editorial positions on the *Forum* and other magazines. For some time he was drama critic for *Harper's Weekly* and later for *Collier's*. Barry wrote novels and plays and was an instructor in the American Academy of Dramatic Arts. From 1910 until his death, he wrote daily columns on social and literary topics for San Francisco newspapers.

      Barry took an early interest in Crane's literary career. At the suggestion of Hamlin Garland,* Crane sent him a copy of *Maggie* soon after its publication, and Barry responded with a frank letter deprecating the novel as "morbid" and "unhealthful." He was more receptive to Crane's poetry. On 14 April 1894 Barry read some of the poems that would comprise *The Black Riders* in front of the Uncut Leaves Society at Sherry's since Crane was averse to public speaking and refused to read them himself. Barry believed that Crane's poetry had been inspired by Emily Dickinson, whose verses, Barry maintained, had been read to him by William Dean Howells.* Barry found a publisher for Crane's poems in Copeland & Day. Barry's 9 January 1896 column in the *Literary World* somewhat unjustly reproached American critics for being slower than the English to recognize Crane's talent. In the 12 November 1896 issue of the *Daily Tattler*, Barry defended *George's Mother* against detractors, but in 1898 he found Crane's Cuban war reporting in the *New York World* "insignificant, at times almost puerile."

Suggested Reading

Barry, John D. "A Note on Stephen Crane." *Bookman* 13 (April 1901): 148.

"Baseball". This unsigned report on the opening games of the baseball season at Claverack College* in the May 1890 issue of the school magazine, *Vidette*,* has been attributed to Crane on the basis of scant stylistic evidence. Witty profiles of "[t]he village dominie" and "the sedate President," whose customary reserve thaws by their absorption in the game, resemble some of Crane's Asbury Park vignettes, but the authorship of this piece is uncertain. Of biographical interest is the statement that "Crane, catcher, was tendered the office of captain, but declining, Jones, 1st base, was elected captain."

Bass, John (1866–1931). A graduate of Harvard College and Harvard Law School, Bass was bureau chief of the *New York Journal* staff during the Greek-Turkish War of 1897. In 1898 he covered the Spanish-American War for *Harper's Weekly* from Manila. He also served as a correspondent in China during the Boxer insurrection, in the Russian-Japanese War, and in World War I. On 30 April 1897, Bass accompanied Stephen and Cora Crane and Richard Harding Davis,* representing the *Times* of London, on a journey from Athens to the sector of combat in Thessaly. On 4 May, Davis and Bass witnessed the first day of fighting at Velestino, the only appreciable military action of the war. Crane, who was ill, saw only the second day of the battle. In a report headed "How Novelist Crane Acts on the Battlefield," printed in the *Journal* on 23 May, Bass narrates that he followed Crane up a steep hill at Velestino to observe how he would act in a real battle. Crane seated himself on an ammunition box "amid a shower of shells" near where the Greek artillery was shelling the Turkish infantry on the plain below "and casually lighted a cigarette." To Bass's question of what impressed him most about the action, Crane responded that it was "the mental attitude of the men." That Crane had sat on an ammunition box with a lighted cigarette while under fire had been previously reported in the *Chicago Post* on 13 May, but the *Post* reporter was less admiring than Bass and commented that Crane apparently "aspired to the championship of inspired idiocy."

"Battalion Notes". A periodic and usually unsigned feature of the *Vidette*,* the student magazine at Claverack College and Hudson River Institute.* The "Battalion Notes" column in the June 1890 issue of the magazine, signed by Crane, includes a description of Memorial Day ceremonies at the school that anticipates his sentimental Memorial Day piece editorially titled "The Gratitude of a Nation" and also a "Special Order" that lists promotions, among them "1st Lieut. Crane, promoted to Captain."

Suggested Reading

Wertheim, Stanley. "Stephen Crane's 'Battalion Notes.'" *Resources for American Literary Study* 6 (1976): 79–80.

"The Battle of Forty Fort". This is the first in chronological order, and probably in order of composition, of Crane's stories set in the Wyoming Valley of Pennsylvania during the Revolutionary War. "The Battle of Forty Fort" appeared in the May 1901 issue of *Cassell's Magazine* and was collected in *Last Words*. The story, based on the Reverend George Peck's *Wyoming*, recounts the

battle between three hundred Continental troops and militia under the command
of Colonel Zebulon Butler and four hundred British troops and Tories with five
hundred of their Indian allies commanded by Colonel John ("Indian") Butler.
It is narrated by Solomon Bennet, the son of John Bennet ("Ol' Bennet"), who
is featured in the series. Solomon relates that at Forty Fort there was friction
between the Continental officers, who wanted to pursue a defensive policy, and
the militia officers, who wanted to attack the enemy at the head of the valley.
On 3 July 1778 the three hundred Continental and militia troops marched out
to meet the enemy. When their left flank collapsed, the Continental regulars held
their ground and were massacred, but the settlers of the militia, Solomon among
them, ran away. Solomon lacks the introspective nature of Henry Fleming of
The Red Badge. He feels no guilt about having run from the enemy, being
convinced that "[i]n my running was wisdom." He is ashamed when he is
forced to tell his father of the defeat, but John Bennet's only reaction is a laconic
statement that he had expected it.

"Bear and Panther". A short Sullivan County hunting sketch printed in the
New York Tribune on 17 July 1892, "Bear and Panther" recounts a story told
by the older inhabitants of the area about a naturalistic struggle to the death
observed by two young hunters between a female panther and a bear that had
entered the panther's den and killed two of her kittens. The panther "sprang
upon the bear, buried her teeth in his throat, and with her powerful claws tore
out his entrails." The hunters then complete the cycle of survival of the fittest
by shooting the panther.

Becker, Charles (1870–1915). As a patrolman assigned to the Nineteenth Pre-
cinct in New York City's Tenderloin district, Becker arrested two women in
Crane's company, Dora Clark* and a chorus girl, for soliciting on the corner of
Thirty-first Street and Broadway in the early morning of 16 September 1896.
He released the chorus girl when Crane gallantly confirmed her claim that she
was his wife, but Dora Clark was charged. This event and its immediate consequences are recounted in Crane's "Adventures of a Novelist." Like Crane,
Becker spent much of his youth in Sullivan County, New York, where he was
born. After working at a series of odd jobs, he became a New York City patrolman in November 1893. In his early days on the force, he modeled his career
on that of Alexander "Clubber" Williams, who gave the Tenderloin its name,
and he thrived in the district's environment of graft and corruption. Becker's
charges against Dora Clark were dismissed after Crane testified in her defense,
and she subsequently filed charges of false arrest against the patrolman. At the
trial on 15–16 October 1896, Becker was exonerated of any offense except
possibly being overly zealous in the performance of his duty. He was promoted
to sergeant in 1907, and a year or two later, when the Police Department was
reorganized, he automatically became a lieutenant. On 30 July 1915 Becker
became the first policeman to be executed in the electric chair at Sing Sing

prison for conspiracy in the murder of his gambling partner, Herman Rosenthal, in front of the Hotel Metropole on the north side of Forty-third Street near Broadway on 15 July 1912. The incident is alluded to in *The Great Gatsby* when Meyer Wolfsheim reminisces about the shooting of Rosenthal. "Four of them were electrocuted," Nick Carraway recalls. "Five," replies Wolsheim, "with Becker."

Suggested Reading

Logan, Andy. *Against the Evidence: The Becker-Rosenthal Affair.* New York: McCall, 1970.

Beer, Thomas (1889?–1940). In his lifetime Crane's first biographer, Thomas Beer, was known primarily as a novelist and a writer of short stories in the *Saturday Evening Post*. Transcending the obscurity into which his literary works have fallen today are his three brilliantly iconoclastic studies of American civilization in the 1890s: *Stephen Crane: A Study in American Letters* (1923), *The Mauve Decade: American Life at the End of the Nineteenth Century* (1926), and *Hanna* (1929), an impressionistic study of William McKinley's presidential campaign manager, Mark Hanna. From the beginning, critics understood that these works contained fictional elements, and subsequent Crane biographers routinely expressed their doubts about Beer's reliability, but they nevertheless continued to treat him as a credible source. Only recently, following the discovery of typescript drafts of *Stephen Crane: A Study in American Letters*, has it been determined that Beer fabricated most of the letters from Crane and other writers and many of the incidents in the book and most likely in the articles he wrote about Stephen and Cora Crane as well. The problem is serious and pervasive because Beer's spurious information has been incorporated in much subsequent Crane biography and criticism, and often its origin has been overlooked or forgotten. Beer interviewed and corresponded with a number of people who knew Crane, but in the absence of documentation it is impossible to determine to what extent he may have elaborated or even invented material. *Stephen Crane: A Study in American Letters* must be considered as essentially a biographical novel; no letters or incidents involving Crane or other authors that derive from Beer's writings should be cited or quoted unless they can be substantiated by more trustworthy sources.

Suggested Reading

Clendenning, John. "Thomas Beer's *Stephen Crane*: The Eye of His Imagination." *Prose Studies* 14 (1991): 68–80.
———. "Stephen Crane and His Biographers: Beer, Berryman, Schoberlin, and Stallman." *American Literary Realism 1870–1910* 28.1 (1995): 23–57.
Wertheim, Stanley, and Paul Sorrentino. "Thomas Beer: The Clay Feet of Stephen Crane Biography." *American Literary Realism 1870–1910* 22.3 (1990): 2–16.

Belasco, David (1853–1931). An actor, dramatist, and producer, Belasco began his career in San Francisco. From 1882 to 1886 he was stage manager of the Madison Square Theater in New York. In March 1900, at the Herald Square Theater, he presented his one-act play, *Madame Butterfly*, adapted from a story by John Luther Long. The play later became famous in Puccini's opera. Belasco wrote many successful melodramas based on his nostalgic memories of California, notably *The Girl of the Golden West* (1905). In 1907 he opened his own theater on Fifty-fourth Street. Belasco contemplated producing Crane's *The O'Ruddy* as a play before it appeared as a novel, although he later insisted that book publication should come first. He also considered dramatizing *The Red Badge of Courage*, but largely because of Cora Crane's vacillations, neither project was carried through to completion.

Suggested Reading

Belasco David. "The Genius of Stephen Crane." *Metropolitan Magazine* 12 (1900): 666.

Bennet, John. Called "Ol' Bennet" by the Indians, John Bennet is the focal character of the Wyoming Valley tales. He is modeled on Thomas Bennet, Stephen Crane's maternal great-great-grandfather. Crane inexplicably changes Thomas's name to John in the stories but preserves the actual names of the other historical characters. Thomas Bennet was one of forty settlers from New England who in 1769 built a fort on the west bank of the Susquehanna River in the Wyoming Valley of Pennsylvania near Wilkes-Barre. The town they established was named Forty Fort in honor of the original settlers.

Bennet, Solomon. The narrator of the Wyoming Valley tales who recounts his own exploits and those of his father, John Bennet.

Bennett, (Arnold) Henry Sanford (1868–1927). While Crane's letters to Bennett are among the most interesting to be found in his correspondence, especially in their references to Ford Madox Ford,* Joseph Conrad,* Mrs. Humphry Ward, and Oscar Wilde, Bennett's very existence remains somewhat problematic. The reason for this anomaly is that anecdotes about him and letters to and from him may be found only in Thomas Beer's* fictionalized Crane biography, *Stephen Crane: A Study in American Letters* (1923), and in his most likely equally spurious periodical publications or in typescripts in Beer's papers in the Sterling Library at Yale University. Considering recent investigations into Beer's fabrications, this circumstance casts doubt on their authenticity. Beer's article "Mrs. Stephen Crane," in the March 1934 issue of the *American Mercury*, also contains excerpts from letters ostensibly written by Cora Crane to Bennett. According to Beer, Harold Frederic* introduced Crane to Bennett. He was a Canadian who spoke French and guided Crane around Paris in early April 1897, when they were both on their way to Greece. Beer described Bennett as a Canadian gentlemen of whom Crane wrote, "Destiny sets an alarm clock so as to be up early and strew banana peels in front of him. If he trusts a friend, he is betrayed. If he starts a journey, he breaks an ankle. If he loves, death comes to her without a smile." His first wife killed herself, for the same reasons as Lucretia. In 1896 he married a charming Frenchwoman who died of puerperal fever in December, 1899. His only son was killed in battle in 1918. In 1925 Mr. Bennett was injured in a motor accident and spent the last two years of his life blind and bedridden. He was so shy that he dropped the name Arnold after the popularity of Arnold Bennett began.

Benson. The third "Kid" in "The Five White Mice" and "The Wise Men," Benson is the odd man out in both stories. In "The Five White Mice," he jostles one of the Mexican pedestrians and provokes the altercation that might have ended fatally if not for the resourcefulness of the New York Kid. In "The Wise Men," Benson doubts the sound judgment of the other two Kids that Pop could outrun Freddie in a foot race and loses his money when he bets on Freddie.

Bierce, Ambrose (1842–1914?). *See* Davis, Robert H.

Bigelow, Poultney (1855–1954). A journalist, author, sportsman, and socialite, Bigelow was the oldest living graduate of Yale when he died at the age of ninety-eight. He was the author of many books of diplomatic and political history, including *White Man's Africa* (1898), *Prussianism and Pacifism* (1919), and *Japan and Her Colonies* (1923). Bigelow and Crane may have met as fellow members of the Authors Club* in New York City in 1896 or as correspondents in Cuba in 1898 when Crane was on the staff of Pulitzer's *New York World* and Bigelow was a correspondent for the *New York Herald* and the *Times* of London. In 1899–1900 Bigelow and his novelist wife, Edith Evelyn, occasionally visited the Cranes at Brede Place.* Cora and Edith Bigelow were members of the Society of American Women in London,* and Crane and Bigelow wrote of their Cuban War experience in consecutive numbers of Lady Randolph Churchill's *Anglo-Saxon Review*. After Crane's death Bigelow engaged his own literary agents, G. H. Perris* in London and John Russell Davidson in New York, to help Cora in publishing Stephen's posthumous work and her own literary efforts. Cora developed an infatuation for Bigelow that was not reciprocated.

Suggested Reading

Wertheim, Stanley. "Cora Crane's Thwarted Romance." *Columbia Library Columns* 36.1 (1986): 26–37.

Big Watson. The cowboy in "Twelve O'Clock" who shoots Placer, the owner of the town's hotel, to death when he attempts to stop a gunfight between Watson and another cowboy.

Bill. The sheepherder protagonist of "A Man and Some Others" (the cowboy in "The Blue Hotel" and a number of other characters in Crane's short stories are also named Bill or Billie) anticipates the Hemingway hero in his foolish but heroic resolution to defend his integrity in the face of inevitable defeat. Bill must either fight or yield his right to common pastureland, and he preserves his manhood but not his life in a brave stand against eight Mexicans who want him off the range.

"Billie Atkins Went to Omaha". Published under this title in the *New York Press* on 20 May 1894 and retitled "An Excursion Ticket" by Crane when he mounted the press clippings for possible book publication, this story remained uncollected in Crane's lifetime. With "A Christmas Dinner Won in Battle," it is one of two Crane stories with Western settings written before his experience of travel to the West for the Bacheller syndicate in early 1895. "Billie Atkins Went to Omaha" is a compulsive Bowery tramp's recounting of his journey on a succession of freight trains from Denver to Omaha. The story seems pointless, and the humor falls flat. Billie boards freight trains and is thrown off them by a number of brakemen, but he is insistent on reaching Omaha and finally succeeds. Finding no place to sleep but a jail, he expresses "a new desire, a sudden born longing. 'Hully mack'rel. I mus' start back fer Denver in th' mornin'.' "

Binks, Phil. The main character in "Mr. Binks' Day Off." Binks is a harried New Yorker who finds a disquieting sense of dread amid the serenity of nature on a day's excursion to the country.

"Biology at Avon-by-the-Sea". A short, unsigned article in the *New York Tribune* on 19 July 1891, probably written by Crane, about the recently opened school of biology at Avon's Seaside Assembly. The report mentions faculty members prominent in their fields, the modern building that houses the school, the library, and other facilities.

"A Birthday Word from Novelist Stephen Crane". A note reproduced in facsimile on page 14 of the 8 November 1896 edition of the *New York Journal*. The page is devoted to congratulatory messages from contributing authors and illustrators on the first anniversary of William Randolph Hearst's acquisition of the newspaper. Crane was a regular contributor of feature articles on a variety of subjects in the *Journal* during 1896. His note consists of a single sentence above his signature: "It is a condition of most of us who are in journalism that we do not know how to define it because your newspaper seems to change and advance each day."

"The Black Dog". Printed in the *New York Tribune* on 24 July 1892, "The Black Dog," subtitled "A Night of Spectral Terror" in its newspaper appearance, has been seen as a parody of Edgar Allan Poe or Ambrose Bierce. Parody is suggested by Crane's double vision in this tale, intermingling humor and terror, a typical rhetorical device in the Sullivan County stories. In "The Black Dog," the four men featured in these tales are lost in the wilds on a stormy night. The little man, determined to find shelter, leads his companions to a cabin in the thickets where they confront a "slate-colored man" dressed in rags who, without further introduction, informs them that his old uncle, Jim Crocker, is "sick ter death" but is unlikely to die until a black dog, a "sperrit" who howls when people in that area are on the verge of death, has appeared. By coincidence (or perhaps not), a starving, mangy dog abandoned by his master smells a beef concoction that the slate-colored man has cooked for his sick uncle and bounds toward the cabin, where he sits howling before the door. As the old man shrieks in terror, the four men and the nephew charge into his room. The little man opens the window and throws utensils and the beef mixture though the window, and the eerie wail of the supposed phantom ceases as he happily consumes the food. The story ends with an admixture of horror and ironic humor: "On the bed, the old man lay dead. Without, the spectre was wagging its tail."

Black, Nora. The Victorian counter-heroine of *Active Service*, Nora is, as her name suggests, a dark figure in the novel. An actress and musical opera singer, Nora is an old flame whom Coleman has jilted. That she goes to the battlefront as a correspondent for the *New York Daylight* suggests that her character is to some extent based on Cora Taylor, and like Cora she has a "past." Independent and liberated, she makes a point of telling Coleman that she makes more money than he does. In accordance with established conventions of nineteenth-century American romantic fiction, Nora is the insidious, sexually experienced woman Coleman must reject in order to win the blond, virtuous Marjory.

The Black Riders and Other Lines. The publication of *The Black Riders* by Copeland & Day in May 1895 was Crane's first serious venture into poetry. Since the sixty-eight free verse poems in this volume and most of the thirty-seven in *War Is Kind* are untitled, as are the thirty-one poems that were uncollected, they are usually identified by first lines or, in the case of *The Black Riders*, by roman numerals that precede the poems. The beginnings of Crane's poetic impulse are obscure, and only two or three uninspired earlier poems are extant. Corwin Linson* recalled that he first saw some of Crane's "lines," or "pills," as he always called them, in mid-February 1894. Among these were "There was a man who lived a life of fire," "The ocean said to me once," "There was a crimson clash of war," and "In Heaven / Some little blades of grass." Less than a month later, Crane brought a sheaf of poetry manuscripts to Hamlin Garland's* New York apartment and, according to one of Garland's not always consistent reminiscences, wrote out "God fashioned the ship of the world carefully" on the spot. Linson, Garland, and others recall Crane's remarks about the spontaneity of his method of composition. He told Linson that the poems appeared to him as pictures. "They came, and I wrote them, that's all."

According to Garland, Crane said they came into his mind "in little rows, all made up, ready to be put down on paper." John D. Barry* states that he saw about thirty poems in manuscript and that Crane told him they had been written in three days. Such accounts have fed into the legend of Crane's inspirational genius, but it is more than likely that his friends were shown fair copies of poems that had been carefully thought out and had undergone previous drafts.

Crane's achievements as a poet were not highly regarded by his contemporaries and have been slighted by modern critics, but Crane at times seemed to have valued his poetry above his accomplishments in fiction. "Personally," he wrote to John Northern Hilliard* in 1897, repeating a sentiment he had expressed a year earlier in letters to other editors, "I like my little book of poems, 'The Black Riders,' better than I do 'The Red Badge of Courage.' The reason is, I suppose, that the former is the more ambitious effort. In it I aim to give my ideas of life as a whole, so far as I know it, and the latter is a mere episode, or rather an amplification." Most of the poems in *The Black Riders* are short, free verse epigrams or parables written in the first person that render a dramatic conflict. They express Crane's worldview—his attitudes toward religion, morality, love, and war—but as many commentators have noted, they also evince a more personal involvement, a confrontation with Crane's spiritual heritage in which, as Amy Lowell put it, he was so steeped "that he could not get it out of his head. He disbelieved it and he hated it, but he could not free himself from it." More specifically, the dramatic encounters subsumed in almost half the poems in *The Black Riders* inquire into the nature of God and the meaning of truth. They counterpoint a vengeful Jehova embodied in the condemnatory theology of Crane's clerical forebears with a more human conception of the divine, an inner voice of tolerance and mercy empathetic to the kinship of fallen humanity.

The lugubrious doctrines of his ancestors assured Crane of the reality of sin, as emphatically set forth in the apocalyptic vision of the title poem:

> Black riders came from the sea.
> There was clang and clang of spear and shield,
> And clash and clash of hoof and heel,
> Wild shouts and the wave of hair
> In the rush upon the wind:
> Thus the ride of Sin.

The wrathful Jehova created man with desires and then proceeded to condemn him for expressing them. Crane's sense of injustice was outraged by this cosmic dilemma. Against the brutal villain of the Old Testament, he set an interior god of human compassion:

> A man went before a strange god,—
> The god of many men, sadly wise.
> And the deity thundered loudly,
> Fat with rage and puffing:

"Kneel, mortal, and cringe
And grovel and do homage
To my particularly sublime majesty."
            The man fled.

Then the man went to another god,—
The god of his inner thoughts.
And this one looked at him
With soft eyes
Lit with infinite comprehension.
And said: "My poor Child!"

Many of the other poems in *The Black Riders* also contrast the jealous, wrathful God of vengeance with a humane, internal God of kindness and mercy. The most explicit of these are "The livid lightenings flashed in the clouds;" and "Blustering god, / Stamping across the sky." A number of critics find the source of the God of transcendent injustice in the narrow religious views of Crane's maternal Peck family and trace the identification with fallen humanity to the more benevolent God of his father, but while Crane in his letters portrayed Jonathan Townley Crane as a kindly man, he died when Stephen was only eight years old, and there is no reason to believe that he held less narrow or condemnatory theological views than George or Jesse Peck. Jonathan Crane was a dour disciple of Saint Paul, whose Epistles it was his particular pleasure to quote. In his books, he portrayed the most innocent popular amusements as machinations of the devil. "He that believeth not is condemned; he that believeth is saved," the elder Crane thundered in *Holiness the Birthright of All God's Children* (1874). Until the penitent passes from unbelief to belief, his condition is "one of inexpressible evil. He is guilty, condemned, corrupt, helpless, the wrath of God resting on him, and hell waiting his coming, with its eternal darkness and despair."

Crane's view of the human condition in *The Black Riders* is generally bleak. God is either an ineffectual blusterer, absent, or nonexistent; nature is indifferent or, more often, threatening, with "angry" mountains, "direful thickets," "snow, ice, burning sand"; love is doomed; and courage and self-sacrifice are unrewarded. Above all, truth in an absolute sense is unattainable, although many persist in thinking it within reach:

I saw a man pursuing the horizon;
Round and round they sped.
I was disturbed at this;
I accosted the man.
"It is futile," I said,
"You can never—"

"You lie," he cried,
And ran on.

"Truth said a traveller" juxtaposes a man for whom the concept of unalloyed truth is "a rock, a mighty fortress" with a second traveler for whom it is "a breath, a wind.'' The narrator identifies with the second traveler since for him truth was also ''[a] breath, a wind, / A shadow, a phantom'' that had never been attainable. In ''A learned man said to me once,'' a character insists to the narrator that he knows the way to truth, and they proceed on together, but when they arrive at a place ''Where my eyes were useless / And I knew not the ways of my feet,'' the seer admits that he is lost. A number of the poems cast doubt on the existence of absolute truth or an external God. ''If I should cast off this tattered coat'' speculates on the possibility that there may be nothing beyond life but ''a vast blue, / Echoless, ignorant,— / What then?'' Even if one assumes the actuality of an impersonal God, his presence cannot be detected in the conception of him created by the church, and Crane dwells on the differences between inward and outward religion. ''Two or three angels'' who come near the earth see people streaming into a church, ''And the angels were puzzled / To know why the people went thus, / And why they stayed so long.'' Correspondingly, God would not recognize the clergymen who have devised the church's representation of Him:

> Walking in the sky,
> A man in strange black garb
> Encountered a radiant form.
> Then his steps were eager;
> Bowed he devoutly.
> ''My lord,'' said he.
> But the spirit knew him not.

Considering the chaotic nature of the universe, if one were to assume the existence of an external God, he would be one who had ''fashioned the ship of the world carefully'' but failed to equip it with a rudder. He became distracted when ''a wrong called,'' and the ship slipped away,

> So that, forever rudderless, it went upon the seas
> Going ridiculous voyages,
> Making quaint progress,
> Turning as with serious purpose
> Before stupid winds.

In this indifferent, hostile, and incomprehensible universe where whatever God may be has lost authority over his creation, human beings must have the courage to admit their unimportance and fall back on an inner moral reality, a sense of human kindness, and a dedication to honesty, justice, and compassion that alone can give meaning to their lives. Truth, consequently, can be found only within the self and not in the institutions in which humanity has traditionally embodied it. In Crane's morality, the greatest sin is the violation of one's own conscience:

> In the desert
> I saw a creature, naked, bestial,

Who, squatting upon the ground,
Held his heart in his hands,
And ate of it.
I said: "Is it good, friend?"
"It is bitter—bitter," he answered;
"But I like it
Because it is bitter,
And because it is my heart."

In contrast to the bombast of the poems dealing with God, absolute truth, and judgmental morality, the few love poems in *The Black Riders* are more given to conventional imagery, sentimentalism, and *fin de siècle** decadence than is usual in Crane's writings. In the world of blackness, deserts, and thickets, romantic love is the one escape the poet can offer. In "I looked here; / I looked there," he finds no woman lovelier than his ideal: "She is none so fair as she / In my heart." In "There was before me," the ideal woman inhabits "a place of infinite loveliness," the antithesis of the world "[o]f snow, ice, burning sand." The best known of Crane's love poems, "Should the wide world roll away," portrays a dissolving world and a fall to doom made bearable by transient pleasure in the white arms of a woman, a synecdoche for beauty that is paradoxically ideal and sensual:

Should the wide world roll away,
Leaving black terror,
Limitless night,
Nor God, nor man, nor place to stand
Would be to me essential,
If thou and thy white arms were there,
And the fall to doom a long way.

In "Places among the stars" the poet reiterates the theme that damnation with the beloved is preferable to a desolate heavenly bliss: "Since she is here / In a place of blackness, / Here I stay and wait." In "Behold the grave of a wicked man," a "stern spirit" prevents a weeping woman from placing flowers on the man's grave. While the spirit's denunciation may have been deserved, the woman's love has discerned the true value of the man who lies beneath the condemnation of society. As in the "Intrigue" series and other love poems in *War Is Kind*, love in *The Black Riders* is associated with two doomed souls bound to one another as well as with sin, despair, and desolation:

Love walked alone.
The rocks cut her tender feet,
And the brambles tore her fair limbs.
There came a companion to her,
But, alas, he was no help,
For his name was Heart's Pain.

There are only three slight poems dealing directly with war in *The Black Riders*, and they center, rather conventionally, on the folly and futility of armed conflict. In "Once there came a man," an arbitrary decision by an individual to arrange everyone in the world in rows provokes hostility: "And blood was shed / By those who would not stand in rows, / and by those who pined to stand in rows." The man who inflamed the combatants with his fatuous demand "went to death, weeping," and those who remain continue the battle without purpose. "There was crimson clash of war" describes a worldwide conflict. When a person inquires about the cause of the conflagration, "a million strove to answer him / There was such an intricate clamor of tongues, / That still the reason was not." The third poem, "Tell brave deeds of war," debunks heroism when the narrator concludes that "there were braver deeds" than those recounted in tales of "stern stands / and bitter runs for glory." For Crane, gallantry in war, unless it occurs in the quiet performance of duty or as a sacrifice for human brotherhood, is usually a manifestation of egotism rather than courage.

Suggested Reading

Blair, John. "The Posture of the Bohemian in the Poetry of Stephen Crane." *American Literature* 61 (1989): 215–29.

Hoffman, Daniel G. *The Poetry of Stephen Crane*. New York: Columbia University Press, 1957.

LaFrance, Marston. *A Reading of Stephen Crane*. Oxford: Clarendon Press, 1971. 129–72.

Miller, Ruth. "Regions of Snow: The Poetic Style of Stephen Crane." *Bulletin of the New York Public Library* 72 (1968): 328–49.

Nelson, Harland S. "Stephen Crane's Achievement as a Poet." *Texas Studies in Literature and Language* 4 (1963): 564–82.

Wertheim, Stanley. "Stephen Crane and the Wrath of Jehova." In *Stephen Crane: Modern Critical Views*. Ed. Harold Bloom. New York: Chelsea House, 1987. 41–48.

Blackwood, William (1836–1912). A Scottish publisher, Blackwood was the third member of his family to bear his name and the fifth editor in line of succession of *Blackwood's Edinburgh Magazine*, established in 1817 by his eponymous ancestor. Through Blackwood's London representative, David Meldrum, Joseph Conrad* arranged a meeting between Blackwood and Crane, and on 15 March 1898 Crane, Conrad, and Blackwood dined together at the Garrick Club. In the first week of April, Conrad and Crane scurried around London visiting publishers in an attempt to raise money for Crane's passage across the Atlantic to report the Cuban War. They met with no success until, finally, at Blackwood's, Crane managed to secure an advance of £60 on "articles to be contributed to Blackwood's Magazine from the seat of war in the event of a war breaking out between the United States of America and Spain." *Blackwood's* published "The Price of the Harness" in its December 1898 issue but rejected "The Lone Charge of William B. Perkins," "The Clan of No Name," and "Marines Signalling under Fire at Guantanamo." On Meldrum's advice, Blackwood also declined "The Blue Hotel," and he refused to advance Crane more money.

Suggested Reading

Conrad, Joseph. *Joseph Conrad's Letters to William Blackwood and David S. Meldrum.* Ed. William Blackburn. Durham, NC: Duke University Press, 1958.

"The Blood of the Martyr". A political satire in the form of a dramatic farce, "The Blood of the Martyr" appeared in the *New York Press Magazine*, 3 April 1898. It was separately published by the Peter Pauper Press in 1940. This playlet lampoons contemporary German imperialistic initiatives in China in which missionaries were used to further economic interests. The first act takes place in Kiachow, where China had signed a treaty with Germany granting railway and mining rights as reparations for the murder of German missionaries. Prince Henry of Prussia, his squadron anchored in the bay, is eager to reap martyrs so that through gunboat diplomacy he can garner more railway concessions and ports. He is delighted to hear that the missionary in Yen Hock may be massacred (as Crane explains in "Opium's Varied Dreams," a yen hock is a needle-like instrument used for cooking opium). In the second act, Prince Henry prematurely announces to a group of assembled mandarins that the missionary at Yen Hock has been murdered, and he demands reparations. They respond by offering Germany a monopoly of the Chinese railway system, but in the third act, Prince Henry is disconcerted when the Yen Hock missionary suddenly appears in Kiachow. Although he remains unimpressed when told that the missionary's parishioners cut off one of his ears, burned off a foot, and sliced out one of his lungs, the missionary's claim that he was also garroted and flayed alive completely mollifies Prince Henry. The railway concessions are ensured.

"The Blood of the Martyr" was probably written shortly after the sinking of the U.S.S. *Maine* in Havana harbor on 15 February 1898 increased the agitation for war with Spain in the jingoist press. Crane was consistently critical of German and English imperialism, but as a correspondent for Pulitzer's *New York World* and Hearst's *New York Journal*, he was supportive of American military intervention in Cuba and in the Philippines, which he believed were justified and idealistically motivated.

Suggested Reading

Gullason, Thomas A. "Stephen Crane: Anti-Imperialist." *American Literature* 30 (1958): 237–41.

"The Blue Badge of Cowardice". Syndicated under diverse headlines by Hearst in newspapers on 12 May 1897, this cable describes the evacuation of the port of Volo, some twenty miles from Velestino, after Crown Prince Constantine unaccountably ordered a retreat while the Greek army was successfully repulsing a Turkish offensive. Crane refers to the dispirited withdrawal of the Greek army from Velestino, the troops bitter at the faintheartedness of their future ruler. There is pandemonium in the resort town of Volo as refugees crowd aboard every available ship in the harbor, and Crane expresses empathy with the plight of the destitute and starving civilians who had crowded into Volo as a sanctuary and are now again forced to flee.

"The Blue Battalions". *See* "When a people reach the top of a hill."

Blue Billie. A character in *Maggie* and *George's Mother*, Blue Billie is the member of Jimmie Johnson's boyhood Rum Alley gang with whom Jimmie scuffles in the opening chapter of *Maggie*. In *George's Mother* Blue Billie, now a young man, is one of a group of street corner hoodlums that George Kelcey joins. In the penultimate chapter of the novel, Kelcey is about to brawl with Blue Billie when he learns that his mother has had a stroke.

"The Blue Hotel". The best of Crane's Western stories and one of his handful of fictional masterworks, "The Blue Hotel" was published in *Collier's Weekly* in two parts, on 26 November and 3 December 1898, having previously been rejected by the *Century*, *Scribner's Magazine*, and the *Atlantic*. The story was collected in *The Monster and Other Stories*.

The setting of "The Blue Hotel" is a bleak prairie town in northern Nebraska named Fort Romper, where the incongruous presence of the Palace Hotel, grotesquely "painted a light blue, a shade that is on the legs of a kind of heron, causing the bird to declare its position against any background . . . was always screaming and howling in a way that made the dazzling winter landscape of Nebraska seem only a gray swampish hush." One morning, Patrick Scully, the proprietor of the hotel, has the deceptive good fortune of securing three guests for his establishment from a train passing through town. One of them is a "shaky and quick-eyed" man known only as the Swede; the second is a cowboy named Bill, who is on his way to a ranch; and the third is an Easterner, meaningfully called Mr. Blanc. From the beginning the Swede evinces a paranoid fear based on fictional representations that the West is a dangerous environment, and in the middle of an afternoon card game he proclaims his conviction that he is in danger of being killed in the hotel and he must leave immediately. In order to allay the Swede's fears and retain him as a guest, Scully affirms that Fort Romper is a civilized community that will soon have electric streetcars and a new railroad line, "Not to mintion the four churches and the smashin' big brick schoolhouse. Then there's the big factory, too. Why, in two years Romper'll be a met-tro-*pol*-is." He takes the Swede into his own room and shows him photographs of his little girl who had died and of his oldest son, who is a lawyer in Lincoln, "an honored an' respicted gintleman." While Scully attempts to reassure the Swede, the Easterner, the cowboy, and Scully's son, Johnnie, sit around the glowing stove in the hotel parlor and reflect on the origin of the

Swede's fears. The Easterner speculates that "this man has been reading dime-novels, and he thinks he's right out in the middle of it—the shootin' and stabbin' and all."

After supper, the card game resumes, while a blizzard rages outside. The scene is seemingly tranquil until the Swede suddenly accuses Johnnie of cheating. Although the game is recreational and no money is involved, this violation of the anachronistic social code of the West, still prevalent despite Scully's disclaimers, is an intolerable insult, and a fistfight ensues outside the hotel in the storm. Johnnie, spurred on by the cowboy, who shouts, "Kill him, Johnnie! Kill him! Kill him! Kill him!" fights valiantly but is badly beaten. The Swede is now obliged to leave the hotel in the midst of the blizzard, and as he struggles down a lonely Fort Romper street, blinded by the wind-driven snow, Crane comments on the hubris of man's failure to apprehend his insignificance in the incomprehensible and indifferent universal scheme, an arrogance that paradoxically makes his brief survival possible:

> He might have been in a deserted village. We picture the world as thick with conquering and elate humanity, but here, with the bugles of the tempest pealing, it was hard to imagine a peopled earth. One viewed the existence of man then as a marvel, and conceded a glamour of wonder to these lice which were caused to cling to a whirling, fire-smote, ice-locked, disease-stricken, space-lost bulb. The conceit of man was explained by this storm to be the very engine of life. One was a coxcomb not to die in it. However, the Swede found a saloon.

The Swede dies in the saloon, a resort of convivial humanity, rather than in the storm, a perceptibly hostile manifestation of nature. In the saloon are a bartender and a group at a table consisting of two businessmen, the district attorney, and a gentlemanly professional gambler, reminiscent of John Oakhurst in Bret Harte's "The Luck of Roaring Camp" and "The Outcasts of Poker Flat," whose veneer of respectability has gained him a limited social acceptance in Fort Romper. The Swede attempts to bully the gambler into drinking with him and when the man refuses grasps him by the throat and drags him from his chair. "There was a great tumult, and then was seen a long blade in the hand of the gambler. It shot forward, and a human body, this citadel of virtue, wisdom, power, was pierced as easily as if it had been a melon. The Swede fell with a cry of supreme astonishment." After the others leave the saloon, the Swede's body remains, "its eyes fixed upon a dreadful legend that dwelt atop of the cash-machine: 'This registers the amount of your purchase,'" implying that the Swede has created the Wild West of his imagination, that his disturbed mental state and his actions have brought about his death, and that his isolation and distortion of reality are ultimately responsible for what occurred.

In a ninth and final section of the story, however, Crane seems to obscure and even obviate this judgment with a different moral view indicating that a failure of community is in large part responsible for the tragedy. The cowboy is frying pork over the stove of a cabin on the Dakota line when the Easterner enters carrying a newspaper and informs him that the gambler has received a mere three-year sentence for the murder of the Swede. The cowboy speculates that the Swede would not have been killed if he had not initiated the series of events that began with his accusation that Johnnie was cheating, again implying that the Swede bears almost exclusive responsibility for his fate. The enraged Easterner denies this by asserting that he knew Johnnie *was* cheating and that there was a conspiracy of silence, a collusion that led to the Swede's death:

> "I let the Swede fight it out alone. And you—you were simply puffing around the place and wanting to fight. And then old Scully himself! We are all in it! This poor gambler isn't even a noun. He is kind of an adverb. Every sin is the result of a collaboration. We, five of us, have collaborated in the murder of this Swede. Usually there are from a dozen to forty women really involved in every murder, but in this case it seems to be only five men—you, I, Johnnie, old Scully, and that fool of an unfortunate gambler came merely as a culmination, the apex of a human movement, and gets all the punishment."

Bewildered and resentful, the cowboy unwittingly affirms his own culpability in the lack of communal action that is responsible for all that occurred by blurting out, "Well, I didn't do anythin', did I?"

Antithetical interpretations have been advanced to explain the speech of the Easterner at the conclusion of "The Blue Hotel." Some critics view it as an affirmation of the Howellsian doctrine of complicity or the existential necessity for human brotherhood in a viable society, a theme also advanced, but not definitively or exclusively, in "The Open Boat." Others find a naturalistic outlook confirming the irresponsibility of the individual in a world he never made and cannot control, and still others see the final section as "tacked on," resulting in a logical gap between the Swede's obvious responsibility for bringing about his own death and the Easterner's insistence on undiminished group culpability. The Easterner's failure to include the Swede as among those responsible for the tragic finale seriously undermines his doctrinaire exposition. Also a subject of debate is the hyperbolic nature of the Easterner's speech, which Crane may have intended as a burlesque of either literary naturalism* or the theory of complicity itself. The contradictory endings of "The Blue Hotel" with their problematic balance of causes for the ultimate tragedy illustrate Crane's modernistic awareness of the multiplicity and partiality of individual perceptions of any event and the futility of attempts to impose coherence on the chaos of existence.

Suggested Reading

Gibson, Donald B. " 'The Blue Hotel' and the Ideal of Human Courage." *Texas Studies in Literature and Language* 6 (1964): 388–97.

Gleckner, Robert F. "Stephen Crane and the Wonder of Man's Conceit." *Modern Fiction Studies* 5 (1959): 271–81.

Kimball, Sue L. "Circles and Squares: The Designs of Stephen Crane's 'The Blue Hotel.' " *Studies in Short Fiction* 17 (1980): 425–30.

Monteiro, George. "Crane's Coxcomb." *Modern Fiction Studies* 31 (1985): 295–305.

Boldin, Major Tom. An ancient worthy in the Civil War story "An Indiana Campaign" who, as the town's only veteran, heads the Migglesville home front.

Borland, Armistead (?–?). Nicknamed Tommie, Borland, who was from Norfolk, Virginia, was the smallest boy in Crane's cadet company at Claverack College and Hudson River Institute.* Borland hero-worshipped Crane; half a century later he described Crane as "a congenital introvert" who was nevertheless attractive to young women and maintained that he learned from Crane "the rudiments of the American game of poker and something more than the rudiments of the ways of a man with a maid."

Suggested Reading

Schoberlin, Melvin H. "Flagon of Despair: Stephen Crane." Unpublished manuscript, Arents Library, Syracuse University. V–9, V–17, V–23.

Boston, Ike. The driver of a stagecoach in "Moonlight on the Snow" who brings a family from the East to the Texas town of War Post. Their arrival interrupts the makeshift hanging of Tom Larpent, and Boston's name ironically suggests the intrusion of Eastern civilization into the West.

Bottles, Jem. A character in *The O'Ruddy*, Jem is a parody of the Robin Hood legend. He is an inept highwayman with "seven ballads of me written in Bristol and three in Bath," but he remains financially and emotionally dependent on his censorious mother and comes to reflect that he "should have remained an honest sheep-stealer and never engaged in this dangerous and nefarious game of lifting purses."

Bowery Tales. Published posthumously only in England by William Heinemann in June 1900, this is a reprinting of *Maggie* and *George's Mother*. William Dean Howells's* introduction to the 1896 English edition of *Maggie* is also reprinted. There is no new material in this volume.

Boyd, Lew (?–?). A famous bear hunter in Sullivan County. Crane chronicles one of Lew Boyd's exploits and the legend that grew out of it in "Hunting Wild Hogs."

Bradley, James A. (1830–1921). The founder of the shore resorts Asbury Park, Ocean Grove, and Bradley Beach, New Jersey, he began his career as a brush manufacturer and retailer in New York City. In 1870 he began to invest in real estate on the New Jersey coast. Bradley sold lots cheaply on the condition that the buyer erect a building of good quality. As mayor of Asbury Park, he imposed his standards of proper behavior on the community. Sabbath closing laws were strictly enforced, and the title deed of each plot stipulated that the property would revert to the original owner if liquor were sold on the premises. Signs were posted on the beach advising bathers that "[m]odesty of apparel is just as becoming to a lady in bathing costume as in silks and satins" and "[a]s a rule respectable people retire from the beach at 10 P.M." Crane ridiculed the priggishness and eccentricities of "Founder Bradley" in some of his shore sketches, such as "On the Boardwalk" and "Asbury Park As Seen by Stephen Crane."

Bradley, Will (1868–1962). A typographer, artist, and author, Bradley served an apprenticeship as a printer and began his career as an artist and engraver working without pay at Rand McNally & Co. in Chicago. In time he opened his own studio, and during his years as a freelance designer, his posters and artwork won great acclaim. In 1895 he moved to Springfield, Massachusetts, where he established the Wayside Press and published a monthly art magazine, *Bradley, His Book*. Bradley designed the title page of Copeland & Day's edition of Richard Le Gallienne's *Robert Louis Stevenson: An Elegy and Other Poems Mainly Personal* (1895) and drew the illustrations for their edition of Archibald Lampman's *Lyrics of the Earth* (1895). In 1899 he undertook the design of Crane's *War Is Kind* for the Frederick A. Stokes Company of New York. The untitled poems are printed on gray cartridge paper in Caslon type, each on the upper portion of the page, with extravagant spaces below, as in *The Black Riders*, and are accompanied by bold art nouveau illustrations. The cover of the book is crowded with images having verbal counterparts in Crane's poems: a drooping tree, flowers, a lyre, an urn, and a long-haired female figure bearing a sword. The design of the book was widely criticized in reviews. Amy Lowell later said that "no man could be taken seriously who had perpetrated a book which looked like this." Bradley went on to become one of the first American art editors, occupying that position at *Collier's*, *Good Housekeeping*, *Metropolitan*, and other magazines. From 1915 to 1917 he was art supervisor for motion pictures produced by Hearst, and after a brief stint writing and directing his own films, he returned to the Hearst organization, where he remained until his retirement in 1930.

Bragdon, Claude (Fayette) (1866–1946). An architect, author, and lecturer who also designed stage sets and wrote books on theosophy. Through his drawings, posters, and poetry, Bragdon came to know Gelett Burgess and Elbert Hubbard.* In his reminiscences, *Merely Players* (1929) and *More Lives Than One* (1938), Bragdon recalled his embarrassment at the ridicule heaped on Crane at the Philistine dinner, a self-promotional celebration sponsored by Hubbard, ostensibly in Crane's honor. Bragdon, who described Crane as "a young ox led to the slaughter," attempted to walk out but was dissuaded from doing so by Crane and Willis Brooks Hawkins.*

Brede Place. An ancient English manor house near Northiam in Sussex constructed in the fifteenth century on the site of a still earlier structure and rebuilt and restored in Tudor and Elizabethan times. The older part of the house was built by Sir Thomas Oxenbridge, who died in 1497, and Sir Goddard Oxenbridge, who died in 1531. Brede Place came into the Frewen family in 1708, when Sir Edward Frewen purchased it from the Oxenbridges. The house was uninhabited for almost a century and frequented by smugglers. Moreton and Clara Frewen* took it over in 1885, after their return from Wyoming, and later bought it from Moreton Frewen's brother, Richard. Like most other old rural houses in Victorian England, Brede Place lacked modern plumbing and electricity, and most of the rooms were uninhabitable. Servants refused to spend the night in the house because of a legend that it was haunted by the spirit of Sir Goddard Oxenbridge, a warlock and ogre who purportedly hanged his wives in a gallows room and ate a child for dinner every night. He was executed on nearby "Groaning Bridge" by local children, who sawed him in half with a wooden saw while he lay in an intoxicated stupor.

Stephen and Cora Crane were dissatisfied with Ravensbrook,* Surrey, their first permanent domicile in England. Before Crane left to report the Cuban War, Edward Garnett* interested him in Brede Place as a suitable residence, and in 1898, while he was in Cuba, the Frewens rented the house to Cora for the nominal sum of £40 a year on the condition that the Cranes undertake restorations specified in an architect's report. Cora planted an extensive rose garden in front of the manor, but the Cranes were never able to afford the repairs they had promised to make and lived in only part of the house. They began to move their household to Brede Place soon after Stephen returned from Cuba and established residence permanently on 19 February 1899, taking with them Cora's companion, Charlotte Ruedy,* and two of Harold Frederic's* children by Kate Lyon.*

The Cranes lived improvidently at Brede Place, with a passel of servants who came with the house that Moreton Frewen insisted they retain and a constant stream of house guests whom Crane derisively referred to as "Indians." Ford Madox Ford* called them "Crane's parasites." The more welcome guests included Joseph Conrad* and his family, Henry James,* and H. G. Wells.* Crane wrote in a room over the porch that Mark Barr* insisted he dissuaded him from painting bright red, and legends about supposedly haunted rooms with defective door latches that mysteriously swung open are recounted by Barr and Edith Richie.* The most notable events of the Cranes' residence at Brede was the extravagant three-day post-Christmas party in 1899 that centered on the production of "The Ghost."

Suggested Reading

Barr, Mark. "The Haunted House of Brede." In Stanley Wertheim. "Stephen Crane Remembered." *Studies in American Fiction* 4 (1976): 45–64.
Hare, Augustus C. *Sussex*. London: George Allen, 1894. 47–48.

"The Bride Comes to Yellow Sky". A comic masterpiece with serious social undertones, "The Bride Comes to Yellow Sky" appeared simultaneously in the

February 1898 issues of *McClure's Magazine* in the United States and *Chapman's Magazine* in England. It was included in both the American and English editions of *The Open Boat*.

The story opens with Marshall Jack Potter and his bride returning by train to his home town of Yellow Sky, Texas, from San Antonio, where they have recently been married. The train is traveling westward, and, as perceived from the windows of the plush Pullman car, "the plains of Texas were pouring eastward," a *coup d'oeil* in which Crane objectifies the precipitous retreat of the Old West before the encroachment of Eastern civilization. For the newly married couple, the elegance of the train with its elaborate dining car and attentive porters epitomizes "the environment of their new estate." They are clearly uncomfortable dressed in their finery in the midst of such splendor. Like the patches of grass on the prairie, the trees and the frame houses are viewed from the train as "sweeping into the east, sweeping over the horizon"; they have, through the fact of their marriage, gone over "a precipice."

As Potter and his bride leave the railroad station platform in Yellow Sky and prepare to slink into town, they fail to notice the station agent running toward them, wildly waving his arms to alert Potter that Scratchy Wilson, the aging town gunfighter, is drunk and has been shooting up the town's watering spot, the Weary Gentleman saloon, where a group of town residents and a visiting drummer cower in terror. At this point Crane shifts the focus of attention and the time to the saloon, twenty-one minutes before the arrival of the train carrying the newly married couple. Through conversation between the drummer and the townsfolk, the history of the confrontations between the aging cowboy and the seasoned marshal is revealed. The point of view shifts again to Scratchy Wilson, futilely attempting to provoke a confrontation at the saloon, and then once again to Potter and his bride, who, seeking to escape the celebration that would be inevitable if the residents of Yellow Sky knew of their marriage, rush through back streets of the town from the station. As they round the final corner of the street leading to Potter's home, they suddenly come upon Scratchy Wilson, who is reloading his starboard revolver. Startled, Scratchy drops the gun and whips out the second revolver dangling from his left hip. The stage is set for the standard Western showdown, but this occurs ironically not in an exchange of gunfire but of speech, the weapon of the more civilized East. Potter announces that he is unarmed, reversing all conventional expectations, and Scratchy Wilson is appalled. " 'If you ain't got a gun, why ain't you got a gun?' he sneered. 'Been to Sunday-school?' " Potter's further revelation that he is married disarms Scratchy even of words. "He was like a creature allowed a glimpse of another world." Nonplussed and dismayed, he backs down. "He was not a student of chivalry; it was merely that in the presence of this foreign condition he was a simple child of the earlier plains."

To a great extent, "The Bride Comes to Yellow Sky" is a satire of the confrontational Western that Crane himself popularized in stories such as "The Five White Mice" and "A Man and Some Others." Also satirized is the Eastern fantasy of the lawman and the gunfighter. Both Potter and Scratchy Wilson are comic anachronisms. Potter is middle-aged and awkward; he does not carry a gun. His bride is neither pretty nor young. By marrying, Potter has violated the traditions of the lone ranger; he has lost his bearings and "gone headlong over all the social hedges." Scratchy is "the last one of the old gang that used to hang out along the river," an ersatz badman whose style of dress and behavior is fashioned by Eastern conceptions. He is a decrepit drunk in Western costume whose decorative flannel shirt has been made by "some Jewish women on the East Side of New York. . . . And his boots had red tops with gilded imprints, of the kind beloved in winter by little sledding boys on the hillsides of New England." Unlike the fast-shooting desperado of Western fiction, Scratchy, who is said to be "a wonder with a gun," is hardly a marksman. He misses the dog lying at the portals of the Weary Gentleman saloon, and he misses the paper target he has nailed to the barroom door. His confrontations with Potter have become a public ritual, a game that everyone understands and accepts as essentially harmless, although Potter's performance once slipped far enough to leave Wilson wounded in the leg. In the anticlimactic conclusion of the story, the expectations of the theatrical showdown Western are reversed as Scratchy drops his gun when confronted by the unarmed marshal. The gunfighter is clumsy and abashed rather than deadly. Potter's marriage introduces a "foreign condition," manifesting the end of the social order as Scratchy has known it and the beginning of a new one. As Scratchy leaves the scene of the failed confrontation, his feet form "funnel-shaped tracks in the heavy sand." Like the sands of an hourglass, time has run out for the classic Wild West confrontation of the lawman and the gunfighter, and human efforts to impose ordered patterns on the vicissitudes of existence are merely imprints on the sands of time.

Suggested Reading

Bergon, Frank. Introduction to *The Western Writings of Stephen Crane*. New York: New American Library, 1979.

Overton, James P. "The 'Game' in 'The Bride Comes to Yellow Sky.'" *Xavier University Studies* 4 (1965): 3–11.

Vorphal, Ben Merchant. "Murder by the Minute: Old and New in 'The Bride Comes to Yellow Sky.'" *Nineteenth-Century Fiction* 26 (1971): 196–218.

Wolford, Chester L. *Stephen Crane: A Study of the Short Fiction*. Boston: Twayne, 1989. 27–30.

The Broadway Garden. A music hall on Broadway between Thirty-first and Thirty-second Streets in New York City sometimes frequented by Crane. The Broadway Garden was a notorious resort of prostitutes, described by a contemporary reporter as "crowded with rum-befuddled patrons. The men were about all very young, while the women were mostly outcasts. These women go in without escorts, but rarely leave alone" (*New York World*, 20 January 1897). Crane describes such a resort in *Maggie* as "a hilarious hall" in which "there were twenty-eight tables and twenty-eight women and a crowd of smoking men.'' Crane was emerging from the Broadway Garden in the early hours of 16 September 1896 with Dora Clark* and two chorus girls when he had the encounter with patrolman Charles Becker* that precipitated the end of his career as an investigative reporter in New York.

"The Broken-Down Van". The first of Crane's New York City sketches, anticipating his later studies of urban life in the *New York Press* in 1894 and the *New York Journal* in 1896, this unsigned Bowery vignette was printed in the *New York Tribune* on 10 July 1892 under the heading ''Travels in New York,'' a caption the *Tribune* used for Sunday feature articles about the city by various writers. The sketch, like much of Crane's other New York journalism, is a genre piece, not a report of a particular incident. It opens with two huge furniture vans, each drawn by four horses, rolling slowly along the horsecar tracks on a busy street with impatient traffic crawling behind them. A wheel falls off the rear van, and an axle goes down. Horsecars pile up behind the van, their drivers yelling, blowing their whistles, and pounding on their dashboards with car hooks. Passengers crane their necks, anxious to learn the reason for the delay. Onlookers crowd the sidewalks, making comments and offering advice. Elevated trains roar overhead. After much confusion, the broken-down van is lifted onto a paving block; the wheel is replaced, and the normal flow of traffic resumes.

The animated impressionistic style of this representation of a seemingly matter-of-fact episode on an urban thoroughfare marks it as distinctly Crane's. There is an excessive concentration of color imagery. The furniture vans are red, and the horsecar immediately behind them is a spectacle in red: ''The car was red, and the bullseye light was red, and the driver's hair was red. He blew his whistle shrilly and slapped the horse's lines impatiently. Then he whistled again. Then he pounded on the red dash board with his car-hook till the red light trembled.'' There are striking similes, such as the ''diamond like an arc-light'' worn by a man in a cab. A horsecar forced to navigate off its tracks pitches ''like a skiff in the swell of a steamer.'' There is the use of improbable adjectives describing ''impossible landscapes'' and a ''prostrated wheel.'' Most of all, there are Crane's oblique glimpses of the inhabitants of the Bowery: the pawnshop owners; the pullers in for clothing stores; the ''ten-cent barber'' who ''eyed a Division-st. girl who was a millinery puller-in and who was chewing gum with an earnest, almost fierce motion of the jaw''; and the foreshadowing of Maggie in ''a sixteen-year-old girl without any hat and with a roll of half-finished vests under her arm'' who ''crossed the front platform of the green car. As she stepped up on to the sidewalk a barber from a ten-cent shop said 'Ah! there!' and she answered 'smarty!' with withering scorn and went down a side street.''

Bronson, Jerozel. In ''An Indiana Campaign,'' Bronson, ''a half-witted lad who comprehended nothing save an occasional genial word,'' exemplifies the unhinged mentality of the crowd of villagers who pursue a supposed "rebel" spy hiding in the woods at the edge of town.

Brown, Curtis (1866–1945). Brown began his career in journalism on the staff of the *Buffalo Express*. From 1894 to 1898 he was on the staff of the *New York Press*. As assistant and successor to the Sunday editor, Edward Marshall,* he shared responsibility for the publication of many of Crane's New York City stories and sketches in 1894, when the young author was living in poverty. The *Press* ran the Bacheller syndicate's abridged version of *The Red Badge of Courage* on Sunday, 9 December 1894. From 1898 to 1916 Brown represented the *Press* and a number of other American newspapers in London. He established his literary agency, Curtis Brown Ltd., in New York and London in 1899 and served as president of the London branch. Among his clients was Ernest Hemingway, for whom he was British and Continental agent. He also founded and headed the International Publishing Bureau.

Suggested Reading

Brown, Curtis. *Contacts*. London: Cassell, 1935. 222–27.

Bryant, Si. A character in "The Knife." He is the Whilomville resident who owns the garden patch containing the watermelons coveted by Peter Washington and Alek Williams.

Burleigh, Colonel John L. Probably an apocryphal character invented by Elbert Hubbard.* In *A Souvenir and a Medley* (1896), an issue of his *Roycroft Quarterly*, Hubbard reprints the regrets in the souvenir menu of the Philistine dinner that he gave in Crane's honor in Buffalo on 19 December 1895, with a few added, of those who could not attend. The last of these added regrets is by Burleigh: "It grieves me greatly to think I cannot be with you at the Feed. I was with Crane at Antietam and saw him rush forward, seize two of the enemy and bump their heads together in a way that must have made them see constellations. When a Rebel general remonstrated with him, Steve, in a red fury, gave him a kick like a purple cow when all at once—but the story is too long to tell now." Most of Crane's biographers have treated this obvious spoof, wholly in tenor with other jesting regrets in the Philistine dinner menu, as an entirely serious if mistaken recollection, despite its hyperbolic mockery of Crane's style and the allusion to Gelett Burgess's comic poem, "The Purple Cow." Taken out of context, Burleigh's "I was with Crane at Antietam" is often cited as evidence for the verisimilitude of *The Red Badge of Courage*.

Suggested Reading

Carruthers, Sharon. " 'Old Soldiers Never Die': A Note on Col. John L. Burleigh." *Studies in the Novel* 10 (1978): 158–60.

Burnham, Luke. The belligerent Western gunfighter who is finally ambushed and shot to death in ''A Freight Car Incident.''

Button, Lucius Lucine (?–?). Nicknamed Budge, (or Budgon, by Crane), he was one of the medical students with whom Crane shared lodgings during the fall and winter of 1892–93 in the boardinghouse on Avenue A in New York City they referred to as the Pendennis Club. Button received one of the first copies of the 1893 *Maggie* inscribed by Crane. Their friendship continued through 1895, and they exchanged a number of letters. Button was from Akron, Ohio, and it was he who took Crane to the tea party on Thirty-fourth Street where he met Nellie Crouse,* who was also from Akron.

C

Cadogan, Caspar. In "The Second Generation," he is the epitome of Crane's satire of the volunteer officer in the Cuban War. Even Caspar's father, a U.S. senator from "Skowmulligan," opines that the army has "got all the golf experts and tennis champions and cotillion leaders and piano tuners and billiard markers they really need as officers." Nevertheless, Caspar becomes a captain on the commissary staff of a general, although he admits that he did not know what a commissary officer was until he became one.

Cadogan, Senator. In early March 1896 Crane went to Washington to study the political life of the city in preparation for a novel to be published by S. S. McClure, but he soon abandonded the project, writing to Ripley Hitchcock* that "These men pose so hard that it would take a double-barreled shotgun to disclose their inward feelings and I despair of knowing them." The depiction of Senator Cadogan "from the great state of Skowmulligan" in "The Second Generation" shows that Crane's experience in Washington was not entirely wasted. Cadogan's successful manipulations to secure a commission for his incompetent and cowardly son and his attempt to pressure officials in the War Department in order to obtain news of Caspar reveal Crane's understanding of insider politics and influence in Washington.

Cahan, Abraham (1860–1951). A labor organizer, fiction writer, and longtime editor of the *Jewish Daily Forward*, a socialist newspaper written largely in Yiddish, Cahan came to the United States from what is now Lithuania in 1882. He wrote articles on urban immigrant life for the *New York Sun* and the *New York Press* and edited Yiddish newspapers. His novel *Yekl: A Tale of the New York Ghetto* (1896) was praised by William Dean Howells* as a model of literary realism* and was a forerunner of Cahan's masterful epic of the Jewish immigrant experience, *The Rise of David Levinsky* (1917). In a 26 July 1896 review essay in the *New York World* entitled "New York Low Life in Fiction," Howells compared *Maggie* and *George's Mother* with *Yekl* and concluded that while Cahan wrote in the comic mood and Crane in the tragic, both were persuasive in their truthful presentation of the slum environment. Crane read *Yekl* and asked Howells to introduce him to Cahan. The two writers met at Howells's summer home in Far Rockaway, New York, on 25 August. On 26 September, along with Hamlin Garland,* they were honored at a dinner at the Lantern Club.* Crane and Cahan were among the first to undermine the sentimental tradition in American tenement fiction.

Suggested Reading

Fine, David M. "Abraham Cahan, Stephen Crane, and the Romantic Tenement Tale of the Nineties." *American Studies* 14.1 (1973): 95–107.

"The Camel". As with its companion sketch, "Art in Kansas City," in what was apparently intended to be a series of tall tales featuring Uncle Clarence, the date of composition of "The Camel" is unclear, and it was not published in Crane's lifetime. It was first printed in *The Complete Short Stories and Sketches of Stephen Crane*, edited by Thomas A. Gullason (Garden City, N.Y.: Doubleday, 1963), 60–61.

"The Camel" appears to be a spoof of the kind of temperance parable illustrating the devastating effects of alcohol that Crane's mother was fond of relating. Uncle Clarence travels to Maine, having contrived a scheme to smuggle whiskey into the dry state. He carries with him three cases of soda water and a dozen bottles of scotch. Using "a wonderful mechanism," he injects the scotch into one of the camel's stomachs and the soda water into the other, forgetting the possible effect this might have on the camel. In the first town he comes to, Uncle Clarence stops for lunch at a hotel. Leaving the camel with the hostler, he strolls out to observe the laying of the cornerstone of a new church. During the ceremony, the camel appears. "He was smiling with an expression of foolish good-nature and his legs were spraddling out in his drunken attempt to keep himself erect." The camel disrupts the ceremony and panics the attending clergymen, who clamber into the treetops. The same day Uncle Clarence finds himself escorted across the borders of the state by a committee of citizens who "courteously informed me that they only carried their shot-guns as a protection against the cold night-air."

"Cantharides". An untraced manuscript of erotic verses supposedly written by Crane that, according to Vincent Starrett in *Stephen Crane: A Bibliography* (Philadelphia: Centaur, 1923), 10–11, was seen by several persons but is probably apocryphal.

"The Captain". There seems to be an autobiographical basis for this slight, humorous sketch that appeared in the *New York Tribune* on 7 August 1892. "The Captain" centers on a group of young people taking a day's outing on a catboat commanded by an aging volunteer fireman. The three young women on the excursion, identified only as a "Baltimore girl," a young woman from New York, and another young woman from Philadelphia, are a composite portrait of Lily Brandon Munroe,* the young married woman with whom Crane was involved that summer in Asbury Park, New Jersey. The sketch consists largely of an exchange of banter replete with double entendres between the excursionists and the laconically witty captain.

The Captain. *See* Murphy, Edward.

"Captured Mausers for Volunteers". Datelined from General William Shafter's* headquarters in Cuba on 7 July, this dispatch did not appear in the *New York World* and the *Philadelphia Press* until 17 July 1898. As in a number of other Cuban War reports, Crane is critical of the arming of regular American troops with rifles that fired black powder ammunition while the Spaniards used smokeless powder in their rifles and field artillery batteries. This resulted in many unnecessary casualties because "the proceedings of the enemy were all shrouded in mystery, while the movements of the Americans were always hopelessly palpable." Crane also deplores the arming of volunteer regiments with outdated Springfield rifles rather than the superior Krag-Jorgensen rifles employed by the regulars. He suggests that the volunteers be given captured Spanish Mausers, which are even better than the Krag-Jorgensens.

[Carleton, Samuel]. A pseudonym Crane used when he registered with the *New York World* staff at the St. James Hotel in Jacksonville on 28 November 1896 on his aborted trip to Cuba to report the insurrection.

Carmichael, Otto (?–?). A Washington correspondent for the *Minneapolis Times*, Carmichael was in Havana in the fall of 1898 observing the activities of the American Evacuation Commission. Carmichael's memoir, "Stephen Crane in Havana," which first appeared in the *Omaha Daily Bee* on 17 June 1900, provides a valuable inside view of the four months from mid-August to late December 1898 when Crane led an underground existence in the Cuban city. Carmichael comments on Crane's irregular life in Havana, calling him "irresponsible and unmanageable" but acknowledging that he was compulsive about writing six hundred words every day.

Suggested Reading

Carmichael, Otto. "Stephen Crane in Havana." *Prairie Schooner* 43 (1969): 200–4.

Carmony, Major Rickets C. In the Cuban War story "Virtue in War," Carmony is a popular volunteer officer who courts favor with his men but proves ineffectual in combat. Crane contrasts Carmony unfavorably with Major Gates, a professional soldier.

"The Carriage-Lamps". In this Whilomville story, published in the February 1900 issue of *Harper's New Monthly Magazine*, Crane seems to be lampooning the romantic boys' adventure fiction exemplified by the works of Robert Louis Stevenson and the dime novels popular in the late nineteenth century. Jimmie Trescott acquires a revolver, and when Peter Washington, the Trescott's black hostler, informs his father of this, Jimmie retaliates by throwing rocks at him. One of the rocks breaks several lamps in the carriage house, and Dr. Trescott sends Jimmie to his room to await punishment. Jimmie's friends, led by Willie Dalzel, who has just been reading a book entitled *The Red Captain: A Tale of the Pirates of the Spanish Main*, contrive an elaborate escape plot reminiscent of the travesty enacted by Tom Sawyer and Huck to free Jim in the last chapters of *Adventures of Huckleberry Finn*. Dr. Trescott enters Jimmie's room when the boys are about to "rescue" Jimmie and is highly amused by their antics; much to the disgust of Peter Washington, Jimmie evades a "trouncin.' "

Carroll, William Waring (?–?). An artist and illustrator who came to New York from Florida, W. W. Carroll was one of Crane's three roommates (with Nelson Greene* and R. G. Vosburgh*) in the old Art Students League building at 143–147 East Twenty-third Street during the autumn and spring of 1893–1894. He later became an illustrator on the *Buffalo Courier* and subsequently a Methodist minister in Georgia. In March 1894 Carroll accompanied Crane on a four-day investigative reporting excursion to the Bowery. His three-page untitled reminiscence, written in 1924 and held in the Thomas Beer Papers (Beer Family Papers) in the Sterling Library at Yale University, attests to the experiential background of "An Experiment in Misery." Carroll recalls the vermin-infested flophouses in which they slept, the Bowery saloons in which they dined on bread and soup with cold beer, and the colorful panhandler who was the original for Crane's character "the assassin" in "An Experiment in Misery."

Suggested Reading

Wertheim, Stanley, and Paul Sorrentino. *The Crane Log: A Documentary Life of Stephen Crane*. New York: Hall, 1994. 97–98.

[Carter, Imogene]. The pen name Cora Crane used for her Greek-Turkish War dispatches in the *New York Journal* and to send her unsigned "European Letters," written in part by Crane, to the *New York Press*. Cora has been called the first woman war correspondent, but Harriet Boyd was also in Greece writing for the *Journal*. Cora's first dispatch, headlined "War Seen Through a Woman's Eyes," is datelined Athens, 26 April, but it did not appear in the *Journal* until

14 May 1897. Written before Cora saw combat, the dispatch renders the view from Athens, the volunteers leaving for the front and the wounded crowding the hospitals. Certain metaphorical phrases—"amid flowers and tears," "as if death were a wine," "an impossible meadow"—suggest that Crane contributed to this piece. On 30 April the *Journal* printed "Woman Correspondent at the Front," datelined 29 April, in which Cora announced that she was leaving for Thessaly. "Imogene Carter's Adventure at Pharsala" survives in two untitled and unfinished manuscripts in the Rare Book and Manuscript Library of Columbia University. The first, an apparent attempt at revision, is in Stephen's hand. Much of this piece was printed by Lillian Gilkes in her biography, *Cora Crane* (Bloomington: Indiana University Press, 1960), 93–96. Cora describes her experience of spending the night of 2 May sleeping on a pool table in Pharsala, where she intended to interview the crown prince whose headquarters were in the town. Stephen had gone on to Volo with other correspondents. "Imogene Carter's Pen Picture of the Fighting at Velestino" is a cable printed in the *New York Journal* and the *San Francisco Examiner* on 10 May in which Cora reports witnessing the retreat of the Greek army at Velestino on 5 May. Her train was shelled on the return to Volo. In manuscript notes, also in the Columbia University Library and published in *Reports of War*, volume 9 of *The Works of Stephen Crane*, edited by Fredson Bowers (Charlottesville: University Press of Virginia, 1971), 272–73, Cora adds that shells flew over her head at Velestino.

Cather, Willa (1873–1947). Born in Virginia, Willa Cather moved with her family to Webster County, Nebraska, in 1883. As a child, she became absorbed in the atmosphere of prairie life and the stories told by her Eastern European and Scandinavian immigrant neighbors. Cather's early schooling was in Red Cloud, Nebraska. She attended the University of Nebraska in Lincoln, graduating in 1895. While in college, she was a drama critic and columnist for Lincoln newspapers. Much of her journalistic and other early writing appeared under various pseudonyms.

Cather left Nebraska in June 1896 for Pittsburgh, where she was an editor on a small magazine and a book reviewer for the *Daily Leader*. Her first separate publication was a collection of poems, *April Twilights* (1903). Her book of stories, *The Troll Garden* (1905), centered on the lives of artists, a subject that she developed further in *The Son of the Lark* (1915). Although she had little interest in social causes, she became an editor on S. S. McClure's muckraking magazine in 1906. Her novel *O Pioneers!* (1913), borrowing its title from Walt Whitman, dramatizes the struggle of early Scandinavian farmers and their rich cultural background. This subject reached its culmination in *My Ántonia* (1918). Cather's later novels sound an elegaic note portraying the end of the frontier era, and following her conversion to the Episcopal Church in 1922, she fused pioneer experiences with theological and historical themes in *Death Comes for the Archbishop* (1927) and *Shadows on the Rock* (1931).

Cather's fascination with the life and work of Stephen Crane extended over

a period of forty years. She first read the syndicated version of *The Red Badge of Courage* in the *Nebraska State Journal*, 4–9 December 1894, when she was a college senior and a drama critic for the *State Journal*, and shortly afterward she met Crane, on his tour of the West and Mexico for the Bacheller syndicate, in the office of the newspaper. Her account of their conversation, first published under one of her pseudonyms, Henry Nicklemann, as an obituary reminiscence titled "When I Knew Stephen Crane" in the *Pittsburgh Leader* of 23 June 1900, is dramatized and fictionalized. Some of the circumstantial facts of the encounter are inaccurate. The description of Crane's disheveled appearance seems true to life, but he is romanticized as having hands resembling those of Aubrey Beardsley and carrying a little volume of Poe in his back pocket. Although the weather in Nebraska in February 1895 was unusually cold and stormy, Cather, in the persona of Nicklemann, describes the night as warm and balmy. Crane's monologue on the writer's trade reveals a deep despondency over the need to subordinate his art to "any sort of stuff that would sell," and his account of his "hide-bound" imagination and need to filter experiences "through my blood" before he can write of them seems more characteristic of Cather's creative processes than Crane's. But Cather concludes memorably, "Now that he is dead it occurs to me that all his life was a preparation for sudden departure."

Cather's comments about Crane's work could be acerbic. Reviewing *War Is Kind* in the *Pittsburgh Leader* on 3 June 1899, she asserts that "[e]ither Mr. Crane is insulting the public or insulting himself, or he has developed a case of atavism and is chattering the primitive nonsense of the apes." Her review of *Active Service* on 11 November 1899 characterizes the novel as "coarse and dull and charmless." Nevertheless, Cather admired Crane's better fiction. Throughout her career, she helped to get his work published in newspapers and magazines where she exerted editorial influence. Her introduction to *Wounds in the Rain* in the Knopf edition of *The Work of Stephen Crane* (1925–27) points out that he was one of the first postimpressionists in literature, and she praises his mastery of detail and powers of description. In an addition to an earlier essay on Sarah Orne Jewett included in *Not under Forty* (1931), Cather concludes, "He died young, but he had done something real. One can read him today."

Suggested Reading

Robinson, Phyllis. *The Life of Willa Cather*. Garden City, N.Y.: Doubleday, 1983.
Slote, Bernice. "Stephen Crane and Willa Cather." *Serif* 6.4 (1969): 3–15.

"The Cat's March". A story about Florinda, the artist's model in *The Third Violet*, that according to Vincent Starrett was written in Cuba (*Stephen Crane: A Bibliography*. Philadelphia: Centaur, 1923, 10). She marries Pennoyer, one of the artists, and they settle in a small town where she experiences social rejection by respectable women. The manuscript is said to have been destroyed.

Centenary Collegiate Institute. The Newark Conference of the Methodist Episcopal Church founded the Centenary Collegiate Institute, which opened its doors

in September 1874 in Hackettstown, New Jersey. Jonathan Townley Crane had been a member of the institution's Building and Educational Committees during its formative years. Stephen Crane's older siblings Agnes, Edmund Luther, and William Howe all attended the institute, which was essentially a high school, but Agnes was the only one who was graduated. The school became Centenary Junior College in 1929. After World War II, it became Centenary College and began to offer full four-year degree programs.

Suggested Reading

Crane, Robert Kellogg. "Stephen Crane's Family Heritage." *Stephen Crane Studies* 4.1 (1995): 42–43.

Chamberlain, Samuel S. (1851–1916). Perhaps William Randolph Hearst's most flamboyant and ostentatious employee, Chamberlain was known for his sartorial splendor as well as his drinking binges. Before working for Hearst, he was a reporter and editor for a number of New York newspapers and executive assistant to James Gordon Bennett in Paris, where he helped to establish the Paris edition of the *New York Herald* and founded a French-language newspaper, *Le Matin*. In 1888 Chamberlain became managing editor of the *San Francisco Examiner*, and from 1895 to 1900 he held that position at the *New York Journal*. Chamberlain hired Stephen and Cora Crane to report the Greek-Turkish War for the *Journal* and played a key role in the sensational coverage that the *Journal* gave to the Spanish-American War. He hired Crane to report the Puerto Rican campaign after Crane had been fired from the *New York World*. Chamberlain was editor in chief of the *New York American* from 1905 to 1907 and continued with Hearst in various editorial positions until his death.

Chap-Book. One of the leading little magazines of the 1890s, the *Chap-Book* was a semimonthly publication founded by Herbert S. Stone and Hannibal I. Kimball in 1894 when they were seniors at Harvard. For a short time it was the house organ of their Chicago publishing firm, Stone & Kimball, but when Kimball took the publishing house to New York in 1896, Stone retained control of the magazine in Chicago. The work of many prominent American authors of the time and also contributions from numerous European writers appeared in the *Chap-Book*. Crane published one of his poems, "In the night," and an appreciative essay on Harold Frederic* in the magazine. The *Chap-Book* suspended publication in 1898.

"Chased by a Big 'Spanish Man-O'-War' ". This sketch, published in the *New York World* on 3 July 1898, is a fast-paced adventure narrative based on an event that occurred on 29 May when seven correspondents, among them Crane, Sylvester Scovel,* Ernest W. McCready,* and Jimmie Hare,* were cruising some 160 miles north of Jamaica aboard the dispatch boat *Somers N. Smith*, chartered jointly by the *World* and the *New York Herald* to search for Admiral

Cervera's fleet. The correspondents are lounging on the deck of the boat when the captain reports a steamer, which they assume to be a Spanish gunboat, headed straight for them. The dispatch boat puts on full steam, but the unidentified ship gains steadily, and since the enemy had proclaimed that newspaper reporters would be treated as spies, the men envision "Spanish prisons and the practice of garroting!" In a sharp anticlimax, the pursuing ship swings to starboard, "and to the eyes of the speechless and immovable crowd on the dispatch-boat was presented the whole beautiful length of the American auxiliary cruiser *St. Paul*." Crane adapted the factual framework of this narrative in his short story "The Revenge of the *Adolphus*."

Chord, Doctor. A character in *The O'Ruddy*, Doctor Chord (a play on *discord*) is a pedantic little scientist and social climber who pretends to befriend the protagonist but betrays his confidences to the Earl of Westport.

"A Christmas Dinner Won in Battle". This story appeared in an unlikely periodical, the *Plumbers' Trade Journal, Gas, Steam and Hot Water Fitters' Review*, on 1 January 1895, because the main character is a plumber. Tom "had set up a plumbing shop in the prairie town of Levelville as soon as the people learned to care more about sanitary conditions than they did about the brand of tobacco smoked by the inhabitants of Mars." With the advent of the railroad, Levelville undergoes transformation into an industrialized metropolis, and Tom rides the wave of progress to become one of its leading citizens. He has a close friendship with Colonel Fortman, the railroad president, and is also in love with the colonel's daughter, Mildred. Although Tom once saved Colonel Fortman's life by pushing him out of the path of a speeding train, Levelville (ironically, considering its name) has become a stratified society, and the Fortmans "mingled warily with the dozen families that formed the highest and iciest grades." The colonel indignantly rejects Tom's proposal of marriage to Mildred and banishes him from his house. When a railroad strike occurs, a mob of enraged workers, comprising a new immigrant underclass of "Slavs, Polacs, Italians, and Hungarians" and reminiscent to Colonel Fortman of the rabble that stormed Versailles in the French Revolution, assails his mansion. Tom resists the mob and rescues the colonel's wife and Mildred. The colonel relents and not only invites Tom to Christmas dinner but now welcomes his proposal of marriage to his daughter. Although not one of Crane's best Western stories, "A Christmas Dinner Won in Battle" illustrates that even before he traveled to the West for the Bacheller syndicate, Crane was already very much aware of the disappearance of the frontier and the emergence of great industrial and social forces that were transforming that section of the country.

Churchill, Lady Randolph (1854–1921). Born in Brooklyn shortly after her parents had returned from Trieste where her father, Leonard Jerome, a wealthy financier and broker, had been U.S. consul, Jennie Jerome married Lord Henry

Randolph Spencer Churchill, second son of the Duke of Marlborough, in 1874. Their eldest son was the future prime minister Winston Leonard Spencer Churchill. Jennie's older sister Clara married Moreton Frewen,* later the owner of Brede Place.* Another sister, Leone, married John Leslie and became mother of the writer Sir Shane Leslie, who wrote a memoir of the Cranes' life at Brede Place. Lord Randolph died in 1895, and in 1910 Jennie married George Cornwallis-West, twenty years her junior. In June 1899 she launched her elaborate quarterly, the *Anglo-Saxon Review*, an expensive miscellany published by John Lane, each volume of which had an finely tooled leather binding that was a facsimile of a celebrated book of the seventeenth or eighteenth century. Each illustrated issue ran about 250 pages and contained literary essays, historical and biographical articles, fiction, and poetry. Henry James,* George Gissing,* and Robert Barr* were among those who contributed short stories. An abridged version of Crane's "War Memories" appeared in the December 1899 number. The miscellany was short-lived, ending publication in September 1901 after ten issues. Through her association with the Society of American Women in London,* of which Cora Crane was a member, Lady Churchill was instrumental in raising funds to outfit a hospital ship, the *Maine*, during the Boer War. Named after the battleship sunk in Havana harbor and staffed largely by American doctors and nurses and an American crew, the ship was a gesture of friendship between the two nations. Lady Churchill and Cornwallis-West were divorced in 1914, and in her late sixties she married Montagu Porch, who was three years younger than her son Winston.

Suggested Reading

Leslie, Anita. *Lady Randolph Churchill: The Story of Jennie Jerome*. New York: Scribner, 1969.

Cinch, Robert F. *See* "A Poker Game."

"The City of Mexico". This report was probably written during Crane's stay in Mexico City in the spring of 1895. It was not published in his lifetime and was first printed from the manuscript by R. W. Stallman in the *Bulletin of the New York Public Library* 71 (1967): 555–57. Crane presents a panorama of life in the city from the tourist's point of view. There is little focus or in-depth analysis. The opening paragraph contrasts the variegated appearance of Mexico City on a typical day, from the commotion of the morning, through the placid siesta hours, to the reawakening bustle of late afternoon, with the "uniform uproar" of days in North American cities. This theme is not extended, and what follows are brief comments on a variety of subjects: the weather, the dress and carriage of Mexican women, the architecture of the buildings and the conversion of the former palaces of Mexican grandees to modern uses, the influence of American business enterprises and amusements, the confident but cruel demeanor of bullfighters, and the portentous and inscrutable faces of priests.

"The City Urchin and the Chaste Villagers". A lame sequel to "The Fight," this Whilomville story appeared in the July 1900 issue of *Harper's New Monthly Magazine*. As in "The Fight," the primary issue in this story is status and supremacy in the juvenile hierarchy of the village. Having defeated Willie Dalzel in a fistfight and thus upset the established social order, Johnnie Hedge's standing remains uncertain. "His fame as a fighter had gone forth to the world, but there were other boys who had fame as fighters, and the world was extremely anxious to know where to place the new-comer." In the course of a game involving an oppressed cabin boy on a pirate ship played by the tribe formerly headed by Willie Dalzel, Johnnie Hedge's younger brother is victimized. Another fight between Willie and Johnnie ensues, and this time Willie seems to have the advantage when Peter Washington, the Trescotts' hostler, intervenes. The fight is resumed after Peter leaves but finally ends when Johnnie's ear is seized by "a dreadful woman," Johnnie Hedge's mother, who drags him off and stampedes the group of boys. The story ends on a comically Darwinian note: "Yes, the war for supremacy was over, and the question was never again disputed. The supreme power was Mrs. Hedge." The autobiographical basis of this story is revealed in Wilbur F. Crane's reminiscence of his brother's childhood. Wilbur describes a fight of Stephen's, "historic in the family, when as a boy of nine he thrashed the bully of Brooklyn Street, Port Jervis, a boy twelve years of age" who had browbeaten him. At the end of the fight, "the bully's mother, who had been watching the scrap, took her hopeful home and finished the thrashing that Stephen had begun."

"The Clan of No-Name". The most complex and cryptic of Crane's Cuban War stories, "The Clan of No-Name" was syndicated in newspapers on 19 March 1899 and collected in *Wounds in the Rain*. The story is preceded by a riddle that the reader is challenged to "unwind." The terms of this riddle, which asserts "a mystic tie" between heroism and treachery, are embodied in the envelope structure of the story. The opening and closing sections concern a beautiful young woman living in Tampa named Margharita, a "privileged belle" who accepts the courtship of a wealthy suitor, Mr. Smith, but simultaneously carries on a clandestine romance with Manolo Prat, a lieutenant with the Cuban insurgents. The body of the story is set in Cuba, where Prat is serving with an expedition that has landed arms from the United States that must be transported through two lines of numerically superior forces of Spaniards and guerrillas (Cubans who remain loyal to Spain) over a steep mountain trail to the main body of insurgents. In a rearguard holding action, Prat is trapped with others in a saucer-like hollow into which he has intentionally thrown himself to aid comrades who are still fighting. He is wounded and the only man still alive when they are overpowered and a guerrilla comes upon the hollow. "He and the young lieutenant exchanged a singular glance; then he came stepping eagerly down. The young lieutenant closed his eyes, for he did not want to see the flash of the machete." In the final episode, which takes place a few months after Manolo's death, Margharita coyly accepts Mr. Smith's proposal and, without regret, destroys the photograph of Manolo on her dressing table.

While Margharita is motivated by greed and Mr. Smith by lust, Manolo's ruling ideals are self-abnegation, duty, and the importance of law and action, themes prevalent in works of Rudyard Kipling such as *Captains Courageous* (1897), which Crane had probably read. Manolo is of a kind, Crane asserts in a refrain that is reiterated at the end of the story, who "needs must obey the law and always with the law there is only one way. But from peak and plain, from dark northern icefields and hot wet jungles, through wine and want, through all lies and unfamiliar truth, dark or light, he heard breathed to him the approval and the benediction of his brethren." Whether this turgid rhetoric asserts the point of the story or ridicules such postulates remains ambiguous. In an 1894 letter to Lily Brandon Munroe,* Crane had rejected the "clever Rudyard Kipling style" and presumably Kipling's maudlin leitmotifs. His admiration of the unassuming mindless courage of the common soldier is evident in the stories of *Wounds in the Rain*, but the "mystic tie" between heroism and treachery in the riddle of "The Clan of No-Name" may be that both are equally absurd in a world of illusions, where all aspects of the human condition, whether manifested in infidelity in love or sacrificial death, are ultimately meaningless.

Suggested Reading

Nagel, James. "Stephen Crane's Stories of War: A Study of Art and Theme." *North Dakota Quarterly* 43.1 (1975): 5–19.
Osborn, Neal J. "The Riddle in 'The Clan': A Key to Crane's Major Fiction?" *Bulletin of the New York Public Library* 69 (1965): 247–58.

Clancy, Martha. A character in "This Majestic Lie." Following the Puerto Rican campaign, Crane virtually secreted himself for some four months in the Havana boardinghouse of Mary Horan, who had previously sheltered the American spy Charles H. Thrall.* She is depicted in "This Majestic Lie" as Martha Clancy, "born in Ireland, bred in New York, fifteen years married to a Spanish captain, and now a widow, keeping Cuban lodgers who had no money with which to pay her."

Suggested Reading

Crane, Helen R. "My Uncle, Stephen Crane." *American Mercury* 31 (January 1934): 24–29.

Clancy, Mrs. In the playlet "At Clancy's Wake," she is the bereaved widow who finds solace in a bottle of rum and discomfits a reporter eager to obtain the basic facts of Clancy's life for an obituary by plying him with drink until he is more hopelessly confused than she is.

Clarence, Uncle. At an undetermined time in his career, but certainly before 1896, Crane projected a series of stories featuring an amiable buffoon named Uncle Clarence. Most likely, only "Art in Kansas City" and "The Camel" were written, and neither of these was published in Crane's lifetime.

[Clark, Dora] (?–?). A notorious Tenderloin prostitute, also known as Ruby Young and Dora Wilkins. Crane interviewed Dora Clark for a series of sketches of the Tenderloin he was writing for the *New York Journal*. In the early morning hours of 16 September 1896, while in Crane's company, she was arrested for soliciting by patrolman Charles Becker* of the Nineteenth Precinct, which was notorious for exacting money from streetwalkers. Crane defended Clark in police court and testified in her behalf when she filed suit for false arrest against the police. The incident brought him under police surveillance and ended his career as an investigative reporter in New York City. *See* also "Adventures of a Novelist."

Claverack College and Hudson River Institute. Crane attended this coeducational high school and junior college near Hudson in Columbia County, New York, from January 1888 to June 1890. The origins of the school were in the eighteenth century, and after its expansion in 1854, it developed rapidly, attracting students from many states and a number of Central American countries who were especially drawn to its exceptional music program. Claverack no doubt appealed to Mrs. Crane because it was a Methodist institution with compulsory chapel attendance and a ban on dancing, gambling, alcohol, and tobacco. Stephen was attracted to Claverack's military cadet corps, compulsory for boys, which consisted of a regiment composed of four companies and a color guard. The president of the school, the Reverend Arthur H. Flack, functioned as colonel of the regiment. Stephen was enrolled in the academic department, as distinguished from the classical or commercial. The course of study that he followed centered on composition, science, history, mathematics, and the Bible.

Crane's first signed publication, a two-column sketch about the explorer Henry M. Stanley, appeared in the February 1890 issue of the Claverack student magazine, the *Vidette*,* and he published one or two other short pieces in the magazine. Crane rose rapidly in the ranks of the cadet corps. The June 1890 issue of the *Vidette* records his promotion from first lieutenant to captain. He was also the catcher of the school's baseball team, one of the positions that he would later play on the Syracuse University* varsity. Claverack had a stimulating cultural and intellectual life. Two of the young women to whom the young Stephen was attracted, Harriet Mattison and Phebe English,* were accomplished in music and art. There were four literary societies for men and three for women. The *Vidette* published poetry and featured articles on literature, history, and art. Crane left Claverack, having completed only two and a half years of the curriculum. The reasons for his departure are not clear, but it is likely, as Cora Crane wrote in notes intended for a biography of Stephen, that he was preparing for West Point and a career as a professional soldier, but his brother William was convinced that there would be no war in Stephen's lifetime and that he would not prosper as an army officer. Crane consequently sought a more practical outlet for his ambitions in the mining-engineering program at Lafayette College,* but he departed from Claverack with deep regret. He wrote to a schoolmate in the fall of 1890, "You will always regret the day you leave old C. C. . . . I have still left a big slice of my heart up among the pumpkin seeds and farmers of Columbia Co."

Suggested Reading

Gullason, Thomas A. "Stephen Crane at Claverack College: A New Reading." *Courier* 27.2 (1992): 33–46.
Pratt, Lyndon Upson. "The Formal Education of Stephen Crane." *American Literature* 10 (1939): 460–71.
Wertheim, Stanley. "Why Stephen Crane Left Claverack." *Stephen Crane Newsletter* 2.1 (1967): 5.

Coke. A character in *Active Service*. Coke is a sophomore at Washurst College and one of the group of students who accompany the Wainwright family to Greece. His father is a millionaire who owns rolling mills, and he is Rufus Coleman's rival for the affections of Marjory Wainright. Nora Black attempts to use Coke in an undefined way to alienate Coleman from Marjory. Nora and Coke "[e]ach had some kind of a deep knowledge that their aspirations, far from colliding, were of such character that the success of one would mean at least assistance to the other but neither could see how to confess it."

Coleman, Rufus. The protagonist of *Active Service*, Coleman is Sunday editor of the *New York Eclipse*. On the one hand, he is a yellow journalist who has no compunctions about publishing stories that focus on sensationalism, slander, and the grotesque. At the same time he is a heroic figure in the Richard Harding Davis* mode. Cool and imperturbable, he resists the temptations of the seductive Nora Black and embarks on a hazardous journey through a war-torn landscape on an improbable mission to rescue his lady love. In the end he is an implausible journalist in whom the obligation of covering a war and the active service of the heart are not convincingly reconciled.

Colles, William Morris (1855–1926). A barrister and prominent member of the Society of Authors, Colles was the founder and managing director of the Author's Syndicate, a British literary agency to which Paul Revere Reynolds sent a number of Crane's Cuban War stories and "The Blue Hotel," which did not appear periodically in England. Colles also tried unsuccessfully to market an earlier story, "A Dark-Brown Dog."

Collins, Fred. The main character of "A Mystery of Heroism," Collins is a private in an infantry company under fire from field artillery. He foolishly accepts a dare by his comrades to cross a meadow under heavy bombardment to obtain some water from a well and returns with a bucket that is either already empty or emptied through an accident. Collins's futile actions illustrate Crane's theme of the unconscious nature and egotistical foundation of what is often called heroism.

"Concerning the English 'Academy' ". Crane intended this piece, one of his very few ventures into literary criticism, as a newspaper article, but it was published in the March 1898 issue of the *Bookman*. Crane derides occasional attempts in England to establish an academy of arts and letters similar to the one in France and also the decision of the London critical journal the *Academy* to award a prize of 100 guineas for the best literary work of 1897 and 50 guineas for the next best to two relatively undistinguished poets, Stephen Phillips and William Ernest Henley. Crane suggests instead that the prizes might better have gone to Henry James* for *What Masie Knew* and Joseph Conrad* for *The Nigger of the "Narcissus."* Crane calls James a "great workman" and opines that Conrad's novel is "the best story of the sea written by a man now alive."

"Coney Island's Failing Days". A newspaper sketch that appeared in the *New York Press* on 14 October 1894, "Coney Island's Failing Days," one of Crane's more significant ephemeral publications, reveals his deep ontological pessimism a short time before the serial publication of *The Red Badge of Courage*. On a Sunday afternoon at the end of the summer resort season, the narrator listens to a stranger, a self-described "very great philosopher," reflecting "with considerable scorn" on the ornate buildings, restaurants, amusement kiosks, music halls, and people on the boardwalk at Coney Island. Although the narrator's attitude toward the stranger's musings is sardonic, Crane's pessimism is evident in the stranger's observations that "humanity only needs to be provided for ten minutes with a few whirligigs and things of the sort, and it can forget at least four centuries of misery" and that in three young men enjoying themselves he sees "revealed more clearly the purposes of the inexorable universe which plans to amuse us occasionally to keep us from the rebellion of suicide."

Conklin, Jim. Henry Fleming's comrade in *The Red Badge of Courage* who dies horribly as a random casualty of war. He is usually referred to as "the tall soldier" in the novel. A considerable critical controversy, overtones of which may still be found today, raged in the 1950s and 1960s about the thematic role of Jim Conklin. In his introduction to the 1951 Modern Library edition of *The Red Badge*, R. W. Stallman interpreted the novel as a religious allegory in which the protagonist's redemption is brought about by the death of Jim Conklin, who, according to Stallman, represents Jesus Christ in such descriptive details as the wound in his side, his torn body, and the initials of his name. The wafer image at his death suggested to Stallman and other interpreters the sacrifice celebrated in communion. The hypothesis of a sacrificial redemption story, however, does not appear to fit the facts of the plot of *The Red Badge*. There is no integral connection between Jim Conklin's death and Henry Fleming's return to the battlefield, which is an accidental consequence of his ignominious wound. Furthermore, there is nothing godlike in the character of the tall soldier. He seems to be a very average man caught in the crosscurrents of battle. To a greater extent than Henry Fleming, Conklin is a hapless victim of war—not a sacrifice but a casualty.

Conklin is again referred to by Henry Fleming in "The Veteran," a story in *The Little Regiment*, as "young Jim Conklin, old Si Conklin's son—that used to keep the tannery," and Fleming's grandson is significantly named "little Jim." There was actually a private James Conklin who served in the 124th New York State Volunteer Regiment, the "Orange Blossoms," that was the model for Fleming's 304th New York and fought at Chancellorsville.

Suggested Reading

Greenfield, Stanley. "The Unmistakable Stephen Crane." *PMLA* 73 (1958): 562–72.
LaRocca, Charles J. Introduction to *The Red Badge of Courage: An Historically Annotated Edition*. Fleishmanns, N.Y.: Purple Mountain Press, 1995.

Conrad, Jessie (George) (1873–1936). One of numerous siblings in a working-class family, Jessie George was a typist when she married Joseph Conrad* in March 1896. They had two children, Borys and John. Jessie Conrad was the author of personal reminiscences, notably *Joseph Conrad As I Knew Him* (1926) and *Joseph Conrad and His Circle* (1935), and she also wrote books on cooking. The Conrads were house guests of the Cranes at Ravensbrook* and Brede Place* on a number of occasions, and Jessie Conrad's recollections are an important source of detailed information on the Cranes' life in England, especially on the close friendship between Crane and Joseph Conrad. These memoirs occasionally reveal flashes of asperity toward Cora. Jessie Conrad's often-quoted anecdote that on the day of Crane's death Cora wired Alfred T. Plant,* "God took Stephen at II.5, make some arrangement for me to get the dog home" (*Joseph Conrad and His Circle*, 75), is most likely apocryphal.

Suggested Reading

Conrad, Jessie. *Joseph Conrad and His Circle*. New York: Dutton, 1935.
Conrad, Mrs. Joseph. "Recollections of Stephen Crane." *Bookman* 63 (1926): 134–37.

Conrad, Joseph (1857–1924). Józef Teodor Konrad Korzeniowski, who wrote under the name of Joseph Conrad, was born in Russian-occupied Poland, the only son of impoverished landed gentry who were ardent Polish nationalists. In 1861 Conrad's father was exiled to a remote Russian province with his wife and son for revolutionary activities. Conrad's mother died in exile when he was seven, and his father, who had been allowed to return to Poland, died when he was eleven. Conrad was raised and supported by his maternal uncle and various other relatives. His formal education was sporadic and desultory, but he was an avid reader. He had an early desire to become a sailor and moved to Marseilles at the age of sixteen to learn seamanship. Conrad made several voyages on French sailing ships, largely to the West Indies. By his own account, he also took part in smuggling operations, transporting arms from France to the Spanish Carlists. In Marseilles Conrad lived a rather dissolute life and acquired debts. In 1878 he attempted suicide by shooting himself in the chest. Having recovered and settling his debts, he shipped out as a common seaman on a British freighter. He tarried aimlessly in London for a time, where he learned to speak English, and then resumed his career as a merchant seaman. For over sixteen years he served on various British merchant ships, especially in the Far East. Conrad secured a master's certificate in 1886, the same year that he became a British subject. His only command was of the *Otego*, which he joined in Bangkok and sailed to Singapore and Australia in 1888. A four-month tour on the Congo River in West Africa provided the setting of his most significant novelette, *Heart of Darkness* (1902). He returned to England in 1891 and took up the life of a writer.

Conrad's first novels, *Almayer's Folly* (1895), *An Outcast of the Islands* (1896), and *The Rescue* (1920; begun in 1896), were based on his experiences in the Malay Archipelago and legends about a trader he had met in Borneo. In 1896 he married Jessie George*; they had two sons. Conrad's third published novel, *The Nigger of the "Narcissus"* (1897), drew on his memory of a stormy sailing from Bombay to London in 1884. His masterpiece, *Lord Jim* (1902), dealt with the abandonment of a ship carrying Muslim pilgrims by the crew and the consequences of this act in the life of a young mate. Political intrigues in South America, London, and Russia formed the background of *Nostromo* (1904), *The Secret Agent* (1907), and *Under Western Eyes* (1911).

Conrad was Stephen Crane's most intimate literary friend in England. They were introduced in London on 15 October 1897 at a luncheon arranged by Sidney Pawling,* the partner of their mutual publisher, William Heinemann. According to Conrad, it was Crane who asked to be introduced to Conrad, but Conrad was also eager to meet Crane. "I *do* admire him. I shan't have to pretend," he wrote to Edward Garnett* the day before the luncheon. Conrad had read *The Red Badge*, which caused him to feel an immediate affinity with Crane as "a man who may understand" what he was attempting to achieve in *The Nigger of the "Narcissus,"* then beginning its serial run in Heinemann's *New Review*. After the luncheon finally broke up at four o'clock, Crane and Conrad tramped through London together and had dinner, discussing each other's work. To Conrad's great surprise, Crane expressed an interest in Balzac, insisting on being told in detail "all about the Comédie Humaine, its contents, its scope, its plan, and its general significance, together with a critical description of Balzac's style." A few weeks later Conrad sent Crane proofs of *The Nigger* *of the "Narcissus"* and a copy of *Almayer's Folly* inscribed to Crane "with the greatest regard and most sincere admiration," a tacit acknowledgment that at that time Crane was the more celebrated writer of the two. Crane responded to *The Nigger of the "Narcissus"* with great enthusiasm, calling the death of James Wait "frightful with the weight of a real and present death. By such small means does the real writer suddenly flash out in the sky above those who are always doing rather well." Conrad was extremely upset when on the book publication of *The Nigger of The "Narcissus"* several reviewers implied that his novel was inspired by *The Red Badge of Courage*. In the *Daily Telegraph* of 8 December 1897, W. L. Courtney wrote that "Mr. Joseph Conrad has chosen Mr. Stephen Crane for his example, and has determined to do for the sea and the sailor what his predecessor had done for war and warriors." In a letter to Crane on 24 December, Conrad called Courtney "a perfidious ass." He must also have been less than pleased by the backhand compliment in the *London Speaker* on 15 January 1898 characterizing his novel as "a worthy pendant" to *The Red Badge*.

The personal relationship between Conrad and the Cranes was close, although the punctilious Conrad always addressed Cora as Mrs. Crane. There are nine surviving letters of Conrad to Stephen and a considerably larger number to Cora. From the beginning, there was great empathy between the two authors. "I write to you as though we had been born together before the beginning of things," Conrad said a month after their first meeting. Jessie Conrad was pleased by "the easy terms of complete understanding" that existed between her husband and Crane when he first visited the Conrads at Stanford-le-Hope on 28 November 1897. In early 1898 Crane proposed that he and Conrad collaborate on a play to be called "The Predecessor,"* but Conrad was reluctant, insisting that he had no gift for drama. On 17 March 1898, Crane sent Conrad the revised manuscript of his story "The Five White Mice" as a token "of my warm and endless friendship for you." Two days later, after dinner at the Savage Club in London, the two writers discussed the plans for "The Predecessor." Conrad, immersed in the composition of *Lord Jim*, reiterated his lack of enthusiasm for the project, and Crane developed his idea into an outline for a novel that he never wrote, although Conrad used it in a later short story, "The Planter of Malta." In early April Conrad helped Crane to secure a £60 advance from William Blackwood & Sons on stories he would write about the Cuban War. When in November Crane, reluctant to return to England, delayed his stay in Havana and pleaded debts as an excuse for being unable to leave, Conrad attempted to secure a loan of £50 from Blackwood, offering his own future work as partial security. After Crane's return from Cuba in early 1899, the Conrads were guests at Brede Place* on a number of occasions. Crane was especially fond of Conrad's infant son, Borys, playing with the child for hours and insisting that Conrad buy a dog for him. When Conrad delayed, Crane provided the dog, as Conrad recalled in *Some Reminiscences* (1912). In the summer of 1899 the two writers bought a sailboat named *Le Reine* from Conrad's friend, Captain G.F.W. Hope, but Crane had difficulty keeping up with his share of the payments. Conrad was himself impoverished at this time. A few weeks before his death, Crane wrote to an influential friend requesting help to get Conrad a government pension. Conrad's last sight of Crane was on 23 May 1900 at the Lord Warden Hotel in Dover, the day before the Cranes crossed the English Channel to Germany in a desperate attempt to save Stephen's life. Conrad recalled that Crane appeared wasted and was barely able to speak, As Conrad left, he had "turned his head on the pillow and was staring wistfully out of the window at the sails of a cutter yacht that glided slowly across the frame, like a dim shadow against the grey sky."

Crane's only published statement on Conrad's work, in his essay "Concerning the English 'Academy' '' in the March 1898 issue of the *Bookman*, expressed unqualified praise for *The Nigger of the "Narcissus."* In his letters to Crane, Conrad was equally approving of Crane's fiction. Writing to Crane on 1 December 1897, he proclaimed admiration "without reserve" for "A Man and Some Others." "The Open Boat" was "immensely interesting. . . . Your temperament makes old things new and new things amazing." Four days later in a letter to Edward Garnett, he severely qualified his delight in Crane's "amazing faculty of vision" with a deprecatory judgment of his surface impressionism*: "While one reads, of course, he is not to be questioned. He is the master of his reader to the very last line—then—apparently for no reason at all—he seems to let go his hold. It is as if he had gripped you with greased fingers. His grip is strong but while you feel the pressure on your flesh you slip out from his hand—much to your own surprise." Notwithstanding these reservations, Conrad encouraged Crane to write "The Monster," which he said had "haunted" him ever since Crane outlined the story to him. In December 1898, when "The Price of the Harness" appeared in *Blackwood's Edinburgh Magazine*, Conrad wrote to Crane and a number of other people that the story was Crane's best work since *The Red Badge*, and he expressed the conviction that he was growing and expanding.

In his December 1919 *London Mercury* essay, "Stephen Crane: A Note without Dates," Conrad restated his appreciation of Crane's "wonderful power of vision" and acknowledged that "His impressionism of phrase went really deeper than the surface." Nevertheless, Conrad did not consider Crane's early death a great loss to literature; there was little likelihood "of any further possible revelation." Conrad's extended introduction to Thomas Beer's* *Stephen Crane: A Study in American Letters* (1923) is largely an idealized and sentimental anecdotal reminiscence, but in reference to "The Open Boat," Conrad expressed his appreciation of Crane's modernistic perspective, "which by the deep and simple humanity of presentation seems somehow to illustrate the essentials of life itself, like a simple tale." In his introduction to the 1925 Heinemann edition of *The Red Badge*, entitled "His War Book," Conrad affirmed Crane's universality: "He dealt with what was enduring, and was the most detached of men."

Critics have noted stylistic and thematic parallels between Crane's fiction and Conrad's, but claims of influence and counterinfluence are largely unsubstantiated. As Ford Madox Ford* put it, what Crane, Conrad, and Henry James*—three foreigners in England—had in common, which set them apart from their contemporaries, is that they rendered rather than told. Conrad's often-quoted statement in the preface to *The Nigger of the "Narcissus"* that his purpose is "by the power of the written word to make you hear, to make you feel—it is, before all, to make you *see*" seems to echo Crane's assertion in an 1896 letter to John Northern Hilliard* that "a man is born into the world with his own pair of eyes and he is not at all responsible for his quality of personal honesty. To keep close to my honesty is my supreme ambition." Although Conrad expressed an aversion to French impressionist painting, his stress on Crane's quality of vision is a counterpart of his own concern with the subjective rendering of experience, the difference being that while Crane most often represented the experiences of his characters directly and immediately, Conrad tended to present experience obliquely through memory and reflection. Both authors considered fiction to be a craft and made use of complex image patterns, suggestion rather than full exposure, irony, and symbolism. Their world perspective was modernistic in depicting man as a creature of limited capacity asserting human values in the face of a nihilistic and mechanical universe. Both were concerned with the relationship of the individual to the group and the moral question of conduct. *The Red Badge of Courage* and *Lord Jim* feature romantic egotists who desert their comrades under conditions of stress and anxiety, attempt to rationalize their cowardly behavior, and finally strive to redeem themselves. Conrad's dense, sometimes turgid and convoluted prose differs radically from Crane's staccato delivery, and his characterizations are more complex and introspective than Crane's, but Crane seems to have been a significant catalyst to Conrad's imagination.

Suggested Reading

Delbanco, Nicholas. *Group Portrait: Joseph Conrad, Stephen Crane, Ford Madox Ford, Henry James, and H. G. Wells*. New York: Morrow, 1982.
Fox, Austin M. "Stephen Crane and Joseph Conrad." *Serif* 6.4 (1969): 16–20.
Galen, Nina. "Stephen Crane as a Source for Conrad's Jim." *Nineteenth-Century Fiction* 38 (1983): 78–96.
Karl, Frederick. *Joseph Conrad: The Three Lives*. New York: Farrar, Straus, and Giroux, 1979.
Nettles, Elsa. "Conrad and Stephen Crane." *Conradiana* 10 (1978): 267–81.
Solomon, Eric. *Stephen Crane in England: A Portrait of the Artist*. Columbus: Ohio State University Press, 1964. 91–118.

The Cook. Unnamed in "The Open Boat," "the cheerful cook" is identified as steward Charles B. Montgomery* in "Stephen Crane's Own Story" and other newspaper accounts of the sinking of the *Commodore*. In the short story, his primary function is to bail out the seawater that threatens to swamp the dinghy.

Copeland & Day. Between 1893 and 1899, Herbert Copeland and Fred Holland Day directed a small publishing firm at 69 Cornhill Street in Boston that emulated private presses in England such as Kelmscott, Ashendene, and Doves, which were devoted to the printing of fine books in limited editions. Other American firms participating in the *fin de siècle** book arts movement were Stone and Kimball in Chicago, Small, Maynard and Company in Boston, and R. H. Russell in New York. In its brief existence, Copeland & Day published ninety-eight books and acted as distributors for a number of other privately printed volumes. Among the publications were works by distinguished British authors including Dante Gabriel Rossetti, Francis Thompson, Oscar Wilde, Robert Louis Stevenson, Elizabeth Barrett Browning, and William Butler Yeats. Copeland & Day was also, until the July 1896 number, the American publisher for *The Yellow Book*, a London quarterly that became the embodiment of the Decadent movement in England and ensured the firm an avant-garde reputation in the United States. The controversial reputation of figures such as Oscar Wilde and Aubrey Beardsley, art editor of *The Yellow Book* until 1895, was a deterrent for prominent American writers, but Copeland & Day gave encouragement to a number of lesser-known American authors whose books they published, particularly Bliss Carman, Richard Hovey, Louise Imogen Guiney,* and Stephen Crane. The firm was dissolved in April 1899.

Crane's poetry was recommended to Copeland & Day by John D. Barry,* assistant editor of the *Forum*. The firm proposed to publish an edition of the Sullivan County tales and also (in 1895) to publish *Maggie* as well as the poems, but these projects were abandoned. Crane proved to be one of Copeland & Day's more contentious authors. He demanded a quick acceptance or rejection of *The Black Riders*, and when the publisher objected to some of the poems, probably more on aesthetic grounds than because they were especially blasphemous, he responded in high dudgeon that he would "absolutely refuse to have my poems printed without many of those which you just as absolutely mark 'No.' It seems to me that you cut all the ethical sense out of the book. All the anarchy, perhaps. It is the anarchy which I particularly insist upon." Copeland & Day partly relented but refused to publish three of the poems and recommended the omission of seven, a suggestion to which Crane agreed. Two of the deleted poems, "To the maiden" and "There was a man with tongue of wood," were published later in *War Is Kind*, "To the maiden" reprinted there from earlier appearances in the *Philistine** (April 1896) and in *A Souvenir and A Medley*. "A god came to a man" and "One came from the skies" remained in manuscript until 1957, when they were printed in Daniel Hoffman's *The Poetry of Stephen Crane*. The other three have been lost.

The Black Riders was published by Copeland & Day in May 1895. The trade edition consisted of five hundred copies on grayish-white laid paper over boards with an adaptation of a rising black orchid design by Frederick C. Gordon* on the front and back covers. There was also a special printing of fifty copies (as was customary with Copeland & Day's books by American authors) in green ink on japan paper with a special binding, a few of these bound in white vellum stamped in gold. The poems were printed entirely in capitals at the top of each

page, leaving an extensive amount of space on each sheet. The poems are identified by roman numerals rather than titles.

Critics who associate Crane with the Arts and Crafts movement in the United
States ignore the fact that Crane had virtually no part in designing the format
of *The Black Riders*. It is inaccurate to maintain, as Christopher Benfey does,
that "[h]e welcomed Copeland and Day's suggestion to print the lines entirely
in uppercase letters—this would further emphasize the materiality of the poems"
(126–27). Indeed, when Copeland & Day advised Crane that they intended to
print the book in a "severely classic" form, Crane mistakenly inferred that they
meant Old English typography. Even the design for the covers of the book was
suggested by the publisher. The design submitted by Crane's friend Frederick
C. Gordon was rejected, and Copeland & Day had their own artist adapt Gordon's drawing of the orchid plant. The publisher did, however, achieve a happy
synergy of content and form in the book, and Crane was enthusiastic about the
eccentric layout that directed the attention of reviewers as much to the format
as to the poems, causing Harry Thurston Peck, in an otherwise favorable notice,
to call Crane "the Aubrey Beardsley of poetry." Nevertheless, *The Black Riders*
was one of Copeland & Day's best-sellers, going into a second and third printing. No copies remained when the stock of the firm was finally sold.

Suggested Reading

Benfey, Christopher. *The Double Life of Stephen Crane*. New York: Knopf, 1992. 123–
    39.
Kraus, Joe W. *Messrs. Copeland & Day*. Philadelphia: MacManus, 1979.
Vanouse, Donald. "The First Editions of Stephen Crane's *The Black Riders and Other
    Lines* and *War Is Kind*." *Courier* 29 (1994): 107–25.

Corcoran, Fidsey. In *George's Mother* Fidsey is one of the most combative
members of the gang of young street-corner toughs that George Kelcey longs
to join.

Corinson. A character who represents Corwin Knapp Linson* in "Stories Told
by an Artist."

The Correspondent. Crane identifies himself by this apt name in "The Open
Boat." The correspondent is the central consciousness of the story, although it
is a third-person narrative, and point of view alternates from the correspondent,
to the narrator, to the four men as a group as they reflect on the unconcern of
nature and society to the circumstances of the individual and the potentialities
of human brotherhood.

Suggested Reading

Nagel, James. "The Narrative Method in 'The Open Boat.' " *Revue des Langues Vi-
    vantes* 39 (1973): 409–17.

The Cowboy. Also called Bill, the cowboy is a functional character in "The Blue Hotel." During the fight between Johnnie and the Swede, the cowboy repeatedly urges Johnnie to "go it! Kill him! Kill him!" but when accused by the Easterner of collusion in the Swede's death, he protests that he "didn't do anythin'," an ironic repetition of Johnnie's insistence that "I ain't done nothin' to 'im," which underscores Crane's theme of malevolent societal indifference.

Crane, Agnes Elizabeth (1856–1884). The younger of Crane's two living sisters, Agnes was an important influence on his early development as a writer. Crane's parents were preoccupied with church and temperance affairs and often neglectful of their youngest son. Fifteen years older than Stephen, Agnes became a surrogate mother to him and, herself a writer, encouraged his youthful literary efforts. Like her brothers Luther, Edmund, and William, Agnes attended the Centenary Collegiate Institute* in Hackettstown, New Jersey (of which her father was a founder), and was class valedictorian upon her graduation in 1880. She worked briefly as a governess in Fort Lee, New Jersey. For a time she taught in the Mountain House School in Port Jervis, New York, which Stephen attended briefly, but she resigned in December 1882 because of disciplinary problems in her class. In 1883–84 she taught in an intermediate school in Asbury Park, New Jersey, where her family had moved. Declining health caused her to leave her teaching position, and she died, like Stephen, at the age of twenty-eight, on 10 June 1884 of cerebrospinal meningitis at her brother Edmund's home in Rutherford, New Jersey. Four of her sentimental, moralistic short stories were published in *Frank Leslie's Illustrated Newspaper.*

Suggested Reading

Gullason, Thomas. "Stephen Crane's Sister: New Biographical Facts." *American Literature* 49 (1977): 234–38.
———. "A Cache of Short Stories by Stephen Crane's Family." *Studies in Short Fiction* 23 (1986): 71–106.
Sorrentino, Paul. "Newly Discovered Writings of Mary Helen Peck Crane and Agnes Elizabeth Crane." *Courier* 21.1 (1986): 103–34.

"Crane at Velestino". The headline "Crane at Velestino" for this syndicated Greek-Turkish War cable was used in the city edition of the *New York Journal* on 11 May 1897. A variant version, "Stephen Crane at Velestino," appeared in the out-of-town edition of the newspaper on same day. On 4 May the Turks launched a major attack at Velestino in Thessaly, having failed in previous attacks to dislodge the defending Greek forces under the command of Colonel Constantine Smolenski. Crane, ill with dysentery, which he told other reporters was a toothache, remained with Cora at nearby Volo and missed the first day of the offensive. He arrived at Velestino on the second day and witnessed his first major battle; he found it exhilarating and described the action in the metaphorical style of his war fiction:

> The roll of musketry was tremendous. From a distance it was like tearing a cloth; nearer, it sounded like rain on a tin roof and close up it was just a long crash after crash. It was a beautiful sound—beautiful as I had never dreamed. It was more impressive than the roar of Niagara and finer than thunder or avalanche—because it had the wonder of human tragedy in it. It was the most beautiful sound of my experience, barring no symphony. The crash of it was ideal.

Crane acknowledges that the men who died there would not have shared his point of view. He attributes the defeat of the Greeks at Velestino to the indecisiveness of Crown Prince Constantine, who inexplicably ordered a retreat and sacrificed both Velestino and Volo, although the Turks had been successfully repulsed for three days. Smolenski was furious at the crown prince's ineptitude, but he obeyed orders and withdrew the army. The Greek retreat in the face of an apparent victory effectually ended the war. Crane's "letter" for the McClure syndicate, "A Fragment of Velestino," offers a more extended and even more subjective account of the campaign in Thessaly and this crucial battle. His cable, "The Blue Badge of Cowardice," describes the Greek retreat on Volo.

[Crane, Cora] (1865–1910). Cora Howorth Murphy Stewart was known as Cora Taylor, the madam of a house of assignation in Jacksonville, Florida, that also featured gambling and other amusements when she and Stephen Crane met at her place of business, the Hotel de Dream, in December 1896. She was born Cora Ethel Eaton Howorth in Boston, the daughter of John Howorth, an artist whose grandfather, George Howorth, had operated an art gallery in Boston and had invented a lucrative method of restoring oil paintings. Cora's father died when she was six years old. Her mother was the daughter of Charles Holder, a piano manufacturer in New York City, to which she returned with Cora when she remarried. By the age of seventeen or eighteen Cora was the mistress of Jerome Stivers, the son of a wealthy New York carriage manufacturer. During the time they lived together, she worked as hostess of a gambling house in the Tenderloin. In September 1886, at the age of twenty-one, she married Thomas Vinton Murphy, a wealthy young man who dabbled in the dry goods business and whose father had been collector of the Port of New York. The marriage was short-lived, and the couple were granted a divorce on the grounds of adultery. In January 1889 in London, Cora married an English aristocrat, Captain Donald William Stewart.* This marriage also quickly soured, but a divorce decree was apparently never granted. By early 1892 Cora had returned to New York and was living in a fashionable town house provided by another wealthy lover, Ferris S. Thompson, whose grandfather had organized the Chase National Bank. Cora affected the name "Lady" Stewart, and the couple traveled extensively, once making the *Orient Express* journey between Paris and Constantinople. The relationship ended in Paris when Thompson left Cora for an actress, and she stabbed him in the arm. Thompson's mother was obliged to go to France and bring her son home. On 15 March 1895 a suit by Captain Stewart against Thompson for alienating Cora's affections was dismissed.

How Cora came to Jacksonville is unknown, but on 21 March 1895, under the assumed name of Cora E. Taylor (local gossip has it that she was the mistress of a townsman named Allen Taylor), she purchased a boardinghouse, called the Hotel de Dreme after its former proprietress, Ethel Dreme. Cora changed the name to Hotel de Dream and transformed it into what her biographer euphemistically refers to as a "pleasure resort" or "nightclub" but it was primarily a place where local residents met their mistresses and where seamen involved in filibustering activities and journalists reporting on the developing insurrection in Cuba could find prostitutes, whether the women lived on the premises or not. The room clerk at the St. James kept a list of "the better houses of ill fame for the intelligent guidance of guests of the hotel," and Cora's establishment had a high rating. Crane was attracted to such places, and soon after he and Cora met, they formed what was to be a lasting relationship. Following the *Commodore* disaster and subsequent failed attempts to reach Cuba, Crane accepted an assignment from the *New York Journal* to report the Greek-Turkish War. He also contracted with the McClure syndicate for a series of reports from Greece, some of which McClure sold to the *Westminster Gazette*. Cora, accompanied by her companion, Mrs. Charlotte Ruedy,* joined Crane in London. In Greece Cora became one of the first identifiable woman war correspondents, sending back dispatches to the *Journal* under the name Imogene Carter* that on the basis of the external evidence of Crane's inscription of a portion of one of the manuscripts and the internal evidence of style seem to have been in part written by him. A series of "letters" from London on topics intended to be of interest to women—fashions, society gossip, travel notes, and the activities of aristocracy and royalty—that were circulated for serialization in American newspapers by Imogene Carter were also a collaborative effort between Stephen and Cora. They appeared unsigned in the *New York Press* between 15 August and 10 October 1897.

In Greece Cora was known as Lady Stewart or Mrs. Stewart, but in June 1897 she and Crane, accompanied by Mrs. Ruedy, two Greek servants, and a dog picked up on the battlefield of Velestino, set up housekeeping in England at Ravensbrook Villa* in Oxted, Surrey, as Mr. and Mrs. Stephen Crane. For Crane, settlement in England meant exile, not expatriation. As a result of his testimony on behalf of Dora Clark* in her suit against the New York police, his career as an investigative reporter in the city was over. His upright Methodist family would never have welcomed the hostess of the Hotel de Dream to their homes, but the literary group among whom the Cranes settled in England had less traditional views of marriage. Harold Frederic,* Ford Madox Ford,* and H. G. Wells* lived with women who were not their wives. Joseph Conrad* and Henry James* were tolerant, if not approving, of unconventional domestic relationships. To conceal his liaison with Cora, Crane gave William Heinemann's return address rather than Ravensbrook in letters to his brothers. When the Cuban War ended, Crane was clearly reluctant to return to England and to Cora. Late in August 1898 he slipped into Havana and went underground. He corresponded regularly with Paul Revere Reynolds but did not disclose his whereabouts to his English friends or to Cora, who was desperately attempting to locate him. After the *New York Journal* discontinued his salary and family pressures increased, he returned to New York on 28 December and sailed for England on New Year's Eve.

While Crane was in Cuba, Cora had negotiated with Moreton and Clara Frewen* to lease Brede Place* at Northiam, Sussex, a rambling, decrepit manor house into which the Cranes moved in mid-February, along with Mrs. Ruedy, two of Harold Frederic's children by Kate Lyon,* and a flock of servants, most of whom came with the house. Here they lived extravagantly, enjoying the company of the many eminent writers who lived in the vicinity and entertaining less welcome house guests—"Indians" Crane called them—for long periods of time while Crane ground out hack work to assuage their ever-mounting debts. Cora was active in the Society of American Women,* of which Lady Randolph Churchill* was the most prominent member. She took over a great deal of Crane's correspondence with his family, agents, and publishers and also acted as his amanuensis, taking dictation and preparing typescripts of articles and stories.

After Crane's final collapse and his death in Germany, Cora accompanied the body home and spent a few weeks with his family. When she returned to England, she and her friend Mrs. Brotherton moved into London apartments, first in Gower Street and then Milborne Grove, South Kensington, where she lived from September 1900 to near the end of April 1901, when she went back to the United States. Cora gathered together manuscripts of Crane's early and late work as well as periodical appearances for *Last Words* (1902). Despite her genuine grief and mourning for Crane, she succumbed to a compensatory infatuation with Poultney Bigelow,* a controversial American journalist and historian who with his novelist wife, Edith Evelyn, had occasionally visited the Cranes at Brede Place. Bigelow resisted Cora's advances but engaged his own literary agents, G. H. Perris* in London and John Russell Davidson in New York, to assist her in publishing Stephen's posthumous work and her own burgeoning literary efforts. Cora's maudlin short story "The Red Chimneys" was accepted by a Chicago literary syndicate, and a prose poem of romantic love on earth that is denied in heaven, "What Hell Might Be," appeared in the *Smart Set* (November 1901). "Cowardice," an incoherent story of the Brede ghost, was published by the Northern Newspaper Syndicate, but Harper's and other publishers rejected "The Lavender Trousers," Cora's attempt to continue Crane's Whilomville series, and her writing career eventually came to nothing.

In May 1902, having apparently spent some ten months with friends in Owensboro, Kentucky, Cora returned to Jacksonville. With money borrowed from bankers and from a loan shark, she built an imposing brothel known as the Court "down the line," Jacksonville's red-light district, at the corner of

Ward and Davis Streets, and, as Cora Taylor, once again took up the life of a madam. In the parlance of the time, the Court was a "sporting house," where gentlemen could enjoy dining, dancing, and other recreations as well as sex. The venture prospered, and in 1905 Cora constructed Palmetto Lodge, a seaside annex of the Court at Pablo Beach, eighteen miles southeast of Jacksonville. In June 1905 she married Hammond P. McNeil, the twenty-five-year-old wayward son of a prominent Georgia family. McNeil was an alcoholic who shortly after the marriage opened a saloon in a Jacksonville hotel. In May 1907 he shot and killed a nineteen-year-old youth he believed to be Cora's lover. Cora refused to testify against her husband at the preliminary hearing, and in October, possibly to prevent her housekeeper, Hattie Mason, an eyewitness to the murder, from being summoned at the trial, she sailed with Hattie for London, where she again took up lodgings in Gower Street. She was welcomed by the Conrads, H. G. Wells and his wife, and other friends, but Henry James snubbed her. McNeil was acquitted in a perfunctory trial since the shooting was an affair of honor, and Cora returned to Jacksonville in December. McNeil divorced her in 1909 and soon remarried. Four years later, he was accidentally killed with his own gun during a brawl with his new wife. Cora died of a stroke at Palmetto Lodge in September 1910. The name Cora E. Crane is engraved on her headstone.

Suggested Reading

Friedmann, Elizabeth. "Cora's Travel Notes, 'Dan Emmonds,' and Stephen Crane's Route to the Greek War: A Puzzle Solved." *Studies in Short Fiction* 27 (1990): 264–65.
———. "Jacksonville's Most Famous Madam." *Jacksonville Magazine* (May–June 1990): 12–20.
Gilkes, Lillian. *Cora Crane: A Biography of Mrs. Stephen Crane.* Bloomington: Indiana University Press, 1960.
Wertheim, Stanley. "Cora Crane's Thwarted Romance." *Columbia Library Columns* 36.1 (1986): 26–37.

Crane, Edith F. (1886–?). One of the daughters of Crane's brother Edmund, Edith Fleming Crane became a librarian in Poughkeepsie, New York. Throughout her life, she was a source of information and misinformation for Crane's biographers (Thomas Beer,* Melvin Schoberlin, John Berryman, and R. W. Stallman), to whom she sent anecdotes, photographs, and copies of letters and memoirs.

Crane, Edmund Brian (1857–1922). Edmund was the brother with whom Stephen had the closest relationship, and his residences in Lake View, New Jersey, and Hartwood, New York, were the closest to what may be called homes that Crane had in the United States. Little is known of Edmund's schooling, except that he attended the Centenary Collegiate Institute,* as did a number of his brothers and his sister Agnes. After the death of Jonathan Townley Crane, Stephen lived for a time with Edmund, then a teacher in Sussex County, New Jersey. When their mother died, Edmund became Stephen's guardian. He was employed in a business establishment on Beekman Street in New York when Stephen was exploring the Bowery between 1891 and 1893. Much of *The Red Badge of Courage* was written in Edmund's house at Lake View in the summer of 1893 when Stephen commuted between Lake View, where he coached a boys' football team on many afternoons, and the old Art Students League building on East Twenty-third Street, where he also did much of his writing. The maiden name of Edmund's wife, Mary L. Fleming, was probably the source for the surname of the protagonist of *The Red Badge*.

In the spring of 1894 Edmund moved to a house on the mill pond in Hartwood as manager of a large tract of land owned by his brother William. He also manufactured and sold ice and functioned as the local postmaster. Crane lived with Edmund and his family for long periods until he left for Florida in November 1896. *The Third Violet* was written at Hartwood and in nearby Port Jervis in the fall of 1895. Contrary to the recollections of Edmund's daughter Edith, Crane did return to Hartwood after the sinking of the *Commodore*, and "The Open Boat" was in part written there. Edmund later moved to Port Jervis, where he was in the coal business.

Suggested Reading

Crane, Edmund B. "Notes on the Life of Stephen Crane by His Brother, Edmund B. Crane." Beer Family Papers, Sterling Library, Yale University.

Crane, George Peck (1850–1903). Stephen Crane had little contact with his oldest living brother, George, who was born in Pennington, New Jersey, where his father was principal of Pennington Seminary.* George Crane was an employee of the Jersey City Post Office and worked for railroad companies in New Jersey. At the time of his death, he lived in New York City.

Crane, (Mary) Helen (1881–1922). At the age of eighteen, William Howe Crane's refractory eldest daughter, Helen, was, at Crane's suggestion, sent to live with Stephen and Cora at Brede Place* because she had, according to her father, acquired a tendency toward irresponsible behavior from her mother and needed the cultivation and guidance of a good home and a European school. Helen arrived at Brede Place in June 1899, and by August she had apparently committed a theft. In September Crane took Helen to the Rosemont-Dézaley School in Lausanne, which Edith Richie* and Mabel Barr had attended. At school Helen extorted a sum of money from her schoolmistress under the pretext that it was a loan to her uncle Stephen. This caused some misunderstanding between Crane and William. Helen accompanied the Cranes to Badenweiler where Stephen died and sailed home with Cora for the funeral. In later life, she was twice married and reportedly died a suicide.

Crane, Helen R. (1889–?). The daughter of Stephen's brother Wilbur, Helen Crane added the "R." to her name to avoid confusion with her cousin, Mary Helen, William Howe Crane's eldest daughter, who also called herself Helen. Her memoir, "My Uncle, Stephen Crane," in the January 1934 issue of the *American Mercury*, touched a raw nerve in the Crane family. Helen R. Crane maintained that Stephen's brothers, including her father, did little to assist him economically in his early struggles and "made no pretense of understanding the queer, uncommunicative boy who used to show up at odd times, often in the middle of the night, and after staying with one or another of them for a few days, would disappear in the same wonderful manner." Her memoir is the first public revelation of Cora Taylor's background as madam of one of Jacksonville's "houses of joy" and also provides valuable particulars of Crane's underground life in Havana in the fall of 1898.

Crane, Jonathan Townley (1819–1880). Stephen Crane's father was born in Connecticut Farms, New Jersey, the descendant of the Stephen Crane who was one of the original settlers of Elizabethtown as early as 1665. The Colonial Stephen Crane (1709–80) was a distinguished member of the New Jersey legislature and served two terms in the Continental Congress. Jonathan Townley Crane was orphaned at an early age and apprenticed to a trunk manufacturer in Newark. His parents had been Presbyterians, but at the age of eighteen he converted to the Methodist faith, purportedly because he could not accept the doctrines of deterministic Calvinism. On graduation from the College of New Jersey (Princeton) he prepared for the ministry, was licensed as a local preacher in 1844, and was admitted to the New Jersey Conference in 1846. In January 1848 he married Mary Helen Peck of Wilkes-Barre, Pennsylvania, daughter of the Reverend George Peck, then editor of the *Methodist Quarterly Review*. They had fourteen children; Stephen was the last. Jonathan Townley Crane was principal of the Conference Seminary at Pennington, New Jersey,* from 1849 to 1858. Dickinson College conferred the degree of Doctor of Divinity on him in 1856. In 1858 he returned to the pastorate as minister for various churches in New York and New Jersey. For eight years he was a church administrator, serving as presiding elder of the Newark district (1868–72) and the Elizabeth district (1872–76). His opposition to the Holiness Movement, which advocated a more spiritual emphasis within the Methodist Church requiring an adult experience of conversion known as "entire sanctification" and was embraced by his father-in-law, George Peck, and his influential brother, Jesse Peck, ultimately led to the loss of his administrative position. He was subsequently pastor of the Cross Street Church in Paterson, and from 1878 until his death, pastor of the Drew Methodist Church in Port Jervis, New York.

Jonathan Townley Crane was the author of numerous essays in the *Methodist Quarterly Review* and the *Christian Advocate* (New York). He tended to focus on social issues, and a number of his books, notably *An Essay on Dancing* (1849), *Popular Amusements* (1869), and *Arts of Intoxication: The Aim and the*

Results (1870), deplored venial sins such as dancing; reading trashy novels; playing cards, billiards, or chess; and drinking alcoholic beverages. Other books such as *Holiness the Birthright of All God's Children* (1874) and *Methodism and Its Methods* (1876) dealt with theological concerns.

Suggested Reading

Benfey, Christopher. "Stephen Crane's Father and the Holiness Movement." *Courier* 25.1 (1990): 27–36.

Crane, Mary Helen. "Rev. Jonathan T. Crane, D. D." *Pennington Seminary Review* 1 (June 1889): 1–5. Reprinted in *Stephen Crane's Career: Perspectives and Evaluations*. Ed. Thomas A. Gullason. New York: New York University Press, 1972. 29–35.

Wertheim, Stanley. "Another Diary of the Reverend Jonathan Townley Crane." *Resources for American Literary Study* 19 (1993): 35–49.

Crane, Jonathan Townley, Jr. (1853–1908). Stephen Crane's brother Townley (pronounced "Toonley") was not as personally close to him as his brother Edmund but was an extremely important influence on his literary career. As a professional journalist, he encouraged Stephen's early writing and was his first employer. Townley's journalistic apprenticeship was on the *Newark Advertiser*. In 1880 he began operating a summer news agency in Asbury Park, New Jersey, for the *New York Tribune* and the Associated Press. Because of his voracity in finding items of interest for his *Tribune* column, he became known as the "Shore Fiend." Townley was married three times. He affected eccentric dress, was a chronic alcoholic, and suffered a number of debilitating emotional breakdowns. Despite his idiosyncrasies, he developed a reputation as a serious reporter, covering important stories and speaking to news organizations on the nature of newspaper work. In 1884 he was elected secretary of the New York Press Club. During the summer months from 1888 to 1892, Stephen was his assistant in the New Jersey Coast News Bureau, gathering society gossip and reporting local events from Asbury Park, Ocean Grove, and other places along the New Jersey coast. In August 1892 the furor caused by Stephen's *Tribune* report on the annual parade of the United Order of Junior American Mechanics in Asbury Park led to his and Townley's dismissal from the *Tribune* staff, although Townley was later rehired and a few months later became the associate editor of the *Shore Press*. In 1899–1900 he lived with his brother and sister-in-law Wilbur and Martha in Binghamton, New York. He died indigent in the Binghamton Asylum for the Chronic Insane.

Crane, Lizzie Archer (?–?). The wife of Crane's oldest brother, George, Lizzie Archer Crane wrote a sketch, "Stephen Crane's Boyhood," that appeared in the *New York World* on 10 June 1900. She had little contact with Stephen as an adult but recalled his boyhood fondness for sports and military affairs.

Crane, Luther Peck (1863–1886). As a boy, Crane's brother Luther assisted his parents in their social and temperance work in Port Jervis, New York. He was librarian of the Sunday school they established for black residents of the town and became secretary of the local chapter of the Women's Christian Temperance Union at the age of fifteen. Like his brothers William, Edmund, and Wilbur, Luther attended the Centenary Collegiate Institute* in Hackettstown, New Jersey, but was forced to drop out when his father died in February 1880. He worked as a flagman and brakeman on the Erie railroad and was killed when he fell beneath the wheels of a moving train.

Crane, Mary Helen Peck (1827–1891). Stephen Crane's mother was born in Wilkes-Barre, Pennsylvania, the daughter of an itinerant Methodist minister. She was graduated from the Rutgers Female Institute, New York City, in 1847 and the next year married Jonathan Townley Crane. They had fourteen children, eight of whom were living when Stephen, their last, was born. After her husband's death in Port Jervis, New York, in 1880, Mrs. Crane moved to Roseville, New Jersey, near Newark, for a short time with some of her children, Stephen remaining with his brother Edmund in Essex County, New Jersey. She returned to Port Jervis for two years and in 1883 removed her family to Asbury Park, a summer resort on the New Jersey coast founded by Methodists. Mrs. Crane and her husband had been active in the temperance cause in Port Jervis, where she had been president of the local branch of the Women's Christian Temperance Union (WCTU), a position she also held in Asbury Park. She represented the local chapter of the WCTU at conventions in St. Louis, Nashville, Atlanta, and Boston. Mrs. Crane lectured frequently and wrote short stories and columns on religious and temperance subjects for local newspapers and perhaps for the *New York Tribune*, although none of her *Tribune* pieces have been identified. She was also a skilled artist and provided sketches for her father's history of the Wyoming Valley (Pennsylvania). In 1885–86 she suffered a nervous breakdown but soon recovered and was active in writing and lecturing on temperance and other civic subjects until her death in Paterson, New Jersey, on 7 December 1891.

Suggested Reading

Gullason, Thomas A. "A Cache of Stories by Stephen Crane's Family." *Studies in Short Fiction* 23 (1986): 71–106.

Crane, Mary Helen Van Nortwick Murray-Hamilton (1849–1933?). Familiarly called Nellie, Crane's eldest sister was an accomplished painter. After the death of her first husband, Cornelius S. Van Nortwick, she established an art school in Asbury Park, New Jersey, in 1887, first in the family home and two years later at an independent location. She continued to maintain her own studio after her marriage to Philip Murray-Hamilton, but only one of her paintings is known to survive. She and Stephen did not have a close relationship, owing probably to the considerable differences in their ages.

Crane, Stephen (1709–1780). Stephen Crane's Colonial progenitor was a third-generation descendant of Stephen Crane (1640?–1710?) of Elizabethtown in what is now New Jersey. Before the Revolution, he was sheriff of Essex County, judge of the Court of Common Pleas, speaker of the New Jersey Assembly, and a trustee of the First Presbyterian Church of Elizabeth. In July 1774 he was elected as one of five delegates from New Jersey to the First Continental Congress, which convened in Philadelphia in September. Although he is portrayed in the painting *The First Prayer in Congress* displayed in Carpenter's Hall, Philadelphia, Stephen Crane did not sign the Declaration of Independence. He had been reappointed by the New Jersey Assembly in January 1775 to attend the Second Continental Congress, but on 22 June the Assembly chose an entirely new slate of delegates, presumably because the former delegates had resigned or were unwilling to sever ties with England. He nevertheless remained active in Revolutionary affairs and is said to have been taken prisoner and bayoneted by British troops passing through Elizabethtown on 23 June 1780 and to have died of his wounds on 1 July. His son Jonathan met a similar fate at the hands of Hessian soldiers. The author of *The Red Badge of Courage* was very proud of his Revolutionary ancestors. "In those old times," he wrote John Northern Hilliard* on 2 January 1896, "the family did its duty," and in the spring he became a member of the Sons of the American Revolution. He made serious attempts to trace his genealogy, and in the summer of 1899 began work on a projected novel about the Revolutionary War in New Jersey, which he never completed.

Suggested Reading

Crane, Robert Kellogg. "Stephen Crane's Family Heritage." *Stephen Crane Studies* 4.1
    (1995): 8–10.

"Crane Tells the Story of the Disembarkment". In this dispatch, published in the *New York World* on 7 July 1898, Crane reports the first landing of U.S. Army regulars commanded by Brigadier General Henry W. Lawton at Daiquirí near Santiago de Cuba on 22 June. The invasion is orderly. The boats from the transport ships systematically disgorge troops, encountering little resistance from the enemy. There is a moment of exultation as the U.S. flag is raised. The only casualties occur when one of the transport boats overturns, and two men of the Tenth Cavalry, a black regiment, weighed down by their blanket rolls and cartridge belts, drown only yards from the shore. Crane fictionalized some of the events of the landing in " 'God Rest Ye, Merry Gentlemen.' "

Crane, Wilbur Fiske (1859–1918). Nicknamed Bert (sometimes written "Burt") in the family, Stephen's brother Wilbur attended the Centenary Collegiate Institute* in Hackettstown, New Jersey, as did his brothers Edmund and Luther and his sister Agnes. In 1881 he enrolled as a medical student at the College of Physicians and Surgeons (Columbia University), which he attended until 1886 without graduating. For a time, as did Stephen, he worked in his brother Townley's news agency in Asbury Park, reporting shore news for local newspapers and the *New York Tribune*. In 1888 he married Martha Kellogg, a servant in the Port Jervis, New York, home of his brother William. This marriage estranged some members of the Crane family from him. Wilbur and his wife lived in Asbury Park and Port Jervis and in 1898 moved to Binghamton, New York, with their four children. His eccentric brother Townley lived with them during the last years of his life. In 1907 Wilbur's wife left him for another man, taking the children with her. In 1915 Wilbur settled in a small town in Georgia, where he lived until his death. Wilbur left a convincing memoir detailing incidents of Stephen Crane's childhood that was published in the *Binghamton Chronicle* on 15 December 1900.

Suggested Reading

Crane, Robert Kellogg. "Family Matters: Stephen Crane's Brother Wilbur." *Stephen Crane Studies* 3.2 (1994): 13–18.
Crane, Wilbur F. "Reminiscences of Stephen Crane." *Binghamton Chronicle* 15 December 1900: 3.

Crane, William Howe (1854–1926). Paterfamilias of the Crane family after the death of his father, Stephen Crane's brother William Howe attended the Centenary Collegiate Institute* in Hackettstown, New Jersey, Wesleyan College, and New York University. He was graduated from Albany Law School in 1880 and established an independent law practice in Port Jervis, New York, in 1883. In 1889, with relatives and friends, he formed the Hartwood Park Association, which in January 1893 incorporated as the Hartwood Club. William Howe Crane was elected as its first president. Stephen often visited this hunting and fishing preserve some twelve miles from Port Jervis and listened to the tall tales of its members. The club served as the setting for his Sullivan County stories and sketches.

In 1890, with his wife and five daughters, William Howe moved into a house on East Main Street in Port Jervis, where Stephen often visited and wrote. He was prominent in community life, serving as district clerk of the board of education, treasurer of the Port Jervis waterworks, and for one year, special judge for Orange County. For the remainder of his life he was known as Judge Crane. William Howe Crane was an ambivalent figure in the life of his bohemian younger brother. Stephen alternately wished to please and placate and at the same time defy him. He frequently borrowed small sums of money from William and never repaid them. On the other hand, Stephen and Cora harbored and cared for William Howe's recalcitrant daughter Helen at Brede Place and attempted to superintend her education. William Howe occasionally dealt with Stephen's legal problems in America and served credibly as executor of his will. In later years he practiced law in New York City and California, where he was president of the American Lithia and Chemical Company. He was the author of one book, *A Scientific Currency* (1910).

Suggested Reading

Katz, Joseph. "The Estate of Stephen Crane." *Studies in American Fiction* 10 (1982): 135–50.
Sorrentino, Paul. "Stephen and William Howe Crane: A Loan and Its Aftermath." *Resources for American Literary Study* 11 (1981): 101–8.

Creelman, James (1859–1915). As a foreign correspondent for James Gordon Bennett, Joseph Pulitzer, and William Randolph Hearst, Creelman covered three wars and a number of minor conflicts in the 1890s. He began his career at age eighteen on the staff of the *New York Herald* and in 1889 was sent to Europe as the *Herald*'s special correspondent. He became editor of the London and Paris editions of the newspaper and gained a reputation for his interviews with distinguished personalities. After briefly editing Bennett's *New York Evening Telegram*, Creelman joined Pulitzer's *New York World* in 1894. He covered the Sino-Japanese War and in February 1896 was sent to Cuba to report the insurrection against Spain. In the spring of 1897 he went to Greece as one of six correspondents, including Julian Ralph and Stephen Crane, for the *New York Journal* to report the Greek-Turkish hostilities. In June 1898 he became one of Hearst's correspondents in Cuba. A believer in activist journalism, Creelman led the charge of American troops at El Caney and was wounded while talking surrender terms with a Spanish officer. Creelman rejoined the *World* in 1900. From 1906 to 1910 he served as special correspondent for the *New York Times*.

Creelman was a forbidding personage, and although he and Crane served together on the *Journal*'s staff in Greece and Cuba, they were not close friends. When Crane remained incommunicado in Havana in September 1898 while Cora's financial plight was growing worse, she attempted through Robert Barr[*] to pressure Creelman, as Hearst's representative in London, to obtain funds for her passage to New York so that she could continue on to Havana to search for Crane. Creelman was willing to contribute a small sum but was otherwise uncooperative. Another quarrel over funds occurred in December when in Creelman's absence from London his wife, Alice, opened a letter to him from Cora asking for a contribution to her private fund for the children of Kate Lyon[*] and Harold Frederic,[*] who had died in October. Alice Creelman refused this appeal, denouncing Kate Lyon "and the evil influence she has exerted over a morally weak man," and Cora replied indignantly condemning Mrs. Creelman's self-righteousness.

Suggested Reading

Creelman, James. *On the Great Highway: The Wanderings and Adventures of a Special Correspondent*. Boston: Lothrop, 1901.

Crocker, Jim. In "The Black Dog" he is the dying man who ironically expires from terror when he mistakes the fortuitous howl of a mangy cur outside his window for the foreboding, unearthly wail of a spectral dog.

Crouse, Nellie Janes (?–1943). A young woman whom Crane met only once and to whom he wrote seven impassioned, self-conscious love letters within a period of three months from December 1895 to March 1896. Crane and Nellie Crouse were introduced by Lucius L. Button* at a tea party on Thirty-fourth Street in New York City in January 1895. Her daughter, Edith Carpenter Lundgren, in a 1953 letter to Lester G. Wells, claimed that Crane visited Nellie Crouse in Akron, Ohio, shortly before her marriage, but this is most unlikely. Born in Akron, Nellie Crouse attended school in Washington, D.C. She married Samuel E. Carpenter in June 1897 and moved to Ridgefield, Connecticut, where her six children were born. In 1914 she was divorced and apparently did not retain custody of her children, who grew up in the Carpenter family home in Philadelphia. She lived in Paris for a time but died in Philadelphia.

Crane's tedious, stilted letters to Nellie Crouse with their forced humor, mannered declarations of principle, and affectations of virtue in the course of a failed attempt to impress a conventional midwestern beauty are often overvalued by scholars, who tend to ignore their context. This is probably because the letters, for all their *fin de siècle** posturing, express some of the moral values and attitudes about life and how it should be lived found in *The Black Riders* and other Crane works: renunciation of cynical pessimism, an affirmation of the importance of human kindness, a commitment to justice, and disdain for popular success. In these embarrassing letters Crane underplays his intellectuality. He attempts to disassociate himself from the bohemian connotations of the word "poet" because he fears that Nellie may "confuse the word 'poet' with various kinds of crazy sentiment." When she playfully expresses "a likelihood of being aghast at being left alone with such a clever person," Crane hastens to assure her that he is "often marvelously a blockhead and incomparably an idiot" and that he is socially inept. On the other hand, he indulges in a good deal of maudlin rhetoric that is found in none of his letters to others: "I will be glad if I can feel on my death-bed that my life has been just and kind according to my ability and that every particle of my little ridiculous stock of eloquence and wisdom has been applied for the benefit of my kind. From this moment to that deathbed may be a short time or a long one but at any rate it means a life of labor and sorrow. I do not confront it blithely. I confront it with desperate resolution." When Nellie Crouse attempts to alleviate the miasma by asserting that she prefers the man of fashion to the young Werther or the "wild shaggy barbarian," as he had described himself, the habitually unkempt Crane performs a volteface and asserts that "[y]our recent confession that in your heart you like the man of fashion more than you do some other kinds of men came nearer to my own view than perhaps you expected," although he acknowledges that "when I see a man of that kind I usually put him down as a kind of an idiot." He rationalizes her pointed remark that she likes "the man with the high aims and things" in her soul but not in her heart. When in March 1896 Nellie finally rejected him, Crane affected "[f]lagons of despair," but his buoyant letters to others at this time reveal that he was not seriously depressed.

Suggested Reading

Stephen Crane's Love Letters to Nellie Crouse. Ed. Edwin H. Cady and Lester G. Wells. Syracuse: Syracuse University Press, 1954.

"Crowding into Asbury Park". An unsigned article in the *New York Tribune*, 3 July 1892, announcing the opening of the summer vacation season in Asbury Park, New Jersey. The hotel keepers "do not put up umbrellas, nor even prices. They merely smile copiously." Crane describes new machines in the amusement park; there is a toboggan slide and a device called the "razzle dazzle." The town's founder, James A. Bradley,* is pursuing his penchant for posting moral maxims on the boardwalk and the beach, and the arrival of a celebrity, the boxer James J. Corbett, is eagerly awaited.

"The Cry of a Huckleberry Pudding". Perhaps the least effective of the Sullivan County stories, "The Cry of a Huckleberry Pudding" appeared in the Syracuse *University Herald* on 23 December 1892. The little man makes a huckleberry pudding for himself and his three friends in their hunting camp, but it is distasteful to the other men and only the little man eats it, feeling that "he must vindicate his work." Later, asleep in their tents, the three men who did not eat the pudding are awakened by a dreadful cry from the thickets and discover their comrade missing. The pudgy man assumes that a ferocious beast has dragged the little man away. They find the little man in the woods writhing in agony from a severe stomachache and giving vent to a harrowing wail described in absurdly hyperbolic terms "like a song of forgotten war," "the scream of a maiden," and "a dog [that] was stabbed in an alley." The savage beast has been the huckleberry pudding. The story ends, as do most of the other Sullivan County tales, with the dispelling of a misleading fear.

D

Dalzel, Willie. Willie appears briefly in "The Monster" as one of the group of boys who joins Jimmie Trescott in taunting Henry Johnson as "the monster" sits on a box behind the Trescott stable, a heavy crepe veil swathed about his head. Willie "was an older boy than Jimmie and habitually oppressed him to a small degree." Willie is prominent in a number of the *Whilomville Stories*. In "Lynx-Hunting" he goads Jimmie into firing the shot that wounds Henry Fleming's cow. As leader of the gang of boys to which Jimmie belongs in "The Trial, Execution and Burial of Homer Phelps," "The Fight," and "The City Urchin and the Chaste Villagers," Willie alternately cajoles and bullies the others, and finally he loses control of his gang to Johnnie Hedge, the boy from Jersey City, who in turn is vanquished by adult authority in the person of his mother.

"Dan Emmonds". A ten-page typescript that is apparently the fragmentary beginning of a novel is preserved in the Rare Book and Manuscript Library of Columbia University. It remained unpublished until printed almost simultaneously by Thomas A. Gullason in his collection *The Complete Short Stories and Sketches of Stephen Crane* (Garden City, N.Y.: Doubleday, 1963) and by R. W. Stallman in "New Short Fiction by Stephen Crane: I. 'Dan Emmonds,' " *Studies in Short Fiction* 1 (1963): 1–7.

On 26 March 1896 Crane wrote Appleton editor Ripley Hitchcock* explaining why he had violated business conventions by offering "Dan Emmonds," which he referred to as "a satirical sketch," to the Anglo-American firm of Edward Arnold rather than to Appleton, which had published *The Red Badge of Courage*. What Edmund Arnold published was *George's Mother*, but from notices that appeared in various publications both before and after the appearance of that novel, it is clear that the firm intended to publish another novel to be entitled ''Dan Emmonds'' (or ''Dan Emmons'') as well. The typescript at Columbia is a transcription of Crane's early manuscript or perhaps a redaction of that manuscript that Cora Crane had professionally prepared in December 1898 while Stephen was in Cuba in the hope of interesting a publisher in the work. It represents all that was written or all that remains of the novel Crane began some time before March 1896 but apparently abandoned. Cora and James B. Pinker attempted to market it as a finished sketch.

The remaining fragment or sketch deals with the adventures of an improvident young Irish immigrant to New York whose father sends him on a long sea voyage to prevent him from ruining the family's successful saloon business. The ship, named the *Susan L. Terwilleger* (possibly after the Terwilleger Funeral Parlor in Port Jervis, New York), founders in a storm off the coast of Australia, and the young man finds himself floating alone on the sea with nothing to buoy him up but a hen coop "and the dead body of a pig named Bartholomew, who had been a great favorite with the ship's cook." He is rescued by a boat from a nearby island that resembles a fishing smack, manned by sailors who are "copper as a door plate," with straight black hair, some of whom are dressed in little kilts. The young man makes a great effort to placate these strange-looking creatures, who fail to understand his long-winded monologue but are obviously delighted by his presence. As the boat nears the island, he begins to suspect that they may be cannibals and becomes very frightened. The story breaks off with Dan's words of farewell to the pig: '' 'Good fortune be with you, Bartholomew,' said I, addressing the distance. 'You are better off than I am indeed, if I am going to be killed after taking this long troublesome voyage.' '' Crane, lost in a cross between a Defoe-like voyage fantasy and a Swiftian satire, evidently found himself unable to bring this work forward.

Suggested Reading

Bowers, Fredson, ed. *Poems and Literary Remains*. Charlottesville: University Press of Virginia, 1975. 292–95. Vol. 10 of *The Works of Stephen Crane*. Ed. Fredson Bowers, 10 vols. 1969–76.

Monteiro, George. ''Stephen Crane's 'Dan Emmonds': A Case Reargued.'' *Serif* 6.1 (1969): 32–36.

———. ''Notes on Stephen Crane's 'Dan Emmonds' '' *American Literary Realism 1870–1910* 18 (1985): 120–32.

''A Dark-Brown Dog''. Crane probably wrote a draft of ''A Dark-Brown Dog'' in the summer of 1893, shortly after the composition of the other two ''Tommie'' stories, ''An Ominous Baby'' and ''A Great Mistake,'' dealing with an unnamed infant based on Maggie's brother who does not survive childhood. The story was revised in December 1899 or the first few days of 1900 when Crane was recycling early, hastily written stories in the hope of marketing them for fast money. ''A Dark-Brown Dog'' received its only contemporary publication in *Cosmopolitan* in March 1901.

The longest and most sophisticated of the baby stories, "A Dark-Brown Dog" embodies an admixture of subtle irony, sensationalism, and sentimentality that was probably introduced to accommodate popular taste. Tommie finds a stray dog and drags him home to his fifth-floor tenement apartment, which closely resembles Maggie Johnson's home. The dog is alternately petted and mistreated by Tommie, to whom he becomes devoted, and learns how to survive violence and abuse by the rest of the family. One day the father comes home more drunk than usual and holds "a carnival with the cooking utensils, the furniture, and his wife." He is "in the midst of this recreation" when Tommie and the dog enter the room, and "in a mood for having fun" he grabs the dog by a leg and flings him out a window. When the family comes looking for Tommie later, they find him "seated by the body of his dark-brown friend." The story ends on a maudlin note uncharacteristic of Crane's slum stories. Crane was fascinated by dogs; he owned and wrote about them throughout his life and mourned when they died. This may account for the unusual empathy evinced in this story.

Davies, Acton (1870–1928). Born in Quebec, Davies came to New York in 1887. He worked as a freelance reporter until 1893, when he became drama critic for the *New York Evening Sun*. During the Cuban War he was a correspondent for the *New York Sun* and, with Crane, covered the marine landing at Guantánamo Bay. Davies was a frequent contributor to magazines. Davies and Crane probably knew one another well, but little reliable evidence of their association survives beyond what has been elaborated or perhaps contrived by biographers. The best-known incident is related by Thomas Beer* in his fictionalized biography of Crane. According to Beer, one day in the spring of 1893, while lounging in the studio of the artist William Dallgren, Crane boasted to Davies, who doted on Zola, that he could write a better war novel than *La Débâcle*. Beer could have derived this story from narrations of similar incidents by Kenneth Herford and Ripley Hitchcock,* who maintain that the conception of *The Red Badge of Courage* originated in the studio of an artist friend when Crane insisted that he could have written a better war story than one that he had just read and was challenged to do so by the artist. Neither Herford nor Hitchcock mentions Dallgren or Davies. Vincent Starrett maintains that in Cuba, Davies typed Crane's manuscript of "The Cat's March," a lost story that was supposedly destroyed.

Suggested Reading

Wertheim, Stanley, and Paul Sorrentino. *The Crane Log: A Documentary Life of Stephen Crane*. New York: Hall, 1994. 90–91.

Davis, Richard Harding (1864–1916). One of the best-known fiction writers and war correspondents of his generation, Davis began his journalistic career with the *Philadelphia Record* and later worked for other Philadelphia and New York newspapers. In 1890 he became managing editor of *Harper's Weekly*. In his *Gallegher and Other Stories* (1891), Davis focused on slum environments, but unlike his mother, Rebecca Harding Davis, whose short stories exposed the inequalities of industrial society, and unlike Crane, he avoided the more sordid aspects of city life. In *Van Bibber and Others* (1892) his protagonist is a news-boy-detective, and the fictive tone is distinctly lighthearted. Davis traveled widely as a journalist and covered all the wars of his time. He reported the Cuban War for the *New York Herald,* the *Times* of London, and *Scribner's* and recorded his experiences in three books: *Cuba in War Time* (1897), *The Cuban and Puerto Rican Campaigns* (1898), and *A Year from a Reporter's Note Book* (1898). Davis served as correspondent for the *Times* of London and the *New York Herald* in the Greek-Turkish, South African, and Russian-Japanese wars. He was a colorful and dramatic correspondent who projected his personality into such books as *With Both Armies in South Africa* (1900) and *With the Allies* (1914). In his best-known work of fiction, *Soldiers of Fortune* (1897), he conveyed an image of himself as the hero of his own romantic adventures.

Davis was an occasional visitor at the Lantern Club,* but his first meeting with Crane was in England at the end of March 1897. Davis had contracted to report the Greek-Turkish conflict for the *Times* of London while Crane, who had been sent to Greece by Hearst's *New York Journal*, stopped briefly in London to meet his English publisher, William Heinemann. On 31 March Davis gave a formal luncheon for Crane at the Savoy that was attended by Harold Frederic,* Anthony Hope, and Sir James Barrie. The next day Crane and Davis left London on the same train, although for different destinations. They were together again in Athens on 28 April, and two days later, accompanied by Cora Crane, John Bass,* and other correspondents, they traveled to the scene of conflict in Thessaly. In a letter to his family, Davis described Cora as "a commonplace dull woman old enough to have been his mother and with dyed yellow hair." The two writers encountered one another on the battlefield of Velestino on 5 May, the second day of the battle, Davis commenting sarcastically that "Crane came up for fifteen minutes and wrote a 1300 word story on that. He was never near the front but dont [*sic*] say I said so."

Crane and Davis covered the major events of the Cuban War and the Puerto Rican campaign together. In his book, *Notes of a War Correspondent* (1910), Davis recalls that on the afternoon of 1 July 1898, the decisive day of the battle for the San Juan Heights, Crane "walked to the crest and stood there as sharply outlined as a semaphore" and refused orders to get down, although he was drawing fire on the American troops: "Crane wore a long India rubber raincoat and was smoking a pipe. He appeared as cool as though he were looking down from a box at a theatre. I knew that to Crane, anything that savored of a pose was hateful, so, as I did not want to see him killed, I called, 'You're not impressing anyone by doing that, Crane.' As I hoped he would, he instantly dropped to his knees. When he crawled over to where we lay, I explained, 'I knew that would fetch you,' and he grinned and said, 'Oh, was that it?' " (125). Davis developed a respect for Crane as a correspondent and an author that he had not had when they served together in Greece. In his May 1899 *Harper's Magazine* article, "Our War Correspondents in Cuba and Puerto Rico," Davis awarded Crane "the first place among correspondents in the late disturbance" and was especially perceptive in his understanding that Crane was a literary reporter who selected incidents and rendered them metaphorically and visually. "Of his power to make the public see what he sees," Davis wrote, "it would be impertinent to speak." Davis called "The Price of the Harness" "the most valuable contribution to literature that the war has produced." Davis served with Crane during the Puerto Rican phase of the war in early August and tells an amusing story in "How Stephen Crane Took Juana Dias" (or "Diaz"), a town near Ponce. According to Davis, Crane strolled into Juana Diaz and was accepted as "the American conqueror." The alcalde surrendered the keys of the town to him, and Crane lined up the men of the community in the plaza and divided them into the "good fellows" and the "suspect." With those he approved of, he held an all-night banquet, and when a regiment of American soldiers entered Juana Diaz in the morning, he blithely informed the colonel that he had taken the town the night before. The character Channing in Davis's story "The Derelict," in the August 1901 issue of *Scribner's Magazine*, bears a circumstantial resemblance to Crane, but the depiction is gently satirical and not unsympathetic.

Suggested Reading

Davis, Richard Harding. "How Stephen Crane Took Juana Dias." *In Many Wars by Many War Correspondents*. Ed. George Lynch and Frederick Palmer. Tokyo: Tokyo Printing Company, 1904. Reprint ed., La Crosse, Wisc.: Sumac Press, 1976.

Lubow, Arthur. *The Reporter Who Would Be King: A Biography of Richard Harding Davis*. New York: Scribner, 1992.

Osborn, Scott C. "The 'Rivalry-Chivalry' of Richard Harding Davis and Stephen Crane." *American Literature* 28 (1956): 50–61.

Davis, Robert H. (1869–1942). Born in Nebraska, Davis was an editor, columnist, and playwright. He began his career in journalism as a compositor on the *Carson Appeal* in Carson City, Nevada. He was a reporter for the *San Francisco Examiner* and the *San Francisco Call*, and from 1895 or 1896 to 1898 he worked for the *New York Journal*. Under the name Bob Davis, he later wrote a series of books that are compilations of his column in the *New York Sun*.

Davis's introduction to *Tales of Two Wars* (1925), the second volume in Wilson Follett's twelve-volume *The Work of Stephen Crane* (1925–27), presents a sensitive but romanticized and unreliable portrait of Crane as "a modern Villon," eager to show a girl of the streets who approaches him on Broadway "the way out" of her degraded existence. Davis dates this incident as occurring in 1896, but since he mentions that it was shortly before Crane's departure for

Greece, the more probable date would be 1897. Davis also reports a conversation with Ambrose Bierce, who purportedly observed that Crane "has the power to feel. He knows nothing of war, yet he is drenched in blood. Most beginners who deal with this subject spatter themselves merely with ink." Actually, Bierce expressed contempt for *The Red Badge of Courage*. In a 25 May 1896 letter to Percival Pollard, who in a *New York Journal* review three days previously had called the novel a crude imitation of Bierce, he congratulated Pollard for exposing "the Crane freak," and on 25 July 1896 the *New York Press* commented that Ambrose Bierce "cannot abear or abide Stephen Crane," quoting Bierce as remarking that Pollard had "dragged to upper day two worse writers than Stephen Crane. I had thought there could be only two worse writers than Stephen Crane, namely two Stephen Cranes."

Davray, Henry D. (1873–1944). Born in Paris and educated at the Sorbonne, Davray was an author, journalist, and London correspondent for a number of French newspapers and magazines. He translated novels by George Meredith, H. G. Wells,* and Joseph Conrad* into French. Crane sent a copy of *The Black Riders* to Davray in the hope that he would translate the poems, but although Davray reviewed the book in the January 1898 issue of *Mercure de France*, there is no record of a French translation. Davray's translation of *The Red Badge of Courage* (with Francis Viellé-Griffin) under the title of *La Conquête du courage* (1911) was uninspired and is sometimes said to be responsible for Crane's lack of reputation in France.

"Death and the Child". Apart from *Active Service*, in which war serves largely as the backdrop for a domestic melodrama, "Death and the Child" is Crane's only fictional representation of his experiences in the Greek-Turkish War of 1897. It is also the first war story Crane wrote after he had actually witnessed combat, and incidents in his dispatch "A Fragment of Velestino" are apparent in the story. Crane began to work on "Death and the Child" in October 1897, dictating a draft to Cora. "Death and the Child" appeared in two parts in *Black and White* (London) under the title "The Death and the Child" on 5 and 12 March 1898 and in *Harper's Weekly* in New York on 19 and 26 March 1898. The story was collected in the American and English editions of *The Open Boat*.

Peza, the protagonist of "Death and the Child," is a young Italian journalist of Greek ancestry who has come to Thessaly as a correspondent. Like Henry Fleming of *The Red Badge of Courage*, Peza is a neophyte to the actualities of war, and his development in the story is from innocence to experience. He differs from Fleming in that he is educated and sensitive, and his decision to join in the fighting is based on empathy and patriotism rather than romantic projections of personal glory. There are relevant if limited parallels between the plot and theme of "Death and the Child" and *The Red Badge*.

The story opens with a scene of terror and confusion that anticipates Hemingway's description in *in our time* (1924) of the Greek retreat from Adrianopolis during a later Greek-Turkish war. A throng of fleeing peasants stream down a mountain trail, "as if fear was a river, and this horde had simply been caught in the torrent, man tumbling over beast, beast over man, as helpless in it as the logs that fall and shoulder grindingly through the gorges of a lumber country." Counterpoised to this turmoil, as in *The Red Badge*, is an indifferent natural universe: a serene bay, a sapphire sky, and majestic mountains. The plight of the people caught up in the maelstrom of the evacuation moves Peza greatly, and he resolves to become a soldier, but he is an intellectual filled with a sense of self-importance, and his view of war is remote and abstract. As a phlegmatic Greek artillery officer leads the impassioned Peza to the arena of combat, into the valley of death, the booming of artillery fire sounds "in regular measures like the beating of a colossal clock, a clock that was counting the seconds in the lives of the stars, and men had time to die between the ticks." In the second section of the story, Crane juxtaposes another perspective on war resembling in its innocence Peza's disengaged attitude. A child, forgotten and abandoned in a mountaintop cottage by his confused parents, views the battle in the valley dispassionately. Engrossed in a game with a stick, he regards it as child's play similar to that in which he is engaged. As for Peza, war is a mystery to the child, and he attempts to interpret it in the familiar terms of shepherding, the occupation of his father.

As Peza approaches the front lines, he encounters wounded men, but at first he does not identify with them: "he cared for the implacable misery of these soldiers only as he would have cared for the harms of broken dolls." Most of the men seem to him to be only "stupid peasants." Climbing from the artillery to the infantry positions, he grows in consciousness as he ascends. Peza comes upon a man whose jaw has been half shot away and whose chest is drenched in blood. The soldier stares at him with "a mystic gaze, which Peza withstood with difficulty." When he announces to an infantry captain that he wishes to fight, he is directed to a group of dead soldiers covered with blankets and is given a bandoleer stripped from one of the bodies and a rifle. The bandoleer feels like "the clutch of a corpse around his neck," and the bodies of the soldiers seem to draw him "slowly, firmly down as to some mystic chamber under the earth where they could walk, dreadful figures, swollen and blood-marked." The emotional distance between Peza and the wounded and dead men dissolves, and, like Henry Fleming, unaware and uncomprehending, he suddenly finds himself bolting to the rear. As the ingenue flees, Crane makes a sharp contrast between his actions and those of experienced soldiers. A bearded man, one of the stolid peasants Peza despises, calmly puts down a piece of bread he has been eating and turns in his trench to face the enemy.

In the final section of the story, the child playing on the mountaintop sees someone who resembles a bloodied animal drag himself to the crest of a hill and fall. Gazing into Peza's upturned face, he inquires, "Are you a man?" This is the basic ontological question that Henry Fleming answers affirmatively at the conclusion of *The Red Badge*: "He had been to touch the great death and found that, after all, it was but the great death. He was a man.'' Sprawled on the hillside, Peza, in contrast, resembles ''a creature'' who gasps ''in the manner of a fish.'' His growth is ironically a descent as he comes to a full realization of his inconsequence, and ''the definition of his misery could be written on a wee grass-blade.'' Having experienced the horror of war, Crane could no longer endow it with any significance as a potential initiation into growth and maturity.

Suggested Reading

Halliburton, David. *The Color of the Sky: A Study of Stephen Crane*. Cambridge: Cambridge University Press, 1989. 159–64.
Holton, Milne. '' 'Death and the Child': The Context of the Text.'' *Stephen Crane Studies* 1.2 (1992): 1–8.

de Camp, Lyda (?–?). Madam of a brothel on Ward Street (''the line'') in Jacksonville, Florida, frequented by Crane at the same time he was involved with Cora. Crane inscribed a copy of the 1896 *Maggie* to Lyda de Camp on 18 February 1897.

De Friese, Lafayette Hoyte (1852–1928). De Friese studied law at Harvard and was admitted to the bar in 1879, He went to England in 1883 and represented a New York law firm in London for a quarter of a century as a specialist in international law. De Friese was an admirer of Crane's work and was introduced to him by Harold Frederic.* His wife, Katherine, was one of the officers of the Society of American Women in London* and sponsored Cora Crane's membership in the organization. The De Frieses were frequent visitors at Brede Place.* De Friese drew up the memorandum of agreement between Cora and Frederick L. Bowen, a young technical engineer, who contributed improvements in the design of a military canteen filter that Cora had invented. Katherine De Friese secured the services of the lung specialist, Dr. J. T. Maclagen, when Crane was stricken with tubercular hemorrhages in early April 1900. After Crane's death, Cora moved to Queen Anne's Mansions, a family hotel where the De Frieses and other friends resided.

Dempster, Billie and Dan. Two reticent brothers who are soldiers in ''The Little Regiment.'' The Dempster brothers hide their anxious concern for one another's safety with pretended indifference.

''A Desertion''. A melodramatic tenement story with echoes of *Maggie*, ''A Desertion'' was written in 1894 but published posthumously in the November 1900 issue of *Harper's Magazine* and included in *Last Words*. The story combines social realism with Poesque horror. A slum girl named Nell returns home to find her overprotective father seated at a table with his back toward her. She launches into a cheerful monologue that reveals the temptations and dangers she faces from a predatory foreman in the sweatshop where she is employed. Believing that her father is sulking, she approaches the chair and embraces him, springing back and shrieking in horror when she discovers he is dead: "The eyes, fixed upon hers, were filled with an unspeakable hatred."

The central episode is enclosed in a choral framework of gossiping neighbors. When the unnamed girl enters the tenement, three women are prattling in a hallway, speculating about the extent to which her father has protected her from the corrosive influences of the urban environment. At the end of the story, the neighbors misinterpret her terrified scream as indicating a brawl between the girl and her father, and a shrewish woman ironically exclaims: "Ah, th' damned ol' fool, he's driven' 'er inteh th' street—that's what he's doin'. He's drivin' 'er inteh th' street."

"A Detail". This cameo masterpiece, first syndicated by Bacheller on 30 August 1896 and reprinted in the Heinemann edition of *The Open Boat and Other Stories*, is an outgrowth of Crane's involvement as an investigative reporter in New York City's Tenderloin district from the spring through the fall of 1896. Although a number of critics have mentioned the striking immediacy of "A Detail," they have tended to dismiss it as a naturalistic depiction of the plight of the helpless in the atavistic environment of the modern city. The sketch involves a confused old lady desperately seeking employment amid the tumult and uproar of Sixth Avenue, the Tenderloin's main thoroughfare. She encounters two overdressed girls wearing "gowns with enormous sleeves that made them look like full-rigged ships with all sails set." The dramatic irony inherent in this meeting emerges only when it is realized that the girls are streetwalkers mistaken for gentlewomen by the naive old lady. She approaches them as they are loitering near a shop and asks them where she might find work. As she becomes more specific in her request, the girls respond with a mixture of sardonic humor and regret to the double entendres implicit for them in her words: "I can sew well and in a house where there was a good many men folks, I could do all the mending. Do you know any place where they would like me to come?" The young women exchange a smile, "but it was a subtly tender smile, the verge of personal grief," at such monumental innocence. " 'Well, no madame,' hesitatingly said one of them at last, 'I don't think I know anyone.' " As the two prostitutes watch the frail old lady walk away from them and merge into the crowd, an essentially ludicrous situation ends on a note of restrained pathos.

Suggested Reading

Wertheim, Stanley. "Stephen Crane's 'A Detail.' " *Markham Review* 5 (Fall 1975): 14–15.

"The Devil's Acre". Accompanied by an illustrator for the *New York World*, Crane inspected the death chamber and the convicts' graveyard at Sing Sing prison in Ossining, New York. His report appeared in the Sunday magazine section of the *World* on 25 October 1896. Crane makes a chilling contrast between the "comfortable and shining [electric] chair," a model of mechanical perfection and structural precision, and its horrific purpose. The chair represents a poetic union of "the terrible, the beautiful, the ghastly." The graveyard on a hillside overlooking the Hudson is the aftermath of death in the chair. The fragile board grave markers, subject to the ravages of nature and the trampling of cattle, are soon obliterated. "It is the fiend's own acre, this hillside."

"Diamonds and Diamonds". A cynical, humorous story about a Tenderloin confidence man nicknamed Jimmie the Mole, who, when "smitten with a financial famine," habitually borrows the same diamond ring from a woman known as the Flasher. He cons his victims into buying an imitation of the ring by allowing them to have it appraised and then substituting an identical paste ring for the valuable diamond the victim believes he has purchased. Jimmie is a concert hall singer with "a Tenderloin voice. This means a tenor well-suited to the air: 'She has fallen by the way-side.' " He is offered a two-week singing engagement in Boston, and the story describes how he deceives a Boston alderman with his favorite sleight-of-hand trick. "Diamonds and Diamonds" was most likely written in 1896 but was not published in Crane's lifetime. It first appeared in R. W. Stallman, "Stephen Crane: Some New Stories (Part II)," *Bulletin of the New York Public Library* 60 (1956): 477–86.

"The Dogs of War". An amusing anecdote published in the *New York Journal* on 30 May 1897 about a puppy Crane picked up on the battlefield of Velestino. John Bass,* in "How Novelist Crane Acts on the Battlefield," states that "amid the singing bullets and smashing shells the novelist had stopped, picked up a fat waddling puppy and immediately christened it Velestino, the Journal dog." In the Greek retreat, the dog was stolen from Crane's servant at Volo and recovered at Chalkis. Later, Cora maintained that it was she who had picked up the dog on the battlefield. Crane's fondness for dogs is evident in this sketch, as it is in his dog stories, "Jack," "A Dark-Brown Dog," and "A Yellow Under-Sized Dog." The puppy died in August at Ravensbrook,* causing Crane considerable distress.

Donovan, Father. A character in *The O'Ruddy*. Father Donovan is a priest from The O'Ruddy's home county in Ireland. They fortuitously meet in London, and Father Donovan accompanies The O'Ruddy to Brede Place* and there performs the wedding ceremony between him and Lady Mary.

Doyer, Swift. The protagonist of "In the Tenderloin: A Duel between an Alarm Clock and a Suicidal Purpose" and also a minor character in "Yen-Hock Bill and His Sweetheart." A Bowery hoodlum, his name is no doubt derived from winding Doyer Street in the Chinatown district of Manhattan. In the New York of the 1890s, a dishonest person might be characterized as being as crooked as Doyer Street.

Dryden. The fear-crazed private in "The Sergeant's Private Mad-House." Dryden's deranged singing ironically averts the Spanish guerrilla attack, the dread of which had driven him mad.

"The Duel That Was Not Fought". A New York City story published in the *New York Press* on 9 December 1894 and collected in the "Midnight Sketches" section of *Last Words*. Patsey Tulligan, a Bowery tough, drops by a saloon on lower Sixth Avenue with two friends after a night of heavy drinking. He provokes a quarrel with a Cuban dandy sitting in the booth behind him. The Cuban threatens a duel with swords, and Patsey, who knows nothing about fencing, is all too willing to accommodate him, ignoring two "peacemakers" in the bar who intervene and attempt to dissuade him. The episode ends when a policeman drags the enraged Cuban out of the saloon. The story satirizes mindless bravado, "For Patsey was not as wise as seven owls, but his courage could throw a shadow as long as the steeple of a cathedral."

Dungen, Carrie. In "The Monster" she is Martha Goodwin's confidante. Her function is to convey the gossip of the town to the reclusive Martha, who makes acidulous comments on Carrie's news that Dr. Trescott has had an altercation with Jake Winters, the father of the girl who had been terrified by Henry Johnson at Theresa Page's party, and that the Hannigans plan to move out of the house next to Dr. Trescott's because he is sheltering Henry.

E

Earl, Dan and Ella. Two children, a brother and sister, in the *Whilomville Stories*. In "The Angel Child" Dan Earl refuses to have his hair cut by William Neeltje, but Ella's "long ash-colored plaits" are shorn. The Earl children are among the picnickers in "Shame," and their mother's sister is the beautiful young woman who dispels Jimmie Trescott's embarrassment over having brought his lunch in a pail. Dan Earl appears as a member of Willie Dalzel's gang in "The Trial, Execution, and Burial of Homer Phelps" and "The City Urchin and the Chaste Villagers."

The Easterner. Significantly named Mr. Blanc, the Easterner represents the failure of human community in "The Blue Hotel." While he recognizes and gives voice to the complicity of the other characters in the Swede's tragedy, he remains a detached observer, and it is this very indifference for which he berates himself and others at the conclusion of the story, asserting that "[e]very sin is the result of a collaboration." He is, if anything, more callous than his fellows because he withholds the vital knowledge that Johnnie was cheating, which might have prevented the Swede's death. Even this is uncertain, for, as the Easterner realizes, "a thousand things might have happened," exemplifying the futility of attempting to impose any pattern of causality on the anarchy of existence.

["The Eastern Question"]. Unpublished in Crane's lifetime, this untitled Greek-Turkish War essay is preserved in manuscript in the Rare Book and Manuscript Library of Columbia University. Most likely it was written in England after the war. The first manuscript page and most of the second are in Cora's hand. It was first published in *The War Dispatches of Stephen Crane*, edited by R. W. Stallman and E. R. Hagemann (New York: New York University Press, 1964), 54–59. Crane concludes that not only has Turkey won the war against Greece but, through devious diplomacy, has outwitted the European powers. Far from being "the sick man of Europe," the Turk has emerged "seated coolly upon a pinnacle of success regarding with a singular smile the nations that have patronized him so long."

Edwards, Elisha Jay (1847–1924). A descendant of Jonathan Edwards and a graduate of Yale College and the Yale Law School, Edwards became a journalist in 1870. He was Washington correspondent for the *New York Sun* from 1880 to 1884 and editor of the *New York Evening Sun* from 1887 to 1889. Beginning in 1889 he wrote a daily column over the signature "Holland" for the *Philadelphia Press*, the *Chicago Inter-Ocean*, and the *Cincinnati Inquirer*. Edwards also reported for the *New York Press* and published articles on diverse subjects in *McClure's* and other magazines.

Edwards occasionally provided Crane with a place to sleep in his West Twenty-seventh Street room during Crane's early vagabond years in New York City. On 22 April 1894 Edwards published a sketch in the *Philadelphia Press* of a forlorn and disillusioned Crane standing in the offices of a New York newspaper with a rejected manuscript in his hand, ready to "chuck the whole thing" and go home "to my brother in New Jersey and perhaps learn the boot and shoe trade." He is given encouragement by a reporter, presumably Edwards, who informs him that William Dean Howells* had read *Maggie* and had compared Crane with Tolstoy. In an interview with Edward Marshall,* published simultaneously in the *New York Press* and the *Philadelphia Press* on 15 April 1894, Howells had called *Maggie* "a wonderful book." Edwards's own opinion of *Maggie* was ambivalent. He recognized the "cold, awful, brutal realism"* of the novelette but found it inadequate in artistry. Next to a clipping of Edwards's article in a scrapbook preserved in the Rare Book and Manuscript Library at Columbia University, Crane wrote: "This is a fake—not only a fake but a wretched, unartistic fake written by a very stupid man. But it was a great benefit."

On 1 May 1894 Edwards published a syndicated piece describing the 14 April reading of Crane's poems by John D. Barry* before the Uncut Leaves Society, and on 8 December 1894, the last day of the serial appearance of *The Red Badge* in the *Philadelphia Press*, Edwards congratulated himself in an editorial column for having recognized the imaginative power of the war novel after a hasty reading of the manuscript that Crane had completed in the spring. Crane liked this editorial comment well enough to make a handwritten copy of it.

Suggested Reading

La France, Marston. "A Few Facts about Stephen Crane and 'Holland.' " *American Literature* 37 (1965): 195–202.

Elliott, George Frank (1846–1931). Elliott was a fifty-two-year-old captain of U.S. Marines commanding Company C in Cuba when he participated in the skirmish at Cuzco on 14 June 1898 reported by Crane in "The Red Badge of Courage Was His Wig-Wag Flag." He served in the Philippines during 1899–1900 and in Panama in 1904. His final promotion was to major general in 1908. Elliott recommended Sergeant John H. Quick* for the Congressional Medal of Honor, which he received, for his heroic actions at Cuzco, described in Crane's "Marines Signalling under Fire at Guantanamo" and in "War Memories." Elliott also wrote an official report that cited Crane for "material aid during the action, carrying messages to fire volleys, etc. to the different company commanders."

"An Eloquence of Grief". On the morning of 14 September 1896 Crane sat beside a magistrate in the Jefferson Market Police Court in Greenwich Village to observe the disposition of justice for a series of articles on urban life he was writing for the *New York Journal*. Later he characterized what he had seen as "a kaleidoscope view," and one of the cases provided the impetus for "An Eloquence of Grief," published as one of the "Midnight Sketches" in the English edition of *The Open Boat and Other Stories*. This sharply focused vignette, dealing with the arraignment of a servant girl accused of stealing clothing from her employer, depicts the drab operation of the machinery of justice but contains sharply focused satire. The courthouse is described as being like a place of worship. The windows are "high and saintly," and the policeman at the door reprimands men who neglect to take off their hats. "He displayed in his voice the horror of a priest when the sanctuary of a chapel is defied or forgotten." But there is no mercy in this church. As the girl is led away after being committed for trial, she screams out her innocence from "a profound depth of woe" at the hopelessness of her situation. Nevertheless, the routine of dispensing "justice" continues undisturbed.

Suggested Reading

Kwiat, Joseph. "Stephen Crane, Literary-Reporter: Commonplace Experience and Artistic Transcendence." *Journal of Modern Literature* 8 (1980): 129–38.

Emerson, Edwin (1869?–1959). Born of American parents in Germany, Emerson went to school in Munich and in Florence. After graduating from Cornell, he undertook further studies at Harvard and was also art and literary critic for the *Boston Post*. At the start of the Spanish-American War, he became a correspondent in Cuba for *Leslie's Weekly* and later for *Collier's*. Emerson's burlesque diary, *Pepys's Ghost* (1900), written in imitation of *The Diary of Samuel Pepys*, amusingly recounts a number of incidents revealing the lighter side of Crane's furtive life in Havana in the fall of 1898. In 1904 Emerson covered the Russo-Japanese War for *Collier's*. He was in San Francisco during the 1906 earthquake and wrote many magazine and newspaper articles on the event. The *New York World* sent him to Europe at the outbreak of World War I. He was interred by the Germans when the United States entered the war, but in the

1930s Emerson was widely perceived as a Nazi sympathizer because he was president of the American Friends of Germany.

English, Phebe (or Phoebe) (?–?). A young girl from Jersey City Heights, nicknamed "Pete," with whom Crane was infatuated at Claverack College and Hudson River Institute.* Crane also carried on flirtations with two other girls, Harriet Mattison and Jennie Pierce. These girls were enrolled in the departments of art and music at Claverack. Phebe was distinguished for her painting. She was also a "special correspondent" for the school magazine, the *Vidette*.*

"An Episode of War". Written specifically for *The Youth's Companion* and submitted to them by Crane in March 1896, this Civil War story was not published by them in Crane's lifetime. *The Youth's Companion* was a family-oriented magazine, which probably considered the story too brutal for its readers and sold the English copyright to *The Gentlewoman*, where it first appeared in the December 1899 issue. It was collected in *Last Words*. *The Youth's Companion* retained the American and Canadian copyright and finally published the story in its 16 March 1916 issue. In an inventory compiled in 1897, Crane listed the story as "The Loss of an Arm," which may have been its original title, with "An Episode of War" as its subtitle. This would correspond in format to *The Red Badge of Courage: An Episode of the American Civil War.*

There are notable resemblances between this short story, one of Crane's best, and the war novel. Many passages in *The Red Badge* suggest that Henry Fleming has been permanently alienated by the traumatic shock of battle and that his adjustment to the regiment that represents his society may be self-delusive and temporary. Like Fleming and like Peza of "Death and the Child," the lieutenant of "An Episode of War" resembles Hemingway's shattered heroes, who can never recover from their physical and emotional wounds. "An Episode of War" opens with a mundane domestic scene in which the lieutenant, fully a part of the community of soldiers, is dividing rations of coffee beans on a blanket with his sword among representatives of the squads in his platoon, when he is suddenly wounded in the right arm by a stray bullet. The wound is simultaneously incapacitating and alienating; it isolates him from his fellow soldiers and from battle. The sword becomes an encumbrance that he transfers awkwardly to his left hand and that someone else must sheath for him. It is a symbol of his transformation from competence and mastery to ineffectuality and dependence. Paradoxically, the lieutenant, like Henry Fleming, acquires a new status and a special vision as he withdraws from the battlefield, a detached objectivity denied to men actively immersed in the turmoil of war that is Crane's metaphor for the struggle of life: "A wound gives strange dignity to him who bears it. Well men shy from this new and terrible majesty. It is as if the wounded man's hand is upon the curtain which hangs before the revelations of all existence—the meaning of ants, potentates, wars, cities, sunshine, snow, a feather dropped from a bird's wing; and the power of it sheds radiance upon a bloody form, and makes the other men understand sometimes that they are little." The lieutenant's new comprehension of his inconsequence is confirmed in the field hospital where his arm is amputated, ironically situated in an old school house, the door of which appears to him "as sinister as the portals of death." His awareness of the insignificance of the individual in the universal scheme is flatly expressed in his understated response to his family's grief at the sight of his empty sleeve. " 'Oh, well,' he said, standing shamefaced amid these tears, 'I don't suppose it matters so much as all that.' "

Suggested Reading

Nagel, James. "Stephen Crane's Stories of War: A Study of Art and Theme." *North Dakota Quarterly* 43.1 (1975): 5–19.
Shaw, Mary. " 'An Episode of War': A Demythologized Dramatization of Heroism." *Studies in Contemporary Satire* 18 (1991–92): 26–34.
Sorrentino, Paul. "Stephen Crane's Sale of 'A Episode of War' to *The Youth's Companion*." *Studies in Bibliography* 37 (1984): 243–48.

Ericson, David (1870–?). One of the artists and illustrators with whom Crane lived in the old Art Students League building on East Twenty-third Street at intervals between 1893 and 1895. Ericson was born in Sweden and studied with William M. Chase at the Art Students League and later with Whistler in Paris. He specialized in murals depicting American historical subjects. An article on Crane's aspirations and achievements in the May 1895 issue of the *Bookman* was illustrated with a pen and ink sketch of Crane by Ericson. In a letter to Ames W. Williams written in 1942, Ericson vividly describes Crane's bohemian life in the old Needham building, his excursion into the Bowery slums with W. W. Carroll,* and his spontaneous and yet deliberate method of writing.

Suggested Reading

Ericson, David. Letter to Ames W. Williams, 4 November 1942. In *Stephen Crane: Letters*. Ed. R. W. Stallman and Lillian Gilkes. New York: New York University Press, 1960. 341–42.

["European Letters"]. Writing to Paul Revere Reynolds in late October 1897 about potential publishing ventures, Crane proposed that Reynolds go to Curtis Brown,* then Sunday editor of the *New York Press*, and tell him "*in the strictest confidence*, that a lady named Imogene Carter* whose work he has been using from time to time is also named Stephen Crane and that I did 'em in about twenty minutes on each Sunday, just dictating to a friend." Crane's reference is not to the dispatches from Greece submitted to the *New York Journal* under Cora's pen name of Imogene Carter but to this group of articles on aspects of European life that were published unsigned in the *Press* between 15 August and 10 October 1897. The manuscripts of these and similar articles not published are now in the Rare Book and Manuscript Library of Columbia University. They are largely in Cora's hand, but stylistic evidence suggests that Crane may have dictated certain portions and revised and corrected others, and they should be considered a collaborative effort. Covering form letters from Cora addressed to the editors of American newspapers reveal that Cora intended them for syndication, but none have been found anywhere but in the *New York Press.*

These European "letters," as Cora called them, generally consist of a disjointed group of paragraphs, apparently culled from English newspapers and magazines, on a variety of topics. They center largely on fashions and society gossip, especially the doings of English and Continental royalty, nobility, and aristocracy, and their appeal seems to be for the most part to a female readership. There are occasional anomalous paragraphs and short essays on divergent subjects, such as the death of a London woman owing to the spontaneous combustion of a petroleum-based hair wash; the gruesome mutilation of Russian children to make them successful beggars; Cora's impressions of a Turkish harem that she visited on her stay in Constantinople with Ferris Thompson; and the announcement that Harold Frederic* has departed from American subjects and completed a novel dealing solely with English characters, *Gloria Mundi,* here identified by an earlier title, "Strawberry Leaves."

Suggested Reading

Bowers, Fredson, ed. *Tales, Sketches, and Reports.* Charlottesville: University Press of
    Virginia, 1973. 943–60. Vol. 8 of *The Works of Stephen Crane.* Ed. Fredson
    Bowers. 10 vols. 1969–76.

"An Experiment in Luxury". A sequel to the more incisive "An Experiment in Misery," this diffuse reflection on the life of the New York wealthy appeared a week after its predecessor in the *New York Press* on 29 April 1894. The second experiment begins, as does the first, with a conversation between two men. Intent on exploring the question posed by an old friend who denies the commonplace that the rich are as burdened with cares as the poor and that "miseries swarm around all wealth," the young man of the earlier sketch visits the home of a wealthy friend named Jack to investigate "[t]he eternal mystery of social condition." The youth is disturbed by his own attraction to the life of luxury but views his friend's family with a great deal of irony. The millionaire father is a banal man fascinated by the antics of a kitten and the dinner-table banter of his children, the mother is a fierce social climber, and Jack's sisters are vapid beauties. There is much bitterness in the youth's final determination of the essential falsehood of the clichés imposed upon the poor, "that riches did not bring happiness" and "that each wealthy man was inwardly a miserable wretch." As in "An Experiment in Misery," Crane avoids commitment to a specific social position. The youth seems to agree with his old friend's statement that "[n]obody is responsible for anything." The rich as well as the poor are creatures of circumstance. Chance, not cosmic or social injustice, determines the unequal distribution of happiness and wealth.

Suggested Reading

Bassan, Maurice. "Stephen Crane and 'The Eternal Mystery of Social Condition.' "
    Nineteenth-Century Fiction 19 (1965): 387–94.

"An Experiment in Misery". When this autobiographically based sketch was
first printed in the *New York Press* on 22 April 1894, it was enveloped by a
framework that begins and ends with a conversation between the young protagonist and an older friend who stand on a sidewalk observing a tramp:

> "I wonder how he feels," said one reflectively. "I suppose he is homeless,
> friendless, and has, at the most, only a few cents in his pocket. And if this is so,
> I wonder how he feels."
>   The other being the elder, spoke with an air of authoritative wisdom. "You can
> tell nothing of it unless you are in that condition yourself. It is idle to speculate
> about it from this distance."
>   "I suppose so," said the younger man, and then he added as from an inspiration:
> "I think I'll try it. Rags and tatters, you know, a couple of dimes, and hungry,
> too, if possible. Perhaps I could discover his point of view or something near it."
>   "Well, you might," said the other, and from those words begins this veracious
> narrative of an experiment in misery.

The introductory frame continues with the young man going to the studio of an
artist friend from whom he borrows an old suit and brown derby hat. "And
then the youth went forth to try to eat as the tramp may eat, and sleep as the
wanderers sleep." As he walks to City Hall Park, small boys taunt him with
cries of "bum" and "hobo." When "An Experiment in Misery" was collected
in the Heinemann edition of *The Open Boat and Other Stories*, the opening
frame was dropped, but some of it was incorporated, in revised form, into the
body of the story itself. The young man is now depicted as a genuine bum
undergoing a real experience, and consequently the title seems inappropriate,
and the sentence, revised from the *Press*, "He was going forth to eat as the
wanderer my eat, and sleep as the homeless sleep," is ambiguous. The closing
portion of the framework was also deleted in book publication since it had
become inapplicable and was in any event redundant to the young man's reflections in the final two paragraphs of the story:

> "Well," said the friend, did you discover his point of view?"
>   "I don't know that I did," replied the young man; "but at any rate I think mine
> own has undergone a considerable alteration."

The removal of the framework changes the perspective of the central character
from that of a dispassionate observer, probably an investigative reporter, to that
of a participant whose detachment is tenuous and who fears that he may also
become submerged in the hapless life of the destitute.
    The structure of "An Experiment in Misery" is geographically circular. The
young man trudges along Park Row, where many of New York's major news-

papers were clustered, to Chatham Square, the southern terminus of the Bowery, where "there were aimless men strewn in front of saloons and lodging-houses," and continues walking up the Bowery, the skid row of New York City extending northward to Cooper Union and St. Marks Place. At the conclusion of the sketch, he returns to City Hall Park along the same route. On a Bowery corner above Chatham Square the youth enters a saloon that serves hot soup with the purchase of a beer. He follows a seedy man, who looks as if he might know of cheap lodging houses, from the saloon, and they discuss the possibilities of shelter for the night. They are approached by a man with the appearance of an assassin who guides them to a seven-cent flophouse. The youth and his companions are led on a Dantesque descent into a charnel-house dormitory by a man wearing spectacles who relegates them to slablike cots. The lockers have the appearance of tombstones; the men lie on their cots like corpses; "there was a strange effect of a graveyard, where bodies were merely flung." The wail of one of the men seems to the youth "the protest of the wretch who feels the touch of the imperturbable granite wheels and who then cries with an impersonal eloquence, with a strength not from him, giving voice to the wail of a whole section, a class, a people." But the morning light dispels this deterministic fantasy as well as the surrealistic atmosphere and gradually makes the room "comparatively commonplace and uninteresting." After they leave the flophouse, the youth buys breakfast for the assassin and discovers that he is not the representative of a downtrodden class but a shiftless tramp who has formed habits of dependency and exploitation. The two men trudge back to City Hall Park, where they sit on benches, ignored by busy, well-dressed people of the business district rushing past them. In the background, the huge commercial buildings appear to the youth as "emblematic of a nation forcing its regal head into the clouds, throwing no downward glances; in the sublimity of its aspirations ignoring the wretches who may flounder at its feet." The youth "confessed himself an outcast, and his eyes from under the lowered rim of his hat began to glance guiltily, wearing the criminal expression that comes with certain convictions." The young man, representative of Crane himself, has been affected by what he has witnessed; his feelings are altered, but he is not moved to sentimental pity for the downtrodden and has not formulated a dogmatic political or economic perspective that views the Bowery denizens as victims of environmental circumstances beyond their control. The journey has been one of descent, discovery, and return. The protagonist's adjustment in attitude has involved a growth in consciousness, a feeling of guilt about his privileged position, and a new awareness of the increasing inequality of social condition in urban America.

Suggested Reading

Bassan, Maurice. "The Design of Stephen Crane's Bowery Experiment." *Studies in Short Fiction* 1 (1964): 129–32.

Giamo, Benedict. *On the Bowery: Confronting Homelessness in American Society.* Iowa City: University of Iowa Press, 1989.

Nagel, James. "Structure and Theme in Crane's 'An Experiment in Misery.' " *Studies in Short Fiction* 10 (1973): 169–74.

Penney, Scott. "The Veracious Narrative of 'An Experiment in Misery.' " *Stephen Crane Studies* 3.1 (1994): 2–10.

"An Explosion of Seven Babies". One of the more bizarre of Crane's Sullivan County stories, "An Explosion of Seven Babies" was not published in his lifetime but appeared under the title "A Sullivan County Episode" in the January 1901 issue of the *Home Magazine of New York*. There seems to be some burlesquing of the fairy tale in this story. The little man, lost in a forest, chances upon a stone wall and looking over it perceives a "brown giantess" working in a potato patch. Nearby on a bench under the eaves of a dilapidated cabin sit seven babies wailing and rubbing their stomachs. When the little man climbs over the wall to ask directions, he is reviled and assaulted by the giantess, who "began to roar like a dragon." The cryptic reason for her hostility is, "It made 'm sick! They ate ut! That dum fly paper!" In the crushing grasp of the giantess, the little man fears he is "going to be eaten." The giantess is momentarily distracted when the pudgy man also scales the wall and unloosens the "talons" that are "squeezing [the little man's] life away." In his panic the little man runs toward the seven babies, and when they "as a unit, exploded," the giantess renews her pursuit. The men escape over the wall and rejoin their companions who are in conversation with a fly-paper salesman for whom the enraged woman had mistaken the little man. Humiliated by his experience—he had not been a giant killer—the little man kicks the salesman in the stomach.

F

Fanhall, Grace. The heroine of *The Third Violet*, Grace Fanhall is a wealthy and aristocratic heiress with whom Billie Hawker falls in love. Like Marjory Wainwright of *Active Service*, she may have been modeled on Crane's conception of Nellie Crouse.* Nevertheless, Grace transcends the stereotype of the genteel Gibson Girl of a later time with her unaffected warmth, frankness, and freedom from class prejudice.

Farragut, Bella. The young woman courted by Henry Johnson in "The Monster." Bella is an example of Crane's stereotyping of African-American characters. A "saffron" beauty, she is delighted to accept Henry Johnson's adoration before he is disfigured. During the courting ritual in Watermelon Alley, Bella, her mother, and Henry "could not have been more like three monkeys." When Henry is transfigured into a faceless "monster," Bella's terror as she struggles to escape him is represented in a burlesque manner.

Ferguson, Jim. The improvident retired sailor in "The Auction" who is derided and humiliated by his parrot as his household goods are disposed of in a public sale.

"The Fete of Mardi Gras". Crane witnessed the Mardi Gras celebration in New Orleans in mid-February 1895, but the Bacheller syndicate delayed publication of this report, which did not appear in newspapers until a year later, on 16 February 1896. It is arguably the most effective of Crane's uneven travel sketches from the West and Mexico. "The Fete of Mardi Gras" captures the excitement and color of Canal Street at the height of the festival. In the expectant crowd can be seen the "gypsy hues of the maskers" and the small boys "arrayed in wondrous garments to represent monkeys, gnomes, imps, parrots, anything but small boys." The king and queen of the Mardi Gras are followed by their resplendent court, and the decorated buildings are illuminated by electric lights by which "[t]he royal colors of green and purple and gold shone forth in bunting and silk and glass." As the procession approaches, there is some jostling in the crowd, and an incongruous voice straight from the Bowery cries out: "Ah, git off de eart' an' give de grass a chanct t' grow." The procession features massive, glittering floats that "looked in the distance like vast confections," and a "luminous smoke" rises from the multicolored fireworks. Crane follows the floats and marchers from the brilliant lights of Canal Street down to the narrow and gloomy streets of the French Quarter, where the procession dissolves in front of the opera house that will be the scene of a grand masked ball in the evening, opened by a person dressed in costume to represent Comus, the young god of festivity and revelry in Greek and Roman mythology.

"The Fight". In this Whilomville story, published in the June 1900 issue of *Harper's New Monthly Magazine*, a newcomer from Jersey City, Johnnie Hedge (an apt name since his position in the children's hierarchy is undetermined), is interposed into the boy's world of Whilomville, where status is defined in trial by combat. "The main thing was his absolute strangeness." Johnnie's foreign condition causes him intense suffering but is not altogether a liability. Utilizing a method of fighting unknown in Whilomville, he achieves a respected place in the scheme of things by defeating in a school yard brawl not only Jimmie Trescott but Willie Dalzel, the hitherto acknowledged chieftain of the town's boyhood society. Like a number of other Whilomville stories, "The Fight" probably has an autobiographical basis. Crane's own childhood as the son of an itinerant Methodist minister obligated frequent moves from town to town and from school to school, and he no doubt often shared Johnnie Hedge's feeling that "[h]e was a stranger cast away upon the moon. None knew him, understood him, felt for him."

"The Filibustering Industry". Written after Crane first sailed for England or perhaps on the voyage to Greece, this article appeared in American newspapers, probably syndicated by Bacheller, on 2 May 1897. Crane comments on the three ships, popularly known as "the Cuban navy," that regularly brought men and munitions to the insurgents on the island in defiance of the blockade by U.S. revenue cutters and warships. The *Commodore*, in which Crane made his abortive attempt to reach Cuba, was little more than a fishing steamer, and the *Dauntless* and *Three Friends* were oceangoing tugs that later became dispatch boats for American journalists. Crane contends that many filibustering expeditions to Cuba in these boats were subverted because correspondents granted passage to Cuban insurgent camps were more loyal to their employers than to the Cuban cause and telegraphed early accounts to newspapers.

Fin de siècle. This French term meaning "end of the century" was often used in the 1890s and generally equated with decadence or the aesthetic movement. Characteristic of the *fin de siècle* temperament in painting and literature was a glorification of art as an end in itself, a demand for cultural change, and a taste for the innovative and even the outrageous. The most prominent theorist of aestheticism was Walter Pater, whose doctrine of art for its own sake explicated in his *Studies in the History of the Renaissance* (1873) influenced a generation of writers at the turn of the century, notably Oscar Wilde and William Butler Yeats. Wilde's novel *The Picture of Dorian Gray* (1891) is probably the most famous exemplar of *fin de siècle* literature, and the art nouveau drawings of Aubrey Beardsley in the magazine *The Yellow Book* (1894–97) convey the essence of the movement in art. Reviewing *The Black Riders* in the May 1895 issue of the *Bookman*, Harry Thurston Peck called Crane "the Aubrey Beardsley of poetry" and opined that his book "has traces of *Entartung*" [Decadence], not only because of the affected format of the volume with its conventionalized orchid in black trailing across both covers but because of its "eccentric verse, skeptical, pessimistic, often cynical." Terms such as *rebellious, modern,* and *blasphemous* were often used to describe Crane's poetry, and this was its primary appeal to Elbert Hubbard* whose *Philistine** imitated *The Yellow Book.* The encapsulated world of Crane's poetry, its rebelliousness, world weariness, strikingly original imagery, synesthesias, personifications, riot of colors, and tendency toward perversity, as epitomized in the posthumously published "A naked woman and a dead dwarf," reveals Crane's affinity with the *fin de siècle* spirit in literature.

"The Fire-Tribe and the Pale-Face". This fragment of a play, the manuscript of which, transcribed in an unidentified hand, is preserved in the Rare Book and Manuscript Library of Columbia University, seems to be a paraphrase of the council of chieftains in the third section of "The Fire-Tribe and the White Face." Internal evidence suggests that the play may have been composed earlier and that Crane despaired of completing a successful dramatic production and recycled his material into the short story.

Suggested Reading

Fine, Lewis H. "*The Fire-Tribe and the Pale-Face*: An Unfinished and Unpublished Play by Stephen Crane." *Markham Review* 3 (1972): 37–38.
Monteiro, George. "Stephen Crane, Dramatist." *American Literary Realism 1870–1910* 19.1 (1986): 42–51.

"The Fire-Tribe and the White-Face". An uncompleted short story preserved in manuscript in the Rare Book and Manuscript Library of Columbia University and published for the first time in *Poems and Literary Remains*, volume 10 of *The Works of Stephen Crane*, edited by Fredson Bowers (1975), 164–186. "The Fire-Tribe and the White-Face" begins as a continuation of the Spitzbergen stories but soon degenerates into farce. The war is over, and the Spitzbergen army is occupying Rostina. Timothy Lean, now a captain, is ordered by Colonel Sponge to subdue a savage tribe in a remote and mountainous part of the country who are fire worshipers "and it is believed that after a successful raid upon their enemies, they celebrate the fact by feasting on boiled prisoners." While Lean's company marches upon their territory, the thirteen chieftains of the fire tribe hold council and, in an exchange of monologues reminiscent of the worst passages of James Fenimore Cooper, vow to defeat the white invader. After a rambling and bathetic address by Rudin, one of the chieftains, Catorce, another chieftain, comments: "O, Rudin, thy wisdom would light a wet log!" Lean's forces and the warriors of the Fire Tribe confront one another and, in negotiations ludicrously garbled by the interpreters, conclude that battle may be avoided if the Spitzbergen force pays each warrior of the tribe four Mexican dollars and a supplement of another Mexican dollar to the women of the tribe for each male child they have borne. Cora Crane attempted to induce Frederic Remington* to complete this fiasco, probably because of the stock characterizations of American Indians, but he wisely declined.

"A Fishing Village". Fourth in the series of "Irish Notes," this sketch was published in the *Westminster Gazette* on 12 November 1897 and collected in *Last Words.* "A Fishing Village" is the most literary of Crane's Irish sketches, opening with the image of an "innocent" little brook that turns "guilty" and sinister with the stain of blood at the site where mackerel are cleaned and packed. There is a picturesque depiction of the preparation of the fish for market, a ceremonial ritual of the community. The mackerel are "beautiful as fire-edged salvers," and the place simulates "a chapel consecrated to labor." An optimistic youth named Denny, "the type that America procures from Ireland," is contrasted with Mickey, a melancholy old fisherman, "bent, pallid, hungry, disheartened," who is likely to remain at home. There is a movement in the sketch from morning, when the fishing boats bring their catch ashore, to evening, when work ends and the brook changes from its ensanguined color to "a tumble of pearly white among the rocks."

"The Five White Mice". Set in Mexico City, this is the best of three stories, with "The Wise Men" and "A Man by the Name of Mud," centering on a point-of-view character known only as the New York Kid and his alter ego, the 'Frisco Kid. "The Five White Mice" was first printed in an abridged version in the Sunday Supplement of the *New York World* on 10 April 1898. It was collected in *The Open Boat* (1898).

The "mice" of the story are dice in a game of seven-up played by a group of brawlers in the Casa Verde, an American bar. When there appears to be nothing left to wager, one man suggests that the loser treat the others to a box at the famous circus, Circo Teatro Orrin. The final bet is lost by the New York Kid despite his supplication to the "five white mice of chance" and his attempt to bluff. Because he must take the gang of rowdies to the circus, he declines an invitation to accompany the 'Frisco Kid and Benson on a drinking binge. Later the New York Kid encounters his friends drunk on a street near the Casa Verde. Benson lurches into a group of Mexican grandees, and there is an immediate confrontation. As the New York Kid, his hand on his holstered revolver, contemplates the knife-bearing Mexicans, his consciousness careens wildly into irrelevancies, such as the hunting scene of a sportsman taking aim at a stag stamped into the black handle of the revolver, and his mind leaps forward, anticipating the reaction of his family to the news of his death. He understands that the consequences of any reaction he makes are as uncertain as the determinations of the five white mice, but despite the "eels of despair [that] lay wet and cold against his back," he suddenly realizes that it is possible to face down the danger. He takes the gamble and this time wins. His revolver "came forth as if it were greased, and it arose like a feather," and the Mexicans retreat. Benson makes a drunken summary of the causative factors leading up to the incident: "Kid shober 'cause didn't go with us. Didn't go with us 'cause went to damn circus. Went to damn circus 'cause lose shakin' dice." But the New York Kid apprehends the ultimate actuality that there is no explanation for the loss or the winning of a game other than the five white mice of chance, a factor that negates Benson's causal sequence, as does the Kid's action in drawing his gun. Calm, poised actions can influence the outcome of an uncertain situation, but Crane's final ironic reflection that "[n]othing had happened" suggests that human events are usually resolved by an inexplicable interplay of cause and effect, decisive action or inaction, and chance.

Suggested Reading

Mayer, Charles W. "Two Kids in the House of Chance: Crane's 'The Five White Mice.' " *Research Studies* 44 (1976): 52–57.

"Flanagan and His Short Filibustering Adventure". Two months after "The Open Boat" appeared in *Scribner's Magazine*, Crane published this second and far less successful short story based on the *Commodore*'s sinking. "Flanagan" was first printed in the *Illustrated London News* on 28 August 1897 and in America in the October 1897 issue of *McClure's Magazine*. Unlike the dedicated captain, Edward Murphy,* of the *Commodore*, Flanagan, whose ship is named the *Foundling*, drifts into filibustering "just for fun, mostly." His ship is in a state of "medieval disrepair," and its engine is "as whimsical as a gas meter." The *Foundling* survives a squall off Savannah and at sea off the southern coast of Florida takes on men and munitions for the Cuban rebels. En route to Cuba there is another storm; the Cuban insurgents are thoroughly seasick, and members of the crew are injured. The cargo and insurgents are successfully landed on the Cuban coast, and Flanagan saves his ship from being captured by ramming a Spanish gunboat. On the return journey, however, a third storm cripples the *Foundling* near the Florida coast, and after inspecting the engine room,

Flanagan orders the boats lowered. The scene in the engine room of the *Found-ling* closely resembles Crane's description in "Stephen Crane's Own Story" of what he saw on the foundering *Commodore*: "Water was swirling to and fro with the roll of the ship, fuming greasily around half-strangled machinery that still attempted to perform its duty. Steam arose from the water, and through its clouds shone the red glare of the dying fires." Flanagan is on one of the boats that leave the ship before it sinks, but like Billy, the oiler in "The Open Boat," he apparently drowns in the surf. His body is found by a group attending a dance at a beachfront hotel, and Crane comments that "[t]he expedition of the *Foundling* will never be historic." Although Flanagan has attained a quiet her-oism, this understated conclusion is inadequately prepared for.

Suggested Reading

Skerrett, Joseph T., Jr. "Changing Seats in the Open Boat: Alternative Attitudes in Two Stories by Stephen Crane." *Studies in the Humanities* 4 (1982): 22–27.

Fleming, Henry. The protagonist of *The Red Badge of Courage*, most often referred to as "the youth." The action of the novel focuses to a great extent on Fleming's mobile and unstable states of consciousness, but the detached, ironic view of the external narrator on his vacillations adds depth and complexity. Consequently much criticism of the novel has engaged the question of Henry's perception of reality and his "real" self, whether he shows psychological or moral development, and, if so, to what extent his transmutation indicates true growth toward maturity or remains self-deception. How the reader perceives the question of Henry's development, or lack of development, depends on the extent to which he or she can reconcile what seem to be two oppositional voices expressing Henry Fleming's affirmations of growth and the narrator's under-cutting commentary, which are counterpoised from the beginning to the end of the novel. The importance of the controversy and how it is resolved centers on the degree to which Crane thought it possible for an individual to achieve a sense of order and understanding in a universe of irrational and contending forces. In a balanced view, the novel may be seen as both a maturation story and an ironic study in self-delusion. Such ambivalence and ambiguity is a hall-mark of Crane's fiction.

Henry Fleming is also a character in two short stories, "The Veteran" and "Lynx-Hunting," in both of which he is depicted as an aged and kindly farmer.

Suggested Reading

Gibson, Donald B. The Red Badge of Courage: *Redefining the Hero*. Boston: Twayne, 1988.

Horsford, Howard C. " 'He Was a Man.' " In *New Essays on* The Red Badge of Cour-age. Ed. Lee Clark Mitchell. Cambridge: Cambridge University Press, 1986. 109–27.

LaFrance, Marston. "Stephen Crane's Private Fleming: His Various Battles." In *Patterns* of Commitment in American Literature. Ed. Marston LaFrance. Toronto: University of Toronto Press, 1967. 113–33.

Reynolds, Kirk M. "*The Red Badge of Courage*: Private Henry's Mind as Sole Point of View." *South Atlantic Quarterly* 52 (1987): 59–69.

Flossie. A demimondaine in "The 'Tenderloin' As It Really Is," Flossie is the subject of an altercation between Billie Maconnigle and Johnnie, "her fellow," who jealously regards her as "me own private snap!"

Flower, Benjamin Orange (1858–1918). An editor, writer, and reformer, Flower was born in Albion, Illinois, and educated in the public schools of Evanston, Indiana, and at Kentucky University. His first venture as an editor was on the *American Sentinel* in Albion. In 1886 he established the *American Spectator*, which he merged with the *Arena* in 1889. Flower edited the *Arena*, a magazine devoted to political, economic, aesthetic, and social change until December 1896. He also founded and edited other magazines dedicated to social issues. He rejoined the *Arena* in 1900 and became editor in chief again in 1904. Flower was cofounder of the American Psychical Society, of which Hamlin Garland* became an active member. From 1909 to 1911 he was founding editor of the *Twentieth–Century Magazine* (Boston), similar to the *Arena* as a forum for discussion of reform issues. In later years, Flower's zeal turned into fanaticism, and he edited the *Menace*, a virulently anti-Catholic magazine.

The forty-one volumes of the *Arena*, published from 1889 through August 1909, contain over four thousand pages of editorials and signed articles from Flower's pen, most of which are social in nature, expressing Flower's empathy with the poor and the oppressed. This concern is also paramount in his books, notable among which is *Civilization's Inferno; or Studies in the Social Cellar* (1893). Flower was a champion of realistic literature, and although he was more interested in messages that would lead to better social conditions than in literary form, the *Arena* supported realistic writers who were yet unknown, including Hamlin Garland, Frank Norris,* Stephen Crane, and Upton Sinclair. Crane was introduced to Flower by Garland, many of whose essays appeared in the *Arena*. The Arena Publishing Company also brought out Garland's books, *Main-Travelled Roads* (1891) and *Jason Edwards* (1892). Garland's June 1893 *Arena* review of *Maggie* was the only notice the novelette received in the year of its publication. Crane's "An Ominous Baby" appeared in the May 1894 issue of the *Arena* accompanied by a commentary in which Flower characteristically stressed the social implications of the story as he saw them. In October 1894, the *Arena* published "The Men in the Storm," also with a commentary by Flower predicting that, "This young writer belonging to the new school is likely to achieve in his own field something like the success Hamlin Garland has attained in his."

Suggested Reading

Dickason, David H. "Benjamin Orange Flower, Patron of the Realists." *American Literature* 14 (1942): 148–56.

"Flowers in [or "of"] Asphalt". A single-page typescript in the papers of Thomas Beer* (Beer Family Papers) in the Sterling Library at Yale University records an anecdote that on the grounds of persuasive circumstantial and intrinsic evidence is usually attributed to James Gibbons Huneker.* Huneker recalls that one evening in the spring of 1894, after attending the theater with Edgar Saltus, he encountered Crane on Broadway, and they started to walk to the Everett House hotel together. In Union Square they were approached by a boy prostitute wearing heavy makeup who was soliciting and followed them to the hotel. "Crane was damned innocent about everything but women and didn't see what the boy's game was," but when he finally understood, "he got interested. He took the kid in and fed him supper. Got him to talk. The kid had syphilis, of course—most of that type do—and wanted money to have himself treated. Crane rang up Irving Bacheller* and borrowed fifty dollars." After questioning the boy at length and, upon Huneker's recommendation, reading Joris Karl Huysmans's *À rebours*, which he thought stilted, Crane began a novel about a boy prostitute. He read the initial episode to Hamlin Garland* who was horrified and begged him to stop. Huneker did not know whether Crane ever finished the book. He was going to entitle it "Flowers of Asphalt."

    Although it is possible that Crane did begin such a book, no trace of the manuscript has been found, and there are several improbable aspects to Huneker's narrative. Given Crane's poverty at this time and that he was as yet unacquainted with Irving Bacheller, it is unlikely that he could or would have borrowed fifty dollars, a considerable sum in the 1890s, to give to a stranger. Huneker told Vincent Starrett that in October 1898 Crane began a book about a boy prostitute with a slightly variant title, "Flowers in Asphalt," that was to be longer than anything else he had written. But Crane was in Havana at this time, and, as John Berryman has suggested, no longer innocent about New York street life.

Suggested Reading

Berryman, John. *Stephen Crane*. New York: Sloane, 1950. 86–88.
Starrett, Vincent. *Stephen Crane: A Bibliography*. Philadelphia: Centaur, 1923. 10.
Wertheim, Stanley, and Paul Sorrentino. *The Crane Log: A Documentary Life of Stephen Crane*. New York: Hall, 1994. 105–6.

Forbes-Robertson, Johnston (1853–1928). One of Britain's greatest classical actors, acclaimed especially for his performances in Shakespearean roles, Forbes-Robertson began his career as a painter. He made his London stage debut in 1874 and for two decades played a great variety of parts. In 1896 he became an actor-manager at the Lyceum Theatre. When Crane sent the manuscript of "The Upturned Face" to James B. Pinker on 4 November 1899, he sent a copy to Forbes-Robertson "in an attempt to make him see that in a thirty-minute sketch on the stage he could so curdle the blood of the British public that it would be the sensation of the year, of the time." Forbes-Robertson did not take up the proposal. Forbes-Robertson was knighted and retired from the stage in 1913. He continued to give occasional performances and lectures in England and the United States.

Ford, Ford Madox (1873–1939). Ford's father was a German immigrant, and he was christened Ford Hermann Hueffer. His mother was the daughter of the pre-Raphaelite painter Ford Madox Brown, who was a formative influence in Ford's early career. In 1897 Ford met Joseph Conrad,* and for the next decade they were literary collaborators. The *English Review*, which Ford founded in 1908, featured modern authors such as Conrad, William James, T. S. Eliot, and Robert Frost. Ford was a prolific writer, producing thirty-four novels alone. His masterpiece, *The Good Soldier* (1915), was a landmark of impressionistic fiction. Ford dropped his middle name before he entered the British army in 1915, and in 1919 he changed his last name to Ford. In Paris after the war Ford launched the short-lived *transatlantic review* to which James Joyce, Gertrude Stein, and Ernest Hemingway contributed. Also in Paris Ford began a tetralogy of novels under the general title of *Parade's End*, centering an Edwardian protagonist named Christopher Tietjens. They comprise *Some Do Not* (1924), *No More Parades* (1925), *A Man Could Stand Up* (1926), and *The Last Post* (1928).

Ford's copious reminiscences are notoriously unreliable, yet they have in large measure been utilized by biographers to represent aspects of Stephen Crane's literary background and views and especially to depict Crane's lifestyle at Ravensbrook* in Surrey, where Ford was a near neighbor, and later at Brede Place.* Ford believed that Crane had read Zola, de Maupassant, and Flaubert in French, although Conrad's pithy observation that he "knew little of literature, either of his own country or of any other" is probably closer to the mark, and Ford is largely responsible for the notion that Crane detested Robert Louis Stevenson. "By God, poor dear!" Ford in *Memories and Impressions* (1911) recalls Crane as commenting on a stilted sentence of Stevenson's. "That man put back the clock of fiction fifty years." This remark was more likely made by Harold Frederic* than by Crane. Ford, however, showed critical acumen in his grouping of Crane with Conrad and Henry James* as progenitors of the fiction of selected incident.

In *Return to Yesterday* (1931), Ford recalls that before meeting Crane he attended a lecture given by him at Limpsfield near Oxted on flag waving or Morse signaling. There is no other record that Crane, who had an abhorrence of public speaking, humorously depicted in his Whilomville story "Making an Orator," ever gave a lecture or addressed an audience other than the Society of the Philistines at the dinner given in his honor on 19 December 1895. He did not learn Morse signaling until his combat experience with the marines in Cuba in 1898. Ford was introduced to Crane by Edward Garnett* in the fall of 1897, and there were occasional visits between Ravensbrook and Gracie's Cottage on Limpsfield Chart, which Ford had rented from Garnett. When Ford and his wife moved to Aldington, Hyth, Kent, in March 1899, he called at Brede to obtain material for a description of the manor for his book *The Cinque Ports* (1900). Ford's melodramatic description of Brede Place in *Portraits from Life* (1937) as "lying, unhealthily beshadowed and low in a Sussex valley" with "[a]ll the mass of the building of grey stone with mullioned, leaded windows, offering a proud and sinister front to sunlight coming through lowering clouds" is contradicted by his early description of Brede in *The Cinque Ports* as standing "upon high ground" with "the park in which it stands a fine tract of rolling country."

In his reminiscences, Ford constantly refers to Crane as "Stevie," or "Steevie," but in *Portraits from Life*, he acknowledges that Crane always addressed him as "Mr. Hueffer," and the salutation in Ford's one extant letter to Crane, written after they had known each other for almost two years, reads very formally, "Dear Mr. Crane." Clearly the personal relationship between the two writers was not close, but Ford is the originator of many of the proverbial anecdotes about Crane's life at Ravensbrook and Brede, especially those that stressed his American gaucherie. At Ravensbrook, Ford maintains in *Thus to Revisit* (1921), Crane loved "to sit about in breeches, leggings, and shirt-sleeves, with a huge Colt strapped to his belt. And he would demonstrate with quite sufficient skill how, on a hot day[,] he could swat a fly on the wall with the bead foresight of his 'gun.' " At Brede, according to Ford in *Portraits from Life*, Crane played lord of the manor, "with his wife in medieval dress and with, on the floors of the banqueting hall, rushes amongst which the innumerable dogs fought for the bones which the guests cast them." There is transparent gothic hyperbole in Ford's portrayal of "[t]he final tragedy of poor Steevie" writing himself to death in his study to support this huge establishment: "The sunlight fell blighted into that hollow, the spectres waved their draped arms of mist, the parasites howled and belched on the banks of Brede." Ford was an imaginative impressionist writer and a brilliant and unabashed fabulist. "Where it has seemed expedient to me," he explains in *Return to Yesterday*, "I have altered episodes that I have witnessed. . . . The accuracies I deal in are the accuracies of my own impressions."

Suggested Reading

Delbanco, Nicholas. *Group Portrait*. New York: Morrow, 1982. 41–81.

Finlayson, Iain. *The Sixth Continent: A Literary History of Romney Marsh*. New York: Atheneum, 1986.

Lindberg-Seyersted, Brita. *Ford Madox Ford and His Relationship to Stephen Crane and Henry James*. Atlantic Highlands, N.J.: Humanities Press International, 1987.

Seymour, Miranda. *Henry James and His Literary Circle, 1895–1915*. Boston: Houghton Mifflin, 1989. 23–44, 199–223.

"A Foreign Policy in Three Glimpses". Crane is often characterized as apolitical, but, while usually avoiding partisan issues, he occasionally commented on international affairs and was especially cynical about the efforts of European powers to justify their expansionist policies. "A Foreign Policy in Three Glimpses" is a dramatized essay written in 1891 or 1892, when feelings against British imperialism ran high in the United States. Its origin may in part have been an essay related to Russia that Crane read at a Delta Upsilon chapter meeting at Syracuse University* in the spring of 1891. The playlet was not published in Crane's lifetime. It was first printed from a faulty typescript in R. W. Stallman, "Stephen Crane: Some New Stories (Part III)," *Bulletin of the New York Public Library*, 61 (1957): 36–46.

The first of the "glimpses" spoofs Britain's economic plundering and brutality toward the natives of the South Sea Islands in the 1870s. In the second glimpse, Britain is ridiculed for its cowardice in the 1884 quarrel with Russia over the annexation of Afghanistan. When faced with a powerful potential foe, England is afraid to fight, but in the third "glimpse" the British press is quick to condemn the United States as a bully that would "never dare to assume such an attitude towards a nation of any importance" for its belligerence toward Chile over the U.S.S. *Baltimore* incident.

Suggested Reading

Gullason, Thomas A. "Stephen Crane: Anti-Imperialist." *American Literature* 30 (1958): 237–41.

Forister, Reginald. The villainous "little black man" in *The O'Ruddy* who is the Earl of Westport's partner in the shipping business. He is reputed to be the finest swordsman in England. By wounding him severely in a duel, The O'Ruddy acquires the reputation of a fierce and dangerous fighter.

Fortman, Colonel. In "A Christmas Dinner Won in Battle," Colonel Fortman is a railroad magnate in the prairie town of Levelville with whose daughter, Mildred, Tom, the protagonist, falls in love. Like Colonel Sherburn in *Huckleberry Finn*, Fortman represents an entrenched aristocracy that soon must give way to the forces of industrial progress, epitomized by Tom, that will "level" social distinctions.

"Four Men in a Cave". The first of the fictional Sullivan County pieces (as distinct from the more reportorial sketches) to be published, "Four Men in a Cave" appeared in the *New York Tribune* on 3 July 1892 and was collected in *Last Words*. In this grotesquerie, the little man is compulsively drawn to explore a cave "because its black mouth had gaped at him." He is reluctantly followed by his companions, the pudgy man, the tall man, and the quiet man. Having initially blustered, the little man grapples with the others as they "fought for last place." The men crawl into the fissure in a hill that forms the mouth of the cave and proceed down a passage that turns abruptly into a sudden decline. Losing their balance, they slide in a body, their torches becoming extinguished as they tumble down some twenty feet, landing "upon a level, dry place in a strong, yellow light of candles. It dissolved and became eyes." They are in a chamber in the midst of which stands a "great gray stone, cut squarely like an altar." Three candles in tin cups suspended from the ceiling illuminate the table, and over it stands the bizarre figure of a man in rustic garments with a long beard who seems to be holding a small volume in his hands. This proves to be a deck of cards, and while the men are speculating whether the figure before them is a vampire, a ghoul, "a Druid before the sacrifice," or "the shade of an Aztec witch doctor," he abruptly announces, "It's your ante." The little man tremulously plays poker with the dread figure and steadily loses. When he announces that he has no more money, the enraged hermit expels them from the cave. At their camp, their guide, John Willerkins, informs them that the man they have encountered is Tom Gardner, a farmer who had become an obsessive gambler and had lost his farm. When his wife died, Gardner became a crazed recluse. The story is a potpourri of impressionistic effects, fantasy, bravado, fear, humor, and bathos. There is a final irony in the fact that a failed gambler wins the little man's money, and the four adventurers are left only with a tale they can tell when they return to the city. The tall tale itself is the focus of most of the Sullivan County stories and sketches.

Suggested Reading

Gibson, Donald B. *The Fiction of Stephen Crane*. Carbondale: Southern Illinois University Press, 1968. 5–7.

"A Fragment of Velestino". The most extended and subjective of Crane's accounts of the Battle of Velestino, this is the second of a series of "letters" syndicated by McClure and printed in the *Westminster Gazette* under the general title "With Greek and Turk." These "letters" are descriptive essays rather than dispatches. "A Fragment of Velestino" appeared in the *Gazette* in three parts on 3, 4, and 8 June 1897 and was separately published in a limited edition entitled *A Battle in Greece*, by the Peter Pauper Press in 1936 with decorations by Valenti Angelo.

"A Fragment of Velestino" evinces the autobiographical overtones of Crane's first important experience of war, as well as many of the impressionistic devices of *The Red Badge of Courage*. There is a certain exhilaration in the encounter with the sights and especially the sounds of war: "Sometimes the pattering of individual firing swelled suddenly to one long beautiful crash that had something in it of the fall of a giant pine amid his brethren of the mountain side. It was the thunder of a monstrous breaker against the hard rocks." In contrast, there is the disjointed nature of experience that reflects the meaninglessness of war, astonishment at the serenity of nature amid the struggles of men, and the juxtaposition of the horrific and the ridiculous that are also evinced in Crane's fictional representation of the Battle of Velestino, "Death and the Child." The sky over Velestino is fair and blue while the guns roar and infantry fire shatters the silence. A roadside shrine at which soldiers are praying is suddenly demolished by an exploding shell. A pompous "tall pale young man in civilian garb" resembling Peza of "Death and the Child" takes offense at what he perceives to be a slight from an artillery captain absorbed in the business of war and demands "satisfaction" amid the carnage. A wounded man trudges toward the rear, the crude bandage around his head stimulating "one's recollection of New England and the mumps." A young Greek volunteer killed by a shot through the chest "had nothing particularly noble in his face." The captain of a field artillery battery sends a man to the rear for a pair of field glasses, and, misunderstanding the order, the soldier returns with a bottle of wine.

"France's Would-Be Hero". One of Crane's rare commentaries on contemporary political affairs, "France's Would-Be Hero" was published in the *New York Journal* and the *San Francisco Examiner* on 15 October 1899. The target of Crane's diatribe against quixotic pretenders to heroism is Jules-Napoléon Guérin (1860–1910), a vulgar street politician and leader of the *Ligue Antisémitque Françes*, who played a major part in the anti-Semitic riots of January and February 1898 in French cities. Guérin was financed by the duc d'Orléans, the pretender to the throne, and attempted to capitalize on the coup attempts of Paul Marie Déroulède. As a result of his activities, Guérin was sought by the French police, who beleaguered him in his luxurious headquarters on the rue de Chabrol in the summer of 1899 and finally arrested him after a siege of forty days on "Fort Chabrol." Crane criticizes past French governments for tolerating flamboyant demagogues and contrasts Guérin with the American reformer Jacob S. Coxey (1854–1951) who led a contingent of unemployed workers (Coxey's Army) that marched on Washington, D.C., in 1894 to protest unemployment and agitate for labor reform. Crane concludes that Coxey was as egotistical as Guérin, but, unlike Guérin, he was at least attempting to benefit people other than himself.

Suggested Reading

Riis, Philip. *Biographical Dictionary of the Extreme Right since 1890*. New York: Harvester Weatsheaf, 1990. 166–67.

Freddie. A character in "The Wise Men" and "The Five White Mice," Freddie is the dapper young proprietor and bartender at the Casa Verde in Mexico City.

Frederic, Harold (1856–1898). Frederic began his career in journalism in his native city of Utica, New York, where he gained a reputation as a reporter of sensational crimes and an enterprising editor. In 1884 he became London correspondent for the *New York Times*. In London he pursued an active social and political life as a prominent member of the Savage Club and, later, the National Liberal Club. He became a champion of home rule for Ireland and was a friend of Charles Stewart Parnell. Frederic's first novel, *Seth Brother's Wife* (1887), was a pioneer work of regionalist fiction, depicting the harshness of farm life in the Mohawk Valley and the crudeness of its population. *In the Valley* (1890) is set in the same region during the American Revolution. *The Lawton Girl* (1890) is a revolt-from-the-village novel set in a small city modeled on Utica. In 1891 Frederic moved his wife, Grace, and four children to a new home outside London and established a second household in the city with Kate Lyon,* an American woman with whom he had three children. In this year he also traveled to Russia, where he reported on the pogroms against Russian Jews in a series of articles for the *New York Times* that were collected as *The New Exodus* (1892). *The Copperhead* (1893) and *Marsena* (1894), a book of stories, deal with the Civil War. The third of Frederic's novels of contemporary upstate New York, *The Damnation of Theron Ware* (1896), a searching character study and trenchant social satire, sustains his reputation today. By 1893 Frederic had moved out of London and centered his life at Homefield in Kenley, Surrey, where he lived with Kate Lyon and their children. Their romance may have inspired *March Hares* (1896). In Frederic's final two years, he completed two novels set in England, *Gloria Mundi* (1898) and the posthumous *The Market Place* (1899). He died in October 1898, having suffered a paralytic stroke two months earlier. Kate, who had called in a Christian Science practitioner to attend Frederic, was tried for manslaughter in his death but was acquitted.

On 26 January 1896, under the heading ''Stephen Crane's Triumph,'' Frederic reported on the phenomenal English reception of *The Red Badge of Courage* in the *New York Times*. He first met Crane at a luncheon at the Savoy on 31 March 1897 given in Crane's honor by Richard Harding Davis* shortly before he and Crane departed London to report the Greek-Turkish conflict. On Stephen and Cora's return in June, Frederic found a home for them at Ravensbrook Villa* in Oxted, Surrey, within commuting distance of London. They became close friends of Frederic and Kate Lyon, who now called herself Kate Frederic. In August the Cranes were injured in a carriage accident while driving to visit the Frederics at Homefield on Harold's birthday. They spent a week at Homefield recuperating, after which they joined Frederic and Kate on a three-week vacation in Ireland, where Frederic had a house lent to him by a wealthy admirer in the village of Ahikista on Dunmanus Bay. Here Crane finished ''The Monster'' and gathered material for his ''Irish Notes.'' The Irish environment, as well as Frederic's satiric *The Return of the O'Mahony* (1892), also inspired Crane's composition of *The O'Ruddy* (1903). Early in the next year Frederic proposed that the two households share the Irish house in order to reduce their living expenses, but the Cranes declined. In one of the ''European Letters'' on which Crane collaborated with Cora published in the *New York Press* on 26 September 1897, Crane (or Cora) praised *Gloria Mundi*, which he had read in manuscript. His essay, ''Harold Frederic,'' one of Crane's very few pieces of literary criticism, was written in November but did not appear in the Chicago *Chap-Book** until

15 March 1898. Frederic reciprocated by lauding *The Open Boat* in the *New York Times* on 1 May.

Frederic introduced Crane to John Hay, the American ambassador to England, and to the prestigious American attorney Lafayette Hoyte De Friese,* at whose home in Queen Anne's Mansions the Cranes were occasional guests. It was probably there that they met the recently widowed Lady Randolph Churchill,* who was a member of the Society of American Women in London* into which Mrs. De Friese introduced Cora. Frederic died while Crane was in Cuba, and Cora took in Kate Lyon and her children: Helen, Héloïse, and Barry. After a time Kate moved to London with Helen, but the two younger children continued to live with the Cranes when they settled at Brede Place.* Cora and John Scott Stokes,* Frederic's secretary and English executor, headed a committee that raised funds for their support. The Cranes considered adopting Barry, but Kate Lyon decided to keep all her children with her when she returned to America.

Suggested Reading

Aaron, Daniel. "Stephen Crane and Harold Frederic." In *The Unwritten War: American Writers and the Civil War*. New York: Knopf, 1973. 210–15.

Fortenberry, George E., Stanton Garner, and Robert H. Woodward, eds. *The Correspondence of Harold Frederic*. Fort Worth: Texas Christian University Press, 1977. 505–6.

Gilkes, Lillian. "Stephen Crane and the Harold Frederics." *Serif* 6.4 (1969): 21–48.

Myers, Robert M. *Reluctant Expatriate: The Life of Harold Frederic*. Westport, Conn.: Greenwood Press, 1995. 537–40.

"Free Silver down in Mexico". In this report, syndicated by Bacheller, Johnson and Bacheller under various headlines in newspapers on 30 June 1895, Crane does not comment on the free silver debate in the United States but compares the Mexican and American prices of miscellaneous items. Although the rate of exchange of Mexican for American dollars is two to one, the American traveler in Mexico will not benefit on anything imported or on railroad fares, which are very expensive. Other than pulque, the national drink, there is little that is not costly in Mexico, and the general standard of living is not comparable to that in the United States. As for the Mexican laborer, "He lives mostly on tortillas, which are like beans. His clothing consists of a cotton shirt, cotton trousers, leather sandals, and a straw hat. For his wages he has to work like a horse."

"A Freight Car Incident". Widely syndicated by Bacheller, Johnson and Bacheller on 12 April 1896, "A Freight Car Incident" is one of Crane's least-known and most undervalued Western confrontation stories. Narrated by a dispassionate railroad man known only as "the major," the setting of the story is a small town, presumably in Texas, where a railroad company is conducting an auction sale of lots, with free beer and sandwiches for the participants. During the sale, the head of the company becomes ill, and the major goes into a freight car where provisions are kept to get ice to put on his forehead. Suddenly the door slams shut, and in the darkness the major perceives that he is trapped in the freight car with another man, "a fellow around there that a good many people wanted to kill." The other man, an aging gunfighter named Luke Burnham whose coarse tone of voice resembles that of Scratchy Wilson in "The Bride Comes to Yellow Sky" and whose fears appear as paranoid as those of the Swede of "The Blue Hotel," believes that his antagonists have shut him into the freight car so they can cut him down in a fusillade when he steps out. With drawn revolvers, he forces the major to open the door of the car. The terrified major faces death from both directions, but when the door is opened, there is "nothing to be seen but blue sky and green prairie, and the little group of yellow board shanties with a red auction flag and a crowd of people in front of one of them." Burnham moves through this deceptively peaceful environment with his guns in hand, threatening the men in the crowd who seem to ignore him. The understated Hemingwayesque conclusion of the story with its succinct elegiac refrain is especially chilling: " 'And so they didn't kill him after all,' said some one at the end of the narrative. 'Oh, yes, they got him that night,' said the major. 'In a saloon somewhere. They got him all right.' " As in a number of Crane's western stories, the trappings of civilized life, exemplified here in the railroad, have not obliterated the identification of the myth of the Wild West with its historical reality.

The French Ball. After the Civil War, concert halls and masked balls became the most public venues for prostitution in New York City. Sponsored by the *Cercle Français de l'Harmonie*, the French Ball was an annual event attended by thousands of people and held at various locations. It was known for its public salaciousness and frequented by prostitutes. Crane was probably present at this affair on a number of occasions. In the early hours of 19 January 1897, when he was leaving the ball at Madison Square Garden with friends, an attempt was made to arrest him for drunkenness. At this time Crane was spending a few weeks in New York following the *Commodore* disaster and was subjected to harassment by the police for his role in the defense of Dora Clark* in the fall of 1896.

Suggested Reading

Gilfoyle, Timothy. *City of Eros: New York City, Prostitution, and the Commercialization of Sex, 1790–1920.* New York: Norton, 1992. 224–25.

French, Mansfield J. (1872–1953). An 1894 graduate of Syracuse University,* French was a pitcher on the varsity baseball team in the spring of 1891, when Crane played catcher and shortstop. His memoir, "Stephen Crane's College Days," in the January 1934 issue of the Syracuse University *Alumni News,* is the most detailed account of Crane's performance as a baseball player and also provides other significant particulars of Crane's single semester at Syracuse. French, an engineer, continued to live in Syracuse after he was graduated from the University and was active in the Alumni Association and the Onondaga County Historical Society.

Frewen, Clara (1853–1924). One of the Jerome sisters of New York, Clara became the wife of Moreton Frewen* and aunt of Winston Spencer Churchill. Both Stephen and Cora Crane corresponded with her.

Frewen, Moreton (1853–1924). The son of a wealthy Sussex squire, Frewen was born at Brickwall in Northiam, Sussex, an estate that included Brede Place* and had been owned by the Frewens for three hundred years. He had the private education of an English gentleman and took a degree at Cambridge. Throughout his life Frewen was an inveterate traveler and entrepreneur, engaging in many speculative ranching and mining enterprises in the United States, Canada, and Kenya and making and losing a number of fortunes. In 1881 he married Clara Jerome, elder sister of Lady Randolph Churchill,* and for a time settled with her on his enormous ranch in Wyoming. He also owned homes in London and in County Cork, Ireland. Active in politics, Frewen championed bimetallism, the theory that currency should be based on a double standard of silver and gold in fixed ratio. He was elected to the House of Commons in 1910 and gave up his seat in 1914.

Cora rented Brede Place, which Moreton Frewen had recently purchased from his brother, in the spring of 1898 while Stephen was in Cuba, but she had discussed the matter with him before he left England. The Cranes had an amiable relationship with Moreton and Clara Frewen, although they defaulted on the nominal annual rent of £40 on the house and failed to undertake the restorations they had agreed to carry out. Frewen, who rented out Brede Place because he could not afford to maintain or live in it himself, contributed to the extravagance of the Crane establishment to some extent by insisting that they retain a group of alcoholic servants long employed in the house, including Mack (William MacVitte), a combination valet-groom and coachman-gardener who headed the staff and finally resigned because the Cranes kept liquor under lock and key; Richard Heather, the old butler; Vernall, the housekeeper and cook; and a serving man. "By the way, we like Mack very much," Crane wrote to Frewen, "but he sometimes complains of the inconveniences, and sometimes longs for five or six footmen which of course we do not need." The fondness that Crane developed for Brede Place and for Moreton Frewen is expressed in the dedication of *Wounds in the Rain* to him as a "friend," a term that Crane used sparingly. When Crane was dying in May 1900, Frewen solicited funds from prominent people such as Joseph Pulitzer* through an appeal signed by Lady Randolph Churchill toward the expense of transporting him to the Black Forest.

Suggested Reading

Andrews, Allen. *The Splendid Pauper*. London: Harrap, 1968.
Leslie, Anita. *Mr. Frewen of England*. London: Hutchinson, 1966. 158–62.
Wertheim, Stanley. "The Stephen Crane Testimonial Fund." *Resources for American
      Literary Study* 9 (1979): 31–32.

The 'Frisco Kid. A character who is the more passive counterpart of the New
York Kid in "The Five White Mice," "The Wise Men," and "A Man by the
Name of Mud." In "The Wise Men," Crane states that the two Kids "resem-
bled each other in appearance" and "were never apart in the City of Mexico."

Fullbil. One of the most successfully realized characters in *The O'Ruddy*, Fullbil
is a parody of the pedantic scholar. A reputed "great literary master," he holds
court for an admiring coterie at the Pig and Turnip Inn in London but is defeated
by The O'Ruddy in an exchange of barbed insults.

G

"Galveston, Texas, in 1895". This travel sketch is a patchwork of impressions and commentary about the island city of Galveston written at different times. Crane visited Galveston in early March 1895 on his trip to the West for the Bacheller syndicate. At that time he wrote to his artist friend James Moser* that "Galveston is a great town," but in this article, probably revised in 1898 from notes made during his visit, he stresses the ordinariness of the city. As in his report from San Antonio, "Stephen Crane in Texas," he is impressed by the rapid modernization or easternization of the West that is becoming one of "the great and elemental facts of American life. The cities differ as peas—in complexion, in size, in temperature—but the fundamental part, the composition, remains." Crane renders his impressions of Galveston as a seaport and resort. This article, not completed in time for syndication by Bacheller, was published posthumously in the *Westminster Gazette* on 6 November 1900.

The Gambler. Otherwise unnamed, the gambler is a character in "The Blue Hotel" to whom Crane devotes a good deal of scrutiny. Like Larpent in "Moonlight on the Snow," he is superficially respectable—a well-dressed, quiet, and genteel man who leads an exemplary home life. The Swede cannot distinguish him from the businessmen and the district attorney with whom he is drinking when the Swede stumbles into the saloon out of the storm and does not comprehend that, like Johnnie Scully, he is a thieving and potentially murderous card player. The gambler becomes the instrument of the Swede's death, but as the Easterner expresses it at the conclusion of the story, he is only a component in the tragedy, "a culmination, the apex of a human movement" that began long before the Swede came to Fort Romper.

Gardner, Tom. In the Sullivan County story "Four Men in a Cave," Tom Gardner is a crazed recluse who, having been ruined in city gambling dens, has retreated to a cave in the wilderness where he compulsively coerces anyone who has the misfortune to encounter him into a poker game.

Garland, Hamlin (1860–1940). Born in a key election year, Hannibal Hamlin Garland was named after Lincoln's running mate, but he soon dropped his first name. Garland is best remembered for his reform journalism and realistic fiction, but he was also a literary critic, a dramatist, and a poet. His childhood was spent on subsistence farms in Wisconsin, Iowa, and the Dakota Territory. At the age of twenty-four he went east to Boston, where he spent twelve hours a day in the public library reading the works of Darwin, Herbert Spencer, Henry George, and Eugène Véron. Garland returned to Iowa and Dakota in the summer of 1887. He was angered by the life of drudgery and impoverishment that he witnessed and felt guilty that he had managed to escape it while his family had not. This conflicting tension and the encouragement of William Dean Howells* led him to write stories for the *Arena* gathered together as *Main-Travelled Roads* (1891) and a companion volume, *Prairie Folks* (1893). These books and the social and aesthetic essays, first published in the *Arena* and the *Forum* and collected in *Crumbling Idols* (1894), were infused with Garland's conception of realism,* the replacing of theoretical knowledge with visual experience, which he called veritism, a term adopted from his reading of Véron's *Aesthetics* (1877). Despite his devotion to literary realism, Garland developed a sustained interest in psychic phenomena in the 1890s and became an official in the American Psychical Society. He moved to Chicago in 1894, and his best novel, *Rose of Dutcher's Coolly* (1895), deals with a Wisconsin farm girl who overcomes her background to graduate from the state university and make a career for herself in Chicago. In 1897 Garland spent a month living among Indian tribes in the West, and in 1898 he joined the hunt for gold in the Yukon. These experiences formed the background of fiction in later years. Desiring a better income, Garland turned to writing historical romances set in the Rocky Mountains, the most popular of which was *The Captain of the Gray-Horse Troop* (1902). He also wrote many reminiscences and family memoirs. Garland gradually became very conservative, but *A Son of the Middle Border* (1917), the first of an autobiographical trilogy, was praised by reviewers as a moving account of his youth and struggles to establish himself as a realistic writer and militant social reformer. Garland moved to Los Angeles in 1930 and died there ten years later.

Crane first met Garland in the summer of 1891 when Garland gave a course of lectures on American literature at Avon-by-the-Sea, New Jersey. Crane, assisting his brother Townley as shore correspondent for the *New York Tribune*, reported Garland's talk on William Dean Howells in the 18 August issue of the newspaper. Crane was forcibly struck with the emphasis on personal experience and vision that Garland ascribed to Howells. When Garland returned to Avon-by-the-Sea in August 1892, he again found Crane reporting shore news. Crane's satiric "On the New-Jersey Coast" article ridiculing the parade of the Junior Order of United American Mechanics had been published in the *Tribune* on 21

August, and about a week later Crane told Garland about being "let out" of his newspaper job. Garland was amused by Crane's naiveté but impressed with his intellectual honesty, and the two men were soon on friendly terms, finding mutual interests in literature and baseball. It was probably at this time that Crane showed Garland an early draft of *Maggie*, and Garland gave Crane a letter of introduction to Richard Watson Gilder,* editor of the *Century Magazine*, who rejected the Bowery novelette when Crane brought him a revised manuscript.

At the time of his friendship with Crane, Garland was publishing his theories of literary realism in the *Arena* and the *Forum*. Garland's essays stressed experimentation, modernism, and a subjective conception of truth in art. Garland praised the French impressionist painters for their emphasis on the emotional effects of color and their efforts to reproduce objects in the external world in the precise manner in which they impress the beholder. Garland's impressionistic conception of realism appealed strongly to Crane. "Art," Garland wrote in an *Arena* essay of November 1892, "after all, is an individual thing. The advice I give to my pupils who are anxious to write is the essence of veritism: 'Write of those things of which you know most, and for which you care most. By so doing you will be true to yourself, true to your locality, and true to your time.'" Garland's statement marks the starting point of literary impressionism,* which stresses the replacing of theoretical knowledge with visual experience as the goal of realistic writing. This aspect of impressionism appealed strongly to Crane and became an integral part of his aesthetic credo. He turned toward the slums of New York in order to test and reconstruct *Maggie* in the light of experience.

Garland's review of *Maggie* in the June 1893 issue of the *Arena* called the book "the most truthful and unhackneyed study of the slums I have yet read, fragment though it is. It is pictorial, graphic, terrible in its directness." Crane was a frequent visitor to Garland's 105th Street apartment in the spring of 1894. He showed Garland some of his poetry and the first part of the holograph manuscript of *The Red Badge of Courage*, and Garland was obliged to lend him fifteen dollars to rescue the second part from the typist. Garland read the manuscript and suggested revisions, especially the normalizing of Crane's incessant use of dialect to standard speech, advice that Crane followed inconsistently. Crane acknowledged his debt to Garland and dedicated *The Black Riders* to him. Their friendship gradually weakened following Garland's move to Chicago, and they had only a few brief and insignificant encounters in 1896 and 1898. Garland became more and more disturbed by the reports that circulated about Crane's alleged immorality. He came to believe the rumors that Crane had become an opium addict, and he did not wish to be associated with what he termed "the shady side of his bohemian life." In his recollections Garland telescoped his meetings with Crane, making them seem casual and few. He gave the impression that he had first seen *Maggie* only in book form after it had been privately printed, obscuring the fact that for a time he had functioned as Crane's mentor, and he made no mention of the significant role he had played in Crane's revision of *The Red Badge of Courage*. In his April 1914 *Yale Review* essay, "Stephen Crane as I Knew Him," Garland's need to condemn was strong. "There was something essentially unwholesome about his philosophy," Garland wrote of Crane. "He was not born for long life and he was not born for development. His work did not change except for the worse." But in the end, a more just view prevailed, and Garland could only conclude that Crane was "a strange, willful, irresponsible boy . . . one that will not soon be forgotten out of American literature."

Suggested Reading

Holloway, Jean. *Hamlin Garland: A Biography*. Austin: University of Texas Press, 1960.
McCullough, Joseph B. *Hamlin Garland*. Boston: Twayne, 1978.
Mane, Robert. "Une rencontre littéraire: Hamlin Garland et Stephen Crane." *Etudes Anglaises* 17 (1964): 30–46.
Pizer, Donald. "The Garland-Crane Relationship." *Huntington Library Quarterly* 24 (November 1960): 75–82.

Garnett, Edward (1868–1937). Both Garnett's grandfather and his father, Richard Garnett, held the prestigious position of Keeper of Printed Books in the British Museum, and his wife, Constance, was renowned for her translations of nineteenth-century Russian novelists into English. Although Garnett was overshadowed much of his life by the greater fame of his father and his wife, he was a prominent critic, playwright, and essayist. He advised and helped to publicize Joseph Conrad,* John Galsworthy, and D. H. Lawrence. He also acted as literary adviser to the publishing firms of Fisher Unwin, Heinemann, and Jonathan Cape. Garnett's essays in the *Academy* and his collection of literary essays *Friday Nights* (1922) offer rich insights into the English literary world of his time. His dramatic works were collected in *The Trial of Jeanne d'Arc and Other Plays* (1931).

When Stephen and Cora Crane returned to England from Greece in early June 1897, they lived for a short time in Limpsfield, Surrey, near Garnett's home, the Cearne at High Court. Garnett introduced them to Ford Madox Ford,* who also lived nearby. Garnett was a close friend of Joseph Conrad, and Conrad's letters to Garnett reveal much of his attitude toward Crane's literary work, especially in the statement in a letter of 5 December 1897 that Crane "certainly is *the* impressionist and his temperament is curiously unique. His thought is concise, connected, never very deep—yet often startling. He is *the only* impressionist and only an impressionist." Garnett echoed this statement in his 17 December 1898 *Academy* essay, "Stephen Crane: An Appreciation," where he concluded that Crane is "the chief impressionist of his age, as Sterne was the great impressionist, in a different manner, of his age." Garnett realized that Crane's impressionism* "makes the surface betray the depths," but he was acutely aware of Crane's limitations and did not believe that he would develop further. Cora Crane resented Garnett's strictures, but the friendship survived, and it was Garnett who found Brede Place* as a residence for the Cranes. In his 9 June 1900 obituary of Crane in the *Academy*, Garnett praised him as ''the man who looked at things with his own eyes, and was unafraid of his prepossessions.''

Suggested Reading

Monteiro, George. ''Stephen Crane: A New Appreciation by Edward Garnett.'' *American Literature* 50 (1978): 465–71.

Gates, Major. In ''Virtue in War,'' Gates is an officer in the regular army who is a battalion commander in a volunteer regiment. He wins the reluctant affection of his men, especially Private Lige Wigram, by his stoical devotion to duty. Gates is fatally wounded in a battle in which his men perform almost as well as regulars. In his Cuban War stories and reports, Crane often lauds professional soldiers and contrasts them favorably with the amateur volunteers.

Gaunt. A meditative painter who dies alone in his studio in ''The Silver Pageant.'' His absent-minded character is based in part on Crane's friend Corwin Knapp Linson.*

George's Mother. Crane began to write a draft of *George's Mother* on the versos of two sheets of his Sullivan County story ''The Holler Tree'' in the spring of 1893, shortly after the appearance of *Maggie*, but he put it aside for *The Red Badge of Courage*. He resumed writing in May 1894 and completed the novelette in November. Mindful of the fate of *Maggie*, which fell stillborn from the press, he did not submit *George's Mother* to the Anglo-American firm of Edward Arnold until the enormous success of *The Red Badge of Courage* had ensured a readership for this second Bowery novelette. It was published in May 1896.

Some contemporary reviewers and a few modern critics like John Berryman have compared certain episodes and themes in *George's Mother* with Zola's *L'Assomoir*, but the mood of the novelette is closer to the everyday realism* of William Dean Howells* than the naturalism* of the French novelist. *George's Mother* lacks the melodramatic intensity and social determinism of *Maggie*; it is more restrained in tone, style, and use of dialect, more convincing in characterization, and less episodically structured. The novelette is a companion piece to *Maggie* and is set in the same Irish neighborhood southeast of Canal Street, with its residue of the descendants of German immigrants. The Kelceys live just two flights below the Johnsons in the same tenement, and Maggie is, ironically, the girl of George's romantic dreams. Blue Billie, the little Rum Alley tough whom Jimmie Johnson battles in the first chapter of *Maggie*, has grown into the swaggering hoodlum George is about to fight when he hears that his mother is dying. To an even greater extent than *Maggie*, *George's Mother* offers graphic descriptions of the slums of lower Manhattan—the crumbling tenements, debris-strewn lots, missions, and cheap boardinghouses. As in *Maggie*, the romantic fantasies of the characters are more important in bringing about their downfall than the destitution of their external world, but here, as elsewhere, Crane does not discount the limitations of the environment as a determinant in human affairs.

Mrs. Kelcey is modeled on Crane's own mother, Mary Helen (Peck) Crane, a strong-willed, moralistic woman dedicated to the temperance cause who held offices in the Women's Christian Temperance Union (WCTU) and struggled, in vain, to keep her bohemian son within the church. The theme of alcoholism as the pervasive degenerative influence of the slums is as omnipresent in *George's Mother* as in *Maggie*. George's mother is depicted as an energetic religiously fanatic who is an occasional lecturer for the WCTU. George is the last survivor among her five sons. Her foremost delusion is blind confidence in his innate superiority and potential. "She rejoiced at qualities in him that indicated that he was going to become a white and looming king among men. From these she made pictures in which he appeared as a benign personage, blessed by the filled hands of the poor, one whose brain could hold massive thoughts and awe certain men about whom she had read." Unable to accept the reality of his alcoholism, she surmises "in a vague way that he was a sufferer from a great internal disease. It was something no doubt that devoured the kidneys or quietly fed upon the lungs." Crane's early title for the novelette was "A Woman without Weapons," without the resources to prevail in the warfare of life. Mrs. Kelcey struggles valiantly to keep George on the narrow path of virtue, temperance, and religion, but she is defeated not so much by the limitations of her circumstances as by her idealization of her weak-willed slothful son.

George is restless under his mother's carping criticism and her insistence that he find regular work and attend church with her, but he also entertains romantic fantasies regarding his place in life and his destiny. An indolent, irregularly employed young drifter recently arrived in the city from a rural town, he conceives of a time when he will become someone "of whom the men, and, more particularly, the women, would think with reverence." In his reveries there are "accessories of castle-like houses, wide lands, servants, horses, clothes." More immediately, he dreams of winning the heart of a magnificent woman whose raison d'être is to wait for him to notice her, and, ironically, he finds her embodied in Maggie, whom he meets one day on the staircase of the tenement "with a pail of beer in one hand and a brown-paper parcel under her arm." To bolster his fragile self-esteem, George frequents a saloon, the names of whose habitués—Jones, Bleeker, O'Connor, Schmidt, Woods, and Zeusentell—reflect the shifting ethnic mixture of the Bowery. When Maggie spurns him in favor of Pete, the rakish bartender, George plunges into debauchery with the middle-aged loafers whose specious brotherhood he has joined. These shabby, working-class alcoholics bolster their shaky self-esteem with elaborately contrived theatrical codes of conduct that induce superficial "brotherly sentiments" and a "fraternal feeling." George comes to believe that he is "a most remarkably fine fellow'' who has established a social position among appreciative gentlemen. This illusion is shattered when George is ejected from the group after a fracas during a drunken party in Bleeker's room, and when he loses his job they find him beneath them in social position and refuse to help him. George also attaches himself to a group of young hoodlums who menace passers-by on a street corner. "Kelcey longed for their acquaintance and friendship, for with it came social safety and ease; they were respected so universally." When his mother's attempt to convert him to religion fails, George's moral slide becomes more precipitous, and as his mother lies upon her deathbed, he is drinking beer and brawling with the gang of young street-corner toughs.

While *George's Mother* embodies the familiar theme of the country boy in the city ruined by drink and degenerate companions, it is not temperance fiction or a serious polemic against the evils of the demon drink in the mode of Jonathan Townley Crane's *Arts of Intoxication* (1870). Nevertheless, Mrs. Kelcey's battle against drink and drunkenness is the metaphor for her struggle to rescue her weak-willed son from his delusions and incapacity to cope with his environment. We first encounter her frenetically cleaning her tenement flat, wielding her broom and dustpan "like weapons" in "a flurry of battle," while in the distance, across the tenement roofs, "an enormous brewery towered over the other buildings. Great gilt letters advertised a brand of beer. Thick smoke came from funnels and spread near it like vast and powerful wings. The structure seemed a great bird flying. The letters of the sign made a chain of gold hanging from its neck. The little old woman looked at the brewery. It vaguely interested her, for a moment, as a stupendous affair, a machine of mighty strength." Other symbols of Mrs. Kelcey's ineffectual struggle are the tiny chapel to which George unwillingly accompanies her that is squeezed "humbly between two towering apartment-houses" confronting the brilliant lights of the city that will eventually overwhelm it and the "swaggering nickle-plated clock" that sits on a mantle in the Kelcey flat, an inexorable reminder of the reality that will destroy her illusions.

Suggested Reading

Brennan, Joseph X. "The Imagery and Art of *George's Mother*." *CLA Journal* 4 (1960): 106–15.

Jackson, Agnes Moreland. "Stephen Crane's Imagery of Conflict in *George's Mother*." *Arizona Quarterly* 25 (1969): 313–18.

Pizer, Donald. "From a Home to the World: Stephen Crane's *George's Mother*." *Papers on Language and Literature* 32 (1996): 277–90.

Solomon, Eric. *Stephen Crane: From Parody to Realism*. Cambridge, MA: Harvard University Press, 1966. 50–67.

Weinstein, Bernard. "*George's Mother* and the Bowery of Experience." *Markham Review* 9 (1980): 45–49.

"The Ghost". Only fragments of the script, seventeen pages including four of music, survive of this musical comedy, farce, and burlesque, performed only once in the Brede village schoolhouse on the evening of 28 December 1899 and never published. The performance was the central event of three days of Christmas festivities at Brede Place* that culminated in Crane's collapse with a tubercular hemorrhage following a ball on the night of 29 December. Crane had begun preparations for "The Ghost" in November, soliciting token contributions from his literary friends that would ostensibly make it a collaboration. As he put it in a letter to H. B. Marriott-Watson* on 15 November, "I have hit upon a plan of making the programmes choice by printing thereon a terrible list of authors of the comedy and to that end I have asked Henry James,* Robert Barr,* Joseph Conrad,* A.E.W. Mason,* H. G. Wells,* Edwin Pugh, George Gisssing,* Rider Haggard* and yourself to write a mere word—any word 'it', 'they', 'you',—any word and thus identify themselves with this crime." Six of these contributions are extant. Marriot-Watson's consisted of a puzzle—words written individually on separate slips of paper that when deciphered read, "Most publishers are d——d fools." Haggard wrote, "Good luck to your playing!" which may have been his contribution or a covering note. Pugh expanded a proverbial express: "A bird in the hand *may* be worth two in the bush, but the birds in the bush don't think so." Gissing contributed a farcical line: "He died of an indignity caught in running after his hat down Picadilly." Conrad's offering was, "The Ghost: This is a jolly cold world." Robert Barr sent a lengthy humorous poem, "The Tiresome Ghost of Somberly Hall, Sussex," that was inspired by Edwin Markham's "The Man with the Hoe" (1899). Only Conrad's words are found in the extant drafts; what James, Wells, and Mason wrote is unknown, although Mason probably contributed more than the others.

The scenario of "The Ghost," composed mostly by Crane with likely refinements by Cora, is centered around the legend that Brede Place was haunted by the ghost of its sixteenth-century owner, Sir Goddard Oxenbridge. The printed program for the performance shows that the Ghost was played by A.E.W. Mason. Among the dramatis personae are characters from Crane's works and the works of some of the collaborators. Rufus Coleman is based on the war correspondent in Crane's *Active Service*. Dr. Moreau comes from the mad biologist of H. G. Wells's *Island of Doctor Moreau*, and the doctor's son, Peter Quint Prodmore Moreau, is a hybrid, owing something also to Henry James's *The Turn of the Screw* and perhaps to Joseph Conrad's *The Nigger of the "Narcissus"* or, more likely, Prodmore, the mortgage holder in James's "Covering End." "Suburbia" may be an oblique reference to Edwin Pugh's *Street in Suburbia* and Tony Drunn to his *Tony Drum, Cockney Boy*. Miranda may derive from A.E.W. Mason's *Miranda of the Balcony* or H. B. Marriott-Watson's *Heart of Miranda*, or perhaps from both. The Three Little Maids from Rye—Holly, Buttercup, and Mistletoe—are allusions to the blowzy Buttercup in *H.M.S. Pinafore* and "the three little maids from school" in *The Mikado*. Barr's poem seems to have been recited by Suburbia. The surviving documents and newspaper accounts of the performance reveal that there were at least two acts, perhaps three, and that these consisted of dialogue, songs, choruses, and dances.

Catherine Wells provided accompaniment on the piano. Conrad, James, Haggard, and Gissing did not attend.

Suggested Reading

Bowers, Fredson, ed. *Tales, Sketches, and Reports*. Charlottesville: University Press of
    Virginia, 1973. 162–79, 835–39. Vol. 8 of *The Works of Stephen Crane*. Ed.
    Fredson Bowers. 10 vols. 1969–76.
Crisler, Jesse S. " 'Christmas Must Be Gay': Stephen Crane's *The Ghost*—A Play by
    Divers Hands." In *Proof: The Yearbook of American Bibliographical and Textual
    Studies*. Ed. Joseph Katz. Vol. 3. Columbia: University of South Carolina Press,
    1973. 62–120.
———. "Crane's *The Ghost* in the *Manchester Guardian*." *Stephen Crane Studies* 4.2
    (1995): 50–52.
Gordan, John D. "*The Ghost* at Brede Place." *Bulletin of the New York Public Library*
    56 (1952): 591–95.

"The Ghostly Sphinx of Metedeconk". Printed in the *New York Press* on 13
January 1895, this article, probably written in 1891 or 1892, recounts the legend
of a specter of a young woman dressed in white who haunts a beach near
Metedeconk, New Jersey, searching for the body of her lover, a ship's captain
who was drowned in 1815. Those who are unable to provide an answer to her
question as to the location of the corpse are themselves found dead on the beach
the next morning. The question the woman asks is rhetorical because she herself
had seen his ship founder off the coast on its return from Buenos Aires and
found his body washed up on the beach. There is a sentimental love story
enclosed within this ghostly tale. The young woman had sulked on her lover's
departure and later regretted her offhand farewell. She is now on an eternal and
futile quest to make amends.

"Ghosts on the New Jersey Coast". With "The Ghostly Sphinx of Metedeconk," this is one of two newspaper sketches based on stories dealing with
legends of spectral manifestations on the New Jersey shore that Crane heard
from local residents during his youth in Asbury Park. "Ghosts on the New
Jersey Coast" appeared in the *New York Press* on 11 November 1894. "In his
cabin," Crane recalls, "many an old fisherman, wagging his head solemnly,
can tell sincere and fierce tales, well calculated to freeze the blood." Most of
the legends have stock plots: A pirate ship sails in only twelve inches of water
with skeletons dangling from the masts; an Indian dead a hundred years searches
for the bride he murdered; at Deal Beach, the ghosts of a youth and a maiden
keep their lovers' trysts; near Barnegat Light, fishermen occasionally see an old
crone who chuckles at them; the phantom of a black dog with a hatchet wound
in his head who died defending the body of his master from despoliation by
pirates is seen by fishermen returning home late at night. Some of the stories
have a basis in historical incidents, such as the bluish light said to float above
the watery grave of the *New Era*, a shipwreck Crane described in a sketch

unpublished in his lifetime, and the tale of the Tory captain who pursues fishermen along a beach where Tories from New York murdered residents of Long Beach during the Revolutionary War.

Suggested Reading

Coad, Oral S. "Jersey Gothic." *Proceedings of the New Jersey Historical Society* 84
       (1966): 89–112.
Mappen, Marc. "Jerseyana." *New York Times* 9 October 1994, New Jersey Section: 15.

"A Ghoul's Accountant". One of the more bathetic of Crane's Sullivan County tales, "A Ghoul's Accountant" appeared in the *New York Tribune* on 17 July 1892. The opening of the story arouses burlesque suspense and dread as the little man, lying asleep with his three comrades by a campfire, is awakened by a phantasmagoric figure whose "skin was fiercely red and his whiskers infinitely black." The intruder threatens the little man with a three-pronged pickerel spear (obviously giving him the aspect of a devil) and marches him through the wilderness into a cabin in which shattered furniture indicates that a violent altercation has occurred. The ghoul hurls the little man into a chair at a table where an older "wild, gray man" is sitting. After an ominous silence, the little man (and the reader) has a deflationary experience when the older man suddenly asks: "Stranger . . . how much is thirty-three bushels of pertatters at sixty-four an' a half a bushel?" When the little man gives the correct answer, the ghoul howls in triumph over the wild, gray man, who had apparently insisted on the wrong sum, and the older man gives a frightful roar, springs forward, and kicks the little man out of the house. While "A Ghoul's Accountant" has little to recommend it as a story, its descriptive style reveals some of the aspects of Crane's later impressionism,* especially personification and synesthesia in which "sunlight is noise"; darkness is "a great, tremendous silence"; a campfire lies "dying in a fit of temper"; and "a mass of angry, red coals glowered and hated the world."

Gibbs, John Blair (1859–1898). A graduate of Rutgers University and Virginia Medical School, Gibbs was the son of an army major killed with Custer at Little Big Horn. Gibbs practiced medicine and surgery in New York City and enlisted in the U.S. Navy early in the Spanish-American War with the rank of ensign. At Key West he was assigned to the First Marine Battalion as acting assistant surgeon. Gibbs was one of the first American casualties in the fighting at Guantánamo Bay on the night of 11–12 June 1898. Crane reports him among the casualties in his dispatch, "In the First Land Fight Four of Our Men Are Killed." Crane was a witness to Gibbs's death, and in "War Memories" he juxtaposes the singular horror of Gibbs's prolonged suffering with the mundane commonality of death in war.

Gilder, Richard Watson (1844–1909). Born in Bordertown, New Jersey, Gilder, like Crane, was the son of a Methodist minister. He served briefly with a Philadelphia cavalry unit during the Civil War and began his journalistic career on the *Newark Advertiser* in 1868. Early in 1869 he was one of the founders of the *Newark Morning Register*. Gilder helped Josiah G. Holland and Roswell C. Smith in establishing *Scribner's Monthly*, and by the mid-1870s he was functioning as de facto editor of the magazine. In 1881 *Scribner's Monthly* was succeeded by the *Century*, the first issue of which appeared in November (the publishing house undertook another magazine named simply *Scribner's Magazine* five years later). Under Gilder's editorship, the *Century* became one of the most esteemed general magazines of the late nineteenth century, on a par with *Harper's* and the *Atlantic Monthly*. Gilder was uncomfortable with the bleak depiction of life set forth by naturalistic authors, but at times he championed realistic writing. The *Century* published excerpted chapters of Twain's *Huckleberry Finn* and *A Connecticut Yankee in King Arthur's Court* and serialized *Pudd'nhead Wilson*. Howells's* *A Modern Instance* and *The Rise of Silas Lapham* and, in a daring departure, Jack London's *The Sea Wolf* were also serialized in the *Century*. The magazine also made known the work of a number of modern poets, notably Edward Arlington Robinson. Gilder published sixteen slim volumes of his own poetry throughout his life and wrote biographies of Abraham Lincoln and Grover Cleveland. In later years, Gilder became more accommodating to the genteel standards of the time. He turned over much of the responsibility for fiction published in the *Century* to his associate, Robert Underwood Johnson, whose tastes tended toward the escapist and sentimental.

Gilder probably knew the Crane family and perhaps the infant Stephen in Newark, but recurring statements in biographical accounts that Gilder founded the *Newark Morning Register* with Crane's uncle, R. Newton Crane, are inaccurate. Robert Newton Crane, an attorney who served as U.S. consul at Manchester from 1874 to 1877, may have been involved in newspaper work in Newark as a young man, but he was a descendant of Jasper Crane, another branch of the Crane family that established itself in New Jersey, and not related to Stephen. When Hamlin Garland* sent Crane to Gilder with the manuscript of *Maggie* in the winter of 1892–93, he considered it necessary to write a note of introduction. Gilder became chairman of the Tenement House Commission in 1894 but showed little interest in realistic fiction dealing with urban life. He rejected *Maggie* for publication in the *Century*, but there is no evidence that he also rejected *The Red Badge of Courage*, as is sometimes alleged, and it seems most unlikely that he would have done so. Crane learned the factual background of the Battle of Chancellorsville that forms the setting of the novel from a highly successful series of recollections by participants that appeared serially in the *Century* from 1884 to 1887 under the general title of "Battles and Leaders of the Civil War." Gilder and Crane were fellow members of the Lantern Club,* but just one of Crane's works, "A Man and Some Others," appeared in the

Century, and that was only after Crane acceded to Gilder's request to render an epithet in the story as "B'G—."

Suggested Reading

Smith, Herbert F. *Richard Watson Gilder*. New York: Twayne, 1970.

Gissing, George (1857–1903). The work of the English novelist George Robert Gissing marks the transition from Victorian fiction to modern realism.* Gissing was expelled from Owens College in Manchester and jailed for having stolen some money to support a prostitute whom he later married, and he recorded his ensuing life of poverty and toil in naturalistic semiautobiographical works such as *New Grub Street* (1891), *The Nether World* (1889), and *The Private Papers of Henry Ryecroft* (1903). His stark realism and pessimistic outlook prevented him from achieving popular success. Gissing, who after two tragic marriages also lived with a woman who was not his wife, was a friend of Harold Frederic* and Kate Lyon,* and after Frederic's death he encouraged his literary acquaintances to donate to the fund that Cora Crane and John Scott Stokes* were raising for the support of Frederic's children with Kate Lyon. Gissing's personal acquaintance with Crane was slight, but he was among the distinguished writers who contributed a token line toward the composition of "The Ghost."

Suggested Reading

Grylls, David. *The Paradox of Gissing*. London: Allen & Unwin, 1986.
Korg, Jacob. *George Gissing: A Critical Biography*. Seattle: University of Washington Press, 1963.

Glenn, Horace. A character in the Whilomville stories "His New Mittens" and " 'Showin' Off.' " In both stories, Horace, who seems somewhat younger than the other boys, suffers a childhood disaster by conforming to group pressures.

" **'God Rest Ye, Merry Gentlemen' ''.** Published simultaneously in the United States in the 6 May 1899 issue of the *Saturday Evening Post* and in England in the May 1899 issue of the *Cornhill Magazine*, this story was collected in *Wounds in the Rain*. Like a number of other stories in that book, " 'God Rest Ye, Merry Gentlemen' '' is a thinly fictionalized account of some of Crane's experiences in the Cuban War. The story debunks the demands of the yellow press to make spectacular news out of the commonplace incidents of war. Two distinct episodes are described here. The first occurred in late May and early June 1898 during the "rocking-chair" period of the war. Crane, named Little Nell in the story, is a reporter for the *Eclipse* (the *New York World*). He spends dreary weeks with other correspondents aboard the dispatch boat *Jefferson G. Johnson* (the *Somers N. Smith*) searching in vain for the Spanish fleet of Admiral Cervera. The correspondents lead "wet, forlorn, half-starved lives," but when they limp into the telegraph station at Mole St. Nicholas in Haiti, Little Nell finds a message from the *Eclipse* upbraiding him for his inactivity.

The greater part of the story deals with events that occurred on 22–24 June. On 22 June six thousand men commanded by General Joseph Wheeler began landing at Daiquirí east of Santiago. In his dispatch to the *World* headlined "Crane Tells the Story of the Disembarkment," Crane reported the landing as uneventful except for the overturning of a boat in the surf in which two men and several horses were killed. Little Nell also is disappointed by the common-place nature of the long-anticipated event: "Like many preconceived moments, it refused to be supreme." Walkley (Sylvester Scovel*), the bureau chief of the *Eclipse*, nevertheless resolves to write a stirring account of the raising of the flag. The next day, Little Nell and the other correspondents—Tailor (Edward Marshall*), Shackles (Ernest W. McCready*), and the photographer Point (Burr McIntosh*)—follow the regular troops and the dismounted Rough Riders on an arduous march to Siboney, where they witness the second phase of the American landing. The final part of the story deals with the fighting near Las Guásimas on 24 June when the Rough Riders were ambushed, as recounted in Crane's dispatch, "Stephen Crane at the Front for the World." That morning Shackles and Little Nell breakfast with a captain and his subaltern. The captain, "old, grizzled—a common type of captain," is the kind of regular army man Crane has come to admire as a result of his combat experiences in Greece and Cuba, a veteran without ideals or ambitions who is later ungloriously killed at the foot of San Juan Hill, a poor subject for the sensational headlines demanded by Pulitzer and Hearst. In the Las Guásimas engagement, Tailor is shot through the lung, and Little Nell overcomes great hardships and the indifference of other correspondents to obtain aid for him, as Crane actually did for the wounded Edward Marshall. The next morning he receives another telegram from the *Eclipse* complaining of his inaction and ordering him home.

Suggested Reading

Wertheim, Stanley. "Stephen Crane Balks: Two New Letters." *American Literary Realism 1870–1914* 29.2 (1997): 76–80.

Goledge, Rose. A classmate of Jimmie Trescott in "The Lover and the Tell-tale," "a vigilant little girl" who discovers Jimmie writing a love letter to little Cora and announces the fact to the school yard.

Goodwin, Clarence N. (?–?) Crane's roommate in the Delta Upsilon fraternity house at Syracuse University,* Goodwin became a lawyer practicing in Chicago. In a letter written to Max Herzberg in 1921, Goodwin described Crane as "unstudious, brilliant, volatile, entertaining and giftedly profane. He was at that time in years about 19 and in worldly experience about 87."

Goodwin, Martha. A character in ''The Monster,'' Martha Goodwin is treated with considerable ambiguity by Crane. Martha is a spinster who lives with her sister Kate, ''who was visibly afraid of her.'' Her only other admirer is a neighbor, Carrie Dungen, who ''sailed across from her kitchen to sit respectfully at Martha's feet and learn the business of the world.'' A dogmatic virago and a gossip whose betrothed had died of smallpox, Martha ''who was simply the mausoleum of a dead passion was probably the most savage critic in town.'' She disapproves of Dr. Trescott's sheltering the defaced and imbecilic Henry Johnson in his home. Yet she is the only person to empathize with Trescott's motives, and when Kate and Carrie contend ''you can't go against the whole town,'' Martha responds that the ''silly people who are scared of Henry Johnson'' are not the whole town. Martha Goodwin's ambivalent attitude mirrors Crane's own uncertainty about the appropriateness of Dr. Trescott's decision.

Gordon, Frederick C. (1856–1924). Born in Canada, Gordon studied art at the Julian and Colarossi Academies in Paris. He began his work as an illustrator in Toronto and came to the United States in 1886. Between 1893 and 1895 Gordon occupied a large studio in the old Art Students League building on East Twenty-third Street on a floor above the crowded loft where Crane roomed with a coterie of illustrators and painters. Crane suggested to Copeland & Day that Gordon design the covers of *The Black Riders*, and on 4 February 1895 Gordon submitted a drawing with an orchid design. The orchid, he explained, ''with its strange habits, extraordinary forms and curious properties, seemed to me the most appropriate floral motive [i.e., ''motif''], an idea in which Mr. Crane concurred before he left New York.'' The publisher asked Gordon to modify this design, but Gordon responded in a letter of 25 February that he was too busy to comply with their request, and Copeland & Day had their own artist adapt Gordon's drawing for the first trade edition of *The Black Riders*. Gordon flourished in his career as a designer of book and magazine formats. In later years he was mayor of Mountainside, New Jersey.

''Grand Opera in New Orleans''. Crane attended two performances by the French Opera Company in New Orleans when he stopped in the city on his way to Mexico in February 1895. This report, syndicated in newspapers by Bacheller on 24 March, extols the quality of the vocalists and the orchestra. Crane gives a brief history of operatic repertory groups in New Orleans, where grand opera is a century-old institution that offers a high quality of entertainment at affordable prices and is patronized by all classes of the population.

''Grand Rapids and Ponce''. Appearing in the *New York Journal* on 17 August 1898, this report resembles Crane's first dispatch from Puerto Rico, ''A Soldier's Burial That Made a Perfect Holiday,'' in that it contrasts American and Puerto Rican attitudes, ''Grand Rapids serenely sitting in judgment upon the affairs of Ponce.'' The inhabitants of Ponce, the chief city of Puerto Rico at this time, are glad that the Spaniards are gone and the Americans have come, but underlying their applause is "a stratum of deceit" since the peasants are convinced that the invincible Spaniards will surely return. The stamp of Spain, Crane concludes, is as indelibly stamped on the temperament of the people of Central America and South America as it is on the architecture.

["The Gratitude of a Nation"]. There is some controversy over this Decoration Day newspaper piece, which was not published until 1957 in Daniel Hoffman's introduction to the Harper edition of *The Red Badge of Courage and Other Stories*. The untitled manuscript, in the Rare Book and Manuscript Library of Columbia University, is appended to Crane's poem, "A soldier, young in years, young in ambitions." On 9 May 1894 Crane wrote to Hamlin Garland,* "I wrote a decoration day thing for the *Press* which aroused no enthusiasm. They said, in about a minute, though, that I was firing over the heads of the soldiers." It seems unlikely that Crane is referring to this manuscript since "The Gratitude of a Nation" is a sentimental and thoroughly conventional tribute to the diminishing number of Civil War veterans, urging that their patriotic contributions be recognized while they are still alive: "Do not then wait. Let not loud and full expression of gratitude come too late to the mind of the nation. Do not forget our heroes, our well-doers, until they have marched to where no little cheers of men can reach them." This could not be characterized as "firing over the heads of the soldiers." More probably, Crane in his letter to Garland is alluding to the sardonic "Veterans' Ranks Thinner by the Year," which appeared anonymously in the *New York Press* on 31 May 1894 in the guise of an eyewitness report of the Decoration Day parade rather than to this manuscript.

Suggested Reading

Hoffman, Daniel. "Crane's Decoration Day Article and *The Red Badge of Courage*." *Nineteenth-Century Fiction* 14 (1959): 78–80.

"A Gray Sleeve". In letters to Nellie Crouse, Crane described this improbable story of the romantic encounter of a Union captain with a Southern belle as "not in any sense a good story" and its central characters as "a pair of idiots." There is no compelling reason to challenge this evaluation. "A Gray Sleeve" was syndicated in a number of newspapers by Bacheller in October 1895 and appeared in magazines in England and the United States before it was collected in *The Little Regiment*. The story opens, as do a number of Crane's other tales of war written immediately following *The Red Badge of Courage*, with an animated and panoramic battle scene. Dismounted Union cavalry troopers sweeping a grove of maple trees in search of Confederate snipers come upon a house in a clearing. A glimpse of an arm in a gray sleeve moving the blinds in an upper window arouses the suspicion of the Union soldiers. Suspecting that fleeing rebels may be hiding in the house, the troopers barge in to confront a comely young woman concealing behind her back what turns out to be an unloaded pistol. She is protecting her brother, a wounded Confederate officer. The dashing Union captain is overcome by the beauty of the shy, weeping young woman and orders his men to ride off without their prisoner. The story ends with banal chatting between the captain and the girl that pointedly suggests romance will follow when the war clouds clear.

Great Battles of the World. A series of eight articles on major battles that first appeared in *Lippincott's Magazine* from March through November 1900, researched and in large part transcribed by Kate Lyon* from historical sources. The American edition was published by J. B. Lippincott in December 1900 and the English edition by Chapman & Hall in June or July 1901. The book is illustrated by John Sloan. The contents are: "The Battle of Bunker Hill"; "Vittoria"; "The Siege of Plevna"; "The Storming of Burkersdorf Heights"; "A Swede's Campaign in Germany" (I. "Leipzig"; II "Lützen"); "The Storming of Badajos"; "The Brief Campaign against New Orleans"; and "The Battle of Solferino."

The idea for the *Great Battles* series originated with Lippincott, and Crane was for some time reluctant to undertake the project because he did not consider himself a historian and had little time to devote to research, but his financial exigencies forced him to attempt a popular series that would require little original writing. On 3 July 1899 Pinker wrote *Lippincott's* editor, Harrison S. Morris, that Crane had agreed to write six sketches for $1,000, and in February 1900 an arrangement was made to expand the series to eight articles. In the fall of 1899 Crane began to gather information about the Battle of New Orleans. "The Brief Campaign against New Orleans," the first battle to appear in *Lippincott's*, seems to be largely his own work, although Kate Lyon had been researching material for him from the start. "The Battle of Solferino" and "The Storming of Burkersdorf Heights" are most likely entirely the work of Kate Lyon, and she probably made the choice of Burkersdorf, the final battle in the series. Her function in the early articles was to write out lengthy quotations from history texts for which Crane provided bridge paragraphs, but as the series progressed, she took a greater part in planning and even writing early drafts of the articles, to be revised by Crane. Crane dictated "The Storming of Badajoz" to Edith Richie* from Kate Lyon's notes. He seems to have taken an active part in the planning and the writing of the series for as long as his declining health would permit, but only fragments, consisting largely of bridge paragraphs, remain of the manuscripts in his hand and the extent of his involvement cannot accurately be determined. The series was not completed until early May 1900. There is little of Crane's distinctive style or his characteristic themes to be found in the articles, and much of the writing consists of direct transcription from sources. While they are for the most part lively narratives, they should be viewed as hack work undertaken solely for the purpose of making money.

Suggested Reading

Bowers, Fredson, ed. *Reports of War*. Charlottesville: University Press of Virginia, 1971. 528–562. Vol. 9 of *The Works of Stephen Crane*. Ed. Fredson Bowers. 10 vols. 1969–76.

Katz, Joseph. "*Great Battles of the World*: Manuscripts and Method." *Stephen Crane Newsletter* 3.2 (1968): 5–7.

"The Great Boer Trek". The surprising military victories of the Boers against the British in the South African War, also known as the Boer War, in late 1899 and early 1900 gave immediacy to this lengthy article, which appeared in the June 1900 issue of *Cosmopolitan*. The history of the Boers was generally less known in the United States than in England, and Crane's article did not achieve British publication. The Great Trek was a series of migrations by Afrikaner farmers (Boers) from the Cape Colony into the interior, beginning in 1835 and lasting into the 1840s. The Boers were motivated by the forced emancipation of their slaves, the failure of the British to protect them from Hottentot raids on their cattle, and interference by missionaries and humanitarian organizations from England in the treatment of their African workers. Stephen and Cora Crane favored the English cause in the war, but the story of the Boer migrations is told with objectivity and compassion in this article. Crane agrees that the Boers were placed in a position that caused them to conclude that "no security existed for life or property on the frontier." Most likely the research for the article was done by Kate Lyon,* who in early 1900 was also providing the source material for *Great Battles of the World*. "The Great Boer Trek" was largely derived from George M. Theale's *History of the Boers in South Africa* (1887) or a later revision of that book.

"Great Bugs in Onondaga". Written when Crane was a stringer for the *New York Tribune* in his single semester at Syracuse University,* this spoof was published simultaneously in the *Tribune* and the *Syracuse Daily Standard* on 1 June 1891. The *Standard* version has additional introductory and concluding paragraphs. The hoax reports a story told by a man who "acted as well as talked strangely and was evidently suffering from alcoholism" about a swarm of insects whose outer shells have a "turtle-like armor" that cover a stretch of railroad track near a limestone quarry and stop the progress of a locomotive between Jamesville and Syracuse. The next day, the *Tribune* and the *Syracuse Daily Journal* extended Crane's *jeu d'esprit* with a tongue-in-cheek apology, probably written by Willis Fletcher Johnson,* which concluded that if the state entomologist expected to serve another term, "he must board a monster of steel and iron, hurry to Syracuse and report on this new bug."

Suggested Reading

Wells, Lester G. "The Iron Monster, the Crackling Insects of Onondaga County, and Stephen Crane." *Courier* 3.1 (1963): 1–7.
William, Ames W. "Stephen Crane's Bugs." *Courier* 3.3 (1963): 22–31.

"A Great Mistake". With "An Ominous Baby" and "A Dark-Brown Dog," this is one of three stories about an unnamed slum child who corresponds to Tommie, Maggie's brother who dies in infancy. It was written in 1893, along with the others, but not published until March 1896 in the *Philistine*.* The urchin in "A Great Mistake" covets the "sweets of the world" sold by an Italian fruit vendor at a corner stand near an elevated train station. When the vendor appears to fall asleep, he snatches a piece of fruit, but he is caught in the act. The story ends on a note of poignancy and irony: "The Italian howled. He sprang to his feet, and with three steps overtook the babe. He whirled him fiercely and took from the little fingers a lemon."

"Greed Rampant". This is a dramatic skit with blatantly anti-Semitic overtones, perhaps dating from Crane's days at Syracuse University* in the spring of 1891 but which may have been composed later. The surviving typescript in the Alderman Library of the University of Virginia indicates that Crane intended to publish it, but there is no evidence that he ever attempted to do so. The first complete printing of the piece is in *Tales, Sketches, and Reports,* volume 8 of *The Works of Stephen Crane*, edited by Fredson Bowers (1973), 7–10. The setting of the scenario is Paradise, New Jersey, and the dramatis personae are St. Peter, a mob of Jews, and a crowd of gentiles. The Jews storm the gate of Paradise, where St. Peter is languidly guarding the turnstile. Through scuffling and devious machinations, they monopolize the front seats. When the gentiles, in contrast, enter in orderly procession behind them, "Every good seat in the house is occupied by a Jew. The entire front is a wriggling mass of big noses and diamonds." A thoughtful gentile devises a trick. He writes a sign on a piece of cloth advertising real estate lots in "Sheol, Cape May County, New Jersey," selling out at 2 percent of cost. The mob of Jews immediately become bargain hunters and reverse their stampede, rushing out of Paradise toward Sheol, and the gentiles move into the front seats. The gentiles are thus not depicted as being without greed. "Greed Rampant," a failed satire, is not entirely an aberration in Crane's work, which occasionally contains traces of anti-Semitism. The "fat foreigner" who employs Maggie is presumably a Jew, but most of the characters in *Maggie* are flat, hackneyed stereotypes of slum dwellers, and the depiction is not inappropriate in this context.

Suggested Reading

Katz, Joseph. "Stephen Crane: The Humanist in the Making." In *William Carlos Williams, Stephen Crane, Philip Freneau: Papers and Poems Celebrating New Jersey's Literary Heritage*. Ed. W. John Bauer. Trenton: New Jersey Historical Commission, 1989. 75–85.

"Greek War Correspondents". This "letter" from the Greek-Turkish War was syndicated under various headlines by McClure on 16 May 1897 but did not appear in the *Westminster Gazette* in the "With Greek and Turk" series. Crane mocks the pretentiousness and arrogance of American and English war correspondents. He refers to one American who "discovered at once that the Parthenon is too little, that it is far smaller than the American Tract Society building in New York'' and another correspondent, ''a wild ass of the desert who wanted a decoration'' from the king. There may well be an element of self-satire in this dispatch since on 10 April Crane had written a pompous, ingratiating letter to his brother William maintaining that he expected ''to get a position on the staff of the Crown Prince'' and would ''try like blazes to get a decoration out of the thing but that depends on good fortune and is between you and I and God. Athens is not much[,] ruins, you know . . . although the Acropolis sticks up in the air precisely like it does in the pictures.''

''Greeks Waiting at Thermopylae''. In this cable, datelined from Lamia on 22 May and syndicated by Hearst under various headlines on 24 May 1897, Crane predicts that the Greek army will retreat from Thermopylae as it has first from Velestino and then from Domoko. The soldiers are willing to fight on, but most officers, enervated by the vacillating policy of Prince Constantine and repeated orders to retreat, wish the war to end. Crane believes that Thermopylae would, as in classical times, be a good place to mount a strong defense, and he ''would like to write a dispatch telling of a full-blown Greek victory for a change.'' This dispatch was obviously written much earlier than its dateline since the Greek army had abandoned its position at Thermopylae during the night of 17 May, and an armistice was signed on 20 May.

Greene, Nelson (1869–1956). An artist, illustrator, journalist, and historian, ''Ned'' Greene shared quarters with Crane in the old Art Students League building on East Twenty-third Street in Manhattan at various times from the autumn of 1893 through the autumn of 1895. Greene came to the city from Fort Plain, New York, in 1893. He studied painting under William M. Chase at the Art Students League and remained living in the old structure when the league moved to its new building on West Fifty-seventh Street. From late fall 1893 through the winter of 1894, Greene was one of Crane's three roommates (with R. G. Vosburgh* and W. W. Carroll*) in one of the cramped studios of the building. Later he roomed upstairs with Frederick C. Gordon,* who drew the original design for the covers of *The Black Riders*. Greene wrote a number of reminiscences of Crane in the 1940s. One of these survives in typescript in the Newark Public Library and two others in holograph in the Schoberlin Collection at Syracuse University. These rambling recollections provide important details of Crane's life at the time he was composing many of his short stories and poems, as well as *The Red Badge of Courage*. Greene describes Crane's appearance, bohemian lifestyle, putative socialist political views, literary idols (de Maupassant, Zola, and Tolstoy), and working habits, and tells a number of colorful anecdotes. He stresses especially the important influence of personal association with artists on the development of Crane's impressionistic literary style. Greene's model Gertrude Selene may have been the prototype for Florinda O'Connor in *The Third Violet*.

Since Greene's memoirs were written in the 1940s, some fifty years after the events they describe, their reliability is not beyond question, especially since Greene wrote under the influence of Thomas Beer's* fictionalized Crane biography. Greene's claim that Crane was "an avowed Socialist," for example, should be viewed in the light of Beer's fanciful attribution to Crane of the flippant remark that he "was a Socialist for two weeks but when a couple of Socialists assured me I had no right to think differently from any other Socialist and then quarrelled with each other about what Socialism meant, I ran away." Crane may have fleetingly adopted socialism as a youthful posture, but comment on any specific economic or political theory is notably absent from his works and letters.

Greene's association with Crane ended in the fall of 1895 when, after a summer in the old Art Students League building, he went back to Buffalo, where he was an illustrator for the *Courier* and the *Sunday Express*. He returned to New York in 1898 and freelanced. Intermittently from 1905 to 1922 Greene was an advertising artist for United Cigar Stores. He did illustrations for *Puck* in 1914–15 and was a political cartoonist for several newspapers in the New York City area during World War I. Greene designed the "Allies United for Liberty" sculpture that stood on the prow of the Flatiron Building from 1918 to 1921. He later became editor of the *Fort Plain Standard* and a prominent historian of the Mohawk and Hudson River valleys.

Suggested Reading

Stanley Wertheim. "Stephen Crane Remembered." *Studies in American Fiction* 4 (1976): 45–64.

Grierson, Billie. The most naive and audacious of the four regular soldiers in the Cuban War story "The Price of the Harness," Grierson had "enlisted for the war." He shields Jimmie Nolan from realizing that he is mortally wounded. At the conclusion of the story, Grierson, in a yellow fever tent, informs Jack Martin of the fate of Nolan and Ike Watkins.

"The Grocer Blockade". In this report, printed in the *New York Journal* on 23 September 1898, Crane explicates a subject that forms the basis of his later Cuban War story, "This Majestic Lie." When the American blockade of Cuban ports was declared, "the grocers of Havana, stirred by a deep patriotism, arose to the occasion and proceeded to soak the life out of the people." The grocers hoarded commodities but pretended that there was a shortage, providing themselves with the opportunity to "gracefully pillage the public pockets." On the mere rumor that the blockade would end, they shamelessly lowered their prices, causing the people to realize that they had been blockaded by the grocers rather than the American warships.

Guiney, Louise Imogen (1861–1920). Born in Boston, the daughter of an Irish immigrant who served as a brigadier general in the Civil War, Guiney began to publish essays and poems in newspapers and magazines in the 1880s. Her first two books of poetry, *Songs at the Start* (1884) and *White Sail and Other Poems* (1887), were conventional Victorian verse with overtones of Tennyson and Browning. Guiney was closely associated with Fred Holland Day, a distant cousin with whom she shared an interest in collecting Keats memorabilia and in Roman Catholic theology and ritual. The fine-printing firm of Copeland & Day published a number of her books, including *Lovers' Saint Ruth's* (1895) and *Patrins* (1897). Fond of classical and medieval subjects, Guiney sometimes wrote in a cryptic fashion reminiscent of seventeenth-century metaphysical poets. *A Roadside Harp* (1893) was stimulated by her foreign travels, and *The Martyrs' Idyll and Shorter Poems* (1899) contained nature lyrics, historical poems, and religious verse. *Happy Ending: Collected Lyrics* (1909) marked the climax of her career. She spent the last decade of her life in England.

Fred Holland Day and his partner, Herbert Copeland, had great confidence in Guiney's literary judgment, and Day asked Guiney to vet the manuscript of *The Black Riders* for the firm. Guiney was favorably impressed by the book and recommended publication, but she made additions to a list of poems Day thought inferior, and Day wrote to Crane requesting that they be excluded. On 9 September 1894 Crane responded with an indignant letter objecting that "you cut all the ethical sense out of the book. All the anarchy, perhaps. It is the anarchy which I particularly insist upon." Day once again submitted the manuscript to Guiney, and she revised the list of poems that she and the editor had targeted for omission. She returned the manuscript to Day on 16 October with the comment that Crane was "extravagantly young, and will out grow his saucy little 'ethical meanings.' " On 17 October she wrote Day that Crane "takes himself too seriously. Perhaps you had better humor him in everything, if you take him at all." Three days later, Day sent Crane a second and much reduced list of poems to be omitted, and this time Crane accepted the suggestions, apparently without demural. Day also sought Guiney's advice about the title. Guiney was unimpressed with Crane's choice of *The Black Riders* but recommended that Day accede to it. The correspondence between Day and Guiney indicates that neither of them was especially offended by the unorthodoxy of Crane's poems but had occasional doubts about his poetic formulations and the maturity of his rebellious expression. Certainly there is as much blasphemy in many of the poems that Copeland & Day did not proscribe as can be found in those they recommended be deleted.

Suggested Reading

Colvert, James B. "Fred Holland Day, Louise Imogen Guiney, and the Text of Stephen Crane's *The Black Riders*." *American Literary Realism 1870–1910* 28.2 (1996): 18–24.
Fairbanks, Henry G. *Louise Imogen Guiney*. New York: Twayne, 1973.

H

Hagenthorpe, Judge Denning. A pivotal character in "The Monster," Judge Hagenthorpe is a neighbor of the Trescotts in Whilomville, and it is to his house that the family and Henry Johnson are taken after the fire that destroys their home. Some critics have viewed Hagenthorpe as a satanic figure reminiscent of Hawthorne's Roger Chillingworth in *The Scarlet Letter*. Hagenthorpe is the unprincipled spokesman for Whilomville. From the beginning, he cautions Trescott, in the interests of "propriety," against following the dictates of his conscience and taking heroic measures to save Johnson's life. Trescott, the judge warns, will become a Frankenstein in the eyes of the community, and Henry will be his creation. "You are making him, and he will be a monster and with no mind." Other critics view Hagenthorpe as a pragmatic foil to Trescott's misguided idealism and consider his final advice that Trescott should not make himself and his family into pariahs by harboring Johnson in his home and imposing him on Whilomville as prudent and ethically correct.

Suggested Reading

Mayer, Charles. "Social Forms vs. Human Brotherhood in Crane's *The Monster*." *Ball State University Forum* 14.3 (1973): 29–37.
Warner, Michael. "Value, Agency and Stephen Crane's 'The Monster.' " *Nineteenth-Century Literature* 40 (1985): 76–93.

Haggard, H. Rider (1865–1925). The prolific author of romantic novels, notably *King Solomon's Mines* (1885) and *She* (1887). Haggard began his career as a British foreign office employee in the Transvaal. He was admitted to the bar in 1885 but devoted much of his energies to parliamentary politics, representing the cause of small farmers. Crane was introduced to Haggard by Robert

Barr,* but they did not develop a close friendship. Haggard contributed a token line to the composition of ''The Ghost.''

Hanham, Smith. In ''Moonlight on the Snow'' he is the man who whirls the roulette wheel in Larpent's casino and urges the residents of the town of War Post to encourage investments in the future of the town by Eastern capitalists.

Hannigan. In ''The Monster'' he is Dr. Trescott's next-door neighbor in Whilomville. When fire breaks out in the Trescott home, it is Hannigan who breaks down the door through which Henry Johnson rushes to save Jimmie and who prevents Mrs. Trescott and Dr. Trescott from entering the burning house, but when Trescott shelters the disfigured Henry in his house, the Hannigans plan to move away.

Hare, James H. (1856–1946). News photographer and war correspondent, Jimmy Hare was born in England, the son of a camera manufacturer. He came to the United States in 1889 as a technical adviser to a New York City camera supplies firm but quit after a year to produce his own hand-made cameras. Hare was a photographer for the *Illustrated American* and a freelance contributor to newspapers and magazines. He was a pioneer in taking snapshots with hand-held cameras. In the spring of 1898 Hare went to Cuba as a photographer for *Collier's Weekly*. With Sylvester Scovel* he made a daring trip into the interior to interview the rebel leader General Máximo Gómez. He later covered events leading to the siege of Santiago and photographed the battles of San Juan Hill and El Caney. In the early years of the twentieth century, *Collier's* sent Hare to report revolutions in Haiti, Venezuela, Panama, and Mexico and the Russian-Japanese War. In 1906 Hare took the first aerial photographs of New York City from a balloon, and two years later he took the first picture of an airplane in flight at Kitty Hawk, North Carolina. He covered World War I for *Leslie's Weekly*.

Hare met Stephen Crane at the end of May 1898 aboard the dispatch boat *Somers N. Smith* on an unsuccessful cruise down the coast of Cuba to search for the Spanish fleet commanded by Admiral Cervera. On 30 June Crane led Hare on a tour of the Las Guásimas battlefield, and on the fateful afternoon of 1 July, Hare accompanied Crane to the ''Bloody Bend'' of the Aguadores River. Later in the day they met again on the crest of San Juan Hill, and Crane introduced Hare to Richard Harding Davis.* Hare considered Crane ''a charming fellow, fond of drink and not too fond of work.'' He maintained that Scovel ''usually found it very difficult to get Crane's copy'' and that Crane told him he had joined the *New York World* staff only to obtain a military pass so that he could gather material for a novel about the Cuban War. Henry M. Cary, manager of the *World* field staff in Cuba, and Don Carlos Seitz, business manager of the *World*, also insisted that Crane was lazy, but the fact is that twenty-four of Crane's dispatches appeared in the newspaper. In a conversation with

Theodore Roosevelt* about *Wounds in the Rain*, after Roosevelt had become president of the United States, Hare made a spirited refutation of Roosevelt's allegation that Crane had been "a man of bad character" who "was simply consorting with loose women" under the guise of reporting on the Tenderloin.

Suggested Reading

Carnes, Cecil. *Jimmie Hare, News Photographer: Half a Century with a Camera*. New York: Macmillan, 1940.

"Harold Frederic". Crane's essay on the personality and writings of his compatriot and friend appeared in the Chicago *Chap-Book** on 15 March 1898. When Crane met Harold Frederic* in London, he expected to find a deracinated expatriate. Instead, "There was a tall, heavy man, moustached and straightglanced, seated in a leather chair in the smoking-room of a club, telling a story to a circle of intent people with all the skill of one trained in an American newspaper school. At a distance he might have been even then the editor of the Albany *Journal*." Crane's focus in this essay is on Frederic's American fiction, especially the Civil War novelettes and stories collected in *In the Sixties* (1897), which Crane considers "a most notable achievement in writing times in America." He makes scant mention of Frederic's masterpiece, *The Damnation of Theron Ware* (1896), because he feels that the acclaim the novel received deflected attention from Frederic's other works set in central New York, especially *Seth Brother's Wife*, *The Lawton Girl*, and *In the Valley*, which Crane believes is "easily the best historical novel that our country has borne. Perhaps it is the only good one." Crane expresses some dissatisfaction that Frederic turned away from American subjects in *March Hares* (1896).

Harriman, Karl Edwin (1875–1935). Harriman's journalistic career began in 1895 as a reporter for the *Detroit Journal*. During 1898 and 1899 he wrote editorials for the *Detroit Free Press*, and in the spring of 1899 the newspaper sent him to England as a correspondent. He was subsequently managing editor of the *Ladies' Home Journal* and editor of the *Red Book*, the *Blue Book*, and the *Green Book* magazines. Harriman contributed short stories and articles to magazines and was the author of a number of novels and short story collections.

Harriman was introduced to Crane by Robert Barr,* and in the summer of 1899 he spent several weeks as a guest at Brede Place.* He was one of the "Indians" who descended on the Cranes and overstayed their welcome, driving Stephen, on occasion, to seek refuge at Brown's Hotel in London, where he could work in peace. Harriman wrote several fanciful reminiscences of his sojourn at Brede Place, and a number of his anecdotes have become part of the apocrypha of Crane biography. Along with Ford Madox Ford,* Harriman is responsible for the legends that Crane's tuberculosis was caused by the deleterious environment of Brede Place; that "The Monster" was written and revised at a single sitting; that Hall Caine earned Stephen's contempt for refusing on moral grounds to contribute to Cora's fund for Harold Frederic's* children by Kate Lyon,* when in fact he gave generously; that Crane's brother Wilbur was a visitor to Brede Place in 1899; and several other doubtful stories. Crane inscribed a copy of *War Is Kind* to Harriman. It is the only known copy of the book with an authorial inscription.

Suggested Reading

Harriman, Karl E. "A Romantic Idealist—Mr. Stephen Crane." *Literary Review* 4 (April 1900): 85–87.
———. Commentary in *Critic* 37 (July 1900): 14–16.
———. "The Last Days of Stephen Crane." *The New Hope* 2 (October 1934): 7–9, 19–21.

Hartwood Club. *See* Crane, William Howe.

"Harvard University against the Carlisle Indians". Crane's narration of the first of two football games in Cambridge, Massachusetts, that he covered in the exceptional role of a sports reporter was printed in the 1 November 1896 issue of the *New York Journal*. The game between Harvard and the Carlisle Indian School had been played the previous day, and the Indians were heavily favored to win. Crane interviewed the Carlisle team at their hotel and found them modest and imperturbable. On the field "the impassive Indians bucked and bucked, and the Harvards went slowly backward," but Harvard scored the only touchdown of the game. Crane's enthused involvement in the action underscores his statement in a letter to John Northern Hilliard* that "I got my sense of rage and conflict on the football field," a reflection on his own experience as a member of the Syracuse University* varsity team.

Hasbrouck. In *The Red Badge of Courage*, Hasbrouck is the lieutenant of Henry Fleming's company and the officer with whom the youth interacts most closely. Hasbrouck represents the military ideal of unreflective courage that stands in contrast to Henry's introspective brooding. "That young Hasbrouck, he makes a good off'cer," one of the soldiers remarks, "He ain't afraid 'a nothin'." In the first engagement Hasbrouck is shot in the hand, but this does not prevent him from seizing a soldier who "had fled screaming at the first volley of his comrades" and driving him back into the ranks "with many blows." When Henry flees, the lieutenant thrusts at him with the sword with which he had earlier beaten him as he lagged behind the company. Even on the second day of the battle, after Henry has distinguished himself among those repulsing an enemy attack, Hasbrouck grapples with him to urge him forward. "It was as if he planned to drag the youth by the ear on to the assault." When Henry himself leads a charge as flag bearer, Hasbrouck forgets his earlier timidity and praises him to the colonel of the regiment as "a jimhickey."

Hathaway, Odell Sneden II (1872–1934). A schoolmate and close friend of Crane at Claverack College and Hudson River Institute,* Hathaway was from Middletown, New York. Some of Crane's earliest known letters were written to Hathaway from Lafayette College* and Syracuse University.*

"Hats, Shirts, and Spurs in Mexico". Bacheller, Johnson and Bacheller syndicated this slight article on Mexican sartorial customs under different headlines in newspapers on 18 October 1896. Crane comments on two extremes of Mexican male attire: the huge sombrero, tight trousers, silver spurs, and adorned jacket of the caballero and the Indian in his serape, cotton trousers, and sandals. In contrast, the majority of Mexican men, especially in the larger cities, wore clothing that, with some local modifications and adornments, was similar to the fashions of New York and London.

Hattie. A young woman in *Maggie: A Girl of the Streets* who is seduced and rebuffed by Jimmie in a manner that parallels Pete's corruption and rejection of Maggie.

"Havana's Hate Dying, Says Stephen Crane". After the signing of the peace protocol ending the hostilities between Spain and the United States, Crane returned to Cuba in late August 1898 and slipped illegally into Havana, still occupied by the Spanish authorities. He registered at the Hotel Pasaje fronting the Prado and frequented the Café Inglaterra with other correspondents. This disjointed report, datelined 25 August, was published in the *New York Journal* on 3 September. Crane makes some cursory observations on conditions in the city, specifically the mood of the people, who now regard Americans without hostility and with a new respect; the inoperative Spanish gunboats in the harbor; and the outrageous prices for provisions.

Hawker, William. The autobiographical protagonist of *The Third Violet*, usually addressed as "Billie," Hawker, as his name indicates, is also in part based on Crane's friend Willis Brooks Hawkins.* Hawker is an observant artist but a bungling ingenue in affairs of the heart. He is obtusely unaware of Splutter O'Connor's feelings for him and inept in expressing his love for Grace Fanhall or understanding whether it is reciprocated. The scion of a poor farm family, Hawker feels inferior to Grace, and whenever he approaches her, his speech and mannerisms become awkward, stilted, and self-conscious. An inept lover who idealizes women as incomprehensible creatures, "strange spirits, as wayward as nature and as pure as nature," Hawker finally blunders into an unanticipated success.

Hawkins, Willis Brooks (1852–1928). A prominent figure in New York publishing circles of the 1890s, Hawkins spent his youth in Aurora, Illinois, where he became acquainted with Abraham Lincoln, a friend of his father. He briefly worked as a telegraph operator in Chicago before turning to journalism. For a time he was a reporter on the *Chicago Daily* News. Hawkins became an associate of Irving Bacheller* in the late 1880s. He wrote for the Bacheller syndicate and was editor of *Brains*, one of first magazines devoted to advertising. He also published children's poetry and fiction. A successful story, "The Boy Recruits," appeared in the March 1902 issue of *St. Nicholas*, a magazine for boys. During the 1920s, Hawkins wrote a series of thirty-five articles, entitled "All in a Lifetime," for an unidentified newspaper. The manuscript is preserved in the Alderman Library of the University of Virginia. Several of these articles are reminiscences of prominent persons he had known, including Lincoln, Eugene Field, James Whitcomb Riley, Lew Wallace, and Stephen Crane. Two of the Crane articles were reprinted in the spring 1967 and fall 1968 issues of the *Stephen Crane Newsletter*.

Hawkins was introduced to Crane by Irving Bacheller, and he and Crane met frequently at the Lantern Club,* of which Hawkins was a founding member and Bacheller the perennial president. Hawkins, almost twenty years Crane's senior, was a paternal figure in the life of the young author and became Crane's closest friend and confidant during 1895 and 1896. When Crane made his will for the first time on 29 November 1896 in Jacksonville, preparatory to what he thought would be his departure for Cuba, he named Hawkins one of his literary executors, along with Hamlin Garland* and William Dean Howells.* Without Hawkins's urging, it is unlikely that Crane would have attended the celebratory banquet given to him by the Society of the Philistines in Buffalo on 19 December 1895 that has been perceived as, for better or worse, a turning point in his literary career. Hawkins reminded Crane that "[t]here is a business side of life that must not be wholly ignored," and when Crane, in a last-minute attempt to avoid a social event about which he felt great trepidation, insisted that he did not have appropriate clothing for the event, Hawkins assured him that he would supply the deficiencies, writing to Crane on 17 December: "I shall express an overcoat to you this afternoon. In Buffalo we will fix up the dress suit question. You bring along your shirt, hat & shoes. I will attend to coat, vest and trousers." When the dinner degenerated into a fiasco and Claude Bragdon* expressed his indignation over the rowdy progress of events by threatening to bolt the room in protest, his way was blocked by Hawkins, who was determined to preserve Crane's dignity if possible. Crane burdened Hawkins with an involvement in an affair more complicated than providing a dress suit when on 25 November 1896, a few days before he left for Florida, he entrusted Hawkins with a check for $500 to disburse in smaller amounts to himself or to Amy Leslie* as needed. Plagued with continual demands by Amy, Hawkins reluctantly performed the role of middleman between her and Crane. In April 1897, Crane sent Hawkins two more checks of $100 for Amy, but, in disgust, Hawkins returned one of them, and he probably never received the other. Hawkins's repudiation of the intermediary function precipitated a lawsuit against Crane by Amy Leslie. With Crane's departure from New York City, the personal relationship between himself and Hawkins was effectively ended. In 1899 the Cranes sent Hawkins a Christmas card but to an address he had long abandoned.

Suggested Reading

Wertheim, Stanley, and Paul Sorrentino, eds. *The Correspondence of Stephen Crane.* New York: Columbia University Press, 1988.

"Hayti and San Domingo Favor the United States". Datelined Porto Plata, San Domingo (Puerto Plata in the Dominican Republic), 15 May, this dispatch was published in the *New York World* on 24 May 1898. Crane reports on the disposition of European settlers and native people in Haiti and San Domingo toward the United States and Spain based on what he heard during the first visit by the *World* dispatch boat *Three Friends* to Cap Haitien, near the site of the cable station at Mole St. Nicholas, and to Puerto Plata. The correspondents found "the French and Germans invariably against us; the English and the natives almost invariably with us, and the more clean and modern the people the more they favor us." Some Haitians, especially soldiers, expressed reservations about the success of American arms: "They feel that the signal for the expansion of the giant republic is also a signal of certain danger to their integrity as an independent nation."

"Heard on the Street Election Night". Expanded from a draft in Crane's notebook, now in the Alderman Library of the University of Virginia, this is apparently a transcription of snatches of direct conversation and debate, slogans, and political jingles dealing with the Tammany Hall defeat in the New York election of November 1894. A newspaper clipping in Crane's scrapbook in the Rare Book and Manuscript Library of Columbia University indicates that the sketch was printed in the *New York Press*, but the edition in which it appeared has not been located. Referred to in this sketch are David Bennett Hill, who had been governor from 1885 to 1891 but was defeated in this election by Republican Levi P. Morton; William L. Strong, the successful Republican candidate for mayor of New York City; John W. Goff, a Republican who was elected city recorder; Hugh J. Grant, the defeated Tammany candidate for mayor; and Richard Crocker, the Tammany Hall boss.

Hearst, William Randolph (1863–1951). One of the most controversial figures in modern American journalism, Hearst was the only child of George Hearst, a mining magnate and a U.S. senator who bought the *San Francisco Examiner* in 1880 to advance his political career. After being expelled from Harvard University, William Randolph Hearst became editor of the *Examiner* in 1887 and rapidly augmented its circulation by sensation-seeking techniques. In 1895 Hearst moved to New York City, where he purchased the failing *Morning Journal* and began the intense competition with Joseph Pulitzer's* *New York World* that characterized the sensationalist trend in newspaper publication of the 1890s known as yellow journalism, a term originating from the "Yellow Kid" cartoon drawn by Richard Felton Outcault. The highlight of the Hearst-Pulitzer feud was their respective coverage of the Spanish-American War. The *Journal* and the *World* achieved circulations of over a million on some days, a new record for American newspapers. After the war, Hearst became involved in politics. He served two terms in the House of Representatives (1903–7) but lost his bid for the 1904 Democratic presidential nomination. For the remainder of his career, Hearst devoted himself to building a media empire that included many major American newspapers and also magazines such as *Cosmopolitan*, *Good Housekeeping*, and *Harper's Bazaar*. To this he added the International News Service, King Features, and broadcasting and motion picture companies. Beginning as a political liberal and populist, Hearst lapsed into a deep conservatism in later years and became an inveterate and outspoken opponent of the New Deal policies of Franklin Delano Roosevelt, the candidate he had strenuously supported for the presidency in 1932.

Crane's extensive reporting for the *New York Journal* and other newspapers in the Hearst syndicate can be divided into three periods. In the fall of 1896 the *Journal* printed Crane's apologia for his part in the Dora Clark* arrest, "Adventures of a Novelist," and his series of sketches on the New York Tenderloin; his reports of the Greek-Turkish War appeared in the *Journal* and the *San Francisco Examiner* in the spring and summer of 1897; during the Spanish-American War, after he had been discharged or had resigned from Pulitzer's *World*, Crane's dispatches from Puerto Rico and from Havana were printed in the *Journal* and at times also in the *Examiner* during the summer and fall of 1898. Periodically, the *Journal* published articles on other subjects by Crane. On 16 August 1896 there was an essay on Asbury Park, New Jersey, and in November of that year Crane reported two Harvard football games. On 18 October 1897 there was an essay on Queenstown, now Cobh, Ireland. Several critical essays on British political and military activities in the Boer War were published in the *Journal* and the *Examiner* in January 1900, and Crane's spoofing article nominating Edward Markham as the sole candidate for an American academy appeared on 31 March 1900. Pieces syndicated by Bacheller were also at times printed in Hearst newspapers. Crane's personal relationship with Hearst was slight, but their professional interactions were generally cordial, although Crane resented the low prices that Hearst paid for his undistinguished reports from Havana and was indignant when the *Journal* cut off his expense account. The *Journal* may have given Crane permission to serialize articles from Cuba on his own initiative, but he did not succeed in doing so. Cora was outraged that James Creelman,* the *Journal's* representative in London, would not forward money to her, and the Hearst press reported more or less accurately that Crane was "hiding" in a Havana rooming house.

Suggested Reading

Swanberg, W. A. *Citizen Hearst: A Biography of William Randolph Hearst*. New York: Scribner, 1961.

Hedge, Johnnie. In "The Fight" and "The City Urchin and the Chaste Villagers," Johnnie is the scrappy outsider from Jersey City who establishes a place in the boyhood society of Whilomville by trouncing the established leaders, Jimmie Trescott and Willie Dalzel. He is finally vanquished by his mother, who takes him by the ear and simultaneously boxes the ears of two of the other boys, asserting the hegemony of adult society in Whilomville.

Heinemann, William (1863–1920). Of German-Jewish ancestry but a practicing Christian, Heinemann was educated in England and Germany. He established the publishing firm of William Heinemann, Ltd. while still in his twenties. In 1893 he went into partnership with Sidney S. Pawling,* and the two were highly successful in attracting authors of high literary merit, some of whom were virtually unknown before Heinemann published their works. Heinemann authors included Joseph Conrad,* H. G. Wells,* Robert Louis Stevenson, Rudyard Kipling, Henry James,* John Galsworthy, and W. Somerset Maugham. Between 1895 and 1897 the firm published the *New Review* under the editorship of W. E. Henley. One of London's most respected publishers, Heinemann played an important part in forming the Publishers' Association of Great Britain, of which he was twice president, and he was president of the National Booksellers' Provident Association from 1913 until his death.

Harold Frederic* was a close friend of Heinemann, and his *In the Valley* was on Heinemann's first list. It was probably Frederic who brought Crane to Heinemann's attention. Heinemann published the English editions of *The Red Badge of Courage, Maggie, The Black Riders, The Little Regiment, The Third Violet, The Open Boat,* and *Active Service* and issued reprints of Crane works under the titles of *Pictures of War* and *Bowery Tales.* Crane's personal relationship with Heinemann was not close, but he was somewhat more amicable with Sidney Pawling.

Suggested Reading

Whyte, Frederic. *William Heinemann: A Memoir.* London: J. Cape, 1928.

"Henry M. Stanley". Crane's earliest known signed publication, this was apparently a classroom exercise culled from an encyclopedia. The piece was printed in the February 1890 issue of the Claverack College* magazine, the *Vidette.** Crane describes the British-American journalist and explorer's expeditions into Africa to find David Livingstone and to trace the Congo River to its source. The hyperbolic conclusion of the essay—that Stanley "should ever rank not only as a great christian explorer, but as a great statesman and a great general"—illustrates Crane's schoolboy admiration for adventurous correspondents.

Hether, Bob. In "Moonlight on the Snow" Hether, the popular barman in Stevenson's Crystal Palace, is the leader of the delegation of the town of War Post residents who come to hang Larpent for disrupting the peace of the town by killing a man who had accused him of cheating at cards. Characterizing Hether as "a damned white-livered coward," Larpent faces down the mob in a manner reminiscent of Colonel Sherburn in *Adventures of Huckleberry Finn*.

Higgins, William. *See* The Oiler.

Higginson, Thomas Wentworth (1823–1911). An influential literary critic in the second half of the nineteenth century, Higginson studied at the Harvard Divinity School and served briefly as minister of nondenominational churches in Massachusetts. A radical abolitionist, he was colonel of a regiment of freed slaves in the Union army. His *Army Life in a Black Regiment* (1870) is a chronicle of this experience. As a critic, Higginson called for an American literature freed from the domination of European traditions and infused with liberal egalitarian values. These views are embodied in *Literature as an Art* (1876), *Youth and the Literary Life* (1892), and *Literature as a Pursuit* (1905). Despite his essentially genteel stand, Higginson admired some of the emerging realists of the post–Civil War period, especially William Dean Howells* and Edith Wharton. He corresponded and with and visited Emily Dickinson, who considered him her "Preceptor," despite his cautious and uncomprehending advice about her poetry. After Dickinson's death, Higginson, with Mabel Loomis Todd, edited the first two volumes of her poems.

On 24 October 1895, Higginson reviewed *The Black Riders* in the *Nation*. He was intrigued by the experimental aspects of Crane's poetry, "the brevity of its stanzas; its rhymelessness and covert rhythm, as of a condensed Whitman or an amplified Emily Dickinson" but cautioned that "so marked a new departure rarely leads to further growth. Neither Whitman nor Miss Dickinson ever stepped beyond the circle they first drew." Higginson commended the verisimilitude of *The Red Badge of Courage* as "A Bit of War Photography" in the July 1896 issue of the *Philistine*,* crediting the novel with presenting a matter-of-fact view of "the daily life of war" from the perspective "not of a commanding general, but of a common soldier—a pawn in the game; a man who sees only what is going on immediately around him, and, for the most part, has the key to nothing beyond." In his 16 November 1899 review of *War Is Kind* in the *Nation*, Higginson despaired of serious analysis, maintaining that his earlier predictions had been fulfilled. Crane had not progressed beyond the novelty of his first poetic impulse, "and the world now finds other experimenters more interesting."

Suggested Reading

Katz, Joseph. "The 'Preceptor' and Another Poet: Thomas Wentworth Higginson and Stephen Crane." *Serif* 5.1 (1968): 17–21.
Tuttleton, James W. *Thomas Wentworth Higginson*. Boston: Twayne, 1978.

Hilliard, John Northern (1872–1935). Largely self-educated, Hilliard lived on a ranch as a boy and came to journalism early in life as a reporter in Chicago and New York City. From 1895 to 1911 Hilliard was literary editor, drama critic, and editorial writer for the *Rochester Union and Advertiser* and the *Rochester Post Express*. He devoted the rest of his life to freelancing and was a contributor to newspapers and magazines and an author of books of poetry and fiction. He also wrote several books on magic and in later years was the advance man for the American illusionist Howard Thurston. Hilliard was a close friend of Crane during his early years in New York and wrote a detailed and convincing memoir of their relationship. Hilliard claimed to have 150 of Crane's letters, as well as manuscripts and inscribed books. Only four of these letters have come to light, and three of them exist only in printed form. They were obviously written for publication and appeared in improvised formats in articles Hilliard wrote on Crane in the *Rochester Union and Advertiser*, the *Rochester Post Express*, and the *New York Times*. Hilliard tampered with Crane's texts, but these letters provide extremely valuable insights into Crane's pride in his ancestry and, more significant, into his literary antecedents and artistic credos.

Suggested Reading

"Establishing the Text of Crane's Letters to John Northern Hilliard." In *The Corre-
    spondence of Stephen Crane.* Ed. Stanley Wertheim and Paul Sorrentino. New
    York: Columbia University Press, 1988. 693–96.
John Northern Hilliard to Thomas Beer. In *Stephen Crane: Letters.* Ed. R. W. Stallman
    and Lillian Gilkes. New York: New York University Press, 1960. 324–26.

Hinckson, Mary. The Southern girl who befriends three Confederate soldiers and an officer and helps them to avoid captivity in "Three Miraculous Soldiers." Mary's resourcefulness meliorates the depiction of her as a conventional romantic heroine.

Hind, C. Lewis (1862–1927). A novelist, essayist, art critic, and writer of memoirs, Hind was an important editor throughout the 1890s. After abortive ventures into a medical career and the lace business, Hind took up music and art criticism. He was editor of the *Studio* in 1893 and was responsible for opening its pages to Aubrey Beardsley. He went on to edit the *Pall Mall Budget*, but his most important editorial position was as head of the *Academy* from 1895 until 1903. Hind wrote some twenty books of art criticism. Among his notable volumes of literary reminiscences are *Authors and I* (1921) and *More Authors and I* (1922). Under Hind's editorship the *Academy* published perspicacious reviews of *The Little Regiment*, *The Third Violet*, and *Active Service*, as well as Edward Garnett's* influential 17 December 1898 essay, "Stephen Crane: An Appreciation." Hind attended the three-day house party at Brede Place* in late December 1899 and saw the sole production of "The Ghost." In its 6 January 1900 issue, the *Academy* reproduced a portion of the title page of the program for "The Ghost" in facsimile with the prescient comment that "[t]he text of 'The Ghost' will never be printed."

"His New Mittens". On 30 May 1898 Crane wrote to Paul Revere Reynolds from a dispatch boat off the coast of Cuba that he was sending him "a short story of boy life in Whilomville—the town of The Monster." "His New Mittens," the first of the Whilomville stories about the lives of children, appeared simultaneously in the November 1898 issues of *McClure's Magazine* in the United States and the *Cornhill Magazine* in England. At Crane's suggestion, it was included with "The Monster" and "The Blue Hotel" in the Harper 1899 American edition of *The Monster and Other Stories* as an expedient to fill out that thin volume.

In "His New Mittens," little Horace Glenn (his last name is not given in this story) is caught between the demands of his matriarchal family and his peers. Horace cannot join the other boys, who are gleefully involved in a snowball fight, because his mother and Aunt Martha had admonished him to come straight home from school so that he will not soil his mittens. His comrades, aware of his plight, pursue him with the taunting chant, "A-fray-ed of his mit-tens!" The boys soon tire of tormenting Horace and turn their attention to a game of warfare between Indians and soldiers, but when Horace rejoins the group, one of the raiding soldiers renews the cry, "A-fray-ed of his mit-tens!" whereupon Horace impulsively makes a snowball and hurls it at him. The game is interrupted by Horace's mother, who drags him home and, finding his mittens soaked, isolates him in the kitchen with his supper while she and his aunt eat in the dining room. In reprisal, Horace refuses to eat, knowing that rejection of food "would work havoc in his mother's heart." Realizing that his mother might not capitulate to this ruse, he resolves to run away to California, but stormy weather causes him to withdraw "for reflection" to the woodshed. As the shawled figure of his aunt runs from the house to alarm the neighbors, Horace rejoices that his absence has caused consternation in his home. Afraid of being punished if he is caught immediately, he decides that his mother's wrath will turn to guilt and contrition if his absence is prolonged, he slips from the woodshed and wanders toward Niagara Avenue, at the head of which is Stickney's butcher shop. In the butcher's window a display of food tempts the famished Horace: "Rows of glowing pigs hung head downward back of the tables, which bore huge pieces of red beef. Clumps of attenuated turkeys were suspended here and there." Having heard the boy's story, Stickney escorts him home. Horace's strategy is vindicated when his mother, "lying limp, pale as death, her eyes gleaming with pain," expresses only relief at his return, and Stickney is rewarded with a glass of homemade root beer. On a minor scale in this story, Crane explores a conflict similar to that experienced by the Swede in "The Blue Hotel" between social conformity—exemplified by family, warmth, and food—and independence for which one must endure the hardships of isolation, cold, and deprivation.

Hitchcock, Ripley (1857–1918). Born James Ripley Wellman Hitchcock in Fitchburg, Massachusetts, where his father was a prominent physician and his mother, for a time, was a professor of Latin at Mount Holyoke, Ripley Hitchcock, as he was professionally known, became one of the first American literary editors who took an active part in working with the manuscripts of authors. Hitchcock edited the works of a number of important writers, including Rudyard Kipling, Arthur Conan Doyle, Zane Grey, Joel Chandler Harris, Stephen Crane, and Theodore Dreiser. Following graduation from Harvard, postgraduate study in art and philosophy, and a year spent as a medical student, Hitchcock joined the staff of the *New York Tribune* as an art critic in 1882. In 1890 he left newspaper work to become literary adviser for D. Appleton & Company, serving in that position for twelve years. After a short time as vice president of A. S. Barnes, he became literary adviser and editor for Harper and Brothers, where he remained from 1906 until his death.

Hitchcock wanted to produce books with popular appeal and was given to active editorial intervention. His greatest success at Appleton was his transformation, with the dying author's consent, of a disorganized and rambling narrative by Edward Noyes Westcott, *David Harum* (1898), into a phenomenal best-seller, and, with the collaboration of his first wife, Martha, Hitchcock wrote a play based on the novel that was also highly successful. *David Harum* was twice made into a film, with Will Rogers starring in the second production. Later, at Harper and Brothers, Hitchcock performed similar if not equally extravagant editorial surgery on Theodore Dreiser's *Jennie Gerhardt* (1911), much to Dreiser's displeasure. There is, however, virtually no evidence, in either manuscript notations or correspondence, that Hitchcock's editorial relationship with Crane was in any way intrusive. Hitchcock was himself the author of a number of books on art and the history of the West. He was a deeply religious and conservative bulwark of the American literary establishment, a member of the National Institute of Arts and Letters, and active in the Century Association and the Authors Club.*

Crane's association with Hitchcock may have begun in late 1892 or early 1893 when, according to a memoir published in 1926 by Willis Fletcher Johnson,* day editor of the *New York Tribune* from 1887 to 1894, Crane offered and Hitchcock rejected his first novel, *Maggie: A Girl of the Streets*, which Crane later had privately printed. Johnson's dating of his relationship with Crane is clearly awry, and some of his material is derived from Thomas Beer's* unreliable biography rather than from personal recollection. Nevertheless, Johnson, who had worked with Hitchcock on the staff of the *Tribune*, is explicit about the circumstances in which he recommended Crane to Hitchcock: ''The man whom I knew best in the New York publishing trade was my very dear friend and former colleague, Ripley Hitchcock, then literary advisor of D. Appleton & Co.; so I sent Stephen to him. He appreciated the merits of the book, but hesitated to recommend its acceptance. He told me, however, that '[t]hat boy has the real stuff in him,' and a few years later eagerly accepted for publication

Stephen's next work, 'The Red Badge of Courage.' '' Johnson dates this event in the summer of 1891, but it was more likely to have occurred in the next summer, when Crane showed him some of his Sullivan County tales. It was later in the summer of 1892 that Crane also showed Hamlin Garland* a manuscript of *Maggie*, and Garland sent Crane with an enthusiastic note to Richard Watson Gilder,* editor of the *Century*. In his preface to the 1900 Appleton edition of *The Red Badge*, however, Hitchcock does not mention any meeting with Crane until December 1894, when he "came to the editorial office of D. Appleton and Company, bringing two short stories as examples of the work he was then doing for the newspapers. The impression made by the stories was so strong that Mr. Crane was asked if he had a story long enough for publication in book form," and Crane sent him the clippings of the serial appearance of *The Red Badge of Courage*.

Before he left New York for the West and Mexico to write feature articles for the Bacheller syndicate, Crane gave Hitchcock a completed manuscript (in the 1890s the word *manuscript* was used indiscriminately to refer to a holograph or a typescript) of *The Red Badge*, which Crane revised while on his trip and after he returned to New York. The nature of the revisions Crane made under Hitchcock's direction have given rise to an extended and spirited scholarly controversy. The issues are technical, but the dispute centers upon whether Crane made the extensive deletions from his holograph manuscript on his own initiative, radically cutting the endings of three chapters and removing the original chapter 12, or whether these changes were mandated by Hitchcock. The deletions contain Henry Fleming's rambling and often incoherent interior monologues rationalizing his cowardice and alternately rebelling against and accepting a deterministic conception of the order of the universe. There are also similar passages, primarily in the original chapters 16 and 25, that were not deleted in the holograph but do not appear in the first Appleton edition, and Hitchcock has also been blamed for insisting that they be excluded.

To a great extent the controversy rests on the question of whether the manuscript Crane revised under Hitchcock's direction was the holograph or a carbon copy of the typescript made for the Bacheller syndicate's serialization of the novel. On the basis of textual evidence, Fredson Bowers, editor of the ten-volume University Press of Virginia edition of *The Works of Stephen Crane*, has concluded that the deleted chapter endings were initiated by Crane and represent his final intention before he had the Bacheller typescript made, the carbon of which was edited by Crane following Hitchcock's suggestions. According to Bowers, Hitchcock never saw the holograph manuscript that reveals the deletions and contains the undeleted passages not present in the Appleton first edition. The evidence Bowers offered to support his assertion is sketchy and inadequate, and consequently this salient issue remains unresolved. In any event, the manuscript is clearly not a finished novel but a draft, and the version edited by Henry Binder in 1979 that has fueled the controversy is not a transcription of any one manuscript, as often stated, but an eclectic text never seen by Crane based on the completed holograph, four recovered pages of the removed chapter 12, an early printing of four lost pages in the August 1895 issue of *Current Literature*, the pages of an earlier draft preserved on the versos of fifty-eight leaves of the final version, and Binder's own emendations. Despite the fact that one or two manuscript-based printings of the novel restoring the deleted passages have appeared, most critics continue to believe that the omitted material was removed because it was heavy-handed, redundant, and out of keeping with the characterization of Henry Fleming and that the first Appleton edition, conservatively edited to emend typographical errors, is the version of *The Red Badge of Courage* that we should and will continue to read.

The revisions that Hitchcock required to make *Maggie* acceptable for publication by Appleton in June 1896 may be more clearly defined since we have Crane's uncorrupted privately printed 1893 version. Crane agreed to remove what he called in a letter to Hitchcock "the words that hurt," and he excised a great deal of profanity and many blasphemous epithets; an Appleton editor probably turned the remaining uses of *damn* and *hell* into the elliptical form of "d——n" and "h——l." Appleton house styling imposed British orthography on words like *honour* and *valour*. The most significant changes were made at the end of the symbolically compressed chapter 17, describing Maggie's descent to the river. Maggie no longer solicits the last two men she meets, and the paragraph describing the "huge fat man in torn and greasy garments" was removed. Editorial patching attempted unsuccessfully to account for the inconsistencies created by the deletions in this chapter. Grammar and style were improved in the 1896 edition and verbal excesses were tempered, but the revisions resulted in an expurgated and incoherent text that has been almost universally rejected by modern editors.

Suggested Reading

Binder, Henry. "The *Red Badge of Courage* Nobody Knows." *Studies in the Novel* 10 (1978): 9–47.

Colvert, James B. "Crane, Hitchcock, and the Binder Edition of *The Red Badge of Courage*." In *Critical Essays on Stephen Crane's* The Red Badge of Courage. Ed. Donald Pizer. Boston: G. K. Hall, 1990. 238–63.

Guemple, Michael. "A Case for the Appleton *Red Badge of Courage*." *Resources for American Literary Study* 21.1 (1995): 43–57.

Parker, Hershel, and Brian Higgins. "The Virginia Edition of Stephen Crane's *Maggie*: A Mirror for Textual Scholars." *Bibliographical Society of Australia and New Zealand Bulletin* 19.3 (1995): 131–66.

Pizer, Donald. "*The Red Badge of Courage* Nobody Knows: A Brief Rejoinder." *Studies in the Novel* 11 (1979): 77–81.

———. "Self-Censorship and Textual Editing." In *Textual Criticism and Literary Interpretation*. Ed. Jerome J. McGann. Chicago: University of Chicago Press, 1985. 144–61.

Hollanden, George. A choral character in *The Third Violet*. In contrast to Hawker, an artist who refuses to sacrifice his integrity to popular success, Hollanden is Crane's caricature of the successful but compromised literary man. An affected and loquacious society writer, Hollanden's primary function in the novel seems to be to deliver long-winded pseudo-philosophical monologues disparaging Hawker's aspirations to win the hand of Grace Fanhall.

"The Holler Tree". This Sullivan County story may have been written somewhat later than others in the series or simply not submitted for publication in 1891 or 1892 since Crane used the versos of some pages of the manuscript later to write the drafts of part of *George's Mother* and the beginning of "The Reluctant Voyagers." The story first appeared in the *Golden Book Magazine* in February 1934. Ridicule of pride and vanity, a theme common to the Sullivan County tales, plays a large role in "The Holler Tree." The four campers featured in the stories are walking along a narrow woodpath when the little man accidentally stumbles against the pudgy man who is carrying a basket of eggs and is admonished for his carelessness. Continuing into the forest, the men see a hollow tree, which the little man imagines is filled with valuable things. When the pudgy man is skeptical, the little man blusteringly proposes a wager that the pudgy man is too egotistical to refuse. The little man climbs up the trunk of the hollow tree and is goaded by the pudgy man to slide into the interior, where he becomes imprisoned. He is enraged with the pudgy man, whom he considers responsible for his predicament. Finally, the frustrated little man tips the trunk. As it falls, "It seemed like a mighty blow aimed by the wrathful little man at the head of the fleeing pudgy man," who bounds away, tumbling into a bush. The little man, grandiloquent in his feat and feeling triumphant over the pudgy man, "resumed his march down the forest pathway. His stride was that of a proud grenadier." The basket of eggs lies crushed under the fallen tree.

Horan, Mary (?–?). *See* Clancy, Martha.

"How the Afridis Made a Ziarat". Only recently attributed to Crane, this short article in the 19 September 1897 issue of the *New York Press* bears the marks of his derisive humor. Crane explains how the Afridis, a fierce tribe in northern India who were still holding the Khyber Pass against the British, established a Ziarat, or place of pilgrimage in their country. What was needed for a Ziarat was a shrine honoring a holy man. The Afridis lacked a holy man to bury because they "had been busy so many centuries robbing caravans and stealing sheep that they had not had time to pay any profound attention to their spiritual welfare." When the mullahs call attention to their great deficiency, the Afridis, known for their resourcefulness, find a saintly man and then murder him, building their shrine over his remains. The British have also contributed to the virtue of the tribe by bribing them to refrain from pillage for two days each week.

"How Americans Make War". Printed as a letter to the *London Daily Chronicle* on 25 July 1899, this piece is actually an animadversion on the failure of the American commander in the Philippines, General Otis, to understand the nature of guerrilla warfare and to modify his tactics in putting down the rebellion against American occupation. In contrast, the Spaniards "had no foolish scruples against learning from the Cubans and then using their experience against the Americans in the Santiago campaign."

"How the Donkey Lifted the Hills". With "The Voice of the Mountain" and "The Victory of the Moon," this fable was written as an aftermath of Crane's Mexican experience. Bacheller, Johnson and Bacheller may have intended to syndicate the piece, but only a single printing has been observed, in the *Nebraska State Journal* on 6 June 1895. It was subsequently published in the June 1897 issue of Bacheller's *Pocket Magazine* and collected in *Last Words*. In keeping with the fable tradition, "How the Donkey Lifted the Hills" uses personified animals to illustrate an adage, in this instance that pride goes before a fall. The donkey, "a proud and aristocratic beast," accepts a wager from the horse that he can duplicate the feat of Atlas by carrying a range of mountains on his back. The animals set out for the mountains and come upon some farmers, who agree to help them by shoveling earth on the donkey's back. When the donkey finds himself buried beneath a weight beyond endurance, he begs for mercy, and the men agree to unearth him but only on the condition that he will henceforth be their slave. "So now, when you see a donkey with a church, a palace, and three villages upon his back, and he goes with infinite slowness, moving but one leg at a time, do not think him lazy. It is his pride."

"Howells Discussed at Avon-by-the-Sea". Crane's report of Hamlin Garland's* 17 August 1891 lecture on William Dean Howells,* one of a series of lectures given by Garland on American literature at Avon's Seaside Assembly, was published in the *New York Tribune* the following day. The report is objective in tenor, quoting Garland with virtually no commentary, but offers substantial evidence of the early influence of Garland and, more especially, Howells on Crane's aesthetic theories and literary practice. Crane quotes Garland as emphasizing Howells's stress on perception and the subjective rendering of experience. The novelist should be "true to himself and to things as he sees them." This impressionistic view of literary realism* corresponds to Garland's theory of "veritism" and was an important factor in the development of Crane's impressionistic* style, which replaced abstract formulations with visual experience as the goal of realistic writing.

Suggested Reading

Pizer, Donald. "Crane Reports Garland on Howells." *Modern Language Notes* 70 (1955): 37–39.

"Howells Fears the Realists Must Wait". Crane's interview with William Dean Howells* in the older novelist's Central Park South apartment was syndicated by McClure in the *New York Times* and other newspapers on 28 October 1894. In this interview Howells reiterated the apothegms of his well-known *Criticism and Fiction* (1891). His dictums that "a novel should never preach" and that a writer must remain "true to his conscience" had a great influence on Crane, who was apparently less impressed with Howells's insistence that "[i]t is the business of the novel to picture the daily life in the most exact terms possible with an absolute and clear sense of proportion." Crane asked Howells whether he had not observed a recent reaction against literary realism,* and both writers agreed that the popularity of romantic fiction, which equated meaningful life with love and courtship, would delay the acceptance of a literature in which these aspects of life were placed in perspective. In *The Rise of Silas Lapham* (1885), Howells had derided the shopworn romance novel as *Tears, Idle Tears* and "slop, silly slop."

"How the Ocean Was Formed". This brief satiric fable appeared in the 7 February 1894 issue of the well-known weekly *Puck* more than a year before Crane's lengthier fables inspired by his Mexican sojourn: "The Voice of the Mountain," "How the Donkey Lifted the Hills," and "The Victory of the Moon." "How the Ocean Was Formed" is a variant of a standard misogynist anecdote. A youth questions a sage as to how the ocean was formed, and the sage replies that once when a man and a woman were alone in the wilderness, the woman asked him to bring her some water to wash her hands. The man brought water, but the woman complained it was too cold; when he fetched warm water, she complained that it was too hot. This sequence was alternatively repeated until "at last the waters which the man had brought, formed the oceans that cover the earth. Whereupon the woman cried with scorn: 'John, you can never do anything rightly. I ought to have gone myself in the first place.' "

Suggested Reading

Andrews, William L. "A New Stephen Crane Fable." *American Literature* 47 (1975): 113–14.

"How Princeton Met Harvard at Cambridge". Crane's second report of a Harvard football game appeared on the first page of the 8 November 1896 issue of the *New York Journal*. Crane's colorful account of the football game between Harvard and Princeton the previous day is centered more on the spectators than the players. The flashing crimson flags of Harvard and "[t]he enthusiasm of the orange and black for their team" overshadow the pedestrian game. Late in the day Harvard is defeated, and "three hundred maniacal chrysanthemums danced weird joy in the gloom." The same issue of the *Journal* contains a page of congratulatory messages from writers and artists on the first anniversary of

Hearst's acquisition of the newspaper, among which is "A Birthday Word from Novelist Stephen Crane."

"How Sampson Closed His Trap". On 19 May 1898 the fleet of Spanish Admiral Pascual Cervera y Topete, having eluded the flying squadron of Commodore Winfield Scott Shley, anchored in the harbor of Santiago de Cuba. From 25–30 May the *World*'s dispatch tug *Three Friends* pursued Admiral William T. Sampson's* flagship, the U.S.S. *New York*, as the American fleet maneuvered near the Santa Maria Keys off the Cuban coast to take up positions that would prevent the escape of Cervera's ships. Crane and the other *World* correspondents, not understanding Sampson's intentions, "debated bitterly the question of why the Admiral clung so closely to this particular spot." This piece, published on 27 May, does not reflect the finality of the *World*'s headline but is instead Crane's report of the fleet's movements and his speculations on the objectives of Sampson and the other American naval commanders.

"How They Court in Cuba". Printed in the *New York Journal* on 25 October 1898, this humorous sketch describes the elaborate courting rituals of Havana. In the upper classes, men and women have traditional social opportunities, but among the masses, a young man is required to attract the attention of his beloved and then follow an elaborate ritual of paying supervised calls on her over a period of some three to eight years to propitiate the demands of her family. In the end, the "interference and trouble and delay and protracted agony and duennas count for nothing, count for nothing against the tides of human life, which are in Cuba or Omaha controlled by the same moon."

"How They Leave Cuba". This sentimental sketch about the distress of a Cuban woman with her child who is deserted at the end of the war by her Spanish lover appeared in the *New York Journal* on 6 October 1898. The woman stands in a boat wailing as the steamer containing the Spanish officer sails from Havana harbor. Crane acknowledges that the woman is to some extent responsible for her situation, but "after all, it is human agony and human agony is not pleasant."

Howells, William Dean (1837–1920). Like Walt Whitman and Mark Twain, Howells was largely self-educated and began his career as a printer. His campaign biography, *Lives and Speeches of Abraham Lincoln and Hannibal Hamlin* (1860), earned him the post of American consul in Venice, which kept him out of military service in the Civil War. From 1866 to 1881, he held editorial positions on the *Atlantic Monthly*, becoming editor in chief in 1871. He became a regular columnist for *Harper's Magazine*, writing "The Editor's Study" from 1886 to 1892 and "The Easy Chair" from 1900 until his death. Howells was a prodigious author, publishing some one hundred books in his lifetime. His range was broad: novels, short stories, plays, poetry, critical essays, and bio-

graphical and literary reminiscences. In his lifetime he was considered the dean
of American letters and the foremost proponent in theory and practice of literary
realism.* As expressed in his collection of essays, *Criticism and Fiction* (1891),
Howells's concept of realism was a decorous verisimilitude to the quotidian
experiences of the common man and "the smiling aspects of life," but the
economic unrest of the 1880s and his devotion to the philosophy of Tolstoy
gradually moved him away from social complacency. Howells's best novels,
such as *A Modern Instance* (1882), *The Rise of Silas Lapham* (1885), and *A
Hazard of New Fortunes* (1889), are infused with ethical and political questions.
A Traveler from Altruria (1894) and *Through the Eye of the Needle* (1907)
embody his vision of a utopian society.

Crane was introduced to Howells by Hamlin Garland,* whose lecture at
Avon's Seaside Assembly on Howells's critical theories and works Crane had
reported in the *New York Tribune* on 18 August 1891. Garland encouraged
Crane to send Howells a copy of the privately printed *Maggie*, and despite its
profanity, violence, and melodrama, Howells praised the slum novelette before
its regular publication in 1896; it remained his favorite among Crane's works.
In April 1893 Crane had tea or dinner with Howells at his home on what is
now Central Park South in Manhattan, and, according to John D. Barry,* Howells at this time read Crane some of the recently published poems of Emily
Dickinson. Although their philosophical perspectives and verse forms are fundamentally dissimilar, the epigrammatic quality and theological concerns of
Dickinson's poems may have influenced the terse lines of *The Black Riders*.
Howells disapproved of free verse poetry, and when Crane sent him a manuscript of the book, Howells responded that the poems were "too orphic" and
that he did not believe "a merciful Providence meant the 'prose poem' to last."
Nevertheless, he attempted, though without success, to help Crane publish some
of his poetry.

In Crane's interview with Howells syndicated by McClure on 28 October
1894, Howells's allusion to "the relation of mother and son" as one of the
important concerns that novelists should deal with may have been a reference
to *George's Mother*, which Crane was then completing. In *Harper's Weekly* on
8 June 1895, Howells predicted that *Maggie* would probably remain unknown
because of its grim subject but that "it embodied perhaps the best tough dialect
which has yet found its way into print." Howells's article entitled "New York
Low Life in Fiction" in the 26 July 1896 *New York World* compared Crane's
work with that of Abraham Cahan.* Howells praised *Maggie* and *George's
Mother* for having "told the truth." Inherent in *Maggie* was "that quality of
fatal necessity that dominates Greek tragedy." But in his 26 October 1895 review of *The Red Badge of Courage* in *Harper's Weekly*, Howells had been
unenthusiastic about the war novel, which he found overly long, incoherent, and
unconvincing in its use of dialect, showing only promise "of the greater things
we may hope from a new talent working upon a high level, not quite clearly as
yet, but strenuously." Congratulating Crane on his English triumph in a letter

on 26 January 1896, Howells could not resist adding that he would "remain true to my first love, 'Maggie.' That is better than all the Black Riders and Red Badges." In the end Howells believed that *The Red Badge* was Crane's "poorest" book. Despite the sensational episodes and apparent nihilism expressed in *The Red Badge*, Howells wanted to believe that Crane would continue to follow in the tradition of commonplace realism that he advocated, stating at a dinner for Crane at the Lantern Club* on 7 April 1896 that "Mr. Crane had taken the right course in looking at and describing men and things as they are." Significantly, Crane did not inscribe a copy of *The Red Badge* for Howells until 17 August 1896, expressing his "veneration and gratitude" for "many things he has learned of the common man and, above all, for a certain re-adjustment of his point of view victoriously concluded some time in 1892." Realizing how far this point of view had diverged from Howells's commonplace realism since that time, he never sent him this inscribed copy. In his obituary essay on Frank Norris* in the December 1902 issue of the *North American Review*, Howells again extolled Crane's accomplishment in *Maggie* and reiterated that " 'The Red Badge of Courage,' and the other things that followed it, were the throes of an art failing with material to which it could not render an absolute devotion from an absolute knowledge. He sang, but his voice erred up and down the scale, with occasional flashes of brilliant melody which could not redeem the errors."

Suggested Reading

Cady, Edwin H. *The Road to Realism: The Early Years, 1837–1885, of William Dean Howells*. Syracuse, N.Y.: Syracuse University Press, 1956.
———. *The Realist at War: The Mature Years, 1885–1920, of William Dean Howells*. Syracuse: Syracuse University Press, 1958.

Hubbard, Elbert (1956–1915). Hubbard worked at a variety of odd jobs in the Midwest before moving to Buffalo, New York, where for fifteen years he was a partner in the Larkin Soap Company. Two years after his marriage in 1881, he settled in East Aurora, a Buffalo suburb. In 1892 he retired from business and early the next year matriculated briefly as an adult undergraduate at Harvard. On a trip to England, Hubbard fell under the influence of William Morris, whose Kelmscott Press produced books and engravings of high artistic merit. On his return, Hubbard resolved to devote himself to literature. He found employment at the Arena Publishing Company, which published his first two novels. His third novel, *No Enemy (But Himself)*, was published in 1894 by Putnam's, which also brought out the first of his *Little Journeys*, a pamphlet on George Eliot. In 1895 Hubbard, with Harry P. Taber,* established at East Aurora the Roycroft Shop, named after the English printers Thomas and Samuel Roycroft (a name that literally means "king's craftsmen") and involved himself in the Kelmscott style of bookmaking, featuring elaborate ornamentation and black-letter typography. In June 1895, he and Taber founded *The Philistine: A Peri-*

odical of Protest,* which was devoted to satire and derision of the literary establishment. Another periodical, the *Fra* (its title derived from Hubbard's sobriquet, "Fra Albertus"), was established by Hubbard in 1908 and was discontinued in 1917. Hubbard wrote six novels and about 170 *Little Journeys*. He contributed some 600 columns to the Hearst Syndicate's *New York American* and was one of the most popular lecturers in the United States. He died in the torpedo sinking of the liner *Lusitania*.

Commentators have magnified the importance of the dinner tendered to Crane by the Society of the Philistines at the Genessee Hotel in Buffalo on 19 December 1895 as a landmark or turning point in Crane's career. Hubbard's own promotion of the event was intended more to publicize his ad hoc Society of the Philistines and its iconoclastic magazine than to celebrate Crane's achievement, and there has been controversy about what actually occurred at the dinner and Crane's reaction to it. Hubbard was a master of advertising. His initial letter of invitation to Crane on 5 November specified that "we will send out invitations to 200 of the best known writers publishers and newspaper men of the United States and England." Writing to a friend shortly after Crane's death, Hubbard maintained that "[t]he banquet started Stevie Crane on the road to fame—there's no doubt about that! We sent out seven hundred invitations to folks we hoped couldn't come. Forty-six came and they acted outrageous—outrageous, Dear, that's what I said." Actually, only twenty-eight men other than Hubbard, Taber, and Crane himself were present, and there is little doubt that what Hubbard intended as a recognition of Crane's "merit as a man" and "genius as a poet" turned into a boisterous roast. Claude Fayette Bragdon,* offended by the ridicule directed at Crane, started to walk out but was restrained by Willis Brooks Hawkins,* who had cajoled the diffident Crane into attending the dinner. Crane apparently accepted the good-natured abuse of the Philistines without resentment. According to Frank Noxon,* he was "having the time of his life." As William MacIntosh, editor of the *Buffalo Evening News*, who attended the dinner reported the next day, Crane responded to Harry Taber's tribute "modestly and gracefully, saying he was a working newspaper man who was trying to do what he could 'since he had recovered from college' with the machinery which had come into his hands—doing it sincerely, if clumsily, and simply setting forth in his own way his own impressions. The poet made a very good impression. He is a young fellow, 24, with a smooth face and a keen eye and doesn't take himself over-seriously." Hawkins felt that Crane was more embarrassed by the praise than disturbed by the ridicule and was "in a blue funk." In honor of the event, Hubbard published *A Souvenir and a Medley*, which, together with the souvenir menu of the dinner, *The Time Has Come*, contains more of Crane's works.

The Philistine banquet did little to further Crane's reputation, since by December 1895 he was already riding the wave of acclaim that followed the English publication of *The Red Badge of Courage*. Whatever occurred during the dinner and despite Hubbard's occasional jeering at Crane in the *Philistine*, their personal and literary relationship remained cordial and mutually beneficial. They maintained an intimate correspondence after Crane went to England, and Hubbard continued to print and promote Crane's work in his publications until long after his death. In his essay on Crane in the March 1896 issue of the *Lotos*, Hubbard concluded that Crane had already "done enough to save the fag-end of the century from literary disgrace; and look you, friends, that is no small matter!"

Suggested Reading

Balch, David. *Elbert Hubbard, Genius of Roycroft: A Biography.* New York: Stokes, 1940.

Hawkins, Willis Brooks. "Stephen Crane Flinches." *Stephen Crane Newsletter* 3.1 (1968): 6–7.

Noxon, Frank. "The Real Stephen Crane." *Step-Ladder* (Chicago) 14 (January 1928): 4–9.

Sorrentino, Paul. "The Philistine Society's Banquet for Stephen Crane." *American Literary Realism 1870–1910* 15 (1982): 232–38.

Hughes, Rupert (1872–1956). The uncle of the reclusive billionaire Howard Hughes and an eccentric figure in his own right, Rupert Hughes established himself in the publishing world as an assistant editor of *Godey's Magazine*, *Current Literature*, and the *Criterion*. His articles in these magazines often appeared over the name "Cheliefer." In May 1901 Hughes settled in London, where his first play, *The Wooden Wedding*, was produced in 1902. Over the next twenty years he wrote more than a dozen plays. Hughes also wrote short stories, many of which were turned into film scripts. By 1923 he was living in Hollywood, where he built a mansion inspired by illustrations from an edition of *Arabian Nights*. Throughout the next two decades, he wrote and directed films. His enduring reputation rests on his three-volume biography of George Washington, the culmination of a lifelong interest.

Convinced from the beginning that Crane was a genius, Hughes, writing as Cheliefer, was assiduous in promoting his work. Hughes's review of *Maggie* was one of the few received by the slum novel before its publication in revised form in 1896. Writing in the October 1895 issue of *Godey's Magazine*, Hughes praised the "great humanity and fearless art" in the novelette and called it "the strongest piece of slum writing we have." After the 1896 *Maggie* appeared, he reiterated his admiration and surpassed William Dean Howells* in the judgment that it had the "inevitableness of Greek tragedy" and the significance of *Medea*. In his extended commentary on Crane's achievement in the September 1896 issue of *Godey's Magazine*, Hughes extolled the verisimilitude of *The Red Badge of Courage* and placed Crane "at the very head of the American story-writers of the younger school." In contrast, Hughes's castigation of Crane's impressionistic style and faulty grammar was acidulous. *The Red Badge*, he asserted, "bristles more with false grammar than with bayonets." In the 3 June

1899 *Criterion*, Hughes condemned *War Is Kind* under the title of "Mr. Crane's Crazyquilting," but his 6 January 1900 summation of Crane's literary career in the *Criterion* credits Crane with "having written some of the best pages America has contributed to literature, in *Maggie*, *The Red Badge*, certain of *The Black Riders* lines, 'The Open Boat,' and in the two books just published from his hand"—*Active Service* and *The Monster and Other Stories*.

Huneker, James Gibbons (1860–1921). A prolific critic of music, art, and literature, Huneker studied piano in Paris and Philadelphia, where he began his career in music journalism. In 1886 he moved to New York City and joined the staff of the *Musical Courier*. From 1887 to 1902 he conducted a column in the magazine that featured critiques, book reviews, parodies, anecdotes, and news items. In these years he also served as music critic of the *New York Recorder*, the *New York Morning Advertiser*, and the weekly magazine *Town Topics*, of which he was associate editor. Subsequently, Huneker was a feature writer for the *New York Times* and *Puck*. From 1919 until his death, he was music critic of the *New York World*. *Ivory Apes and Peacocks* (a comma after the first word was inadvertently omitted), published in 1915, contained essays on Whitman, Conrad,* Dostoyevski, Tolstoy, and Jules Laforgue. Huneker's only novel, *Painted Veils* (1920), was intended for private circulation. *Steeplejack* (1920), his autobiography, is a sweeping analysis of the artistic world of his time.

Crane and Huneker became friends during Crane's early years in New York. An unsigned typescript in the papers of Thomas Beer,* Crane's first biographer, is probably a copy sent to Beer by Vincent Starrett of an anecdote by Huneker recalling an incident in the spring of 1894 that ostensibly motivated Crane to begin an untraced novel about a boy prostitute entitled "Flowers in [or "of"] Asphalt."* In *Steeplejack* Huneker states that it was Crane who first made him aware of the fiction of Joseph Conrad,* which Crane believed was the finest being written in English at the end of the nineteenth century. In the *Musical Courier* of 3 August 1898, Huneker parodied Crane's war correspondence, especially his overuse of color words.

Suggested Reading

Schwab, Arthur T. *James Gibbons Huneker: Critic of the Seven Arts*. Stanford: Stanford University Press, 1963.

"Hunger Has Made Cubans Fatalists". Written in late June 1898 during an interlude in the action of the Cuban War, this report was not published in the *New York World* and other newspapers until 12 July. Crane is acutely aware of the demand for sensational news created in the American public by the yellow press and rebukes "the bulletin board crowds who fancy that war is not a complication composed of heat, dust, rain, thirst, hunger and blood," stressing that "it is impossible for the army to move faster than it does at present." In order to compensate for the lack of fresh information, Crane relates the story of how on 17 and 18 June he and Sylvester Scovel* swam two horses ashore from the *Triton* and, escorted by Cuban insurgents, made their way through Spanish lines to ascend a mountain from the summit of which they could view the Spanish fleet in Santiago Harbor, an experience he also describes in "War Memories." In this report he dwells on the stoical character of the insurgents, their meager diet of mangoes and occasional horseflesh, and the mutual lack of regard that they and the American soldiers have for one another. Here, as in other Cuban War dispatches and stories, Crane laments that the press has neglected the accomplishments of regular troops in favor of the exploits of volunteer regiments.

"Hunting Wild Hogs". A Sullivan County sketch more reportorial than literary in tone, "Hunting Wild Hogs" was printed in the *New York Tribune* on 28 February 1892. This is a matter-of-fact account of the pursuit by Crane's brother William Howe Crane and the hunter Lew Boyd* of a number of European wild hogs that escaped from an enclosure in Sullivan County owned by a wealthy New York banker who had imported them. In some of the Sullivan County sketches, such as "Sullivan County Bears" and "The Way in Sullivan County," Crane ridicules the courage of hunters, but in this sketch, his admiration for Boyd, who chased and killed a wounded wild hog for two hundred miles, seems unqualified.

Huntington, Robert W. (?–1917). Commander of the First Battalion of the U.S. Marine Corps, the assault force that invaded Cuba on 10 June 1898. He entered service in 1861, was promoted from lieutenant colonel to colonel less than two months after the Guantánamo Bay incursion, and retired in 1900. Huntington figures in a number of Crane's Cuban War dispatches and in the sketch "Marines Signalling under Fire at Guantanamo."

I

"I'd Rather Have—". Written when Crane had just turned eight, this amusing and highly literate little doggerel about a young boy's desire for a dog refutes the canard, often repeated by biographers, that he could not read or did not attend school until the age of eight. The diary of Stephen's father, Jonathan Townley Crane, reveals that he began his public school education in Port Jervis, New York, on 2 September 1878, when he was six years old. On 18 March 1879, the *Port Jervis Evening Gazette* lists him on the honor roll of a class in the Main Street School, so presumably he could read and write.

["If the Cup Once Gets Over Here ... "]. An untitled news commentary unpublished in Crane's lifetime dealing with the 1899 America's Cup yachting competition in which the English sloop *Shamrock* was defeated by the American *Columbia*, this report was first printed from a manuscript in the Rare Book and Manuscript Library of Columbia University in *Tales, Sketches, and Reports*, volume 8 of *The Works of Stephen Crane*, edited by Fredson Bowers (1973), 755–57. Crane remarks that "the British government and people have a sort of constitutional inability to admit anything," so instead of acknowledging that an English sailing champion has been outraced, they tend to tell Americans in England that "[i]f the Cup once gets over here, you'll never get it back."

"An Illusion in Red and White". Syndicated by the *New York World* on 20 May 1900, "An Illusion in Red and White" was included in the English edition of *The Monster and Other Stories*. Crane's prologue attributes the origin of the story to a New York journalist who narrated it to fellow correspondents on a dispatch boat to wile away a boring evening on the Cuban blockade. As in "War Memories," this seems to be Crane's stratagem for distancing himself from the first-person narrative, a point of view he used infrequently. The story hinges on the indeterminacy of perception. The internal narrator cautions that "this is the way I imagine it happened. I don't say it happened this way, but this is how I imagine it happened." A farmer in New York State named Jones murders his wife by striking her over the head with an ax in the presence of their four children and burying her in the woods. When the children are questioned, they insist that their mother was killed by a stranger with red hair, white teeth, and white hands. What the narrator imagines is that Jones gradually insinuates to the children that this is what they have seen until they are determined to believe it. The oldest child, Freddy, has a mind that "began to work like ketchup," and long after his father has been hanged for the murder by a disbelieving jury, "he hopes to meet the man with the red hair, big white teeth, and white hands, whose image still remains so distinct in his memory that he could pick him out in a crowd of ten thousand."

"An Impression of the 'Concert' ". Crane's first report of the Greek-Turkish War was published in the *Westminster Gazette* on 3 May 1897, the first in a series headed "With Greek and Turk." The dispatch is datelined "On Board French Steamer *Guadiana*," the ship on which Crane left Marseilles for Piraeus on 3 April, most likely accompanied by Cora and Mrs. Ruedy.* On 7 April, the *Guadiana* changed course and diverted to Suda Bay on the northern coast of Crete to deliver mail to the European fleet, the "Concert" that was blockading the Cretan ports. The *Guadiana* remained in Suda Bay for three hours, and Crane describes the various European warships on blockade duty, the launches plying between them, and the officers who come aboard to collect mail. Despite its shipboard dateline, this report was probably written later in Athens.

Suggested Reading

Stallman, R. W. "How Stephen Crane Got to Crete." *American Literature* 44 (1972): 308–13.

Impressionism. In painting, this term describes a movement, rather than a specific technique, that originated in Paris following the Franco-Prussian War and encompassed a diverse group of artists, the more significant of whom were Edouard Manet, Claude Monet, Camille Pissarro, Pierre Renoir, and Edgar Degas. These artists held in common the conviction that art should be subjective, reproducing the object perceived as closely as possible. Rather than a static, preconceived reproduction of reality, a painting should render the immediate and fluctuating sensory impression of light and color on the eye. The impressionist renders experience as the subjective and fleeting deposit of the moment. Impressionism was an attempt to show the effects produced by masses of form and color in movement before the eye. Of primary importance was the matter of focus. Since the eye obviously could not rest on two things simultaneously, impressionists gave detailed treatment of only a specific portion of a scene, while the foreground or background was filled with shadow or masses of confused color.

Applying these techniques to fiction, Henry James,* Ford Madox Ford,* and Joseph Conrad* maintained that the novel that truly reflected life would be a filament of impressions episodically presented rather than a continuous narrative, that personality is most truly revealed in moments of crisis, and that the recounting of apprehended experience is preferable to a detached, omniscient point of view. The appeal of fiction, Conrad wrote in his preface to *The Nigger of the "Narcissus"* (1897), "must be an impression conveyed through the senses. . . . All art, therefore, appeals primarily to the senses, and the artistic aim when expressing itself in written words must also make its appeal through the senses."

Crane was familiar with artists in childhood. His mother and his older sister Mary Helen were accomplished painters. Many of his friends during his early years in New York were painters and illustrators, notably Frederick Gordon,* R. G. Vosburgh,* David Ericson,* Nelson Greene,* W. W, Carroll,* Edward S. Hamilton, Corwin Knapp Linson,* Henry McBride,* and Gustave Verbeek.* None of these was an impressionist, but by the late 1880s the impressionist movement in art and literature was a frequent subject of discussion among American artists and writers, and exhibitions of French impressionist pictures were common. In April 1887 the American Art Association exhibited over three hundred paintings in New York, most of them by Degas, Monet, Pissarro, and Renoir. More directly, Crane was exposed to the literary aesthetics of Hamlin Garland,* who believed that the impressionistic stress on individual sense experience was in accord with his own "veritism." In a letter of 1891 he wrote: "I am . . . an impressionist, perhaps, rather than a realist. I believe, with Monet, that the artist should be self-centered, and should paint life as he sees it. If the other fellow doesn't see the violet shadows on the road, so much the worse for him."

Crane experimented with impressionistic techniques in his earliest writing. The density of color imagery in the Sullivan County stories and in his first New York City sketch, "The Broken-Down Van," is almost as great as in *The Red Badge of Courage.* His first novel, *Maggie,* is not a continuous narrative but a series of short, dramatic episodes in which incidents are filtered through the limited point of view of the characters and their distorted sense impressions of the flux of reality. This fragmentary, episodic structure is evident in *The Red Badge.* Although the ironic stance of the third-person narrator is always palpable, the essential movement in the war novel consists of emotional transitions in the mind of the protagonist. The appearance of the outer world is modulated in conformity with Henry Fleming's fleeting sensations. There are numerous personifications, largely in the form of descriptive adjectives such as those that describe wagons as "terror-stricken," smoke as "lazy and ignorant," and woods as "lowering." *The Red Badge* is saturated with color imagery and synesthesia used in realistic descriptions and metaphorically to suggest states of mind. "The Open Boat" also employs painterly scenes, terse dialogue, and a detached narrator with an ironic perspective that is juxtaposed to the encompassed, fearful preoccupation of the men in the dinghy whose eyes are so fixated on the sweeping waves that threaten to swamp the boat that ''[n]one of them knew the color of the sky.'' This contrast between an objective narrator and apprehensive, fearful characters unable to discriminate between distortive sensory experience and objective reality conjoined with episodic structure and fragmented dialogue are correspondingly evident in ''The Blue Hotel'' and ''Death and the Child.''

Crane's experience as a war correspondent probably had a great deal to do with his movement away from impressionism in his later fiction. Newspaper writing requires an objective point of view and an emphasis on facts rather than impressions. It became necessary to replace pictorially conceived, disconnected configurations with sustained chronological narratives. Crane became interested in describing the life of the common soldier in as detailed a manner as possible and sacrificed his subjective impressionism to this end. His later war stories consequently are more concerned with ascertaining the nature of reality than with the problem of perceiving it and resemble his newspaper dispatches in being less intense and less carefully executed than *The Red Badge of Courage*.

Suggested Reading

Nagel, James. *Stephen Crane and Literary Impressionism*. University Park: Pennsylvania
    State University Press, 1980.
Overland, Orm. ''The Impressionism of Stephen Crane: A Study in Style and Technique.'' *Americana Norvegica* 1 (1966): 239–85.
Perosa, Sergio. ''Naturalism and Impressionism in Stephen Crane's Fiction.'' In *Stephen Crane: A Collection of Critical Essays*. Ed. Maurice Bassan. Englewood Cliffs, N.J.: Prentice-Hall, 1967. 80–94.
Rogers, Rodney O. ''Stephen Crane and Impressionism.'' *Nineteenth-Century Fiction* 24 (1969): 292–304.
Wertheim, Stanley. ''Crane and Garland: The Education of an Impressionist.'' *North Dakota Quarterly* 35 (1967): 23–28.

"In the Broadway Cable Cars". Syndicated in newspapers by McClure on 26 July 1896, this humorous New York sketch dramatizes a day in the life of the city from the outlook of the cable cars proceeding down Broadway in the early morning and returning to their stations a few hours before dawn. ''In the gray of the morning they come out of the uptown bearing janitors, porters, all that class which carries the keys to set alive the great downtown.'' Later they carry the clerks and the shoppers. Toward dusk, the tide of travel sets northward, and people in evening dress headed toward the restaurants and theaters of the Tenderloin are added to the throng. Late at night, drunks emerging from the saloons on Sixth Avenue board the cars and entertain passengers with their banter. ''It is a great ride, full of exciting action. Those inexperienced persons who have been merely chased by Indians know little of the dramatic quality which life may hold for them. These jungles of men and vehicles, these cañons of streets, these lofty mountains of iron and cut stone—a ride through them affords plenty of excitement.''

"In the Depths of a Coal Mine". One of the most incisive of Crane's Sunday feature articles, this dramatically rendered study of working conditions in the Pennsylvania coal mines was the product of an investigative trip by Crane and his illustrator friend C. K. Linson* for the McClure syndicate in May 1894 to the coal fields near Scranton, Pennsylvania. Crane wrote a preliminary draft of his article that reveals McClure deleted material from the printed text that he considered overly critical of business interests. The nature of what was cut is suggested by passages in the draft in which Crane excoriates the mine owners and the coal brokers, ''wondering why it is that coal-barons get so much and these miners, swallowed by the grim black mouths of the earth day after day get proportionately so little.'' Ironically, on the death of his mother, Crane had inherited stock in coal mines in Kingston, Pennsylvania, a short distance from Scranton. In a deed dated 24 January 1893, Stephen sold his shares in the mine to his brother William, probably to pay for the printing of *Maggie*. ''In the Depths of a Coal Mine'' was syndicated by McClure in various newspapers on 22 July 1894 and included in the August 1894 issue of *McClure's Magazine* with illustrations by Linson.

Despite the excisions, ''In the Depths of a Coal Mine'' still contains strong social criticism that anticipates *McClure's* muckraking in the first decade of the twentieth century. Writing about the young boys yet at ''the spanking period,'' whose task it is to separate the slate from the coal, Crane observes cynically that ''when they have grown to be great big men they may become miners, real miners, and go down and get 'squeezed,' or perhaps escape to a shattered old man's estate with a mere 'miner's asthma.' They are very ambitious.'' The struggle between the miners and the coal-laden earth is seen in terms of a war that the men will inevitably lose through disaster or disease: ''They have carried the war into places where nature has the strength of a million giants. Sometimes their enemy becomes exasperated and snuffs out ten, twenty, thirty lives. Usually she remains calm, and takes one at a time with method and precision.'' Crane's empathy with animals is evident in his compassion for the mules doomed to lifelong toil in the mines. Unlike the men, they do not go into the mines willingly but value their freedom and ''go mad with fantastic joy'' when brought up to the sunshine. As in *The Red Badge of Courage*, which he had recently completed, Crane depicts the man in the mines as ''in the implacable grasp of nature. It has only to tighten slightly and he is crushed like a bug.''

Suggested Reading

Bowers, Fredson, ed. *Tales, Sketches, and Reports*. Charlottesville: University Press of Virginia, 1973. 923–32. Vol. 8 of *The Works of Stephen Crane*. Ed. Fredson Bowers. 10 vols. 1969–76.

Katz, Joseph. "Stephen Crane: Muckraker." *Columbia Library Columns* 17:2 (1968): 3–7.

"In the First Land Fight Four of Our Men Are Killed". Although the dateline of this dispatch reads "On Board the World Dispatch Boat *Triton*," Ernest McCready,* Ralph Paine,* and others who were present state that it was composed aboard the *Three Friends*. The dispatch appeared in the *New York World* on 13 June 1898, unsigned, probably because it was put together by McCready from notes dictated by Crane. It deals with the fighting between marines and Spanish guerrillas at Guantánamo Bay on 11 and 12 June. Among the four men reported killed was Doctor John Blair Gibbs,* an assistant surgeon in the navy. Crane renders a harrowing account of his death in "War Memories." This dispatch notes that the bodies of two marines killed in the fighting "were stripped of shoes, hats and cartridges and horribly mutilated," but in a correction, "Only Mutilated by Bullets," printed in other newspapers the next day, Crane denied that this had occurred.

Suggested Reading

McCready, Ernest W., to B.J.R. Stolper, 22 January 1934. Stephen Crane Collection, Columbia University Libraries.
Paine, Ralph W. *Roads of Adventure*. Boston: Houghton Mifflin, 1922. 243–47.

"In Havana As It Is To-day". In his report " 'You Must!'—'We Can't!' " Crane had expressed admiration for the combat performance of the insurgents in the Havana area. This article, printed in the *New York Journal* on 12 November 1898, focuses on these revolutionary bands. Crane, with other correspondents, visited some of the insurgent units scattered along a road still interspersed with Spanish outposts, although the war was long over. In one of the camps, they encountered an American who had become an officer on the staff of General Mario García Menocal, a Cornell University graduate who became president of Cuba. Later they visited Menocal himself. Crane comments favorably on Menocal's demeanor and achievements in the war and critiques the armaments, food, and horses in the insurgent camps.

"In a Park Row Restaurant". A burlesque sketch that appeared in the *New York Press* on 28 October 1894, two weeks after its predecessor, "Coney Island's Failing Days," which also features the ruminations of a character identified only as "the stranger." In this later sketch, the stranger sits with the narrator at lunch time in a crowded restaurant on Park Row, the center of New York City's newspaper and financial district, and reveals that he was at one time sheriff of one of the most undomesticated counties in Nevada. In a parodic tone, he compares the hurly burly of the restaurant with the Wild West. Written before Crane's trip to the West in 1895, "In a Park Row Restaurant" reveals his interest in the undomesticated concept of the West as a distinctly American phenomenon.

"In the 'Tenderloin' ". The *New York Journal* carried this second of a series of sketches written specifically for the newspaper about the residents of Manhattan's infamous entertainment district in its Sunday *American* magazine section on 1 November 1896. This is a slight journalistic piece detailing snatches of conversations among people who are late-night diners in a Tenderloin restaurant. Two men who come to the edge of a fight reconcile when they recall a common experience, and "cafe historians" tell anecdotes about other diners. The din of conversation continues until the morning hours when "[i]nto the street came the clear, cold blue of impending daylight, and over the cobbles roared a milk wagon."

"In the Tenderloin: A Duel between an Alarm Clock and a Suicidal Purpose". Published in *Town Topics* on 1 October 1896, part of the dialogue of this story originates in a draft in Crane's 1894 notebook preserved in the Alderman Library of the University of Virginia, but the Tenderloin setting was no doubt added later. Swift Doyer and "his girl" have an altercation about her lack of truthfulness, during which he "grabbed an alarm clock from the dresser and banged her heroically on the head with it." When she recovers from this blow, she informs him that she has taken a fatal dosage of morphine. Swift drags her to a sideboard in the dining room of the flat and revives her with successive measures of whiskey followed by coffee. As she emerges from her stupor, the girl's attention becomes fixated on a fly she has accidentally killed. Swift realizes that she is not going to die since her preoccupation does not conform to his theatrical conception of death: "Why in the name of the gods of the drama did she not refer to her past? Why, by the shelves of the saints of literature, did she not clutch her brow and say: 'Ah, once I was an innocent girl'? What was wrong with this death scene?" As the girl continues to babble, Swift falls asleep, and the dawn finds them sleeping opposite each other at the dining room table with her hand entwined in his hair. In this story of a Tenderloin pimp and a prostitute whose despair "seemed almost as real as the woe of good people," although Swift Doyer "knew as well as the rest of mankind that these girls have no hearts to be broken," Crane offers implicit social commentary through realistic depiction of a sordid episode of life in the Tenderloin as well as satire of the romantic and melodramatic modes of popular literature and theater in his time.

Suggested Reading

Solomon, Eric. *Stephen Crane: From Parody to Realism*. Cambridge: Harvard University Press, 1966. 19–22.

"Inaction Deteriorates the Key West Fleet". Written aboard the *New York World*'s dispatch boat *Triton* off Havana, this short telegram appeared in the *World* and other newspapers on 6 May 1898. Crane emphasizes the wear to the ships and the listlessness among the men of Willaim T. Sampson's* North Atlantic Squadron blockading the coast of Cuba and waiting to intercept the ships of Spanish Admiral Cervera in order to make it safe for the navy to transport troops across the Straits of Florida.

"An Indiana Campaign". A Civil War story only in the broadest sense of the term, "An Indiana Campaign" anticipates the lighthearted communal misunderstandings of the *Whilomville Stories*. When the able-bodied men of Migglesville, a sleepy Indiana town, march away to war, they leave old Major Tom Boldin, a Mexican War veteran, in charge of the community. Nodding on his bench in front of the Migglesville tavern one warm summer day, the major is startled by a frowzy-headed boy who reports having seen a Confederate soldier, who has stolen some of his mother's chickens and run into the woods at the edge of town. The major takes his antiquated smoothbore rifle from its pegs on the wall and goes in pursuit of the rebel. He is followed by another ancient worthy, Peter Witheby; Jerozel Bronson, a mentally retarded young man; and a crowd of terrified women. In a skillful metaphor, Crane compares this disoriented throng to a flock of chickens "who had been scratching intently near the major's feet. They clamoured in an insanity of fear, and rushed hither and thither seeking a way of escape, whereas in reality all ways lay plainly open to them." The major and Witheby pursue the ostensible rebel through a cornfield and into the woods, to find that he is really only "ol Milt' Jacoby," the town drunk. "An Indiana Campaign" was syndicated by Bacheller in various newspapers in two parts on 23 and 25 May 1896 and appeared in magazines in England and the United States. It was collected in *The Little Regiment*.

"Intrigue". *See War Is Kind.*

"Irish Notes". A series of five travel sketches ensuing from Crane's trip to Ireland with Harold Frederic* and Kate Lyon* in August and September 1897 that appeared in the *Westminster Gazette* in October and November. They include: "Queenstown," "Ballydehob," "The Royal Irish Constabulary," "A Fishing Village," and "An Old Man Goes Wooing."

J

"Jack". Three fragmentary manuscripts have survived of a dog story involving a camping trip in Sullivan County, New York, or in the Adirondacks. The first two fragments are untitled; the third, in the Alderman Library of the University of Virginia, is titled "Jack." Frank Noxon* recalled that while a student at Syracuse University* Crane wrote a story about a dog named Jack that was praised but rejected by the editor of the *St. Nicholas Magazine*. Based on the fragments, the story probably involved an attack by a bear on a little boy in a hunting camp and the defense of the boy by a large black mastiff called Jack.

Suggested Reading

Bowers, Fredson, ed. *Poems and Literary Remains*. Charlottesville: University Press of Virginia, 1975. 95–97, 306–8. Vol. 10 of *The Works of Stephen Crane*. Ed. Fredson Bowers. 10 vols. 1969–76.

"A Jag of Pulque Is Heavy". In this Mexican sketch, syndicated under various headlines by Bacheller, Johnson and Bacheller on 10 and 11 August 1895, Crane makes facetious comments about the popular fermented drink pulque, which resembles "green milk" and tastes like "some terrible concoction of bad yeast perhaps. Or maybe some calamity of eggs." The addiction of the poorer class of Mexican Indians to pulque is not catastrophic unless it is mixed with mescal or tequila, since its usual effect on those who consume it is a feeling of genial conviviality. A more serious consequence of the addiction to pulque is the impoverishment, both economic and spiritual, that also afflicts the alcoholic denizens of the slums in American cities. "The Indian, in his dusty cotton shirt and trousers, his tattered sombrero, his flapping sandals, his stolid dark face, is of the same type in this regard that is familiar to every land, the same prisoner, the same victim."

Jake. A cowboy who provokes the fatal gunfight in ''Twelve O'Clock.''

James, Henry (1843–1916). Born near Washington Square in New York City, the son of Henry James, Sr., and the younger brother of the philosopher and psychologist William James, Henry James, Jr., was schooled to lead a life of cosmopolitan leisure. From the age of twelve he accompanied his family on extended sojourns across the Atlantic, spending peripatetic years in France, England, Germany, and Switzerland, a pattern that he continued in his adult life. A back injury kept him out of the Civil War. In 1875 James settled permanently in Europe, first in Paris, where he became acquainted with Gustave Flaubert, Guy de Maupassant, Émile Zola, and especially Ivan Turgenev, who was an important formative influence on his writing. In 1876 he moved to London, where he met Alfred Lord Tennyson, Robert Browning, George Eliot, and other English writers. Although he had a long and productive literary career in England and gained international fame, James was never entirely comfortable with his expatriation, and many of his earlier works, such as *Roderick Hudson* (1876), *The American* (1877), *Daisy Miller* (1879), and *The Portrait of a Lady* (1881), reflect his concern with national identity.

The long novels James wrote in the 1880s on social subjects, such as *The Bostonians* (1886) and *The Princess Casamassima* (1886), were commercial failures, and the plays he wrote in the 1890s were generally not well accepted. *What Masie Knew* (1897) and *The Spoils of Poynton* (1897) are representative of complex psychological studies that continue to appeal only to discerning readers. A number of extended short stories or novelettes composed at this time, notably ''The Aspern Papers,'' ''The Lesson of the Master,'' ''The Jolly Corner,'' and ''The Real Thing,'' have proved to be among his most enduring creations. From 1898 to 1903 James lived at Lamb House in Rye, Sussex. Here he produced by dictation the three complex novels that comprise what many critics consider the major phase of his career: *The Wings of the Dove* (1902), *The Ambassadors* (1903), and *The Golden Bowl* (1904). In his last years, James traveled in the United States, assembled a twenty-six-volume edition of his novels and tales with critically important prefaces, and wrote reminiscences such as *A Small Boy and Others* (1913) and *Notes of a Son and Brother* (1914). In 1915, as an act of protest against America's failure to enter the war, he became a British subject.

The contemporary record for the friendship between Crane and James is meager, and the sources for much of what is written about their personal and literary relationship, largely Ford Madox Ford* and Thomas Beer,* are extremely unreliable. The circumstances of their meeting, probably in early 1898, are obscure. Beer's story that Crane salvaged James's top hat after a fantastic woman named Madame Zipango had poured champagne into it at a London party and the two retreated into a corner together to discuss literary style is probably apocryphal, and the claim that James later submitted manuscripts to Crane for criticism or editorial help is equally dubious. When Crane moved to Brede Place,* Sussex, in February 1899, he became a proximate neighbor of James, who was living in Rye. James had an intense interest in the Civil War and had read *The Red Badge of Courage*, the only Crane book known to have been in his library, but there is no specific mention of the war novel or other Crane works in James's letters or criticism. No letters of Crane to James survive, and all that remain of James's written communications to Crane are a short note addressed to both Stephen and Cora and an inscription torn from a book, most likely *The Awkward Age* (1899). Crane admired James's fiction. His and Cora's library at Brede Place contained copies of several James novels and collections of short stories. Commenting on *What Masie Knew* in his essay "Concerning the English 'Academy,' " Crane characterized James's novel as "alive with all the art which is at the command of that great workman." Both writers were modernist in their concern with fiction as an art and as an impression of life, point of view, and shifting psychological states, but the differences between the style and content of their work are more apparent than the similarities.

The personal relationship between James and Crane was not intimate. When James came to live at Lamb House in June 1898, he embraced the life of a country gentleman. He bicycled, attended flower shows and cricket matches, entertained a cavalcade of visitors, bought a pew in a local church, and snobbishly maintained a distance from those he regarded as social inferiors. James was more at ease with patrician New Englanders and English aristocrats than with Crane, Joseph Conrad,* and H. G. Wells.* Crane and Cora exchanged visits with James on occasion, and James was fond of Crane, although occasionally embarrassed by his rambunctious Americanism. There is a well-known photograph of James enjoying one of the doughnuts made by Cora's cook, Vernall, at a party in the rectory garden of the Brede village church in August 1899. James did not attend the production of "The Ghost" in the Brede Village schoolhouse on 28 December 1899, but among the dramatis personae of that musical farce is Peter Quint Prodmore Moreau. The name Moreau is that of the mad scientist in H. G. Wells's *The Island of Dr. Moreau*, but Peter Quint is from "The Turn of the Screw" and Prodmore from James's story "Covering End." James contributed £5 toward Cora's fund for the support of Harold Frederic's* orphaned children by Kate Lyon,* and on the day Crane died at Badenweiler, James sent Cora £50 for "whatever service it may best render my stricken young friend." Two days later he wrote her: "What a brutal, needless extinction—what an unmitigated unredeemed catastrophe! I think of him with such a sense of possibilities and powers." James remained cordial to Cora while Crane was alive, but he disapproved of her extravagance and irresponsibility. When Cora returned on a visit to England in 1907, in the midst of the scandal over her new husband's shooting to death a man he believed to be her lover, James snubbed her.

Suggested Reading

Delbanco, Nicholas. *Group Portrait: Joseph Conrad, Stephen Crane, Ford Madox Ford, Henry James, and H. G. Wells.* New York: Morrow, 1982.
Edel, Leon. *Henry James, 1901–1916: The Master.* Philadelphia: Lippincott, 1972.
Seymour, Miranda. *A Ring of Conspirators: Henry James and His Literary Circle, 1895–1915.* Boston: Houghton Mifflin, 1989.
Solomon, Eric. *Stephen Crane in England: A Portrait of the Artist.* Columbus: Ohio State University Press, 1964.

Jimmie the Mole. The Tenderloin confidence man in "Diamonds and Diamonds." He is also mentioned in "Yen-Hock Bill and His Sweetheart."

Johnnie. The main character in "This Majestic Lie," Johnnie is a fictional depiction of Charles H. Thrall.* Formerly the manager of a sugar plantation in Pinar del Rio, Johnnie flees to Key West when war breaks out between Spain and the United States and is reduced to the position of "a little tan-faced refugee without much money." Although he is sympathetic to the insurgents, the "sentimental tenderness" in his nature is tempered by an "irony of soul," and he becomes an American spy in Havana for reasons of expediency rather than patriotism.

Johnson, Henry. The black hostler in "The Monster" who saves the life of Dr. Trescott's son Jimmie in a fire at the Trescott home. He is horribly burned when he falls at the foot of a desk and chemicals from exploded vials spill over, dripping onto his upturned face. He becomes monstrous because "he now had no face. His face had simply been burned away," and he is transformed into an unknown quantity—a person who no longer fits into the defined scheme of things. Ironically, Johnson had been an invisible man in Whilomville before the catastrophe that rendered him physically faceless since he had previously been identified by the townspeople only in terms of their stereotyped conception of young black men.

Suggested Reading

Church, Joseph. "The Black Man's Part in Crane's *Monster.*" *American Imago* 45 (1989): 375–88.
Cooley, John. "The Savages: Stephen Crane." In *Savages and Naturals: Black Portraits by White Writers in Modern American Literature.* Newark, Del.: University of Delaware Press, 1982. 38–49.

Johnson, Jimmie. Maggie's brother Jimmie proves the most adaptive character in the struggle for survival that pervades *Maggie: A Girl of the Streets*, although his resolutions of physical and ethical conflicts are couched in relentlessly ironic terms. As a little boy, he perches on a heap of gravel, repulsing the aggression of neighborhood roughnecks from Devil's Row "for the honor of Rum Alley." He is subjected to violent assaults from both his parents, and he resists them with kicks and curses. Growing into manhood, Jimmie "studied human nature in the gutter, and found it no worse than he thought he had reason to believe it." He develops a sneer that "turned its glare upon all things." When he becomes a truck driver, foot passengers are "mere pestering flies" to him. He fights with other drivers and dominates the streets, regardless of whatever stands in the way, unless, like a fire engine, it threatens him with destruction. Morally, he is equally ambivalent. His anger at Pete for seducing Maggie is briefly tempered by his realization that his behavior with young women has been no different, but he dismisses his reservations with a characteristic, "What deh hell?" He quickly backs off when his mother rejects his suggestion that Maggie be allowed to return home, and he draws back in feigned revulsion from her approach: " 'Well, now, yer a hell of a t'ing, ain' yeh?' he said, his lips curling in scorn. Radiant virtue sat upon his brow and his repelling hands expressed horror of contamination." Like his mother, he can always manage to rationalize and reconcile the discrepancies in his attitude and behavior.

Johnson, Maggie. The central character of *Maggie: A Girl of the Streets* is more a type than a fully developed personality. Her fate is no doubt determined to a great extent by the corrosive influences of the slum and the sweatshop, as well as the indifference of social institutions such as the home and the church, but she remains strangely untouched by her physical environment. Maggie "blossomed in a mud puddle. . . . None of the dirt of Rum Alley seemed to be in her veins." She is as sentimental as any other romantic heroine of her time who fulfills the nineteenth-century stereotype of a naive girl seduced and abandoned, and she retains this monumental innocence even after she becomes a prostitute. Maggie is a victim less of slum conditions than of lack of knowledge, intelligence, and sensibility; most of all, she is the victim of her irrepressible illusions. Despite the daily destruction of furniture by her drunken parents, Maggie steadfastly attempts to restore appearances. Even before she leaves with Pete, she makes a final effort to reestablish some order in her home. She idealizes Pete, a drunken Bowery brawler, as a "golden sun," a "knight," and "an ideal man," who "brought forth all his elegance and all his knowledge of high-class customs for her benefit," and she cannot distinguish between the sentimental melodramas to which he takes her and the realities of the life around her. Maggie's life complies, if only temporarily, with her self-delusions. Even as a prostitute she is well dressed, with a "handsome cloak" and "well-shod feet," "daintily lifting her skirts" as she threads her way among the comfortable, theatergoing crowd around her. In her blind materialism, Maggie believes she is rising out of the degradation of the Bowery when in fact she is poised on the edge of a precipice.

Suggested Reading

Hapke, Laura. "Stephen Crane and the Deserted Street Girl." In *Girls Who Went Wrong: Prostitutes in American Fiction, 1885–1917.* Bowling Green, Ky.: Bowling Green University Popular Press, 1989. 45–67.

Minks, Tamara. "Maggie Johnson: An American Eve in a Fallen Eden." *Revisiting Literature* 16 (1988): 23–35.

Johnson, Mary. A depraved alcoholic steeped in hypocrisy, the mother of Maggie and Jimmie in *Maggie: A Girl of the Streets* is an animalistic character with massive shoulders and huge arms and hands that whirl in a continual frenzy. Her utterances are confined to screams and curses or disoriented sentiments. Mary Johnson's violence and brutality alternate with sanctimoniousness moralizing and maudlin self-pity. When she is not "poundin' a kid," smashing furniture, or prostrate and in a drunken stupor in a corner of her flat, she is advising Maggie to "Go teh hell an' see how yeh likes it," and subsequently condemning her for following this advice. She is the insincere voice of middle-class morality in the Darwinian circumstances of Devil's Row. Crane pursues the theme of Mary Johnson's pretense of virtue with relentless irony that sometimes borders on the comical—for example, when she says of Maggie's behavior, "Ah, who would t'ink such a bad girl could grow up in our fambly, Jimmie, me son," or when confronted with the news of Maggie's death she "continued her meal. When she finished her coffee she began to weep."

Johnson, Tommie. Maggie's brother who dies in infancy in *Maggie: A Girl of the Streets.* Tommie is a grubby child whom Maggie drags along the street while he makes "heroic endeavors to keep on his legs, denounce his sister and consume a bit of orange peeling which he chewed between the times of his infantile orations." Crane's staccato observation on Tommie's brief existence, "The babe, Tommie, died. . . . She and Jimmie lived," is a commentary on the Darwinian theme of the survival of the fittest in an urban jungle. The infant Tommie is resurrected as slightly older in three later slum stories: "An Ominous Baby," "A Great Mistake," and "A Dark-Brown Dog."

Johnson, Willis Fletcher (1857–1931). Johnson was graduated from Pennington Seminary* in Pennington, New Jersey, in 1875 and was thereafter active in the school's affairs, eventually becoming president of the alumni association. The Reverend Jonathan Townley Crane had been principal of Pennington for almost a decade before the Civil War, and Stephen had been a student at the school for more than two years. Johnson became an editor of the *New York Tribune* in 1880 and was day editor from 1887 to 1894. He remained an editorial writer for the *Tribune* until 1917, when he became literary editor, a position he held until 1920. Johnson was also a contributing editor of the *North American Review* and a lecturer on foreign relations at a number of schools and colleges.

   Johnson's memoir, "The Launching of Stephen Crane" (*Literary Digest In-*

ternational Book Review 4 [1926]: 288–90), provides important information about Crane's early journalistic and literary career. Johnson recalls that Crane began writing for publication in the summer of 1888 when he assisted his brother Townley in reporting news of events in resorts on the New Jersey coast for the *Tribune*. Until 1890 Townley did not inform Johnson that some of the material he sent to the *Tribune* was written by his younger brother but paid Stephen from his own pocket. In the fall of 1890, Johnson, probably through Townley, engaged Stephen as the *Tribune's* correspondent in Syracuse, New York. Johnson considered Crane qualified for the job based on his work at Asbury Park, New Jersey, and because he "felt a warm personal interest in both of the Crane boys on account of my former friendship with their father," but Crane sent back only one known piece to the *Tribune*, the hoax "Great Bugs in Onondaga."

Johnson met Crane again for the first time since Crane's early childhood in the summer of 1891, when Johnson spent the summer at Asbury Park and had almost daily contact with him. Crane showed Johnson two of his Sullivan County pieces, which he accepted for publication in the Sunday supplement section of the *Tribune*. Fourteen of Crane's Sullivan County sketches and stories appeared in the *Tribune* between February and July 1892. At this time Crane also showed Johnson an early draft of *Maggie*. Johnson's dating of this event has been disputed, but a number of Crane's friends at Syracuse University* attest to the composition of a version of *Maggie* in the spring of 1891 that Johnson may well have seen. Impressed with the verisimilitude and vitality of *Maggie*, Johnson maintains that he sent Crane to Appleton's literary adviser, Ripley Hitchcock,* with the manuscript, but Hitchcock rejected the book.

Johnson also attempts to correct misconceptions about the circumstances surrounding the publication in the 21 August 1892 issue of the *Tribune* of Crane's report on the American Day Parade of the Junior Order of United American Mechanics, "Parades and Entertainments," in which Crane ridiculed both the uncouth march of the workingmen and the smug complacency of the middle-class Asbury Park onlookers. Johnson maintains that Crane was not fired by the *Tribune*, whose owner, Whitelaw Reid, the Republican candidate for vice president, was politically damaged by Crane's satire, but the paper never published any of his work after 1892.

Jones, Charley. In *George's Mother*, Jones is an acquaintance from George Kelcey's home town of Handyville who introduces him to the group of middle-aged barflies among whom he seeks to establish a sense of identity.

Jones, Edith Richie. *See* Richie, Edith.

Jones, Freddy, Lucy, and Martha. The elder three of the four children in "An Illusion in Red and White" whose father convinces them that it was not he but a man with red hair, big white teeth, and white hands who murdered their mother. The youngest child, Henry, is an infant and "was not concerned with the fact that his mother had been murdered."

José. In "One Dash—Horses" José is Richardson's terror-stricken guide. The leader of the Mexican sheepherders who drive Bill off the range in "A Man and Some Others" is also named José. Neither character rises above Crane's derogatory stereotype of Mexicans as cowards and sneaks.

"Joys of Seaside Life". A sardonic report on the amusements offered to summer vacationers in Asbury Park and Ocean Grove, New Jersey, printed in the *New York Journal* on 17 July 1892. Crane describes the tintype galleries, the mechanical contrivances "to tumble-bumble the soul and gain possession of nickles," the Ferris wheel and the "razzle-dazzle," the hucksters selling cheap and gaudy women's apparel, the frankfurter man, the camera obscura, and the entertainers, including a singer and dancer of undetermined gender whose costume is "a chromatic delirium of red, black, green, pink, blue, yellow, purple, white, and other shades and colors not known."

"The Judgment of the Sage". A brief fable dubunking intellectual pretentiousness, "The Judgment of the Sage" was published in the January 1896 issue of the *Bookman*. Two men each give a beggar a loaf of bread of the same size and quality. The first does this act of charity because it is the will of God and the second because the man is hungry. An argument breaks out among the men of the town as to which motive is superior, and they consult a philosopher, who readily responds to being greeted as "most illustrious sage." When confronted with the conundrum, the philosopher can only respond with an "Eh?" and protest that "you mistake me for an illustrious sage. I am not he whom you seek. However I saw a man answering my description pass here some time ago. With speed you may overtake him. Adieu."

Julie. In "Yen-Hock Bill and His Sweetheart," she is Bill's masochistic girlfriend who seems to thrive on his abuse of her.

K

Kelcey, George. The main character in *George's Mother*, Crane's "brown young man" is an aimless drifter from a small-town background whose romantic dreams and ideals, like those of his mother, fail to be realized. Disaffected from his mother's religious zealotry and unable to achieve the love, understanding, and companionship he craves, George seeks consolation in alcohol. "Drink and its surroundings were the eyes of a superb green dragon to him. He followed a fascinating glitter, and the glitter required no explanation." George loses his job and slides into depravity among alcoholics and street brawlers. The death of his mother leaves him desolate and isolated in an urban environment with which he is unable to cope.

"Kellar Turns Medium". Syndicated in newspapers on 12 July 1896 over the signature of H. F. (or H. T.) Jokosa, this sketch is the only known publication other than *Maggie* for which Crane used a pen name. The reason that he concealed his identity is obscure since the piece is a straightforward account of how the famous illusionist Harry Kellar utilized his skill to disabuse a wealthy old man of his confidence in the spurious advice of a spiritualistic medium. Crane's authorship is not in dispute; the item appears on one of his inventory lists.

Kenealy, Alexander C. (1865–1915). Born in England and educated there and in France, Kenealy emigrated to the United States and served his journalistic apprenticeship on the *New York Herald* and the *Philadelphia Press*. In 1887 he rejoined the *Herald* and was its correspondent on Robert E. Peary's first Arctic expedition. He also covered the Homestead and Buffalo riots. Later he was Paris and London correspondent for the *Herald*. Kenealy joined the staff of the *New York World* in 1895 and was in charge of the dispatch boat *Triton* during the Cuban War. With Crane and Sylvester Scovel,* Kenealy covered the marine landing at Guantánamo Bay and the Santiago campaign in June 1898. He returned to London to become news editor of the *Daily Express* from 1901 to 1904, and in 1904 he became founding editor of the *Daily Mirror*, the first English half-penny daily.

"The Kicking Twelfth". This is the first in order of composition and publication of the four episodes that comprise the Spitzbergen tales. The protagonist of the story, Lieutenant Timothy Lean, also appears in "The Shrapnel of Their Friends" and "The Upturned Face." "The Kicking Twelfth" was first published in the February 1900 issue of the *Pall Mall Magazine* and collected in *Last Words*. The story describes the first battle of the "Kickers," the Twelfth Regiment of Spitzbergen Infantry, in which they charge up a hill and take a formidable stronghold while suffering a loss of five hundred men. They then continue their assault down the other side of the hill under even greater fire and more losses, but the enemy retreats and the Twelfth secures its position. Lieutenant Lean is the antiheroic hero of the affair, and the charge, conducted by a "mob of panting men," has an "unromantic aspect." There is nevertheless a good deal of stereotyping and more than a touch of farce. Nearest to Lean in the melee are two stock characters, "an old grizzled sergeant who would have gone to hell for the honour of the regiment and a pie-faced lad who had been obliged to lie about his age in order to get into the army." Colonel Sponge, named after Crane's dog, is "breathless but resolute," and General Richie, named after Edith Richie* (Jones) who transcribed the manuscript from Crane's dictation, is "cold-eyed, stern, and grim as a Roman." The battle cry of "Kim Up the Kickers" seems as incongruous and puerile as a football cheer in the midst of the carnage, and the burlesque tone of this story makes a travesty of conventional notions of war and heroism.

Suggested Reading

Shaw, Mary N. " 'The Kicking Twelfth': Stephen Crane's Demythologized Dramatization of War and Heroism." *Short Story* 1.1 (1993): 84–93.

"Killing His Bear". In this Sullivan County story, published in the *New York Tribune* on 31 July 1892, Crane comes closer to the impressionistic style and thematic concerns of *Maggie* and *The Red Badge* than in any other in this group of rural tales, especially in the use of animism, color imagery and synesthesia, and references to blood, death, and battle. The opening tableau shows a group of pine trees "huddled together" that "sang in quavers. . . . Icicles dangled from the trees' beards, and fine dusts of snow lay upon their brows." As the sun sinks, "red rays retreated" and "armies of shadows stole forward." The little man, separated from his three companions, stands motionless at a hunting post holding a rifle and listening to the yelping of a hound chasing a bear through the forest toward his position. "The animal heard only the crying behind him. He knew nothing of the thing with death in its hands standing motionless in the shadows before him." As the bear approaches, the little man becomes intense and excited. His entire being is concentrated in the shot that will fell the bear: "When the rifle cracked it shook his soul to a profound depth. Creation rocked and the bear stumbled." The bear is mortally wounded and the little man pursues it for a few hundred yards. When he comes on the body, he experiences ecstatic triumph, and the story ends in a conflation of images of love and war: "He ran up and kicked the ribs of the bear. Upon his face was the smile of the successful lover." This is the most subjective of the Sullivan County stories, exhibiting virtually none of their characteristic spoofing, with the exception of some hyperbolic language exemplifying the little man's inflated ego, which may also be found in much of Crane's more serious fiction.

"The King's Favor". Crane probably met the tenor Albert G. Thies (later Gerard-Thiers) at Avon's Seaside Assembly, where Thies and his wife, Louise Gerard, gave a number of performances in the summer of 1890. In his *New York Tribune* report "Avon's School by the Sea," Crane devoted a paragraph to an anecdote about Thies's performance before Chief Cetewayo, self-styled king of the Zulus but at that time a prisoner of the British, who was so delighted with Thies's performance that he offered to give him one of his four wives as a reward, a gift that Thies found difficult to refuse diplomatically. Crane may have heard this story from Thies himself. In "The King's Favor," published in the May 1891 issue of Syracuse University's* *University Herald*, he expands his account of the episode into a humorous sketch that combines journalism with fictional techniques of direct and indirect dialogue and hyperbolic narrative. "The King's Favor" may consequently be considered Crane's first signed short story.

Kitchell, John (?–?). At the conclusion of his newspaper report on the sinking of the *Commodore*, "Stephen Crane's Own Story," Crane recounts the heroic rescue efforts of John Kitchell of Daytona, who, as the dinghy overturned in the surf, "came running down the beach, and as he ran the air was filled with clothes." Kitchell dashed into the water and helped the cook and Crane to reach shore. In "The Open Boat" Crane does not mention Kitchell by name but uses almost the identical language of the report to describe his actions, adding metaphorically that "He was naked—naked as a tree in winter; but a halo was about his head, and he shone like a saint."

"The Knife". This is the only one of Crane's *Whilomville Stories* that does not involve children and is the most complex and balanced of the series in its narrative structure. "The Knife" was published in the March 1900 issue of *Harper's New Monthly Magazine*. Unfortunately, the story hinges on the tired canard of the American black's fondness for watermelons, which Crane himself acknowledges is an "effete joke," but Crane's attitude toward blacks in "The Knife" and elsewhere does not often transcend the stereotypes of the 1890s.

Nevertheless, Crane's unsparing depiction of a Northern black community and his rendition of African-American dialect in "The Knife" are more convincing than the idealized representations of Joel Chandler Harris and Thomas Nelson Page.

In "The Knife," Peter Washington, who has succeeded the late Henry Johnson of "The Monster" as Dr. Trescott's hostler, and Alek Williams, who for a time harbored Johnson in his demented state after his face had been burned away and is now a respected deacon in the church, covet the delectable watermelons in the garden of Si Bryant, a white resident of Whilomville. Both independently scheme to steal one of the melons by cutting it from its stalk with a knife. They accidentally encounter one another at midnight in Bryant's watermelon patch, and Peter opportunely deceives Alek into thinking he has caught him in the act and takes him prisoner. When Alek's hound, Susie, sinks her teeth into Peter's leg and is beaten down by Alek, Peter in gratitude releases the old man. The next morning, Alek is confronted and interrogated by Si Bryant, who has found a knife in his watermelon patch that Alek immediately recognizes belongs to Peter Washington. Alek realizes that he has been tricked and that Peter is as culpable as he, but when pressed by Bryant to identify the owner of the knife, the quick-witted Alek loyally outmaneuvers and frustrates the white man with a "white lie" by naming an unrecognizable black man in Oswego, a community that would be a great distance from the mythical Whilomville.

L

Lafayette College. Crane was a student enrolled in the mining engineering curriculum of this college in Easton, Pennsylvania, for a single semester in the fall of 1890. Lafayette was controlled by the Presbyterian Synod of Pennsylvania and had a religious ambiance, with mandatory Bible study and daily chapel attendance. Crane was enrolled in seven required courses: algebra, chemistry, French, industrial drawing, Bible, elocution, and theme writing. Crane participated actively in the intellectual and social life of Lafayette. He was a member of two literary societies, joined Delta Upsilon fraternity, and played intramural and varsity baseball. Crane received no grades in three of his courses, and aside from a 92 in elocution, his other grades were low. In theme writing, a course devoted entirely to scientific topics, he was given a zero. Nevertheless, Crane was not expelled from Lafayette but withdrew "without censure" in December. Much has been made of a hazing incident in which Crane purportedly confronted a group of sophomores who invaded his room in East Hall with a revolver. Hazing was a problem at Lafayette, but the only recollection of the incident involving Crane is in a reminiscence published by a fellow freshman student more than forty years later. It is most unlikely that this episode, if it occurred at all, had anything to do with his transfer to Syracuse University* in January 1891. Crane was probably motivated by the prospect of a more liberal curriculum than the restrictive engineering program at Lafayette and the scholarship advantages he would receive as the great-nephew of Bishop Jesse Peck, principal founder of Syracuse University.

Suggested Reading

Gullason, Thomas. "Stephen Crane at Lafayette College: New Perspectives." *Stephen Crane Studies* 3.2 (1994): 2–12.

Robertson, Michael. *Stephen Crane at Lafayette*. Easton, Pa.: Friends of the Skillman
  Library, 1990.
Sloane, David E. "Stephen Crane at Lafayette." *Resources for American Literary Study*
  2 (1972): 102–5.

The Lantern Club. According to the reminiscences of its prime mover and
perpetual president, Irving Bacheller,* the Lantern (alternatively spelled Lanthorn or Lanthorne) Club was probably founded in 1893. The first clubhouse
was on Monkey Hill over an old ironmonger's shop on William Street, near the
newspaper buildings of Park Row in lower Manhattan. After this property was
acquired by William Randolph Hearst,* the club moved to a historic building,
126 William Street, said to be the oldest house in New York and ostensibly the
house in which Captain Kidd lived when he was in the city. The members were
young journalists and aspiring writers, such as Post Wheeler,* Edward Marshall,* Richard Watson Gilder,* Willis Brooks Hawkins,* and John Langdon
Heaton, but distinguished guests, among them William Dean Howells,* Mark
Twain, and Theodore Roosevelt,* occasionally visited the group. Bacheller recalls that a lunch was served every day, and literary banquets were held on
Saturday evenings. Each week at the banquet, one of the members read a short
story he had written. Only negative criticism was permitted, and "the highest
tribute that a story could receive was complete silence." In memoirs by some
of his acquaintances, Crane is listed as being one of the organizers of the club,
but it is more likely, as Bacheller recalls, that he did not become a participating
member until after he returned from Mexico in mid-May 1895. The Lantern
Club honored Crane on a number of occasions, notably at a dinner given for
him on 7 April 1896 at which Howells was the principal speaker. Crane's story
"The Wise Men" occupies most of the space of the club's only known publication, *The Lanthorn Book* (1898).

Suggested Reading

Bacheller, Irving. *From Stores of Memory*. New York: Farrar and Rinehart, 1933. 111.
Marshall, Edward. "Authors' Associations." *Manuscript* 1 (May 1901): 32–34.

The Lanthorn Book. Subtitled "Being a Small Collection of Tales and Verses
Read at the Sign o' the Lanthorn," this elaborate gift book was printed, probably
in the fall of 1898, by the Lantern (Lanthorn or Lanthorne) Club* at 126 William
Street in New York City in an edition limited to 125 copies, most of which are
signed by the contributors following their contributions. Willis B. Hawkins's*
signature is in facsimile. Crane's story, "The Wise Men," is first of seven pieces
and occupies more than half the space in this slim volume. Most of the other
contributors are undistinguished journalists, but among them are a number of
Crane's friends and literary associates, including Willis Brook Hawkins, Post
Wheeler,* and Irving Bacheller.*

Larpent, Tom. The central character in "Moonlight on the Snow," Larpent is a gentlemanly gambler—an educated, well-spoken point-of-view character who resembles the genteel but deadly gambler of "The Blue Hotel." Larpent cynically agrees with the residents of the town of War Post that random violence and killing must end and the perpetrators of such deeds must be hanged before Eastern investors will be attracted to the town. But the next morning he shoots to death a man who had accused him of cheating at cards. The town's citizens are torn between their greed and their affection for a favorite citizen when Sheriff Jack Potter fortuitously steps in to resolve their dilemma.

"The Last of the Mohicans". The first of the Sullivan County sketches to appear, "The Last of the Mohicans" was printed in the *New York Tribune* on 21 February 1892. This sketch is more of a sardonic assault on the conventions of romantic literature than an account of life in rural Sullivan County. In a manner similar to Mark Twain's essay, "Fenimore Cooper's Literary Offenses," Crane debunks Cooper's *The Last of the Mohicans* (1826). Unlike the genteel readers of Cooper's novels, "Few of the old, gnarled and weather-beaten inhabitants of the pines and boulders of Sullivan County are great readers of books or students of literature." They know that the real last of the Mohicans was not Cooper's Uncas, "that bronze god in a North American wilderness, that warrior with the eye of the eagle, the ear of the fox, the tread of the cat-like panther, and the tongue of the wise serpent of fable." He was, in contrast, a hapless alcoholic who dressed in rags and "wandered listlessly from village to village and from house to house, his only ambition being to beg, borrow or steal a drink." This sketch anticipates Crane's later method of puncturing ideals with realities and undercutting illusions with insights. In the light of this depiction of "a veritable 'poor Indian,' " it seems significant that Crane frequently employed the epithet "Indian" to characterize the impoverished artists with whom he boarded in his early years in New York and the journalists who later imposed on his hospitality at Ravensbrook* and Brede Place.*

Suggested Reading

Stallman, R. W. "Stephen Crane and Cooper's Uncas." *American Literature* 39 (1967): 393–96.

"The Last Panther". Printed in the *New York Tribune*, 3 April 1892, this sketch is subtitled "An Ancient Memory of Sullivan County" since it deals with early nineteenth-century hunting legends. In part a straightforward journalistic account of the extermination of dangerous predatory animals, the sketch also demonstrates Crane's predilection to relish the yarn and the tall tale. There is the story of Nelson Crocker who saw seven panthers at once and slew three of them; Cyrus Dodge, who saw six panthers near a pond and dashing into the pond stood in water up to his waist and shot four of them; and, most elaborate of all, legends of Calvin Bush, "the prince of panther-killers," who once aimed a blow with a hatchet at the head of a panther that was attacking his dog. The animal wrenched away the hatchet with his teeth, and following this encounter Bush "always carried a crooked finger, which was made by the panther's teeth when it grasped the hatchet-handle."

Last Words. This volume was compiled by Cora Crane following Stephen's death. A melange of early and late short stories and fables previously uncollected, it is thus inappropriately titled. Although Paul Revere Reynolds sold the book to the Philadelphia publisher Henry T. Coates, no American edition appeared. The English edition was published in May 1902 by Digby, Long & Co., probably because it was declined by Crane's usual publishers. A few of the pieces appear under changed or modified titles. Contents: "The Reluctant Voyagers"; "The Kicking Twelfth"; "The Upturned Face"; "The Shrapnel of Their Friends"; " 'And If He Wills, We Must Die' "; "The Surrender of Forty Fort"; "Ol' Bennet' and the Indians"; "The Battle of Forty Fort"; "London Impressions"; "Great Grief's Holiday Dinner"; "The Silver Pageant"; "A Street Scene"; "Minetta Lane"; "Roof Gardens"; "In the Broadway Cars"; "The Assassins in Modern Battles"; "An Old Man Goes Wooing"; "Ballydehob"; "The Royal Irish Constabulary"; "A Fishing Village"; "Four Men in a Cave"; "The Mesmeric Mountain"; "The Squire's Madness"; "A Desertion"; "How the Donkey Lifted the Hills"; "A Man by the Name of Mud"; "A Poker Game"; "The Snake"; "A Self-Made Man"; "A Tale of Mere Chance"; "At Clancy's Wake"; "An Episode of War"; "The Voice of the Mountain"; "Why Did the Young Clerk Swear?"; and "The Victory of the Moon."

Lawrence, Frederic M. (?–?) Crane's mother and Lawrence's father, a physician in Middletown, New York, had worked together for the temperance cause in Port Jervis, New York, but Crane and Lawrence were not acquainted until they met as Delta Upsilon fraternity brothers at Syracuse University* in January 1891. That summer and for four or five years afterward in August, Crane and Lawrence camped together with a number of friends in Pike County, Pennsylvania, usually at Twin Lakes near Milford. At intervals they also went on shorter camping trips in Sullivan County, New York, and from these experiences came the inspiration for Crane's Sullivan County tales in which Lawrence would figure as "the pudgy man." In the fall of 1891 Lawrence went to New York City to attend medical school. During the autumn and winter of 1892–93, Crane and Lawrence roomed together. With a number of other medical students, they shared a boardinghouse at 1064 Avenue A in Manhattan, directly across from Blackwell's Island, where a city prison was located; the lines of marching convicts are impressionistically depicted in the opening episode of *Maggie*. In his recollections, Lawrence insists that the slum novelette was based on experiences he and Crane had in the surrounding neighborhoods and in the Bowery and entirely composed in the house on Avenue A. Other contemporaries of Crane at Syracuse University, however, recall drafts of what would eventually become *Maggie* that were written earlier in the Delta Upsilon house. In the spring of 1893, at the end of the medical school semester, the boardinghouse group that had sardonically called themselves the Pendennis Club broke up, and that fall Lawrence went to Philadelphia to complete his studies. He was graduated from Hahnemann Medical College in May 1894 and practiced medicine in Philadelphia, where Crane visited him from time to time, the most notable occasion being in October 1896 when Crane fled New York City to escape the pressure of publicity generated by his involvement in the Dora Clark* case.

Suggested Reading

Lawrence, Frederic M. *The Real Stephen Crane*. Ed. Joseph Katz. Newark, N.J.: Newark Public Library, 1980.

Lean, Timothy. A first lieutenant in the Twelfth Regiment of the Spitzbergen army, Timothy Lean appears in three of the four Spitzbergen stories. In "The Kicking Twelfth," Lean leads a charge up a hill against an entrenched Rostina position and wins the praise of his colonel. In "The Shrapnel of Their Friends," he is captain of a company that retreats under friendly fire, and in "The Upturned Face," he and an adjutant apprehensively bury a dead officer.

"Legends". A group of five short poems published in the May 1896 issue of the *Bookman*, with marginal illustrations by Melanie Elisabeth Norton. The poems are: "A man builded a bugle for the storms to blow," "When the suicide arrived at the sky," "A man said: 'Thou tree!,' " "A warrior stood upon a peak and defied the stars," and "The wind that waves the blossoms." The general title was probably supplied by the magazine. Each poem deals with Crane's familiar theme of the absurdity of human conceit in the face of the indifference of nature.

[Leslie, Amy] (1855–1939). Born Lillie West in West Burlington, Iowa, one of two daughters of Albert Waring West and Kate (Webb) West, Amy Leslie, as she came to be known, received most of her education in Catholic schools, although she was a Protestant. After musical training in Europe and Chicago, she embarked on a singing career, and by the mid-1880s she had achieved considerable fame as a light soprano. In 1880 she married Harry Brown, a fellow performer. They had one son, who died at the age of four. Her husband abandoned her, and she secured a divorce. Depressed by the death of her son, she left the stage in 1899, never to return, and in 1890, under the name of Amy Leslie, began her forty-year career as drama critic for the *Chicago Daily News*. In 1901, while living at the Virginia Hotel in Chicago, she met and married Frank Buck, later to become famous as a jungle adventurer, who was then a bellboy in the hotel and more than twenty-five years younger than she. Amy Leslie was the author of two books: *Amy Leslie at the Fair* (1893), an account of the World's Columbian Exposition, and *Some Players* (1899), a collection of sketches of actors and actresses reprinted from the *Chicago Daily News*.

When and under what circumstances Crane and Amy Leslie first met is unknown, but she was invited to attend the Philistine dinner in his honor in Buffalo on 19 December 1895, and a comment in her *Chicago Daily News* column on 22 July 1896 reveals that she and Crane had been on very friendly terms before the end of 1895. When on 16 October 1896 Crane appeared at police headquarters on Mulberry Street in New York City as a witness for Dora Clark* at the hearing into her charges of harassment and assault against patrolmen Martin Conway and Charles Becker,* it was revealed that Crane had lived with Amy Leslie (who may have been using the name Traphagen or Huntington, or both) in a house on West Twenty-seventh Street notorious for drugs and prostitution. Amy Leslie's activities in the Tenderloin are obscure, but Amy Huntington and Sadie Traphagen were well-known prostitutes, and when Becker's lawyer asked Crane whether he ever smoked opium "with this Sadie or Amy" in the house on West Twenty-seventh Street, Crane denied it on the ground that "it would tend to degrade or incriminate" him (*New York World*, 16 October 1896). Crane's involvement in the life of the New York Tenderloin was, in any event, deeper than that of simply an observer and investigative reporter. It is also possible that Amy Leslie was pregnant with or gave birth to a child by Crane, although the evidence is far from convincing.

When Crane left New York for Jacksonville, Florida, at the end of November 1896 to report the Cuban insurrection for the Bacheller syndicate, he was accompanied by Amy Leslie, who traveled with him as far as Washington, D.C. From Florida he sent her a series of impassioned letters unique in his correspondence for their expression of devotion and loyalty, but, significantly, he avoided addressing her by name or subscribing his own name with anything more than an initial. Shortly before leaving, Crane deposited $500 with his friend Willis Brook Hawkins,* ostensibly part of a sum of $800 that was derived from Amy Leslie and was doled out to her in part by Hawkins. On 3 January 1898 she obtained a warrant against Crane's property in the amount of $550 for "a breach of contract express or implied, other than a contract to marry." The case was apparently settled out of court by Crane's brother William, who was an attorney, and Amy Leslie's lawyer, Louis Mabon. Crane corresponded with her again in 1897, but with his absence from America, their personal relationship ended.

Suggested Reading

Conway, John D. "The Stephen Crane–Amy Leslie Affair: A Reconsideration." *Journal of Modern Literature* 7 (1979): 3–14.

Katz, Joseph. "Some Light on the Stephen Crane–Amy Leslie Affair." *Mad River Review* 1.1 (1964–65): 43–62.

Monteiro, George. "Amy Leslie on Stephen Crane's *Maggie*." *Journal of Modern Literature* 9 (1981–82): 147–48.

Parker, Hershel. "The Dates of Stephen Crane's Letters to Amy Leslie." *Papers of the Bibliographical Society of America* 75 (1981): 82–86.

Wertheim, Stanley. "Who Was 'Amy Leslie'?" *Stephen Crane Studies* 2.2 (1993): 29–37.

Lewis, Robert (?–?). A black man who was lynched in Port Jervis, New York, on 2 June 1892, purportedly for raping a local girl. A mob pulled Lewis out of a wagon taking him to jail and dragged him up Sussex Street to East Main Street where he was twice hanged from a maple tree in front of the Reformed church opposite the home of William Howe Crane. Crane was foremost among several men in the crowd who vainly attempted to stop the lynching. Stephen Crane was not present but was undoubtedly aware of this horrendous event since detailed accounts appeared in the *Port Jervis Gazette* and the *New York Tribune*, for which he was a shore correspondent. Very likely, the lynching remained in Crane's mind and the brutal murder of Robert Lewis may have foreshadowed the defacing and social extinction of Henry Johnson in "The Monster."

Suggested Reading

Marshall, Elaine. "Crane's 'The Monster' Seen in the Light of Robert Lewis's Lynching." *Nineteenth-Century Literature* 51 (1996): 205–24.

The Lieutenant. Many characters in Crane's war fiction are identified only as "the lieutenant." The most important of these is the lieutenant in "An Episode of War" who is shot in the arm while doling out the day's ration of coffee to his men and whose life is forever changed by his wound.

Linson, Corwin Knapp (1864–1959). A painter, illustrator, and photographer, Linson received his professional training in Paris, studying at the Académie Julian and the École des Beaux Arts under Jean-Leon Gérôme and Jean-Paul Laurens. Paul Gauguin was a fellow pupil. Linson was an illustrator for the *Century*, *Scribner's Magazine*, and *Cosmopolitan*. *Scribner's* sent him to Athens to make sketches of the first modern Olympic Games, and he won a bronze medal for his depictions. He accompanied the Barnum and Bailey Circus to sketch animals for the McClure syndicate and spent two years in Palestine drawing illustrations for John Watson's *Life of the Master* (1901). His paintings were exhibited at the Pan-American Exhibition of 1901, the St. Louis Exhibition of 1904, and in a number of museums. He painted landscapes and oil portraits, among them those of Crane, Mark Hopkins, and Edmund Wilson.

Linson, who had spent part of his boyhood in Port Jervis, New York, and Sullivan County, New York, was introduced to Crane by his cousin Louis C. Senger* in the winter of 1892–93, shortly before the publication of *Maggie*. They remained personal friends until Crane left to report the Greek-Turkish War in March 1897, although their association was close only in 1893–94. Linson is depicted as Corinson in "Stories Told by an Artist," and his self-absorption is satirized in the character of Gaunt in "The Silver Pageant." Hawker, in *The Third Violet*, may also in part be based on Linson. In May 1894 Linson accompanied Crane on a trip to the coal mines near Scranton, Pennsylvania, and drew the illustrations for "In the Depths of a Coal Mine" (*McClure's*, August 1894). Linson's memoirs of his relationship with Crane are extremely valuable, especially for the background they provide for the circumstances under which his Bowery sketches and other early stories and poems were written, the publication and reception of *Maggie*, and the literary sources of *The Red Badge of Courage*. Linson's "Little Stories of 'Steve' Crane" is an early, firsthand account of Crane's apprenticeship days living in poverty in the old Art Students League building on East Twenty-third Street and the explorations in the Bowery that resulted in "The Men in the Storm" and "An Experiment in Misery." In Linson's studio Crane read the accounts by veterans in *Century Magazine's* series "Battles and Leaders of the Civil War" and, finding only narrations of external events, was inspired to write of how men "*felt* in those scraps" rather than only "what they *did*." Linson's later elaborations of these experiences, edited as *My Stephen Crane*, must be approached with caution because they were written to a large extent under the influences of Thomas Beer's* fictionalized biography of Crane, Hamlin Garland's* recollections, and Crane's own fictional works.

Suggested Reading

Linson, Corwin Knapp. "Little Stories of 'Steve' Crane." *Saturday Evening Post* 11 April 1903: 19–20.
———. *My Stephen Crane*. Ed. Edwin H. Cady. Syracuse: Syracuse University Press, 1958.

Linson, L. S. (?–?). Brother of Corwin Knapp Linson.* Crane inscribed a copy of *Maggie* to L. S. Linson on 17 May 1894. During the Cuban War, Linson was captain of Company D in the Seventy-first Infantry Regiment, New York Volunteers. He and Crane met at the port of Siboney during the disembarkation of American troops in late June 1898 and later at Santiago. In letters to his brother, Captain Linson reflected on the different aspects of Crane's personality as an artist and a war correspondent. At Siboney, Crane appeared "animated and jolly . . . the spirit of the fighter in him. When I met him in your studio he seemed of an entirely opposite disposition, rather somber." At Santiago Linson characterized Crane as "a hustler."

Linton, Jack. The main character of "The Squire's Madness," Linton seems in his reclusiveness, obsession with death, and fear of insanity to be a parodic representation of Roderick Usher in Edgar Allan Poe's "The Fall of the House of Usher." Like Usher, Linton improvises verses that reflect his macabre concerns.

Little Cora. A character in two of the *Whilomville Stories*, "The Angel Child" and "The Stove," Little Cora is also the object of Jimmie Trescott's preadolescent romantic longings in "The Lover and the Telltale." She is the enterprising, mischievous child of an unworldly, indulgent artist and his domineering wife. Her character may have been based on stories that Cora Crane told Stephen about her childhood.

Little Nell. A war correspondent in the short story " 'God Rest Ye, Merry Gentlemen.' " One of Crane's little men, he is an autobiographical character who reflects Crane's disillusionment with the demands of the yellow press, specifically Pulitzer's *New York World*, during the Cuban War.

Little Pennoyer. A character, also called Penny, who represents Crane himself in "Stories Told by an Artist," "The Silver Pageant," and *The Third Violet*.

"A Little Pilgrimage". First published in the August 1900 issue of *Harper's New Monthly Magazine* under the title "A Little Pilgrim," this story was retitled "A Little Pilgrimage," as in Crane's holograph manuscript, when collected in the Harper edition of *Whilomville Stories*. The church in Whilomville is the subject of the story. The Trescotts are "consistently undenominational," but Jimmie regularly attends the Presbyterian Sunday school. One November, at the instigation of the superintendent of the school, the children, "in a burst of virtuous abandon," vote to forgo their Christmas tree and donate the funds usually allocated to holiday festivities for the relief of victims of an earthquake in Charleston. Deeply disappointed, Jimmie, using a specious justification, convinces his father to allow him to transfer to the Sunday school of the Big Progressive Church, another Protestant denomination. After enduring an inane lesson in his new Sunday school, the doldrums of which suggest to him the martyrdom of St. Stephen as depicted in a lithograph behind the superintendent's chair, Jimmie learns that the Big Progressive Church, not to be outdone by the Presbyterians, will also sacrifice its Christmas tree. Speechless and morose, Jimmie resolves to banish the question of Christmas trees from his mind, and "[i]f he remembered Sunday-school at all, it was to remember that he did not like it."

Embedded in this deceptively simple plot is an indictment of those in Whilomville for whom the institutional embodiment of religion has replaced its essence. The Sunday school superintendent of the Big Progressive Church exhibits the sanctimonious hypocrisy of the clergymen in *Maggie* and in some of the poems of *The Black Riders*. He is "one who had never felt hunger or thirst or the wound of the challenge of dishonor." The biblical verse expounded by the teacher in the class Jimmie attends is Jeremiah 7:4, in which the prophet admonishes Judah: "Trust ye not in lying words, saying, The temple of the LORD, the temple of the LORD, The temple of the LORD *are* these." The Sunday-school teacher's fatuous interpretation of this verse as meaning "that we should be good, very good indeed," is punctured by a boy who, overhearing a nearby discussion of Daniel in the lion's den, responds to her question about the significance of the verse with, "It means that they were in the wrong place." The answer she expects, as given by Clarence, "the professional bright boy of the class," is that "it means church, same as this." The exchange between the teacher and the boys is an ironic reflection on Jeremiah's preaching to Judah about the distinction between true and false religion.

Suggested Reading

Monteiro, George. "Whilomville as Judah: Crane's 'A Little Pilgrimage.' " *Renascence* 19 (1967): 184–89.

"The Little Regiment". The title story of *The Little Regiment and Other Episodes of the American Civil War* appeared in the June 1896 issue of *McClure's Magazine* and simultaneously in England in *Chapman's Magazine*. Crane began writing "The Little Regiment" before he went to Fredericksburg, Virginia, to research the site of what he called in a letter to John S. Phillips* "the most dramatic battle of the war" for a projected but never written series of historical articles on the Civil War requested by the McClure syndicate. The story, completed after his return, is loosely patterned on the events of that battle. "The Little Regiment" is rich in description of the fighting, but its plot line is thin. Dan Dempster and his brother Billie are soldiers in an infantry regiment engaged in fierce combat around a southern town, probably Fredericksburg. Billie and Dan are rivals who quarrel constantly and pretend to despise each other, but their experiences of battle have uncovered depths of feeling, and whenever they are separated the one worries about the other's welfare. First, Billie fears for Dan when he is sent on a dangerous assignment. After a desperate, failed assault on a hill that only veteran soldiers sustain, the men rename their command "the Little Regiment." Billie is wounded and missing in the engagement, and Dan is immersed in gloom, but when they are reunited the brothers greet each other in a matter-of-fact manner with no show of emotion. Crane's theme, as in *The Red Badge* and "A Mystery of Heroism," centers on the contrast between public and private emotion, but here he deals with it less successfully.

Suggested Reading

Ives, C. B. " 'The Little Regiment' of Stephen Crane at the Battle of Fredericksburg," *Midwest Quarterly* 8 (1967): 247–60.

The Little Regiment and Other Episodes of the American Civil War. A gathering of six short stories, all but one of which, "The Veteran," have a Civil War setting, published in the United States by D. Appleton in November 1896 and William Heinemann in England in February 1897. Contents: "The Little Regiment"; "Three Miraculous Soldiers"; "A Mystery of Heroism"; "An Indiana Campaign"; "A Gray Sleeve" ("Grey" in the English edition); and "The

Veteran." This is a mixed collection. Some of the stories, written before Crane had experienced battle, are bids for popular success and are sentimental and romantic or feature buffoonery; others continue the study of individual fear and isolation that is the central concern of *The Red Badge of Courage*.

Suggested Reading

Solomon, Eric. "Stephen Crane's War Stories." *Texas Studies in Literature and Language* 3 (1961): 67–80.

"The Little Stilettos of the Modern Navy Which Stab in the Dark". A feature article first published in the *New York Journal* on 24 April 1898 and collected in *Last Words* under the title "The Assassins in Modern Battles." This article on torpedo boats built at Yarrow on the Isle of Dogs, near London, is a commonplace piece of journalism written to finance Crane's transatlantic trip to report the Cuban War. The title derives from the bow of the torpedo boat, which is shaped "like a dagger." Crane details the configuration, ordnance, and maneuverability of torpedo boats, naval weapons that have become "knives for the nations," but whose usefulness is limited to swift nighttime attacks on other ships.

"London Impressions". A series of eight short humorous sketches of London street life that appeared serially in three successive issues of Frank Harris's *Saturday Review* on 31 July, 7 August, and 14 August 1897 and were collected as "chapters" in *Last Words*. The impressions are successive representations of scenes observed on Crane's first arrival in the city and encompass his reflections on a porter and a cabman at a railroad station, the quiet of London streets in contrast to the bedlam of New York City, the fall of a cab horse and efforts to raise it, top hats and their relative significance in London and the American West, the surprise of encountering an aged elevator operator in a hotel, and reflections on London street signs and advertisements. The humor in these sketches is somewhat forced, but their central theme, the limitations of individual apprehensions of reality, is a definitive element in Crane's more serious writing. As the cab rolled out of the railroad station, the London fog seemed so enveloping that "In it each man sat in his own little cylinder of vision, so to speak. It was not so small as a sentry-box nor so large as a circus-tent, but the walls were opaque, and what was passing beyond the dimensions of his cylinder no man knew."

"The Lone Charge of William B. Perkins". More of a sketch than a fully developed short story, "The Lone Charge of William B. Perkins" is a barely fictionalized rendition of an incident involving Ralph Paine,* the correspondent for the *Philadelphia Press*, at the provisional Camp McCalla set up by the First Marine Battalion after their landing at Guantánamo Bay on 10 June 1898. The story was published in the *Westminster Gazette* on 2 January 1899 and collected in *Wounds in the Rain*. Like Collins of "A Mystery of Heroism," Perkins is an amateur at war who foolishly exposes himself to danger because of a dare and survives his bravado, having accomplished nothing. Perkins "could not distinguish between a 5-inch quick-firing gun and a nickle-plated ice-pick, and so naturally he had been elected to fill the position of war correspondent." He lands from a dispatch boat on the third day of the marine encampment and attempts to ingratiate himself with two young lieutenants by offering to bring them a bottle of scotch from his dispatch boat. As he proceeds downhill toward the shore, a private fires his rifle into the air to discharge a clogged cartridge, precipitating a hail of fire from the Spaniards and guerrillas. The marines respond, and Perkins, imagining that he sees a Spaniard hiding behind a bush, borrows a rifle from a wounded marine and mindlessly rushes toward the supposed enemy. "Four seconds elapsed before he discovered that he was an alms-house idiot plunging through the hot crackling thickets on a June morning in Cuba." The Spaniard turns out to be a dried palm branch, and Perkins is caught in the crossfire. He takes shelter in an abandoned sugar boiler that is peppered with fire until the shooting stops. When he returns to his tug, he is "wearing a countenance of poignant thoughtfulness," reflecting his initiation into the absurdity of war.

Suggested Reading

Paine, Ralph D. *Roads of Adventure*. Boston: Houghton Mifflin, 1922. 251–56.

The Lotus. One of the little magazines of the 1890s, *The Lotus* (not to be confused with another little magazine, *The Lotos*) was published for only two years, from November 1895 through November 1897. Walter Blackburn Harte was the second of its three editors. *The Lotus* published satire of Elbert Hubbard,* Stephen Crane, and other writers, taking particular jabs at Crane's poetry.

"A Lovely Jag in a Crowded Car". A fictional episode depicting street life in New York similar to "When Man Falls, a Crowd Gathers," this piece appeared in the *New York Press* on 6 January 1895. It offers a humorous contrast of perspectives and characterizations. A crosstown horsecar bound for the shopping district, whose passengers are a number of women "preserving their respectability with fierce vigilance" and a single man slumped in a corner, is boarded by a raucous drunk, "a wild red demon of drink and destruction." Ignoring admonishments and threats to expel him by the conductor, the drunk destroys the frigid decorum of the car with his antics. In his inebriated fantasies, he is in a saloon and the conductor is a bartender, and he orders drinks all around for the passengers. Finally, after the car has passed the neighborhood of the large stores and the women are gone, he realizes that he has traveled beyond the place he intended to get off and demands that the car be halted. As the car stops suddenly, he tumbles to the pavement but quickly recovers and begins to run back up the route over which the car had taken him. From the rear platform, the male passenger and the phlegmatic conductor observe his retreating form, "and they remained there deep in reflection, absorbed in contemplation of this wavering figure in the distance, until observation was no longer possible."

"The Lover and the Telltale". A Whilomville story published in the October 1899 issue of *Harper's New Monthly Magazine*. Little Cora of "The Angel Child" and "The Stove" does not appear in this story but is the object of an infatuation by Jimmie Trescott (the lover). He is observed writing an orthographically chaotic but impassioned letter to her in the school room during recess by little Rose Goldege (the telltale), who runs into the yard, where she announces this peccadillo to the other children. Enraged at being goaded, Jimmie strikes out, and a general brawl ensues. Jimmie is told by his teacher that he will be kept after school for refusing to divulge the names of the boys with whom he has been fighting. "When he took his seat he saw gloating upon him the satanic black eyes of the little Goldege girl."

"The Lover and the Telltale" is an essentially comic story about the volatile world of childhood, and one should resist interpreting Crane's hyperbolic metaphors for the children who taunt Jimmie, a "yelping demonic mob" and "blood-fanged wolves," as serious social commentary on the plight of the individual in a conformist society. Crane does introduce an incongruous and somewhat incoherent didactic element into the story when he comments on Rose Goldege's family, "which numbered few males." For these embittered women, as for the vituperative gossips of "The Monster" and *The Third Violet*,

> the principal and indeed solitary joy which entered their lonely lives was the joy of talking wickedly and busily about their neighbors. It was all done without dream of its being of the vulgarity of the alleys. Indeed it was simply a constitutional but not incredible chastity and honesty expressing itself in its ordinary superior way of the whirling circles of life, and the vehemence of the criticism was not lessened by a further infusion of an acid of worldly defeat, worldly suffering and worldly hopelessness.

Suggested Reading

Solomon Eric. *Stephen Crane: From Parody to Realism*. Cambridge: Harvard University Press, 1966. 213–16.

"Lynx-Hunting". This Whilomville story, the first of the series written by Crane, appeared in the September 1899 issue of *Harper's New Monthly Magazine*. "Lynx-Hunting" marks the third and last appearance of Henry Fleming in Crane's fiction and is set at a time between the end of the Civil War and Henry's death in "The Veteran." In "Lynx-Hunting, Jimmie Trescott, Willie Dalzel, and another boy set out to explore the countryside around Whilomville. There is an Emersonian quality in the foray of Jimmie Trescott and his companions into nature that "spoke some great inspiring word, which they knew even as those who pace the shore know the enigmatic speech of the surf.'' Willie Dalzel, envied by the other boys for his possession of a gun, resolves to shoot a lynx, an animal that he had reluctantly learned about at school. Willie manages to shoot a bird ''into a mere rag of wet feathers,'' and the second boy has a turn at another bird. When Jimmie's turn comes, he takes aim at a chipmunk but manages instead to hit a cow grazing in Henry Fleming's pasture. Fleming's Swedish farmhand—also a character in ''The Veteran''—collars the boys, who clamorously protest their innocence when they are brought before Fleming. Finally, Jimmie admits that he fired the shot that wounded the cow, and when Fleming asks him why, he replies confusedly, ''I thought she was a lynx,'' a retort that convulses Henry and the Swede, and presumably the nineteenth-century reader, with laughter but now seems rather pointless.

Lyon, Kate (1856–?). Harold Frederic's* mistress and mother of his three younger children, Kate Lyon was born in Oswego, New York, and graduated from Cook County Normal School in Chicago, where she had moved with her family. She taught for a time in a grammar school there. The date that she and Frederic met is conjectural. She may have known Frederic as a young woman and renewed her acquaintance with him in 1890, when he was on vacation in the United States. According to family legend, they met in the British Museum in that year, and their meeting was the occasion for Frederic's novel *March Hares*. Kate's mother was an O'Mahony, and it is likely that Frederic named his book *The Return of the O'Mahony* and its heroine after her. Kate probably came to England with her sister May, helping to take care of her four young children, one of whom was Edith Richie* (later Jones), who was a house guest of the Cranes at Brede Place* and wrote a notable memoir about them. By 1891 Kate Lyon and Frederic established a home together in London, moving in 1893 to Homefield, in Kenley, Surrey, where Kate was known as Mrs. Frederic. When Stephen and Cora Crane settled in Oxted, Surrey, in the spring of 1897, they became close friends of Harold and Kate.

Kate Lyon was a believer in Christian Science and when Frederic was dying called in a Christian Science practitioner, Mrs. Althie Mills, to treat him. At Cora Crane's insistence, physicians were also summoned, although Frederic himself detested doctors. After Frederic's death on 19 October 1898, Cora took in Kate and her children, Helen, Héloïse, and Barry. The younger two continued to live with the Cranes after they settled at Brede Place. Kate and Mrs. Mills were widely execrated in the press, and in November a coroner's jury indicted them for manslaughter. Cora Crane testified in their behalf at the trial in the Croydon County Police Court; the charges were withdrawn, and they were formally acquitted in London's Central Criminal Court on 13 December. Cora Crane, with the help of John Scott Stokes,* Frederic's secretary and English executor, raised a private fund for the support of Kate Lyon's children with Frederic. To distinguish this fund from a public appeal on behalf of Frederic's legitimate wife and children, Kate adopted the family name of Forman.

From late 1899 until their completion shortly before Crane's death, Kate Lyon functioned as his researcher for the series of battle articles published in *Lippincott's Magazine* and later collected as *Great Battles of the World*. After Crane became seriously ill in April 1900, she did much of the actual writing of first drafts to be revised by Crane, and the final articles in the series, "The Battle of Solferino" and "The Storming of Burkersdorf Heights," are probably entirely her work. Kate Lyon returned to Chicago with her children in 1904.

Suggested Reading

Bowers, Fredson, ed. *Reports of War*. Charlottesville: University Press of Virginia, 1971. 527–40. Vol. 9 of *The Works of Stephen Crane*. Ed. Fredson Bowers, 10 vols. 1969–76.

Gilkes, Lillian. "Stephen Crane and the Harold Frederics." *Serif* 6.4 (1969): 21–48.

M

McBride, Henry (1867–1962). An artist, illustrator, and art critic, McBride founded the Educational Alliance of New York City in 1900 and served as its director. He was an early champion of modernism and the Stieglitz group and one of the first to rediscover the painter Thomas Eakins. McBride worked for the *New York Sun* from 1912 to 1950 and for *Art News* from 1950 to 1955. His reminiscence, "Stephen Crane's Artist Friends," in the October 1955 issue of *Art News*, gives a lively description of the group of artists, including McBride, Charles J. Pike* and his brother, Gordon,* Edward S. Hamilton, and Gustave Verbeeck,* with whom Crane shared dinners at a table d'hôte in New York's Tenderloin district, probably on occasion from early 1895 to late 1896. McBride's memoir is a notable record of Crane's association with artists.

McCalla, Bowman Hendry (1844–1910). A naval officer known for his innovative ideas on naval administration, McCalla was commander of the *Marblehead*, one of the U.S. Navy ships on the Cuban blockade, and was in charge of landing the First Marine Battalion at Guantánamo Bay on 10 June 1898. The following day McCalla sent in reinforcements, and the headquarters they established was named Camp McCalla. Crane describes the defense of the camp against intense resistance by the Spaniards in "Marines Signalling under Fire at Guantanamo." McCalla was promoted to the rank of captain for his Cuban service. He later took part in suppressing the insurrection in the Philippines and commanded an American force during the Boxer rebellion in China.

McClure, Samuel Sidney (1857–1949). S. S. McClure, as he was generally known, was born in Ireland and emigrated to the United States with his family at the age of nine. He attended school in Valparaiso, Indiana, and after trying a variety of odd jobs enrolled in Knox College, Galesburg, Illinois, from which he was graduated in 1882. In 1884 McClure founded a literary syndicate that was well established by 1887 when he hired his college classmate John S. Phillips* to work with him. While Phillips managed the home office, McClure traveled frequently throughout the United States and across the Atlantic to engage writers. Among those with whom he contracted were Robert Louis Stevenson, Rudyard Kipling, A. Conan Doyle, Henry James,* Walt Whitman, and Jack London. At the height of a national recession, McClure and Phillips founded *McClure's Magazine*, which published its first issue in June 1893. With its combination of serialized biographies of Napoleon and Lincoln by Ida Tarbell, fiction by popular writers such as Stevenson and Kipling, engaging articles on scientific subjects, wild animals and exploration, great personalities, and railroads, all set off with numerous halftone illustrations, *McClure's* flourished, achieving a circulation of 370,000 by 1900, greater than that of any other general monthly magazine except *Munsey's*. In 1897 McClure joined with Frank Doubleday to establish the book publishing firm of Doubleday & McClure Company. After Doubleday left the firm, it was continued as McClure, Phillips & Company. The January 1903 issue of *McClure's* featured initial articles of series on the Standard Oil Company by Ida Tarbell, corruption in American cities by Lincoln Steffens, and labor unions, rackets, and the railroads by Ray Stannard Baker that established *McClure's* as the leading muckraking magazine in the first decade of the twentieth century. S. S. McClure relinquished control of the magazine in 1911, although he continued to act as editor intermittently until 1926. Much of the rest of his life was devoted to writing dubious political philosophy (he was an admirer of fascism in Italy) and to lecturing.

Crane's involvement with S. S. McClure's newspaper syndicate, his magazine, and his book publishing firm was extensive throughout his career. In early January 1894, Hamlin Garland* sent Crane to McClure's office with a recommendation that McClure hire him as a feature writer, and in late April, shortly after completing *The Red Badge of Courage*, Crane submitted the manuscript for publication either by the McClure syndicate or in the newly formed *McClure's Magazine*, but financial exigencies caused McClure to keep his options open, and he declined to commit himself to either accept or reject the novel. On 15 November Crane complained to Garland that "McClure was a Beast about the war-novel." He had kept it for six months until the exasperated Crane offered it to the Bacheller syndicate. Nevertheless, McClure had given Crane employment, sending him and his illustrator friend, Corwin Knapp Linson,* to Scranton, Pennsylvania, in May 1894 to report on conditions in the coal mines of the region. Crane's pioneering muckraker article, "In the Depths of a Coal Mine," was syndicated in newspapers by McClure in July and appeared in *McClure's Magazine* in August. McClure syndicated a number of other feature articles by Crane, notably his graphic Tenderloin sketch, "Opium's Varied Dreams" (17 May 1896), and some of his 1897 Greek-Turkish War "letters" and also his novels *The Third Violet* (1896–97) and *Active Service* (1899–1900). In mid-January 1896, McClure's sent Crane to Virginia to tour the battlefields preparatory to writing a series of historical pieces on major Civil War battles, but nothing came of this effort. A number of Crane's short stories appeared in *McClure's Magazine*, including "The Little Regiment" (June 1896), "The Veteran" (August 1896), "Flanagan and His Short Filibustering Adventure" (October 1897), "The Bride Comes to Yellow Sky" (February 1898), "His New Mittens" (November 1898), "Marines Signalling under Fire at Guantanamo" (February 1899), and "The Lone Charge of William B. Perkins" (July 1899). Crane sometimes felt himself in thralldom to McClure, who had a habit of holding stories as collateral against advance payments, even if he had no intention of publishing them. *McClure's Magazine* foolishly rejected two of Crane's best stories, "Death and the Child," and "The Monster," but *The Open Boat and Other Tales of Adventure* was published by Doubleday & McClure Company in 1898.

Suggested Reading

Lyon, Peter. *Success Story: The Life and Times of S. S. McClure*. New York: Scribner, 1963.
Mott, Frank Luther. *A History of American Magazines*, Vol. 4. 1885–1905. Cambridge, Mass.: Belknap Press of Harvard University Press, 1957. 589–607.
McClure, S. S. *My Autobiography*. New York: Magazine Publishers, 1914. (Ghostwritten by Willa Cather*)

McClurg, Alexander C. (1832–1901). A prominent Chicago publisher and bookseller and an outspoken conservative and patriot, McClurg had enlisted in the Union army as a private and served through the Chickamauga and Chattanooga campaigns. He attained the brevet rank of colonel, afterward raised to brigadier general, in three years. McClurg's publishing firm owned the *Dial*, which in a curt review in the 1 February 1896 issue dismissed *The Red Badge of Courage* as unconvincing in its representation of the mind of a young soldier in battle. On 11 April 1896 McClurg wrote a lengthy letter to the editor of the *Dial*, printed in the 16 April issue, that condemned the acclaim that *The Red Badge* had received in English periodicals and newspapers. McClurg mistakenly assumed that the novel had first been published in England and had been puffed by the undeserved praise of English critics, bringing it to the attention of American reviewers, who were then slavishly subservient to English opinion. McClurg held that the British were enthusiastic about the book because it is "a vicious satire upon American soldiers and American armies." Although he considers it a negative factor, McClurg is actually perceptive in discerning that Crane's protagonist is motivated not by ethical considerations but by unconscious reactions to environmental conditions: "Under the influence of mere excitement, for he does not even appear to be frightened, he first rushes madly to the rear in a crazy panic, and afterward plunges forward to the rescue of the colors under exactly the same influences. In neither case has reason or any intelligent motive any influence on his action." Devoid of patriotism or courage,

McClurg concludes, *The Red Badge* is "a mere work of diseased imagination," praised by English reviewers despite its bad grammar and outrageous diction solely because of their animus against anything American.

In the 1 May 1896 issue of the *Dial*, J. L. Onderdonk, a lawyer, newspaper editor, and Idaho state legislator, supported McClurg's attack on *The Red Badge*, characterizing the novel as "realism run mad, rioting in all that is revolting to man's best instincts, and utterly false to nature and to life" and giving further examples of its grammatical peccadilloes. On the same page appeared a letter from D. Appleton & Company replying to McClurg, probably written by Ripley Hitchcock,* correcting McClurg's mistaken conceptions of the novel's publishing history and citing many American reviews that had preceded its appearance in England. The controversy in the *Dial* ended with the publication of a letter in the 16 May issue by the English critic Sidney Brooks, who had written a highly favorable notice of *The Red Badge* in the 11 January 1896 issue of the *Saturday Review*. Brooks ridicules McClurg's assumption that British reviewers were motivated by anti-American bias in praising the novel and calls McClurg's letter "a compound of misjudged patriotism and bad criticism." McClurg's diatribe and the responses to it set the tone for a number of subsequent controversial discussions of *The Red Badge* in American magazines and newspapers.

McCready, Ernest W. (1869?–1950). A lifelong reporter and editor, McCready was a correspondent for the *New York Herald* during the Cuban War. In May 1898 he was with Crane and other *New York World* correspondents on their first visit to Haiti aboard the *Three Friends*, and in June he was among the correspondents who covered the marine landing at Guantánamo Bay and the march to Siboney. McCready left a detailed account of Crane's activities during this campaign in letters written to B.J.R. Stolper, now in the Rare Book and Manuscript Library of Columbia University. Crane depicts McCready as Shackles in " 'God Rest Ye, Merry Gentlemen,' " "The Revenge of the *Adolphus*," and "Virtue in War" and as McCurdy in "War Memories."

McIntosh, Burr (1862–1942). Like Crane, McIntosh attended Lafayette College* but did not graduate. In 1882–83 he studied at Princeton. A prominent actor at the turn of the century, McIntosh created the role of Taffy in *Trilby* and appeared in many Broadway plays. In 1898 he went to Cuba as a correspondent and photographer for *Leslie's Weekly*. He contracted yellow fever and returned to the United States after the fall of Santiago, but in 1905 he went as official photographer on Secretary of War Taft's trip to the Philippines. In 1910 McIntosh founded his own movie company in California. During World War I he served as a YMCA entertainer in France. McIntosh's book, *The Little I Saw of Cuba* (1899), contains valuable eyewitness accounts and photographs of Crane's activities during the landing of American troops at Daiquirí, east of Santiago, on 22 June 1898 and the capture of the fortifications of San Juan on 1 July. McIntosh was with Crane, Frederic Remington,* and Henry J. Wigham of the *Chicago Tribune* on the vantage point of El Pozo, where they were able to observe all aspects of the decisive battle of San Juan.

McNab, Reuben (?–?). A former Claverack College* schoolmate whom Crane found badly wounded at a dressing station known as the "Bloody Bend" on the Aguadores River near Santiago de Cuba on 1 July 1898. The incident is recorded in "War Memories."

Maconnigle, Billie. In "The 'Tenderloin' As It Really Is," he is a belligerent tough, derisively known as a "celebrated cavalier," who provokes a brawl in a dance hall.

Maggie: A Girl of the Streets. Crane's Delta Upsilon fraternity brothers at Syracuse University,* Frank Noxon* and Henry Phillips, who edited the *University Herald*, and his friend Clarence Loomis Peaslee* recall that Crane began to sketch out a draft of *Maggie* in the spring of 1891. Other classmates also remember his fascination with the underbelly of Syracuse society, his frequenting of music halls, his interviews with prostitutes in the Syracuse police court, and his explorations of the shabby tenement districts of the city as local correspondent for the *New York Tribune*. Nevertheless, *Maggie* is clearly, as its subtitle indicates, "A Story of New York," and Crane's unsigned sketch in the *New York Herald* (5 July 1891) "Where 'De Gang' Hears the Band Play," with its Tompkins Square setting, Bowery dialect mixed with standard English, sharp delineations of immigrant groups, "tough girl and her tough brother" named Maggie and Jimmy, and Maggie's factory employment, reveals that Crane was already familiar with the Bowery environment and was writing an early version of *Maggie* while still a student at Syracuse University. From the vantage point of his brother Edmund's home in Lake View, New Jersey, Crane roamed the tenement districts of New York in the autumn and winter of 1891–92, reconstructing his conception of *Maggie* in the light of these experiences. The novelette was extensively revised or perhaps entirely rewritten in the fall of 1892, when Crane shared a room with another Delta Upsilon fraternity brother, Frederic M. Lawrence,* in a boardinghouse inhabited by a group of medical students on Avenue A near Fifty-seventh Street in Manhattan overlooking the East River and Blackwell's Island (now Roosevelt Island) that they sardonically christened the Pendennis Club. The neighborhood was an immediate environmental source for *Maggie*. In an 1898 article on torpedo boats, "The Little Stilettos of the Modern Navy Which Stab in the Dark," Crane refers to the Isle of Dogs as "an ordinary, squalid, nauseating slum of London, whose streets bear a faint resemblance to that part of Avenue A which lies directly above Sixtieth street in New York."

After being rejected by a number of publishers, *Maggie: A Girl of the Streets* was privately printed under the nom de plume of Johnston Smith in late February or early March 1893 with money that Crane derived from the sale of coal stock that he had inherited, supplemented perhaps by a loan from his brother William. The pseudonym was probably intended to spare Crane's prominent Methodist family embarrassment since Crane acknowledged authorship of the book from the first. Post Wheeler* recalls proposing it to Crane as a joke. According to Frederic M. Lawrence, the jest consisted in elevating the plebeian Johnson into a more aristocratic surname. Crane told Willis Fletcher Johnson* that he took the two most common names in the New York City telephone directory and later whimsically inserted the "t" into the first. He told Corwin K. Linson* that "the alias was a mere chance. Commonest name I could think of. I had an editor friend named Johnson, and put in the 't,' and no one could find me in the mob of Smiths." *Maggie* was produced, according to Lawrence, at "a little printing shop on lower Sixth Avenue whose sign we had often noticed." Crane mailed a small number of inscribed copies to friends and potential reviewers, but few if any were sold beyond those that guests were cajoled into buying at a Pendennis Club party, and the novelette was almost totally ignored by the critics. Hamlin Garland's* short review in the *Arena* (June 1893) was the only notice that *Maggie* received in the year of its publication. An expurgated version of *Maggie* was published by D. Appleton & Company in June 1896 and was more widely reviewed. The English edition published that September was entitled *Maggie: A Child of the Streets* to avoid invidious implications and had an introduction by William Dean Howells.*

Critics have proposed literary as well as experiential sources for *Maggie*. Émile Zola's *L'Assomoir* and its sequel, *Nana*, are sometimes mentioned, and while it is possible that Crane read Zola's studies of the underworld of Paris, it is more likely that the documentary background of *Maggie* is to be found not in European fiction but in the mass of social literature on slum life produced by Americans after the Civil War that warned of the problems consequent to a rapid growth in the immigrant population of cities, the proliferation of industry, and the rising rates of urban crime and disease. Crane could have learned more details about the slums and prostitutes by reading books such as Thomas DeWitt Talmage's *The Night Sides of City Life* (1878) and James D. McCabe's *New York by Sunlight and Gaslight* (1882) than from *L'Assomoir*. Crane was familiar with Jacob Riis's* *How the Other Half Lives* (1890) and *Children of the Poor* (1892) and probably read some of the reformist editorials and essays by B. O. Flower,* Edgar Fawcett, and others in the *Arena*, in which he published "An Ominous Baby" (May 1894) and "The Men in the Storm" (October 1894), denouncing the owners of tenements and sweatshops and deploring the circumstances of working girls in the city. There were also fictional representations of life of urban poverty in popular magazines of the period, but writers like James Sullivan, Julian Ralph, and Edward Townsend usually portrayed slum dwellers in terms of romantic and sentimental nineteenth-century literary conventions, avoiding the harsh realities. Fawcett's *The Evil That Men Do* (1889) resembles *Maggie* in that Fawcett's Cora is a poor girl with repulsive, drunken, and brawling parents who is seduced and deserted by a man of the middle class, becomes a prostitute, and is finally murdered in an alley by a working-class lover. Verisimilitude in this novel is, however, much weakened by melodrama, bombast, and cardboard characterizations, faults that also damage *Maggie*.

Maggie has traditionally been viewed as one of the earliest examples of literary determinism in American fiction, and indeed the novelette delineates a milieu in which the lives of its characters seem to be rigidly circumscribed in a physical and moral universe hostile or indifferent to their survival. As Crane wrote, with minor variations, in inscriptions to friends on the mustard-yellow covers of the book, "it tries to show that environment is a tremendous thing in the world and frequently shapes lives regardless. If one proves that theory, one makes room in Heaven for all sorts of souls, notably an occasional street girl, who are not confidently expected to be there by many excellent people."

Violence is the characteristic mode of communication in this atavistic arena, where moral judgments either do not apply or are viewed from an ironic perspective. The novelette opens with a brawl between two gangs of street urchins, and Maggie's brother Jimmie is the "little champion of Rum Alley." Pete, a lad of sixteen, saunters down the street and vanquishes the contingent of boys from Devil's Row out of boredom rather than partisanship. "Ah, what deh hell," he comments as he strikes "one of the most deeply engaged" of the Devil's Row children. Maggie upbraids Jimmie for fighting because "it puts mudder out when yehs come home half dead, an' it's like we'll all get a poundin'." When Jimmie hits Maggie, his father admonishes him to "leave yer sister alone on the street." Maggie's father complains to her mother that he "can't git no rest 'cause yer allus poundin' a kid." The mother remonstrates with the father for not stopping Jimmie from fighting because "he tears 'is clothes, yeh damn fool." Jimmie's father drinks the pail of beer Jimmie has fetched for an old woman on the tenement floor beneath and hits him over the head with the empty pail. Jimmie and Maggie fight with their parents, who in turn battle each other with a prodigious smashing of furniture. When Jimmie grows older, he "menaced mankind at the intersections of streets." As a truck driver he disputes the right of way "with two sets of very hard knuckles" and "would have derided, in an axle-wide alley, the approach of a flying ferry boat." But unconsciously regardful of the naturalistic doctrine of survival of the fittest, "he achieved a respect for a fire engine. As one charged toward his truck, he would drive fearfully upon a side-walk, threatening untold people with annihilation." When Jimmie and a companion engage in a fistfight with Pete after Maggie's seduction, their combat is couched in animal metaphors: "The glare of a panther came into Pete's eyes," and the men "bristled like three roosters." Their faces express "[t]he bravery of bull-dogs," and when Pete swings at him Jimmie ducks "Bowery-like, with the quickness of a cat." One of Pete's most attractive attributes for Maggie is that "he was invincible in fights." In this climate of violence, Maggie's options are narrow indeed. Her growing beauty adds to her peril. When the young men of the neighborhood begin to notice her, Jimmie explains the alternatives open to her: "Mag, I'll tell yeh dis! See? Yeh've edder got teh go teh hell [or, more explicitly in the 1896 revision of the novelette, "go on d' toif"] or go teh work!". Whereupon Maggie goes to work in a collar-and-cuff factory, "a dreary place of endless grinding," in contrast to which, combined with "[t]he broken furniture, grimy walls, and general disorder and dirt of her home," Pete's "aristocratic person" takes on the aspect of an irresistible allure. The violent environment of *Maggie* with its rigorously circumscribed choices, profanity, prostitution, and hostility is a radical departure from the genteel realism* of the late nineteenth century.

Corollary to the unremitting violence of the Bowery world is the unconcern of its social institutions. The residents of Maggie's tenement house observe the pandemonium of her home with mere dispassionate curiosity and offer nothing more than a choric commentary on her plight. The immigrant owner of the sweatshop in which Maggie works, among "twenty girls of various shades of yellow discontent," sees her only as an instrument of production: "What een hell do you sink I pie fife dolla a week for? Play? No, py damn!" When Jimmie seeks refuge from a home that has become a "reg'lar livin' hell" by "happening hilariously in at a mission church where a man composed his sermons of 'yous,' " he and his companion "confused the speaker with Christ." After her seduction and rejection by Pete, Maggie encounters a dignified clergyman. Having "heard of the Grace of God," she approaches him, whereupon "he gave a convulsive movement and saved his respectability by a vigorous side-step. He did not risk it to save a soul. For how was he to know that there was a soul before him that needed saving?"

Despite the emphasis on struggle, survival of the fittest, and social indifference, *Maggie* is neither simply naturalistic fiction in the manner of Zola nor a conventional nineteenth-century melodrama of a blameless girl seduced and abandoned. Irony is the pervasive tone of the novelette, and Maggie's downfall is attributable less to the pressures of the external environment than to the projection by herself and her family of theatrical romantic illusions and middle-class moral values on the atavistic world of the slums. Swaggering Pete is Maggie's "beau ideal of a man. . . . Under the trees of her dream-gardens there had always walked a lover." His bullying and coarse Bowery rudeness impress her as "elegance" and "high-class customs." In order to impress Pete, she attempts to improve the appearance of her home by making a lambrequin of flowered cretonne that she hangs over the kitchen mantle. Pete fails to notice it, and shortly afterward the lambrequin is destroyed by Maggie's mother in one of her drunken rampages. Pete and Maggie attend melodramatic plays "in which the brain-clutching heroine was rescued from the palatial home of her guardian, who is cruelly after her bonds, by the hero with the beautiful sentiments." For Maggie and the rest of the audience, the final "triumph for the hero, poor and of the masses," is "transcendental realism." Maggie's mother has driven her from home and into Pete's arms, but she is astounded and affronted by Maggie's downfall and wonders, "When a girl is bringed up deh way I bringed up Maggie, how kin she go teh deh devil?" And although Pete rejects Hattie, a "forlorn woman'' he has impregnated, he also cannot ''conceive how under the circumstances his mother's daughter and his sister could have been so wicked.'' Maggie's destruction is ensured by the hypocritical and false moral poses of her family and her Rum Alley neighbors who, as in Greek tragedy, form a chorus that represents the community, but rather than offering commentary and interpretation, they condemn and ostracize her.

The structure of *Maggie* has been regarded as loose and episodic, but patterns of thematic development are apparent. The three music halls to which Pete takes Maggie, described at the beginnings of chapters 7, 12, and 14, reflect the degenerating quality of their relationship. The ''green-hued hall,'' where Pete begins his seduction, has an orchestra of ''yellow silk women and bald-headed men'' who play a waltz while little boys dressed as French chefs vend fancy cakes. The ''hall of irregular shape'' that they frequent when their liaison is established has a ''submissive orchestra'' directed by ''a spectacled man with frowsy hair and a dress suit.'' There is a ballad singer in a scarlet dress who does a striptease, encouraged by men who pound the tables with their beer glasses. The third hall, where Pete abandons Maggie to run off with Nell, the ''woman of brilliance and audacity,'' is described as ''a hilarious hall'' with twenty-eight women seated at twenty-eight tables, and ''[v]aliant noise'' is made by ''an orchestra composed of men who looked as if they had just happened in.'' There are soiled waiters who cheat their customers and a bouncer who has a great deal of business. Parallel incidents occur in chapter 15, where Jimmie rejects Hattie, and chapter 16, where Pete rejects Maggie. Both Jimmie and Pete give the same parting advice, ''Oh go teh hell!'' In chapter 12 Maggie draws back her skirts in revulsion from two painted prostitutes, and in chapter 15 Jimmie and the tenement women hastily draw back at Maggie's approach. At the conclusion of chapter 18, the prostitutes Pete has been entertaining ''screamed in disgust and drew back their skirts'' as he lurches to the floor in a drunken stupor. In these redundant episodes, the theatrical posturing and sanctimonious self-righteousness of the characters reinforce Crane's theme of the basic amorality of slum life.

Chapter 17, in which Maggie descends from the splendor of brightly lit avenues to the darkness of the river, is a brilliant tour de force with a dual time scheme. Maggie's life as a prostitute is telescoped into the events of a single evening. She is not mentioned by name but referred to only typically as ''[a] girl of the painted cohorts of the city.'' She has apparently been successful in her career, since she wears a ''handsome cloak'' and has ''well-shod'' feet, but as she progresses in a linear movement from the entertainment district of the city through the more squalid neighborhoods, the men she solicits and who reject her are increasingly degraded. She no longer importunes the well-dressed men of the theater district for whom she has lost attraction and who spurn her, and as she passes the ''more glittering avenues'' and goes into ''darker blocks'' she is rejected by a number of men progressively lower in the social scale, until the final encounter with ''a huge fat man in torn and greasy garments'' who follows her to the "deathly black hue" of the river and presumably murders her or, more likely, provides the symbolic motivation for her suicide. Crane is not explicit about how Maggie dies. Maggie's death is followed by a chapter depicting Pete's demise into drunken debauchery and by the highly theatrical last chapter in which Maggie is mourned in a burlesque antiphony by her mother and a woman in black whose vocabulary "was derived from mission churches." The novelette ends in a parody of misplaced culpability as Mary Johnson screams, "Oh yes, I'll fergive her! I'll fergive her!"

Suggested Reading

Brennan, Joseph X. "Ironic and Symbolic Structure in Crane's *Maggie.*" *Nineteenth-Century Fiction* 16 (1962): 303–15.
Colvert, James B. Introduction to *Bowery Works*. Charlottesville: University Press of Virginia, 1969. Vol. 1 of *The Works of Stephen Crane*. Ed. Fredson Bowers. 10 vols. 1969–76.
Gandal, Keith. "Stephen Crane's 'Maggie' and the Modern Soul." *ELH* 60 (1993): 759–85.
Gullason, Thomas A. "Tragedy and Melodrama in Stephen Crane's *Maggie.*" In *Maggie: A Girl of the Streets*. Ed. Thomas A. Gullason. New York: Norton, 1979. 245–53.
Graff, Aida Farrag. "Metaphor and Metonymy: The Two Worlds of Crane's *Maggie.*" *English Studies in Canada* 8 (1982): 422–36.
Pizer, Donald. "Stephen Crane's *Maggie* and American Naturalism." *Criticism* 7 (1965): 168–75.

"Making an Orator". This satirically titled short story was published in the December 1899 issue of *Harper's New Monthly Magazine* and collected in *Whilomville Stories*. Its origins seem to be autobiographical in that Crane had a lifelong fear of speaking to groups. At Claverack College* he was excused from declaiming, although the school considered the development of oratorical skills essential in a proper nineteenth-century education. When some years later he was invited to read a selection of his poetry before the Uncut Leaves Society, Crane declined to do so, asserting to John Barry,* who read the poems for him, "that he would 'rather die than do it.' " Ford Madox Ford* maintained that he heard Crane give a lecture on military signaling with flags, but it is unlikely that Crane ever spoke in public.

"Making an Orator" opens with an unusual didactic attack on the cruel educational requirement of elocution that "operated mainly to antagonize many children permanently against arising to speak their thoughts to fellow-creatures." Jimmie Trescott dreads being placed in a class at the Whilomville school, where every Friday afternoon is devoted to declamation. When he is "somehow sent ahead into the place of torture," he tries further delaying tactics to avoid the assignment of having to recite "the incomprehensible lines" of Tennyson's "The Charge of the Light Brigade." He manages to feign sickness for two successive Fridays, but on the third Friday, escape becomes impossible.

He is preceded to the lectern by three children who also dread the reciting of words that have no relevance to their lives. Johnnie Tanner opens the ceremony with a fervent peroration about the loyalty of Ireland to Great Britain. He is followed by Susie Timmens, who "would be Queen of the May," and by the Trass boy, who "calmly spoke some undeniably true words concerning destiny." When Jimmie's turn comes, he is almost entirely unable to recall the lines of Tennyson's poem and enrages the teacher, who orders him back to his seat with the admonition that she will expect a better recitation from him the next week. Jimmie is temporarily relieved, but he does not realize that "on this day there had been laid for him the foundation of an unfinished incapacity for public speaking which would be his until he died."

"Making an Orator" is infused with Crane's irony since "The Charge of the Light Brigade" (1854) is based on an incident in the Battle of Balaklava during the Crimean War in which an English brigade charged Russian troops against odds they knew were hopeless and were slaughtered. In a Victorian devotion to duty, the men of the brigade did not question a command they knew was foolish: "Theirs not to reason why, / Theirs not to make reply, / Theirs but to do and die, / Into the valley of Death / Rode the six hundred." Tennyson's lines were intended as praise; Jimmie had been told that the brigade of over six-hundred men "were performing something there that was very fine." Jimmie is metaphorically also being subjected to a trial by fire that is irrational and unprofitable. In juxtaposing Jimmie's childhood ordeal with Tennyson's poem on unquestioned obedience to unrealistic military orders, Crane is again mocking abstract conceptions of heroism, as he had in *The Red Badge of Courage*.

Suggested Reading

Monteiro, George. "With Proper Words (or without Them) the Soldier Dies: Stephen Crane's 'Making an Orator.' " *Cithera* 9.2 (1970): 64–72.

"A man adrift on a slim spar". Arguably Crane's finest poem, "A man adrift on a slim spar" was inexplicably omitted from *War Is Kind* and was first published posthumously in the April 1929 issue of the *Bookman*. The poem echoes the theme of cosmic isolation symbolized by the "high cold star on a winter's night" in "The Open Boat." As in the short story, where none of the men in the dinghy "knew the color of the sky," point of view in the first two and last two four-line stanzas of "A man adrift," all of which end with the refrain "God is cold," is that of the drowning man who is the focus of the poem. There is a middle stanza of nine lines representing the reflections of an observer or perhaps the inner thoughts of the drowning man himself who can see only "[a] horizon smaller than the rim of a bottle" or "[a] horizon smaller than a doomed assassin's cap." He or the observer reflects that the merciful, omnipotent God of Christian tradition putatively watches over his creation ("The seas are in the hollow of the Hand") and could save the drowning man, but Crane's creative force is remote and controls neither nature nor the fate of humanity. He is the indifferent, inaccessible spectator of "God fashioned the ship of the world carefully." In the final stanza, the dying man relinquishes his hold on the spar, and all that is left is the meaningless, incessant motion of the waves, "A weary slow sway of a lost hand / And the sea, the moving sea, the sea. / God is cold."

Suggested Reading

Monteiro, George. "Crane's 'A Man Adrift on a Slim Spar.' " *Explicator* 32 (1973): Item 14.

"A Man and Some Others". First printed in the February 1897 issue of the *Century* with a full-page illustration by Frederic Remington* and collected in *The Open Boat*, this is one of three stories, along with "The Wise Men" and "The Five White Mice," that Crane wrote in the spring and summer of 1896 based on his experiences in Mexico. Crane considered "A Man and Some Others" to be among his best works. Joseph Conrad* admired it "without reserve," and although he called it "an amazing bit of biography," the story should not be viewed as verifiable personal history but as an imaginative projection embodying two of Crane's favorite themes: the destruction of innocence through confrontation with ineluctable and brutal circumstance and the unconscious, unassuming nature of true courage.

The plot concerns a sheepherder in southwestern Texas who is being forced off the range by a gang of Mexican rivals whose spokesman, a man named José, warns him that he will be killed if he does not get out. Bill is making his last stand, having descended in the social scale from being a mine owner in Wyoming ruined by one disastrous hand of poker, a cowboy who was forced to flee after he "killed the foreman of the ranch over an inconsequent matter as to which of them was a liar," a brakeman on the Union Pacific railroad, and, finally, before retreating to an isolated existence on the prairie, a bouncer in a Bowery saloon who was fired after being undone in a brawl with some sailors. The story centers not on Bill but on a naive young "stranger" from a northern city who wants to share his camp and who, after hearing Bill's story of the Mexicans' threats to kill him, displays great innocence by suggesting that Bill summon the sheriff. Bill and five of the Mexicans are killed in two shoot-outs that ensue that evening and the following morning before the eyes of the astounded stranger, who has not previously been involved in or even imagined confrontations in which death is the outcome. Stupefied by his experience and remote from the comforting illusions of civilization, he covers Bill's body with a blanket and moves gingerly around one of the bodies into a natural world where "the bushes, nodding and whispering, their leaf-faces turned toward the scene behind him, swung and swung again into stillness and the peace of the wilderness." The stranger learns that in an indifferent universe whatever relevance human life has must be created through individual qualities such as honesty, stoicism, and courage. This theme, contrasting with the determinism and

cynicism of *Maggie* and *The Red Badge of Courage*, becomes increasingly evident in Crane's later fiction, especially his war stories, and anticipates the Hemingway ethos of grace under pressure.

A number of commentators on this story and Crane's other Mexican short
stories and reports have pointed out that his attitude toward Mexicans, as even
the title "A Man and Some Others" implies, is often more than a little condescending. Like the defenders of the Alamo in Crane's dispatch from San
Antonio, "Stephen Crane in Texas," Bill has fought a courageous battle against
insuperable odds while the Mexicans are portrayed as predatory, treacherous,
and cruel.

Suggested Reading

Deamer, Robert Glen. *The Importance of Place in the American Literature of Hawthorne,*
  Thoreau, Crane, Adams, and Faulkner. Lewiston, N.Y.: Mellen Press, 1990. 139–
  52.
Gibson, Donald. *The Fiction of Stephen Crane.* Carbondale, Ill.: Southern Illinois University Press, 1968. 118–20.
Paredes, Raymund A. "Stephen Crane and the Mexican." *Western American Literature*
  6 (1971): 31–38.

"A Man by the Name of Mud". A third story, with "The Wise Men" and
"The Five White Mice," involving the New York Kid and his counterpart, the
'Frisco Kid, although which Kid is which is never made clear in this story,
giving support to the idea that the kids are actually opposite sides of the same
person. The setting is a city, perhaps New York, and the verve shown by the
Kids in Mexico City where the two other stories take place is notably missing.
One of the Kids is sitting morosely self-absorbed in an armchair being ragged
by his friends about the second Kid, who is pursuing a chorus girl at the Co-
mique. The woman has "come between the two Kids," and they are no longer
inseparable. The first Kid is not brooding on the absence of his friend, but he
seems lost without the presence of his alter ego and lapses "into a state of
voiceless dejection." The woman encourages the advances of the second Kid,
who becomes increasingly infatuated with her. When she gives excuses for not
being able to see him at times, the Kid becomes jealous and confronts her. The
offended girl rebukes him, and the Kid loses his dignity, "surrenders and pleads
with her—pleads with her. Kid's name is mud." The outline form of the conclusion suggests that the story may have been hastily finished or remained unfinished. It appeared only posthumously in *Last Words*.

"The Man from Duluth". An unsuccessful story of New York life whose date
of composition is uncertain, "The Man from Duluth" was either completed or
revised by Cora Crane and first published in the February 1901 issue of *Metropolitan Magazine*. The point of view of Crane's Western stories is reversed
as a man from the West observes New York night life on a Sunday night and

finds it boring. His New York friends agree, lamenting that since the decline of the Tenderloin, "the town is about dead now, anyhow." Seeking excitement, the men go to "a little French concert hall" in Greenwich Village. There is much singing and dancing, but the man from Duluth considers it "dead slow." He becomes somewhat more interested when a fight breaks out in the middle of the hall, but since the participants are not hurting each other very much, he contemptuously regards them as "a pair of birds." The turmoil increases when "a little, fat, tipsy Frenchman" interjects himself into the fight and is attacked by a woman with hands "outstretched like the claws of an eagle" because he has threatened her lover. The man from Duluth becomes electrified and cheers the woman on, but she turns on him with her face "red and fierce" and her hands "held in the same peculiar claw-like manner." At this point, the man from Duluth realizes that he has found more excitement than he sought. "He made a flying leap and ran for the door. The woman made a grab at his coattails, but she missed him."

"The Man in the White Hat". Published on 18 June 1897 as the seventh and last "letter" of Crane's "With Greek and Turk" series in the *Westminster Gazette* and later circulated by McClure in American newspapers, this article depicts a mob in front of the royal palace on Constitution Square in Athens in late April addressed by a fiery orator, an editor and parliamentary deputy wearing a tall white hat, "the hat of insurrection," who proposes to confront the king and ask, "Why was Greece shamed? Whose fault was it?" He is easily rebuffed at the door of the palace by a servant who coolly informs him that "[t]he King does not receive to-day," and an evzone on guard duty contemptuously flings a handful of pebbles in the face of the mob. Richard Harding Davis* and John Bass* also observed and reported this incident but, like Crane, did not identify the deputy. Bass refers to him as "Gannadius" (*New York Journal*, 30 April 1897), but this is a satirical allusion to the fifteenth-century Greek monk George Scholarios, a great orator who later became patriarch of Constantinople.

The Man of the Cheery Voice. A character who appears midpoint in *The Red Badge of Courage* to guide Henry Fleming back to his regiment after he has been wounded. Unlike the confused and conflicted Henry, the stranger is audacious and assured. He is a guide in the wilderness (the Battle of Chancellorsville was fought in an area known as the Wilderness), who "seemed to the youth to possess a wand of a magic kind. He threaded the mazes of the tangled forest with a strange fortune." He anticipates the courageous, self-possessed soldier Henry will become in the second part of the novel.

"Manacled". The earliest publication of "Manacled" was, posthumously, in the English magazine *Argosy* (August 1900). It appeared in the United States in the November 1900 issue of *Truth** with two illustrations by R. G. Vosburgh,* Crane's friend and roommate in the old Art Students League building. The story was collected in the English edition of *The Monster and Other Stories*. Although written in England in 1899, "Manacled" has some of the impressionistic* touches of Crane's early fiction. The story concerns an actor who is abandoned on the stage chained in real handcuffs and anklets when fire breaks out in a theater during the second act of a melodrama. The fierce colors of the flames in the burning theater, of which "some were crimson, some were orange, and here and there were tongues of purple, blue, green," complement the quiet colors of the sidewalk outside where "[t]he gleam of lights made the shadowed pavements deeply blue, save where lay some yellow plum-like reflection." "Manacled" has been described as a fantasy, but the disordered flight of the audience from the burning theater, the frantic charge of a policeman on the corner fire alarm box, the unnamed actor's futile struggle to escape, and his agonizing death are rendered in excruciatingly realistic detail. Crane's fascination with fire is apparent in his newspaper feature, "When Every One Is Panic Stricken," as well as in "The Veteran" and "The Monster."

Margate, Eldridge. In "The Angel Child" he is the grandfather of the twins whose golden locks are shorn by the crazed barber, William Neeltje. Amid the general hysteria of Whilomville parents, he remains unperturbed by this mock tragedy. Trescott observes that old Eldridge Margate is one of the few residents of the town "who wore his brains above his shoulders."

The Margate Twins. Reeves Margate and his brother, Wolcott, are characters in the *Whilomville Stories*. In "The Angel Child," they are despoiled of their long golden curls, "the heart-treasure and glory of a mother, three aunts, and some feminine cousins," by the demented barber William Neeltje. The twins appear as members of Willie Dalzel's gang in "The Trial, Execution, and Burial of Homer Phelps" and are among the Whilomville children who attend the town picnic in "Shame."

Margharita. The Tampa belle in "The Clan of No-Name" whose deceitful behavior forms the framework of the story. In the first section, Margharita accedes to her "commercially excited" mother's wish that she allow herself to be courted by the wealthy Mr. Smith, although she is carrying on a romance with Manolo Prat. In the last section she displays a callous indifference to the fate of her dead lover and accepts Mr. Smith's proposal.

"Marines Signalling under Fire at Guantanamo". More of a sketch than a short story, this Cuban War piece deals with the practice of military signaling with flags by day and lanterns at night. It was printed in the February 1899 issue of *McClure's Magazine* and collected in *Wounds in the Rain*. The events depicted are those that occurred in the earliest engagements of the war, at Guantánamo Bay in mid-June 1898 and especially in the fighting at Cuzco on 14

June at which Crane was present and which he reported in his *New York World* dispatch, "The Red Badge of Courage Was His Wig-Wag Flag." Crane was fascinated by the stoic courage of the signalmen who stood exposed and defenseless, performing their duty under heavy fire, the quality that Ernest Hemingway would later call "grace under pressure." He is especially impressed by the workmanlike behavior of Marine Sergeant John H. Quick,* mentioned in Crane's *World* report as "a spruce young sergeant of marines," whose flag signals directed the fire from the U.S.S. *Dolphin* offshore. Quick was awarded the Congressional Medal of Honor for his actions at Cuzco, as was another marine signalman to whom Crane refers under the fictional name of Clancy. Most of the other characters in this sketch—Lieutenant Colonel Robert Huntington,* Commander Bowman H. McCalla,* Lieutenant Herbert L. Draper, and Captain George F. Elliott*—are identified by their real names.

Marriott-Watson, Henry Brereton (1863–1921). Born in New Zealand, Marriott-Watson published more than forty novels and collections of short stories between 1888 and 1919. As a journalist he worked on the *St. James Gazette*, the *Scottish* (later *National*) *Observer*, *Black and White*, and the *Pall Mall Gazette*. He was coauthor of a play, *Richard Savage*, with J. M. Barrie. Now largely forgotten, Marriott-Watson was associated with some of the most prominent English literary circles in the late 1890s. He wrote one of the earliest and most influential English reviews of *The Red Badge of Courage*; it appeared in the *Pall Mall Gazette* on the day of the novel's English publication, 26 November 1895. Crane's Western story "Twelve O'Clock" was published in the December 1899 issue of the *Gazette*. Marriott Watson made a cryptographic contribution to "The Ghost," and the character of Miranda in the comedy is in part an echo from his *Heart of Miranda*. After Crane's death, Cora asked Marriott-Watson to complete *The O'Ruddy*, a work not unlike much of his own fiction, but he declined to undertake the task.

Marshall, Edward (1869–1933). A lifelong journalist and a prolific playwright, Marshall was news editor of the American Press Association from 1885 to 1889 and Sunday editor of the *New York Press* from 1890 to 1895. In 1897 he served as foreign correspondent for the *New York Journal* and for a time was Sunday editor of the *New York World*. He rejoined the *Journal* staff in June 1897 and was sent to Cuba as a correspondent at the outbreak of the Spanish-American War. He was shot through the body at Las Guásimas on 24 June 1898. Marshall's book *The Story of the Rough Riders* (1898) is an eyewitness account of the exploits of that famous volunteer regiment. Afterward Marshall was a newspaper writer on tenement reform in Europe and New York. In 1914 he organized the Edward Marshall Newspaper Syndicate, which purchased the Curtis Brown* News Bureau in London in 1916.

Marshall and Crane became close friends in 1894, when the *Press* published a number of Crane's New York City tales and sketches as Sunday feature items.

It was at Marshall's suggestion that Crane brought the manuscript of *The Red Badge of Courage* to Irving Bacheller.* In an early review of the novel in the *Press*, Marshall extolled Crane's impressionistic descriptions. Marshall was one of the organizers of the Lantern Club,* a group of New York journalists that Crane joined shortly after its formation. Marshall and Crane served together as correspondents for rival newspapers in Cuba, and when Marshall was wounded at Las Guásimas, Crane supervised his removal to a field hospital and trudged back to Siboney to cable Marshall's dispatch to the *Journal*, an act much resented by Crane's employers at the *World*.

Martin, Jack. One of the regular soldiers in "The Price of the Harness," Martin is shot in the arm in the charge at San Juan and joins his comrade Billie Grierson in the yellow fever tent.

Mason, A.E.W. (1865–1948). An English romance novelist, playwright, and author of detective fiction, Alfred Edward Woodley Mason began his career as an actor. Mason first wrote historical fiction but turned to novels of contemporary life. His *Miranda of the Balcony* (1899) was produced as a drama in New York in 1901. Mason was a frequent visitor to Brede Place.* He contributed to "The Ghost" and played the lead role in the single performance of the farce. After Crane's death, Cora asked Mason to complete *The O'Ruddy*, after a number of other writers had declined the project, and he held the manuscript for two years without working on it. For his best-known novel, *The Four Feathers* (1902), Mason journeyed to Egypt to absorb local color, and *The Broken Road* (1907), a novel set in India, was esteemed for the faithful atmosphere of its literary scene. Mason was a member of the House of Commons from 1906 to 1910.

"Meetings Begun at Ocean Grove". Crane's authorship of this unsigned account of the annual meting of Methodist ministers at Ocean Grove, New Jersey, in the *New York Tribune*, 2 July 1892, is indicated by the ironic tenor of the opening sentence describing the "sombre-hued gentlemen" who arrive "with black valises in their hands and rebukes to frivolity in their eyes." The ministers attend various lectures, including one by "Big Frank" Carr, who "went considerably into the details when describing the lives and methods of 'crooks.' "

The Members of the Society. A promotional pamphlet issued by the Society of the Philistines comprising a letter dated 10 November 1895 signed by Elbert Hubbard,* Henry P. Taber,* and a number of journalists constituting the Committee for the Society inviting Crane to attend a dinner in his honor in East Aurora, New York, and requesting to know "upon what date you could conveniently come to us" and also containing Crane's reply dated 15 November accepting the invitation and designating 19 December as a convenient date.

Because of the inconvenient location of East Aurora, the site was changed to Buffalo—first to the Iroquois and then to the Genesee Hotel.

"Memoirs of a Private". The subheading of this bitter invective printed in the *New York Journal* on 25 September 1898 reads "Dictated to and Taken Down by Stephen Crane." This is, of course, a fiction. Crane, speaking in the voice of a private in the regular army, castigates the public for their indifference as to who occupies the office of secretary of war, "a highly honorable post which is the proper loot of some faithful partisan." Crane's diatribe is probably directed against Russell Alger,* who occupied the position during the Spanish-American War and was often blamed for the inadequacy of supplies and armaments, poor-quality food, poor sanitary conditions, and other liabilities that burdened the American troops in Cuba.

"The Men in the Storm". A companion piece to "An Experiment in Misery," this sketch was based on a personal experience that Crane had in the Bowery on a night in late February 1894 when a blizzard engulfed New York City, covering the streets with almost a foot and a half of snow. It was first published in the *Arena* (October 1894), reprinted in the *Philistine** (January 1897), and collected in the English edition of *The Open Boat and Other Stories*.

"The Men in the Storm" opens with an impressionistic montage of great swirls of snow sweeping along a street as pedestrians hurry by, their faces buried in their coats. Vehicles and streetcars slip and slide along while elevated trains rumble overhead. As the afternoon darkens into evening, the lights from shops illuminate "the force and discomfort of the storm" and the "scores of pedestrians and drivers, wretched with cold faces, necks and feet, speeding for scores of unknown doors and entrances, scattering to an infinite variety of shelters, to places which the imagination made warm and familiar with the familiar colors of home."

A crowd of wretched homeless men, their number increasing as the hour grows later, huddle in a freezing mass before the closed door of a five-cent lodging house, waiting for the time when they will be admitted. Crane distinguishes two character types among these men: those temporarily "vanquished in the race" for survival in the midst of the depression of 1893 and "others of the shifting, Bowery lodging-house element," social outcasts for whom this is a familiar circumstance. As the winds and cold grow fiercer, the men squash one another against the door. In sharp social contrast, the window of a dry goods shop across the street reveals a mocking spectacle of opulence and comfort:

> In the brilliantly lighted space appeared the figure of a man. He was rather stout and very well clothed. His whiskers were fashioned charmingly after those of the Prince of Wales. He stood in an attitude of magnificent reflection. He slowly stroked his moustache with a certain grandeur of manner, and looked down at the snow-encrusted mob. From below, there was denoted a supreme complacence in

him. It seemed that the sight operated inversely, and enabled him to more clearly regard his own environment, delightful relatively.

When the lodging house door finally opens, the crowd surges forward, the men becoming less frenetic and more complacent as they approach the entrance, and the diminishing mass slowly filters in, "one by one, three by three, out of the storm."

Crane had little interest in humanitarian causes or didactic reform literature and considered his Bowery tales and sketches to be psychological analyses and realistic works of art. "The Men in the Storm" is one of his more naturalistic works since the forces of the external environment embodied in the whirling snowstorm combined with the social circumstance of economic depression seem to annihilate the existential individuality of the men, breaking down the distinction between honest workingmen temporarily down on their luck and the habitual derelicts of the Bowery. Although Crane does not engage in social commentary, there is explicit recognition in this sketch that free will is circumscribed in a universe of human indifference in the face of the manifest hostility of nature.

Suggested Reading

Monteiro, George. "Society and Nature in Stephen Crane's 'The Men in the Storm.' " *Prairie Schooner* 45 (1971): 13–17.

"The Mesmeric Mountain". The most evocative and hallucinatory of the Sullivan County stories, "The Mesmeric Mountain" was published posthumously in *Last Words*. The story opens with the little man sitting with his back against a pine tree on a hillock near his camp. He becomes intrigued with an irregular opening into a forest at the foot of the hill and wonders what it leads to. The pudgy man scoffs at his curiosity, but dissatisfied with his mundane response that it simply leads "to ol' Jim Boyd's over on the Lumberland Pike" and convinced that "it leads to something great," the little man walks through the opening in the forest wall. Unable to get his bearings on the tangled floor of the forest, he climbs a tall pine tree and sees Jones' Mountain. He heads away from the mountain, but when he emerges from the wood, he finds himself at the mountain's foot. Staring at the peak in bewilderment, he sees eyes glaring back, and suddenly the mountain seems to be approaching. He flees but after a time finds himself once again confronting the mountain, as if it had been following him. Enraged he grabs a handful of pebbles and flings them at the mountainside: "The little man then made an attack. He climbed with hands and feet, wildly. Brambles forced him back and stones slid from beneath his feet. The peak swayed and tottered and was ever about to smite with a granite arm. The summit was a blaze of red wrath." He reaches the top in triumph and sees familiar landmarks. He imagines that he has triumphed over a challenge to his ego, but in reality "[t]he mountain under his feet was motionless," suggesting that victory, like defeat, is merely a subjective construct.

The little man engaged in strife with mountains representing an apparently antagonistic nature is a recurrent image in Crane's fiction and poetry. Conceiving of himself as a hero in chapter 17 of *The Red Badge of Courage*, Henry Fleming reflects that "he had overcome obstacles which he had admitted to be mountains." Poems in *The Black Riders*, such as "Once I saw mountains angry" and "On the horizon the peaks assembled," also counterpoise a little man against seemingly hostile mountains. The conquest of Jones' Mountain and the spurious sense of triumph achieved by the little man in "The Mesmeric Mountain" over an obstacle created by his imagination is Crane's ironic comment on humanity's colossal egotism.

Suggested Reading

Colvert, James B. "Stephen Crane's Magic Mountain." In *Stephen Crane: A Collection of Critical Essays*. Ed. Maurice Bassan. Englewood Cliffs, N.J.: Prentice-Hall, 1967. 95–105.

Michelson, Charles (1868–1948). A journalist and political publicist, Michelson was born in Virginia City, Nevada, and began newspaper work on the *Virginia City Chronicle*. In about 1887 he moved to San Francisco, where he was a reporter on the *San Francisco Evening Post* and Hearst's *San Francisco Examiner*. In 1896 Hearst sent Michelson to cover the Cuban revolt against Spanish rule. He was briefly imprisoned by the authorities in Havana's Morro Castle. During the Spanish-American War, Michelson spent a good deal of time on Hearst dispatch boats but saw no action. Subsequently he served in editorial capacities on Hearst newspapers in New York, San Francisco, and Chicago. In 1917 he joined the *New York World* as chief Washington correspondent and for twelve years wrote a pro-Democratic column, "The Political Undertow." In 1929 he became publicity director for the Democratic party and was highly effective as a ghostwriter for many politicians.

Michelson's introduction to *The Open Boat and Other Tales* (1927), the last volume of Wilson Follett's twelve-volume edition of *The Work of Stephen Crane* (1925–27), is rich in details of Crane's physical appearance, activities, and personality during the earlier and later phases of the Cuban War. Crane and Michelson met in Jacksonville in the fall of 1896. "Crane always disappeared on his arrival at a new town," Michelson notes. "He dived into the deep waters of society and stayed under." In Ponce, Puerto Rico, Crane submerged into the underworld of the city almost immediately upon arrival: "We found him, where we knew to look for him, in a back-street cantina, with the wastrels of Ponce— drunkards, drabs, and tin-horn gamblers." Shortly afterward in Havana, Crane would repeat this pattern of disappearance. Michelson tells a somewhat different story from Richard Harding Davis* about Crane's supposed "capture" of the town of Juana Diaz. After Crane's death, Michelson returned the saddle bags

Crane had left in his care to Cora; one of them contained a manuscript of Crane's poem "The Battle Hymn."

Mickey. In the Irish sketches "A Fishing Village" and "An Old Man Goes Wooing," he is a lachrymose elderly man. Unable to sustain himself in his native land and too old to join the mass of immigrants to America, he becomes part of the detritus of a declining society.

"Miss Louise Gerard—Soprano". Crane may have met Louise Gerard and her husband, the tenor Albert Thies, in the summer of 1890 at Avon's Seaside Assembly, where the couple participated in a number of concerts. His report "Avon's School by the Sea" and the later sketch "The King's Favor" describe Thies's performance before Chief Cetewayo of the Zulus. Crane's interest in Thies may account for his authorship of this blurb for Louise Gerard's singing, derived apparently from press notices of her performances in England and the United States and published in the December 1894 issue of the *Musical News* and the 26 December 1894 *Musical Courier.*

"The Monster". Although "The Monster" is one of Crane's fictional master-pieces that aroused considerable controversy at the time of its first publication, it has been given relatively scant critical attention. Crane wrote the novelette in the summer of 1897, completing it at Harold Frederic's* house in Ireland. "The Monster" appeared in the August 1898 issue of *Harper's Magazine* with illustrations by Peter Newell and was collected, along with "The Blue Hotel" and "His New Mittens," in *The Monster and Other Stories.* The setting of "The Monster" is Whilomville, apparently modeled on Port Jervis, New York, where Crane lived at the time his age corresponded with that of Jimmie Trescott, and some of the details of the novelette may have had literal origins in his life. In the fourth section of "The Monster," a factory whistle fire alarm scatters the crowd gathered in a little park to hear a concert at the very instant the bandmaster is about to bring down his baton. In Orange Square, the focal point of Port Jervis, a fountain and a bandstand stood along the Sussex Street side of the park where Jonathan Townley Crane's parsonage was located. Thomas Beer,* if he is to be given any credence, thought at one time that he had traced the prototype of Henry Johnson to a Port Jervis teamster by the name of Levi Hume, but he could find no one to confirm the suggestion. Edna Crane Sidbury said that her father, William Howe Crane, believed a local carter who hauled ashes, "his face eaten by a cancer," to be the original. He was an object of fear to the children, "for it could truthfully be said of him, 'He had no face.' "

In "The Monster" a black hostler named Henry Johnson rescues Jimmie, the son of his employer, Dr. Edward Trescott, a prominent Whilomville physician, from a fire in the Trescott home and is horribly deformed in the process by a spilled jar of molten chemicals in Dr. Trescott's laboratory that burns away his face and leaves him mentally incapacitated as well. In gratitude for having saved his son's life, Dr. Trescott shelters Johnson in the house of Alek Williams, another black resident of Whilomville, but he escapes and unwittingly terrifies the townspeople. Thereafter Trescott harbors him in his own home, and as a result the doctor's medical practice deteriorates; his neighbors, the Hannigan family, plan to move; and he and his wife are ostracized by the community. The novelette culminates in one of Crane's most effective deflationary endings. Returning home on a Wednesday, the day that his wife "receives," Trescott finds that only one of the wives of Whilomville's influential citizens has had the temerity to attend her afternoon tea. As he attempts to console his wife, Trescott's attention is irresistibly centered on the unused tea cups:

> The wind was whining round the house, and the snow beat aslant upon the windows. Sometimes the coal in the stove settled with a crumbling sound, and the four panes of mica flashed a sudden new crimson. As he sat holding her head on his shoulder, Trescott found himself occasionally trying to count the cups. There were fifteen of them.

A number of recent commentators have attempted to modernize "The Monster" by reductively centering on Henry Johnson's blackness, but race is a tangential factor in the novelette, and Crane in his treatment of it no way transcended the stereotypes of his time and place. Throughout his writings, black characters are almost invariably represented as comics and fools, minstrel show figures like the clownish Peter Washington and Alek Williams in "The Knife," Black John Randolph in "Billy Atkins Went to Omaha" who shines shoes to make money for gingerbread, the dancing teamster at the beginning of *The Red Badge of Courage*, or the Pullman car porter and dining car waiter who cajole and bully Marshall Potter and his wife in "The Bride Comes to Yellow Sky." Before his single act of heroism, Henry Johnson is also depicted as a ludicrous character in lavender trousers and a straw hat with a bright silk band who woos his saffron beauty in Watermelon Alley with shuffles, bows, and stilted diction hyperbolically imitative of the conventional mannerisms of courting in the 1890s. The Zeitgeist racist image is ameliorated only by Johnson's courage when he saves Jimmie Trescott from the fire, and even this is represented not as a moral act but as an unconscious reflexive reaction to circumstance.

However pejoratively depicted, the hackneyed image of blackness originally gives Henry Johnson his only identity in Whilomville, and the true horror that confronts the town is that through his trial by fire he has lost even this adventitious hallmark of identity and has been socially as well as physically defaced. The patrons of Reifsnyder's barbershop, including Young Griscom, a lawyer, and Bainbridge, a railroad engineer, are the choral voice of the community. "Well, what makes him so terrible?" asks one of the gossips of the barbershop. " 'Because he hasn't got any face,' replied the barber and the engineer in duet. 'Hasn't got any face!' repeated the man. 'How can he do without any face?' " The destruction of the peony in Dr. Trescott's garden sideswiped by Jimmie's play cart in the opening episode of the novelette, for which, in Crane's words, he "could do no reparation," is a foreshadowing of the malformation of Henry Johnson that leads to his banishment from the Whilomville community. Kindly, well-meaning Judge Denning Hagenthorpe is the pragmatic, unprincipled spokesman for Whilomville. When he learns from Dr. Trescott that Johnson's facial structure is destroyed and that he is likely to be an imbecile, the judge immediately suggests that he should be allowed to die. Although he is aware of the ethical problem posed by Trescott's rejoinder, "He saved my boy's life," and the accountability of a physician to his patient, Hagenthorpe considers Trescott's resolve to shelter Henry Johnson "a questionable charity . . . one of the blunders of virtue." Martha Goodwin, the village virago, is one of the few rational minds in the aroused community. She scorns "these silly people who are scared of Henry Johnson" and takes a commonsense attitude toward the psychological damage that her neighbor Carrie Dungen maintains was done to little Sadie Winter, who was terrified by glimpsing Henry's face at the window during Theresa Page's party. But even Martha is skeptical about the wisdom of Trescott's quixotic defiance of the community and makes no response to her sister Kate's outburst that it "[s]erves him right if he was to lose all his patients."

The first part of "The Monster" creates the broken, misshapen outcast adumbrated by the symbol of the peony; the second part is given over to the creation of a composite monster as Crane gradually transfers this image to the collective citizenry of Whilomville. The spokesman for the group of prominent citizens who make a final effort to salvage Dr. Trescott's reputation by attempting to persuade him to send Henry Johnson away bears the unusual name of John Twelve, a transparent reference to the twelfth chapter of the Gospel of John, which contains repeated references to the raising of Lazarus from the dead. Trescott is not Christ, but his relationship to Henry is manifestly godlike, perversely so in the eyes of the respectable citizenry of Whilomville: "He will be your creation, you understand," warns Judge Hagenthorpe. "He is purely your creation. Nature has very evidently given him up. He is dead. You are restoring him to life. You are making him, and he will be a monster, and with no mind." Dr. Trescott accepts the central motif of John 12, which extols rectitude over expediency.

The basic theme of "The Monster" is the futility of any attempt to reconcile ethical values and social norms in the moral facelessness of the Whilomvilles of America. A good many works of fiction dealing with the realities of small-town life in the tradition that Carl Van Doren described as the "Revolt from the Village," such as Edward Eggleston's *The Hoosier Schoolmaster* (1871), Edgar Watson Howe's *The Story of a Country Town* (1883), Hamlin Garland's* *Main-Travelled Roads* (1890), and, most significant for Crane, Harold Frederic's *The Damnation of Theron Ware* (1896), form the literary background of "The Monster." These books were frank in their presentation of the stifling restrictiveness of provincial prejudices, social dogmas, and religious beliefs but tended to affirm the essential goodness of small-town life despite their exposure of its underlying cruelty and hypocrisy.

There is no compromise with nostalgia in "The Monster." The novelette is a study of prejudice, fear, and isolation in an environment traditionally associated with neighborliness and goodwill. Critics who complain that "The Monster" lacks unity often cite the slow pace and repetitiousness of the later sections. The plot is, however, carefully controlled and organized and simply and clearly constructed. The first nine sections comprising the Whilomville background and the events of the burning of the Trescott home are fast paced, filled with descriptive background and action. After the climactic fire, attention is focused on the ethics of Dr. Trescott's decision to save the ghastly remnant of what was once Henry Johnson and the inability of the townspeople to comprehend or accept a person who no longer fits into the defined scheme of things. The focus of the last fifteen sections is on the inability of society to transcend convention. The pace is slower, and narration gives way to the analysis of motives. There is a certain dragging inevitability and hopelessness that succeeds the climax of the physical drama. The decisions of the ethical drama are more complex, the results less easy to fathom. The destruction of a man by prejudice is more insidious than the destruction of a house by fire.

Suggested Reading

Ellison, Ralph. "Stephen Crane and the Mainstream of American Literature." In *Shadow and Act*. New York: Random House, 1964. 60–76.

Gullason, Thomas. "The Symbolic Unity of 'The Monster.' " *Modern Language Notes* 75 (1960): 663–68.

Hafley, James. " 'The Monster' and the Art of Stephen Crane." *Accent* 19 (1959): 159–65.

Mitchell, Lee Clark. "Face, Race and Disfiguration in Stephen Crane's 'The Monster.' " *Critical Inquiry* 17 (1990): 174–92.

Wertheim, Stanley. "Stephen Crane's *The Monster* as Fiction and Film." In *William Carlos Williams, Stephen Crane, Philip Freneau: Papers and Poems Celebrating New Jersey's Literary Heritage*. Ed. W. John Bauer. Trenton: New Jersey Historical Commission, 1989. 97–105.

The Monster and Other Stories. The American edition of this book, published by Harper and Brothers in December 1899, was an incongruous collection comprising the title novelette, "The Blue Hotel," and "His New Mittens." The English edition, not published by Harper until February 1901, added four stories: "Twelve O'Clock," "Moonlight on the Snow," "Manacled," and "An Illusion in Red and White."

Montgomery, Charles B. (?–?). The steward of the *Commodore* who shared the open-boat experience with Crane, William Higgins,* and Captain Edward Murphy.* Newspapers in Florida and New York on 4 January 1897 printed Montgomery's claim that the *Commodore*'s sinking had been caused by sabotage and that the Cubans on board had behaved in a cowardly manner during the crisis. The *New York Press* quoted Montgomery as stating that "[o]ne of the Cubans got rattled and tried to run out one of the boats before time, and Crane let him have it right from the shoulder, and the man rolled down the leeway, stunned for the moment." In "Stephen Crane's Own Story" and in "The Open Boat," Crane is vague about the cause of the oiler's death in the surf, but in the *Boston Globe* Montgomery is quoted as stating that Higgins was struck on the head by the heavy oars as he fell from the boat. Other newspapers gave different and contradictory accounts of the oiler's death.

"Moonlight on the Snow". Composed at Brede Place* in 1899, "Moonlight on the Snow" was published in the United States in the April 1900 issue of *Frank Leslie's Popular Monthly* and collected as the second of four stories added to the English edition of *The Monster and Other Stories*. It is a sequel to "The Bride Comes to Yellow Sky," not only because two characters reappear—Jack Potter, who had been a marshal in Yellow Sky and is now the sheriff of the county, and Scratchy Wilson who has, most improbably, become his deputy— but because there are thematic parallels between the stories.

The west Texas town of War Post has "an evil name for three hundred miles in every direction" as a center for gunfighters and thieves. The town's main function is to prey on the cowboys of the area, who, "when they had been paid, rode gaily into town to look for sin." As in "The Bride," Easternization is rapidly advancing. There is a real estate boom in the area, but because of the town's notoriety, Eastern investors and settlers have been frightened off. The citizens of War Post are worried that Wild West violence will ruin their opportunity for real estate speculation. The Old West's concern for individuality capitulates to a new concern for capital. Under pressure from leading citizens such as Bob Hether, Smith Hanham, and Billie Simpson, the residents decide that the reputation of the town must be ameliorated through the imposition of law and order and that the next person to kill another person will be hanged. This is agreed to by Tom Larpent, the soft-spoken proprietor of the town casino. Larpent voices Crane's cynical attitude toward the commercialization of the West. He sardonically comments that "[t]he value of human life has to be established before there can be theatres, water-works, street cars, women, and babies," but the next morning he shoots and kills a man who had accused him of cheating. Faced with the prospects of hanging one of their most prominent neighbors, the residents of War Post are reluctant to carry out their decree. Just before they are about to hang Larpent from a crane in front of the general store—symbolic of the new commercialism since, significantly, there are no trees left in War Post—a stagecoach driven by a man symbolically named Ike Boston pulls up to the store, also meaningfully named Pigrim's (Pilgrim's). An Eastern clergyman and his family, a beautiful girl and two small children, emerge from the coach, "And the rough West stood in naked immorality before the eyes of the gentle East." This incident interrupts the hanging, which is rescheduled, but

War Post is spared further embarrassment when Jack Potter and Scratchy Wilson ride into town and arrest Larpent for grand larceny, removing him from the jurisdiction of the town, to the great relief of the residents. "Moonlight on the Snow" is a gloss on "The Bride Comes to Yellow Sky" but falls short of being one of Crane's better Western stories because of stock situations and Larpent's unbelievable detachment and heavy-handed ironic monologues.

Suggested Reading

Monteiro, George. "Stephen Crane's 'Yellow Sky' Sequel." *Arizona Quarterly* 30 (1974): 119–26.

Moser, James Henry (1854–1913). Although he was almost twice Crane's age, the Canadian-born Moser was a close friend during the young writer's early years in New York. Moser was a landscape painter in oil and watercolors, an author of children's poetry, and an illustrator. With Frederick S. Church, he illustrated the first edition of Joel Chandler Harris's *Uncle Remus, His Songs and Sayings* (1881). Crane wrote one of his most exuberant inscriptions in a copy of *Maggie* (1893) to Moser, and an intimate and equally enthusiastic letter written by Crane to Moser in March 1895 survives in which Crane describes separate drinking bouts in a single day with the mayor of Galveston, Texas, and the editor of the *Galveston Daily News*.

Suggested Reading

Wertheim, Stanley. "Stephen Crane in Galveston: A New Letter." *Stephen Crane Studies* 5.1 (1996): 2–4.
Wertheim, Stanley, and Paul Sorrentino. *The Crane Log: A Documentary Life of Stephen Crane*. New York: Hall, 1994. 115–16, 128, 130.

"Mr. Binks' Day Off". Printed in the *New York Press* on 8 July 1894, this story was not collected in Crane's lifetime. Phil Binks, a bookkeeper in a New York City office, glimpses green grass in Madison Square Park from the cable car carrying him back to his Harlem apartment and yearns for a vacation in the country. Unable to afford more than a short trip, Binks and his wife and three children depart by train that Saturday afternoon to spend the weekend with the wife's aunt in the Ramapo hills of New Jersey. In the rural peace, they experience the contrast between their lives and those of the inhabitants of the little New Jersey village: "The sense of a city is battle. The Binkses were vaguely irritated and astonished at the placidity of this little town." Amid the fields and hills, they feel an Emersonian identification with "the mighty and mystic hymn of nature, whose melody is in each landscape." The children revel in mindless enjoyment, but as Binks and his wife sit on a fallen tree near the edge of a cliff at sunset, they experience a disquieting sense of the death of the day that is a portent of universal death. The sighing of the wind in the trees "was a wail telling the griefs, the pains of all ages," and "[t]he sun was dead." The bustle of city life has served to suppress the troubling reality that is ironically brought into consciousness through the tranquility of nature.

Suggested Reading

Johnson, Clarence O. "Mr. Binks Reads Emerson: Stephen Crane and Emerson's 'Nature'." *American Literary Realism 1870–1910* 15 (1982): 104–10.

"Mr. Crane of Havana". Printed in the *New York Journal* on 9 November 1898, this report from Havana criticizes the behavior of some of the American troops occupying Santiago who since the surrender have comported themselves in a rowdy and even indecent manner toward the populace. Gossip about the indecorous conduct of American troops in Santiago has caused apprehension in Havana, which has not yet been occupied. Crane realizes that individual soldiers do not fully comprehend that they are regarded as representatives of a nation and also that their peccadilloes have been exaggerated in the press and by rumor, but this is "what occurs in the lives of individuals, crowds, nations. A man spills some claret down his cuff and the report goes out that he has been drowned in a wine vat."

Mr. Slick. In the playlet "At Clancy's Wake," Slick is a caricature of the intrusive and insensitive investigative journalist, "attired in a suit of gray check [with] a red rose in his buttonhole."

"Mr. Stephen Crane on the New America". In this interview at Ravensbrook,* printed in the London *Outlook* on 4 February 1899, Crane denies that the people of the United States had imperialistic intentions in the Spanish-American War. "The idea would probably never have occurred to them had it not been for foreign statements and definitions." Cuba will be given its independence, although the common American soldier, who is the average man, resents the inadequate performance of the Cuban insurgents in the war. Crane expresses great skepticism about proposals made by the foreign minister of Czar Nicholas II of Russia to hold an international conference on the reduction of armaments and the preservation of peace. The conference was held in the Hague on 18 May 1899, with twenty-five nations represented.

Munroe, "Lily" Brandon (1870?–?). Alice Augusta Brandon, nicknamed Lily, was born in Brooklyn and in her childhood lived in London for about six years. She returned to New York at the age of ten or eleven and there attended public and private schools. In 1891 Lily Brandon married Hersey Munroe. They lived in Washington, D.C., and had a son but were divorced in the late 1890s. In the spring of 1892, while vacationing in Asbury Park, New Jersey, Lily was introduced to Crane by her mother-in-law at the Lake View Hotel, where Townley Crane's press bureau was located. Hersey Munroe, an employee of the Geological Survey, was often away on trips, and the couple was estranged. Crane and

Lily spent a great deal of time together in Asbury Park that summer. In the fall Crane took Lily to his artist friend David Ericson* to sit for a portrait, which was never completed. Crane gave Lily the manuscript of *Maggie* in 1894 or 1895. It was presumably destroyed by her jealous husband. Many letters were exchanged between the two, but only a few of Crane's letters to Lily have survived. Despite her subsequent disclaimers, it is apparent from the tenor of these letters that they had an intimate relationship. The last meeting between Crane and Lily Brandon Munroe occurred at the Library of Congress when he asked her to run off with him. She refused, and they never saw one another again. The date of this encounter is uncertain, but it was probably in April 1898, when Crane stopped in Washington on his way to Cuba. In 1901 Lily married George Frederick Smillie, chief engraver of the Bureau of Engravings and Printings, with whom she also had a son, Frederick Brandon Smillie, born in 1904.

Murphy, Edward (?–?). A filibustering sea captain operating out of Jacksonville, Florida, in the early years of the Cuban rebellion and during the Spanish-American War, Murphy was commander of the *Commodore* when it foundered on the morning of 2 January 1897. He is identified only as the captain in "The Open Boat," and in the story the "patient captain" retains a steadfast command of the dinghy despite his injured arm. Crane checked his factual details with Captain Murphy while writing "The Open Boat." In the 5 January 1897 issue of the *New York Press*, Murphy praised Crane's conduct throughout the *Commodore* disaster, stating that he behaved like a born sailor and calling him "a thoroughbred . . . and a brave man, too, with plenty of grit." Crane reciprocated in his syndicated report, "Stephen Crane's Own Story," declaring that "the captain gave orders amid the wildness of the breakers as clearly as if he had been on the quarter deck of a battleship."

"My Talk with 'Soldiers Six' ". The *Westminster Gazette* printed this McClure "letter" under the title "Some Interviews" as the fifth and sixth parts of its "With Greek and Turk" series on 14–15 June 1897. It was later syndicated in American newspapers. Perhaps referring to James Creelman's* celebrated interviews for the *New York World*, Crane comments that since many people have interviewed the king, the crown prince, and Colonel Constantine Smolenski on the reasons for the defeat of the Greek army, it might be worthwhile to ascertain the opinions of common soldiers. The soldiers Crane interviews in and around Lamia to a man blame the crown prince and the king for ordering premature retreats from Velestino and Domoko, with one expressing the dissenting opinion that defeat at Domoko was inevitable. An evzone exclaims that the royal family are "cowards. They are not Greeks. They are foreigners." The *Gazette*, apparently disturbed by the attacks on Queen Victoria's royal relatives and the revolutionary sentiments of some of the soldiers interviewed, appended a note to Crane's article observing that defeated soldiers invariably blame their commanders: "So it is natural that the Greek soldier who is conscious of having done his best should turn and upbraid the King and the Crown Prince. It does not follow that either is to blame, and it is certain that if they are in any respect to blame the burden laid upon them is infinitely heavier than they deserve."

"A Mystery of Heroism". Written in the spring of 1895, before the publication of *The Red Badge of Courage*, this episode of the Civil War, subtitled "A Detail of an American Battle" in its newspaper appearances, is closer to the war novel in tone and incident than the other stories collected in *The Little Regiment*. The story was first syndicated by Bacheller in various newspapers, generally in two parts, on 1 and 2 August 1895. It opens, as many of Crane's other war stories do, with an overview of a battlefield. An infantry regiment is sheltered in the bank of a hill on the top of which a Union artillery battery is engaged in a fierce duel with an opposing Confederate battery. Fred Collins of Company A decides to obtain water for himself and his comrades from a well near a house located across a meadow that is under heavy bombardment. After he receives permission from the captain of his company and the colonel of the regiment, who "could not for the life of them tell whether Collins wanted to go or whether he did not," he realizes that he has impulsively exposed himself to enormous danger. His pride and the jeers of his comrades will not allow him to back down. Realizing that he feels no fear, he wonders whether he is a hero but finally concludes that he is merely "an intruder in the land of fine deeds."

Collins is one of Crane's little men, a captive of his actions. Any illusions about heroism as an act of will or intention are dispelled when, after scampering across the meadow and flinging himself down near the well, "he was suddenly smitten with the terror. It came upon his heart like the grasp of claws." As he fills a canteen a shell bursts near the house, and he abandons the slow process of filling canteens and instead fills the well bucket and scurries back with it across the meadow. Like Henry Fleming fleeing from battle, he is in a state of "quaking apprehension. His cap was gone and his hair was riotous. His clothes made it appear that he had been dragged over the ground by the heels. He ran on." A wounded artillery lieutenant who had fallen in the meadow asks him for some of the water. Collins, "mad from the threats of destruction," ignores him and runs on. Reacting to another involuntary impulse, he veers around and tries to give the dying man a drink, but his shaking hands cause him to splash water over the officer's face. Upon his return to the regiment, Collins gives the bucket to "two genial, sky-larking young lieutenants." When one tries to drink, the other jostles his elbow, and the bucket falls. "The two lieutenants glared at each other. The bucket lay on the ground empty." Whether there had still been any water in it by the time Collins brought it back is left uncertain. As in *The Red Badge*, Crane in this story debunks the romantic conception of battle, exposes the unconscious nature of heroism, the absurdity of pride, and the essentially senseless nature of war. The final emptiness of the bucket constitutes the ultimate value of Collins's action.

Suggested Reading

Gargano, James. "Crane's 'A Mystery of Heroism': A Possible Source." *Modern Language Notes* 74 (January 1959): 22–23.

Monteiro, George. "After the *Red Badge*: Mysteries of Heroism, Death, and Burial in Stephen Crane's Fiction." *American Literary Realism 1870–1910* 28.1 (1995): 66–79.

Shaw, Mary N. "Apprehending the Mystery in Stephen Crane's 'A Mystery of Heroism.' " *CLA Journal* 39 (1995): 94–103.

Witherington, Paul. "Stephen Crane's 'A Mystery of Heroism': Some Redefinitions." *English Journal* 58 (February 1969): 201–4, 218.

N

"A naked woman and a dead dwarf". This poem was published posthumously in the April 1929 issue of the *Bookman*, but it seems to provide some justification for Harry Thurston Peck's dictum in the May 1895 issue of the magazine that Crane was "the Aubrey Beardsley of poetry" and to ally him with the perversity of the Decadent movement. The patently outrageous juxtaposition of the naked woman and the dead dwarf nevertheless highlights a theme recurrent in Crane's poems that women in the late nineteenth century were often constrained into oppressive role playing, "—the eternal clown— / a naked woman."

"Narrow Escape of the Three Friends". Printed in the *New York World* on 29 May 1898, this sketch relates an incident also mentioned in "War Memories" when the *World*'s dispatch tug *Three Friends* was accidentally rammed by the gunboat *Machias* (named after a town in Maine) while returning to Key West after a first visit to Haiti and Santo Domingo on or about 19 May. The correspondents are especially rueful about the incident because in their previous encounter with the *Machias*, they had given up their "last spud to the country's defenders" who had been on station for three weeks. Crane specifically recalls "splintered timbers," on the *Three Friends*, but Ralph Paine* remembers only that the *Machias* fired a warning shot that nicked the funnel of the tug.

Suggested Reading

Paine, Ralph. *Roads of Adventure*. Boston: Houghton Mifflin, 1922. 215.

Naturalism. A widespread literary philosophy in Europe and the United States in the latter part of the nineteenth and early twentieth centuries, naturalism is conventionally considered to be an extension or elaboration of realism.* As epitomized in the fiction and literary theory of William Dean Howells,* its leading American exponent, realism stressed "the truthful treatment of material" with a focus on the commonplace and a reliance on an objective view of human experience, to the extent that objectivity can be attained by a writer. Naturalists depicted the same world of everyday occurrences but emphasized the aberrant or abnormal within this milieu, centering on acts of violence and passion, the extraordinary, and the excessive. Under the influence of Charles Darwin's theory of evolution, which showed man to be a changing animal conditioned by environmental circumstances, Hippolyte Taine in his *History of English Literature* (1863–64; English translation, 1871) viewed the individual as a creature shaped by forces of heredity and environment beyond his control. Émile Zola, the foremost European exponent of literary naturalism, expounded his ideas in *The Experimental Novel* (1880; English translation, 1893). Zola regarded free will and moral choice as illusions and considered it the task of the novelist to place characters, often those with inherited temperamental deficiencies, in well-defined, usually adverse, social circumstances and to observe the effects of hereditary and social contingencies on their behavior as a scientist might observe the interaction of substances in a laboratory. Zola's ideas were embodied in a series of twenty novels collectively titled *Les Rougon-Macquart* (1871–93) that chronicled the degeneration of two branches of a working-class family plagued by drunkenness, sloth, and homicidal tendencies through five generations. In the United States the most prominent writers influenced by the central philosophical and stylistic conceptions of literary naturalism were Hamlin Garland,* Stephen Crane, Frank Norris,* and Theodore Dreiser in the late nineteenth and early twentieth centuries and, later, John Dos Passos, Richard Wright, James T. Farrell, and John Steinbeck. These writers developed their own distinctive artistic methods and individual philosophical approaches to the problems of the human condition; none of them was committed to a single-minded monistic determinism.

Crane's *Maggie: A Girl of the Streets* and *George's Mother* are often cited as the first exemplars of naturalistic situations and themes in American fiction. Both novelettes depict characters weak in personality development and apparently below average in intelligence who are at least in part destroyed by environmental conditions, specifically inadequate families, the pervasiveness of alcohol, and the corrosive influence of the slums. Crane is, however, not a simple determinist; false moral imperatives and personal illusions play as large a part in undermining Maggie and George Kelcey as external surroundings. Conversely, Henry Fleming in *The Red Badge of Courage* and the correspondent of "The Open Boat" survive because they develop the mental and physical resources to comprehend and struggle with the circumstances of the external world that threaten them. Crane is a naturalistic writer in that he emphasizes the importance of natural and social environments in deciding the destiny of men and women, but more often than not, sheer chance determines the outcome of any given situation in his fiction. He falls short of being a doctrinaire pessimistic determinist since he believes it at least possible for the individual, through effort and struggle, to acquire internal capabilities, a sense of selfhood that will ensure survival even in a universe of chaotic and contending social and natural forces. Stylistic devices such as Crane's impressionistic technique, ironic tone, and use of symbolism also contribute to the indeterminacy in his work.

Suggested Reading

Conder, John J. *Naturalism in American Fiction: The Classic Phase*. Lexington, Ky.: University of Kentucky Press, 1984.

Howard, June. *Form and History in American Literary Naturalism*. Chapel Hill: University of North Carolina Press, 1985.

Mitchell, Lee Clark. *Determined Fictions: American Literary Naturalism*. New York: Columbia University Press, 1989.

Pizer, Donald. *Realism and Naturalism in Nineteenth-Century American Literature*. Rev. ed. Carbondale: Southern Illinois University Press, 1984.

————. *The Theory and Practice of American Literary Naturalism*. Carbondale: Southern Illinois University Press, 1993.

"Nebraska's Bitter Fight for Life". The first of Crane's reports for the Bacheller newspaper syndicate on his trip to the West and Mexico, this account of the devastation in the northwestern counties of Nebraska caused by drought and wind storms in the summer of 1894 and blizzard conditions in early 1895 was widely circulated by the syndicate on 24 February 1895. Crane's report is to some extent a response to an alarming series of fifteen articles appearing in an Omaha newspaper in December that described widespread destitution in the state. Crane stresses that only certain counties were laid waste by the weather of the previous summer. He quotes at length from an interview with Governor Holcomb, who is anxious to assure prospective settlers that Nebraska remains a rich and fertile territory. Crane's dispatch is datelined from Eddyville, Dawson County, in the heart of the stricken area where he spent three days, from 6 to 8 February. A twenty-four-hour storm occurred on the first day. At Kearny, a likely model for the Fort Romper of "The Blue Hotel," the temperature ranged from fourteen to eighteen degrees below zero on the three days Crane stayed in the region. Crane viewed the storm from his unheated hotel room and vividly depicts the whirling snowflakes, "fleeing into the south, traversing as level a line as bullets, speeding like the wind." Throughout the piece, he illustrates the unyielding endurance and courage of the farmers who remain steadfast amid repeated disasters. When he asks a Lincoln County farmer who failed to receive relief supplies, "How did you get along?" the man replies laconically, "Don't git along, stranger. Who the hell told you I did get along?"

Suggested Reading

Slote, Bernice. "Stephen Crane in Nebraska." *Prairie Schooner* 43 (1969): 192–99.

Neeltje, William. The fatuous barber who shears off the locks of little Cora and the other children in "The Angel Child." Neeltje escapes any retribution for his foolishness. His foreign name and his vacuity make him, like Henry Johnson of "The Monster," a faceless outsider, but in "The Angel Child," the townspeople manifest benign curiosity and common sense rather than malevolence. As the grandfather of the Margate twins, representative of a more tolerant Whilomville, reflects, "this here Neel-te-gee, er whatever-his-name-is, is a plumb dumb ijit, but I don't see what's to be done, now that the kids is full-well cropped. I might go and burn his shop over his head but that wouldn't bring no hair back onto the kids."

Nell. A foil to Maggie in *Maggie: A Girl of the Streets*. Nell is a prostitute but "wore no jewelry and was painted with no apparent paint. She looked clear-eyed through the stares of the men." Unlike the passive, docile Maggie she is a "woman of brilliance and audacity." Nell has learned to manipulate men like Pete, and rather than being their prey, she preys on them. When Nell is present, Maggie is astounded by "an air of submission about her leonine Pete." In the penultimate chapter of the novelette, Nell abandons Pete as he has abandoned Maggie. She steals Pete's money as he lies in a drunken stupor in the corner of a saloon. " 'What a damn fool,' she said, and went."

Nell. The Bowery girl in "A Desertion" who finds her father dead in their tenement flat. In contrast to Nell, the "woman of brilliance and audacity" in *Maggie*, she is a hapless victim of her slum environment.

"New Invasion of Britain". Syndicated by McClure in a number of American newspapers on 9 May 1897, this humorous article was written in Greece and sent from Athens to London to be forwarded to the United States. Crane reflects "upon elasticity and point of view" in the employment of slang terms, specifically the imprecise British use of the epithet "bounder." The "bounders," he writes, "have taken London's attention by assault." Crane's definition of slang is a commentary on his own much-criticized tendency to employ it in his fiction: "Good slang is subtle and elusive. If there is a quick equivalent for a phrase it is not good slang, because good slang comes to fill a vacancy. It comes to cover some hole in the language."

["New York Boarding House Tale"]. An unfinished and untitled story or beginning of a novel about a New York City boardinghouse. The manuscript, in the Rare Book and Manuscript Library of Columbia University, was first published by R. W. Stallman and E. R. Hagemann in *The New York City Sketches of Stephen Crane* (1966). The editors believe that Crane here recasts his own experience and that the piece was written in the period 1893–94, but there is no reliable evidence that Crane ever lived in a boardinghouse, and this fragment was undoubtedly written in 1896 or later since it contains a reference to the Raines law, passed in 1896, which prohibited the sale of liquor on Sunday except by a hotel having at least ten bedrooms. The story deals with a number of boarders, including Thorpe, an old bookkeeper; Trixell, a clerk in a Broadway flower shop, the landlady and her beautiful daughter with whom all the young men in the boardinghouse are infatuated; and a mysterious young man who takes a room in the house and is also entranced by the landlady's daughter.

The New York Kid. A character in "The Wise Men," "The Five White Mice," and "A Man by the Name of Mud," the New York Kid illustrates the controlling role of chance in human affairs. In "The Five White Mice" he loses at dice and must take the winners to the circus. Consequently he remains sober when the other "kids," Benson and the 'Frisco Kid, become intoxicated and saves their lives in a potentially fatal confrontation with three Mexican grandees. In "The Wise Men," he and the 'Frisco Kid win an improbable bet that Pop, the aging bartender of the Café Colorado, can beat Freddie, the young proprietor of the Casa Verde, in a foot race.

"New York's Bicycle Speedway". This tongue-in-cheek report of the transformation of New York's Western Boulevard, slanting from Columbus Circle to Riverside Drive, into a bicycle path was syndicated in newspapers by McClure on 5 July 1896. The sudden popularity of bicycle riding transformed a once-quiet residential street into a thoroughfare for thousands of bicycles. Crane comments on the bicycle shops that sprang up on Columbus Circle and the new bicycle police who chase speeding "scorchers." Most interesting are the bloomers worn by young women riders in a "bewildering variety" of styles and colors. Bicycles and bloomers, he concludes, will assume economic and social importance in the future.

"A Night at the Millionaire's Club". A broadly satirical sketch published in the 21 April 1894 issue of *Truth** and linked to "An Experiment in Luxury," which appeared a little more than a week later in the *New York Press*. In this sketch, a dozen members of the Millionaire's Club are relaxing in the library, "where the decorations cost seventy-four dollars per square inch" and each chair occupied $2,000 worth of floor, listening to Chauncey Depew tell jokes at ten-minute intervals. The last one had smashed a $7,000 vase, "and Mr. Depew was hesitating. He had some doubt whether, after all, his jokes were worth that much commercially." At this point, a lackey announces the arrival of a group of visitors consisting of Ralph Waldo Emerson, Nathaniel Hawthorne, George Washington, and Alexander Hamilton. The members are puzzled as to who these people might be, and Erroll Van Dyck Strathmore gives an elaborately worded order to the servant to dismiss them. When the clock indicates that another ten minutes have passed, Mr. Depew begins to tell a new joke, but the members are asleep. In a burst of rage, "he hurled a champagne bottle at the clock and broke it to smithereens. Its cost was $4,675." Depew awakens William C. Whitney, and the two millionaires make a hasty departure from the club.

While keeping score for a poker game in 1896, Crane repeatedly scribbled his name and that of Chauncey M. Depew on a sheet of note paper. Depew (1834–28) was at this time president of the New York Central Railroad. He later became a U.S. senator. For Crane, Depew's rise to wealth and power was emblematic of a rapidly changing American social milieu about which he expressed concern in "An Experiment in Misery."

"Night Attacks on the Marines and a Brave Rescue". Datelined from Guantánamo on 4 July and printed in the *New York World* on 16 July 1898, this brief dispatch reminisces about events that occurred in the mid-June invasion of the Guantánamo Bay area by U.S. Marines. Crane centers on the matter-of-fact courage of volunteers from Company C, among them a man named Nolan, who rescued two groups of advance guards who were surrounded by Spanish guerrillas during a night attack on the marine encampment. Crane used the name Nolan in his dispatch "Regulars Get No Glory" and in his short story "The Price of the Harness."

Noguchi, Yone (1875–1947). Educated at Keio Gijuku University in Tokyo, where he was later professor of English literature, Noguchi spent three years in San Francisco from 1893 to 1896 living with Joaquin Miller, whose poetry he greatly admired. During this period, he published his first poems in the *Lark*, a little magazine edited by Gelett Burgess. Noguchi published many books of poetry and a noteworthy study of Japanese verse, *The Spirit of Japanese Poetry* (1934). The epigrammatic nature of Noguchi's poetry evoked comparison to Crane, and on 28 November 1896 he wrote to Crane: "I regret verily much, some uneducated (in poetry) people compares me with you—I don't like such comparison, as perhaps you don't."

Suggested Reading

Noguchi, Yone. *The Story of Yone Noguchi, Told by Himself.* London: Chatto & Windus, 1914.

Nolan, Jimmie. Crane's prototype of the regular army enlisted man in his Cuban War dispatch "Regulars Get No Glory" (as Michael Nolan) and in the short story "The Price of the Harness," where Nolan is shot and bleeds to death on the battlefield, unaware that he has been seriously wounded.

Norris, Frank (1870–1902). Benjamin Franklin Norris, Jr., was born in Chicago on 5 March 1870. The family moved to Oakland, California, in 1884 and to San Francisco the following year. Norris studied painting at the San Francisco Art Association and at the Académie Julian in Paris. He entered the University of California in 1890 and in 1891 published *Yvernelle*, a lengthy romantic poem that reflects his interest in medieval culture. After his parents divorced, Norris left the University of California without a degree. In 1894–95 he attended Harvard University where he experimented with realistic fiction in a writing class taught by Lewis E. Gates. In 1895 he traveled to South Africa as a correspondent for the *San Francisco Chronicle*. From 1896 to 1898 he wrote short stories, book reviews, and articles for the *Wave*,* a San Francisco literary weekly. His first novel, *Moran of the Lady Letty*, was serialized in the *Wave* in 1898. In the same year Norris left San Francisco for employment in New York City with *McClure's Magazine* and went to Cuba as a war correspondent for the McClure newspaper syndicate. *McTeague*, begun at Harvard, was published in 1899 and is Norris's earliest extended venture into naturalistic fiction. *Vandover and the Brute* (1914) was probably completed by 1900. *The Octopus* (1901) was intended as the first volume of a trilogy centered on the production, distribution, and consumption of Western wheat. The flow of wheat eastward is the background of the second volume, *The Pit* (1903), but before the serialization of this novel was concluded, Norris died of peritonitis following an appendectomy, and the third volume, to be entitled "The Wolf," was never written.

When Norris met Stephen Crane in mid-May 1898 on a two-day cruise in a dispatch boat, the *Three Friends*, off the coast of Cuba, he was already very familiar with Crane's work. He had written a trenchant parody of *Maggie*, *The Red Badge of Courage*, "The Open Boat," and Crane's poetry entitled "The Green Stone of Unrest" that had appeared in the *Wave* on 18 December 1897 under the general title of "Perverted Tales." A disparaging review of *Maggie* and *George's Mother*, "Stephen Crane's Stories of Life in the Slums" (*Wave*, 4 July 1896), long attributed to Norris, was probably written by John O'Hara Cosgrave, editor of the *Wave*. Cosgrave was most likely also author of another unflattering review essay, "Stephen Crane in London" (*Wave*, 18 September 1897), formerly thought to have been written by Norris.

Norris observed Crane closely during the cruise of the *Three Friends*, drawing an acerbic but accurate portrait of him as "the Young Personage" in a dispatch, "On the Cuban Blockade," that appeared posthumously in the *New York Evening Post*, 11 April 1914. He describes Crane as "wearing a pair of duck trousers grimed and fouled with all manner of pitch and grease and oil. His shirt was guiltless of collar or scarf, and was unbuttoned at the throat. His hair hung in ragged fringes over his eyes, his dress suit-case was across his lap and answered him for a desk. Between his heels he held a bottle of beer against the rolling of the boat, and when he drank was royally independent of a glass." Crane and Norris witnessed the disembarking of the troops at Daiquirí on 22 June, and both reported the slaughter and devastation at El Caney, described by Norris in "Comida: An Experience in Famine" (*Atlantic Monthly*, March 1899) and by Crane in "War Memories" (*Anglo-Saxon Review*, December 1899). Norris spent relatively little time in Cuba, and his reporting of the war was slight. He and Crane never met again. Although Crane's anarchistic worldview is fundamentally different from Norris's evolutionary theism, there are traces of Crane's influence in Norris's later fiction, especially in *The Octopus*, in which one of the main characters reflects on "the colossal indifference of nature."

Suggested Reading

McElrath, Joseph R., Jr. *Frank Norris and The Wave: A Bibliography*. New York: Garland, 1988. 11, 87–90, 140.
———. *Frank Norris Revisited*. New York: Twayne, 1992.
Wertheim, Stanley. "Frank Norris and Stephen Crane: Conviction and Uncertainty." *American Literary Realism 1870–1910* 24.1 (1991): 54–62.
———. "Frank Norris's 'The Green Stone of Unrest.' " *Frank Norris Studies*, no. 5 (Spring 1993): 5–8.

"Not Much of a Hero". This Sullivan County sketch, printed in the *New York Tribune* on 1 May 1892, is one of the first instances of Crane's employing the ambiguity and juxtaposition of contradictory perspectives that distinguish his best fiction. Crane examines the legends surrounding "Tom" Quick,* the famous Indian slayer who has become a hero to the boys of the area. In Quick's alleged biography, "He is a paragon of virtue and slaughters savages in a very high and exalted manner." A dispassionate study of Quick's exploits made by a Port Jervis writer who was asked to create a drama based on Quick's life demonstrates a historical reality that must be set against the legendary reality. After the ambush, shooting, and scalping of his father during the French and Indian War, Quick became a merciless avenger who slaughtered Indian men, women, and children in a cowardly manner. He was a killer rather than a fighter of Indians. Crane leaves the reader with three views of "Tom" Quick from which to make a choice:

> The deeds which are accredited to him may be fiction ones and he may have been one of those sturdy and bronzed woodsmen who cleared the path of civilization. Or the accounts may be true and he a monomaniac upon the subject of Indians as suggested by the dramatist. Or the accounts may be true and he a man whose hands were stained with unoffending blood, purely and simply a murderer.

Noxon, Frank (1873–1945). Crane's Delta Upsilon fraternity brother at Syracuse University,* Noxon was poet of the class of 1894 and published stories and poems in the *University Herald*. In 1892–93 he worked as a reporter for the *Syracuse Herald*. From 1893 to 1900 he was drama critic for the *Boston Record* and until 1905 served as managing editor of several other Boston and Providence newspapers. For most of his subsequent career, Noxon was secretary of the Railway Business Association. He was active in the Presbyterian church and wrote several books on religion and on government. Noxon's memoir, "The Real Stephen Crane," originally a letter to Max Herzberg, president of the Stephen Crane Society in Newark, was published in the January 1928 issue of the Chicago *Step-Ladder*. It is an extremely valuable reminiscence centering on Crane's college days and the Philistine banquet, at which Noxon was present.

O

O'Connor, Florinda ("Splutter"). The artist's model in *The Third Violet* who is hopelessly in love with Billie Hawker. According to Vincent Starrett in *Stephen Crane: A Bibliography* (Philadelphia: Centaur, 1923, 10), Crane wrote a story in Cuba entitled "The Cat's March" about Florinda in which she marries Pennoyer, another artist character in *The Third Violet*, "and settled down with him in a small town, where the respectable women gave her a bad time of it" (10). The manuscript of "The Cat's March" was supposedly destroyed.

"The Octopush". The humorous and the frightful are intermingled in "The Octopush," as in the other seriocomic Sullivan County tales. The story, printed in the *New York Tribune*, 10 July 1892, deals with the four city men of the tales journeying into the wilderness to go pickerel fishing in a pond that contains numerous tree stumps. They encounter a person designated only as "the individual" who demands that they hire him as a guide. He provides "a blunt-ended boat, painted a very light blue, with yellow finishings, in accordance with Sullivan aesthetics" and rows them out to four stumps, on each of which he deposits one of the fisherman, planting himself on a fifth stump. The fishermen enjoy a plentiful catch, but when evening comes and they wish to be taken back to shore, the individual, who has been drinking heavily all afternoon, waves "a great yellow-brown bottle" and exclaims, "You fellersh—hic—kin all go—hic—ter blazersh." As night descends with wind and cold, the four men become increasingly more uncomfortable on their stumps, which seem to be alive with creeping insects. Their importunities have no effect on the individual until, for no apparent reason, he suddenly springs up, paddles out to the little man's stump, and cowers at his feet. " 'Stump turned inter an octopush. I was a-settin' on his mouth,' he howled." The enraged little man begins to kick the drunken guide, but the others dissuade him. They in turn are rescued, and since the nearest house is four miles away spend the remainder of the night enduring the individual's ravings about the "octopush."

While the humor in this story does not go beyond the traditional anecdote of the city slicker outdone by the backwoodsman, imagery and themes distinctive in Crane's more serious work are apparent. The situation of four fishermen marooned on stumps in the middle of a pond is essentially comical but conveys the impression of a more abysmal and profound human isolation: "Suddenly it struck each that he was alone, separated from humanity by impassable gulfs." At night a threatening animism suffuses the bucolic ambiance of daylight. As in "An Experiment in Misery," there is a terrifying contrast between illusion and reality when a commonplace journey with a disreputable but harmless guide suggests a descent into death. The individual has "a voice from a tomb," and he speaks "in graveyard accents." As darkness falls, "[a] ghost-like mist came and hung upon the waters. The pond became a grave-yard. The grey tree trunks and dark logs turned to monuments and crypts."

Suggested Reading

Church, Joseph. "Reading, Writing, and the Risk of Entanglement in Crane's 'Octo-
    push.' " *Studies in Short Fiction* 29 (1992): 341–46.

Oglethorpe, Jem. A character in *The Third Violet*. Oglethorpe is a handsome and wealthy friend of the Fanhall family. Hawker believes he is his rival for Grace Fanhall's affections.

The Oiler. In "The Open Boat" Crane identifies the oiler only as "Billie," but in his news report, "Stephen Crane's Own Story,"* he gives his full name as William or Billy Higgins. The oiler was the only fit sailor in the dinghy since the captain had a broken arm and the cook and the correspondent were inexperienced seamen. In "The Open Boat" the oiler does the greater part of the rowing, and it is he who steers the frail craft over the parlous sea. Higgins drowned in the surf when the dinghy was beached. The *New York Herald* reported that he had been injured when he fell into the dinghy from the deck of the *Commodore*. According to the *Florida Times-Union*, he was struck in the head by the dinghy as it overturned, and in the *Boston Daily Globe* the steward, Charles Montgomery,* maintained that Higgins's injuries had been caused by striking his head against the oars. Striving for ambiguity, Crane gives no specific reason, either in his news report or the short story, why the oiler, "a wily surfman," drowns.

Suggested Reading

Billingslea, Oliver. "Why Does the Oiler Drown?: Perception and Cosmic Chill in 'The
    Open Boat.' " *American Literary Realism 1870–1910* 27.1 (1994): 23–41.
Going, William T. "William Higgins and Crane's 'The Open Boat': A Note about Fact
    and Fiction." *Papers on English Language and Literature* 1 (1965): 79–82.

" 'Ol' Bennet' and the Indians". First published in the December 1900 issue of *Cassell's Magazine*, this is the last story in the chronological progression of the Wyoming Valley tales. Solomon Bennet relates how his father, John ("'Ol' Bennet''), and his brother Andrew leave the shelter of Forty Fort to plow some of their outlying fields. They are abducted by a roving band of four Indians. Returning to their camp with the captives, the party joins forces with two other Indians who have a prisoner named Lebbeus Hammond and in time with another band of forty Indians commanded by a loyalist who recognize "'Ol' Bennet'' as their implacable foe and rejoice in his capture. The Indians split into two groups, with seven men guarding the prisoners while the loyalist takes the remainder of the band into the valley to harass the settlers. As they approach their camp, the seven Indians become careless, and while they doze, the captives rise up and slaughter five of them with their own weapons. The other two run away, and "'Ol' Bennet,'' Andrew, and Hammond gather up their weapons and begin the return journey to Forty Fort.

Old Man Crumford. A cowboy in "Twelve O'Clock'' who doubts that a clock could contain "a wooden bird a-tellin' ye th' time!''

"An Old Man Goes Wooing". The fifth and last of the "Irish Notes,'' this impressionistic sketch of life in an Irish fishing village appeared in the *Westminster Gazette* on 23 November 1897 and was collected in *Last Words*. "An Old Man Goes Wooing'' has more serious social undertones than the other local color episodes in this series. Mickey, a melancholy and emaciated old fisherman, enters the kitchen of an inn that he regards as a "paradise'' and asks for a tupenny glass of stout. He is treated rudely by the cook, a robust, strapping girl named Nora, "with her towering figure and bare brawny arms,'' and her mistress, the proprietress of the inn, but attention is lavished on a group of wealthy pig buyers feasting in the parlor. When the old man falls asleep after finishing his bottle, Nora drags him from his seat and thrusts him into the street. Avarice and the contempt of the younger generation for the old, benchmarks of a modern commercial spirit that rejects traditional Irish values, wear an especially ugly aspect in this bucolic setting.

Oliver, Arthur (?–?). A classmate of Crane at Lafayette College* and a New Jersey journalist who served his apprenticeship on the *Daily Spray*, Oliver operated an Asbury Park shore correspondence agency with Post Wheeler.* On 17 August 1892 Oliver and Crane witnessed the annual parade in Asbury Park of the United Order of Junior American Mechanics that resulted in Crane's *New York Tribune* report "Parades and Entertainments.'' In his memoir "Jersey Memories,'' published in the *Proceedings of the New Jersey Historical Society* 16 (1931): 454–63, Oliver relates the details and consequences of Crane's inauspicious report, but his implication that it may have been a primary factor in the defeat of the Republican party in the national election of 1892 is unwarranted. He also provides valuable insights into Crane's early literary philosophy. "You've got to feel the things you write if you want to make an impact on the world," Crane told Oliver.

"An Ominous Baby". With "A Great Mistake" and "A Dark-Brown Dog," this is one of three "Tommie" stories about Maggie's brother who dies in infancy in *Maggie: A Girl of the Streets*. A small child from the slums, "ominous" in that he constitutes a threat outside the Bowery environment, wanders into an upper-middle-class neighborhood. In rags and dragging a frayed piece of rope with nothing attached to it behind him, he encounters a well-dressed child playing with "a tiny fire engine painted brilliantly in crimson and gold." When the wealthy child refuses to allow him to play with it, the slum child wrests the toy from him and runs off with it. The contest between the children is expressed in terms of established right—" 'It's mine! It's mine!' cried the pretty child"—in conflict with desperate need—" 'I want it,' roared the wanderer." The social implications of this struggle were not lost on B. O Flower,* the crusading editor of the *Arena* in which this story was published in May 1894. In an accompanying editorial, Flower commented: "The little chap who had acquired the engine and who refused the gamin the pleasure of even playing with it for a few moments, places the toy behind him the moment there is danger. The 'divine right' of property, as practically held by modern plutocracy, finds a striking expression in the involuntary action of the little aristocrat, who risks a thrashing by placing himself between the toy and danger." Flower makes explicit the implication in Crane's story that violent conflict may be inevitable in a society that fails to rectify gross material inequalities. "An Ominous Baby" was first collected in the Heinemann edition of *The Open Boat and Other Stories*.

Suggested Reading

Hall, Dean. "Stephen Crane's Glittering Possession." *American Notes and Queries* 19 (1981): 147–48.

"On the Boardwalk". A feature article in the *New York Tribune*, 14 August 1892, with humorous depictions of the strollers on the boardwalk in Asbury Park, New Jersey, and typical summer guests: the businessman from the city and his family, the "summer girl," and the "golden youth." James A. Bradley,* the founder of Asbury Park, "has lots of sport with his ocean front and boardwalk. It amuses him and he likes it. It warms his heart to see the thousands of people tramping over his boards, helter-skeltering in his sand and diving into that ocean of the Lord's which is adjacent to the beach of James A. Bradley."

Suggested Reading

Elconin, Victor A. "Stephen Crane at Asbury Park." *American Literature* 20 (1948): 275–89.

LaFrance, Marston. "The Ironic Parallel in Stephen Crane's 1892 Newspaper Correspondence." *Studies in Short Fiction* 6 (1968): 101–3.

"One Dash—Horses". Syndicated by Bacheller, Johnson and Bacheller in American newspapers during the first week of January 1896, this story first appeared in England in the February issue of Heinemann's house organ, the *New Review*, under the title "Horses," probably because the slang use of the term "one dash," referring to a single throw of the dice, would not be understood by English readers. Crane's biographers have accepted "One Dash— Horses" as a more or less accurate account of an experience that Crane had in Mexico in the spring of 1895. In his fictionalized biography, Thomas Beer* provided the names Ramón Colorado for the fat bandit who led the gang that pursued Crane and Miguel Itorbide for Crane's guide, a name Beer probably adapted from the Hotel Iturbide in Mexico City where Crane stayed in the latter part of April. Corwin Knapp Linson* remembers Crane's giving him a vivid account of the episode on his return from Mexico, but in his expanded memoirs Linson was very much under the influence of Beer's book, where the narrative of events that ostensibly happened to Crane follows "One Dash—Horses" very closely.

When Crane was writing the story in September 1895, he told Willis Brook Hawkins* that he was "engaged at last on my personal troubles in Mexico," but whatever the factual basis of "One Dash—Horses" may be, it follows the plot line of stalking, pursuit, and rescue familiar in Western fiction. An Eastern ingenue named Richardson and his guide, José, take refuge for the night in the back room of an adobe tavern in the Mexican hinterlands. They are awakened by a noisy party in the main room of the inn and hear voices threatening to kill Richardson for his pistol, spurs, money, and saddles. The blanket that separates their shelter from the tavern, a symbol of veiled reality, is thrust aside, and the bandits enter the room and beat José. Richardson, his hand on a revolver concealed under his blanket, faces them down, and when a group of women arrive at the tavern, the bandits return to their party. At dawn Richardson and José sneak out of the adobe and mount their horses. They are immediately pursued by the gang, and there is a frantic chase until they are saved from the wild group of marauders by a detachment of *rurales*, the cavalry corps of the Mexican army that patrols the plains. Through his experience, Richardson, like other Crane initiates, learns that calmness and the detached assessment of reality are essential to survival in the social as well as the natural wilderness.

Suggested Reading

Beer, Thomas. *Stephen Crane: A Study in American Letters*. New York: Knopf, 1923. 116–17.

Linson, Corwin Knapp. *My Stephen Crane*. Ed. Edwin H. Cady. Syracuse: Syracuse University Press, 1958. 87–88.

"Only Mutilated by Bullets". A correction to the dispatch by Crane and Ernest W. McCready* in the 13 June 1898 *New York World*, "In the First Land Fight Four of Our Men Are Killed," that maintained that two of the marines killed in the fighting at Guantánamo Bay on 11–12 June had been mutilated by the enemy. Crane cites a surgeon's report that the wounds were caused by bullets only and concludes that there was "positively and distinctly no barbarity whatever." This report, which was originally sent to the *World*, appeared in the *Boston Globe* on 16 June and the *Philadelphia Press* the following day. The *World* did not publish it, perhaps because the editors were reluctant to refute a story they had prominently featured in their 15 June edition under the headline "Mutilation of Our Marines Too Horrible for Description" without further assurance that it was untrue.

"The Open Boat". Crane's finest short story and one of the masterworks of late nineteenth-century American literature, "The Open Boat" is, as its subtitle indicates, "A Tale Intended to Be after the Fact. Being the Experience of Four Men from the Sunk Steamer 'Commodore.' " Crane had recounted the circumstances leading to the sinking of the filibustering steamer *Commodore* in his 7 January 1897 *New York Press* report, "Stephen Crane's Own Story." "The Open Boat" is a fictional reworking of subsequent events that occurred in the thirty hours he spent with the ship's captain, the cook, and an oiler in a ten-foot dinghy on the Atlantic off the coast of Florida before the craft capsized in the surf at Daytona Beach on the morning of 3 January and William Higgins,* the oiler, drowned. Crane intended "The Open Boat" to be accurate, but rather than a simple rendition of experience, he strove for an interpretation that had broad social and metaphysical significance. The story appeared in the June 1897 issue of *Scribner's Magazine* and was collected in the American and English editions of *The Open Boat*.

The initial sentence, "None of them knew the color of the sky," evokes the question of the subjective nature reality central to the story. There is a detached narrator, but the focus is on perception and the individual and collective consciousness of the four men in the dinghy as they react to their ordeal. In danger of imminent death, their attention is fixated on the "walls of water," the "barbarously abrupt" waves sweeping toward them that threaten to swamp their frail craft. The men are relative strangers, but in the face of their common danger, they establish an unexpected community, a "subtle brotherhood" on the sea. "They were a captain, an oiler, a cook, and a correspondent, and they were friends—friends in a more curiously iron-bound degree than may be common." In the microcosmic world of the dinghy, a collaborative society with divided functions is established. The oiler and the correspondent row; the cook bails the invading seawater out of the boat; and the captain, whose arm is broken, mans the tiller. Counterpointed to and contrasted with this theme of human solidarity that is developed in early sections of the story is what seems to be an overwhelming stress on the isolation of the individual in an irrational physical and social universe at first perceived by the men in the dinghy as malevolently hostile, then as mindlessly hostile, and finally as indifferent to their existence. Through self-abnegation, courage, and endurance the men strive to find meaning in events that seem to deny the significance of human aspirations and efforts. Their illusions of an ordered, justifiable framework of being are revealed in a refrain used three times in the narrative that runs through the collective mind of the men in the dinghy when they are within sight of land: "If I am going to be drowned—if I am going to be drowned—if I am going to be drowned, why, in the name of the seven mad gods who rule the sea, was I allowed to come thus far and contemplate sand and trees?" The chaos of existence seems to be an "abominable injustice," a fundamental condition that they are powerless to either affirm or deny: "When it occurs to a man that nature does not regard him as important, and that she feels she would not maim the universe by disposing of him, he at first wishes to throw bricks at the temple, and he hates deeply the fact that there are no bricks and no temples." As if to underscore the insignificance of the individual, only the oiler is given a name, Billie. Confronted by this cosmic detachment, symbolized by a shark that menacingly circles the dinghy and "[a] high cold star on a winter's night," the correspondent recalls, somewhat inaccurately, the first stanza of Caroline Norton's "Bingen on the Rhine," a lachrymose ballad he had been required to memorize as a child in which "a soldier of the Legion lay dying in Algiers." The correspondent had never before empathized with the plight of this self-pitying sentimental hero: "It was less to him than the breaking of a pencil's point." Now even this bathetic jingle arouses in him a sense of the importance of human community.

Ironic circumstances seem to obviate this theme of mortal interindebtedness. In the fourth section, midpoint in the story, before night falls, individuals and groups of people are seen by the four men in the dinghy performing actions on the remote shore that they interpret as pertinent to their situation. Two men are walking aimlessly on the beach. They are joined by a third man who waves a coat around his head as if it were a signal, but the men in the boat finally apprehend that he is "just playing." A hotel omnibus crawling along the beach is first perceived to be a lifeboat and then seems to be collecting a rescue crew. No help is forthcoming from the people on the shore, who apparently are merely involved in the recreational activities of a resort. A "house of refuge" purportedly north of the Mosquito Inlet Light never materializes. In the morning the beach is deserted, and only a few cottages on the dunes with a tall white windmill rearing above them are visible. The men realize that they will have to attempt a run through the surf without assistance:

> The correspondent wondered if none ever ascended the tall wind-tower, and if then they never looked seaward. This tower was a giant, standing with its back to the plight of the ants. It represented in a degree, to the correspondent, the serenity of nature amid the struggles of the individual—nature in the wind, and nature in the vision of men. She did not seem cruel to him then, nor beneficent, nor treacherous, nor wise. But she was indifferent, flatly indifferent.

Chance and "the unconcern of the universe" are the dominant motifs in the concluding section of "The Open Boat." When the dinghy is swamped in the surf, the oiler swims "strongly and rapidly" toward the shore. The cook floats on his back and paddles toward the beach with one of the oars. The captain is saved by clinging to the keel of the dinghy with his one good hand, and the correspondent is miraculously hurled over the boat to safety by a huge wave and lands far beyond it in water that reaches only to his waist. Perversely, for reasons Crane purposefully leaves unexplained, the oiler, who is the only competent sailor in the dinghy, drowns, a circumstance that denies the simplistic Darwinian doctrine of the survival of the fittest as well as the lifesaving efficacy of the bond of human brotherhood. Despite the cooperative union established in the dinghy, each man must swim to shore alone when the moment of crises comes. A would-be rescuer who appears to have a halo around his head and who "shone like a saint" sheds his clothing and dashes into the surf to proffer assistance, but he is powerless to prevent the final tragedy. In the death of the oiler is symbolized not only the indifference of nature but the ultimate isolation of man.

There is thematic development in "The Open Boat" that is evident in the growth of perception from the first statement that "[n]one of them knew the color of the sky" to the conclusion that the surviving men "felt that they could then be interpreters." But this ambiguous statement seems to refer only to their increased understanding of perceptual realities and the problematic nature of interpretation; it does not confer any particular meaning on their experience or imply that human beings can achieve a rational understanding of their fate.

Suggested Reading

Buitenhuis, Peter. "The Essentials of Life: 'The Open Boat' as Existentialist Fiction."
    Modern Fiction Studies 5 (1959): 243–50.
Colvert, James B. "Style and Meaning in Stephen Crane's 'The Open Boat.' " *Texas
    Studies in English* 37 (1958): 34–45.
Halliburton, David. *The Color of the Sky: A Study of Stephen Crane*. Cambridge: Cam-
    bridge University Press, 1989. 236–54.
Marcus, Mordecai. "The Three-Fold View of Nature in 'The Open Boat.' " *Philological
    Quarterly* 61 (1962): 511–15.
Metress, Christopher. "From Indifference to Anxiety: Knowledge and the Reader in 'The
    Open Boat.' " *Studies in Short Fiction* 28 (1991): 47–53.
Rath, Sura P., and Mary Neff Shaw. "The Dialogic Narrative of 'The Open Boat.' "
    College Literature 18.2 (1991): 94–106.

The Open Boat. Published by Doubleday & McClure in April 1898, the American edition of this volume of short stories is titled *The Open Boat and Other Tales of Adventure*. The book has a dedication, "To the Late William Higgins and to Captain Edward Murphy and Steward C. B. Montgomery of the Sunk Steamer Commodore." Contents: "The Open Boat"; "A Man and Some Others"; "One Dash—Horses"; "Flanagan and His Short Filibustering Adventure''; ''The Bride Comes to Yellow Sky''; ''The Wise Men''; ''Death and the Child''; and ''The Five White Mice.'' The English edition, published simultaneously with the American by William Heinemann, is titled *The Open Boat and Other Stories* and bears the same dedication. The stories of the American edition appear under the general heading ''Minor Conflicts.'' There is an added section of New York City (and Asbury Park) stories under the heading ''Midnight Sketches'' that includes ''An Experiment in Misery''; ''The Men in the Storm''; ''The Duel That Was Not Fought''; ''An Ominous Baby''; ''A Great Mistake''; ''An Eloquence of Grief''; ''The Auction''; ''The Pace of Youth''; and ''A Detail.''

''Opium's Varied Dreams''. This study of the opium dens of New York City, and especially those in the Tenderloin district, was widely circulated under different headlines in newspapers by the McClure syndicate on 17 May 1896. Crane's detailed descriptions of the dens, how the opium habit is contracted, the instruments used in the preparation of opium, the manner in which the drug is ingested, and its effects upon sensation smokers and addicts, or ''hop fiends,'' gave rise to unwarranted speculation that he was himself addicted to the drug. On 11 October 1896, the *New York Journal* reported that the police of the Tenderloin district threatened to prosecute Crane for maintaining an opium den in his apartment if he testified on behalf of Dora Clark* in her court action for false arrest against patrolman Charles Becker.* Crane responded that while he had an opium layout in his rooms, it was tacked to a plaque on the wall as a souvenir of his research for ''Opium's Varied Dreams.'' Crane's report is notable not only for its detailed descriptions of the milieu of opium addiction but also for its empathy with ''the people of the Tenderloin, they who are at once supersensitive and hopeless, the people who think more upon death and the mysteries of life, the chances of the hereafter, than any other class, educated or uneducated.''

The O'Ruddy. Burdened by debt and illness, Crane wrote his final novel, *The O'Ruddy*, in the last year of his life. His motives were primarily pecuniary. The publication of a popular historical romance, he believed, would provide the money he needed to work with composure on the kind of finely crafted fiction— great stories such as ''The Monster,'' ''The Bride Comes to Yellow Sky, ''Death and the Child,'' and ''The Blue Hotel''—that he wrote shortly after he settled in England and before his financial burdens forced him into hack work. In the hope of a quick financial return, Crane abandoned the laborious research necessary for a novel on the Revolutionary War he was writing under contract with Frederick A. Stokes and in the fall of 1899 began work on *The O'Ruddy*. The serious lung hemorrhage he suffered in late December slowed progress on the work, and after further hemorrhages in April 1900 he wrote virtually nothing more, having completed twenty-five chapters, or over three-quarters of the novel. Even on his deathbed he continued to dictate notes to Cora.

Robert Barr* read the manuscript of *The O'Ruddy* at Dover a few days before the Cranes crossed the English Channel to Calais on the final journey to Bad-enweiler. Crane told him that he intended the book to end at Brede Place,* where it had been written, and Barr reluctantly agreed to finish the novel. After Crane's death, he had second thoughts about his commitment and suggested that Stewart Edward White or Cora herself undertake the task. H. B. Marriott Watson* and Rudyard Kipling declined the project, and A.E.W. Mason* held the manuscript for two years without working on it. Finally, in the autumn of 1902, James B. Pinker and Barr reached a mutually satisfactory understanding, but terms were made final only in June 1903, when Stokes and William Howe Crane signed a contract that incorporated Stokes's arrangement with Barr to finish the book. Barr wrote the last eight of the thirty-three chapters, and after considerable wrangling over his payment, the way was finally clear for *The O'Ruddy* to appear. Copyright deposit in the Library of Congress was made on 2 November 1903 and publication announced in *Publishers' Weekly* on 5 December. A variant and shortened version of the novel was serialized in *The Idler* in seven installments in 1904. *The O'Ruddy* was published in book form in England in July.

In her memoir, "Stephen Crane at Brede," Edith Richie Jones* suggested that one purpose of the Cranes' short trip to Ireland in October 1899 was to gather local color for *The O'Ruddy*, but only the opening paragraphs of the novel are set in Ireland. *The O'Ruddy* is simultaneously a swashbuckling romantic novel in the manner of Alexander Dumas and Sir Walter Scott and a burlesque caricature of that genre. In development it is a picaresque novel in the tradition of Cervantes' *Don Quixote* and Le Sage's *Gil Blas*, describing the adventures in England of the scion of a family of Irish brigands and pirates from Glandore in County Cork who have assumed the trappings of aristocracy. The main character, Thomas O'Ruddy, known simply as The O'Ruddy, is enjoined by his dying father to travel to England to return some valuable papers given to him by the Earl of Westport during a military campaign in France in return for his lending the earl "a pair of breeches or he would have gone bare." The O'Ruddy's father does not know the import of the papers because he is illiterate, and since The O'Ruddy disdains to read them, the reader is also not informed of their contents or the actual reason that the earl gave them to The O'Ruddy's father until well into the story.

In obedience to his father's wishes, The O'Ruddy sails from Cobh to Bristol, where at an inn, in one of the many incredible coincidences of the novel, he encounters Lord Strepp, the son of the Earl of Westport, and two of his friends, Colonel Royale and Forister, who are recounting their version of the story of how the earl lost his papers. When the colonel maintains that the noble earl "found it necessary, after fording a stream, to hang his breeches on a bush to dry" when "a certain blackguard of a wild Irishman in the corps" came along and stole them, The O'Ruddy gives the lie to this account and as a matter of course is challenged to a duel by the colonel. When Forister derides the Irish as savages, The O'Ruddy kicks him into the courtyard of the inn, making a duel with Forister inevitable as well. Searching for a second to represent him for his duel with Colonel Royale, The O'Ruddy acquires his Sancho Panza in the person of Paddy, a red-haired Irish rogue whom he finds begging at the roadside. In the duel he wounds Royale slightly and returns triumphant to the inn, only to discover that the valuable papers have disappeared from his luggage. The O'Ruddy suspects Forister of the theft. Forister has fled to Bath, and The O'Ruddy sets out in pursuit, leaving Paddy behind. On the road he is challenged by Jem Bottles, an inept highwayman with pretensions to being a celebrated knight of the road, who is enlisted as another follower of The O'Ruddy. The two men proceed to Bath, where they find that Forister has returned to Bristol. They double back and at an inn five miles from Bristol find Forister, who has been barricaded in his room by Paddy, but The O'Ruddy discovers that Forister does not have his papers. Returning to Bristol, the O'Ruddy has an interview with the ailing Earl of Westport, who denies that the papers have any value at all and denounces The O'Ruddy as a scoundrel who is intent upon ruining him. In a flash of insight, the O'Ruddy realizes that it is the earl himself who has stolen the papers. An altercation ensues in which the papers fall out of the earl's bedding. In a noble gesture, The O'Ruddy turns them over to the earl's daughter, Lady Mary, with whom he has fallen in love.

The O'Ruddy gains great reputation when, in his duel with Forister, he seriously wounds the evil little man who is reputed to be the finest swordsman in England. All fear him except the countess, the wife of the Earl of Westport, who chases him around a table of the inn, using language "which would not at all suit the pages of my true and virtuous chronicle; but indeed it was no worse than I often heard afterward from the great ladies of the time." When Lady Mary is taken to London by her family, The O'Ruddy sets out on a new quest: "The first had been after my papers. The second was after my love." Within a few miles of Bath he is reunited with Paddy and Jem Bottles. The highwayman has robbed the Earl of Westport's coach, and with other spoils has taken the papers from Lady Mary, so they are in The O'Ruddy's possession once again.

The second part of the novel is set primarily in London, where The O'Ruddy, assisted by his faithful henchmen and a pedantic, comically Machiavellian old scientist named Doctor Chord, experiences many adventures in his pursuit of Lady Mary. Through various machinations, he gains entrance into the Earl of Westport's garden, where in an interview with Lady Mary he learns that his love for her is reciprocated. The O'Ruddy plots with Dr. Chord to gain entrance into the Westport mansion itself in order to advance his courtship of Lady Mary. He does not know that the treacherous Doctor Chord is in the employ of the earl, who is plotting to lay hands on the papers once again. Having suborned Strammers, the earl's gardener, The O'Ruddy and his followers are admitted for a second time to the earl's grounds. No sooner are they beyond the gate when the earl's servants, accompanied by the earl, the countess, and Doctor Chord, attack Paddy and Jem Bottles. The O'Ruddy eludes them and finds his way to

Lady Mary's room, where he lays the papers at her feet and learns from her that they are title deeds to great estates in Sussex. The earl, afraid that he would be captured and held for ransom, had given them into the care of The O'Ruddy's father, who "always intended to come over to England and return the papers to the earl; but he got lazy-like, by sitting at his own fireside, and seldom went farther abroad than to the house of the priest; but his last injunctions to me were to see that the earl got his papers, and indeed he would have had them long since if he had but treated me like the son of an old friend." Lady Mary suggests that for the time being, The O'Ruddy keep the papers and consult an attorney as to his rights. She also proposes a strategy that will lead to the union of the two lovers, advising The O'Ruddy to take possession of the earl's estate at Brede Place and surrender the papers to her father only when he consents to allow them to marry. The attorney counsels The O'Ruddy that while he may have no legal right to Brede Place, possession is nine points of the law. Accompanied by Paddy, Jem Bottles, and Father Donovan, a priest from Glandore on his way to Rome, whom he has encountered in a London church, The O'Ruddy proceeds to Rye, where he enlists a group of local men to aid him in the occupation of Brede Place. Once in the manor house, they utilize an underground tunnel formerly used by smugglers to entrap a group of the earl's men led by Lord Strepp who are attempting to retake the manor house. Thoroughly defeated, the earl and the countess agree to trade the hand of their daughter for the papers, and The O'Ruddy and Lady Mary are married by Father Donovan in the chapel of Brede Place.

The spontaneity, zest, sardonic humor, and lively dialogue of *The O'Ruddy* belie the circumstances under which it was written. Despite some repetitiousness, the plot is fast paced and surprisingly well integrated, notwithstanding its episodic structure. Generally neglected by Crane's critics, the novel displays the satiric acumen of his more serious works of fiction in stripping away the facade of egotism, pretentiousness, vanity, and hypocrisy of characters on every level of society. If Crane had been granted the time and leisure to complete and polish the novel, it might have marked a new phase of his career as a masterful comedic storyteller and ironist.

Suggested Reading

Bradshaw, James Stanford. "Completing Crane's *The O'Ruddy*: A New Note." *ANQ* 3 (1990): 174–78.
Knapp, Bettina. *Stephen Crane*. New York: Ungar, 1987. 121–26.
Levenson, J. C. Introduction to *The O'Ruddy*. Charlottesville: University Press of Virginia, 1971. xiii–lxxiv. Vol. 4 of *The Works of Stephen Crane*. Ed. Fredson Bowers. 10 vols. 1969–76.

O'Ruddy, Thomas. Referred to only once as Tom, the eponymous hero and narrator of *The O'Ruddy* is an inconsistently developed character reminiscent of the picaroons of Henry Fielding's *Tom Jones* and Tobias Smollett's *Roderick*

Random. A swashbuckling Irish lad, The O'Ruddy is often witty, sometimes obtuse, diversely a clown and a sage. Like Huckleberry Finn, his radical innocence gives him a neoteric perspective that allows him to be, unknown to himself, a perceptive critic of the foibles of his society.

"Ouida's Masterpiece". Ouida was the pseudonym of the English writer Marie Louise de la Ramé (1839–1908). She lived in Italy from 1870. Many of her forty-five novels, which include *Under Two Flags* (1867) and *Moths* (1880), deal with romantic exploits, but she also wrote the children's classic *A Dog of Flanders* (1872). *Under Two Flags* was reissued in a two-volume illustrated edition in 1896, and Crane's appreciation of the book appeared in the January 1897 *Book Buyer*. Apart from his appraisal of Harold Frederic's* work, this is the only book review Crane wrote, and it is doubly curious that he did so since Ouida was an unabashedly sentimental writer specializing in fast-paced stories of English upper-class and military life that stressed adventures and intrigues. In *Under Two Flags*, Crane writes, the characters "abandon themselves to virtue and heroism as the martyrs abandoned themselves to flames." These would appear to be the sentiments that Crane usually ridiculed, but he admired Ouida's stress on personal integrity and her ideal of sacrifice, although he confesses that he finds the flawed secondary character in her book more satisfying than the impeccable heroine.

"Our Sad Need of Diplomats". In this piece printed in the *New York Journal* on 17 November 1898, Crane continues his discussion of the inadequacies of the American military commissions in Cuba supervising the Spanish evacuation that he began in his 8 November *Journal* article, " 'You Must!'—'We Can't!' " Crane believes the inefficiency of the Evacuation Commission is based on its unwieldy size and the Spanish policy of delay. Colonel Frank J. Hecker, who is in charge of selecting camp sites for the occupying American army, is exceptional in that he usually carries out what he proposes to do. Crane feels that the subordinate officer, the "wheel horse," invariably is responsible for whatever is accomplished but never receives the slightest credit for anything.

P

"The Pace of Youth". Crane's friend, the painter and illustrator Corwin Knapp Linson,* recalls that this story was composed in the spring of 1893, when Crane still lived in the boardinghouse on Avenue A in Manhattan that he called the Pendennis Club. Bacheller, Johnson and Bacheller syndicated it in two parts in various newspapers on 17–18 and 18–19 January 1895. It was collected in the English edition of *The Open Boat.* The setting of "The Pace of Youth" is an amusement park in a resort reminiscent of Asbury Park, New Jersey, and the plot of the story revolves around the stock situation of a father's attempting to thwart a romance between his daughter and a young man of whom he disapproves. John Stimson owns a carousel, very much like the one described by Crane in his Asbury Park sketch "Joys of Seaside Life" (*New York Tribune,* 17 June 1892). His daughter, Lizzie, works as his cashier, and Frank, her lover, sorts and affixes the iron and brass rings on the contrivance. Stimson is an avaricious little man who wants to end the flirtation between Lizzie and Frank, at least in part because he is afraid of losing his daughter's unpaid services. Despite his vigilance, the lovers find ways to communicate and to meet. Finally they elope in a buggy drawn by a high-spirited young horse while Stimson pursues them in a rented hack drawn by an aged horse that is quickly outpaced. There is a seriocomic, universalized ending to the story as Stimson comes to realize that "his whole expedition was the tottering of an old man upon the trail of birds" and that the vehicle pursued in vain "was youth, with youth's pace, it was swift-flying with the hope of dreams." The highway on which the pursuit is conducted seems to symbolize the road of life. As the hackman gives up the chase, "Stimson made a gesture of acquiescence, rage, despair." He realizes that he has been "defied by the universe."

Suggested Reading

Schellhorn, G. C. "Stephen Crane's 'The Pace of Youth.' " *Arizona Quarterly* 25 (1969): 334–42.

Paddy. In *The O'Ruddy* Paddy is the servant of the protagonist. A resourceful, picaresque rogue, he shares in the defeats and the achievements of his master and with unconscious wit offers discerning commentary on the personal foibles of the other characters in the novel and the social, political, and religious questions of the time.

Page, Walter Hines (1855–1918). A graduate of Randolph-Macon College in Ashland, Virginia, Page went on to graduate work at Johns Hopkins University. He was a freelance writer for a number of newspapers and held various editorial positions. From 1891 to 1895 he was editor of the *Forum*. In 1895 Page became literary adviser and associate editor of the *Atlantic Monthly*. He functioned as editor of the magazine from mid-1896, although Horace Scudder retained the title for two more years. Page was named sixth editor of the *Atlantic* in 1898, but in December 1899 he resigned the position and formed a partnership with Frank Doubleday in the publishing firm of Doubleday, Page and Company. In the following year he founded *The World's Work*, a magazine of politics and business that he edited until 1913, when he became U.S. ambassador to Britain.

   None of Crane's works appeared in the *Atlantic Monthly*. On 2 March 1896 Page asked Crane for a contribution to the magazine. Crane sent "An Indiana Campaign" and asked Hitchcock to forward the manuscript of *The Third Violet* to Page, who rejected them both. Page also rejected "The Blue Hotel" when Reynolds submitted it to the *Atlantic* in March 1898; what he really wanted from Crane was a group of stories or a novel that could be published by Houghton Mifflin & Company, the sponsor of the *Atlantic*, after appearing in the magazine.

Paine, Ralph Delahaye (1871–1925). Paine began his career as a journalist in Florida, where his father was a clergyman. He was a graduate of Yale and received an M.A. from the University of New Hampshire. Paine joined the staff of the *Philadelphia Press* in 1894 and served as its correspondent during the Cuban War and the Boxer rebellion. He headed the *New York Herald*'s campaign against the beef trust in 1902 and served as a special correspondent with the Allied naval forces in World War I. After a brief stint as managing editor of the *New York Telegraph*, Paine embarked on a prolific career as a novelist and author of books dealing with ships and sailors. He was also a frequent contributor of articles and stories to magazines. His *Roads of Adventure* (1922) is a lively, subjective account of his experiences in three wars.

   Paine first met Stephen Crane at Asbury Park, New Jersey, where during summer vacations both reported shore news for metropolitan newspapers. They encountered one another again in Jacksonville, Florida, in December 1896. Unlike Crane, who sailed on the ill-fated *Commodore*, Paine was successful in reaching Cuba aboard the *Three Friends*, which in 1898 became a dispatch boat shared at times by the *New York World*, the *Philadelphia Press*, and the *New York Herald*. Paine vividly recalls Crane's reading his manuscript of "The Open Boat" to the *Commodore*'s captain, Edward Murphy,* in a Jacksonville restaurant in February 1897 to verify that it was indeed, "After the Fact," as Crane stipulated in the subtitle of the story. In the spring of 1898, Paine and Crane were among the reporters who spent monotonous days lounging in the lobby of the Key West Hotel while waiting for the Cuban War to begin. In mid-May, with Harry Brown of the *Herald*, they were together aboard the *Three Friends* visiting Haiti and Santo Domingo and pursuing the American fleet to ascertain news of the impending war. In *Roads of Adventure*, Paine offers a valuable account of Crane's activities during the Guantánamo Bay invasion in June, and one of Paine's own experiences is amusingly fictionalized in Crane's story, "The Lone Charge of William D. Perkins."

Suggested Reading

Paine, Ralph D. *Roads of Adventure*. Boston: Houghton Mifflin, 1922. 162–75, 192–93, 221–28, 236–38, 243–46, 251–56.

"Pando Hurrying to Santiago". This short cable, datelined from Playa Del Este on 30 June, appeared in the *New York World* on 1 July 1898. Crane reports on rumors that Spanish General Luis Manuel de Pando y Sanchez is advancing toward Santiago with 8,400 men. Cubans doubt that he can reinforce the Spanish garrison in the city, but the number of insurgents standing between his forces and Santiago is unknown.

"Parades and Entertainments". This brief, unsigned report on the 1892 annual American Day parade of the Junior Order of United American Mechanics (JOUAM), a nativist social organization, in Asbury Park, New Jersey, resulted in a breach between Crane and his brother Townley and earned Crane the enmity of the *New York Tribune*. While Townley was temporarily absent, Crane covered the parade for the New Jersey Coast News Bureau, of which Townley was president and he was secretary. Crane's report appeared in the *Tribune* on 21 August under the series headline "On the New-Jersey Coast." It described the marchers as "the most awkward, ungainly, uncut and uncarved procession that ever raised clouds of dust on sun-beaten streets. . . . Their clothes fitted them illy, for the most part, and they had no ideas of marching. They merely plodded along, not seeming quite to understand, stolid, unconcerned and, in a certain sense, dignified—a pace and a bearing emblematic of their lives." Crane satirized the middle-class residents of Asbury Park and the summer visitors even more bitterly than their working-class counterparts. "Asbury Park," he wrote, "creates nothing. It does not make; it merely amuses." The Asbury Park hotel and shop owner "is a man to whom a dollar, when held close to his eye, often shuts out any impression he may have had that other people possess rights. He is apt to consider that men and women, especially city men and women, were created to be mulcted by him." Nevertheless, the indignation that Crane's piece aroused did not come from the expected sources in Asbury Park. It was the JOUAM that protested in a letter to the *Tribune* printed on 24 August, and the *Tribune* apologized. Whitelaw Reid, the owner of the newspaper, was the Republican vice-presidential nominee, and opposition papers took political advantage of Crane's gaffe. Both Townley and Stephen were fired by the *Tribune* for this indiscretion, but Townley was later rehired. None of Crane's work appeared in the newspaper after 1892, and the *Tribune* became his nemesis. The *Tribune* condemned *The Black Riders*, *The Red Badge*, *Maggie*, and *George's Mother*, but the paper's reviews of some later Crane books were more favorable.

Suggested Reading

Gullason, Thomas A. "Stephen Crane and the *New York Tribune*: A Case Reopened." *Resources for American Literary Study* 22 (1996): 182–86.
Oliver, Arthur. "Jersey Memories—Stephen Crane." *Proceedings of the New Jersey Historical Society* 16 (1931): 454–63.
Johnson, Willis Fletcher. "The Launching of Stephen Crane." *Literary Digest International Book Review* 4 (1926): 288–90.
Wertheim, Stanley, and Paul Sorrentino. *The Crane Log: A Documentary Life of Stephen Crane*. New York: Hall, 1994. 77–80.

Parker, Alton Brooks (1852–1926). A graduate of Albany Law School, Parker practiced in Kingston, New York, and served as a judge in several divisions of the New York Supreme Court. In 1897 he was elected chief justice of the New York State Court of Appeals. In 1904 Parker was chosen as the presidential candidate of the Democratic party. He lost the election to Theodore Roosevelt* and spent the remainder of his career practicing law in New York City. Parker was American executor of Harold Frederic's* will and administered the proceeds of his American copyrights and royalties, which were left to Kate Lyon* and her children. Cora Crane corresponded with Parker over the possible adoption of Barry Frederic under American law, which did not provide for adoption in another country. Parker drafted an amendment to the statute to be introduced into the Senate, but nothing came of plan since Kate Lyon decided to keep her children, and the Cranes' matrimonial status would probably have posed insuperable difficulties.

Parker, Walter (?–?). Shortly after the blockade of Havana was lifted in mid-August 1898, Crane slipped into the city illegally, evading the Spanish authorities who had temporarily imprisoned some of his fellow journalists. With other correspondents, including Walter Parker of the *New Orleans Times Democrat*, he stopped for a time at the Hotel Pasaje adjoining his center of operations, the

American Bar. Parker's eight-page typescript, "Re: Stephen Crane," in the H. L. Mencken Collection of the New York Public Library, is the only extended eyewitness account of Crane's experiences in Havana, where he reported the final phases of the Cuban War for the *New York Journal*. Parker's memoir describes incidents of Crane's life in Havana so dramatic that they might be thought apocryphal were it not for the verisimilitude with which they are narrated, especially those concerning Crane's involvement with a volatile Cuban he putatively saved from drowning in the wreck of the *Commodore*. There are also some startling disclosures about the possible biographical sources of the "Intrigue" poems that Crane wrote in Havana and later incorporated into *War Is Kind*. Parker's memoir is printed by Stanley Wertheim in "Stephen Crane Remembered," *Studies in American Fiction* 4 (1976): 45–64.

Parkin, Thomas (1845–?). A local magistrate in Hastings, Sussex, and author of numerous essays on ornithological subjects, Parkin was an ardent "grangerizer," a bibliophile who extra-illustrates books. The Cranes occasionally visited Parkin's estate, Fairseat, High Wickham, and on 2 February 1900 Parkin gave a luncheon in Crane's honor. Crane sent Parkin an inscribed copy of *George's Mother* (now in the Berg Collection of the New York Public Library) in which Parkin inserted clippings from local newspapers that provide details of Crane's activities in his last months at Brede Place.*

Pawling, Sidney Southgate (1862–1922). Orphaned while an infant, Pawling was raised by his uncle, Charles Edward Mudie, founder of Mudie's library, and worked in his uncle's book trade until 1893, when he became a silent partner of William Heinemann. It was Pawling who accepted Joseph Conrad's* *The Nigger of the "Narcissus"* for publication and established the firm's first contact with Crane after Heinemann had acquired English rights to *The Red Badge of Courage* from D. Appleton & Company. Crane was so pleased with Pawling's praise for the "actuality—virility & literary distinction" of the novel that he copied out Pawling's letter in his own hand. Crane met Conrad at a luncheon arranged by Pawling on 15 October 1897.

Pease Family. Edward and Margery Pease and their children lived at the Pendicle in Limpsfield, Surrey, a mile away from Ravensbrook,* the Cranes' first home in England. Edward Pease was secretary of the local branch of the Fabian Society, while Margery Pease was active in Labour party politics. Cora Crane gave Mrs. Pease the manuscripts of "The Lover and the Telltale" and "The Angel Child" as a gift because these stories were partly based on a childhood infatuation that their son Michael had for Helen Frederic, the oldest child of Harold Frederic* and Kate Lyon.* In a 27 November 1948 letter to Melvin Schoberlin, now in the Alderman Library of the University of Virginia, Michael Pease recalls Crane's frequent visits to the Pendicle because he liked to be shaved by the twin brother of Adoni Ptolemy, a servant in the Pease household.

Peaslee, Clarence Loomis (1871–?). Crane's fellow student and friend at Syracuse University,* Peaslee was graduated from Syracuse and received an M.A. in 1896. He was admitted to the Pennsylvania bar in 1897 and practiced law in Williamsport. Peaslee was an aspiring writer in the 1890s. His only book publication was a collection of poems, *Tomorrow* (London: Fowler Wright, n.d.), but he contributed short stories to magazines. In 1894–95 Peaslee corresponded with Crane about his writing, and Crane sent him a series of letters advising him to avoid the phenomenal or unusual and concentrate on the average life of simple people. Peaslee's memoir, "Stephen Crane's College Days," in the August 1896 *Monthly Illustrator* provides important contemporary support for a Syracuse version of *Maggie* but is based more on Crane's letters and on published sources than memory.

Suggested Reading

Wertheim, Stanley. "Stephen Crane to Clarence Loomis Peaslee: Some New Letters." *Resources for American Literary Study* 22 (1996): 30–36.

Peasley, George H. The marine sergeant in "The Sergeant's Private Madhouse," Peasley typifies the regular soldier of Crane's later war stories whose primary virtues are discipline and stoical courage, but in this story he is baffled by "a lunatic asylum" at the front in the person of Dryden, the mad private.

Peck, George (1797–1876). Crane's maternal grandfather was one of five brothers who were clergymen of the Methodist Episcopal Church. George Peck was ordained in 1816 and in 1819 married Mary Helen Myers, whose given names would descend as a family tradition to Stephen's mother, one of his sisters, and a number of other women in the Crane family. In 1824 Peck was appointed presiding elder of the Susquehanna (Pennsylvania) District, which included the territory of the Wyoming Conference, and was elected a member of the General Conference of the Methodist Church. In 1840 he became editor of the *Methodist Quarterly Review* and eight years later assumed the editorship of the influential *Christian Advocate* (New York), a position he held for four years. In 1852 he returned to the active ministry in Pennsylvania and was a pastor in Wilkes-Barre, Scranton, Providence, and Dunmore. He subsequently served for eight years as presiding elder of the Lakawanna and Wyoming districts. George Peck was a prolific author of polemical and historical works. Among his books are *The Scripture Doctrine of Christian Perfection, Stated and Defended* (1842), *Wyoming: Its History, Stirring Incidents, and Romantic Adventures* (1858), and *Our Country: Its Trial and Its Triumph* (1865). Peck retired in 1873 and the next year published his autobiography, *The Life and Times of Reverend George Peck, D.D.*

Peck, Jesse Truesdell (1811–1883). Crane's maternal great uncle was one of five sons of the Reverend Luther Peck (1767–1848), all of whom who became

Methodist ministers. For many years he served as an itinerant pastor and principal of Methodist seminaries. In 1844, at a meeting of the General Conference of the Methodist Episcopal Church, he made a speech on the slavery question that brought him into prominence. In 1848 he became president of Dickinson College in Carlisle, Pennsylvania, a position he retained for four years. For much of the rest of his career, he served as a pastor of churches and presiding elder in Washington, D.C., California, and New York. For a time he was editor of the Tract Society of the Methodist Church and contributed many essays to church periodicals. His hortatory tract *What Must I Do to Be Saved?* (1858) was in Stephen Crane's library from 1881 until his death and exerted a significant influence on his mind and imagination. Among Jesse Peck's books are *The Central Idea of Christianity* (1856) and *The History of the Great Republic Considered from a Christian Standpoint* (1868). At the General Conference of 1872 he was elected bishop. In the remaining years of his life, he presided at eighty-three conferences in the United States and in Europe. He was one of the founders of Syracuse University* and first president of its board of trustees.

Pennington Seminary. Crane attended this school, sponsored by the New Jersey Conference of the Methodist Episcopal Church and located near Trenton, from September 1885 through 1887. His father had been Pennington's third principal, from 1849 to 1858. Pennington had several curriculums that included literary, classical, and scientific studies, but no records survive of what courses Stephen took. The school was active in preparing young men for the ministry. Students were required to attend two religious services daily in the chapel and a service at either the Methodist or Presbyterian church in the town of Pennington on Sunday. Drinking, gambling, smoking, participation in popular amusements, and even recreational walking on the Sabbath were forbidden. This regime may have been too confining for the rebellious young Crane and may in part account for his leaving Pennington. He was also probably attracted to the military training program at Claverack College,† to which he transferred in January 1888. Stephen's brother Wilbur, in a memoir published in the *Binghamton Chronicle* on 15 December 1900, cites a more immediate reason for his abrupt departure from Pennington. One of the teachers charged him with involvement in a hazing incident and when he denied it accused him of lying. "Stephen went to his room, packed his trunk and went home to Asbury Park where he told his story, adding that 'as the Professor called me a liar there was not room in Pennington for us both, so I came home.' Nothing would induce him to return to the seminary."

Suggested Reading

Gullason, Thomas A. "The Cranes at Pennington Seminary." *American Literature* 39 (1968): 530–41.

Pent. Commander of the *Chicken* in "The Revenge of the *Adolphus*."

Perkins, William B. The inept but courageous war correspondent in "The Lone Charge of William D. Perkins," Crane's satiric short story based on an experience of Ralph D. Paine* of the *Philadelphia Press* at Guantánamo Bay during the initial military action of the Cuban War.

Perris, George H. A London literary agent with whom Cora Crane began to deal in August 1901 in marketing her own short stories and, subsequently, Crane's posthumous literary works. Perris sold *Last Words* to the English house of Digby, Long and Co. for £50, but, like James B. Pinker, he was unsuccessful in selling serial rights to the uncompleted *The O'Ruddy*.

Pete. In *Maggie: A Girl of the Streets*, Pete is the vulgar, flamboyant bartender by whom Maggie is seduced. A conventional Bowery villain, Pete is a pugnacious dandy, his face set in a "chronic sneer," hair curled in an oiled bang, and patent shoes that shine "like weapons." Maggie's illusions cause her to think that this crude tough is a "knight," an "aristocratic person." Pete appears to Maggie "like a golden sun," but in the Darwinian world of the slums, he is finally victimized by prostitutes as he has deceived Maggie and caused her to become a prostitute. To the more sophisticated Nell, Pete is only another "damn fool."

Peza. The focal character of "Death and the Child," Peza, an Italian correspondent in the Greek-Turkish War of 1897, progresses from an observer to a participant and finally to a victim in the course of the story. Like Henry Fleming of *The Red Badge of Courage*, Peza's ideals of war are shattered by its realities, and he is overpowered by the apprehension of death. The seeming purposefulness of the happenings in which he involves himself are reduced to absurdity and inconsequence by the sight of badly wounded soldiers, and, similar to the perspective of the baffled child observing the battle from a mountaintop, his ultimate realization is that "[i]t was mystery."

The Philistine: A Periodical of Protest. Printed at Elbert Hubbard's* Roycroft Shop in East Aurora, New York, the *Philistine* was the most successful of the refractory little magazines of the 1890s and remained in publication until July 1915. It reached a peak of popularity with Hubbard's "A Message to Garcia," a moral preachment from the Gospel of Work in the March 1899 issue of the *Philistine* that stressed duty and perseverance. Over a million copies of this essay were printed in pamphlet form by the New York Central Railroad, and it was translated into many languages and circulated throughout the world. Although Hubbard wrote much and sometimes all of the contents of the *Philistine*, the magazine also published the original work or reprints of some two hundred writers, of whom Crane was the most prominently featured. Hubbard reviewed *The Black Riders* in the first, June 1895, number of the *Philistine* and sent a copy to Crane with a request for a contribution. Crane submitted "The chatter of a death-demon from a tree-top'' and "Each small gleam was a voice," which appeared, respectively, in the August and September issues of the *Philistine*. As Hubbard wrote Crane in July 1895, he considered Crane's poetry "all live wire" but did not have "an unqualified liking" for it. Consequently, although the *Philistine* published much of Crane's poetry, a good many parodies and much snide commentary on his literary productions also appeared in the periodical. Altogether, the *Philistine* was an important conduit for Crane's work. Hubbard published twenty-one of Crane's poems in his various publications, some of them more than once. Fifteen of these poems appeared in the *Philistine*, ten for the first time. These include: "The chatter of a death-demon from a tree-top," "Each small gleam was a voice," "A slant of sun on dull brown walls," "What says the sea, little shell?" "To the maiden," "The impact of a dollar upon the heart," "You tell me this is God?" "On the desert," "When a people reach the top of a hill," and "Rumbling, buzzing, turning, whirling Wheels." Six of Crane's stories appeared in the *Philistine*, two of them, "A Great Mistake" and "At the Pit Door," for the first time. Crane's minidrama, "A Prologue," was reprinted from another Hubbard publication, *A Souvenir and a Medley*.

Suggested Reading

White, Bruce A. *Elbert Hubbard's* The Philistine: A Periodical of Protest (*1895–1915*). Lanham, Md.: University Press of America, 1989.

Phillips, John S. (1861–1949). A magazine editor and publisher, Phillips was a graduate of Knox College in Galesburg, Illinois, and received a second B.A. from Harvard in 1885. After a year of further study in Germany, Phillips returned to New York and worked as an editor. In 1887 he became manager of the newspaper syndicate founded by his Knox College classmate S. S. McClure. In 1893 McClure and Phillips launched *McClure's Magazine*, with Phillips as manager of the home office. In 1900 Phillips became a partner in the publishing firm of McClure, Phillips & Company. The journalistic staff Phillips brought together for *McClure's* began an investigative series on political, corporate, and union corruption in 1903 that identified the magazine with the muckraking movement. Phillips broke with McClure in 1906 and, along with Ida Tarbell, Ray Stannard Baker, and Lincoln Steffens, purchased the *American Illustrated Magazine*, which they transformed into the *American Magazine*. In 1911 the group sold its interest to the Crowell Publishing Company. Phillips resigned in 1915 but continued as advisory editor until 1938.

Shortly after the publication of *The Red Badge of Courage*, Phillips asked Crane to write a series of articles about Civil War battlefields for the McClure syndicate or for *McClure's Magazine*. Crane was initially reluctant to undertake the project, but in mid-January 1896 he traveled to northern Virginia to study the sites of the major battles. He was especially interested in Fredericksburg since, as he wrote Phillips on 9 January, the battle "was fought in December and no doubt the color of things there now would be the very same color of things of the days the battle was fought.'' Caught up in the composition of the short stories of *The Little Regiment*, Crane wrote no battlefield sketches, but the title story of the book and ''The Veteran'' appeared in *McClure's* and the Mc-Clure syndicate sold a shortened version of ''Three Miraculous Soldiers'' to a number of newspapers. In England Crane usually dealt with McClure's son Robert, London agent for the firm, and he relied on Paul Revere Reynolds ''to get me out of the ardent grasp of the S. S. McClure Co.,'' which sometimes held his work as collateral for advances, but he was especially unhappy about McClure's reluctance to either publish or relinquish ''The Monster,'' writing in desperation to Phillips in October 1897, ''Did I write a story called *The Monster*? Did I deliver it to you? And what happened after that?''

Pictures of War. A collection of *The Red Badge of Courage* and the stories of *The Little Regiment* published only in England by William Heinemann in July 1898. George Wyndham's* January 1896 review essay on *The Red Badge* in the *New Review*, retitled ''An Appreciation,'' is reprinted as an introduction. There is no new material in this volume.

Pike, Charles J. (1866–1931), and **Pike, Gordon** (1865–1925). Charles Pike was a sculptor of busts and statues who studied in New York City at the National Academy of Design and under Augustus Saint-Gaudens. From 1890 to 1895 he continued his studies in Paris at the Académie Julian and the École des Beaux Arts. On his return to the United States, he taught for a time and then established his studio in New York. His brother, Gordon, was a graduate of Yale, where he played on the football team. He studied architecture at MIT and Columbia University and then went to Paris, where he studied painting and life drawing. He returned to the United States in early 1895 and entered architectural practice in New York. For some years, he was assistant to Stanford White. The Pike brothers were part of Crane's coterie in New York from 1895 until he left for Florida in November 1896. They were the center of a group that ate dinners and gambled for small stakes in a Tenderloin basement restaurant run by two elderly French women. Crane inscribed a copy of *The Black Riders* to Gordon Pike shortly after its publication. He roomed occasionally in Charles Pike's studio on West Thirty-third Street, and in 1896 inscribed a copy of the 1893 *Maggie* to him that had his ownership signature and that Pike believed was the last copy of the book Crane ever owned.

Pike County Puzzle. For almost a month in the summer of 1894, Crane camped with Frederic Lawrence,* Louis C. Senger,* Corwin Knapp Linson,* Wickham W. Young, and other friends, mostly from Port Jervis and Middletown, New York, at Twin Lakes in Pike County, Pennsylvania. The trip was organized by Mrs. Charles M. Lawrence to celebrate the graduation of her son Frederic,* Crane's Delta Upsilon fraternity brother at Syracuse University,* from the Hahnemann Medical College in Philadelphia. The group named their camp

Camp Interlaken to distinguish it from the nearby encampment of Edgar Wells and his family, Port Jervis neighbors of the Lawrence family who owned the property at Twin Lakes. It was the custom of campers at Twin Lakes to commemorate their summer experience with a keepsake, and the *Pike County Puzzle*, a four-page burlesque newspaper written by Crane with Senger's assistance on their return to Port Jervis, was the souvenir for the Lawrence group in 1894. It is dated 28 August 1894, the day that the campers returned, and was privately printed by the job department of the *Port Jervis Union.*

In format the *Pike County Puzzle* is a parody of small-town newspapers that recorded trivial events in detail, working in as many of the names of residents as possible and chastising their rivals for inaccuracies. There are jibes in the *Puzzle* at the ''Weekly Hearth-Rug,'' the ''Manayunk Cloud-burst,'' the ''Curry Ear-Trumpet,'' and the ''Misleading Record.'' There are spoofs of concerts, baseball games, and other events at the camp. Campers are at times identified by nicknames; Crane's was ''Pan-Cake Pete,'' presumably because of his liking for pancakes. Crane's penchant for singing is satirized, as well as his intellectualism: ''As Stephen Crane was traversing the little rope ladder that ascends the right hand side of the cloud-capped pinnacle of his thoughts, he fell and was grievously injured.'' There are also mocking allusions to forthcoming events. Linson, who was going to Germany for *McClure's Magazine*, is pictured as devouring all the brown bread and water in the country. He is briefly imprisoned for debt, but in the end ''[t]he Reichstag, at a special session, unanimously voted him the war budget as a testimonial of his worth and capacity. It was handsomely engraved with the American and German arms.'' Crane and Senger are respectively identified as ''Office Boy'' and ''Associate Office Boy'' of the newspaper because they were designated to provide the memento for the group's experience.

Suggested Reading

Katz, Joseph. ''Solving Stephen Crane's *Pike County Puzzle.*'' *American Literature* 55 (1983): 171–82.

Pinker, James B. (1864?–1922). Pinker was a London literary agent who represented many English authors and American authors living in England, among them Henry James,* Joseph Conrad,* Stephen Crane, John Galsworthy, and Compton Mackenzie. He traveled frequently to the United States on their behalf and died in New York City on one of his business trips.

Pinker wrote to Crane in late August 1898 offering to sell serial rights to his short stories in England, but Crane was in Cuba at the time and Pinker's letter did not reach him until November. From that time on, Pinker was Crane's British literary agent, assuming control of his American affairs as well in July 1899 when Crane broke with Paul Revere Reynolds. In Crane's absence, Pinker's first arrangements were made through Cora. Apart from selling Crane's short stories, Pinker secured a contract with Methuen for an unspecified novel that Crane had not yet begun to write. When Crane returned to England in January 1899, he began work on a Revolutionary War novel, but he abandoned it some six months later. *Active Service*, which would not be completed until May, was already committed to Stokes in the United States and to Heinemann in England. Pinker attempted but failed to sell the serial rights of the Greek War novel. In July 1899 Pinker negotiated a new contract with Methuen for an unspecified novel that eventually became *The O'Ruddy*. He also arranged for the serial and book publication of *Wounds in the Rain* in England and *Great Battles of the World* in the United States. The relationship between Crane and Pinker was often strained by Crane's frequent demands for advances on stories that had not yet been sold or even written and by his attempts to circumvent his agent and make separate arrangements with publishers. Pinker was also obliged to lend Crane money for overdue rent on Ravensbrook* and to satisfy the claims of other debtors. After Crane's death, Cora, hounded by creditors and unable to obtain further advances from Pinker, ended her business relationship with him and turned to G. H. Perris* to market Crane's literary works as well as her own.

Placer. The hotel owner in "Twelve O'Clock" who is shot to death when he attempts to prevent a gunfight between two cowboys.

"Plans for Story". Crane was extremely proud of his Revolutionary War heritage. He became a member of the Sons of the American Revolution in 1896, and in April of that year he reminded the editor of the *Newark Sunday Call* in a letter that "[d]uring the Revolution the Cranes were pretty hot people." In the summer of 1899, he resolved to write a novel about the Revolution in New Jersey and secured a contract with Frederick A. Stokes for its American publication. Crane made desultory attempts to gather background material, but lacking the leisure and the facilities for historical inquiry, he soon abandoned the idea. All that remains are these sketchy plans, which reveal he intended to work his ancestors and also Henry Fleming's grandfather into the story and another group of notations headed "Plans for New Novel" that reveal his projected research methods. The manuscripts of these notes, written in Cora's hand from dictation, are in the Rare Book and Manuscript Library of Columbia University and are published in *Poems and Literary Remains*, volume 8 of *The Works of Stephen Crane*, edited by Fredson Bowers 1975, 158–60.

Plant, Alfred T. (?–?). An English solicitor recommended to Crane by Moreton Frewen in early 1899 to help ward off Crane's importunate creditors. Plant served as the English executor of Crane's estate and was also instrumental in helping Cora to settle some of her debts.

["Play Set in a French Tavern"]. An untitled and unfinished script for a dramatic farce satirizing the swashbuckling romantic style of Alexander Dumas whose setting is "a little inn in old France." Four carousing soldiers, identified only by the initial letters of their names, engage in banter about duels and intrigues with the landlord, a "Stranger," and a "villainous old doctor." The style, setting, and characterizations in this play suggest that it was composed at the same time Crane was writing *The O'Ruddy*. A typescript of the first act is preserved in the Rare Book and Manuscript Library of Columbia University. It is published in *Poems and Literary Remains*, volume 8 of *The Works of Stephen Crane*, edited by Fredson Bowers (1975), 129–38.

Suggested Reading

Fine, Lewis H. "Two Unpublished Plays by Stephen Crane." *Resources for American Literary Study* 1 (1971): 200–16.

Point. An artist on the *Eclipse* (the *New York World*) in " 'God Rest Ye, Merry Gentlemen,' " Point is a fictionalized depiction of *Leslie's Weekly* photographer Burr McIntosh.*

"A Poker Game". A slight, satiric tale that reflects Crane's interest in the tall tale and in poker itself, one of his favorite pastimes. "A Poker Game" may be an early work, but it appeared only posthumously in *Last Words*. Young Bobbie Cinch of Chicago, heir to $22 million, comes to New York and joins a poker game with a group of men including old Henry Spuytendyvil, who had been a friend of his father and who owns "all the real estate in New York save that previously appropriated by the hospitals and Central Park." Cinch wins heavily while Spuytendyvil loses a considerable amount. In the final hand, both draw straight flushes, which "are not as common as berries on a juniper tree," but Spuytendyvil's is higher than Cinch's. Hoping to draw Bobby in and to recover his losses, Spuytendyvil opens with a moderate bet, but Cinch, unwilling to take advantage of an opponent with "a sure thing," merely calls the bet rather than raising the ante and frustrates the old man's bluff. As in some of Crane's Western stories, chance and a generous impulse combine to prevent a misadventure.

"The Porto Rican 'Straddle' ". This dispatch from Juana Diaz, Puerto Rico, appeared in the *New York Journal* on 18 August 1898. Crane relates the experience of a group of correspondents who preceded five companies of American troops marching into the hills beyond Juana Diaz to reinforce the advance guard of the U.S. Army. The Puerto Rican natives they encounter, caught between the American and Spanish lines, are "as tongue-tied and sullen as a lot of burglars met in the daytime," but when they see a significant body of American soldiers and a general, they become happy and excessively polite. The cynical correspondents "told them they were a lot of honest men. And, after all, who knows?"

["A Portrait of Smolenski"]. Unpublished in Crane's lifetime, this Greek-Turkish War report survives as a manuscript in Cora's hand, with a few corrections by Crane, in the Rare Book and Manuscript Library of Columbia University, but it is most likely entirely Crane's work, dictated by him to Cora. It was first published in *Reports of War*, volume 9 of *The Works of Stephen Crane*, edited by Fredson Bowers (1971), 72–75. Crane opines that if a hero is to emerge from the conflict, it will be Colonel Constantine Smolenski, who held off the Turks at Velestino for three days and inflicted heavy losses on them before he was ordered to retreat. At this point in the war, "Smolenski is the man of whom a romantic people would make a natural idol."

Potter, Jack. The superannuated marshal in "The Bride Comes to Yellow Sky" who arrives in town armed with a wife rather than a gun. Potter does not fully realize that Yellow Sky has also entered into a "new estate" until the final confrontation with Scratchy Wilson, in which conversation replaces the gunfight of the mythical Wild West. Potter appears again in "Moonlight on the Snow" as sheriff of the county, with Wilson as his deputy.

Prat, Manolo. The young insurgent lieutenant in "The Clan of No-Name" whose actions are the central drama of the story. Prat conforms to a rigid Kiplingesque code of behavior that demands the subordination of self-interest to duty and the service of others. Whether Crane is extolling such altruism or mocking it as a jejune illusion is left ambiguous in the conclusion.

"The Predecessor". Shortly after Crane met Joseph Conrad,* he proposed that Conrad collaborate with him on a play. Conrad was reluctant from the start, writing to Crane in mid-January 1898 that "collaborating with you would be either cheating or deceiving you. In any case disappointing you. I have no dramatic gift." In his introduction to Thomas Beer's* *Stephen Crane: A Study in American Letters* (1923), Conrad recalls that on 19 March, after the two writers had dinner together at the Savage Club, they went to a café, where Crane described a story that he believed would make a good play, to be called "The Predecessor." As Conrad remembered Crane's proposal, the play would be set in the American West and would involve "a man personating his 'predecessor' (who had died) in the hope of winning a girl's heart. The scenes were to include a ranch at the foot of the Rocky Mountains . . . and the action I fear would have been frankly melodramatic." Crane conceived of one scene in which the man and girl would stand on a prairie by the carcasses of their horses, which they had ridden to death. Conrad commented that it was unlikely that a London theater manager could be induced to deposit two stuffed horses on his stage. Although the project was discussed further from time to time, the play was never written.

In early April Crane and Conrad visited a number of London publishers in an effort to raise money for Crane's passage across the Atlantic to report the Cuban War. At the office of C. Arthur Pearson, publisher of *Pearson's Weekly* and other magazines, Crane showed a prospectus of "The Predecessor," now recast as a novel, to the book department, but no contract or advance was offered. Crane then gave his prospectus to George Brown Burgin, the literary adviser of the department and subsequently the author of some ninety forgettable novels, telling Burgin that he was welcome to write the book himself if Crane failed to return from Cuba. Burgin retained Crane's plot outline and printed it twenty-five years later in a book of reminiscences, *More Memories (and Some Travels)*.

The outline is much more elaborate but only a little more plausible than the scenario that Conrad recalled for the play. In Crane's conception of the novel, a young officer in the Life Guards who has become involved in a financial scandal exiles himself to America and with a partner begins a new life on a ranch in the West. He is cleared of any wrongdoing but dies without knowing this. His fiancée, a girl of noble family, follows him to America accompanied by her father to reestablish their relationship. Near the ranch they meet the partner of the Guardsman, who instantly falls in love with the girl and in order to detain her tells her that the Guardsman is still alive but away on a journey to one of the cattle camps. "The partner lies and lies. He engages in a terrible conflict with the memory of the dead man—in his own mind and in the girl's mind." Finally, "he is driven to the absurdity of arranging an elopement from the Guardsman. He has defeated the shade, but the girl cannot face the man with whom she has apparently broken faith." The lovers flee on horseback across the prairie. When they see a cloud of dust raised by the wind behind them, the girl imagines they are being pursued by the Guardsman. The partner confesses his deception, and their relationship resumes on a new footing. Crane's proposal for this absurd romantic fantasy is an indication of the desperation to which his financial problems were driving him before he left for Cuba. Conrad questioned him about the novel when he returned to England, but Crane seems to have made no effort to develop it further.

Suggested Reading

Garner, Stanton. "Stephen Crane's 'The Predecessor': Unwritten Play, Unwritten Novel." *American Literary Realism 1870–1910* 13 (1980): 97–100.

Price, Carl F. (?–?). Price was apparently not personally acquainted with Crane but interviewed a number of people who knew him. Price's overview of Crane's career, "Stephen Crane: A Genius Born in a Methodist Parsonage," *Christian Advocate* 98 (1922): 866–67, provides some convincing and amusing anecdotes about Crane's life as a child and as a student at Syracuse University.*

"The Price of the Harness". Crane's most successful Cuban War story, "The Price of the Harness" was written in Havana in September 1898 and appeared simultaneously in December in *Blackwood's Edinburgh Magazine* and in the *Cosmopolitan*. The editor of the *Cosmopolitan*, John Brisben Walker, published the story under the title, "The Woof of Thin Red Threads," adapted from a phrase in the fifth section. Crane's objection to the editorially supplied title reflects his thematic intentions. "Damn Walker," he wrote to Paul Revere Reynolds. "The name of the story is 'The Price of the Harness' because it *is* the price of the harness, the price the men paid for wearing the military harness, Uncle Sam's military harness; and they paid blood, hunger and fever." Joseph Conrad* was especially appreciative of this story, considering it the best of Crane's works since *The Red Badge of Courage*. "The Price of the Harness" was collected as the lead story of the posthumous *Wounds in the Rain*.

"The Price of the Harness" is a fictional extension of Crane's last report for the *New York World*, "Regulars Get No Glory" (20 July 1898), for there is no glory in the combat experiences of Jack Martin, Jimmie Nolan, Billie Grierson, and Ike Watkins, the four private soldiers who participate in the storming of the fortifications of San Juan on the eastern outskirts of Santiago. Unlike Henry Fleming of *The Red Badge* or Collins of "A Mystery of Heroism," the common soldiers of "The Price of the Harness" entertain no illusions about the exalted nature of personal courage in battle. With "marvellous impassivity," they view themselves as companions in duty, performers in a mechanistic enterprise in which the individual is a sprocket or gearwheel of "a great machine set to running frantically in the open air. . . . It reminds one always of a loom, a great grand steel loom, clinking, clanking, plunking, plinking, to weave a woof of thin red threads, the cloth of death." In the course of what Crane described in "War Memories" as "the spectacle of the common man serenely doing his work, his appointed work," Martin is hit in the arm and, after marching in Crane's ubiquitous procession of the wounded, joins Grierson in the yellow fever tent; Watkins is shot through the lung, probably fatally; and Nolan dies on the field, unaware that his wound is mortal.

Crane's more mature view that war is an imposed social responsibility rather than an individual enterprise that may be either personally ennobling or humiliating is reflected in the opening of the story, where the four comrades are part of a group digging and smoothing a path on a hillside so that field artillery batteries will be able to advance. Their drudgery "gains no encrusted medals from war. The men worked like gardeners." The battle that commences on the following day is also depicted in terms of work, encompassing the chores of dressing, finding something to eat, and marching through muddy fields and paths overgrown with shrubbery. The death and injury that will destroy the group is prefigured by the sight of a Cuban insurgent borne in a litter who has been shot through the groin. His "doleful sobbing cry, 'Madre mia,' was a tangible consequent misery of all that firing on in front into which the men knew they were soon to be plunged." Nolan's death is prosaic. He feels as if he had been punched in the stomach and thinks of lying down to rest as he falls. Not realizing that he is bleeding, he insists that the ground is damp: "He did not know he was dying. He thought he was holding an argument on the condition of the turf."

While Crane's admiration for the sustained interdependence of common men in the face of danger and death is evident in "The Price of the Harness," there is no blatant chauvinism or unalloyed admiration for mindless devotion to duty, and the story is not devoid of his distinctive irony. A young officer passing the column of wounded insurgents is deaf to the wails of the wounded man because he is "bound by traditions of fidelity and courage," which inure him from the sufferings of humanity and ensure that he is "guided by an ideal which he has himself created." The story ends sardonically with a delirious soldier in the fever tent where Martin and Grierson are confined, "wringing from the situation a grim meaning by singing the Star-Spangled Banner with all the ardour which could be procured from his fever-stricken body." This final episode was almost without doubt derived from Edward Marshall's "A Wounded Correspondent's Recollections of Guasimas" (*Scribner's Magazine*, September 1898). Marshall, lacking Crane's irony, concludes his account with a group of soldiers lying in a field hospital quaveringly singing "My country 'tis of thee," their voices "punctuated by groans and made spasmodic by pain."

"The Private's Story". Printed in the *New York Journal* on 26 September 1898, this report is sometimes treated as if it were a protofictional account by Crane's archetypal regular soldier in the Cuban War, Private Nolan, the central character of "Regulars Get No Glory" and "The Price of the Harness." It is actually a recounting of incidents that occurred when Crane himself arrived from Cuba at Fortress Monroe, located at Old Point Comfort, Virginia, in mid-July 1898 on the hospital transport *City of Washington*. Incidents in this report such as the little woman on a launch circling the incoming ship who is searching for her husband (actually Colonel Liscum of the Twenty-fourth Infantry), the women weeping at the sight of the procession of wounded men, and the narrator's obsessive longing for an ice cream soda are repeated almost verbatim in "War Memories."

"A Prologue". A cryptic dramatic scenario, sometimes mistaken for a poem because of its presentation format, which is entirely in capital letters, like the poems of *The Black Riders*, and its single stanzaic form. "A Prologue" was first printed in *A Souvenir and a Medley*, the May 1896 issue of Elbert Hubbard's* *Roycroft Quarterly*. On a gloomy stage, a table with an unopened book on it stands before a window through which a moonbeam falls on the book. There is a moment of silence, and then from an adjacent room come sounds of drinking, laughter, quarreling and a fight. After a pause a woman screams "AH, MY SON, MY SON," and there is another moment of silence. "A Prologue" seems to be a melodramatic temperance vignette, unique in the Crane canon. A similar dramatic passage with a temperance theme in Thomas de Witt Talmage's *The Night Sides of City Life* (1878), a book with which Crane was probably familiar, may have been a source for "A Prologue."

Suggested Reading

Stallman, R. W. *Stephen Crane: A Biography*. Rev. ed. New York: Braziller, 1972. 545–46.

Prospectus for *The Black Riders*. In March 1895, at Crane's request, Copeland & Day issued this announcement for the publication of *The Black Riders* printed on the same paper that would be used for the trade edition of the book. The leaflet contains excerpts from Hamlin Garland's* June 1893 *Arena* review of *Maggie* and the first printing of *The Black Riders* XXVIII, "Truth, said a traveller."

Ptolemy, Adoni (?–?). One of a pair of Greek twins, war refugees, whom the Cranes brought from Greece to England. Adoni served for a time as butler at Ravensbrook.* When the Cranes moved to Brede Place,* the Frewens insisted that their own servants be retained in the house, so Adoni went to work temporarily for the Mark Barrs* and then joined his brother as a servant in the Pease* household.

Pulitzer, Joseph (1847–1911). A powerful editor and publisher in St. Louis and in New York City, Joseph Pulitzer was born in Hungary and emigrated to the United States at the age of seventeen. He served briefly in the Union army during the Civil War and in 1868 went to St. Louis, where he started his journalistic career with a German-language newspaper. In 1869 he was elected as a Republican to the Missouri legislature and became active in national politics. Pulitzer took advantage of the rapid growth in communication concomitant with American industrial and population expansion in the late nineteenth century. In 1878 he purchased the *St. Louis Dispatch* and combined it with the *Post* to create the *St. Louis Post-Dispatch*. Under his direction, the newspaper linked sensational news coverage with an assertive editorial policy, and its circulation rapidly increased. In 1883 Pulitzer assumed ownership of the marginal *New York World*. During the Spanish-American War, the *World* engaged in jingoistic competition, which came to be known as yellow journalism, with Hearst's *New York Journal* and boosted the circulation of both newspapers. Pulitzer's will left funds to establish a school of journalism at Columbia University and to endow the Pulitzer Prizes in American journalism and literature and later in music. His son Joseph (1885–1955) and grandson of the same name (1913–93) succeeded him as publishers of the *Post-Dispatch*.

In late April 1898 Crane contracted with Pulitzer's *New York World*, which on 10 April had printed an abridged version of his Western story "The Five White Mice," to report the Cuban phase of the Spanish-American War, ostensibly for a fee of $3,000. In July, when Crane returned to New York stricken with malaria, he was discharged by the *World* under circumstances that remain unclear. Don Carlos Seitz, business manager of the *World* at the time, maintained erroneously that Crane "sent only one dispatch of any merit and that, accusing the Seventy-first New York regiment of cowardice at Santiago, imperilled the paper." Actually, Crane wrote almost twenty-five dispatches that appeared in the *World*, dealing with military actions from the marine landing at Guantánamo Bay to the battle of the San Juan hills, some of them of very high quality. The report of the rout of the Seventy-first New York Regiment was written by his bureau chief, Sylvester Scovel.* More likely, Crane was discharged by the *World* because Pulitzer was angry that on 24 June when Edward Marshall,* correspondent for Hearst's *New York Journal*, the *World*'s arch rival, was severely wounded in an ambush of the Rough Riders at Las Guásimas, Crane carried Marshall's dispatch to back to the coast and cabled it for him. Later Seitz asserted that Crane left the *World* staff when the financial manager contemptuously refused his request for a salary increase.

Suggested Reading

Juergens, George. *Joseph Pulitzer and the "New York World."* Princeton, NJ: Princeton University Press, 1966.
Seitz, Don Carlos. *Joseph Pulitzer: His Life and Letters*. New York: Simon & Schuster, 1924.
———. "Stephen Crane: War Correspondent." *Bookman* 76 (1933): 137–40.
Swanberg, W. H. *Pulitzer*. New York: Scribner, 1967.

Purple Sanderson. A character in "Stories Told by an Artist" and *The Third Violet* representing Nelson Greene.*

Q

"Queenstown". The first of the series of five "Irish Notes" written for the *Westminster Gazette*, "Queenstown" appeared in the *New York Journal* on 18 October 1897 and in the *Gazette* the next day. It is the only sketch in the group that was not collected in *Last Words*. Crane describes his arrival by ship at the town of Cobh in Cork Harbor, which was renamed Queenstown in honor of a visit by Queen Victoria in 1849 and retained this name until 1922. Queenstown is viewed impressionistically through torrents of rain. "Cork was weeping like a widow." The "pinnacled position" of the town above the harbor and the imaginative quality of its Irish inhabitants give the residents of Queenstown an original and timeless quality of vision that is lacking in staid and provincial Englishmen. The agile mind of an Irishman could "attempt forty games of chess at one time and play them all passably well," but the white pennant of the British warship *Howe* in the harbor, a symbol of British domination, is an "emblem of the man who can play one game at a time."

Quick, John H. (1870–?). Sergeant in the U.S. Marine Corps during the Cuban War and recipient of the Congressional Medal of Honor. *See also* "The Red Badge of Courage Was His Wig-Wag Flag" and "Marines Signalling Under Fire at Guantanamo."

Quick, "Tom". A legendary Indian slayer in Sullivan County during the French and Indian War. Crane deflates Quick's fabled reputation in "Not Much of a Hero."

R

"Raft Story". *See* "Six Years Afloat."

Randolph, Black John. A black hobo in "Billie Atkins Went to Omaha" who Billie said was " 'the whitest pardner' he ever had.'' Black John rescues Billie from some boys who are throwing stones at him, and the two tramps ride together in an east-bound freight car.

Ravensbrook Villa. On Stephen and Cora's return to England from Greece in June 1897, Harold Frederic* found a home for them at Ravensbrook Villa in Oxted, Surrey, within commuting distance of London. Frederic's Homefield at Kenley was some seven miles away. Ravensbrook was a sprawling plain brick and tile house at the bottom of a hill, with a culvert through which a brook flowed. There were a drive, a gatekeeper's lodge, and a garden. The house was located just over the Oxted line, with the village of Limpsfield, where Edward Garnett* and Ford Madox Ford* lived, adjoining. Crane's expenses at Ravensbrook exceeded his income, and he began to experience the pressures of financial indebtedness that would plague him for the rest of his life. Ravensbrook was sparsely furnished, and the Cranes ran up enormous debts to refurbish the house that they never entirely repaid. Before they moved to Brede Place* in February 1899, the Oxted butcher, grocer, and dairy served summonses. A year's rent was due on Ravensbrook, and a bill of £98.9s for Cora's piano had not been settled. Despite these concerns and the annoyance of crowds of tourists, fledgling writers, and journalists who crowded into the villa so that Crane had to sequester himself in a London hotel room in order to work, he wrote prolifically during his time at Ravensbrook, composing a great deal of remunerative hack work and some of his finest stories: "The Bride Comes to Yellow Sky," "Death and the Child," "The Blue Hotel," and "The Monster."

Suggested Reading

Wertheim, Stanley, and Paul Sorrentino, eds. *The Correspondence of Stephen Crane.* New York: Columbia University Press, 1988.

Rea (alternatively spelled Rhea), George Bronson (1869–1936). Informally trained as an engineer, Rea was special correspondent of the *New York Herald* in Cuba in 1895–97. After the sinking of the *Maine*, he became a war correspondent for the *New York World*. With Crane he reported on the battle at Las Guásimas and the ambush of the Rough Riders on 24 June 1898. On 8 July, Rea put Crane, who was suffering from malaria, aboard the transport *City of Washington* to return to the United States for medical treatment. After the Cuban campaign, Rea went to Manila, where he founded the *Far Eastern Review*. In 1906 he moved to Shanghai. He was a strong supporter of the Chinese Republic but later became an advocate for Japanese interests. Rea was author of *Facts and Fakes about Cuba* (1897), *The Case for Manchoukuo* (1935), and a number of other books and monographs.

Suggested Reading

Laval, C. J. "George Bronson Rea." *Far Eastern Review* 32 (1936): 469–73.

Realism. As a movement in the late nineteenth century, American literary realism was a reaction, influenced by figures such as Balzac, Flaubert, and Zola in France and Turgenev, Tolstoy, and Chekhov in Russia, against the idealized vision of life inherent in the romanticism of writers like Edgar Allan Poe, Nathaniel Hawthorne, and Herman Melville, as well as a host of minor sentimental escapists, who were concerned with the ideal and the transcendent and whose works incorporated the imaginative elevation of mystery, terror, ideality, and sublimity. The development of empirical Darwinistic science led realistic American writers to a positivistic factualism that stressed careful observation and depiction of the outer world, a concern with the mundane lives of common people, a concentration on the modern and the regional, a dramatic method of presentation that distanced the author from the scene of the work, mimetic dialogue, and a transparent narrative style. As somewhat tautologically defined by William Dean Howells* in *Criticism and Fiction* (1891), realism is "nothing more and nothing less than the truthful treatment of material" whose essential conditions are "fidelity to experience and probability of motive." Among important American writers usually considered realists are Hamlin Garland,* William Dean Howells,* Mark Twain, Henry James,* John W. De Forest, Harold Frederic,* Bret Harte, and Sarah Orne Jewett.

Crane identified himself with the realists early in his career but denied that he had developed his literary tenets under the personal influence of Garland and Howells. "You know, when I left you, I renounced the clever school in literature," he wrote in an often-quoted letter to Lily Brandon Munroe* in the spring of 1894. "It seemed to me that there must be something more in life than to sit and cudgel one's brains for clever and witty expedients. So I developed all alone a little creed of art which I thought was a good one. Later I discovered that my creed was identical with the one of Howells and Garland and in this way I became involved in the beautiful war between those who say that art is man's substitute for nature and we are the most successful in art when we approach the nearest to nature and truth, and those who say—well, I don't know what they say." He implied a similar common vision with the realists later in his career when he wrote to a magazine editor that since the age of sixteen he felt that "the most artistic and the most enduring literature was that which reflected life accurately. Therefore I have tried to observe closely, and to set down what I have seen in the simplest and most concise way." Yet despite his fidelity to observed experience and rejection of romantic sentimentality, Crane fits uneasily under the rubric of literary realism. While he thanked Howells in an inscription written in a copy of *The Red Badge of Courage* that he never sent to him "for many things he has learned of the common man," Crane's characters were seldom common men, and he rarely wrote about ordinary experiences. His almost pervasive irony, use of symbolistic techniques, narrative ambiguities, and sometimes deterministic, sometimes nihilistic view of the natural and social universe also place his fiction beyond the commonly understood taxonomy of literary realism.

Suggested Reading

Bell, Michael Davitt. "Irony, Parody, and 'Transcendental Realism': Stephen Crane." In *The Problem of American Realism: Studies in the Cultural History of a Literary Idea*. Chicago: University of Chicago Press, 1993. 131–48.
Cady, Edwin H. *The Light of Common Day: Realism in American Fiction*. Bloomington: Indiana University Press, 1971.
Kaplan, Amy. *The Social Construction of American Realism*. Chicago: University of Chicago Press, 1988.
Kolb, Harold H. *The Illusion of Life: American Realism as a Literary Form*. Charlottesville: University Press of Virginia, 1968.

The Red Badge of Courage. Traditionally considered Crane's greatest achievement as a writer and unquestionably the most realistic novel about the American Civil War, albeit the work of a man born six years after it had ended, the personal and literary antecedents of *The Red Badge of Courage* remain obscure. Critics have speculated that previous to writing the novel Crane may had read or at least familiarized himself with European works of war fiction, notably Stendhal's *Charterhouse of Parma* (1839), Tolstoy's *Sebastopol* (1855), Emile Erkmann and Alexandre Chatrian's *The Conscript* (1864) and *Waterloo* (1865), Kipling's *The Light That Failed* (1890), and Zola's *La Débâcle* (1892). Others have emphasized that Crane's works and letters indicate that he was ill-read in nineteenth-century English and Continental fiction and that the literary origins of Crane's war novel are where one should first expect to find them—in the magazine articles, personal narratives, and fiction dealing with the American Civil War.

The Red Badge is primarily an internal narrative concerned with changing emotional states and little attention is devoted to tactical and circumstantial matters, but the occasional descriptions of places and events that comprise the factual background of the novel follow closely the details of the Battle of Chancellorsville, fought in late April and early May 1863 on the banks of the Rappahannock River in northern Virginia. The movements of Crane's fictional 304th New York roughly correspond to those of the 124th New York State Volunteer Regiment, known as the Orange Blossoms, which had its first experience of combat at Chancellorsville. Crane most likely chatted with some of the veterans of this regiment under the impressive Civil War monument in Port Jervis's Orange Square, but his immediate written source for the actualities of the battle was the series "Battles and Leaders of the Civil War" that appeared in the *Century Magazine* from November 1884 to November 1887 and was published in four volumes by the Century Company in 1887. In early 1893 Crane spent many hours in the studio of his artist friend Corwin Knapp Linson* and in the old Art Students League building poring over old copies of the *Century*. He must have been especially impressed by the eyewitness accounts of the Chancellorsville campaign in "Battles and Leaders" written by enlisted men, such as Warren Lee Goss's "Recollections of a Private" and John L. Collins's "When Stonewall Jackson Turned Our Right." These narratives contain many parallels to specific episodes and environmental particulars in *The Red Badge*. Crane's reading no doubt also included some of the many personal narratives published during and after the Civil War that traced the experiences of a young recruit from the time of his enlistment through his battle experiences, usually as a member of a particular brigade or regiment. It is likely that he originally conceived of *The Red Badge* as an outgrowth of the genre that included such books as Alonzo F. Hill's *Our Boys: The Personal Experiences of a Soldier in the Army of the Potomac* (1864), Wilbur F. Hinman's *Corporal Si Klegg and His "Pard"* (1887), and Frank Wilkeson's *Recollections of a Private Soldier in the Army of the Potomac* (1887). Since these chronicles evolve the maturation theme of a recruit into a veteran, usually through an entire military campaign, Crane first entitled his manuscript "Private Fleming/His various battles," but he became increasingly concerned with the question touched on in most of the autobiographical narratives—the private soldier's fear of death—and restricted his subject to one soldier's struggle to achieve emotional stability in a single battle of the Army of the Potomac. Changing his title to *The Red Badge of Courage: An Episode of the American Civil War*, he shifted the conception of the book from a traditional Civil War chronicle to a complex internal narrative. This was probably what Crane was referring to when he told Louis Senger, "I deliberately started in to do a pot-boiler . . . something that would take the boarding-school element—you know the kind. Well, I got interested in the thing in spite of myself, and I couldn't, I couldn't. I *had* to do it my own way." A few works of fiction, especially John W. De Forest's *Miss Ravenel's Conversion from Secession to Loyalty* (1867), Joseph Kirkland's *The Captain of Company K.* (1891), and Ambrose Bierce's *Tales of Soldiers and Civilians* (1891), may have help Crane to integrate circumstantial realism* with introspective narration.

Crane probably began the composition of *The Red Badge of Courage* in June 1893 and worked intensively on the manuscript at his brother Edmund's home in Lake View, New Jersey, that summer. In the fall he moved into the old Art Students League building on East Twenty-third Street in New York, where he completed the novel in April 1894. Shortly afterward he submitted it to S. S. McClure for publication by his newspaper syndicate or in *McClure's Magazine*. McClure refused to commit himself, and in mid-October, at the suggestion of Edward Marshall,* Crane brought the manuscript of *The Red Badge* to Irving Bacheller.* An abridged and truncated version of the novel was published in early December 1894 by the Bacheller, Johnson and Bacheller syndicate in an undetermined number of newspapers; only seven printings have been observed. In mid-December Crane showed the newspaper clippings to Ripley Hitchcock,* then literary adviser to D. Appleton & Company. Appleton formally accepted the novel in February, but publication was delayed because Crane was traveling in the West and Mexico for the Bacheller syndicate. The first American edition of *The Red Badge of Courage* was published on 27 September 1895, according to Appleton records.

The distinctive style of *The Red Badge*, as well as of most of Crane's early fiction, is often identified as impressionistic. The ideal of impressionism,* in literature as well as in painting, is not the close reproduction of reality but the rendering of experiences in the instant they pass through the mind. The primacy of change and chance implies the superiority of the passing mood over the permanent qualities of life and the Heraclitean outlook that reality is not a state of being but a becoming, not a condition but a process. The essence of Crane's impressionism is in the metaphorical use of color, the subjective point of view, and intertwined patterns of personification and animal imagery.

No other American novel is as saturated with color imagery as *The Red Badge*. For the most part it is used in realistic descriptions. There are the blue and gray of uniforms, the red of campfires, the yellow and orange of sunlight, and the green of forests. More important is the use of color to suggest emotional states. Red is associated with war and rage and, at times, with both fear and courage. Blue remains conventionally indicative of sadness. Green and brown, the colors of the earth, reflect the serenity of nature; gray is the color of death and is seen in the ashen hue of corpses. Yellow is primarily associated with truth or the world of objective reality, as when the mother of the protagonist, Henry Fleming, casts a deflating "yellow light" on the romantic vagaries of his martial ambitions. The bright yellow sunlight shining on the battlefields reveals the cold indifference of nature to the bloody affairs of men. The fragmentary, episodic structure of *The Red Badge* reflects the detached nature of Henry's experience. There is an extraordinary precision in that which he views directly, but the background is broken and filled with shadows. The essential movement in the novel consists of emotional transitions in the mind of the protagonist. Crane modulated the appearance of the outer world in conformity with Henry's fleeting sensations. He is more often the object of the action than its subject. The entire world of his perceptions is vividly alive. There are numerous personifications: wagons are "terror-stricken"; smoke is "lazy and ignorant"; woods are "lowering"; the cannon are "surly" and "restless"; they squat in a row "like savage chiefs" and they argue "with abrupt violence." Closely related to these instances of the pathetic fallacy is the pervasive use of animal images. Henry perceives the enemy and even formations of Union soldiers as "huge crawling reptiles" and "serpents." As the Confederate attack becomes imminent, the colonel of the youth's regiment begins "to scold like a wet parrot," and Henry feels "the acute exasperation of a pestered animal, a well-meaning cow worried by dogs." A soldier who flees screaming at the first volley and is apprehended stares at the lieutenant "with sheeplike eyes." As the enemy attacks for the second time, a man near Henry throws down his gun and runs "like a rabbit," and Henry himself flees "like a proverbial chicken."

Structurally and thematically, *The Red Badge of Courage* is an initiation or maturation story—a tale in which a young protagonist passes from ignorance of his own soul to self-discovery or from ignorance of the external world to some vital knowledge through immersion in a communal experience. At the initial stage of the traditional initiation journey, the protagonist is summoned to adventure by a destiny that transfers his spiritual center of gravity from his familiar environment to unknown and mysterious regions. The call to adventure comes to Henry Fleming from the ringing church bells and the newspapers—the spiritual and social heralds of the community. The land is stirred by "[t]ales of great movements," and Henry's unconscious desire to become a hero "had drawn for him large pictures extravagant in color, lurid with breathless deeds." His first disappointment begins when his mother casts a "yellow light" of reality on the fervent enthusiasm of his ambitions. He had envisioned an affecting parting scene, but when the moment comes, he can blurt out only a pathetic, "Ma, I've enlisted," and his mother disappoints him by "saying nothing whatever about returning with his shield or on it." She doggedly continues to peel potatoes and shatters his dream of personal glory by reminding him of his unimportance: "Yer jest one little feller amongst a hull lot of others, and yeh've got to keep quiet an' do what they tell yeh." Crane underscores this antiheroic lack of individual significance by most often referring to Henry simply as "the youth"; Jim Conklin is "the tall soldier"; Wilson, "the loud soldier," has no first name; and "the tattered soldier" has no name at all.

Henry nevertheless marches away to war with his romantic-chivalric conception of the nature of reality still relatively undisturbed. "On the way to Washington his spirit had soared. The regiment was fed and caressed at station after station until the youth had believed that he must be a hero." Disillusionment sets in when the regiment is marched from one post to another and spends months in a camp. With time for reflection, Henry begins to develop doubts about his potential reaction to the stresses of combat. In his earlier visions of "broken-bladed glory," he had prudently repressed any suspicions of cowardice, but now he is forced into the realization that he is merely an untried adolescent and that as far as war is concerned he knows nothing of himself. The apathetic reactions of his comrades to his problem reinforce Henry's sense of isolation. Neither Conklin nor Wilson is a sensitive, introspective person. Instead, they typify the common run of humanity. Conklin represents the phlegmatic man who docilely accepts his situation, while Wilson is an aggressive blusterer whose resistance is unintelligent and ineffectual. In the course of the novel, they undergo dramatic change, but at this point, they merely serve as foils to Henry's self-doubt. Having lost confidence in his ability to control his own actions, Henry begins to practice self-delusion and to view himself as a victim, not of his own fantasies and misconceptions but of the government: "He had not enlisted of his free will. He had been dragged by the merciless government. And now they were taking him out to be slaughtered."

Henry's reaction to the first attack of the enemy is entirely unconscious. There is no question of a decision to fight but merely a reflexive action toward self-defense. This is accompanied by a feeling that he is breaking through the wall of isolation and merging his individual identity with the corporate personality of the regiment. This sense of solidarity gives way to the "red rage" of battle, and he fires wildly into the smoke. As soon as the enemy charge has abated and Henry is given time to reflect, his delusions of grandeur again assume control, and he deceives himself into thinking that he has acted deliberately and even heroically. This confidence is quickly dissipated when the enemy attacks again. Fatigued, disoriented, and frightened, Henry sees men scamper away. Suddenly, without reflection, he finds himself speeding toward the rear. "His rifle and cap were gone. His unbuttoned coat bulged in the wind. The flap of his cartridge box bobbed wildly, and his canteen, by its slender cord, swung out behind. On his face was all the horror of those things which he imagined."

Isolation becomes more intense as the youth, now literally cut off from his comrades by his defection, attempts to justify his cowardice by finding philosophical rationalizations for his completely instinctive reactions. He first conceives of himself as an enlightened individual whose flight was motivated by superior powers of perception. "He had done a good part in saving himself, who was a little piece of the army. . . . His actions had been sagacious things. They had been full of strategy. They were the work of a master's legs." The fallacy in this line of reasoning soon becomes apparent when he learns that the Union line has withstood the enemy attack. Filled with self-pity and despair, Henry next turns to nature for a vindication of his conduct. He throws a pine cone at a squirrel, and when the animal runs, he perceives in this an exhibition of the law of self-preservation: "Nature had given him a sign." The irony of this fatuous analogy is apparent, but it is doubled a moment later when the youth sees a small animal pounce into a swamp pond and emerge with a fish and when he enters "a place where the high, arching boughs made a chapel" and finds as the altarpiece of this natural church a dead soldier with his back against a tree. "The corpse was dressed in a uniform that once had been blue, but was now faded to a melancholy shade of green. The eyes, staring at the youth, had changed to the dull hue to be seen on the side of a dead fish. The mouth was open. Its red had changed to an appalling yellow. Over the gray skin of the face ran little ants. One was trundling some sort of a bundle along the upper lip." The law of nature is that life feeds on death; it is not self-preservation but survival of the fittest.

Abandoning hope of finding solace in nature and stripped of his intellectual defenses, the youth joins a ghastly procession of the wounded. He encounters a tattered man who deepens his guilt with the question, "Where yeh hit?" and a spectral soldier who turns out to be Jim Conklin, ensanguined and raving. Henry, trailed by the tattered soldier, follows Jim into a field and witnesses the prolonged agony of his death:

> As the flap of the blue jacket fell away from the body, he could see that the side looked as if it had been chewed by wolves.
> The youth turned, with sudden, livid rage, toward the battlefield. He shook his fist. He seemed about to deliver a philippic.
> "Hell———"
> The red sun was pasted in the sky like a wafer.

Not even the horror of Conklin's death or the sense of guilt he feels among these wounded men causes Henry to feel contrite or to return to duty. Instead, he compounds his guilt by deserting the tattered man, who is also on the verge of death, and resuming his aimless wanderings. Midpoint in the novel, Crane still makes us see Henry as an emotional puppet. His passivity in the face of experience is most apparent in the eleventh chapter. Henry interjects his environment, becoming what he sees, unconscious of the contradictions in which his vacillations involve him. As he watches a retreat, he feels a sense of comfort. If this were a general rout, he would be vindicated. When a forward column of infantry appears, he is downcast, imagining these men who are riding toward the front to be "chosen beings" and intensely aware of the emotional distance between them and himself. As he contemplates their bravery, he reverts back to the same type of romantic fantasy that characterized his reveries before the first experience of battle: "Swift pictures of himself, apart, yet in himself, came to him—a blue desperate figure leading lurid charges with one knee forward and a broken blade high—a blue, determined figure standing before a crimson and steel assault, getting calmly killed on a high place before the eyes of all. He thought of the magnificent pathos of his dead body."

Henry's return to his regiment at nightfall on the first day of the battle is not a volitional act. Wandering in a field, he suddenly finds himself engulfed by a wave of soldiers running out of the woods "like terrified buffaloes." They are oblivious to Henry's incoherent questions until he clutches one of them by the arm, and, when he attempts to detain him, the terrified man smashes his rifle down on Henry's head. This is the culminating irony of the novel: Henry receives his wound, his "red badge of courage," not from the front end of the rifle of a charging Confederate soldier but from the butt end of the rifle of a retreating Union soldier. He is led back to the regiment in a dazed condition by an individual identified only as "the man of the cheery voice" and is greeted as a hero. Moments before being clubbed, he had debated the question and decided not to return to the front lines at all. Furthermore, Crane still views his protagonist as a deluded youth, and Henry is still the subject of a good deal of ironic comment in the last half of the book. He rejoices that Wilson, who has actually been sobered by his battle experiences, had displayed fear by entrusting him with a packet of letters for relatives in the event of his death, and he feels superior to his friend, adopting toward the loud soldier an attitude of patronizing good humor. His own pride "was now entirely restored. . . . He had performed his mistakes in the dark, so he was still a man." He remembers how some of the other soldiers had fled from the firing line. "As he recalled their terror-struck faces he felt a scorn for them. They had surely been more fleet and more wild than was absolutely necessary. They were weak mortals. As for himself, he had fled with discretion and dignity."

Nevertheless, the youth fights bravely on the second day of battle. His doubts and fears seem to be resolved, and he immerses himself completely in the business of war. In the regiment's first charge, he carries the flag, assuming the position of symbolic center of the group and in every way manifesting the attitude and bearing of a courageous soldier. Once again, however, his actions are not the result of conscious moral determination but of rage and animal fury. "Yesterday, when he had imagined the universe to be against him, he had hated it, little gods and big gods; to-day he hated the army of the foe with the same great hatred." In the grip of animalistic feelings, Henry Fleming becomes a hero, finally leading a bayonet charge that results in the taking of prisoners. What Crane is saying is that heroism as well as cowardice is an instinctive emotional reaction and not a virtue based on conscious moral effort and resolve. At times, of course, Henry seems to be making ethical choices. He and Wilson lead a charge despite the fact that they have heard a general say that few in the regiment will survive it. When the two friends simultaneously rescue the flag from the hands of a falling color sergeant, Henry pushes Wilson away as an indication of his willingness to assume the danger of carrying the banner. Yet even Henry's capacity for self-sacrifice is explained by Crane as an emotional reaction lacking volition. It is "the delirium that encounters despair and death, and is heedless and blind to the odds. It is a temporary but sublime absence of selfishness." The culminating dramatic irony of the novel is in the paradoxical resolution of the hero quest. Henry Fleming becomes a hero, but he does so not by the exercise of those qualities that formed the subject of his fantasies but by debasing his human qualities to become an animal in battle. In terms of a change in character—in the sense that this means the transformation of moral resolution into action—the youth makes little if any progress.

In view of the counterpointing of instinctive behavior and self-delusion with which Henry is treated in the course of the novel, critics have found his sudden attainment of insight and development toward maturity in the final chapter difficult to accept. It seems as poorly motivated as his bravery in battle after his return to the regiment or Wilson's sudden transformation from a loud soldier into a humble one. The problematic nature of the conclusion, however, is consistent with Crane's dedication to psychological verisimilitude in fiction. Henry is proud of his "public deeds" but ashamed of those he has concealed from his comrades. He realizes that he has incurred guilt through his desertion of his comrades in the ranks and his abandonment of the tattered soldier, but he fails to accept responsibility for his actions, and he has not lost his tendency to rationalize. Therefore, "gradually he mustered force to put the sin at a distance," and in his youthful mind, "[s]cars faded as flowers." Henry's maturation is primarily experiential and epistemological rather than moral. He has attained neither spiritual salvation nor full maturity, but he has gone through the fires of experience and has acquired some degree of self-knowledge and understanding of his environment. "He had dwelt in a land of strange, squalling upheavals and had come forth. He had been where there was red of blood and black of passion, and he was escaped." In the nineteenth-century conception of courage and manhood, he has met the test of battle, found favor in the eyes of his comrades, and survived: "He was a man." Henry has also gained some insight into the true meaning of fear, courage, and the nature of combat and has learned that the heroic ideal is false since human behavior is largely determined by emotional reactions to external conditions. "He found that he could look back upon the brass and bombast of his earlier gospels and see them truly. He was gleeful when he discovered that he now despised them. With this conviction came a store of assurance. He felt a quiet manhood, nonassertive but of sturdy and strong blood." No longer will he attempt to predicate his future on fantasy or specious rationalizations, for he realizes that the lot of humanity is to accept the uncertainty and ambiguity that is symbolized in the final image of the novel by the sun shining through hosts of leaden rain clouds.

Suggested Reading

Beaver, Harold. "Stephen Crane: The Hero as Victim." *Yearbook of English Studies* 12 (1982): 186–93.

Beidler, Philip D. "Stephen Crane's *The Red Badge of Courage*: Henry Fleming's Courage in Its Contexts." *Clio* 20 (1991): 235–51.

Curran, John E., Jr. " 'Nobody seems to know where we go': Uncertainty, History, and Irony in *The Red Badge of Courage*." *American Literary Realism 1870–1910* 26.1 (1993): 1–12.

Delbanco, Andrew. "The American Stephen Crane: The Context of *The Red Badge of Courage*." In *New Essays on "The Red Badge of Courage."* Ed. Lee Clark Mitchell. Cambridge: Cambridge University Press, 1986. 49–76.

Fryckstedt, Olaf W. "Henry Fleming's Tupenny Fury: Cosmic Pessimism in Stephen Crane's *The Red Badge of Courage.*" *Studia Neophilologica* 33 (1961): 265–81.

Kent, Thomas. "Epistemological Uncertainty in *The Red Badge of Courage.*" *Modern Fiction Studies* 27 (1982): 621–28.

LaRocca, Charles J. "Stephen Crane's Inspiration." *American Heritage* 42.3 (1991): 108–9.

Limon, John. *Writing after War: American War Fiction from Realism to Postmodernism.* New York: Oxford University Press, 1994. 32–58.

Rechnitz, Robert M. "Depersonalization and the Dream in *The Red Badge of Courage.*" *Studies in the Novel* 6 (1974): 76–87.

Swann, Charles. "Stephen Crane and a Problem of Interpretation." *Literature and History* 7 (1981): 91–123.

Wertheim, Stanley. "*The Red Badge of Courage* and Personal Narratives of the Civil War." *American Literary Realism 1870–1910* 6 (1973): 61–65.

"The Red Badge of Courage Was His Wig-Wag Flag". Published in the *New York World* on 1 July 1898, this Cuban War dispatch deals with events that occurred on 14 June when Crane accompanied a detachment of U.S. Marines and Cuban insurgents commanded by Captain George F. Elliott* on a mission to Cuzco, six miles down the coast from Guantánamo Bay, to destroy a guerrilla encampment guarding the only well in the area. This is Crane's most personal account of combat in Cuba, and it employs a technique found often in his war fiction: the contrast of the serenity of nature amid the chaos of human struggle. As the marines prepare for the march, they contemplate "the dash and death there would presently be on the other side of those hills—those mysterious hills not far away, placidly in the sunlight veiling the scene of somebody's last gasp." During the short but fierce battle, the sky is cloudless; "the sun blazed out of it as if it would melt the earth," and the bay is "a vast expanse of blue sea." The editorially supplied title of the dispatch is a reference to Sergeant John H. Quick,* whose flag signals directed fire from the *Dolphin* offshore. Quick is mentioned only briefly here, but his courageous actions are extolled in Crane's sketch, "Marines Signalling Under Fire at Guantanamo."

Redmond, Dr. The psychiatrist in "The Squire's Madness" who surprisingly concludes that it is Linton's wife, not Linton, who is insane.

Reeves, Earl T. (?–?). Crane's closest friend at Claverack College and Hudson River Institute. Nicknamed "Sioux" or "the Rushville Indian" by Crane because he came from Rushville, Indiana, Reeves was rumored to be the richest boy in the school.

Suggested Reading

Starrett, Vincent. "Stephen Crane at Claverack." *Stephen Crane Newsletter* 2.1 (1967): 4.

"Regulars Get No Glory". This is Crane's last Cuban War dispatch for the *New York World*, which printed it on 20 July 1898 (it had appeared in the *Philadelphia Press* and the *Boston Globe* on the previous day). Datelined from Siboney on 9 July, the dispatch is a bitter diatribe against the neglect by the American press of the regular soldier in favor of the more socially prominent men who comprise the volunteer regiments such as Theodore Roosevelt's* Rough Riders. Crane does not disparage the courage of the volunteers but is indignant that the public is informed only "of the gallantry of Reginald Marmaduke Maurice Montmorenci Sturtevant, and for goodness sake how the poor old chappy endures that dreadful hard-tack and bacon. Whereas, the name of the regular soldier is probably Michael Nolan and his life-sized portrait was not in the papers in celebration of his enlistment." Nolan, Crane's archetypal regular soldier, is described as "[t]he ungodly Nolan, the sweating, swearing, overloaded, hungry, thirsty, sleepless Nolan, tearing his breeches on the barbed wire entanglements, wallowing through the muddy fords, pursuing his way through the stiletto-pointed thickets, climbing the fire-crowned hill—Nolan gets shot." Private Jimmie Nolan is the character who is shot to death in a charge up a hillside in Crane's later Cuban War story, "The Price of the Harness," and an actual marine named Nolan is listed among those who volunteered for a rescue party in Crane's dispatch "Night Attacks on the Marines and a Brave Rescue," datelined from Guantánamo on 4 July 1898.

Reifsnyder. The garrulous proprietor of a Whilomville barbershop that serves as a social center in "The Monster." To those "who looked through the glass from the yellow glamour of Reifsnyder's shop . . . the people without resembled the inhabitants of a great aquarium that here had a square pane in it." Reifsnyder and his customers are a choric voice in the story commenting on the ethics and propriety of Dr. Trescott's actions in saving the deformed Henry Johnson. In "The Angel Child," Reifsnyder is the representative of the Whilomville barbers' union who approves the credentials of the demented barber William Neeltje. One of Crane's Delta Upsilon fraternity brothers at Lafayette College* was named Samuel K. Reifsnyder, which is probably the source of the name.

Reigate. Commander of the *Holy Moses* in "The Revenge of the *Adolphus*."

"The Reluctant Voyagers". The grotesque characterizations, overstated dialogue, and bathetic humor in this lengthy story and the fact that a fragment of the opening text was written on a leaf of the manuscript of "The Holler Tree" suggest a date of composition contemporaneous with the Sullivan County tales, but a draft of the opening of *George's Mother* also appears on two leaves of "The Holler Tree" manuscript, indicating that "The Holler Tree" may have been composed later than some of the other Sullivan County stories that were published in the summer of 1892. Corwin Knapp Linson* recalls that Crane brought "The Reluctant Voyagers" to his studio in the spring of 1893 and asked him to draw illustrations for it. Linson did so, and the manuscript was submitted to a "responsible magazine," where it languished for six months before being returned to Crane for some minor revisions. When it was resubmitted, Linson's drawings were lost, and the magazine failed to publish the story. "The Reluctant Voyagers" did not appear until it was syndicated in two parts on 11 and 18 February 1900 in American newspapers through an English agency, Tillitson's (the Northern Newspaper Syndicate). It was collected in *Last Words*.

The two main characters in "The Reluctant Voyagers" are given nondescript names (Tom Sharp and Ted) but are usually identified only as "the tall man" and "the freckled man." They are at a beach resort and decide to go swimming. A bathhouse attendant miscalculates the physical dimensions of the freckled man and rents him a bathing suit that is much too large. Embarrassed to be seen in this ridiculous-looking outfit, the freckled man dashes into the water followed by the tall man. They crawl aboard a raft floating near the beach and succumb to a relaxed drowsiness. Suddenly they realize that the raft has been swept out to sea. After much time spent in bickering and recriminations, they are finally rescued by a sailing vessel that, after a series of misadventures, lands them in New York City; still dressed only in their bathing suits, they hail a cab and ride off to the apartment of a friend who lives in Park Place. There is a comic reversal at the end of the story when the freckled man lectures the tall man on his deficiencies of temperament and blames him for their plight, when at the beginning the tall man had hectored his freckled friend.

Attributes of style and theme in this seemingly pointless story anticipate Crane's later and better works. The subjectivity of experience and the limitations of perception are stressed. The bathhouse clerk looks at the world "with superior eyes through a hole in a board." Three ships seen by the men in the distance "fell off the horizon." The external world is insistently personified and animated. The sea "heaved painfully, like a lost bosom"; "A moon came and looked at them." The insignificance of the individual in an indifferent universe is epitomized in the freckled man's exclamation, "I feel like a molecule," and the deflation of self-delusion is a major element in the story. The tall man fantasizes that they "will be rescued by some ship bound for the golden seas of the south" with "[k]ind sailors in blue and white" and a "handsome, bearded captain with gold bands all around." Instead, they are picked up by a commonplace merchant vessel sailing from Little Egg Harbor, New Jersey, to Athens, New York, whose barefooted captain wears "[f]earful trousers" supported by a solitary suspender that seems on the point of snapping and whose bronzed face sports a solitary whisker. The shock of confrontation with reality leaves the two men baffled but no wiser.

Suggested Reading

Wolford, Chester L. *Stephen Crane: A Study of the Short Fiction*. Boston: Twayne, 1989. 14–17.

Remington, Frederic (1861–1909). An American artist who recorded the rapidly disappearing Wild West in paintings, drawings, and sculpture, as Crane did in fiction, Remington worked for a time as a cowboy. He studied at the Art Students League and in 1891 established his studio in New Rochelle, New York. He was also an illustrator for magazines and supplied a full-page drawing for Crane's ''A Man and Some Others'' in the *Century*. During the Spanish-American War, Remington was employed as a correspondent and artist in Cuba, sketching illustrations for a number of magazines. He and Crane were together on dispatch boats off the Cuban coast and on the vantage point of El Pozo on the morning of 1 July 1898, at the beginning of the fateful battle for the San Juan hills. After the Cuban campaign, Remington returned to his favorite subject, the artistic exploration of the old West.

Suggested Reading

Samuels, Peggy, and Harold. *Frederic Remington: A Biography*. Garden City, N.Y.: Doubleday, 1982.

''A Reminiscence of Indian War''. Because of its time and place of publication in the *New York Tribune* on 26 June 1892 and because it focuses on a skirmish in Sullivan County, New York, this piece has sometimes been grouped among Crane's Sullivan County sketches. Unlike them, its subject is not hunting or folklore but a campaign in July 1779 during the Revolutionary War by a group of Tories and Indians who conducted a murderous rampage in the Delaware Valley in which many civilians were slaughtered. Crane also dealt with the subject of massacre during the Revolution in his later Wyoming Valley (Pennsylvania) stories, and both this sketch and the stories are based on *Wyoming* (1858), a book by his maternal grandfather, George Peck. Crane's paternal ancestry—two Stephen Cranes fought in the Revolutionary War—also predisposed him to a lifelong interest in the subject of the American Revolution. ''A Reminiscence of Indian War'' recounts events at the Battle of Minisink and a foolhardy attempt by a militia group to pursue the retreating Indians who had devastated the Delaware Valley. The sketch ends on a note of typical Craneian irony. The officer who had urged the suicidal venture was one of a group of men cut off from the main American force and was not involved in the battle in which many of his comrades were killed.

''The Revenge of the *Adolphus*''. A fictionalized account of the experience of correspondents aboard a dispatch boat off the Cuban coast during the early phase of the Spanish-American War, this story is loosely related to Crane's reportage, especially his *New York World* dispatch, ''Chased by a Big 'Spanish Man-O'-War.' '' The story was first printed in *Collier's Weekly* on 28 October 1899 from a text Crane sent to the magazine before he received a list of corrections of naval terms he had requested from Commander J. C. Colwell, the U.S. naval attaché in London. Crane incorporated many of Colwell's suggestions in the text of "The Revenge of the *Adolphus*" that appeared in the *Strand Magazine* in December 1899. The story was collected in *Wounds in the Rain*.

Fictional names for naval officers are used in "The Revenge of the *Adolphus*." The only correspondent aboard the dispatch boat specifically identified is Shackles, the designation Crane also used for Ernest W. McCready* in " 'God Rest Ye, Merry Gentlemen' " and "Virtue in War." Two of the American naval ships, the *Hudson* and the *Winslow*, are named the *Chicken* and the *Holy Moses*, adding a note of spoofery to the story. There are occasional flashes of Crane's best sea writing suggestive of "The Open Boat." When the correspondents perceive that the *Adolphus* is being pursued by two Spanish gunboats against which the dispatch boat is helpless, one of them "bitterly accused himself, the others, and the dark, sightless, indifferent world." The "certainty of coming evil" simultaneously isolates the correspondents and causes them to seek a common bond, and "each man looked at the others to discover their degree of fear and did his best to conceal his own, holding his crackling nerves with all his strength." The unconcern of nature with the human condition is affirmed by the sea over which the gunboats race, "a glowing blue plain with the golden shine dancing at the tips of the waves." Otherwise, the story is an uncomplicated and only slightly fictionalized account of a naval battle in Cardenas Harbor. The American cruiser *Wilmington*, here named the *Chancellorville*, rescues the dispatch boat from the two Spanish gunboats and drives them into a shallow port, where the cruiser is unable to pursue them. Two smaller American ships, the *Chicken*, a converted harbor tug, and the *Holy Moses*, the former yacht of a Philadelphia millionaire, enter the bay through a ruse and in a spirited exchange of fire destroy the gunboats.

Reynolds, Paul Revere (1864–1944). Born into a family of Boston Brahmins, Reynolds was graduated in 1887 from Harvard, where he studied philosophy and psychology under William James. In 1892, a year after the passage of the international copyright law, he began to sell publication rights of English books to American publishers on behalf of the firm of Cassell & Company, Ltd. Later he represented other English publishers, and in 1895 he established himself as America's first professional literary agent, acting on behalf of authors independently by selling their manuscripts to magazine editors and publishers and charging them a commission for his services. Among the American writers Reynolds represented were Paul Lawrence Dunbar, Hamlin Garland,* Joel Chandler Harris, Stephen Crane, Frank Norris,* Willa Cather,* and Jack London. Foreign authors included Émile Zola, Leo Tolstoy, George Bernard Shaw, Joseph Conrad,* and H. G. Wells.*

Crane and Reynolds met at a luncheon given by Irving Bacheller* at the Lantern Club* in early 1896. The extensive correspondence between them, sometimes through Cora, is a chronicle of Crane's literary career in the years following the publication of *The Red Badge of Courage*. At first Crane apparently used Reynolds as a means of obtaining more money for his work by breaking prior commitments to publishers. In September Crane wrote to him requesting that he arrange the sale of "A Man and Some Others" but cautioning him not to approach Bacheller or McClure, to both of whom he was financially indebted. Reynolds placed the story with the *Century Magazine*. In October Crane attempted to circumvent his obligation to the McClure syndicate by having Reynolds sell serial rights of *The Third Violet* directly to the *New York World*. In March 1897 Reynolds sold "The Open Boat" to Scribner's. In October of that year, Crane established a regular relationship with Reynolds as his literary agent, largely, as he wrote him, "to get me out of the ardent grasp of the S. S. McClure Co.," since McClure was holding "The Monster" and "The Bride Comes to Yellow Sky" as collateral on a loan advance made in March. By mid-December, his financial situation declining, Crane tried to circumvent the exclusive agency rights he had granted Reynolds by selling the English rights to "The Five White Mice" and "Death and the Child," but Reynolds's protest caused him to abandon this effort, and Reynolds sold "Death and the Child" to *Harper's Weekly*. In early 1898 Reynolds arranged the sale of "The Monster," finally relinquished by McClure, to Harper and Brothers and "The Blue Hotel," which had been rejected by the *Atlantic Monthly*, to *Collier's Weekly*.

When the Spanish-American War ended, Crane lived a virtually underground existence in Havana for almost four months, but he corresponded regularly with Reynolds, sending him the manuscripts of poems for *War Is Kind* and Cuban War stories. At Crane's insistence, Reynolds persuaded Harper and Brothers to publish "The Monster," "The Blue Hotel," and "His New Mittens" in one volume, comprising the American edition of *The Monster and Other Stories*, and he sold Crane's Whilomville stories to *Harper's Magazine* and the book rights for these stories to Harper and Brothers. In November 1898 Crane turned his English affairs over to James B. Pinker, and in July 1899 he broke with Reynolds, making Pinker his literary agent on both sides of the Atlantic. Nevertheless, relations between Crane and Reynolds were resumed in January 1900, and even after Crane's death, Reynolds occasionally sold his stories to American magazines. In the spring of 1901 he sold *Last Words* to Henry T. Coates of Philadelphia and secured an advance, but the American edition of the book was never published.

Suggested Reading

Allen, Frederick Lewis. *Paul Revere Reynolds*. New York: Privately printed, 1944.
Wertheim Stanley, and Paul Sorrentino, eds. *The Correspondence of Stephen Crane*. New York: Columbia University Press, 1988.

Richardson. The main character and central consciousness of "One Dash—Horses," through whom Crane registers the emotions of anxiety and fear similar to those apprehended by Henry Fleming in *The Red Badge of Courage*. Like Henry, Richardson demonstrates courage and exerts considerable control over his situation, but he is twice saved from death by chance rather than his own enterprise—first when the arrival of a group of women interrupts a potentially deadly confrontation between him and a group of Mexican bandits and again when he and his servant are rescued from the pursuing bandits by a detachment of *rurales*. That Richardson is "a New Yorker" supports the contention that there is an autobiographical foundation for the story.

Richie, Edith (?–?). The niece of Kate Lyon* and the sister of Mark Barr's* wife, Mabel, nineteen-year-old Edith Richie came to Brede Place* in July 1899 as a companion for Crane's niece, Helen, and stayed as a house guest until January 1900. She was an important part of the Crane household, traveling with Stephen and Cora to Paris and Ireland and taking dictation for a number of Crane's stories and sketches. Under her married name of Edith Richie Jones, she left a lively and detailed, if somewhat idyllic, memoir of life at Brede Place that highlights the familiar stories of the haunted room, Crane's association with Joseph Conrad* and Henry James,* and the genesis of works such as "Manacled," "The Ghost," and *The O'Ruddy*. Unlike Conrad and Ford Madox Ford,* Edith Richie insists that she never heard money mentioned at Brede and never saw an uninvited guest.

Suggested Reading

Jones, Edith Richie. "Stephen Crane at Brede." *Atlantic Monthly* 194 (July 1954): 57–61.

Richie, Major General. A character in the Spitzbergen tales, General Richie is commander of the 7,500-man force of the Spitzbergen army invading Rostina. He is playfully named after Edith Richie.*

Riis, Jacob (1849–1914). A journalist, author, and photographer, Riis was born in Denmark and, like Crane, was one of fourteen children. He emigrated to America in 1870 at the age of twenty-one and worked at odd jobs that brought him into contact with the New York City poor. Often in the early years he slept in shelters provided for vagrants by the police. Riis was a reporter for several newspapers. In 1877 he began to cover the police beat for the *New York Tribune*, a job he shared with Lincoln Steffens. Later he transferred to the *New York Sun*, with which he was associated until 1899. In the late 1890s he lectured on the living conditions of New York tenement dwellers, using slides made from a flash photography process that he perfected. Immersion in the slums led to the writing of his best-known book, *How the Other Half Lives* (1890). *The Children of the Poor* (1892) exposed the exploitation of minors in tenement factories. Among his other important social studies are *Out of Mulberry Street* (1898) and *The Battle with the Slums* (1902). Riis's books were illustrated with his own photographs. His pictures as well as his words exposed the squalid living conditions of the poor. Riis's books, magazine articles, and lectures anticipated the muckrakers and made him one of the most important figures in the reform movement of the late nineteenth century. Theodore Roosevelt* was a consistent supporter of his causes.

In the 24 July 1892 issue of the *New York Tribune*, Crane reported that a few days earlier Riis had given an illustrated lecture in Asbury Park, New Jersey, on the plight of tenement dwellers. While Crane learned most of what he knew about New York City's slums from personal observation, most likely his final redaction of *Maggie: A Girl of the Streets* was influenced by Riis's lectures and writings. The ethnically divided neighborhoods of the underclass are closely described in *How the Other Half Lives*, where Crane might have read about "The Problem of the Children," "The Reign of Rum," "The Working Girls of New York," and the "toughs" from Battle Row and Poverty Gap, who closely resemble the brawling urchins of Devil's Row and Rum Alley in the opening paragraphs of *Maggie*. *Children of the Poor* emphasizes the degenerative effects of the tenements, sweatshops, saloons, and gangs on young people in the slums. Riis's depictions and graphic photographs of the living conditions of the immigrant poor were probably as important a part of Crane's background as direct personal experience. Crane had occasional social contacts with Riis through 1896, but their personal relationship was never close, and they were temperamentally very different. In contrast to Crane's detached individualism, Riis was essentially a moralist who held an ideal of the city as a Christian community. He articulated traditional family values not practicable for the polyglot ethnic enclaves of New York in the 1890s, and there is an unmistakable nativist tone to his writings. Crane focused on perception and self-awareness as catalysts of social change, while Riis stressed tenement reform, better schools, moral guidance, and community involvement.

Suggested Reading

Fried, Lewis F. *Makers of the City*. Amherst: University of Massachusetts Press, 1990. 3–63.

Ware, Louise. *Jacob Riis: Police Reporter, Reformer, and Useful Citizen*. New York: Appleton-Century, 1938.

Robins, Elizabeth (1862–1952). An American actress, playwright, and novelist and a friend of Henry James,* Elizabeth Robins emigrated to England in 1888 following the suicide of her husband. She won acclaim in the 1890s for her London performances in Henrik Ibsen's plays. Her best-selling novel, *The Magnetic North* (1904), was based on her experience in Alaska, and her controversial play, *Votes for Women* (1907), was a valuable contribution to the suffrage movement. It was recast in novel form as *The Convert* (1907). Robins came to know Cora Crane through the Society of American Women in London* and was a visitor to Brede Place.* She declined to contribute to Cora's fund for Kate Lyon's* children because of "a prior & most imperative claim" on her funds, probably one of the women's rights causes to which she was dedicated.

Suggested Reading

Gates, Joanne E. *Elizabeth Robins, 1862–1952: Actress, Novelist, Feminist*. Tuscaloosa:
    University of Alabama Press, 1994.
John, Angela V. *Elizabeth Robins: Staging a Life, 1862–1952*. London: Routledge, 1995.

Roddle, Ben. A character in "Twelve O'Clock" who rightly fears that the reputation for gunfighting in his western town would frighten away any "eastern capiterlist" and wants to organize the citizens in an effort to make the cowboys lay down their weapons.

Rogers, Jimmie. In *The Red Badge of Courage*, Rogers is a soldier in Henry Fleming's company. He is shot through the body on the second day of battle, and his agonies underscore the horrors of war.

"The Roof Gardens and Gardeners of New York". This Sunday feature piece, syndicated in newspapers by McClure on 9 August 1896, portrays the grand summer roof garden restaurants that flourished in New York in the late nineteenth century. Crane focuses on two recently opened roof gardens, one at the top of Grand Central Palace, "large enough for a regimental drill room," and Oscar Hammerstein's gaudy and dazzling Olympia on Broadway, with "real swans swimming in real water." Contrasted to the splendor of these watering places for the affluent are the roofs of tenements to which the denizens of the slums are driven on hot summer evenings. "An evening upon a tenement roof with the great golden march of the stars across the sky and Johnnie gone for a pail of beer is not so bad if you have never seen the mountains nor heard, to your heart, the slow sad song of the pines."

Roosevelt, Theodore (1858–1919). Educated at Harvard from which he was graduated in 1880, Roosevelt served three one-year terms in the New York Assembly (1882–84). He lived as a rancher in the Dakota Territory for two years, returning in 1886 to run unsuccessfully for mayor of New York City. An early interest in American history turned Roosevelt to authorship, beginning with *The Naval War of 1812* (1882). His devotion to heroic action and literary narrative is exemplified in *The Winning of the West* (1889–96) and *The Strenuous Life* (1900). In 1895 Roosevelt became president of New York's Board of Police Commissioners. Two years later he was appointed assistant secretary of the navy by President William McKinley. During the Spanish-American War, Roosevelt achieved distinction in Cuba as a lieutenant colonel and subsequently the colonel of the Rough Riders, a volunteer regiment that he had helped to organize. He was elected governor of New York State in 1898 and vice president of the United States in 1900. After the assassination of McKinley on 14 September 1901, Roosevelt became the twenty-sixth president. He was elected to that office in his own right in 1901, serving until 1909. In 1912 Roosevelt, as leader of the Republican Party's progressive wing, again sought the nomination for the presidency but was defeated by William Howard Taft. He subsequently established his own National Progressive Party, popularly known as the Bull Moose Party, and zealously advocated social and economic reforms.

Roosevelt met Crane at the Lantern Club* in late 1895 or early 1896. He admired Crane's fiction, especially *The Red Badge of Courage*. He read *Maggie*, and Crane sent him an inscribed copy of *George's Mother* and a typescript of "A Man and Some Others," to which Roosevelt reacted with characteristic ethnocentrism, writing to Crane: "Some day I want you to write another story of the frontiersman and the Mexican Greaser in which the frontiersman shall come out on top; it is more normal that way!" When in the summer of 1896 Crane began to investigate conditions of life in the Tenderloin for a series of articles in the *New York Journal*, Roosevelt was at first cooperative. In his capacity as chairman of the Board of Police Commissioners, he agreed to be interviewed, and he arranged for Crane to observe proceedings in the Jefferson Market Police Court, but when Crane began to criticize the conduct of the New York City police, Roosevelt became defensive. To preserve his relationship with Roosevelt, Crane published his most scathing attacks on the police in an obscure newspaper, the *Port Jervis Gazette*, rather than in the *Journal*. Nevertheless, when in October 1896 Crane defended a notorious prostitute, Dora Clark,* and testified in her behalf when she brought charges of false arrest against two members of the police department, Roosevelt was outraged, and his resentment never slackened. Jimmie Hare* recalled an incident aboard a train in September 1902 when Roosevelt was president. Hare maintained that Crane's problems in New York resulted from his investigations as a reporter, and Roosevelt retorted: "Nonsense! . . . He wasn't gathering any data! He was a man of bad character and he was simply consorting with loose women." Crane, on the other hand, retained his journalistic objectivity toward Roosevelt. When during the Las Guásimas battle Roosevelt was accused of leading his men into an ambush, Crane's report of the incident in the 26 June 1898 *New York World* was headed "Roosevelt's Rough Riders' Loss Due to a Gallant Blunder."

Suggested Reading

Miller, Nathan. *Theodore Roosevelt: A Life*. New York: Morrow, 1993.
Moers, Ellen. "Teddy Roosevelt: Literary Feller." *Columbia University Forum* 6.3 (1963): 10–16.
Cairnes, Cecil. *Jimmie Hare, News Photographer: Half a Century with a Camera*. New York: Macmillan, 1940. 128–29.

"Roosevelt's Rough Riders' Loss Due to a Gallant Blunder". In this short telegram, published in the *New York World* and the *Philadelphia Press* on 26 June 1898, Crane defends Lieutenant Colonel Theodore Roosevelt* against the charge that he led the Rough Riders into an ambush on the road to Las Guásimas on 24 June. There is nevertheless an implicit criticism in Crane's statement that the regiment "marched noisily through the narrow road in the woods, talking volubly" and suffered heavy losses "due to the remarkably wrong idea of how the Spaniards bushwhack." Crane handles this incident more fully in his dispatch "Stephen Crane at the Front for the World."

"The Royal Irish Constabulary". The third in the series of "Irish Notes," this sketch was published in the *Westminster Gazette* on 5 November 1897 and collected in *Last Words*. Crane views the Irish constabulary force as a veritable occupying army, the representatives of the British empire. The life of the constable amid hostile neighbors, he insists, is "lonely, ascetic, and barren." Constables are as imprisoned by their isolation as lighthouse keepers or "conspiring monks." The *New York Sun* on 6 November cast scorn on Crane's depiction of the Irish constable, and in the 3 December *Westminster Gazette* Michael F. Morahan, a retired constable, wrote a good-natured rejoinder, refuting Crane's claim that constables were socially ostracized in Ireland.

Royale, Colonel. A character in *The O'Ruddy*. Colonel Royale is defeated in a duel by The O'Ruddy and, in turn, serves as his second in his duel with Forister.

Ruedy, Charlotte (?–?). A native of Akron, Ohio, Mrs. Ruedy, Cora's unobtrusive companion and assistant from the Hotel de Dream, accompanied her to Greece and lived with the Cranes in England at Ravensbrook* and Brede Place.* Her status in the Crane household is obscure, but allusions to her in letters from Harold Frederic* and others, such as Joseph Conrad,* who referred to her as "the good Auntie Ruedy," indicate that she was a friend and not a lady's maid. Mrs. Ruedy returned to the United States in June 1899. After Crane's funeral, Cora went back to England with another companion, Mrs. Brotherton, about whom even less is known than Mrs. Ruedy.

S

"Sailing Day Scenes". A short sketch in the *New York Press*, 10 June 1894, depicting the sailing of an ocean liner bound for Europe from a New York pier. Like "When Every One Is Panic Stricken" and "The Broken-Down Van," this is a genre piece, not a report of a specific event. Crane realistically evokes the bustle, confusion, and excitement of imminent departure. With unusual sentimentality, he focuses on the emotions of families that are being separated, especially women whose husbands are sailing.

"Sampson Inspects Harbor at Mariel". Because of the friendship of Crane's *New York World* bureau chief, Sylvester Scovel,* with Acting Rear Admiral William T. Sampson,* commander of the North Atlantic Squadron, Crane spent two days aboard the, U.S.S. *New York*, an armored cruiser that served as the flagship of the American naval force, on an inspection trip of the Spanish defenses at Mariel, a harbor and city west of Havana. In this dispatch, published in the *World* and other newspapers on 1 May 1898, Crane describes the trip down the coast and a minor engagement involving an exchange of fire between the musketry of a troop of Spanish cavalry and the four-inch guns of the *New York*.

Sampson, William T. (1840–1902). A graduate of the U.S. Naval Academy, Sampson attained the rank of captain in 1889. In 1890 he took command of the U.S.S. *San Francisco*, the first modern steel cruiser in the U.S. Navy. Acting rear admiral commanding the North Atlantic Squadron in 1898, Sampson was not present when the ships under his command destroyed Admiral Cervera's fleet on 3 July, Commodore Winfield S. Schley having taken command. In "War Memories," Crane called Sampson "the most interesting person of the war." On first acquaintance, Crane thought that Sampson seemed immensely bored by the conflict, but he finally concluded that "hidden in his indifferent, even apathetic, manner there was the alert, sure, fine mind of the best sea-captain that America has produced since—since Farragut? I don't know. I think—since Hull."

Sawyer, Captain. The captured Confederate officer in "Three Miraculous Soldiers." In order to rescue him, one of the Confederate soldiers rushes out of hiding and knocks out a Union guard. The sight of the prostrate guard evokes Mary Hinckson's sympathy.

"Sayings of the Turret Jacks in Our Blockading Fleets". Published in the *New York World* on 15 May 1898, this sketch reproduces fragments of conversation on the American warships blockading the Cuban coast. There is banter between sailors as to which ship and which captain is superior; a monologue by a sailor who is reprimanded by a deck officer for bringing his launch back to the ship when the officer learns, to his embarrassment, that he had forgotten to haul down the signal flag that recalled an earlier launch; an anecdote about a woman aboard a captured Spanish ship who spurns the spurious gallantry of an American naval lieutenant; and a final mocking question: "Where is the *Vizcaya*? That's what I want to know. She came over here feelin' so brash, and had all them people in Havana cheerin' themselves to death. But where is she now? That's what I want to know." The Spanish cruiser *Vizcaya* was bombarded while attempting to slip out of Santiago harbor. Having hauled down its colors, it ran aground and exploded, with great loss of life.

"The Scotch Express". In August 1897, en route to visit Harold Frederic* and Kate Lyon* in Ireland, the Cranes took the Scotch Express from London's Euston Station to Glasgow and from there the River Clyde steamer to Cobh, then named Queenstown. By the fall Crane was under contract to write an article about the train ride for S. S. McClure, but publication of "The Scotch Express" was delayed until January 1899, when it appeared simultaneously in *McClure's Magazine* in the United States and in *Cassell's Magazine* in England with illustrations by William L Sonntag, Jr., who accompanied the Cranes to Glasgow. Crane rode in the cabs of the successive engines employed on the three major parts of the trip: the "monster painted a glowing vermilion" that brought the train from London to Crewe, a tandem of engines for the journey to Carlisle, and the smaller engine of the Caledonian Railway that completed the journey to Glasgow, all at an average speed of almost fifty miles an hour. This essay offers an impressionistic sweep of vistas from the suburbs of London, through "the clear-shining English scenery" and the forests of Scotland, to "the long prison-like row of tenements" on the outskirts of Glasgow that resemble the slums of New York. There is more focus on the train itself and its operations than on the countryside through which it passes, with commentary on the signal and switching systems, the decor of the engine cabs, the dining cars and passenger compartments, and the roadbeds, tunnels, and stations as compared to their American counterparts.

Scovel, Henry Sylvester (1869–1905). Son of a Presbyterian minister who became president of the University of Wooster (now the College of Wooster), Sylvester Scovel, as he always called himself, attended the University of Michigan but dropped out in his sophomore year and embarked on a series of jobs in engineering and entertainment promotion firms. In 1895 he began his career as a journalist, reporting the growing insurrection in Cuba for the *New York Herald* and the *Pittsburgh Dispatch*. In 1896 he was briefly imprisoned by the Spanish authorities for consorting with the rebels and carrying false credentials but escaped and was hired as a correspondent for the *New York World*. For almost a year Scovel lived with insurgent groups and became a trusted confidant of their leader, General Máximo Gómez. In February 1897 he was again captured by the Spaniards but released at the insistence of the U.S. government. In April 1897 Scovel married Frances Cabanné. After covering the brief Greek-Turkish War and undertaking an expedition to the Klondike accompanied by his wife, to report the gold rush for the *World*, Scovel was sent back to Cuba. At the outbreak of the war between the United States and Spain, he became bureau chief of *World* correspondents with the American forces. At the ceremony marking the Spanish surrender in Santiago de Cuba on 17 July 1898, Scovel was involved in a scuffle with the commanding general, William R. Shafter,* that resulted in his expulsion from Cuba and almost ended his career as a reporter, but he returned to Havana and until 1902 served as a *World* correspondent and as a consulting engineer to the U.S. military government. After he resigned this position, he engaged in several promotional enterprises in Havana, where he lived for the remainder of his life.

Crane accompanied Scovel and other *World* reporters to Jacksonville, Florida, in late November 1896, where Scovel headed the efforts to find a filibustering boat to take the *World* staff to Cuba. He did not sail on the doomed *Commodore* with Crane but on another boat. Scovel met Cora in Jacksonville and encountered her again with Crane in Athens, in May 1897. From Athens, Scovel wrote to his wife that he had feared Cora "would ruin [Crane], but really her influence has, so far, been the reverse." In Cuba Scovel and Crane were close collaborators in their work for the *World*. Scovel's friendship with Admiral Sampson* enabled Crane to spend two days at the end of April 1898 aboard the flagship *New York*, resulting in Crane's 1 May *World* dispatch, "Sampson Inspects Harbor at Mariel," and on 4 May Scovel and Crane took the spy Charles H. Thrall* to the flagship in their dispatch boat. Crane's interview with Thrall was printed in the *World* on 8 May. Scovel or his wife took the well-known photographs of a disheveled Crane dressed in pajamas aboard the *Three Friends*. On 17 June, Scovel, Crane, and Alexander Kenealy* established *World* headquarters near Santiago, and Crane accompanied Scovel on a mission to ascertain the deployment of the Spanish fleet in Santiago Harbor. Crane reported this adventure in a 12 July *World* dispatch, "Hunger Has Made Cubans Fatalists." Scovel and Crane were also together at the storming of the San Juan hills on 1 July, and it was most likely Scovel who wrote the unsigned report, printed in the *World* on 16 July, accusing the officers of the Seventy-first New York Volunteer Regiment of cowardice that was attributed to Crane and resulted in his severance from the newspaper. Scovel appears as a character in some of Crane's Cuban War stories, as Walkely in " 'God Rest Ye, Merry Gentlemen' " and under his own name in "War Memories."

Suggested Reading

Milton, Joyce. *The Yellow Kids: Foreign Correspondents in the Heyday of Yellow Journalism.* New York: Harper & Row, 1989.
Wertheim, Stanley, and Paul Sorrentino. *The Crane Log.* New York: Hall, 1994.

Scully, Johnnie. The son of Patrick Scully in "The Blue Hotel," Johnnie is an important character in the story. He is similar to the gambler, who preys "solely upon reckless and senile farmers," in that he attempts to deceive a gullible farmer by cheating at cards, even though money is not involved in the game. His cheating and his defense of his false sense of honor initiate the violence that ultimately results in the murder of the Swede, but like the cowboy and the Easterner, he repeatedly disavows responsibility, professing to his father that "[w]e didn't do nothin' at all."

Scully, Patrick. The proprietor of the Palace Hotel in Fort Romper, Scully plays an ambivalent role in "The Blue Hotel." He represents at once the voice of society and the failure of that society to form a viable community. Scully joins the Easterner in attempting to assure the Swede that the Wild West exists only in his imagination. He is ingratiating and placating, but after his son Johnnie is defeated by the Swede in a fistfight, he joins the others in expressing murderous impulses toward him: " 'I'd loike to take that Swade,' he wailed, 'and hould 'im down on a shtone flure and bate 'im to a jelly wid a shtick.' "

"The Seaside Assembly's Work at Avon". A report printed in the *New York Tribune*, 29 August 1892, that gives an account of lectures and entertainment at the Seaside Assembly's summer school and a plan to deepen the channel of Shark River to make it navigable for yachts and passenger vessels. A sequel, "The Seaside Assembly," appears in the *Tribune* on 6 September and gives a more detailed description of the departments or "schools" of the assembly. These are fairly straightforward articles, lacking the bantering sarcasm evident in many of Crane's reports from the New Jersey shore.

"The Seaside Hotel Hop". A sketch in the *New York Tribune*, 11 September 1892, describing a typical Saturday evening dance in a New Jersey shore summer hotel. In a bantering tone Crane describes the "types" usually seen at such events: the avaricious hotel proprietor, the little girls with short white dresses demonstrating skills learned in dancing school, the "summer girl," the young men in tennis shirts, and the inevitable spinsters in the front row who sit in judgment.

"The Second Generation". A Cuban War story published simultaneously in the December 1899 issue of *Cornhill Magazine* and the *Saturday Evening Post* (2 December 1899) and collected in *Last Words*, this story was apparently written in such haste that Crane confused it with "Virtue in War," writing several times to James Pinker that he was not certain that the two titles did not refer to the same story. "The Second Generation" is a critique of the nepotism and class privilege that produced the inadequate gentleman officer. The story deals with two "cads": Senator Cadogan "from the great State of Skowmulligan, where the war fever ran very high," and his son, Caspar, who is "resolved to go to the tropic wars and do something." Through political chicanery and manipulation, the senator secures a commission for Caspar as a captain and commissary of an army corps. Crane comments that the practice of appointing a large number of well-bred young men without military experience as officers has "all the logic of going to sea in a bathing-machine." Senator Cadogan has few illusions about his son, who he realizes "couldn't successfully run a boarding house in Ocean Grove," but he desperately hopes that Caspar will not disgrace himself. Caspar's brigade, under the command of General Reilly, an old friend of the senator, lands at Siboney, and from the first Caspar neglects his duties, occupying himself with searching for his misplaced saddle bags and stuffing himself with potted ham and crackers from the brigade stores he is supervising. A colonel on Reilly's staff characterizes him as a "selfish young pig." The brigade takes part in the 1 July 1898 attack on the San Juan hills overlooking Santiago. Casualties are very high, especially among the officers. At the War Department, the senator is rebuffed when he attempts to obtain news of Caspar and seems to come to some awareness of the impropriety of obtaining special privileges for his son. Caspar has survived, but during the long encampment, he becomes the object of scorn when he refuses a drink of water from his full canteen to a fever-stricken young lieutenant. On his return to the family estate in Long Island, Caspar buckles under the intense interrogation of his father, admitting that he performed his duties barely competently and that he was not in good repute with his fellow officers. Reluctantly, the senator, who still retains perfidious ambitions to make Caspar a general, concludes that he is simply "no damn good."

"Seen at Hot Springs". A pedestrian report syndicated by Bacheller on 3 March 1895 of Crane's brief stop in Hot Springs, Arkansas, on his way to New Orleans. Crane finds this watering place of the mid-South, basking in its eternal spring, less than picturesque, reminding him of the resorts on the New Jersey shore with their heterogeneous population and nondescript hotels that he had written about previously. The report meanders into an apparently meaningless anecdote of Crane, picturing himself as "the youthful stranger with the blonde and innocent hair" eluding entrapment in a local con game.

"A Self-Made Man". A parody of the Horatio Alger rags-to-riches success story, "A Self-Made Man" was first published in the March 1899 issue of *Cornhill Magazine* and collected in *Last Words*. Walking aimlessly down Broadway, an impoverished youth named Tom encounters an illiterate old man for whom he reads a letter from a lawyer in Tin Can, Nevada, which reveals that the old man's son George has swindled him out of the proceeds of the sale of some western property. Posing as the old man's lawyer, Tom confronts the embezzler, a stock villain with "a diamond in his shirt front and a bit of egg on his cuff," and forces him to return the stolen money. As a result, the old man concludes that Tom has "all the virtues mentioned in high-class literature" and since he "knew a man who knew another man," he secures a position for Tom that helps him to become "Thomas G. Somebody." Subsequently, Tom "writes long signed articles to struggling young men, in which he gives the best possible advice as to how to become wealthy." Crane satirizes in this story the popular American conception that the way to wealth is through luck and audacity rather than hard work.

Suggested Reading

Solomon, Eric. *Stephen Crane: From Parody to Realism*. Cambridge, Mass.: Harvard
    University Press, 1966. 49–50.

Senger, Louis C., Jr. (?–?). A childhood friend of Crane in Port Jervis, New York, Senger was a cousin of Corwin Knapp Linson,* to whom he introduced Crane in the winter of 1893. Senger frequently accompanied Crane on camping trips in the area around Port Jervis and was the prototype for the "tall man" of the Sullivan County stories. He was with Crane and the other campers at Twin Lakes, Pike County, Pennsylvania, in August 1894, and he helped Crane with the composition of *The Pike County Puzzle*. Senger was one of the first people to whom Crane showed the manuscripts of *Maggie*, *The Red Badge*, and his early poems. Senger himself was an aspiring writer, but his work came to nothing. In later years he was a claims agent for the Erie Railroad and a member of the Port Jervis Board of Education.

Suggested Reading

Louis C. Senger to Hamlin Garland, 9 October 1900. In *Stephen Crane: Letters*. Ed. R.
    W. Stallman and Lillian Gilkes. New York: New York University Press, 1960.
    318–19.

"The Sergeant's Private Madhouse". Printed in the 30 September 1899 issue of the *Saturday Evening Post* with illustrations by George Gibbs and Howard

Chandler Christy and collected in *Wounds in the Rain*, "The Sergeant's Private Madhouse" is a Cuban War story that hinges on Crane's familiar theme of the primacy of chance in human affairs. Sergeant George H. Peasley, a U.S. marine at an outpost of some forty men entrenched near a camp on the Cuban coast, discovers that Dryden, one of his sentries, has become maddened with fear while on duty. When a skirmish breaks out, Peasley drags Dryden back to the outpost but loses sight of him in the confusion of the fighting. Throughout the night, the small marine detachment is besieged by a large force of guerrillas (Cubans loyal to Spain). The marines are almost out of ammunition when the guerrillas attack in force. Suddenly a voice is heard singing loudly above the battle din; it is Dryden, the "madhouse." Both sides stop firing in amazement, not knowing what to make of the anomalous occurrence. The guerrillas do not renew their charge, and the marines are saved. Dryden is entirely unaware that he has played a part in the action, but the sergeant ironically informs the officials on the hospital ship that will take him home that he is "the most useful ———— crazy man in the service of the United States."

Shackles. A war correspondent in " 'God Rest Ye, Merry Gentlemen,' " "The Revenge of the *Adolphus*," and "Virtue in War." Shackles is a fictional representation of Ernest W. McCready.*

Shafter, William R. (1835–1906). Commander of U.S. forces in Cuba during the Spanish-American War, Shafter entered the army as a volunteer in the Civil War. He was promoted to brigadier general in 1897 and to major general in June 1898. Subsequent to his Cuban experience, he commanded the Departments of the East and California. A huge man afflicted with gout, Shafter quarreled repeatedly with reporters, notably Richard Harding Davis* and Sylvester Scovel,* and he was often ridiculed in the press. Theodore Roosevelt* called him "criminally incompetent." Crane alludes to him dispassionately in his dispatches and in "War Memories."

"Shame". A Whilomville story published in the January 1900 issue of *Harper's New Monthly Magazine*, "Shame" is a corollary to "The Lover and the Telltale," where Jimmie Trescott had been detected writing a love letter to Little Cora, "the angel child," and had defended himself physically when ridiculed by his schoolmates. In this story, Jimmie is again subject to derision by the group for having brought his sandwiches to a picnic of his middle-class friends in a working-class lunch pail provided by the distracted Trescott family cook. Jimmie is "made a social leper" by the children for his blunder. This time he cannot resort to fisticuffs because adults are present. The priggishness of Whilomville's adults is mirrored in their children's being conditioned to follow group behavior. Even the boys, "who were not competent to care if he had brought his luncheon in a coal bin . . . all immediately moved away from him." Jimmie is rescued from this ostracism by a beautiful young lady who shares her picnic lunch with him, and he enjoys a brief fantasy of acceptance in contemplating future marriage to her. The story ends on a farcical note when Jimmie disposes of the contents of his pail beneath a heap of blankets in the Trescott stable, where they are found by the astounded hostler, Peter Washington.

Sharp, Tom. A character in ''The Reluctant Voyagers,'' also identified as ''the tall man.'' He irrationally blames his friend Ted, ''the freckled man,'' for having abducted him when the raft on which they are lounging drifts out to sea.

Sheridan, Clare (1885–1970). The eldest daughter of Moreton and Clara Frewen,* Clare Sheridan turned to sculpting portrait busts as a mingled livelihood and career after her husband, Wilfred, a direct descendant of the dramatist Richard Brinsley Sheridan, was killed in World War I. In 1921 she came to the United States, then returned to Europe as a correspondent for the *New York World* in Russia and Turkey, among other places. She wrote a number of travel books, including *Russian Portraits* (1921) and *My American Diary* (1922). Her reminiscences of Brede Place* in *Nuda Veritas* (1927), published as *Naked Truth* (1928) in the United States, provide intimate details of the Cranes' life at Brede Place.

'' 'Showin' Off' ''. One of the less effective of the Whilomville stories, '' 'Showin' Off' '' appeared in the November 1899 issue of *Harper's New Monthly Magazine*. The story is a childhood version of ''A Mystery of Heroism,'' ridiculing the emptiness of foolish bravado. Jimmie Trescott, smitten once again by an infatuation as in ''The Lover and the Telltale,'' follows the object of his adoration home, accompanied by a retainer named Clarence whom he bullies to impress the girl. They meet Horace Glenn, the protagonist of ''His New Mittens,'' on a velocipede, an early bicycle, and Jimmie argues with him over who can ride it faster. Seeking to find favor with the girl and her friends, each boasts of his ability to ride the velocipede down a dangerous ravine and dares the other to attempt this feat. Jimmie is saved from having to fulfill his boast because Horace will not lend him his velocipede, but Horace, having moved to the edge of the ravine, is impelled down it inadvertently, and the story ends with Jimmie and Clarence watching Horace trudge home bawling as he pushes his shattered velocipede before him.

''The Shrapnel of Their Friends''. A deflating sequel to ''The Kicking Twelfth,'' this Spitzbergen tale appeared in the May 1900 issue of *Ainslee's Magazine* and was collected in *Last Words*. The losses of the ''Kickers'' have been so great that Lieutenant Timothy Lean is given command of his own company, but he does not play a central role in the story. The focus instead is on the regiment, which in its second engagement makes a long, slow advance over difficult terrain. The irrationality of war appears more evident as the men, at rest in trenches recently occupied by Rostina forces, come under the artillery fire of one of their own batteries. When the regiment scatters, the soldiers are denounced by General Richie as "white-livered cowards," "swine," and "curs." Colonel Sponge is enraged by these insults, but the general does not apologize. When Richie learns that the soldiers had retreated under friendly fire, he compensates for his insults by commending the regiment and decorating the colonel. "Richie knew that it is hard for men to withstand the shrapnel of their friends."

Sidbury, Edna Crane (1886–1927). One of five daughters of William Howe Crane, Enda Crane married Kirby Sidbury and had three children. Her memoir, "My Uncle, Stephen Crane, As I Knew Him," in the March 1926 issue of the *Literary Digest International Book Review*, is a warm, sympathetic retrospection of Crane's relationship with his nieces in Port Jervis, New York, and offers a convincing depiction of the town as the setting for "The Monster," "His New Mittens," and the *Whilomville Stories*.

"Siege". Reported by Vincent Starrett in *Stephen Crane: A Bibliography* (Philadelphia: Centaur, 1923, 10), to have been a story Crane wrote about Brede Place* in Cromwellian times. The manuscript is supposed to have been destroyed.

"The Silver Pageant". First printed in *Last Words*, this brief story of studio life in the old Art Students League building probably dates from late 1894 when "Stories Told by an Artist" was written, but unlike its insouciant companion piece, "The Silver Pageant" is essentially tragic. Great Grief, Wrinkles, and Little Pennoyer visit the studio of Gaunt, another artist living in the building, and criticize a painting on which he is working. Gaunt is a depressed dreamer who, the young men believe, could be a great artist "if he would only move faster than a pyramid." Wrinkles considers Gaunt to have "pictures in his eyes," that is, great powers of imagination. One day Gaunt bursts into the room shared by the three young men and announces that he is going to paint an important picture, but when they again visit his studio, he is lying dead on the floor. Wrinkles concludes that "[t]here is a mistake. He couldn't have had pictures in his eyes."

Simpson, Billie. In "Moonlight on the Snow" he is the alcoholic former Baptist preacher who acts as the unofficial spokesman of the town of War Post in announcing to Larpent that the town intends to hang him. The disreputable nature of Simpson and Bob Hether causes Larpent to comment sarcastically that they lend "a certain dignity to this outing of real-estate speculators."

"Six Years Afloat". Circulated by the McClure syndicate, this curious tall tale was printed in a few newspapers on 2 August 1896. Because Crane designated it as "Raft Story" in a corner of the manuscript now in the Berg Collection of the New York Public Library, it is sometimes referred to by that title and also occasionally confused with "The Reluctant Voyagers." "Six Years Afloat" tells the story of an enormous raft built to transport logs. According to a person employed in its construction, it was "six hundred feet in length—longer than any liner," and weighed 10,000 tons. Lost at sea, it was discovered six years later off the coast of Labrador. Despite the report format of this story, it is fiction loosely allied to Crane's ghost and shipwreck narratives.

["Sixth Avenue"]. An untitled manuscript fragment of the opening paragraph of a Tenderloin sketch that would have described the "dual existence" of Sixth Avenue, a decorous shopping street during the day, but at night a sleazy thoroughfare devoted to gambling, drinking, and prostitution. This may have been a draft of the piece that Curtis Brown,* Sunday editor of the *New York Press*, recalls as having been submitted to him which "was entitled 'Sixth Avenue,' and there was little left of it after the crossing-out of comments and descriptions that would have caused sorry inroads on the newspaper's Sixth Avenue advertising receipts, to say nothing of libels. Then the editor read the remainder and threw it away too, as not being exciting enough" (*Contacts* [London: Cassell, 1935], 222).

Skinner, Ernest B. (?–?). Following a ball at Brede Place* on Friday evening, 29 December 1899, Crane collapsed with a lung hemorrhage. H. G. Wells,* who had suffered from a tubercular condition himself at one time, bicycled to Rye to summon the local general practitioner, Dr. Ernest B. Skinner, who was also the primary care physician for Henry James.* Skinner was involved in Crane's medical treatment until shortly before his death and at first took what may have been an overly optimistic view of his condition. When Crane suffered more hemorrhages in early April 1900, Skinner recommended the salubrious air of Bournemouth. Crane and Cora entertained the possibility of a working trip to Gibraltar or even to St. Helena. Dr. Skinner corresponded with William Howe Crane and Moreton Frewen,* probably to explain that Crane's illness was becoming more serious and that funds were needed to transport him to the Continent. On 21 April Skinner was one of two witnesses to Crane's will, and he may have been the physician who was with the Crane party in Dover in May, although it is doubtful that he accompanied them to the Black Forest, as James believed he did. James was outraged that Cora failed to pay Skinner for his services, but she was debt ridden and practically destitute after Crane's death.

Suggested Reading

Miles, Peter. "Ernest Skinner, Henry James, and the Death of Stephen Crane: A Cora Crane Inscription." *ANQ* 8.2 (1995): 19–26.

Smith, Harry Bache (1860–1936). Based on his own estimate, Smith wrote at least three hundred operettas and musical comedies. Early in his career, he was a music and drama critic for Chicago newspapers. He wrote four extravaganzas for the Chicago Opera House. One of them, *The Crystal Slipper*, ran for eight hundred performances. After the success of *The Fencing Master* in 1892, Smith gave up newspaper work in Chicago and settled in New York. In his reminiscence, Smith recalls that one evening in the fall of 1895 he accompanied Willis Brooks Hawkins,* a former colleague on the *Chicago Daily News*, for a poker game at the loft on West Twenty-third Street where Crane roomed with Post Wheeler.* Crane slept in a partitioned-off bedroom.

> We played cards till two or three o'clock in the morning and, as we started for home, we passed the window of the partitioned bedroom. A girl was asleep in the bed.
> "Gosh!" said Crane. "I didn't hear her come in."
> There were facetious comments. "Is it *Maggie*?" asked one of the ribald, referring to Crane's story.
> "Some of her," said Crane.

Suggested Reading

Smith, Harry B. *First Nights and First Editions*. Boston: Little, Brown, 1931. 177–78.

Smith, Mr. Manolo Prat's ultimately successful rival for the hand of Margharita in "The Clan of No-Name." Smith is a wealthy Tampa businessman whose avarice and lust are contrasted to Prat's self-abnegation and devotion to duty.

Smithers, Bill. In *The Red Badge of Courage*, Smithers is a private in Henry Fleming's company who is a subject of conversation and amusement for other soldiers. He is first encountered, although not named, in the second chapter of the novel, when a comrade accidentally treads on his hand as he stumbles in the march and gropes for his rifle. In a disjointed conversation in the fourth chapter, a soldier comments that Smithers's fingers had been crushed, "So he went t' th' hospital disregardless of th' fight." In chapter 6, a soldier dismayed by a renewed charge of the enemy exclaims: "I wish Bill Smithers had trod on my hand, insteader me treddin' on his'n," and in the final chapter another man repeats Smithers's comment that the field hospital was more dangerous than the front lines. In contrast to Fleming, Smithers is an average soldier, untroubled by speculations about courage, cowardice, or the nature of the universe.

Suggested Reading

Stone, Edward. "Introducing Private Smithers." *Georgia Review* 6 (1962): 442–45.

"The Snake". At times incorrectly identified as a Sullivan County sketch, "The Snake" was probably based on an incident that occurred in August 1894, when Crane and Louis Senger* killed a large black rattlesnake that crossed their path near Parker's Glen in Pike County, Pennsylvania. The sketch was syndicated by Bacheller, Johnson and Bacheller on 14 June 1896. "The Snake" is informed by the primal apprehension also experienced by characters in *The Red Badge of Courage*. As in the war novel, a commonplace event is endowed with metaphysical significance. A young man with a dog named Rover encounters a rattlesnake on a narrow path through the woods. Both man and snake confront one another with instinctive, primitive feelings of hatred and fear, a "deadly repulsion" that was "another detail of a war that had begun evidently when first there were men and snakes." A vicious battle ensues, the man battering the snake with a stick and the snake striking out with its fangs. Finally, the snake is beaten to death, and the sketch ends on an incongruously lighthearted note: " 'Well, Rover,' said the man, turning to the dog with a grin of victory, 'we'll carry Mr. Snake home to show the girls.' "

The Society of American Women in London. A group devoted to social and cultural activities formed in 1898 by upper-class American women living in London. Cora Crane was probably introduced into the society by Katherine De Friese and Clara Frewen,* whose sister, Lady Randolph Churchill,* was also a member. Cora was active in the affairs of the group, raising funds and helping to procure new members and speakers.

"A Soldier's Burial That Made a Native Holiday". Crane's first report to the *New York Journal* from Puerto Rico appeared in the newspaper on 15 August 1898. Crane contrasts the "calm, stoical, superior" demeanor of the members of an American infantry company at the funeral of a soldier with the "monkeyish" behavior of an uncomprehending throng of natives. The babble of the crowd "beat like waves upon the hearse; noisy, idle, senseless waves beating upon the hearse, the invulnerable ship of the indifferent dead man." Such condescending contrasts of Americans and Cubans are not unusual in Crane's Cuban War dispatches and stories.

"Some Curious Lessons from the Transvaal". The South African War (1899–1902), a conflict between Britain and the two Afrikaner governments of the Transvaal and the Orange Free State, provoked Crane's thoughts about the role of war correspondents. Crane had a strong desire to report the war, but his declining health and financial indebtedness prevented him from undertaking the enterprise. This essay, the first of a series on South Africa Crane wrote for the *New York Journal*, appeared in that newspaper and in Hearst's *San Francisco Examiner* on 7 January 1900. Crane surmises that because of modern advances in communication, censorship of military engagements is inevitable, but the censors must remain aware that the public is entitled to authentic reports. British bravado has been punctured by news of heavy losses suffered by some crack regiments "at the hands of bewhiskered farmers," the Boers. Although English pride has been somewhat humbled by the news of these defeats, there is a general determination to carry the war to a successful conclusion.

"Some Hints for Play-Makers". Crane despised the popular romantic plays of his time, replete with inauthentic situations and false emotions, such as those to which Pete takes Maggie in *Maggie: A Girl of the Streets*. "Some Hints for Play-Makers," printed in the 4 November 1893 issue of the humor magazine *Truth*,* presents "a few valuable receipts" for such plays. A prefatory statement explains that "we have followed models which have received the sanction of tradition, and are upheld at the present day by a large and important portion of the public." Among the parodies mockingly presented for emulation are an Irish melodrama featuring a standard hero, heroine, and villain; a society play; an aborted international intrigue; and a musical comedy of young love initially frustrated but finally requited.

A Souvenir and a Medley: Seven Poems and a Sketch by Stephen Crane. The first number of Elbert Hubbard's* short-lived *Roycroft Quarterly*. This booklet, issued in May 1896, is a souvenir of the dinner given to Crane by Hubbard's ad hoc Society of the Philistines in Buffalo on 19 December 1895. The pamphlet consists of regrets by those unable to attend this event reprinted, with some additions, from the dinner menu, *"The Time Has Come"*; an essay on Crane by Hubbard that was previously published in the *Lotos*; seven Crane poems, all of which had appeared in the *Philistine*,* except "Fast rode the knight," which is printed here for the first time, as is Crane's dramatic vignette, "A Prologue"; the "Tommie" story, "A Great Mistake"; and a smattering of newspaper reviews of the Philistine dinner. Since "I have heard the sunset song of the birches" is printed as a preface, the booklet actually contains eight of Crane's poems. The design by Dwight R. Collin for *"The Time Has Come"* is reproduced on the front cover of *A Souvenir and a Medley*.

"Spaniards Two". In this article printed in the *New York World* on 11 November 1898, Crane criticizes two Spanish officials in Havana, which had not yet been occupied by American forces. General Manuel de Pando y Sanchez, one of General Blanco's lieutenants in Cuba, apparently boasted to the press about the insufficiency of the American army, causing Crane to recall that after Waterloo some of Napoleon's officers "wrote pamphlets proving that the English knew nothing of the art of war." Crane's second target is Rafael Montoro, the treasury secretary and member of the Evacuation Committee, whose cupidity extends to insisting that 25 percent of the profits from a fair to benefit hospitals that the Americans intend to establish for sick soldiers be remitted to the government.

["Spanish-AmericanWar Play"]. Cora Crane tried in vain to interest the actors Nat Goodwin and William Gillette in this untitled and uncompleted two-act comic play, probably written in late 1899. The typescript, in the Rare Book and Manuscript Library of Columbia University, was first published by R. W. Stallman in the *Bulletin of the New York Public Library* 67 (1963): 498–511.

The setting of the play is a sugar plantation in the province of Santiago de Cuba at the close of the Cuban War. In the first act, an Englishman named John Stilwell, his two daughters, Marjorie and Lucy, and a Spanish colonel named Mavida are at dinner in the dining room of Stilwell's house. They are interrupted by Henry Patten, an American army officer whose men capture Mavida. The colonel refuses to take Patten's word that the Spanish army has surrendered, but Patten nevertheless releases him on his own recognizance. In the second act, Mavida returns with his battalion to attack the plantation. The Americans are trapped by a force with superior firepower, but a troop of U.S. cavalry intervenes in the nick of time to rout the Spaniards. There is a great deal of strained verbal banter throughout, and Sylvester Thorpe, an apathetic war correspondent for the *New York Eclipse*, Rufus Coleman's newspaper in *Active Service*, takes notes on the proceedings.

"Spanish Deserters among the Refugees at El Caney". Datelined from El Caney, Cuba, on 5 July, this report was printed in the *New York World* on 8 July 1898. A stream of refugees, most of them civilians from Santiago fearful of an American bombardment, poured into El Caney, itself a site of great carnage. Crane commends the American military authorities for providing aid to the refugees and especially for setting up a hospital to treat wounded enemy soldiers. He condemns the Spanish guerrillas who pursued the opposite course: firing on the line of American wounded going to the rear and on Red Cross workers and doctors.

["The Spirit of the Greek People"]. This report, datelined Athens, 17 April 1897, the day that Greece declared war on Turkey, may be Crane's first writing about the Greek-Turkish War. The untitled manuscript is in the Rare Book and Manuscript Library of Columbia University. It was first published in R. W. Stallman and E. R. Hagemann, eds., *The War Dispatches of Stephen Crane* (New York: New York University Press, 1964). The title was adapted by the editors from a phrase in the dispatch. Crane describes the exuberance of the crowd clamoring for war in front of the royal palace on Constitution Square in Athens. He is convinced that the outnumbered Greeks are determined to support the rebellion of Crete against Turkey, even if only because they feel that "it is better to be defeated than shamed."

The Spitzbergen Tales. This general heading was used for the first time in *Last Words* for four stories written in 1899 about an imaginary infantry regiment in a war between fictitious countries, Spitzbergen and Rostina, the causes of which are not given. The regiment bears the sobriquet of the "Kicking Twelfth" because during a civil war in Spitzbergen, the king, lacking confidence in the Twelfth Regiment from which there had been many defectors, sent the remnant to guard a dockyard in a distant corner of the kingdom, causing some of the officers to express strenuous disapproval. The stories, in narrative order but not in order of composition or publication, are: "The Kicking Twelfth"; "The Shrapnel of Their Friends"; " 'And If He Wills, We Must Die' "; and "The Upturned Face." Crane left uncompleted at his death the manuscript of a fifth Spitzbergen Tale, "The Fire-Tribe and the White-Face," a long, fanciful story about the occupation by the Spitzbergen army of a section of Rostina whose inhabitants resemble American Indians, and also the related fragmentary manuscript of a play, "The Fire-Tribe and the Pale-Face."

Sponge, Colonel. A character in the Spitzbergen tales named after Crane's favorite dog. Colonel Sponge is commander of the "Twelfth Regiment of the Line—The Kicking Twelfth." An old man with stumpy legs, the colonel is an intrepid officer who is given a high decoration because he and his regiment were wrongly reprimanded by General Richie when they retreated under friendly fire in "The Shrapnel of Their Friends."

"The Squire's Madness". Left uncompleted by Crane and finished by Cora from instructions he had dictated to her, "The Squire's Madness" was published first in England in the October 1900 issue of *Crampton's Magazine* and was collected in *Last Words*. The setting of this parody of gothic fiction is an English manor house in Sussex, much like Brede Place,* where it was written. The main character, Jack Linton, returns to Oldrestham Hall with his wife after ten years of "an incomprehensible wandering." Much to the dismay of his neighbors, who long for a rugged, fox-hunting squire to inhabit the four-hundred-year-old hall, Linton prefers the solitude of his study, where he is writing a tortured poem he cannot finish about a poisoned lover dying at the feet of a woman. There are disturbing autobiographical elements in Crane's description of the study and Linton's emaciated physique. Linton's awkwardness, erratic temper, and peculiar habits (or lack of habits) lead some of the villagers to conclude that he is mad. This sentiment is shared by his wife, who insists that Linton is ill and finally persuades him to visit a London brain specialist, Dr. Redmond. The doctor asks first to consult with Linton's wife who "almost ran into the room which the doctor pointed toward as his study." When the doctor emerges, he informs Linton, "I have never met a man more sound mentally than yourself . . . but it is my painful duty to tell you the truth—It is your WIFE WHO IS MAD. MAD AS A HATTER!" The story ends on this farcical note.

"Stephen Crane Fears No Blanco". The title of this dispatch, which appeared in the *New York Journal* on 31 August 1898, refers to General Ramon Blanco y Erenas who in October 1897 replaced General Valeriano Weyler as Spanish governor in Cuba. Crane reports on the rumors circulating in Havana about what the American commissioners will do once they occupy the city. The Spaniards are indifferent to the few Americans in Havana, mostly tobacco buyers, Red Cross officials, and correspondents. Crane discloses that he "came into Havana without permission from anybody. I simply came in. I did not even have a passport. I was at a hotel [the Hotel Pasaje] while the Government was firmly imprisoning nine correspondents on a steamer in the harbor. But no one molested me.''

"Stephen Crane at the Front for the World". This report deals with events that occurred during the fighting around Santiago de Cuba on 24 June 1898 but was not published until 7 July, when it appeared in the *New York World* and the *Boston Globe*. Crane was with the dismounted Rough Riders, the First Volunteer Cavalry under the command of Colonel Leonard Wood and Lieutenant Colonel Theodore Roosevelt,* on the jungle trail from Siboney to Las Guásimas, when they were ambushed. The Rough Riders suffered heavy losses, and Edward Marshall,* an old friend from Park Row and a fellow member of the Lantern Club,* was wounded. Although Marshall was a correspondent for a rival newspaper, the *New York Journal*, Crane trudged back to the coast and filed his dispatches for him, a generous act that was in part responsible for his being fired from the *World*. Crane wrote about this event in two of the fictionalized sketches of *Wounds in the Rain*, '' 'God Rest Ye, Merry Gentlemen' '' and "War Memories." In this dispatch Crane praises the courage of the Rough Riders but is critical of their amateurish carelessness. Unlike regular infantry troops experienced in the tactics of Indian warfare, the volunteers "wound along this narrow winding path, babbling joyously, arguing, recounting, laughing; making more noise than a train going through a tunnel."

Suggested Reading

Marshall, Edward. "Stories of Stephen Crane." *Literary Life* n. s. 24 (December 1900): 71–72.

"Stephen Crane in Havana". Forced humor permeates this slight sketch printed in the *New York Journal* on 9 October 1898. Crane comments on the inability of the residents of Havana to "comprehend public navigation." The sidewalks are so narrow that only acrobats can negotiate them, and this circumstance frequently results in quixotic quarrels over the right of way.

"Stephen Crane in Mexico (I)". The first of two pieces headlined "Stephen Crane in Mexico," this sketch was syndicated by Bacheller, Johnson and Bacheller, with variant titles in some newspapers, generally on 19 May 1895. Crane describes aspects of street life in Mexico City: the use of porters and donkeys to carry staggering amounts of freight; the usually reasonable prices charged by cabs, hotels, and restaurants; and the deceits practiced by many street vendors. He comments that "[t]he men who sell opals are particularly seductive. They polish their wares and boil them in oil and do everything to give them a false quality." Crane was evidently taken in by this scam. Shortly after his return from Mexico, he visited Corwin Knapp Linson's* studio and handed him "a half a dozen or more opals with the lambent flames of sunsets in their depths.

He freely gave me the choice of the lot." Crane gave the rest of his "pretty pebbles" to his journalist friends at the Lantern Club.*

Suggested Reading

Linson, Corwin Knapp. *My Stephen Crane.* Syracuse: Syracuse University Press, 1958. 88–89.

"Stephen Crane in Mexico (II)". The second of Crane's reports from Mexico City with this editorially supplied title (and variant titles such as "Ancient Capital of Montezuma") was syndicated in newspapers by Bacheller, Johnson and Bacheller on 21 July 1895. The dateline of 14 July from the "City of Mexico" was arbitrarily inserted by the syndicate, as was the dateline of 18 May in the first article, since Crane returned to New York on 17 or 18 May. Although two of his travel letters from Mexico had already appeared, Crane, representing himself as a Boston archaeologist, recounts his two-day train ride from San Antonio to Mexico City with a fellow traveler whom he identifies only as a Chicago capitalist. Changing colors of the landscape and the clothing worn by people delineate the trip. As the train rolls over an "astonishing brown sea of mesquite" toward Laredo, foreshadowings of Mexico begin to appear with the sight of a Mexican woman crouched in the doorway of a hut and a sheepherder wearing a sombrero. At the border, the men exchange American currency for "new bills which were quite gay with red and purple and green." In Nuevo Laredo there is "a preliminary picture painted in dark colors" in the throng of women muffled in old shawls and men wrapped in dark-hued serapes. Later, "the purple, the crimson and the other vivid hues became the typical colors, and even the trousers of dark cloth were replaced by dusty white cotton ones. A horseman in a red serape and a tall sombrero of maroon or pearl or yellow was vivid as an individual, but a dozen or two of them reposeful in the shade of some desert railway station made a chromatic delirium." In the morning hours the train leaves the sagebrush- and cactus-filled valleys and begins the ascent to Mexico City. The peak of Nevado de Tolca is "sun smitten with gold," and the travelers are thrilled at the sight of the two great mountains, Popocatepetl and Iztaccihuatl, "clothed in snow that was like wool." In the distance is the "vast green plain" leading to the city of the Aztecs.

"Stephen Crane in Minetta Lane". This is Crane's last Sunday feature sketch about New York City. It was written shortly before he left on his ill-fated trip to report the Cuban War for the Bacheller Syndicate and was printed in a number of newspapers on 20 December 1896. Built over what had been Minetta Brook, Minetta Lane is now, as it was in the nineteenth century, a winding residential Greenwich Village alleyway that connects McDougal Street with Sixth Avenue. Crane describes a sordid interim period in the lane's history, recounting how "Minetta Lane, and Minetta Street, which leads from it southward to Bleecker Street, were, until a few years ago, two of the most enthusiastically murderous thoroughfares in New York." The lane was set apart for the most infamous element of the city's black population. Crane relates anecdotes about the more notorious of these individuals with quaint names like Bloodthirsty, No-Toe Charley, Black-Cat, and Guinea Johnson. Interviews with older residents of the lane, such as Mammy Ross, Pop Babcock, and Hank Anderson who knew it well "in its direful days," evoke recollections of well-known murders and thefts. The sketch concludes with the almost doleful reflection that the black population is gradually being displaced by Italian immigrants, "and there are no cutting affrays among them worth mentioning."

"Stephen Crane in Texas". This travel article, circulated by the McClure syndicate and printed in newspapers on 8 January 1899, is based on impressions of San Antonio and the Alamo formed by Crane on his trip to the West and Mexico in early 1895. Crane makes an uncharacteristically nostalgic contrast between modern San Antonio with its rows of business blocks and trolley car lines and the pathetic remnants of an earlier time, "little old buildings, yellow with age, solemn and severe in outline, that have escaped by a miracle or by a historical importance, the whirl of the modern life." Inevitably, "the unprotected mass of them must get trampled into shapeless dust which lies always behind the march of this terrible century. The feet of the years will go through many old roofs." Foremost among the monuments that have survived is the Alamo mission, where in 1836 fewer than two-hundred Texans resisted Santa Anna's invading army for twelve days and were finally overcome and massacred. Crane implicitly praises the resoluteness of the Alamo defenders, but he is also impressed by the "strange inverted courage" of a man who refused to remain in the fortification and die with his comrades.

"Stephen Crane Makes Observations in Cuba's Capital". Datelined Havana, 20 September, this bitter invective against the slowness of the peace negotiations between the United States and Spain did not appear in the *New York Journal* until 2 October 1898. Crane expresses impatience with the delay in expelling the Spanish from Cuba and forming a stable government. In our next war, he suggests, the armed forces should first attack Washington: "If we could once take and sack Washington the rest of the conflict would be simple."

"Stephen Crane on Havana". The printing of this article in the *New York Journal* on 6 November 1898 marks the beginning of a new arrangement between Crane and the newspaper, which had discontinued his salary. Crane's previous dispatches from Havana were copyright by W. R. Hearst, but this "letter" and most of those following it bear the imprint, "Copyright by Stephen Crane, 1898." Crane's intent was to syndicate the articles, but Paul Revere Reynolds failed to sell them to other newspapers. In this article Crane makes desultory comments on the bell ringers of Havana, the lack of opportunity for American workers or small entrepreneurs in Cuba, and the intransigence of the

Spaniards remaining on the island who grouse over their loss of the war and hope that through some miracle Cuba may once again come under Spanish domination.

"Stephen Crane Says: The British Soldiers Are Not Familiar with the 'Business End' of Modern Rifles". A short article on the South African War printed in the *New York Journal* on 14 February 1900 at a time when Boer forces had gained some surprising victories over the British and were laying siege to Mafeking, Kimberley, and Ladysmith. Crane is mildly derisive of the British claim to superior knowledge of firearms, maintaining that "the proud British soldier has never known the range of the modern rifle—not when it was pointed at him."

"Stephen Crane Says: Edwin Markham Is His First Choice for the American Academy". A late newspaper spoof printed in the *New York Journal*, 31 March 1900. As in "Concerning the English Academy," Crane derides the idea of an established institution that would evaluate literary merit. An American academy, he quips, would be feasible because in a group photograph "we can show more fine old litterateurs with manes of snow white hair than any country on the face of the globe." Since most of our better writers appear too respectable to convey the image of the virile American, Crane suggests Edwin Markham as an academy of one. Markham had attained international fame with the publication of his moralizing poem "The Man with the Hoe" (1899), inspired by Millet's painting of the same title: "[G]ive him a constitution and a set of by-laws; let him convene himself and discuss literary matters. Then we have an American Academy."

"Stephen Crane Says Greeks Cannot Be Curbed". During the Greek-Turkish War, Crane first saw action in Epirus, the southwestern province of Turkey where the war began, but he soon returned to Athens and from there went to Thessaly in northeastern Greece, where he heard there was more intense fighting. In the capital he witnessed "another popular outburst of the Athenians" as crowds massed in front of the palace of King George I and in other parts of the city. In contrast to some journalists who reported widespread disaffection from the war, Crane maintains that "[p]ractically every man in Athens is arming to go and fight the Turks." But the Greeks are not overconfident: "No nation ever had a truer sense of the odds." This dispatch, datelined 29 April 1897, appeared in a number of Hearst newspapers the next day. It was printed on the front page of the *New York Journal* with four other articles bearing the same dateline by Imogene Carter,* John Bass,* Julian Ralph, and Julius Chambers under the headline "War in the East as Seen by the Journal's Correspondents."

"Stephen Crane Says: Watson's Criticisms of England's War Are Not Un-patriotic". In this article printed in the *New York Journal* on 25 January 1900,

Crane defends the poet William Watson, who has been accused in the *London Daily News* of being unpatriotic because of his disapproval of British imperialism in South Africa. Crane supports Watson's contention that individuals may love their country and yet not condone all of its actions, and he applies this apothegm to the American situation in coping with the Philippine resistance to annexation: "One has the burning wish for the quick success of American arms in the Philippines. At the same time, one has a still more burning wish that the Filipinos shall see us as just men, willing, anxious to deal fairly, govern with studious equity; depart, if need be, with honor." On the other hand, Crane, always ambivalent about American imperialism, makes the oblique suggestion that the activities of the Anti-Imperialist League, formed in Boston in November 1898, are contributing directly to the death of American soldiers in the Philippines.

"Stephen Crane Sees Free Cuba". This short cable from Havana was printed in the *New York Journal* and the *San Francisco Examiner* on 28 August 1898. Crane reports that the Cuban inhabitants and even the Spaniards will welcome the entrance of American troops into the city. There is no famine in Havana, but in Matanzas, about sixty miles to the east, there is hunger among the poor. In that city, as well as in Havana, sentiment for annexation is growing.

"Stephen Crane Tells of War's Horrors". On 18 May 1897 Stephen and Cora Crane watched the abandonment of Stylidia by the Greek army and helped evacuate civilian refugees before departing for Chalkis. At Chalkis, the Cranes boarded the *St. Marina*, an ambulance ship returning to Athens crammed with soldiers wounded at Domoko. This cable, written aboard the ship on 22 May and syndicated in newspapers by Hearst the next day under different headlines, depicts the horrific plight of wounded soldiers and civilians and concludes characteristically that "[t]here is more of this sort of thing in war than glory and heroic death, flags, banners, shouting and victory."

"Stephen Crane's Own Story". Crane's report on the sinking of the *Commodore* did not appear in newspapers until 7 January 1897, when it was, at least in part, syndicated by Bacheller four days after many other newspapers had carried the full story of the misadventure. The title, "Stephen Crane's Own Story," is taken from the version in the *New York Press*. Although Crane's graphic account was delayed, it remains extremely important in its own right as an artistically crafted first-person narrative and as the experiential background of "The Open Boat," which is, as its subtitle indicates, "A Tale Intended to Be after the Fact. Being the Experience of Four Men from the Sunk Steamer 'Commodore.' " The news report deals with the circumstances of the sinking itself and telescopes the aftermath into two final paragraphs, referring briefly to the bravery of Captain Edward Murphy* and Billy Higgins (spelled Billie in

"The Open Boat"), the swamping of the dinghy in the surf, and the death of the oiler.

In this report, Crane recounts the circumstances under which the filibustering ship *Commodore* sailed from the port of Jacksonville on the evening of 31 December 1896 with reinforcements and a cargo of supplies and ammunition for the Cuban insurgents from Spanish rule. The *Commodore* was seemingly in violation of U.S. neutrality laws, but American sentiments were with the rebels, and the shipment had been cleared by the secretary of the treasury. Crane, who according to the *Florida Times-Union* had been shipped as a seaman, was representing the Bacheller syndicate as a writer of feature articles on the situation in Cuba. The *Commodore* was beached twice on sandbars in the St. John's River before, with the help of the revenue cutter *Boutwell*, it attained the open sea, and on the morning of 2 January 1897 the ship foundered following a mysterious leak in the engine room that could not be contained. Crane describes how three lifeboats left the vessel, but one of them sank and the seven men on the lost boat returned to the *Commodore* and built rafts. The first mate was killed when he leapt from the boat toward one of the rafts and plunged into the sea, and three other men remained on board when the *Commodore* went under at 7:00 A.M. The three on the improvised rafts also lost their lives. Captain Edward Murphy; William Higgins, an oiler; the cook, Charles B. Montgomery*; and Crane were the last to leave the ship in a ten-foot dinghy. They remained alongside all night until the *Commodore* sank.

The most harrowing incident Crane describes in "Stephen Crane's Own Story" occurred when the men in the dinghy tried to save those on one of the rafts. A stoker on the first raft threw a line to the dinghy, which then attempted to tow the raft, a task that proved to be impossible. The stoker, eager to board the dinghy, which was already only six inches above the water's edge, began to rein in the line. According to Crane, "He had turned into a demon . . . and we knew that his hand on our gunwale doomed us. The cook let go of the line." When the *Commodore* went down, "the rafts were suddenly swallowed by this frightful maw of the ocean." Crane forbears to tell the story of the thirty hours spent in the dinghy before it came to shore on Daytona beach, reserving this tale for "The Open Boat." As in the short story, he is vague about what occurred when the dinghy was swamped in the surf, but when the men reached shore, "we saw Billy Higgins lying with his forehead on sand that was clear of the water, and he was dead." Crane comments that he will reserve the "history of life in an open boat for thirty hours" for a later story, and "The Open Boat" picks up where "Stephen Crane's Own Story" leaves off.

Suggested Reading

Day, Cyrus. "Stephen Crane and the Ten-foot Dinghy." *Boston University Studies in English* 3 (1957): 193–213.

Frus, Phyllis. "Two Tales 'Intended to Be after the Fact': 'Stephen Crane's Own Story'

and 'The Open Boat.' " In *Literary Nonfiction: Theory, Criticism, Pedagogy*. Ed. Chris Anderson. Carbondale: Southern Illinois University Press, 1989. 125–51.
Hagemann, E. R. " 'Sadder Than the End': Another Look at 'The Open Boat.' " In *Stephen Crane in Transition*. Ed. Joseph Katz. De Kalb: Northern Illinois University Press, 1972. 66–85.
Stallman, R. W. "Journalist Crane in That Dinghy." *Bulletin of the New York Public Library* 72 (1968): 261–77.

"Stephen Crane's Pen Picture of C. H. Thrall". On 4 May 1898 Crane was aboard the *New York World*'s dispatch tug *Triton*, which was to take the American spy (and ostensible *World* reporter) Charles H. Thrall* off the gunboat *Wilmington*, which had picked him up from a beach east of Havana, and take him back to Key West. Thrall, in Havana since 13 April, had gathered valuable information about the city's defenses. Admiral Sampson* ordered that Thrall be put aboard the *Leyden* and transferred to his flagship, but Crane managed to interview him while the *Triton* was alongside the *Wilmington*. Crane's report appeared in cut form in the *World* on 8 May on the same page as Thrall's own narrative, "Thrilling Adventures of World Scout in Cuba." It was printed in full in other newspapers. Crane describes Thrall and relates his account of the confusion among the population of Havana as they await an American attack. Crane recast Thrall as Johnnie, an American spy in Havana, in his short story "This Majestic Lie."

"Stephen Crane's Views of Havana". This telegram was printed in the *New York Journal* on 7 September 1898. Crane offers some general observations on conditions in Havana before American occupation. Spanish merchants in the city had raised $800,000 for the purchase of a warship for the Spanish navy, but they now want their money back. They have "discovered that a Spanish warship is not a good investment." A half-dozen unarmed men from a relief ship in American army uniforms are in Havana and have attracted much attention. A few Spaniards are speculating on the disposition of what they suppose are the bones of Columbus in the local cathedral. The harbor is growing lively with shipping, but there are still no indications of the Spanish army's embarking.

"Stephen Crane's Vivid Story of the Battle of San Juan". Crane's comprehensive account of the decisive military engagement of the Cuban War, the capture of the fortifications on the San Juan hills and the village of El Caney northeast of Santiago on 1 and 2 July 1898, is datelined "In Front of Santiago, July 4, via Old Point Comfort, Va., July 13." It was filed on the day that Crane arrived in the United States on the transport *City of Washington* suffering from exhaustion and malaria. The dispatch was printed in the *New York World* and other newspapers on 14 July and in *Harper's Weekly* on 23 July. This dispatch belies its editorially supplied headline since it is detached and objective rather than vivid. Crane recounts the main events of the battle: the shelling of the

Spanish trenches by the batteries of Captain Allyn Capron and George S. Grimes; the destruction of the observation balloon that drew fire on the troops marching down the Santiago road; the charge up the hills of San Juan, "hills that resembled the sloping orchards of Orange County [New York] in summer"; the wounded straggling back from the front and the improvised field hospital at the ford of the Aguadores River; and the struggle to overcome stiff enemy resistance at El Caney. These events are depicted more dramatically and more concisely in "War Memories."

Stewart, Donald William (1860–1905). The son of Sir Donald Martin Stewart, commander in chief of British forces in India, Donald William Stewart joined the Gordon Highlanders in 1879 and served as an army officer in the Afghan War, in India, and in the Sudan. He resigned his captain's commission in 1888. Stewart met Cora Ethel Eton Howorth (Cora Crane) on a visit to New York City, and they were married in London in January 1889. The couple took up residence at the town house of Stewart's father in South Kensington, London, and lived together in New York City, where by 1892 Cora had left Stewart for a lover. The Stewarts were Presbyterians of Scottish lineage, but Donald Stewart held religious strictures against divorce, and a decree was never granted. Before settling in England with Crane, Cora continued to call herself Lady Stewart whenever convenient, although Donald Stewart was not knighted until 1902. He served as a political officer in Africa and at his death was commissioner of Kenya, then known as the East African Protectorate.

Stickney. A character in "His New Mittens," Stickney is a Whilomville butcher who returns little Horace Glenn to his home after he has run away.

Stimson, John. The owner of the merry-go-round in "The Pace of Youth" who futilely attempts to thwart the love affair between his daughter, Lizzie, and Frank, his young assistant.

Stokes, Frederick Abbot (1857–1939). After graduating from Yale in 1879, Stokes worked briefly for Dodd Mead and was a partner in various publishing ventures. In 1887 he established a firm with his brother, which he continued as the Frederick A. Stokes Company when the partnership was dissolved three years later. His publishing house issued works by Anthony Hope, H. G. Wells,* John Masefield, and Maria Montessori, among others, and was notable for its list of popular works and children's books. He is credited with discovering Edna Ferber and Louis Bromfield. Stokes wrote essays and for a time edited his own periodical, the *Pocket Magazine*. Through his London agent, Stokes established contact with Crane in February 1899. Crane bypassed his own agent, Paul Revere Reynolds, by selling the book rights of *Active Service* directly to Stokes, and the negotiations for *Wounds in the Rain* were stormy because of Crane's contractual misunderstandings and continuous demands for advance payments.

Crane signed a contract with Stokes for the American edition of a Revolutionary War novel that he never completed and substituted *The O'Ruddy* for this proposed book. Stokes published *War Is Kind* and the American edition of *Active Service* in 1899. After Crane's death, Stokes published the American editions of *Wounds in the Rain* and *The O'Ruddy*.

Stokes, John Scott (?–1918). Harold Frederic's* literary assistant, secretary, and English literary executor, Stokes was a resident of Surrey where Frederic settled with Kate Lyon* in 1893. Stokes attended to Frederic's affairs during his last illness, and advised Kate Lyon, an adherent to Christian Science, to summon medical aid for Frederic. He nevertheless supported her when she was charged with manslaughter after Frederic's death. With Cora Crane, Stokes established a fund soliciting private subscriptions for the three children of Frederic and Kate Lyon. Stokes helped to bring Crane home from Havana by securing a £50 advance from Heinemann and arranging to have it forwarded to Crane through Major General J. F. Wade.

"Stories Told by an Artist". A group of fragmentary stories about studio life in the Old Art Students League building where Crane lived at various times between 1893 and 1895 that in revised form were incorporated into chapters 19 and 20 of *The Third Violet*. Crane and his roommates, Nelson Greene,* R. G. Vosburgh,* and William W. Carroll,* are represented, respectively, as Little Pennoyer (Penny), Purple Sanderson, Warwickson (also known as Great Grief), and Wrinkles. The cynical but successful artist Corinson, who has compromised his craft by drawing crayon portraits in order to survive, is clearly based on Crane's friend Corwin Knapp Linson.* The three stories are: "A Tale about How 'Great Grief' Got His Holiday Dinner," "As to Payment of the Rent," and "How Pennoyer Disposed of His Sunday Dinner." This trilogy is a light-hearted treatment of the bohemian hand-to-mouth existence of these young painters and illustrators. "Stories Told by an Artist" was published in the *New York Press* on 28 October 1894 and collected in *Last Words* under the title "Stories Told by an Artist in New York."

"The Stove". Little Cora of "The Angel Child" is once again the central character of this Whilomville story, published in the April 1900 issue of *Harper's New Monthly Magazine*. In "The Stove" simple childhood rituals upset elaborate adult rituals. Little Cora and her parents are visiting the Trescotts for the Christmas holidays, and Cora has brought along her favorite toy, a small but functional stove that soon captivates the fancy of Jimmie Trescott as well. The children cook potatoes on the stove in the yard; when it begins to snow, they relocate the stove in the cellar of the Trescott house and heap turnips that they pretend are puddings for a large hotel party into it. In the meantime, Mrs. Trescott is giving a tea party upstairs that is a microcosm of the social rivalry and pretentiousness of Whilomville. At a Whilomville tea party a small picked company of latent enemies would meet. There would be a fanfare of affectionate greetings, during which everybody would measure to an inch the importance of what everybody else was wearing. Those who wore old dresses would wish then that they had not come; and those who saw that, in the company, they were well-clad, would be pleased or exalted, or filled with the joys of cruelty. Then they had tea, which was a habit and a delight with none of them, their usual beverage being coffee with milk.

While the tea party is in progress, the imperious little Cora urges Jimmie to shovel more and more turnips into the stove. The stench of the burning turnips soon rises to the Trescott parlor, and the tea party is dispersed. Dr. Trescott persuades the angel child's ineffectual father to spank her, to the consternation of her overindulgent mother, but the social farce in the cellar has clearly been more innocent than the fiasco in the parlor. Dr. Trescott seems to sense this paradox at the conclusion of the story when he extends his hands over the scene "in a quiet but magnificent gesture of despair and weariness."

Suggested Reading

Brown, Bill. "American Childhood and Stephen Crane's Toys." *American Literary History* 7 (1995): 443–76.

Strepp, Lord. The son of the Earl of Westport in *The O'Ruddy*. Before he inherited his title, the earl was also named Lord Strepp.

Sturgeon. Proprietor of the *Eclipse* in *Active Service*, Sturgeon is a yellow journalist whose character is based on Joseph Pulitzer and William Randolph Hearst. Like Hearst and Pulitzer, Sturgeon is "some kind of a poet using his millions romantically, spending wildly on a sentiment that might be with beauty or without beauty, according to the momentary vacillation."

"Sullivan County Bears". Printed in the *New York Tribune* on 1 May 1892, this sketch is similar in theme to "Not Much of a Hero," another Sullivan County piece that appeared in the *Tribune* on the same day. The sketch begins with an extended description of the living and feeding habits of bears in Sullivan County and continues with a narrative of the roles of men and dogs in the pursuit of what is "the shyest of all the animals" that live in the woods. Crane emphasizes that "it is difficult to reconcile the bear of fiction with the bear of reality. The black bear of the hunter's tales was a fighter. He had a fashion of rearing upon his hind legs and crushing men and guns in a passionate embrace." But the actual bear fights only when cornered, and the prowess of bear hunters is vastly exaggerated. In this early sketch Crane deals with two themes that would become pervasive in his fiction: the contrast between illusion and reality and the deflation of the myth of the hero.

"Sullivan County Sketches". This title was first used by Cora Crane as a heading for two early pieces, "The Mesmeric Mountain" and "Four Men in a Cave," in the Contents of *Last Words* (1902), a mistitled compilation of Crane works early and late that had not previously appeared in book form. In 1949, Melvin Schoberlin edited *The Sullivan County Sketches of Stephen Crane*, a collection of ten short fictional episodes very loosely based on the camping experiences of four friends in the Hartwood Club area northwest of Port Jervis in Sullivan County, New York, mostly in the summer of 1891. Five of the tales were first published in the Sunday supplement of the *New York Tribune* in July 1892; one of them appeared in *Cosmopolitan* and another in the *Syracuse University Herald* in December of that year; three were published posthumously. The stories printed by Schoberlin are: "Four Men in a Cave"; "The Octopush"; "A Ghoul's Accountant"; "The Black Dog"; "Killing His Bear"; "An Explosion of Seven Babies"; "A Tent in Agony"; "The Cry of a Huckleberry Pudding"; "The Holler Tree"; and "The Mesmeric Mountain." These stories feature the fantastic experiences of four men from the city who are hunting, fishing, and camping in a surrealistic rural environment. Most of them have a similar plot dealing with the dispelling of an illusionary fear. The men are generally nameless (the little man is sometimes called "Billie") and distinguished only by epithets. Louis C. Senger, Jr.,* identified their real-life counterparts as Louis E. Carr, Jr., the little man; Frederic M. Lawrence,* the pudgy man; Louis C. Senger, Jr., the tall man; Stephen Crane, the quiet man. Only the little man and the pudgy man are individuated, and it is evident since Crane was approximately five feet, seven inches in height and the little man plays the predominant role in the stories that Crane identifies with him more than with the quiet man.

In a June 1895 letter to Copeland & Day, Crane referred to a group of stories that he wished them to publish as a book as "eight little grotesque tales of the woods which I wrote when I was clever." They were written, he had told Lily Brandon Munroe* the previous year, in "my clever Rudyard-Kipling style," although there is little in the distended prose of these tall tales to suggest Kipling. Notwithstanding Crane's claim that he had "renounced the clever school in literature" to develop "a little creed of art" that "was identical with the one of Howells and Garland," it is notable that he was composing these Sullivan County fantasies at the same time that he was revising *Maggie: A Girl of the Streets*. The tales are as preoccupied with contrasts between self-importance and self-actualization, illusion, and reality as Crane's later works. Also significant is that while Crane may have learned a good deal about impressionism* in art and literature from his studio associates in the years 1893–95, the dense use of color imagery, synesthesia, synecdoche, metaphor, personification, and startling similes and qualifiers that distinguish his style is already evident in these stories.

In his *Stephen Crane: Sullivan County Tales and Sketches* (1968), R. W. Stallman adds to the stories six nonfictional or semifictional sketches concerned largely with Sullivan County folklore, legend, and myth and with hunting that also appeared in the *Tribune* in 1892: "The Last of the Mohicans"; "Hunting Wild Hogs"; "The Last Panther"; "Sullivan County Bears"; "The Way in Sullivan County"; and "Bear and Panther." Stallman includes "Across the Covered Pit" because he mistakenly believes that it deals with a cave in Sullivan County rather than the famous Mammoth Cave in Kentucky, and he erroneously follows previous editors in classifying "The Snake," which is based on a well-documented experience Crane had returning from a camp in Pike County, Pennsylvania, to be a Sullivan County tale. Stallman acknowledges that the fable "How the Donkey Lifted the Hills" is not a Sullivan County sketch, but he includes it here also because he believes that it has a thematic link with "The Mesmeric Mountain" and functions as a coda to the volume. Thomas A. Gullason, in a periodical essay that appeared shortly before the publication of *Stephen Crane: Sullivan County Tales and Sketches*, independently identified Crane's authorship of the six *Tribune* sketches and added three other Sullivan County pieces from the *Tribune* not in Stallman's book: "Not Much of a Hero"; "A Reminiscence of Indian War"; and "Two Men and a Bear." For the journalistic sketches, Crane utilized historical legends of Sullivan County that he derived from the yarns of older residents and from historical chronicles of the region.

Suggested Reading

Gibson, Donald B. *The Fiction of Stephen Crane*. Carbondale: Southern Illinois University Press, 1968. 3–24.

Gullason, Thomas A. "A Stephen Crane Find: Nine Newspaper Sketches." *Southern Humanities Review* 2 (1968): 1–37.

Schoberlin, Melvin. Introduction to *The Sullivan County Sketches of Stephen Crane*. Ed. Melvin Schoberlin. Syracuse: Syracuse University Press, 1949. 1–20.

Stallman, R. W. Introduction to *Stephen Crane: Sullivan County Tales and Sketches*. Ed. R. W. Stallman. Ames, Iowa: Iowa State University Press, 1968. 3–24.

Wolford, Chester L. *Stephen Crane: A Study of the Short Fiction*. Boston: Twayne, 1989. 3–12.

"Summer Dwellers at Asbury Park and Their Doings". An unsigned report in the "On the New-Jersey Coast" column of the *New York Tribune*, 24 July 1892, juxtaposing events at Asbury Park such as the shutting down of the Ferris wheel because residents complained that its engine spread ashes and also "disturbed their pious meditations on the evils of the world," the first annual convention of the Christian alliance, a glut on the weak fish market because of an abundant catch, and an illustrated lecture on the urban poor by Jacob Riis.*

"The Surrender of Forty Fort". First published in the Wyoming Valley Tales section of *Last Words*, this is the most mundane of that generally uninspired series. Solomon Bennet narrates the story of what happened in Forty Fort after its capture by the British and the Indians, although he and his younger brother, Andrew, and their father, Ol' Bennet, had fled over the mountains to the Delaware settlements and were not present during the occupation. The British declined to ensure the safety of the Continental troops, who consequently fled, leaving the militia commander, Colonel Denison, in charge. For several days the Indians obeyed the British officers and kept out of the fort, but they gradually infiltrated and plundered everything of value. Even the colonel literally lost his shirt, a fringed hunting shirt made of fine linen. When the British learned that General Washington intended to send a strong force to retake the valley, they abandoned Forty Fort, leaving only small bands of Indians to burn whatever cabins remained. Solomon and his father and brother returned with the first company of Continental regulars, and they began the job of rebuilding the valley settlement.

The Swede. Otherwise unnamed, the Swede is the focal character of "The Blue Hotel," and the pivotal thematic argument of the story is to what extent his distorted perception of reality or the complicity of the other characters who have failed to form a viable community is the causal factor in his death. The Swede has come to Nebraska from New York, where he worked as a tailor for a decade. His conceptions of the West have been formed by popular literary conventions, and his paranoid behavior provokes aggressive behavior in those around him that gives substance to his delusions. From another perspective, the Swede strips away the domesticated veneer of Fort Romper; it is still a frontier town—a fort, as its name implies. The Swede's conception of the town as imperfectly civilized and potentially dangerous is borne out by his violent death at the hands of the deceptively genteel gambler. He is in the end both a creator and a victim of his tragedy. Henry Fleming's farmhand in "Lynx-Hunting" and the drunken hired man in "The Veteran" who cause the conflagration that results in old Henry Fleming's death are also known only as "the Swede."

Suggested Reading

Beards, Richard D. "Stereotyping in Modern American Fiction: Some Solitary Swedish Madmen." *Moderna Sprak* 63 (1969): 329–37.
Church, Joseph. "The Determined Stranger in Stephen Crane's 'Blue Hotel.' " *Studies in the Humanities* 16 (1989): 99–110.
Wolford, Chester L. *The Anger of Stephen Crane*. Lincoln: University of Nebraska Press, 1983. 101–14.

Syracuse University. Crane's short time as a nondegree student in the College of Liberal Arts at Syracuse University from January to June 1891 was an extremely important period in his life and literary career. Syracuse, like Pennington Seminary* and Claverack College,* was a Methodist-sponsored institution, with many students preparing for the ministry. Religious observance was required, and there were prohibitions against alcohol, smoking, gambling, and idle amusements. Notwithstanding such strictures, Crane thoroughly enjoyed his Syracuse experience. He roomed in the Delta Upsilon fraternity house and participated actively in its literary program, and he played catcher and shortstop on the varsity baseball team. As a stringer for the *New York Tribune*, Crane explored the tenement districts and the music halls of Syracuse and observed the underbelly of society in the city's police court. Based on these experiences, he sketched out an early version of the novel that he later developed into *Maggie: A Girl of the Streets*. In a lighter vein, Crane published "The King's Favor" and "Great Bugs at Onondaga" while a student at Syracuse and wrote other stories and sketches, including "A Foreign Policy in Three Glimpses" and perhaps "Greed Rampant."

Academically, Crane's accomplishments at the university were few. He participated in Chancellor Charles N. Sims's English literature class and attended Professor Charles J. Little's class on the French Revolution. The often repeated statement that Crane received an A+ in English literature is based on a mistaken interpretation of the records. Syracuse did not give grades at this time, so his progress in these and other courses was not reported. As he wrote to John Northern Hilliard* in 1895, "I did little work at school, but confined my abilities, such as they were, to the diamond. Not that I disliked books, but the cut-and-dried curriculum of the college did not appeal to me. Humanity was a much more interesting study. When I ought to have been at recitations I was studying faces on the streets, and when I ought to have been studying my next day's lessons I was watching the trains roll in and out of the Central Station."

Suggested Reading

Gullason, Thomas A. "Stephen Crane at Syracuse University: New Findings." *Courier* 29 (1994): 127–40.
Jones, Claude. "Stephen Crane at Syracuse." *American Literature* 7 (1935): 82–84.
Sorrentino, Paul. "New Evidence on Stephen Crane at Syracuse." *Resources for American Literary Study* 15 (1985): 179–85.

T

Taber, Harry Persons (1865–?). Born in East Aurora, New York, Taber was a journalist, printer, and author. From 1892 to 1894 he was on the staff of the *Denver Republican*. He returned to East Aurora and in 1895, under the inspiration of Elbert Hubbard,* he founded the Roycroft Shop, devoted to fine printing in the manner of William Morris's Kelmscott Press. In June 1895 Hubbard and Taber also established *The Philistine: A Periodical of Protest,** for which Hubbard did most of the writing. Taber is credited as editor in the July through December issues and as copyright holder from the September through January 1896 issues. In the January issue he is listed as "Datary" instead of editor. Taber had sold his share in the Roycroft Shop and the *Philistine* to Hubbard in November 1895. In February 1896, after a disagreement with Hubbard over editorial and business matters, Taber and a group of journalists associated with him formed a stock company and attempted to form a competing publishing company and buy the *Philistine*. While Hubbard vacillated, Taber and his associate Eugene White met with Crane at the Hotel Imperial in New York and proposed to become his publisher. Crane evidently agreed to give them one of the books on which he was working, probably *The Little Regiment*, but when Hubbard finally decided not to sell the *Philistine*, the new publishing venture was dissolved.

After his association with Hubbard ended, Taber repeatedly claimed that he was the exclusive founder of both the *Roycroft Shop* and the *Philistine* and that Hubbard was a mere interloper, but the contents of the periodical and extant correspondence between Hubbard and Crane and other authors show that Hubbard's was the guiding and controlling hand from the first. Taber was editor of the *Buffalo Times* in 1896. In 1897 he served as a foreign correspondent, and from 1901 to 1903 he edited the *Springfield* (Massachusetts) *Union*. With Carolyn Wells, he was the author of two novels: *The Gordon Elopement* (1904) and *The Matrimonial Bureau* (1905). His fictionalized reminiscences, *Ezra and Me*, appeared in 1943. Taber's unpublished reminiscences, "Chant after Battle," are in the George Arents Research Library at Syracuse University.

Suggested Reading

Stallman, R. W. *Stephen Crane: A Critical Bibliography*. Ames, Iowa: Iowa State University Press, 1972. 298–301, 310–12, 356–58.

"A Tale of Mere Chance". Apart from the Wyoming Valley stories, this is Crane's only work of fiction narrated directly in the first person (fictional narrators are created in "An Illusion in Red and White" and "War Memories"). "A Tale of Mere Chance" was syndicated by Bacheller, Johnson and Bacheller on 15 March 1896. While the Ides of March publication date is no doubt adventitious, this grotesque story of murder and detection seems to be a parody of Edgar Allan Poe's "The Tell-Tale Heart," with overtones of "Bernice" and "The Purloined Letter." The neurasthenic narrator, a self-described "delicate and sensitive person," visits the home of a rival in love and shoots him to death in the drawing room. As his victim falls, the narrator experiences a hallucination in which objects in the room become personified and animated. The white tiles of the floor that had "whispered one to another" and looked at him as he entered the room "huddled and covered their eyes" from the rain of blood. The clock stops ticking, and a chair throws itself in his way as he springs toward the door. From that point on, he is pursued by the blood-stained tiles, which scream out his guilt to the world, and "great, round, vividly orange spots" appear on his coat, which he is unable to shed despite his struggles. Clearly it is no great feat for even the most obtuse detective to apprehend "a man in a coat of spotted orange, followed by shrieking blood-stained tiles," which continue to plague him even in his prison cell.

"The Talk of London". The last of Crane's series for the *New York Journal* on the Boer War, this short report appeared in the *Journal* and in Hearst's *San Francisco Examiner* on 11 March 1900. Crane discusses the effects of the war on other European nations in their relationship to Great Britain. France, Russia, and Germany are undertaking imperialist ventures that they would not attempt if the British were not engaged in South Africa, and the Irish nationalists in the House of Commons are taunting the opposition and being insulted in turn so that the best efforts of Prime Minister Arthur Balfour are required to preserve order.

"Tarantula". According to Vincent Starrett in *Stephen Crane: A Bibliography* (Philadelphia: Centaur, 1923, 10), this was a Mexican story said to have been written at Brede Place* in September 1899 and to have been destroyed.

The Tattered Man. A wounded soldier in *The Red Badge of Courage*, the unnamed tattered man becomes the personification of Henry Fleming's conscience. The tattered man's question, "Where yeh hit?" humiliates Henry into a realization of the necessity of atonement, especially when it is reinforced by the observation that "it might be inside mostly, an' them plays thunder." Henry abandons the tattered man, and at the conclusion of the novel the guilt over this desertion undercuts his elation at having fought bravely. "Yet gradually," the narrator comments ironically, "he mustered force to put the sin at a distance."

Ted. The "freckled man" in "The Reluctant Voyagers." A passive butt of the "tall man's" ridicule for much of the story, he provides comic relief in a role reversal at the conclusion.

"The 'Tenderloin' As It Really Is". Appearing on 25 October 1896, this is the first of a series that Crane wrote for the *New York Journal* about the residents of Manhattan's tawdry entertainment district. The Tenderloin, an area extending roughly from Twenty-third to Forty-second Streets between Fourth and Seventh Avenues, contained most of New York's theaters, hotels, gambling houses, and brothels. A pedestrian piece of fictional journalism, "The 'Tenderloin' As It Really Is" purports to refute those "who have mistaken the departure of their own youth for the death of the Tenderloin" with two anecdotes that are intended to illustrate the spirit is still alive, although Crane acknowledges that there is more show than substance in what remains. In the first anecdote, which takes place in a boisterous dance hall on Seventh Avenue, Billie Maconnigle, "one of the greatest society leaders that the world has produced," dances with Flossie, whose "fellow," Johnnie, objecting that she is "me own private snap," interrupts the dance. A brawl ensues in which Flossie joins, and the three are ejected. In the second, shorter episode, five men enter a more sedate café on Broadway and drink into the morning hours. Crane maintains that despite its up-to-date garishness "the Tenderloin is more than a place. It is an emotion," but he fails to bring it alive in this sketch.

"A Tent in Agony". This slight Sullivan County story in the December 1892 issue of the *Cosmopolitan* is Crane's first publication in a commercial magazine. The little man of the tales is left to guard a fishing camp while his three companions trudge to a farmhouse for supplies. A bear appears, and when the little man ducks into the tent to escape, the bear pursues him. The little man escapes through a flap in the tent and crouches fearfully in the branches of a tree. The bear in his rampage knocks down the center pole of the tent and becomes entangled in the canvas. When the little man's companions return, they are terrified by the sight of the "canvas avalanche" sweeping past them. The story ends on this insipid farcical note.

"Tent Life at Ocean Grove". Circumstantial evidence supports Melvin Schoberlin's attribution to Crane of this prolix piece printed in the *New York Herald*
on 19 July 1891. Crane wrote feature articles for the *Herald* in the summer of
1891. His family owned a lot on the Ocean Grove campground where Methodist
ministers conducted revival meetings in a resort environment, and in his childhood Stephen often visited during the summer. Mrs. Crane was president of the
Women's Christian Temperance Union (WCTU) of Asbury Park and Ocean
Grove, and in the *New York Tribune* on 2 August 1890 Townley Crane defended
the Ocean Grove Camp Meeting Association against charges of puritanism for
its ban on alcohol and tobacco and strictures against card playing, dancing, and
other diversions. Stephen wrote a number of articles about shore life at Asbury
Park, Ocean Grove, and Avon-by-the-Sea in 1890–92, but these appeared in the
Tribune to which Townley's New Jersey Coast News Bureau regularly sent
shore news. Crane's authorship of "Tent Life at Ocean Grove" is conjectural.
The article is lengthier, more discursive, and less satirical than his *Tribune* reports but reflects his concerns in criticizing the "absolute despotism" and lack
of privacy at the meeting ground. It also dwells on the hypocrisy of the Methodist ministers and their families, especially their lack of modesty and the ease
with which alcohol and tobacco are obtained in defiance of the stringent regu-
lations.

Suggested Reading

Gullason, Thomas A. "The 'Lost' Newspaper Writings of Stephen Crane." *Courier* 21.1
     (1986): 57–87.

"The Terrible Captain of the Captured Panama". Written only a few days
after he had arrived in Key West, this is the first of Crane's Cuban War dispatches as a special correspondent for the *New York World*. It appeared in the
28 April 1898 issue of the newspaper. With considerable hyperbole, Crane reports that Key West is thronged with some 250 correspondents awaiting the
American invasion of Cuba and eager for news. The most noteworthy event is
the capture of the Spanish steamer *Panama*, whose captain wishes to go ashore
and consult with the British consul but is terrified of the Key West population,
which is sympathetic to the insurgent cause. When he and his chief engineer
are taken ashore in the *World's* launch, "[n]othing happened. Key West, enervated from too much excitement, slept in the dusk-thickened sunshine."

The Third Violet. Crane's motivation in writing this conventional romantic
novel of manners was no doubt largely pecuniary, an attempt to capitalize on
the success of *The Red Badge of Courage* with another best-seller. Crane was
well aware of the limitations of *The Third Violet*. "I think it is as well to go
ahead with The Third Violet. People may just as well discover now that the
high dramatic key of The Red Badge cannot be sustained," he wrote on 27
January 1896 to his editor, Ripley Hitchcock,* who was apparently asking for

further revisions. "The Third Violet is a quiet little story but then it is serious work and I should say let it go." A few weeks earlier, writing to Curtis Brown, he had been more frank: "It's pretty rotten work. I used myself up in the accursed 'Red Badge.' "

The germ of *The Third Violet*, first tentatively entitled "The Eternal Patience," dates from the fall of 1894 when Crane wrote the goup of vignettes about bohemian life in the old Art Students League building, "Stories Told by an Artist," much of which in revised form is incorporated into chapters 19 and 20 of the novel, with traces appearing in chapters 21 and 25, and "The Silver Pageant," where the young artists drawn from his studio acquaintances also appear. Most of *The Third Violet* was written in the fall of 1895 at the home of Crane's brother Edmund in Hartwood, New York. The Hartwood Club and the August encampment Crane shared with friends in Pike County, Pennsylvania, probably contributed to the Howellsian vacation resort environment that forms one of the two major settings in the novel. There are also overtones of "In a Park Row Restaurant," which appeared in the same issue of the *New York Press* as "Stories Told by an Artist" (28 October 1894), in the café episode that forms chapter 27 of the novel. *The Third Violet* was syndicated in newspapers by McClure in the fall of 1896 and was published in book form by Appleton in New York and Heinemann in London in May 1897.

The Third Violet is the most directly autobiographical of Crane's novels. In the opening episode, a young painter, William (Billie) Hawker, the name obviously a play on that of Crane's close friend Willis Brooks Hawkins,* returns by train to a village in the vicinity of which his family has a farm on which he grew up. This setting resembles Hartwood, New York, the home of Crane's brother Edmund, where much of the novel was written. He shares a stagecoach, whose final destination is a resort sardonically called Hemlock Inn, with a family that includes a young woman, Grace Fanhall, and her sister, who is accompanied by her two children and the children's nursemaid, all of whom are staying at the inn. Hawker instantly falls in love with Grace, a droll but thoroughly conventional society girl resembling Nellie Crouse* with whom Crane became enamored after a single meeting and who ultimately rejected his epistolary courtship. Hawker has a friend, a cynical, worldly writer named George Hollanden who for some unexplained reason is spending the summer at Hemlock Inn. This adventitious circumstance gives Hawker access to Miss Fanhall. Hollanden is a compromised artist, "a trained bear of the magazines, and a juggler of comic paragraphs" who caters to the public demand for romantic fiction. Hawker strives to remain true to Crane's ideal of artistic sincerity, but his stilted declarations of integrity convey the false note of Crane's posturing to Nellie Crouse, and Hollanden's sardonic remarks often puncture his illusions. Hollanden and Hawker both incorporate different aspects of Crane's fractured personality: the aspiring journalist and seeker after popular success and the thwarted artist.

Hawker calls at Hemlock Inn and courts Grace under the watchful eyes of fifteen middle-aged ladies "of the most aggressive respectability," resembling Martha Goodwin and her gossips in "The Monster" and the lonely spinsters of "The Lover and the Telltale," who, according to Hollanden, "have come here for no discernible purpose save to get where they can see people and be displeased at them. They sit in a large group on that porch and take measurements of character as importantly as if they constituted the jury of heaven." Hawker is a diffident suitor, and his lovemaking with Grace consists largely of a great deal of verbal fencing, conducted with her and with Hollanden who offers sarcastic observations on his effrontery in courting an heiress and on his lack of progress, noting especially Hawker's surreptitious retrieval of a violet that Grace drops at the side of the tennis court.

Hawker has a rival in Jem Oglethorpe, a socially prominent playboy who is a friend of the Fanhalls and who, Hollanden maliciously assures him, is popular and wealthy, while Hawker, as one of the chorus of porch sitters informs another, comes from "the commonest kind of people, my dear, the commonest kind. The father is a regular farmer, you know. He drives oxen." Returning to Hemlock Inn from pickerel fishing one day, Hawker and Grace encounter his father, John, driving a wagon hauled by this team of oxen. To Hawker's embarrassment, Grace enthusiastically accepts a ride back to the inn in the oxcart. This further titillates the porch sitters, one of whom pointedly comments to Grace that only people of wealth and position can afford to indulge in such unconventional behavior. The incident is important because Hawker is himself acutely aware of the social distance between himself and Grace, although she seems to be remarkably free from class prejudices.

Oglethorpe reinforces Hawker's conflict over his artistic sincerity since he expresses a philistine attitude toward literature, maintaining that "the men who made the most money from books were the best authors" while even Hollenden "contended that they were the worst." As the summer ends, Oglethorpe departs from the resort, apparently vanquished. Grace also returns to New York City, leaving Hawker, who confesses that he will miss her desperately, with only an uncommitted, formal goodbye and a second violet that she has plucked from a cluster on her gown and given to him. Hawker follows her the next week, and the setting of the novel shifts abruptly and awkwardly to the building in which his studio is located and the struggle for survival of his impecunious artist friends who share a loft in the building: Warwickson (familiarly known as Great Grief), Wrinkles, Purple Sanderson, and Pennoyer (Penny). Added to this coterie, clearly drawn from Crane's roommates in the old Art Students League building depicted earlier in "Stories Told by an Artist," is a model, Florinda O'Conner (Splutter), probably inspired by Nelson Greene's* model, Gertrude Selene, who often drops into the studio and is desperately in love with Hawker. She and the artists soon notice that Hawker is in a distracted mood and moping over two violets that he conceals in an envelope. There is a good deal of speculation by the artists about Hawker's relationships with Splutter and with the unknown young woman with whom he is clearly infatuated. Hawker, paying careful attention to his wardrobe, which features a pair of gray gloves at which the artists scoff, calls repeatedly at Grace Fanhall's mansion with its "great windows" and "colossal chandelier," and they chat aimlessly about their resort experiences. During one of these visits Hawker relates the story of his impoverished youth and his struggles to gain stature as an artist. She reassures him that "[p]overty isn't anything to be ashamed of," but Hawker, who remains painfully aware of his social inferiority, is unconvinced. The novel ends abruptly in a melodramatic reversal during Hawker's final visit in which he tells Grace that he is leaving the city because he is despondent over his futile love for her. In a maudlin farewell, he mentions the two violets that he will take with him, and she petulantly flings a third violet at him. When she cries, "Oh, do go! Go! Please! I want you to go!" he understands that she means the exact opposite of this, Hollanden having pompously informed him about the total irrationality of women, and he suddenly realizes that his courtship will be successful.

The Third Violet was widely condemned as trivial and inane when it was published in book form in the spring of 1897, although English reviews tended to be more favorable than the American, and the novel has been more or less dismissed or ignored by modern critics, whose commentary has centered on external factors. *The Third Violet* has been variously viewed as Crane's most resolute but failed effort at realism* in the manner of William Dean Howells,* as a critique of artistic success and failure in America, as a Jamesian study of class distinctions, or as a satire of romantic fiction and the demands of the literary marketplace. Conventional in its plot and stock characters as *The Third Violet* may be, it contains some lively dialogue and descriptions of nature, such as the "brawling, ruffianly little brook" that "swaggered from side to side down the glade, swirling in white leaps over the great dark rocks and shouting challenge to the hillsides." There are also occasional striking images, as when a stovepipe in the studio shared by the artists "wandered off in the wrong direction and then turned impulsively toward a hole in the wall." Even contemporary critics commented on the book's most engaging personality, Hawker's orange and white setter Stanley, who romps through the farm and resort episodes in the novel. According to a reminiscence by Edna Crane Sidbury,* a daughter of Crane's brother William, Stanley's progenitor was a dog named Chester owned by her family in Port Jervis at the time Crane was writing *The Third Violet* in nearby Hartwood:

> When Chester was a pup, father was teaching him to lie down at the command, "Charge!" One of his brothers began to quote:
>
> > "Charge, Chester, charge!
> > On, Stanley, on!"
>
> Thereupon the dog was named Chester, and when he appears in "The Third Violet," he is called Stanley.

Suggested Reading

Andrews, William L. "Art and Success: Another Look at Stephen Crane's *The Third Violet*." *Wascana Review* 13.1 (1978): 71–82.
Gullason, Thomas A. "The Jamesian Motif in Stephen Crane's Last Novels." *Personalist* 42 (1961): 77–84.
Levenson, J. C. Introduction to *The Third Violet* and *Active Service*. Charlottesville: University Press of Virginia, 1976. xi–xl. Vol. 3 of *The Works of Stephen Crane*. Ed. Fredson Bowers. 10 vols. 1969–76.
Sidbury, Edna Crane. "My Uncle, Stephen Crane, As I Knew Him." *Literary Digest International Book Review* 4 (1926): 248–50.

"This Majestic Lie". Published posthumously in two parts in the *New York Herald* and in other newspapers, on 24 June and 1 July 1900 in most of the papers, and collected in *Wounds in the Rain*, this Cuban War story is an intermixture of autobiographical and fictional elements. In part the story is based on the experiences of Charles H. Thrall,* an American spy posing as a reporter for the *New York World* who spent the early weeks of the war in Havana and whom Crane had interviewed for his report, "Thrilling Adventures of World Scout in Cuba." From September 1898 until shortly before American troops occupied Havana, Crane lived a virtually underground life in the boardinghouse of Mary Horan,* who had previously harbored Thrall. She is fictionalized in "This Majestic Lie" as Martha Clancy.

The story opens with a virtual tirade against the jingoistic press in Havana and the United States during May 1898. The Havana newspapers reported the destruction of the Spanish fleet in Manila Bay as a great victory for Spain, while American newspaper editors demanded reports from Cuba and pressured correspondents into inflating the significance of mundane events. "This happened and that happened and if the news arrived at Key West as a mouse, it was often enough cabled north as an elephant." Johnnie, an American spy who had been the manager of a sugar plantation, searches out intelligence on the fortifications of Havana while secreted in Martha Clancy's boardinghouse. His efforts to gather information and his failed attempt to deliver it to the American fleet ultimately prove futile because an attack on Havana is not part of the American war strategy. Food is expensive in the blockaded city, largely because of the extortion described in Crane's dispatch, "The Grocer Blockade." When Johnnie decides to eat at the Café Aguacate, where he had frequently enjoyed a meal, the proprietor, who knows he is a spy, extorts $50 in gold from him for bread, coffee, and two eggs and then compounds the injury by failing to serve up this sparse fare. In October, when the fighting has ended, the narrator of the story meets Johnnie in Havana. They share a sumptuous meal at the Café Aguacate and leave without paying. For Johnnie "the war is now over."

Thompson, Harry (?–?). A Claverack College* schoolmate of Crane, Thompson became American manager of the Anglo-American publishing firm of Edward Arnold. Explaining to Ripley Hitchcock* why he had broken his commitment to D. Appleton & Company in allowing Arnold to publish *George's Mother*, Crane jestingly commented that Thompson "conducted such a campaign against me as is seldom seen. He appealed to my avarice and failing appealed to my humanity."

Thrall, Charles H. (1871–1950). A Yale graduate, prominent businessman, and spy for the U.S. government, Thrall slipped in and out of Havana, ostensibly as a *New York World* reporter, in April and early May 1898. He reported his experiences in a 8 May *World* dispatch, "Thrilling Adventures of World Scout in Cuba." Crane's interview, "Stephen Crane's Pen Picture of C. H. Thrall," appeared in the same issue of the newspaper. Thrall is depicted as Johnnie in "This Majestic Lie." After the Spanish-American War, Thrall continued to live in Havana, where he became president of his own electrical supply company.

"Three Miraculous Soldiers". One of the six Civil War stories collected in *The Little Regiment*, "Three Miraculous Soldiers" was first syndicated in a shortened form by S. S. McClure in a number of newspapers, generally on 15 March 1896. The story concerns the adventure of a young southern belle named Mary Hinckson who aids three Confederate soldiers by hiding them in a feedbox in her barn and then assisting them in effecting their own escape and that of a Confederate officer who has been captured and held prisoner in the barn by Union sentinels. Like Henry Fleming, the girl has romantic aspirations toward heroism acquired from popular fiction, but she is more sensible than the protagonist of *The Red Badge*. Although she knows that stock heroines "severed the hero's bonds, cried a dramatic sentence, and stood between him and his enemies until he had run far enough away," she realizes that her own conduct will require more circumspection. Nevertheless, she weeps over the Yankee sentry knocked unconscious in the escape, and the story ends with the sentimental reflection of a Union officer that "[w]ar changes many things; but it doesn't change everything, thank God!" Crane apparently reined in his irony to achieve a popular success with this story.

Suggested Reading

Mayer, Charles W. "Stephen Crane and the Realistic Tradition: 'Three Miraculous Soldiers.' " *Arizona Quarterly* 30 (1974): 127–34.

Shaw, Mary. "Stephen Crane's 'Three Miraculous Soldiers': A Satire on Romanticized Notions of Traditional Heroism." *Studies in Contemporary Satire* 17 (1990): 58–63.

"The Time Has Come". A souvenir menu issued by the Society of the Philistines to commemorate the dinner given in Crane's honor at Buffalo on 19 December 1895. Its title is adopted from a line in Lewis Carroll's "The Walrus and the Carpenter." The menu prints humorous regrets from thirty-seven invited guests who could not or would not attend, probably because they did not want to involve themselves in one of Elbert Hubbard's* self-promotional ventures. Among those who declined are notable figures in Crane's literary career, including Irving Bacheller,* Ripley Hitchcock,* William Dean Howells,* Hamlin Garland,* Louise Imogen Guiney,* Richard Harding Davis,* and S. S. McClure. As McClure put it, he preferred to "admire the valiant Philistines—from a safe distance." One of the unintentionally facetious commentaries was made by Hitchcock when a misprint resulted in the word *puppets* being substituted for *prophets*, resulting in the statement, "I am glad to know that our puppets, when they prove themselves prophets, are not without honor in their own country." "Confusion to the printers!" Hitchcock wrote to Crane. "I used no such word, and I am disgusted." On the front cover of this pamphlet is a drawing by Dwight R. Collin of a man chasing the horizon and a sky filled with black riders on rocking horses. The back cover contains the first printing of Crane's poem, "I have heard the sunset song of the birches."

"To Use in Stephens Life". Posthumous notes made by Cora for a proposed biography of Crane inscribed in a shorthand notebook preserved in the Rare Book and Manuscript Library of Columbia University. The distraught handwriting and the incoherence of the notations indicate that they were made shortly after Stephen's death. The notebook contains anecdotes of Crane's youth but is more important for the fine points of Crane's personal appearance and temperament in his last year of life and the manner of his death. The first publication of these notes was in *Poems and Literary Remains*, volume 10 of *The Works of Stephen Crane*, edited by Fredson Bowers (1975), 343–46.

Tom. The enterprising plumber in "A Christmas Dinner Won in Battle." Crane contrasts his instinctively courageous actions in saving his beloved from a mob with the false heroics depicted in the popular fiction and drama of his time, "that magnificent fortitude, that gorgeous tranquillity amid upheavals and perils which is the attribute of people in plays."

Tom. In "A Self-Made Man" Tom is a parodic Horatio Alger hero who, according to the subtitle of the story, is "An Example of Success That Anyone Can Follow."

Tounley, Peter. A character in *Active Service*. One of the group of Washurst College students who accompany the Wainwright party to Greece, Tounley is a forthright and courageous young man who serves as a foil to Coke, another Washurst student. His name, but not his personality, is similar that of Crane's brother Townley.

"Tramps and Saints". Vincent Starrett in *Stephen Crane: A Bibliography* (Philadelphia: Centaur, 1923), 10, reports that this was a projected book about which nothing is known.

Travis, Abram Lincoln (?–?). A schoolmate of Crane at Claverack College and Hudson River Institute* and later at Syracuse University,* Travis taught for a year at Claverack after graduation in 1894 and then established the Travis Classical School in Syracuse. In 1930 Travis wrote a memoir of Crane's experience as a baseball player and a student at Claverack in response to Mansfield J. French's request for information about Crane. His letter is in the George Arents Research Library at Syracuse University. Of particular interest is Travis's account of Crane's reading: "He was a prodigious reader of all the nineteenth century English writers and reveled in the classics of Greece and Rome. Plutarch's Lives was his constant companion and even at this age he was familiar with the English and American poets. He would frequently quote from Tennyson's 'In Memoriam' and Bryant's 'Thanatopsis.' " Since Travis's recollections were written more than forty years after the event, they may be somewhat idealized.

Trescott, Dr. Edward. The protagonist of "The Monster," Dr. Trescott also appears as Jimmie's father in several of the *Whilomville Stories*. In "The Monster" Trescott assumes moral responsibility toward Henry Johnson, who has been rendered faceless and mentally incompetent in a fire while saving Trescott's son, by preserving Henry's life and receiving him into his home. In consequence Trescott is isolated and ostracized in Whilomville. He maintains his integrity but alienates his friends and neighbors and loses his medical practice. Critics have raised the question of whether Trescott's ethical idealism in sheltering Johnson is not motivated more by pride than compassion or prudence in that Henry Johnson would be better served in an institution than in Trescott's home and that Trescott needlessly sacrifices the peace of the community and his family to an abstract conception of virtue as foolish as Collins's blind courage in "A Mystery of Heroism."

Suggested Reading

Dooley, Patrick. *The Pluralistic Philosophy of Stephen Crane*. Urbana: University of Illinois Press, 1993. 97–104.

Trescott, Jimmie. A character in all but one of the thirteen *Whilomville Stories*, Jimmie also appears in "The Monster." Of uncertain age (he seems to be four or five in "The Monster" and eight or nine in *Whilomville Stories*), Jimmie is a "bad" boy in the sense that *Tom Sawyer* (1876) and Thomas Bailey Aldrich's *The Story of a Bad Boy* (1870) represent boys who fall short of the saccharine ideal of Frances Hodgson Burnett's *Little Lord Fauntleroy* (1886). Jimmie is mischievous and often pugnacious, not averse to lying or violence, and subject to peer pressure. In "The Monster" he teases the defaced Henry Johnson, who had saved his life. In "Lynx-Hunting" he attempts to deceive his companions into believing that he is able to borrow his father's gun. He lies "as naturally as most animals swim." In "The Lover and the Telltale," he reacts to teasing by charging blindly into a group of boys and "striking out frenziedly in all directions." In " 'Showin' Off' " Jimmie boastfully taunts a rival into driving a velocipede down a steep hill and causes a potentially serious accident, and in "The Carriage-Lamps" he wrathfully hurls stones at Peter Washington who has informed Jimmie's father that the boy possesses a pistol. In "A Little Pilgrim-age" Jimmie deceives his parents into believing that spiritual rather than venial reasons are behind his desire to attend a different Sunday school. The character of Jimmie Trescott undermines the ideal of innocent boyhood and stresses the similarities in the worlds of children and adults.

"The Trial, Execution, and Burial of Homer Phelps". A Whilomville story published in the May 1900 issue of *Harper's New Monthly Magazine*, this light-hearted tale of boyhood initiation has been rather speciously compared by critics to Crane's grim burial story, "The Upturned Face," written some six weeks later. Homer Phelps fails to respond with the proper password when challenged by one of the Margate twins during a war game played by Willie Dalzel's gang in the woods near Whilomville. He refuses to participate in the mock trial and execution that is the designated punishment for his offense, and Jimmie Trescott stands in as a substitute for him. Ostracized for his refusal to "play it the right way," Homer realizes that regaining acceptance in the group requires him to submit to feigned burial, the last act of the ritual and, despite his reluctance, allows the boys to immure him in a grave of hemlock boughs. Willie Dalzel delivers a eulogy over Homer, whom he has imaginatively transformed into "Bowie-knife Joe." Overcome by his own eloquence, he pauses, "and the still-ness was only broken by the deep manly grief of Jimmie Trescott."

Trudeau, Edward Livingston (1848–1915). A pioneer in the treatment of tu-berculosis in America, Trudeau was a graduate of the College of Physicians and Surgeons (Columbia University). In 1878 he was stricken with a severe case of pulmonary tuberculosis and moved to the Adirondacks, where he established the first sanitarium for the treatment of the disease in the United States, the Adirondack Cottage Sanitarium, later called the Trudeau Sanitarium, at Saranac Lake, New York. In 1904 he became president of what came to be known as the National Tuberculosis Association and in 1910 president of the Congress of American Physicians and Surgeons. Two of Trudeau's children died of tuber-culosis, and eventually he himself succumbed to the disease.

Crane probably became aware in Cuba that he had contracted tuberculosis. In late July 1898, before he went to Puerto Rico for the *New York Journal*, he visited Saranac Lake and consulted Dr. Trudeau, who diagnosed his condition as "not serious." Crane was never registered at the sanitarium but was a private patient of the eminent lung specialist. Writing to Cora on 16 September 1898, Trudeau states, "I have only examined him once," but the wording of his letter suggests a previous visit and perhaps a later consultation. The Nordrach treat-ment for consumptives developed by Dr. Otto Walther at Nordrach in the Black

Forest, which Crane sought shortly before his death, was based on Trudeau's principles of a "cottage" sanitarium.

Truth. A New York humor magazine in which Crane published "Some Hints for Play-Makers," "A Night at the Millionaire's Club," "Why Did the Young Clerk Swear?" and the posthumous "Manacled." Frequent satirical critiques of Crane's work appeared in *Truth* as well as in other ephemeral humor magazines of the 1890s, such as the *Philistine*,* the *Chap-Book*,* the *Fly Leaf*, *Life*, the *Lotus*,* and *Chips*.

Suggested Reading

Linneman, William R. "Stephen Crane's Contributions to *Truth*." *American Literature* 31 (1959): 196–97.

Tulligan, Patsey. A pugnacious Bowery hoodlum in "The Duel That Was Not Fought." His blustering almost precipitates him into a potentially tragic confrontation with an equally bellicose Cuban who challenges him to a duel with swords.

"The Turkish Army". This incomplete article is preserved in a manuscript partly in Crane's hand and partly in Cora's hand, no doubt from Stephen's dictation, in the Rare Book and Manuscript Library of Columbia University. It was first published in *Reports of War*, volume 9 of *The Works of Stephen Crane*, edited by Fredson Bowers (1971), 72–75. Writing at the end of the Greek-Turkish War, Crane reflects that the Turkish army, while not up to modern standards, won the war handily and belied its reputation. The Turk "had been called the sick man of Europe so long that he began to believe it himself. However he has discovered that he is quite well."

Twelve, John. In "The Monster" he is the spokesman for the group of concerned citizens who calls on Dr. Trescott and urges him to institutionalize Henry Johnson, His name is clearly a reference to the twelfth chapter of the biblical book of John in which Jesus extols the virtue of principle over expediency: "He that loveth his life shall lose it; and he that hateth his life in this world shall keep it unto life eternal," or, as more familiarly stated in Mark 8:36: "For what shall it profit a man, if he shall gain the whole world, and lose his own soul?"

"Twelve O'Clock". An undistinguished Western story, "Twelve O'Clock" appeared only in an English periodical, the *Pall Mall Magazine* (December 1899), and was the first of four additional stories in the English edition of *The Monster*. "Twelve O'Clock" involves a shoot-out over a cuckoo clock, a symbol of the mechanical age and Eastern civilization, in the hotel lobby of a town that, as a leading citizen named Ben Roddle warns the residents, Eastern capitalists have shunned because of its reputation for violence. A cowboy named

Jake who sees the clock in Placer's Hotel is amazed by the mechanism and tells his friends in a local bar about it. He is mocked and ridiculed, even by those familiar with cuckoo clocks, as being a victim of bad whiskey. Jake persuades the skeptics and pretended skeptics to return to the hotel with him. When they arrive, he becomes involved in an altercation with a belligerent cowboy named Big Watson, and a gunfight ensues in which Big Watson shoots and kills Placer, the proprietor of the hotel, as he stands ''behind his absurd pink counter with his two aimed revolvers in his incompetent hands.'' Jake fells Big Watson with the butt of his revolver, and another cowboy is killed in the shooting. When the smoke clears, the doors of the clock fly open and the bird cries ''cuckoo'' twelve times. The grotesque environment of the hotel lobby, a scene of senseless ferocity and death, with its improbable pink counter and cuckoo clock, suggests, although less effectively, the similar setting and theme of ''The Blue Hotel.''

"Two Men and a Bear". A short Sullivan County hunting sketch printed in the *New York Tribune* on 24 July 1892. After some commentary on the bear ''as a pugilist'' who can readily destroy dogs with forceful sweeps of his paws, Crane recounts a story of two men chopping logs in the woods who encountered a bear and rushed upon him with uplifted axes. The bear deftly destroyed the ax helve of the foremost man with his paw and clipped the second man on the head, knocking him unconscious. The men fortunately survived the incident when the bear unaccountably shambled off.

U

Uncle Clarence. The narrator of "Art in Kansas City" and "The Camel," he is an affable bumpkin who tells tall tales about fabulous animals, a cow that paints in watercolors, and a camel that stores whiskey and soda water in its two stomachs.

"Uncle Jake and the Bell-Handle". According to a notation made by Cora on the manuscript, this story was written in 1885 when Crane was thirteen or fourteen, which would make it his earliest known prose composition. It was not published in his lifetime but appeared first in *The Complete Short Stories and Sketches of Stephen Crane*, edited by Thomas A. Gullason (New York: Doubleday, 1963). "Uncle Jake and the Bell-Handle" deals with an old farmer and his niece Sarah who come to the city to sell a crop of turnips and buy supplies for the farm. Uncle Jake conceives of himself as a sophisticate, but he is bilked by everyone he encounters, from the dealer who purchases his turnips to the owner of the livery stable where he quarters his horses. Their purposes accomplished, Uncle Jake and Sarah check into a hotel and await the dinner gong. While exploring the splendors of the hotel parlor, Uncle Jake comes upon an object he perceives as a bell handle. Coincidentally, he pulls on it at the precise instant that "a waiter of the hotel made a terrific onslaught on a gong that was sure to make any horses in the vicinity run away and awaken all the late sleepers for blocks around." Uncle Jake mistakenly believes that he has caused this commotion and that, having falsely "called out the fire department, or the police force or the ambulance corps or something else that's awful!" he has become "a fergitive from justice, a critir hounded by the dogs of the law!" Uncle Jake and Sarah furtively leave the hotel, take a circuitous route to the livery stable, and drive home in panic. The ironic stance of the narrator of this story toward his characters, the emphasis on self-delusion, and the contrast between perception and reality anticipate in an elemental way themes that are developed in Crane's later fiction.

"The Upturned Face". Often considered apart from the other Spitzbergen stories because of its superior quality, this stark, terse episode is the culmination of the Spitzbergen series, as well as the emblem of Crane's final commentary on the ugliness and ignobility of war. It was published in the March 1900 issue of *Ainslee's Magazine* and collected in *Last Words*. Lieutenant Timothy Lean, an adjutant, and two soldiers are shown burying an officer of their regiment, identified only as "old Bill," under intense fire from Rostina sharpshooters. While the soldiers, who are as frightened by the body as they are by enemy bullets, dig a shallow grave, Lean removes the dead officer's effects from his pockets, his finger fumbling with the blood-stained buttons, and he and the adjutant tumble him into the grave. Before the grave is filled in, with the sound of bullets singing in their ears, Lean and the adjutant stammer through a garbled, half-remembered burial service, which is entirely inappropriate because it is the burial service for the dead at sea. Then one of the privates begins to shovel earth onto the corpse, "which from its chalk-blue face looked keenly out from the grave." Immediately afterward the man with the shovel is shot in the arm, and Lean orders both privates to the rear. Lean continues filling in the grave, working upward from the feet, under the scrutiny and nervous expostulations of the adjutant. Lean's own nervousness and repugnance intensifies as the shovelfuls of earth, each striking the corpse with an insistent and irreverent plop, approach the chalk-blue face. The adjutant beseeches him to finish. "Lean swung back the shovel. It went forward in a pendulum curve. When the earth landed it made a sound—plop."

Much has been written about the significance of the repeated images of upturned faces in Crane's fiction. In the New York City sketch "When Man Falls, a Crowd Gathers," the attention of the spectators is riveted on the contorted face of the man who has suffered an epileptic seizure, arousing both curiosity and mortal terror. The ashen face of the "invulnerable dead man" in *The Red Badge* is Henry Fleming's first presentiment of death. Henry Johnson in "The Monster" is violently disfigured by the molten chemicals that pour onto his upturned face and leave him socially as well as physically faceless. Peza in "Death and the Child" is relentlessly drawn to the uncovered faces of dead soldiers, "dreadful figures, swollen and blood-marked," and his final face-to-face confrontation with the uncomprehending child on the mountaintop causes him to question his humanity. "The Upturned Face" is a starkly economical horror story in which the face of the dead officer materializes the finality of death. It is the macabre, appalling center of concentration from which other physical details are excluded. Timothy Lean, who in other Spitzbergen stories found purpose and self-justification in war, finally confronts its ultimate frightful and nihilistic reality in the synesthetic image of the "plop" of earth on the dead face of his comrade.

Suggested Reading

Christopherson, Bill. "Stephen Crane's 'The Upturned Face': An Expressionist Fiction." *Arizona Quarterly* 38.2 (1982): 147–61.

Dillingham, William B. "Crane's One-Act Farce: 'The Upturned Face.' " *Research Studies* 35 (1967): 324–30.

Fried, Michael. *Realism, Writing, Disfiguration: On Thomas Eakins and Stephen Crane.* Chicago: University of Chicago Press, 1987. 93–161.

V

Van Petten, John B. (1827–?). A well-known raconteur of Civil War stories, Van Petten was professor of history and elocution at Claverack College and Hudson River Institute* at the time Crane attended the school. Van Petten, an ordained Methodist minister, had been principal of Fairfield Academy in Herkimer County, New York. He resigned in 1861 to serve as chaplain of the 34th New York Volunteers, a number suggestive of Henry Fleming's fictional 304th Regiment in *The Red Badge of Courage*. In September 1863 at Antietam, Van Petten witnessed confusion and panic on the battlefield, and the 34th suffered heavy casualties. Almost immediately after Antietam, Van Petten became lieutenant colonel of the 160th New York Volunteer Regiment and was soon appointed its permanent commander. In his new post Van Petten was no longer a chaplain but a combat officer, and at the Battle of Winchester in September 1864, he witnessed a rout in which he saw foot soldiers running in terror from the enemy and was himself severely wounded. In 1866 he returned to Fairfield to serve another four years as principal. During this period he was briefly a New York State senator. From 1877 to 1882 he was principal of a Methodist seminary in Sedalia, Missouri, and in 1885 he came to Claverack, where he stayed for sixteen years. In 1889, at the age of sixty-two, Van Petten received an earned doctorate in history from Syracuse University.*

Van Petten had reason to remember his Civil War experiences well, and it is probable that he spoke of them to his military-minded young charges at Claverack. Crane was always interested in personal combat reminiscences, and the oral tradition embodied in the tales of veterans apparently made an early impression on him. He would have listened intently to Van Petten's accounts of bloody engagements at Antietam and Winchester. However, it seems unlikely that as a Union general, a minister of the Gospel, and a teacher of American history Van Petten would dwell on the cowardice of Union soldiers on a battlefield before boys in whom he was attempting to instill the virtues of fortitude and patriotism. The direct influence of Van Petten's personal accounts on specific incidents depicted in *The Red Badge* seems unlikely.

Suggested Reading

O'Donnell, Thomas F. "John B. Van Petten: Stephen Crane's History Teacher." *American Literature* 27 (1955): 196–202.
Pratt, Lyndon Upson. "A Possible Source of *The Red Badge of Courage*." *American Literature* 11 (1939): 1–10.

"Vashti in the Dark". An untraced short story identified by Vincent Starrett in *Stephen Crane: A Bibliography* (Philadelphia: Centaur, 1923), 10, as having been written in 1895 and rejected by *Harper's*. Starrett maintains that Crane had the story, which concerned a rape, with him in Cuba; that it was seen by some of his associates; and that Crane destroyed it in 1898. While Thomas Beer* in his *Stephen Crane: A Study in American Letters* (1923) asserts that Starrett's bibliography "contains all my information as to Crane's unpublished work" (248, n.1), he elaborates considerably on the sketchy information given by Starrett. According to Beer, "Vashti in the Dark," which Crane revised on the Cuban blockade in the spring of 1898, "tells how a young Methodist preacher from the South killed himself after discovering that his wife had been ravished by a negro in a forest at night. To Acton Davies* who typed the manuscript, this was one of Crane's best stories but no magazine ever bought it and Crane burned it in one of his rare fits of pique" (183). It is possible that Beer, perhaps intentionally, confused the external circumstances of "Vashti in the Dark" with another untraced Crane story, "The Cat's March," that according to Starrett was written in Cuba, typed by Acton Davies, and subsequently destroyed.

Ver Beck, William Francis (1858–1933). Born in England, "Frank" Ver Beck was a prolific writer and illustrator of childrens' stories and one of Crane's earliest friends in New York City.

Verbeek, Gustave (1867–1937?). Born in Nagasaki, Japan, to a missionary family, Verbeek was a painter, etcher, and later a cartoonist. His portraits of prim ladies were considered avant-garde at the turn of the century, according to Henry McBride.* Verbeek was one of Crane's artist friends in New York in the period 1894–96 and a fellow member of the Lantern Club.*

Vernall. The narrator of "War Memories," who is a fictional voice for Crane himself. He is satirically named after the housekeeper and cook at Brede Place.*

"The Veteran". First published in *McClure's Magazine* (August 1896), "The Veteran" is the only short story collected in *The Little Regiment* that is not, strictly speaking, a Civil War tale, although it is a sequel to *The Red Badge of*

Courage. The story begins in a pastoral setting. Henry Fleming, grown old, has become a cracker-barrel raconteur, relating his war experiences to an awed group, including his grandson Jimmie, in the grocery of his village, perhaps the Handyville from which George Kelcey of *George's Mother* originates since a farmer named Sickles is mentioned in both works. We learn that having fought bravely, Henry had attained the rank of orderly sergeant, but he now freely admits, much to Jimmie's chagrin, that he ran from the enemy in his first engagement. "That was at Chancellorsville." He remembers a former comrade, Jim Conklin, who "went into it from the start just as if he was born to it. But with me it was different. I had to get used to it." The second part of the story takes place on Henry Fleming's farm. One of the hired men, identified only as "the Swede," and, like the Swede of "The Blue Hotel," characterized as "a maniac," has gotten drunk and overturned a lantern, setting the barn on fire. Fleming rescues some horses and cows but forgets the colts trapped in the barn. Ignoring the warnings of his farmhands, he again rushes into the barn at the moment that the roof caves in. There is at least an implication in the final paragraph of the story that Fleming has achieved a kind of immortality through heroism: "When the roof fell in, a great funnel of smoke swarmed toward the sky, as if the old man's mighty spirit, released from its body—a little bottle— had swelled like the genie of fable. The smoke was tinted rose-hue from the flames, and perhaps the unutterable midnights of the universe will have no power to daunt the colour of this soul." Since Fleming's act was impulsive and unconsciously determined, however, some critics have suggested that Crane is once again, as in *The Red Badge*, ironically undermining moralistic conceptions of heroism.

Suggested Reading

Solomon, Eric. "A Gloss on *The Red Badge of Courage.*" *Modern Language Notes* 75 (1960): 111–13.

"Veteran's Ranks Thinner by a Year". Crane's authorship of this sardonic Decoration Day parade report that appeared in the *New York Press* on 31 May 1894 is debatable. Like "The Gratitude of a Nation," not published until 1957, this article deals with the thinning ranks of Civil War veterans marching in the parade, but "Veteran's Ranks Thinner by a Year" seems closer than the report unpublished in his lifetime to Crane's description of the piece he submitted to the *New York Press* that he told Hamlin Garland* the editors said was "firing over the heads of the veterans."

Suggested Reading

Gullason, Thomas A. "Additions to the Canon of Stephen Crane." *Nineteenth-Century Fiction* 12 (1957): 157–60.

"The Victory of the Moon". With "The Voice of the Mountain" and "How the Donkey Lifted the Hills," this is one of Crane's Mexican fables. Presumably syndicated by Bacheller, its appearance has been noted only in the *Nebraska State Journal* on 24 July 1895. Bacheller reprinted the fable in the July 1897 issue of the *Pocket Magazine*, and it was collected in *Last Words*. In this cynical fable the moon's victory is pyrrhic since there can be no decisive victor in the conflict between man and nature.

The Strong Man of the Hills has lost his wife and consults a young philosopher, who advises him to bathe, eat, and gaze at the loveliness of the earth and sky rather than engage in a futile struggle to regain her. The Strong Man ignores this advice and mounts an assault on the moon, which he is led to believe by "the little men of the valley" is mocking him. In the home of the moon, the Strong Man finds his wife, who scorns his blandishments, causing the battered moon to reflect on the vanity of human concepts like victory or defeat.

The Vidette. The magazine of Claverack College and Hudson River Institute,* *The Vidette* (meaning "mounted sentry") was published monthly during the school year. The magazine featured student essays on art and literature, historical figures, philosophers, poets, and inventors. There was original poetry by students and a written debate feature, as well as notices of school events. Crane published his essay on Henry M. Stanley in *The Vidette* (February 1890) and the "Battalion Notes" column in the June 1890 issue. He was perhaps also the author of a report on the opening of the baseball season (May 1890).

"The Viga Canal". Probably written in April 1895 during Crane's stay in Mexico City, this sketch was not published in his lifetime. It was printed from the manuscript by R. W. Stallman in the *Bulletin of the New York Public Library* 71 (1967): 557–60. "The Viga Canal" is the most coherent and intense of Crane's writings about Mexico City. The sketch opens with a cab ride to the embarkation point on the canal for the two-mile boat trip to the so-called floating gardens and the resort village of Santa Anita. After the hubbub caused by the boatmen seeking to secure the patronage of the tourists, the journey commences through placid scenes of rural life over which tower the imposing peaks of Popocatepetl and Iztaccihuatl. At Santa Anita there is a babbling crowd in front of the pulque shops. A policeman remonstrates with a drunken caballero; a boatman admonishes some youths who had neglected to pay him; four men seated around a table roar with laughter at a joke told by a fifth man; beggars importune everyone. In the midst of this turmoil stands "a little white church, stern, unapproving, representing the other fundamental aspiration of humanity, a reproach and a warning." On the return trip, the tourists procure two musicians to entertain them as they float under the emerging stars, but the music serves only to evoke memories of other nights in each traveler, "the emotional and tender voices of his past." Pervasive in this sketch is the contrast between the serene indifference of nature, embodied in the mountains and the stars, and the eternal verities exemplified by the church with the transient and inconsequential preoccupations of humanity.

Suggested Reading

Katz, Joseph. Introduction to *Stephen Crane in the West and Mexico.* Kent, Ohio: Kent
State University Press, 1970. 20–22.

Villa Eberhardt. The house in which Crane died on 5 June 1900 at Badenweiler, Baden, a health spa situated on the edge of the Black Forest. The Villa
Eberhardt, named after its owner, Albert Eberhardt, was one of the buildings of
a cottage sanitarium modeled on that of Dr. Edward L. Trudeau* in the Adirondacks. Here Crane was attended by Dr. Albert Fraenkel, himself a victim of
tuberculosis.

Suggested Reading

Hagemann, E. R. "The Death of Stephen Crane." *Proceedings of the New Jersey
Historical Society* 77 (1959): 173–84.

"Virtue in War". First published in the November 1899 issue of *Frank Leslie's
Popular Monthly* under the title of "West Pointer and Volunteer; Or Virtue in
War," this Cuban War story was collected in *Wounds in the Rain.* As in *The
Red Badge,* the question of what constitutes heroism or virtue in war is the
theme of this story and is ambivalently reflected in the oppositional characters
of its two protagonists, Major Gates and Private Lige Wigram. Gates, a West
Point graduate, had left the regular army and taken a position with the Standard
Oil Company, which "differs from the United States Government in that it
understands the value of the loyal and intelligent services of good men and is
almost certain to reward them at the expense of incapable men." But Gates's
heart remains in the barracks, and when war breaks out in 1898, he enlists as a
major in a volunteer infantry regiment and imposes regular army discipline on
his unruly battalion. Unlike another battalion commander in the regiment, Major
Rickets C. Carmony, a former hardware dealer who wins the affection of his
men by serving ice cream at the battalion mess, Gates administers "more kicks
than ice cream, and there was no ice cream at all." When Lige Wigram, an
unrestrained bumpkin, attempts undue familiarity, the major icily rebuffs him,
but Wigram remains insubordinate. In combat in Cuba, a large number of Carmony's men follow Gates, preferring to be led by a professional soldier. Gates
is mortally wounded, and Wigram attempts to save him by quixotically attempting to stem the flow of blood with his hat, although the major orders him to
the rear. "The man bleeding to death was the same man to whom he had once
paid a friendly visit with unfriendly results. He thought now that he perceived
a certain hopeless gulf, a gulf which is real or unreal according to circumstances." Lige once again refuses to obey orders and remains with the major
until he dies. In the final section of the story, three correspondents, among whom
is Shackles of " 'God Rest Ye, Merry Gentlemen' " and "The Revenge of the
Adolphus," with equal detachment, discuss the manner of Gates's death and
argue about where the best mint juleps are made. They are interrupted by Lige

Wigram who is looking for an empty bottle to mark Gates's grave. Crane seems
to be once again burlesquing the very concept of heroism, whether it be the
disciplined stoicism of Gates or the deep-felt loyalty of Wigram. Neither has
more consequence than the notion that the best mint juleps are made in Kentucky, which is "only a tradition."

"Visitor's Book". Hitherto unused by Crane biographers other than Jean Cazemajou, this guest book in the Rare Book and Manuscript Library of Columbia
University contains important information about the time spent at Brede Place*
by Edith Richie,* Edwin Pugh, A.E.W. Mason,* H. G. Wells* and Catherine
Wells, C. Lewis Hind,* and others. Cora Crane's dates of arrival and final
departure are given, respectively, as 19 February 1899 and 2 August 1900. The
book opens with a notation in Crane's hand that "[t]his book dates from November 8, 1899 and one regrets that it doesn't date earlier since the names of
many charming people are thus lost—unless they come again. God save all
here." There are, however, some earlier entries dating back to 22 July 1899 that
recall previous visits.

"The Voice of the Mountain". This fable was syndicated in newspapers by
Bacheller on 22 May 1895, but the only appearance that has been observed is
in the *Nebraska State Journal* under the heading "Mexican Tales." It was reprinted in the November 1896 issue of the *Pocket Magazine* and collected in
Last Words. The mountain in the fable is Popocatepetl, a quiescent volcano in
central Mexico about forty-five miles south of Mexico City. Crane commented
on the beauty of Popocatepetl and its companion mountain, Iztaccihuatl, in the
second of his reports from Mexico City, "Stephen Crane in Mexico (II)." In
"The Voice of the Mountain" Popocatepetl is very hungry. He asks advice
from a little eagle as to how he might seek his food since the King of Everything
has forbidden him to walk for fear that his feet will make holes in the earth.
The eagle foolishly proposes that the "little animal with two arms, two legs,
one head, and a very brave air" should be summoned to relieve Popoctepetl's
distress. The little animal appears and agrees to build wings for the mountain
if he and his kind are allowed to live on the plain that surrounds the mountain.
Popocatepetl agrees and human beings settle on the plain, but they make no
wings for the mountain. The image of the little man against the mountain, representing the eternal struggle between humanity and nature in which neither
prevails for long, is common in Crane's work.

Vosburgh, R. G. (?–?). An artist and illustrator, Vosburgh was one of Crane's
three roommates, with W. W. Carroll* and Nelson Greene,* in a small studio
of the old Art Students League building on East Twenty-third Street during
1893–94. Vosburgh's account of their life together, "The Darkest Hour in the
Life of Stephen Crane," published in the *Criterion* in February 1901, contributes

important details of Crane's methods of composition and literary theories in the period in which he was writing *The Red Badge of Courage*. Vosburgh provided two illustrations for Crane's posthumous horror story "Manacled," in the November 1900 issue of *Truth*.*

W

Wainwright, Harrison B. Professor Wainwright, Marjory's father in *Active Service*, is a stereotypical, self-righteous pedant whose personality is epitomized in his writing style, replete with sentences "ponderous, solemn and endless, in which wandered multitudes of homeless and friendless prepositions, adjectives looking for a parent, and quarreling nouns, sentences which no longer symbolized the language forms of thought but which had about them a quaint aroma from the dens of long-dead scholars." As a husband and father, the professor is overbearing and authoritarian. He asserts his power by removing his family and some deserving students to Greece in order to separate his daughter Marjory from Coleman, but when Coleman miraculously finds the Wainright party behind enemy lines and guides them to safety, the professor looks on him as their protector, leader, and savior. Humbled by his experience of helplessness and having a new appreciation for Coleman, the professor gradually comes to accept him as Marjory's suitor.

Wainwright, Marjory. The vacuous heroine of *Active Service*, Marjory is a shadowy figure in the novel. A young, naive girl torn between conventional expectations of maidenly behavior and her love for Rufus Coleman, she lives, however uncomfortably, in a patriarchal world, gradually moving from dependence on her father to dependence on Coleman.

Wainwright, Mary. Wife of Professor Wainwright and Marjory's mother in *Active Service*, Mrs. Wainwright, "a fat woman who was said to pride herself on being very wise and if necessary sly," is actually a rather dim-witted conventional harridan concerned mainly with preserving social respectability even in the midst of mortal danger by refusing to associate with Nora Black and obsessively condemning Coleman's association with her.

Walkley. In " 'God Rest Ye, Merry Gentlemen,' " Walkley is a correspondent for the *Eclipse* (the *New York World*). A fictional representation of Sylvester Scovel,* he typifies the correspondents of the yellow press who try to transform mundane military events into stirring heroic actions for newspaper headlines.

War Is Kind. Crane began to assemble the poems collected in *War Is Kind* in England before he went to Cuba; the book, completed while he was living in Havana, was published by Frederick A. Stokes in April 1899. Heinemann deposited an advance copy of the Stokes edition in the British Museum, but there was no English edition of *War Is Kind*. Crane's second volume of poetry lacks the coherence of *The Black Riders*. Written intermittently from the fall of 1894 but mostly after 1897 when Crane had moved to England, more than half of the thirty-seven poems are not first printings, and many of those that are presented here for the first time were not written for the volume. As in *The Black Riders*, two-thirds of the poems in *War Is Kind* are free verse epigrams, but several have conventional stanzaic and rhythmic patterns, and there are occasional refrains and approximate rhymes, as well as an increased use of metaphor.

Thematically most of the poems of *War Is Kind* reiterate and define the attitudes set forth in *The Black Riders*. As in the earlier book, there is little visual imagery in the poems, and the voice is moral and didactic. There are renewed assaults on conventional religion and further deprecations of man's failures and expressions of sympathy for his pathetic existence, as in a poem recast in slightly variant form from an earlier version in *The Black Riders*:

> There was one I met upon the road
> Who looked at me with kind eyes.
> He said: "Show me of your wares."
> And I did,
> Holding forth one.
> He said: "It is a sin."
> Then I held forth another.
> He said: "It is a sin."
> Then I held forth another.
> He said: "It is a sin."
> And so to the end.
> Always He said: "It is a sin."
> At last, I cried out:
> "But I have none other."
> He looked at me
> With kinder eyes.
> "Poor soul," he said.

In the absence of a God external to the human spirit, nature is apart from man and as indifferent to his concerns as the waves that threaten to swamp the men in the dinghy in "The Open Boat" or the bright sunshine and blue sky that looks down on the carnage of the battlefield in *The Red Badge of Courage*.

Human beings such as the individual in "I stood musing in a black world," who rather than looking within himself looks toward the sky, the stream and the hills for moral guidance and cries, "I see nothing! Oh, where do I go?" is answered only by the invective of nature: "Fool! Fool! Fool!" "A slant of sun on dull brown walls," whose first appearance was on the front wrapper of the December 1895 *Philistine** and "In the night," first published in the March 1896 issue of the *Chap-Book,** resemble in method and theme a number of other poems in *War Is Kind*, notably, "What says the sea, little shell?"; "I have heard the sunset song of birches"; and "Each small gleam was a voice." In these poems, natural objects are personified and equated with the utterance of humanity desperately seeking supernal knowledge and personal salvation in a universe where such insights remain ineffable, emphasizing the futility of man's search for ultimate knowledge of God through the manifestations of natural phenomena. Morally neutral, nature takes on the attributes with which it is endowed:

> To the maiden
> the sea was blue meadow,
> Alive with little froth-people
> Singing.

> To the sailor, wrecked,
> The sea was dead grey walls
> Superlative in vacancy,
> Upon which nevertheless at fateful time
> Was written
> The grim hatred of nature.

Man's conceit and the unconcern of the universe toward his existence is epitomized in one of Crane's shortest and most frequently anthologized ironic epigrams:

> A man said to the universe:
>   "Sir, I exist!"
> "However," replied the universe,
> "The fact has not created in me
> "A sense of obligation."

This theme is elaborated more fully in "The Open Boat" when the men in the dinghy, incredulous that an indurate fate would casually drown them, are confronted with the insignificance of the individual in the scheme of things: "When it occurs to a man that nature does not regard him as important, and that she feels she would not maim the universe by disposing of him, he at first wishes to throw bricks at the temple, and he hates deeply the fact that there are no bricks and no temples."

War Is Kind includes Crane's most explicit social poems. The title poem, which first appeared in the February 1896 issue of the *Bookman*, contains three stanzas of ironic understatement addressing a maiden, a child, and a mother who have lost loved ones in battle, each stanza ending with the admonition, "Do not weep. / War is kind." These enclose two stanzas of seemingly conventional rhetoric blazoning the glory of war that are also undercut by irony implying the attitude is false. The poem satirizes the bombast of Tennyson's "The Charge of the Light Brigade," which is likewise ridiculed in the Whilomville story, "Making an Orator." Crane's experience as a reporter for the most notorious practitioners of yellow journalism, Joseph Pulitzer* and William Randolph Hearst,* is reflected in the bitterness of "A newspaper is a collection of half-injustices," which echoes the contempt expressed in a poem in *The Black Riders*, "In a lonely place," for the vulgarity and sensationalism of the press and for the mass market in which newspapers have become "the wisdom of the age." Two poems, "The impact of a dollar upon the heart," first printed in bowdlerized form on the back wrapper of the February 1898 *Philistine*,* and "The successful man has thrust himself / Through the waters of the years," are acerbic satires critical of the worship of burgeoning wealth and power in the Gilded Age.

"I explain the silvered passage of a ship at night" first appeared in the October 1896 issue of the *Bookman* under the title "Lines." Shortly afterward Crane paraphrased the poem in a book inscription he wrote to Cora Taylor in Jacksonville. The inscription makes clear that the ship symbolizes love, which is mutable and transient, as in Longfellow's "Ships that pass in the night" from *Tales of a Wayside Inn*. Crane's poem is, however, more symbolistic than sentimental, and the vanishing ship, "The dwindling boom of a steel thing's striving / The little cry of a man to a man," suggests the cosmic isolation of his more trenchant poem on this theme, "A man adrift on a slim spar."

The "Intrigue" sequence of ten turgid, maudlin love poems that ends *War Is Kind* is indefensible as poetry and has been given various biographical interpretations. Manuscript evidence indicates that the first five "Intrigue" poems were completed in December 1896 or early 1897, almost a year after the collapse of Crane's epistolary love affair with Nellie Crouse.* The last five "Intrigue" poems were written or revised in Havana in the fall of 1898. The poems reveal the tormented love of a man for a woman with whom he has been passionately involved but who has betrayed him, or he fears may deceive him, and his jealousy of another man who has secured her favors or with whom she may become involved in the future. The "Intrigue" title suggests the complexities of a love that is not mutually spontaneous but entangled in personal and social conflict. Biographers have proposed Nellie Crouse, Lily Brandon Munroe,* Cora, and an unknown woman in Havana as the inspiration for one or another of the poems. Little evidence is available, but the passion and anguish manifest in them make it evident that they deal with a very personal involvement.

Suggested Reading

Hoffman, Daniel. "Many Red Devils upon the Page: The Poetry of Stephen Crane." *Sewanee Review* 102 (1994): 588–603.

Marcus, Mordecai. "Structure and Irony in Stephen Crane's 'War Is Kind.' " *College Language Association Journal* 9 (1966): 274–78.
Vanouse, Donald P. "Schoberlin's Annotated Copy of *War Is Kind.*" *Courier* 21.1 (1986): 89–102.

"War Memories". Collected with Crane's Spanish-American War fiction, "War Memories" is in part a more or less factual synoptic account of his experiences as a correspondent for the *New York World* in Cuba during the spring and summer of 1898. The piece was first published in cut form in the third volume of Lady Randolph Churchill's* *Anglo-Saxon Review* in December 1899 and printed in full in *Wounds in the Rain*. Crane names his autobiographical protagonist Vernall and distorts the name of Ernest W. McCready* of the *New York Herald* to McCurdy, but other correspondents such as Edward Marshall,* Sylvester Scovel,* and Ralph Paine* are identified by their real names. Jimmy Hare* of *Colliers Weekly* is referred to as "Jimmie, the photographer." Officers who played crucial roles in the Cuban campaign, including Admiral William T. Sampson,* General William R. Shafter,* Brigadier General Henry Lawton, and Lieutenant Richmond P. Hobson, are also identified. Crane renders subjective impressions of some of the important events he witnessed and in which he participated during the Cuban conflict and reported in his dispatches: the time he spent in April and May in dispatch boats off the coast of Cuba attempting to garner news of the stalled war; the incident in May narrated in Crane's dispatch "Narrow Escape of the Three Friends" when the correspondents' boat was sideswiped during the night by the gunboat *Machias*; the landing at Guantánamo Bay on 10 June and the death of assistant surgeon John Blair Gibbs* two days later; Crane's ascent with Scovel on 17 and 18 June of a mountain peak from which they viewed the Spanish fleet in Santiago Harbor; the wounding of Marshall, a correspondent for the *New York Journal*, on 24 June at the Battle of Las Guásimas; the American advance on the fortifications of San Juan on 1 July; the evacuation of civilians from Santiago to El Caney on 5 July; and the ceremonial exchange of Lieutenant Hobson and the men of the *Merrimac* for three Spanish officers the next day. Finally, Crane describes his return to Hampton Roads, Virginia, aboard a hospital ship laden with wounded soldiers.

What distinguishes "War Memories" from Crane's Cuban War dispatches is a deliberate relinquishing of objectivity and an attempt to render experiences expressionistically. Vernall is frustrated by the impossibility of capturing "the real thing" because "war is neither magnificent nor squalid; it is simply life, and an expression of life can always evade us. We can never tell life, one to another, although sometimes we think we can." The essential absurdity of war is illustrated by the juxtaposition of the sublime and tragic with the trivial and ridiculous. On the dispatch boat from Key West, a bunch of bananas hung from a chandelier in the center of the cabin swings wildly, knocking down one of the correspondents and causing the others to scurry for safety: "You see? War! A bunch of bananas rampant because the ship rolled." Immediately after the excruciating death of Doctor Gibbs at Guantánamo Bay, a bustling adjutant asks, '' 'Where's the doctor? There's some wounded men over there. Where's the doctor?' A man answered briskly: 'Just died this minute, sir.' It was as if he had said: 'Just gone around the corner this minute, sir.' '' Amid the intense fighting a marine turns from the firing line and attempts to buy a drink of whiskey from Vernall, pleading, ''if I don't get a drink I'll die.'' When Vernall attempts to get help for the wounded Marshall at Siboney, another correspondent to whom he appeals insists that ''Marshall isn't in Cuba at all. He left for New York just before the expedition sailed from Tampa.'' During the attack on the San Juan Heights, the correspondents observe ''a man in a Panama hat strolling to and fro behind one of the Spanish trenches, gesticulating at times with a walking stick.'' Among the scores of wounded at a dressing station on a ford of the Aguadores River known as Bloody Bend, Crane (and here he drops all pretense of being Vernall) finds Reuben McNab,* a schoolmate from Claverack College,* shot through the lung. Crane had viewed hundreds of corpses with indifference, ''but the apparition of Reuben McNab, the schoolmate, lying there in the mud, with a hole through his lung, awed me into stutterings, set me trembling with a sense of terrible intimacy with this war which theretofore I could have believed was a dream—almost.'' The symbolic import of this immediacy is rendered by a figure on an operating table in the doorway of a church in El Caney that has been converted into a hospital for wounded Spanish prisoners. ''Framed then in the black archway was the altar table with the figure of a man upon it. He was naked save for a breech-clout, and so close, so clear was the ecclesiastical suggestion, that one's mind leaped to a phantasy that this thin, pale figure had just been torn down from a cross.'' Despite the ''overwhelming, crushing, monstrous'' nature of the circumstances, the limitations of language cause Vernall to despair that the writer can render the senseless horror of war convincingly in mere words, and in the end he concludes that ''you can depend upon it that I have told you nothing at all, nothing at all, nothing at all.''

Warwickson. A character in ''Stories Told by an Artist,'' ''The Silver Pageant,'' and *The Third Violet* often called by ''his popular name of Great Grief.'' Warwickson is a fictional representation of R. G. Vosburgh.*

Washington, Peter. A character in *Whilomville Stories*, specifically ''Shame,'' ''The Knife,'' ''The Carriage-Lamps,'' and ''The City Urchin and the Chaste Villagers.'' He has succeeded Henry Johnson as Dr. Trescott's hostler. Crane's depiction of Peter Washington, who also appears briefly in ''The Monster,'' does not transcend his usual stereotypes of African-Americans.

Watkins, Ike. One of four regular army soldiers in ''The Price of the Harness'' who become casualties in the battle for the San Juan hills. At the end of the story Grierson informs Martin that Watkins ''ain't dead, but he got shot through the lungs. They say he ain't got much of a show.''

The Wave. The San Francisco weekly magazine *The Wave* commented on Crane's work throughout much of his literary career. In an extensive review of *The Red Badge of Courage* on 19 October 1895, the editor, John O'Hara Cosgrave, disparaged Crane's poetry as "an issue of the esthetic craze" but considered the war novel evidence that Crane might be "one of the young men who may lift our literature out of its rut, and provide reading for England as London is now doing for us." The unsigned review of *Maggie* and *George's Mother*, "Stephen Crane's Stories of Life in the Slums," that appeared in *The Wave* on 4 July 1896 was formerly attributed to Frank Norris,* but is now believed to be by another *Wave* editor, probably Cosgrave. Here the praise is more qualified, the reviewer complaining that "the author is writing, as it were, from the outside. There is a certain lack of sympathy apparent. Mr. Crane does not seem to *know* his people." The 18 September 1897 of "London Impressions" entitled "Crane In London," also formerly attributed to Norris, is signed "Justin Sturgis," a name used by a number of *Wave* editors, and was most likely written by Cosgrave as well. *The Wave* could be severely critical of Crane, calling his *New York Journal* feature article "The 'Tenderloin' as It Really Is" "the veriest filth" (7 November 1896), but its praise for "The Monster" in an article by Cosgrave (13 August 1898) was unqualified.

Suggested Reading

McElrath, Joseph R., Jr. *Frank Norris and* The Wave: *A Bibliography.* New York: Garland, 1988 11, 87–90, 140.
———. "Stephen Crane in San Francisco: His Reception in *The Wave* " *Stephen Crane Studies* 2.1 (1993): 2–18.

"The Way in Sullivan County". The subtitle of this Sullivan County sketch, printed in the *New York Tribune* on 8 May 1892, is "A Study in the Evolution of the Hunting Yarn." The tone of the sketch is essentially humorous, lampooning in the manner of Mark Twain the tall tale and the backwoods liar. In a deeper sense, "The Way in Sullivan County" is a commentary on the nature of creativity. A hunter, like a writer, should not "tell just exactly what he did. He should tell what he would have liked to do or what he expected to do, just as if he accomplished it." Embellishing reality requires creative genius, and Crane ends this short sketch with two tales of accomplished liars. The first is "one of great execution done by the liar," in which some six men tell the same story of shooting at and killing three bears when they thought they were shooting at only one. In the second, "in which the liar figures as one who saw great things," two men observe a bear and a panther tending to themselves some distance apart. One man shoots the bear, and the other shoots the panther. Each animal thinks the other has caused its pain, and they battle until the panther overcomes the bear. The hunters observe the combat passively until the end, and then, in an irony that would become a hallmark in Crane's later stories, "they shot the victor."

Wells, Anna E. (?–?). Daughter of Edgar Wells of Port Jervis, New York, one of the owners of the land at Twin Lakes near Milford in Pike County, Pennsylvania, on which Crane and his friends camped in summers from 1891 through 1895 or 1896. Anna Wells, who became librarian of the Poughkeepsie, New York, public library, left a slight unpublished memoir, written in about 1951 and preserved in the Arents Library of Syracuse University, about the experiences of the campers in 1894 and the origins of *The Pike County Puzzle*.

Wells, H. G. (1866–1946). Herbert George Wells's class origins and scientific training distinguished him among the English novelists of his time. Wells was born into an impoverished home in Bromley, Kent, and received a desultory education until he entered the Normal School of Science (later Royal College) in South Kensington, where he studied under the social Darwinist Thomas Henry Huxley. In 1880 he was graduated with a degree in biology from London University. For a brief time he was a tutor, but he soon turned to writing. Wells produced more than one hundred books, the most distinctive being his science fiction classics *The Time Machine* (1895), *The Island of Dr. Moreau* (1896), and *The War of the Worlds* (1898). He also wrote comic novels, three of which—*Love and Mr. Lewisham* (1900), *Kipps: The Story of a Simple Soul* (1905), and *The History of Mr. Polly* (1910)—have become minor classics. Wells moved restlessly from one social movement to another, envisioning a perfectible society through religion in *Mr. Britling Sees It Through* (1916) or through science in *The World of William Clissoid* (1926). Theories of social progress and education dominated Wells's later writing, *The Shape of Things to Come* (1933) being the most mature expression of his speculations. He also wrote encyclopedic treatises such as his ambitious *An Outline of History* (1920). Wells's *Experiment in Autobiography* (1934) is a subjective and lively account of his life.

Wells prided himself in being among the first in England to express appreciation of Crane's work. He was probably the author of the 5 September 1896 *Saturday Review* essay, "The New American Novelists," that praised *George's Mother* and compared Crane favorably with Tolstoy for his narrative power and psychological acumen. On 19 December Wells reviewed *Maggie* in the *Saturday Review*, but more ambivalently, speculating on "whether we have not been hasty in assuming Mr. Crane to be a strong man in fiction." Nevertheless, when the *Academy* recorded the votes of prominent English authors for the best books of 1896, Wells included *Maggie* and *George's Mother* in his list. The review of *The Open Boat* in the 11 June 1898 issue of the *Saturday Review* may also have been authored by Wells. While Wells tended to disdain aestheticism and conceived of literature primarily as a vehicle for ideas, he admired Crane's increasing mastery of structure and style in his short stories, especially "The Bride Comes to Yellow Sky" and "The Open Boat," although he characteristically urged him to deal with "more passionate issues."

Crane and Wells most likely met shortly after the American author settled with Cora at Ravensbrook,* Oxted, Surrey, in early June 1897, but their personal relationship was largely confined to Crane's final year at Brede Place* in Sussex, which was near Sandgate, where H. G. and Catherine Wells were living. Wells was one of the contributors to Crane's musical farce, "The Ghost," and attended the three-day celebration at Brede Place at the end of December 1899. He left an amusing account of the event in his *Experiment in Autobiography*. When Crane collapsed with a tubercular hemorrhage after a gala ball on 29 December, it was Wells who bicycled to Rye through a freezing rain to summon the local physician, Dr. Ernest Skinner.* Wells, who had suffered a bout with tuberculosis himself in youth, was seriously concerned and corresponded with both Crane and Cora, although not always with sensitivity, about Crane's declining health. He paid a last visit to Crane in May 1900 in the Lord Warden Hotel at Dover, where Crane was resting before crossing the English Channel to Calais. In his memorial tribute, "Stephen Crane from an English Standpoint," in the August 1900 issue of the *North American Review*, Wells bemoaned the fact that Crane wrecked his health in Cuba. Wrongly believing that Crane suffered shipwreck returning from Cuba rather than while attempting to reach Cuba from Florida, Wells conjectured that "it was the sea that had taken his strength" and reaffirmed his conviction that "The Open Boat" was "the crown of all his work." Wells considered Crane to be the forerunner of the modern literary era and called him "one of the most brilliant, most significant and most distinctly American of all English writers." Despite his proclivity for the literature of ideas, it was the artistry, restraint, and discipline in Crane's work that Wells admired. "In style, in method and in all that is distinctively *not* found in his books, he is sharply defined, the expression in literary art of certain enormous repudiations."

Suggested Reading

MacKenzie, Norman, and Jeanne MacKenzie. *The Life of H. G. Wells: The Time Traveller*. London: Hogarth 1987.
Solomon, Eric. *Stephen in England: A Portrait of the Artist*. Columbus: Ohio State University Press, 1964. 41–50.
Wertheim, Stanley. "H. G. Wells to Cora Crane: Some Letters and Corrections." *Resources for American Literary Study* 9 (1979): 207–12.

Westport, the Countess of. Wife of the Earl of Westport in *The O'Ruddy*, the countess is a more sharply individuated character than her husband, whom she dominates. A shrill, brawling harridan, she engages in violent altercations on more than one occasion, attacking The O'Ruddy, Paddy, and Jem Bottles in fiery rages reminiscent of the maddened giantess in Crane's Sullivan County story "An Explosion of Seven Babies." Like the earl, she is motivated almost solely by avarice and is willing to grant permission for her daughter to marry The O'Ruddy, whom she loathes, when she feels that the earl's rights to Brede Place* might be compromised if The O'Ruddy retains the title papers to the manor.

Westport, the Earl of. A character in *The O'Ruddy*, the aged Earl of Westport is a gouty miscreant motivated almost entirely by self-interest. Although he knows that The O'Ruddy has no legal claim on his estates in Sussex, he apprehends that his property rights may be called into question and steals the title deeds that he had in a moment of panic during a battle in France given to The O'Ruddy's father to safeguard because "[h]e feared capture, and knew the ransom would be heavy if they found evidence of property upon him." When he has once again lost the papers, the earl engages in nefarious schemes to regain them, but he shows a flash of integrity at the conclusion of the novel when he supports his daughter's wily ruse of refusing to marry the O'Ruddy, whom she falsely claims that she does not love.

Westport, Lady Mary. The beloved of the title character in *The O'Ruddy*, Lady Mary is a pallid, conventional romantic heroine. In the concluding section of the novel written by Robert Barr,* she steps out of character when she concocts a wily scheme that will lead to the union of the two lovers, and in order to overcome her shrewish mother's objections to her marriage to The O'Ruddy she pretends that she does not love him, knowing that her avaricious mother will be easily duped into opposing what appear to be her wishes.

Wheeler, (George) Post (1869–1956). Often called America's first career diplomat, Wheeler's background was similar to Crane's in that his father was a Methodist minister and his mother a proselytizer for the Women's Christian Temperance Union (WCTU). Wheeler was educated at Princeton, the University of Pennsylvania, and the Sorbonne. In 1895 he became editor of the *New York Press*. He began his diplomatic career in 1906 as second secretary of the American embassy in Tokyo. He subsequently held diplomatic posts in the embassies at St. Petersburg, Rome, Stockholm, London, Madrid, and Rio de Janeiro. At his retirement in 1934, he was minister to Albania. Throughout his diplomatic career, Wheeler continued to write. He published Russian folk tales, biblical stories, and Japanese legends. Among his books are *Russian Wonder Tales* (1912), *The Golden Legend of Ethiopia* (1936), and *The Sacred Scriptures of the Japanese* (1952).

Wheeler and Crane became acquainted in childhood, when in the summer of 1878 their mothers brought them to a WCTU meeting addressed by Frances Willard.* Mrs. Crane and Stephen were guests of Wheeler's parents a few days later in Wyoming, Pennsylvania, at the centenary commemoration of the British and Indian attack on Forty Fort. Wheeler recalls that before the age of seven, Crane was already drinking beer and smoking cigarettes. Wheeler's father was a member of the Ocean Grove Association, and in 1888 he and Crane renewed their friendship in Asbury Park, New Jersey, when Wheeler was preparing for admission to Princeton and Crane was beginning to help his brother Townley in reporting New Jersey shore news for the *New York Tribune*. In 1895–96 Wheeler and Crane were again associated as members of the Lantern Club.*

Wheeler, at this time editor of the *New York Press*, shared a large loft with Victor Newman at 165 West Twenty-third Street near Seventh Avenue, and Crane often roomed with them. In his reminiscences, Wheeler maintains that *The Black Riders* and much of *The Red Badge of Courage* were written in the loft, but these works had been completed previously. Crane and Wheeler saw little of one another after Crane left for Florida in November 1896, but in January 1900 Crane seconded Wheeler's nomination for membership in the Authors Club.*

Suggested Reading

Wheeler, Post, and Hallie E. Rives. *Dome of Many Coloured Glass*. Garden City, N.Y.: Doubleday, 1955.

"When Every One Is Panic Stricken". One of Crane's most vivid Sunday feature sketches, this account of an imaginary midnight fire in a tenement on a street west of Sixth Avenue was published in the *New York Press* on 25 November 1894. The sketch is sometimes referred to as "The Fire," a title Crane gave it in an 1897 inventory list of his writings. It is also occasionally misidentified as either a report of a real fire or a hoax. As in "When Man Falls, a Crowd Gathers," Crane dramatizes this tour de force by having a number of voices commenting on the action, including a "stranger" who accompanies the narrator. The stranger is imparting "some grim midnight reflections upon existence" to the narrator when he is interrupted by a woman's scream. A policeman runs by and activates a firealarm box at the corner. There is an awakening of the street as a crowd forms in front of No. 135, where a fire in a bakery on the first floor spreads rapidly through the building. A stream of fire engines descend on the structure. Crane emphasizes the impotence and insignificance of human beings before the onslaught of natural forces. A woman who had fled the burning house suddenly realizes that she has forgotten her baby. In her hand she clutches a little bamboo easel worth about thirty cents that she has rescued from the flames. The policeman who turned in the alarm rushes into the house to save the baby, but there is no mention of whether he reemerges. The narrator and the stranger resume their walk toward the avenue while ladders are placed against the side of the building and "firemen went slowly up them, dragging their hose. They became outlined like black beetles against the red and yellow expanses of flames. A vast cloud of smoke, sprinkled thickly with sparks, went coiling heavily toward the black sky."

Suggested Reading

Bergon, Frank. *Stephen Crane's Artistry*. New York: Columbia University Press, 1975. 38–41.
Mayfield, John S. "Stephen Crane's Curious Conflagration." *American Book Collector* 7.4 (1956): 6–8.

"When Man Falls, a Crowd Gathers". A generic study of city life, this Sunday feature sketch was printed in the *New York Press* of 2 December 1894. When collected in *Last Words*, it was entitled "A Street Scene in New York," the title under which it appeared in the *Westminster Gazette*. Two Italian immigrants, a man and a boy, are walking along an East Side street leading to one of the ferries when the man collapses in an epileptic seizure. The man's infirmity, like the wound of the lieutenant in "An Episode of War," immediately depersonalizes him and sets him apart from the stream of humanity. A crowd quickly gathers, and people push forward and jostle each other to view the prone form. "Their eyes . . . were held in a spell of fascination. They seemed scarcely to breathe. They were contemplating a depth into which a human being had sunk and the marvel of this mystery of life and death held them chained." Crane emphasizes the isolation and insignificance of the afflicted individual as normal life continues undisturbed around the scene. Streetcars and elevated trains pass by routinely. "Over the heads of the crowd hung an immovable canvas sign. 'Regular dinner twenty cents.' " When a policeman disperses the mob and an ambulance takes the stricken man away, many in the crowd feel that they have been denied a further glimpse into the enigma of mortality, and the curtain "suddenly intervening between a suffering creature and their curiosity, seemed to appear to them as an injustice."

"When a people reach the top of a hill". One of the most cryptic of Crane's poems, "When a people reach the top of the hill" was omitted from *War Is Kind*. The poem was first published in the June 1898 issue of the *Philistine*,* where it was entitled "Lines," and then in Sidney A Witherbee's *Spanish-American War Songs: A Complete Collection of Newspaper Verse during the Recent War with Spain* (1898) under the title "The Blue Battalions," a title that Crane also used in a holograph list of his poems. Manuscript evidence shows that this poem was written before the Spanish-American War and most likely was an outgrowth of Crane's experience in the Greek-Turkish War of 1897. Crane reported the war from the Greek lines and was clearly sympathetic to the valiant, if foolish, struggle of the Greek forces throughout the short-lived war. The Greek infantry wore blue uniforms while the Turks remained "shadows on the plain—vague figures in black, indications of a mysterious force," as Crane told John Bass.*

The specifically religious and apocalyptic imagery of this poem, with allusions to God, Christ, and the church, indicates that its significance goes beyond a particular event and is symbolistic and allegorical. The conquest of hills in Crane's poetry and prose often bespeaks spiritual triumph. The poem suggests that when humanity in its struggles approaches truth or insight, "Then does God lean toward them" and provide help in the endeavor for ultimate insight or salvation. The battalions seem to be marching toward a regeneration of humanity symbolized by their final victory when they have overcome the limitations of mortality:

A sword will come at the bidding of the eyeless,
The God-led turning only to beckon.
Swinging a creed like a censer
At the head of the new battalions
    —Blue battalions—

Suggested Reading

Katz, Joseph. " 'The Blue Battalions' and the Uses of Experience." *Studia Neophilologica* 38 (1966): 107–16.

"Where 'De Gang' Hears the Band Play". Identified by Melvin Schoberlin in his uncompleted biography of Crane, "Flagon of Despair" (George Arents Research Library, Syracuse University), as one of four unrecorded pieces by Crane printed in the *New York Herald* in 1891, this sketch appeared in the newspaper on 5 July and may well be a segment or a redaction of the version of *Maggie* that Crane had written at Syracuse University* that spring. The setting is the Bowery, and the central characters are Maggie and her brother Jimmy. Maggie works in a factory and has a boyfriend named Fred, a "dude mash," as Jimmy calls him, who is suggestive of Pete, the suave bartender who betrays the innocent heroine of the novelette. The Maggie of this piece is a "tough girl" in contrast to the naive and passive Maggie Johnson, but the character of the hardened and cynical Jimmie is already developed. The Bowery dialect and banal, repetitive dialogue, the ethnic mix of Germans, Irish, and Italian immigrants, the "growlers" of beer, and the band concerts in Tompkins Square all anticipate the environment of *Maggie: A Girl of the Streets*.

Suggested Reading

Gullason, Thomas A. "The 'Lost' Newspaper Writings of Stephen Crane." *Courier* 21.1 (1986): 57–87.

Whilomville Stories. Crane's stories of Whilomville, an imaginary town whose name conveys a suggestion of timelessness or "once-upon-a-time," are based on his boyhood in Port Jervis, a town in Orange County, New York, where he lived from the ages of six to eleven. The term *Whilom* may have a more specific family connotation since Crane's maternal grandfather, the Reverend George Peck, and his brothers organized a fife and drum corps known as the "Whilom drum corps" that performed at a number of family reunions from 1814 through 1874. Even if Crane did not attend these reunions or was too young to remember them, he could have heard about the old fife and drum corps from relatives or read his cousin Jonathan K. Peck's book, *Luther Peck and His Five Sons* (1897), which described the activities of the corps at family reunions.

With the exception of the "The Monster" and "The Knife," the stories with Whilomville as their setting are devoted to the world of childhood. "The Monster" and "His New Mittens" were published previously in *The Monster and*

Other Stories. The thirteen stories in the volume entitled *Whilomville Stories* appeared in successive issues of *Harper's New Monthly Magazine* from August 1899 to August 1900, with illustration by Peter Newell. They were published in book form by Harper and Brothers in New York in August 1900 and in February 1901 (dated 1900) in London. Contents: "The Angel Child"; "Lynx-Hunting"; "The Lover and the Telltale"; " 'Showin' Off' "; "Making an Orator"; "Shame"; "The Carriage-Lamps"; "The Knife"; "The Stove"; "The Trial, Execution, and Burial of Homer Phelps"; "The Fight"; "The City Urchin and the Chaste Villagers"; and "A Little Pilgrimage."

The Whilomville of these stories is vaguely delineated; neighborhoods, streets, and houses are not given specific independent actuality. While Jimmie Trescott and his family appear in all the stories except "The Knife," this is not the Whilomville of "The Monster," which is a small city of the 1890s with a number of churches and fire companies, an electric streetcar system, and a theater. The Whilomville depicted in *Whilomville Stories* is an arcadian American village of the 1870s or 1880s, as insular and provincial as the St. Petersburg of *Tom Sawyer* a generation earlier, but in the staid, uneventful, middle-class life of Whilomville, populated by conventional families with well-meaning if bungling parents and children isolated in their communal concerns, there is little of the romance and melodrama of Twain's novel or of the nostalgia found in the stories of Sarah Orne Jewett and George Washington Cable. The stories are uneven in quality, and their pervasive tone is gentle comic irony. Larger and more serious social issues are sometimes suggested. These are not children's stories but stories about children written for adults, and the jealousies, fears, conflicts and cruelties, and violence in the world of the children reflect on the lives of their parents. There are also suggestions of darker questions involving racial and ethnic prejudice, religion, and the pressures of group conformity on the individual, but the *Whilomville Stories* are focused for the most part on the interrelationships of seven or eight year olds with their families and with their peers in an idyllic environment. The attempts of some critics to interpret them as allegorical studies of social conflict seem strained and unconvincing.

Suggested Reading

Brown, Ellen A., and Patricia Hernlund. "The Source for the Title of Stephen Crane's *Whilomville Stories*." *American Literature* 50 (1978): 116–18.
Jacobson, Marcia. *Being a Boy Again: Autobiography and the American Boy Book*. Tuscaloosa: University of Alabama Press, 1994.
Levenson, J. C. Introduction to *Tales of Whilomville*. Charlottesville: University Press of Virginia, 1969. xi–lx. Vol. 7 of *The Works of Stephen Crane*. Ed. Fredson Bowers. 10 vols. 1969–76.
Solomon, Eric. *Stephen Crane: From Parody to Realism*. Cambridge, Mass.: Harvard University Press, 1966. 201–28.

"Why Did the Young Clerk Swear?" This story, published in the humor magazine *Truth** (18 March 1893) and reprinted in *Last Words*, offers persuasive evidence that Crane was familiar with French naturalistic fiction, especially the works of Émile Zola, at the time he was writing *Maggie*. Crane parodies the hallmarks of Zola's techniques. In the story, a bored clerk in a haberdashery is reading a lurid French novel on a rainy day. At strategic intervals he is interrupted by customers, none of whose desires he can satisfy, as his desires are not satisfied by the novel he is reading, which deals with the heated passion of a young man named Silvere for Eloise, a virginal girl whom he fails to seduce. Zola's spurious eroticism is lampooned in Silvere's prurient innuendoes, repeated swooning, and passionate exclamations. Zola's atavism and fondness for enumeration is mocked by constant allusions to barnyard animals:

> Through the open door to the kitchen came the sound of old Marie shrilly cursing the geese who wished to enter. In front of the window, two pigs were quarreling over a vegetable. Cattle were lowing in a distant field. A hay-wagon creaked slowly past. Thirty-two chickens were asleep in the branches of a tree. This subtle atmosphere had a mighty effect upon Eloise. It was beating down her self-control. She felt herself going. She was choking.

Crane satirizes Zola's fondness for superfluous detail in allusions to well-known occurrences in his novels as the clerk skips "some seventeen chapters descriptive of a number of intricate money transactions, the moles on the neck of a Parisian dressmaker, the process of making brandy, the milk-leg of Silvere's aunt, life in the coal-pits and scenes in the Chamber of Deputies." The clerk's expectations of salacious episodes are frustrated as Eloise wrenches herself from Silvere's passionate embrace and escapes. "He madly hurled the novel with the picture on the cover from him. He stood up and said 'Damn!' "

Suggested Reading

Solomon, Eric. *Stephen Crane: From Parody to Realism*. Cambridge, Mass.: Harvard University Press, 1966. 7–8.

Wickham, Harvey (?–?). A schoolmate of Crane at Claverack College and Hudson River Institute,* Wickham, who was from Middletown, New York, spent a single year at Claverack. He was a special music student and sometimes served as organist and choirmaster of the village Methodist church, where Crane, a tenor, reputedly liked to sing. Wickham's memoir of Crane at Claverack is an explicit account of Crane's activities on the campus and the drill field, but Wickham, who disliked Crane's bohemianism, is not entirely reliable. "Only women and other hero worshippers ever really liked him," he wrote of Crane. "He wanted to be a democrat and yet a dictator. Hence that contradiction, self-depreciation coupled with arrogance, which has puzzled so many." Wickham became a professional musician.

Suggested Reading

Wickham, Harvey. "Stephen Crane at College." *American Mercury* 7 (March 1926): 291–97.

Wigram, Lige. In "Virtue in War," Lige is private in a volunteer regiment who is reprimanded for undue familiarity by Major Gates, a West Pointer. When Gates is fatally wounded in battle, Lige refuses to leave his side, paradoxically showing his allegiance by disobeying an order. This devotion continues after the major's death when Lige buries his body with a note in a bottle containing his name and regiment.

Willard, Frances Elizabeth (1839–1898). An educator and reformer, Frances E. Willard was a university administrator before she devoted herself fully to the temperance cause in 1874. She appeared on lecture platforms throughout the United States and conducted prayer groups on street corners and in saloons. From 1879 to 1898 she was president of the national Women's Christian Temperance Union, and from 1891 to 1898 she served as president of the World's WCTU. Frances Willard aided in forming the Prohibition party and was first president of the National Council of Women. She was the author of *Women and Temperance* (1883) and other books.

Both Crane's father and mother had a lifelong devotion to the temperance cause, and Mrs. Crane was a leading member of the WCTU in New Jersey. As a child, Stephen was taken by his mother to hear Mrs. Willard lecture in Atlantic City. On later visits to Asbury Park, she occasionally stayed with Mrs. Crane and her family at Arbutus Cottage.* Her influence on the young Stephen Crane, however, was apparently negligible.

Willerkins, John. In "Four Men in a Cave" he is the hunting guide who discloses to the four campers the series of events that caused Tom Gardner to become a crazed recluse.

Williams, Alek. A black resident of Whilomville in "The Monster" in whose home Dr. Trescott briefly shelters the maimed Henry Johnson. Henry escapes from the Williams cabin and frightens a child attending a party given by little Theresa Page. He also terrorizes a group of black residents in Watermelon Alley. Thereafter Dr. Trescott is obliged to harbor Johnson in his own home. Alek appears again as a comical character in "The Knife," one of the *Whilomville Stories*.

Williams, Herbert P. (1871–?). A journalist who was graduated from Harvard and studied at the Harvard Law School, Williams was assistant editor of the *Boston Herald* from 1893 to 1895 and literary editor from 1895 to 1903. From 1903 to 1906 he was head of the literature department at the Macmillan Company. Williams's interview with Crane, "Mr. Crane as a Literary Artist," in the 18 July 1896 issue of the *Illustrated American* provides an intimate view of Crane's method of fictional composition and his attitude toward the reading public. Williams made perceptive comparisons between Crane's work, the paintings of Vasilii Verestschagin, and Tolstoy's fiction.

Williams, Talcott (1849–1928). Born in Turkey the son of a Congregational missionary, Williams was graduated from Amherst College in 1873. That same year he joined the staff of the *New York World*. In 1877 he went to Washington, where, as correspondent for the *World* and later for the *San Francisco Chronicle* and the *New York Sun*, he emerged as the outstanding political reporter of his day. In 1881 Williams became an editorial writer for the *Philadelphia Press* and subsequently managing editor and editor in chief. Williams supervised the newspaper publication of *The Red Badge of Courage* in the *Press*, 3–8 December 1894. Subsequently he reviewed a number of Crane's works in *Book News*. In the November 1895 issue he extolled the verisimilitude of *The Red Badge*, and in the July 1896 issue he concluded that *Maggie* was "a better piece of work" than the war novel because it was "truer." Williams reviewed *The Open Boat* in the May 1898 issue, and while he considered Crane "[i]n many respects, today the most original and interesting prose figure in American letters," he felt that the stories in the volume suffered "under the limitations of the photograph." In the December 1899 issue, Williams found little good to say about *Active Service*, calling it "a story which opens with interest and closes with confused dull talk and incident." Williams left the *Philadelphia Press* in 1912 to become the first director of the Columbia University School of Journalism.

Wilson. Known as "the loud soldier" and "the blatant soldier" in *The Red Badge of Courage*, Wilson is a contentious braggart who in the last half of the novel is transformed into a quiet, courageous soldier, presumably as a result of his initial experience of combat. His rancorous complaints of the inaction of the army in the early chapters exasperate the tall private, but when the regiment is about to go into action, Wilson is suddenly filled with trepidation and, convinced that he will be killed, begs Henry Fleming to take a packet of personal papers for his family. When Henry returns to the regiment, shaken and wounded, Wilson accepts his spurious badge of courage as authentic. On the second day of battle, he fights side by side with Henry and helps him to rescue a flag from a falling standard-bearer, sharing with Henry the plaudits of the colonel of the regiment. In a subsequent charge, Wilson captures a Confederate flag, at which he springs "as a panther at prey" when the enemy color bearer falls.

Wilson, Scratchy. The aging gunfighter and town drunk in "The Bride Comes to Yellow Sky," whose seriocomic appearance and demeanor suggest that, like the funnel-shaped tracks his feet make in the sand at the conclusion of the story, the hourglass is running out for the mythical Wild West. Scratchy appears again as Sheriff Potter's deputy in "Moonlight on the Snow."

Suggested Reading

Marovitz, Sanford E. "Scratchy the Demon in 'The Bride Comes to Yellow Sky.' " *Tennessee Studies in Literature* 16 (1971): 137–40.

"The Wise Men". An undistinguished story with much the same setting and characters as "The Five White Mice," "The Wise Men" is, as its subtitle indicates, little more than "A Detail of American Life in Mexico." H. G. Wells,* however, called it "a perfect thing. . . . I cannot imagine how it could possibly have been better told." The story appeared in an abridged form in *The Lanthorn Book* and complete in the April 1898 issue of the *Ludgate Monthly*. It was collected in *The Open Boat*.

The New York Kid and the San Francisco Kid make apparently foolhardy bets with a number of people that Pop, the old and overweight bartender of the Café Colorado who claims to be a great runner, can defeat Freddie, the young and trim bartender at the Casa Verde, in a foot race. The third Kid, Benson, derides them as "a pair of asses." The denizens of the American colony flock to the Paseo de la Reforma where the race is run; improbably, Pop wins. If taken seriously, the story illustrates the significance of chance in human events, and the calm, understated reaction of the Kids to unlikely happenings reinforces this theme.

"With the Blockade on Cuban Coast". Datelined aboard the *New York World* tug *Three Friends* off the Cuban coast on 6 May 1898, this dispatch was printed in the *World* and in the *Philadelphia Press* on 9 May. Crane describes the monotony of daily life on the blockading warships strung along the Cuban coast near Havana. Officers are at breakfast; some sailors are asleep on the gun deck, while others are writing letters, talking, or pacing back and forth. The flagship *New York* steams inshore until the houses of Havana are clearly visible. The dispatch boats filled with correspondents are close in her wake anticipating action, but the *New York* keeps out of range of the defensive batteries and heads out to sea again. "It was a peaceful scene. In fact it was more peaceful than peace, since one's sights were adjusted for war."

Witheby, Peter. A character in "An Indiana Campaign." Peter is an aged resident of Migglesville who expresses skepticism about Major Boldin's claim that a Confederate soldier is hiding in the woods near the town but nevertheless accompanies him in the chase.

Wounds in the Rain. A posthumous gathering of Cuban War stories published in September 1900 by Frederick A. Stokes in the United States and Methuen in England. The dedication, written in April, is to Moreton Frewen.* For the most part this collection consists of fictionalized reworkings of Crane's journalism. The soldiers represented in these stories are stoical, battle-hardened professionals, lacking in the introspection and concern with heroics that preoccupy the inexperienced amateurs of Crane's earlier war stories, and the writing is low key and realistic. Contents: "The Price of the Harness"; "The Lone Charge of William B. Perkins"; "The Clan of No-Name"; " 'God Rest Ye, Merry Gentlemen' "; "The Revenge of the *Adolphus*"; "The Sergeant's Private Mad-

house''; ''Virtue in War''; ''Marines Signalling under Fire at Guantanamo'';
''This Majestic Lie''; ''War Memories''; and ''The Second Generation.''

Suggested Reading

Gullason, Thomas A. ''The Significance of 'Wounds in the Rain.' '' *Modern Fiction
    Studies* 5 (1959): 235–42.

''The Wreck of the 'New Era' ''. This essay, unpublished in Crane's lifetime,
was probably written in 1891. It deals with the destruction of a packet ship
sailing from Bremen to New York with 380 passengers in steerage, many of
them German immigrants, that ran aground on a sandbar near Asbury Park, New
Jersey, in November 1854 and foundered within sight of the shore. The captain
and crew deserted the ship, leaving the passengers to drown in the flooded hold
or to be swept from the rigging by keen winds. Nearly 230 lives were lost. The
one lifeboat to reach shore capsized three times in the surf, and only five of the
fourteen aboard it survived. ''The Wreck of the 'New Era' '' reveals Crane's
early interest in shipwreck and in acts of courage and cowardice in the midst
of disaster. It anticipates ''The Ghostly Sphinx of Metedeonck,'' as well as
''Stephen Crane's Own Story'' and ''The Open Boat,'' with its final imagery
of bodies washed up on the beach. The essay was first printed in R. W. Stallman,
''The Wreck of the 'New Era': (An Unpublished Sketch by Stephen Crane),''
Connecticut Campus Fine Arts Magazine [University of Connecticut] 28 April
1956: 1–2, 19–20.

Suggested Reading

Benfey, Christopher. ''Shipwreck.'' *Pequod* 32 (1991): 134–45.
Gullason Thomas A. ''Wreck of New Era Graphically Described.'' *Asbury Park Sunday
    Press* 19 January 1969: 61.

Wrinkles. A character who represents W. W. Carroll* in ''Stories Told by an
Artist,'' ''The Silver Pageant,'' and *The Third Violet*. Wrinkles lives in a loft
shared with other artists in a structure that resembles the old Art Students League
building on East Twenty-third Street in New York City, where Crane roomed
intermittently from 1893 to 1895.

Wyndham, George (1863–1913). Educated at Eton and Sandhurst, Wyndham
joined the Coldstream Guards in 1883; he served through the Suakin campaign
of 1885. He was private secretary to Arthur Balfour and in 1889 was elected to
the House of Commons. In 1892 the Conservatives went into opposition, and
for the next five years Wyndham devoted himself to literature. He wrote for the
Heinemann house organ, the *New Review*, and for the *National Observer*, and
he edited a collection of Shakespeare's poetry. In the autumn of 1899 Wyndham
was appointed parliamentary undersecretary in the War Office. In 1900 he became chief secretary for Ireland.

Wyndham's review of *The Red Badge of Courage* in the January 1896 issue of the *New Review* was extremely influential and set the tone for much of the British acclaim of the novel. Wyndham called Crane "a great artist" and *The Red Badge* "a masterpiece." Crane's portrayal of war was "more complete than Tolstoi's, more true than Zola's." Wyndham noted Crane's originality in viewing war from the limited perspective of a private soldier in contrast to the strategic and tactical concerns of commanders and his immersion in the emotional aspects of war. Above all, Wyndham realized that Crane went beyond the surface realism* "to recognise all life for a battle and this earth for a vessel lost in space." Crane was delighted with Wyndham's encomiums, but it was his insight into the artistic and philosophical aspects of *The Red Badge* that pleased and reassured Crane most. As he wrote William Heinemann on 27 January 1896, "Mr Wyndham has reproduced in a large measure my own hopeful thoughts of the book when it was still for the most part in my head." Joseph Conrad* and Harold Frederic* also praised Wyndham's insight. Wyndham's essay, retitled "An Appreciation," was reprinted as the introduction to *Pictures of War*. When the Cranes settled at Brede Place,* Wyndham was an occasional visitor.

Wyoming Valley Tales. This is a general heading for three stories grouped together in *Last Words* that deal with the massacre of settlers and its aftermath on 3 July 1778 in the Wyoming Valley of Pennsylvania. In logical sequence they are "The Battle of Forty Fort," "The Surrender of Forty Fort," and " 'Ol' Bennet' and the Indians." These stories as we know them were written in the fall of 1899, but they may have been conceived earlier when Crane was writing "A Reminiscence of Indian War." Crane's source is a book authored by his maternal grandfather, the Reverend George Peck, entitled *Wyoming: Its History, Stirring Incidents, and Romantic Adventures* (1858), two copies of which were in his library at Brede Place.* Mary Helen Peck Crane, Stephen's mother, drew one of the illustrations in this book. Three chapters in Peck's *Wyoming* are: "Incidents and Adventures Related by Mrs. Martha Myers," "Captivity and Escape of Thomas and Andrew Bennet and Lebbeus Hammond," and "Providential Deliverance of Rufus Bennet on the Fatal 3rd of July." Crane followed his source closely for the historical circumstances but reordered events and modified characterizations. In turn, Dr. Peck, who was presiding elder of the Wyoming district, relied heavily on the narrative written by his mother-in-law, Martha (Bennet) Myers, the daughter of Thomas Bennet, Stephen Crane's maternal great-great-grandfather, who is Ol' Bennet in the stories. Crane changes Thomas's name to John but does not deviate from his source in the use of other names. The narrator of the Wyoming Valley stories is Solomon, Thomas Bennet's sixteen-year-old son, but the focus of the stories never strays far from the character of Ol' Bennet, a laconic and stoical old settler.

Suggested Reading

Arnold, Hans. "Stephen Crane's 'Wyoming Valley Tales.': Their Source and Their Place in the Author's War Fiction." *Jahrbuch Für Amerikastudien* 4 (1959): 161–69.

Y

"Yale Man Arrested". A short report syndicated by Hearst on 14 May 1897 about the arrest of George R. Montgomery, a correspondent for the *London Standard* who later became a lecturer in the Divinity School and assistant professor of French at Yale. Montgomery and a correspondent for an Austrian newspaper had been wandering between the lines. According to Crane, Montgomery wore a Turkish fez and had a Turkish servant, causing people in Athens to treat the two men as if they were spies, but they were later released.

"A Yellow Under-Sized Dog". An amusing but simple sketch syndicated by McClure on 16 August 1896 about a small dog that frequents a construction site in Harlem. The dog is "yellow and under-sized; not very intellectual in appearance," but he learns to imitate in his fashion the actions of a man in a red shirt who warns residents of nearby apartment houses when a blast is about to be set off. The dog makes the man's job superfluous by howling and leaping frantically into the air: "He will endure no carelessness; he is there to see that the windows are closed, and he will submit to no quibble. The task of the man in the red shirt is now an easy one. He merely goes along and superintends the dog."

"Yen-Hock Bill and His Sweetheart". Bill is an opium addict, and the term "Yen-Nock," used by the *New York Journal* in the title and text of this minor Tenderloin story printed on 29 November 1896, is a misreading for "Yen-Hock." In "Opium's Varied Dreams," Crane defines a yen-hock as a needle-like instrument used in cooking opium. In "Yen-Hock Bill and His Sweetheart," Julie, a devoted girlfriend, spirits Bill, who is ill with pneumonia, away from his avaricious landlady to whom he owes back rent and nurses him in her own apartment, although he continually abuses and bullies her. Swift Doyer, the protagonist of "In the Tenderloin: A Duel between an Alarm Clock and a Suicidal Purpose," and Jimmie the Mole, the protagonist of "Diamonds and Diamonds," briefly appear in this story.

" 'You Must!'—'We Can't!' ". The peace protocol signed by the United States and Spain on 12 August 1898 required that the Spanish "immediately evacuate" Cuba. The two commissions appointed to secure this end fell into bickering about the precise meaning of evacuation. In this article, printed in the *New York Journal* on 8 November 1898, Crane reports that "the two commissions are engaged in a sort of a polite and graceful deadlock. The Americans say: 'You must!' The Spaniards reply: 'We Can't.' " Crane is caustic about the Spanish commissioners, whom he considers "liars and men of delay." He is especially empathetic to the stateless plight of the Cuban insurgents for whom he had shown small regard in previous dispatches, but he explains this by interpolating that "the Havana province insurgents are very different from those patriots who so successfully did little or no fighting at Santiago." Crane discusses the problems besetting the American military commissioners further in his 17 November *Journal* piece, "Our Sad Need of Diplomats."

Young Griscom. In "The Monster" he is a lawyer who patronizes Reifsnyder's barbershop and derides Henry Johnson's resplendent appearance and cake-walk stride.

"Youse Want 'Petey,' Youse Do". The Bowery vernacular and satirical tone of this unsigned report in the 4 January 1892 *New York Herald* indicates that it was probably written by Crane. It deals with three young boys arraigned at the bar of the Jefferson Market Police Court on the charge of breaking into a street stand on lower Broadway and stealing several brushes and a can of corn. The seven-year-old leader of the group declares that the boys merely accompanied "Petey," identified as "a mug wot lives in Thompson street," who actually "did der swipen."

Selected Bibliography

BOOKS

Beer, Thomas. *Stephen Crane: A Study in American Letters*. New York: Knopf, 1923.

Benfey, Christopher. *The Double Life of Stephen Crane*. New York: Knopf, 1992.

Bergon, Frank. *Stephen Crane's Artistry*. New York: Columbia University Press, 1975.

Berryman, John. *Stephen Crane*. New York: Sloane, 1950.

Bloom, Harold, ed. *Stephen Crane: Modern Critical Views*. New York: Chelsea House, 1987.

Bowers, Fredson, ed. *The Works of Stephen Crane*. 10 vols. Charlottesville: University Press of Virginia, 1969–76.

Brown, Charles H. *The Correspondents' War: Journalists in the Spanish-American War*. New York: Scribner's, 1967.

Cady, Edwin H. *Stephen Crane*. Revised ed. Boston: Twayne, 1980.

Cazemajou, Jean. *Stephen Crane (1871–1900): Écrivain journaliste*. Paris: Librairie Didier, 1969.

Cervasco, G. A., ed. *The 1890s: An Encyclopedia of British Literature, Art, and Culture*. New York: Garland, 1993.

Colvert, James. *Stephen Crane*. San Diego: Harcourt, 1984.

Delbanco, Nicholas. *Group Portrait: Joseph Conrad, Stephen Crane, Ford Madox Ford, Henry James, H. G. Wells*. New York: William Morrow, 1982.

Dooley, Patrick K. *The Pluralistic Philosophy of Stephen Crane*. Urbana: University of Illinois Press, 1993.

———. *Stephen Crane: An Annotated Bibliography of Secondary Scholarship*. New York: Hall, 1992.

Fried, Michael. *Realism, Writing, Disfiguration: On Thomas Eakins and Stephen Crane*. Chicago: University of Chicago Press, 1987.

Frus, Phyllis. *The Politics and Poetics of Journalistic Narrative*. Cambridge, England: Cambridge University Press, 1994.

Gale, Robert. *The Gay Nineties in America*. Westport, Conn.: Greenwood, 1992.

Gibson, Donald B. *The Fiction of Stephen Crane*. Carbondale: Southern Illinois University Press, 1968.

Gilkes, Lillian. *Cora Crane: A Biography of Mrs. Stephen Crane*. Bloomington: Indiana University Press, 1960.

Gross, Theodore L., and Stanley Wertheim. *Hawthorne, Melville, Stephen Crane: A Critical Bibliography*. New York: Free Press, 1971.

Gullason, Thomas A., ed. *Stephen Crane's Career: Perspectives and Evaluations*. New York: New York University Press, 1972.

Halliburton, *The Color of the Sky: A Study of Stephen Crane*. Cambridge: Cambridge University Press, 1989.

Hoffman, Daniel G. *The Poetry of Stephen Crane*. New York: Columbia University Press, 1957.

Holton, Milne. *Cylinder of Vision: The Fiction and Journalistic Writing of Stephen Crane*. Baton Rouge: Louisiana State University Press, 1972.

Katz, Joseph, ed. *The Poems of Stephen Crane*. New York: Cooper Square, 1971.

———. *Stephen Crane in Transition: Centenary Essays*. De Kalb: Northern Illinois University Press, 1972.

Kindilien, Carlin T. *American Poetry in the Eighteen Nineties*. Providence: Brown University Press, 1956.

Knapp, Bettina. *Stephen Crane*. New York: Ungar, 1987.

LaFrance, Marston. *A Reading of Stephen Crane*. Oxford: Clarendon Press, 1971.

Lindberg-Seyerstedt, Brita. *Ford Madox Ford: His Relationship to Stephen Crane and Henry James*. Oslo: Solum Forlag, 1987.

Linson, Corwin Knapp. *My Stephen Crane*. Ed. Edwin H. Cady. Syracuse: Syracuse University Press, 1958.

Lubow, Arthur. *The Reporter Who Would Be King: A Biography of Richard Harding Davis*. New York: Scribner's, 1992.

Morgan, H. Wayne. *New Muses: Art in American Culture, 1865–1920*. Norman: University of Oklahoma Press, 1978.

Nagel, James. *Stephen Crane and Literary Impressionism*. University Park: Pennsylvania State University Press, 1980.

Orvell, Miles. *The Real Thing*. Chapel Hill: University of North Carolina Press, 1989.

Parrish, Stephen Maxfield. *Currents of the Nineties in Boston and London: Fred Holland Day, Louise Imogen Guiney, and Their Circle*. New York: Garland, 1987.

Pizer, Donald, ed. *Critical Essays on Stephen Crane's* The Red Badge of Courage. Boston: Hall, 1990.

Seymour, Miranda. *A Ring of Conspirators: Henry James and His Literary Circle, 1895–1915*. Boston: Houghton, 1988.

Solomon, Eric. *Stephen Crane in England: A Portrait of the Artist*. Columbus: Ohio State University Press, 1964.

———. *Stephen Crane: From Parody to Realism*. Cambridge: Harvard University Press, 1966.

Stallman, R. W. *Stephen Crane: A Biography*. Rev. ed. New York: Braziller, 1972.

———. *Stephen Crane: A Critical Bibliography*. Ames, Iowa: Iowa State University Press, 1972.

Stallman, R. W., and E. R. Hagemann, eds. *The New York City Sketches of Stephen Crane*. New York: New York University Press, 1966.

————. *The War Dispatches of Stephen Crane*. New York: New York University Press, 1964.

Trachtenberg, Alan. *The Incorporation of America: Culture and Society in the Gilded Age*. New York: Hill and Wang, 1982.

Weatherford, Richard M., ed. *Stephen Crane: The Critical Heritage*. London: Routledge & Kegan Paul, 1973.

Wertheim, Stanley, and Paul Sorrentino. *The Crane Log: A Documentary Life of Stephen Crane*. New York: Hall, 1994.

————, eds. *The Correspondence of Stephen Crane*. New York: Columbia University Press, 1988.

Williams, Ames, and Vincent Starrett. *Stephen Crane: A Bibliography*. Glendale, Calif.: John Valentine, 1948.

Wolford, Chester. *The Anger of Stephen Crane*. Lincoln: University of Nebraska Press, 1983.

————. *Stephen Crane: A Study of the Short Fiction*. Boston: Twayne, 1989.

GENERAL BIOGRAPHICAL REFERENCES

Artist Biographies Master Index
Biography and Genealogy Master Index
Dictionary of American Biography
Dictionary of Literary Biography
The Dictionary of National Biography
A Dictionary of North American Authors
The National Cyclopedia of American Biography
The New York Times Obituaries Index: 1868–1968
Twentieth Century Authors
Who's Who
Who Was Who
Who's Who in America
Who Was Who in America
Who Was Who in American Art

Index

Boldface page numbers indicate location of main entries.

About the Author

STANLEY WERTHEIM is Professor of English at William Paterson University. His books include *The Crane Log* (1994) and *The Correspondence of Stephen Crane* (1988). His articles have appeared in journals such as *Hemingway Review*, *American Literary Realism*, and *Stephen Crane Studies*. An internationally re-spected Crane scholar, Wertheim was president of the Stephen Crane Society from 1992 to 1994.

ISBN 0-313-29692-8

EAN

9 780313 296925

90000>

HARDCOVER BAR CODE